PRAISE FOR
MADEMOISELLE
BY RHONDA GARELICK

"Broadly focused and beautifully written."

—*The Wall Street Journal*

"Garelick paints a detailed, wry and nuanced portrait of a complicated woman that leaves the reader in a state of utterly satisfying confusion—blissfully mesmerized and confounded by the reality of the human spirit."

—*The Washington Post*

"Writing an exhaustive biography of Chanel is a challenge comparable to racing a four-horse chariot.... This makes the assured confidence with which Garelick tells her story all the more remarkable."

—*The New York Review of Books*

"Garelick can convincingly, and engagingly, illuminate a succession of parallels between fashion and politics."

—*The New York Times Book Review*

"A true coup de grâce ... a vital entry in the extensive library of Chanel scholarship."

—*Yale Alumni Magazine*

"With more rigor and less hyperbole than its predecessors, this exhaustively re-searched yet highly readable biography secures a prominent place among count-less books on Chanel."

—*Library Journal* (starred review)

"A fascinating, meticulously researched biography"

—*Maclean's* magazine

"This is the definitive biography of Chanel. It is also the life of one of the most suc-cessful world conquerors who has ever imposed her will on a vast subject popula-tion. It is gripping, astute, and elegantly written."

—Judith Thurman, author of the National Book Award–winning
Isak Dinesen: The Life of a Storyteller

"In this magisterial, affecting portrait, Rhonda K. Garelick traces Chanel's history as a woman and as a designer and in doing so illuminates the troubling contradictions of twentieth-century Europe. Her book is a masterwork of original research and psychological nuance, remarkable in combining insight into her subject with insight into modernity entire. It's a Jamesian portrait of the curious mix of sadness and sadism that loneliness can hatch. It is also a deeply moving exploration of a damaged, unhappy genius striving vainly for an elusive wholeness, and, by sheer force of will and vision, remaking the world's notion of elegance in her own image."

—Andrew Solomon, author of the National Book Award–winning
The Noonday Demon

"A stylish book about style, based on meticulous research and a deep understanding of French culture. Rhonda Garelick tells this extraordinary story with just the right blend of sympathy and judgment, in an utterly readable account."

—Peter Brooks, author of *Reading for the Plot* and
Henry James Goes to Paris

"Garelick expertly illuminates the forces that created one of the world's most iconic brands. *Mademoiselle* is a fascinating account of the grit as well as the glamour behind the rise of Coco Chanel."

—Amanda Foreman, author of *Georgiana* and *A World on Fire*

"Garelick explores the world of Coco Chanel in intimate—and intricate—detail, revealing the life and times of the woman she astutely describes as 'understanding how the right labels can govern desire.' This is a must-have book for followers of fashion and social history devotees alike."

—Lindy Woodhead, author of *War Paint* and
Shopping, Seduction & Mr. Selfridge

"Definitive … offers a fine psychological portrait of the poor orphaned girl [who] … succeeded smashingly on her own terms."

—*Kirkus Reviews*

"Garelick deftly situates Chanel in political and cultural history; in addition, the book's extensive archival sources and new interviews make it a valuable resource for scholars."

—*Publishers Weekly*

BY RHONDA K. GARELICK

Mademoiselle: Coco Chanel and the Pulse of History

Electric Salome: Loie Fuller's Performance of Modernism

Rising Star: Dandyism, Gender, and Performance in the Fin de Siècle

Fabulous Harlequin: ORLAN and the Patchwork Self (editor)

Mademoiselle

Mademoiselle

COCO CHANEL
AND THE
PULSE OF HISTORY

RHONDA K. GARELICK

RANDOM HOUSE NEW YORK

Published in the United States by Random House, an imprint and division
of Penguin Random House LLC, New York.

RANDOM HOUSE and the HOUSE colophon are registered trademarks of
Penguin Random House LLC.

Originally published in hardcover in the United States by Random House,
an imprint and division of Penguin Random House LLC, in 2014.

Library of Congress Cataloging-in-Publication Data
Garelick, Rhonda K.
Mademoiselle : Coco Chanel and the pulse of history / Rhonda K. Garelick
pages cm
Includes bibliographical references and index.
ISBN 978-0-8129-8185-8 (paperback) — ISBN 978-0-679-60426-6 (ebook)
Chanel, Coco, 1883–1971. 2. Fashion designers—France—Biography. 3.
Fashion design—History—20th century. I. Title.
TT505.C45G37 2014
746.9'2092—dc23
[B]
2014006844

Printed in the United States of America on acid-free paper

www.atrandom.com

2 4 6 8 9 7 5 3 1

Book design by Liz Cosgrove

For Daniel

To know her, or any one, one must seek out the people who completed them.

—VIRGINIA WOOLF, *MRS. DALLOWAY*

CONTENTS

INTRODUCTION

I dressed the universe.

—COCO CHANEL, 1947

What is Chanel? What every woman is wearing without knowing it.

—*L'EXPRESS* MAGAZINE, 1956

Corporate headquarters for the House of Chanel occupies an anonymous building on a cul-de-sac in Paris's fashionable first arrondissement. Stepping inside the lobby, one enters a high modernist temple—a hushed, windowless cavern of gleaming cream-colored marble, smoked glass doors, and Eames chairs for waiting guests.

Patience is required here, since even after being announced by security guards, all visitors are personally ushered upstairs by a Chanel employee who must penetrate an elaborate series of high-security checkpoints with an electronic badge. For convenience, badges are worn on elastic strings around the neck, often hidden beneath the long ropes of Chanel pearls worn by so many of the (mostly female) employees here, along with chain-link belts, bouclé suits, jersey separates, quilted purses, beige-and-black shoes, and hundreds of other iconic objects, which, together with the wafting clouds of Chanel No. 5, conjure the goddess who haunts this temple still. She may have passed away more than forty years ago at the age of eighty-seven, but within these marble walls, the founder of the empire is ever-young, ever-present, and referred to simply as "Mademoiselle."

Ask nearly any woman in the developed world if she is familiar with "Chanel" and you get an instant reaction—a little "whoosh" of breath, a deep awareness. Most men know who she is, too, or rather what *it* is, since part of what is being recognized is an identity that transcends fashion and even the person herself. For one hundred years and counting, Gabrielle "Coco" Chanel has exerted global influence as a designer, a businesswoman, a corporate brand, and, finally, as a symbol of feminine privilege and style.

Although Chanel was born in rural poverty and raised in an orphanage with little formal education, by the time she was thirty her name was a household word in France. At the age of thirty, she expanded her business into the international market; thanks in part to the wild success of her perfume, Chanel No. 5 (the first synthetically created fragrance in history), she became a multimillionaire before the age of forty. By 1930, when Chanel was forty-seven, she employed 2,400 people and was worth at least $15 million—close to $1 billion in today's currency. To this day, every three seconds a bottle of Chanel No. 5 is sold; it is the most successful perfume in history. The Chanel corporation, founded in 1910, is the highest-earning privately owned luxury goods manufacturer in the world.

Chanel's influence extends beyond the long life of her company; it has been woven deeply into global consciousness. Her name remains as recognizable today as it was a century ago, known not only to the millions of customers who buy Chanel merchandise at all price points (from perfume to couture), but also to those who wish they could, and to the millions more who buy the infinitely available copies. Every day, on nearly any urban street corner in the world, a constant *défilé* of Chanel products (genuine and imitation) streams by—the famous initial motif, those interlocking Cs, emblazoned on handbags and scarves, dangling from necklaces and earrings. Not all of the women sporting these accessories necessarily know that they are wearing someone's initials or that "Chanel" was once a real person, so completely has Chanel the woman blended into Chanel the brand. But they all have faith in the talismanic power of those Cs, in their ability to conjure a little magic, to cast an aura of chic and privilege over their wearer.

I know this because I have been stopping CC-wearing strangers for years to ask them what the letters mean to them. Regardless of social class or whether the "Chanels" are real, the answers rarely vary. When asked why she had chosen her oversize, rhinestone double-C earrings, one inner-city teenager (who was surprised to learn that "Chanel" was the name of a real woman) responded: "I don't know; it's just classy. I like the brand." When asked about her black Chanel sunglasses, an affluent college student first assured me they were "real," and then said, "It just makes me feel better to have them on." A Chanel executive offered little more in the way of explanation, stating simply that the double-C logo was *"un vrai sésame de luxe"*—a French expression roughly translatable as "a truly magical passport [more literally, an 'open sesame'] to luxury."

Chanel would not have minded this odd admixture of fame and anonymity. On the contrary, she would have loved it, for she devoted her life to transcending the personal, to transforming herself (and her name) into an icon of feminine desirability and luxury. She would probably be equally pleased to learn that "Chanel" has gained popularity in the twenty-first century as a first name for baby girls in the United States. (A few young women now even bear the hyphenated first name "Coco-Chanel.")

Through her unique blend of overt and anonymous influence Chanel forged the look of modern womanhood as we know it. Even now, every day, millions of women awake and costume themselves as some version of Coco Chanel, choosing from a vast array of simple and reproducible items that created the streamlined look designed and worn first by Chanel, then by her vast army of customers: skirt suits in neutral colors, trousers, cardigan sweaters, jersey knits, T-shirts, flat shoes, the little black dress, and about a hundred other items we consider wardrobe staples.

Chanel was among the very first to wear her hair short, to wear eyeglasses without shame, even to sport a suntan—formerly scorned as a sign of peasant labor. (Later, when she learned about skin-damaging UV rays, she counseled caution in the sun and developed a lotion with sunscreen.)

Look around you—on the street, in the subway, at the office—at women of all ages and social classes and you will see a kind of retinal afterimage of Coco Chanel. So deeply has the Chanel aesthetic been impressed upon us that we no longer see it—like the air we breathe, it is everywhere but invisible. Even during her lifetime and at the height of her fame, Chanel's style operated more by stealth than by fanfare.

How can we explain the power and longevity of this one individual's vision? Certain lives are at once so exceptional and so in step with their historical moment that they illuminate cultural forces far beyond the scope of a single person. Such is the case with Gabrielle "Coco" Chanel, whose life, while fascinating in its details, becomes even more compelling when studied in relationship to European history, especially the interwar period—the era that launched her to stardom.

Despite the world's fascination with Coco Chanel, no one has truly broached the subject of her relationship to the sweeping currents of political change in her lifetime; indeed, it has been shunned. "Mention Chanel and politics," one prominent museum director warned me in ominous tones, "and they will shut you down."

"They"—the tenders of the Chanel corporate flame—"will sully your reputation." This may be true, for Chanel's role in political history remains the curiously blank space around which many other books have been written. Biographies and films about Chanel tend to focus on her personal glamour and on her rags-to-riches story; histories of fashion recount her design work as if it had no political resonance beyond her (quite genuine) liberation of women's bodies via her easy, relaxed style. Conversely, the books that do look at fashion politically tend to omit Chanel in favor of a literal idea of "political" fashion, tracing, for example, the history of Nazi uniforms, or studying fashion's role as a wartime morale booster. The references to politics that do appear in Chanel biographies focus on revelations about her friends and lovers, or on a few of her own questionable political actions. What remains to be considered is how her work and art themselves partook of European politics, and what her many intriguing love affairs might offer beyond their anecdotal value.

To discover the historical we must sometimes look to the personal.

Chanel came alive in relation to other people, the lovers and friends through whom she absorbed and synthesized every aspect of the world around her—art, history, politics. The key to her global importance lies in those intimate relationships. Chanel approached those closest to her with a uniquely ferocious hunger, a nearly vampiric desire to swallow whole and incorporate whatever appeared most delicious in them—their social status, athletic grace, talent, or style. Her fierce desire to absorb the desirable attributes of others—to borrow from them to enhance herself—sustained her through her early years. But it is also precisely the quality she understood best and appealed to in her own customers. Chanel knew from personal experience how deeply women can yearn to slip, as it were, into *someone* more comfortable, to burnish their own identities by borrowing someone else's.

In response, she used fashion to create perhaps the world's most easily borrowed persona, a persona so attractive on so many levels that other women longed to incorporate it, much as Coco herself had subsumed (and creatively reinterpreted) the influential people in her own life. In this, she demonstrated her strangely flexible, self-aware talent: She could play equally well both—apparently opposite—roles in the drama of emulation. She could, that is, discern and emulate vastly different creative models and then turn around and serve as just such a model for others, becoming arguably the most copied woman of the twentieth century.

Through her personal aesthetics, which evolved out of her own longings, Chanel tapped into other women's deepest yearnings, whose scope—as Coco always knew—far exceeded the sartorial. Her brilliant grasp of the psychological and social forces driving celebrity emulation led Chanel to create what one might call "wearable personality"—which we are all still wearing today.

From the moment she arrived in Paris, Chanel was playing on the world stage, meeting and befriending some of the most influential and well-connected figures of the twentieth century—members of European royalty, artists and intellectuals, politicians, spies, and criminals. These relationships granted her intimate familiarity with large swaths of history, known to most people only through the pages of books. Coco's lover

Grand Duke Dmitri, for example, regaled her with his family stories—of the Romanov dynasty, the Bolshevik Revolution, and his personal role in the assassination of Rasputin. A later companion, Hugh Grosvenor, the 2nd Duke of Westminster, had participated in the Second Boer War—where he befriended Churchill—and contributed significant financial support to the establishment of British-ruled South Africa and its apartheid system. Artist Paul Iribe, to whom Chanel was briefly engaged, championed protofascist, archconservative, and racist causes, yet also had a deep, familial connection to the Paris Commune, the radical worker uprising of 1871. Iribe's politics, which evolved in direct opposition to his father's participation in that Communist revolt, profoundly informed Chanel's own worldview, which veered ever rightward as time went on. Both personally and through her work, Chanel participated in a particular strain of politics that was heavily inflected with the mass movements of interwar Europe and their manipulations of human desires and insecurities. And yet, ever contradictory, Chanel was most tenderly attached to the memory of her lover, Boy Capel, a committed internationalist, and to her longtime intimate friend—and sometime lover—poet Pierre Reverdy, a staunch leftist who introduced her to classical French literature.

As readily as she took in and assimilated aesthetic influence, Chanel absorbed and filtered elements of European history that she discovered through her social and erotic encounters. Then, through an alchemical process unique to her, she transformed these filaments of history into her designs, creating an aesthetic that now functions as a kind of style DNA for virtually every woman in the industrialized world. Whether we know it or not, we are all now wearing Chanel's distillation of European history, as she absorbed it through her relationships. No other single individual has ever wielded anything comparable to this degree of aesthetic influence on so many, or for so long.

Chanel herself had a complex personal relationship to the genre of biography: She found it at once frightening and compellingly attractive. Having sought all her life to hide her true origins—the poverty, her orphaned childhood, her lack of education—she replaced her life story with a series of ever-changing fictions, as carefully tailored as her clothes. She destroyed her own letters and begged (or bribed) her correspondents to do the same. Some say that her poor education left her with imperfect written French, which embarrassed her enough to keep her from writing many letters in the first place. Yet those few letters that do remain, in both French and English, while simply written and containing some minor errors, are far from embarrassing. And she famously lied constantly to everyone, about everything—even trivial matters—never bothering even to keep her many fictions consistent.

Yet as much as Chanel wished to hide her story, she yearned to tell it, too, and did—repeatedly—to various potential biographers, only to deny later what she'd recounted, withdraw approval for publication, or simply abandon the endeavor in midstream. This happened with a wide variety of writers (many of them her friends) who attempted to tell her story, including Jean Cocteau, novelist Louise de Vilmorin, journalist Michel Déon, and Edmonde Charles-Roux. Michel Déon sat for hours with Chanel interviewing her for his book, which she adamantly rejected afterward. Bowing to her wishes, he never published it and claims to have destroyed the manuscript. Even Chanel's lifelong best friend, Misia Sert, encountered similar resistance. When Sert was about to publish her own memoirs, Chanel insisted at the last minute that she excise the entire section devoted to their friendship. Charles-Roux's biography, *L'Irrégulière,* remains among the best, although Chanel angrily repudiated both the book and her friend, Madame Charles-Roux, upon its publication. Chanel's longtime friend, assistant, and chief stylist Lilou Marquand told me that Chanel wanted to make it illegal for anyone to write her biography, and tried to have her attorney René de Chambrun draw up an official document to formalize this impossible injunction. A few other writers and one movie producer told me that they, too, had begun and later given up on projects about Chanel's life, so difficult did it become both legally and personally (even long after Mademoiselle's death).

Among some of the biographers who succeeded in publishing their work on Chanel, a curious—even eerie—phenomenon prevails: The authors seem to permit their subject to overtake them entirely, almost as if through spirit possession. Jean Cocteau's brief essay on Chanel features this stylistic oddity; it is written in the first person, as if spoken by Coco herself. But his is not the only one. Paul Morand, whose book *The Allure of Chanel* also stands among the finest (for its style rather than accuracy), results from a series of interviews between them (published only after Chanel's death), but is written, as is Cocteau's essay, in the first person, as if Coco had told the story herself.

Louise de Vilmorin, who'd been a close friend of Chanel's, produced her *Memoirs of Coco* in 1971, and here, once more, the text is written in the first person, in the voice of Mademoiselle, though Chanel withdrew her approval of the manuscript when it was done and tried to block its publication legally. And while Justine Picardie's 2010 biography, *Chanel: The Legend and the Life*, does not indulge in that peculiar, ventriloquized Chanel voice, Picardie does tiptoe into the realm of the occult.

Picardie, who received permission to spend a night in Chanel's suite at the Ritz, has recounted a possible encounter with the ghost of Mademoiselle. According to Picardie, after she retired for the night in Chanel's bed, all kinds of eerie mischief broke loose: A bulb burst out of a wall sconce; lights in the room began flickering on and off by themselves; doors rattled; voices murmured; and mysterious footsteps echoed in the corridor. Although told in a slightly tongue-in-cheek style, the episode seems designed to convey Chanel's ongoing unearthly power, her tendency to invade anyone who dares write of her.

It may be that, faced with the depths of obfuscation Chanel practiced to shield the truth of her life, some biographers simply gave over their voices to Coco to signal that they could not determine an objective truth—that they were yielding to Chanel's ongoing theatrical monologue about her life. But something more happens in these books; their transmission of Coco's voice is too absolute, too startling, and happens too often to be the result of a mere stylistic coincidence. On the contrary, this biographical ventriloquism is nothing less than the literary version of Chanel's stylistic revolution. That is, just as Chanel succeeded in making half the world wish to copy her, she seduced her biographers into channeling her voice. Chanel wills herself (sometimes even posthumously) to be reproduced by and through others. She truly embodies the spirit of mimetic contagion.

No one writing about Chanel proves completely immune to this seductive force of hers, and I confess I've had my moments. Few women raised on fashion magazines could mount the famous mirrored spiral staircase at the House of Chanel without a little inward gasp, without stopping for a moment to compose themselves as I did when climbing those noiseless, plush, beige-carpeted stairs. And thanks to the gracious staff of the Conservatoire Chanel (renamed in 2011 the Direction du Patrimoine Chanel), I have also experienced the thrill of examining Coco's personal jewelry collection, handling (and yes, trying on) her giant emerald ring (the stone a gift from the Duke of Westminster) and ruby-encrusted bracelet.

I have donned one of Romy Schneider's original Chanel jackets, and I have spent time in the famous rue Cambon studio and adjacent apartment. There, I even tried on Mademoiselle's spectacles and experienced firsthand their vertiginously strong prescription.

I knew I had to rein myself in, though, the night I interviewed Chanel's longtime friend Lilou Marquand at her home in Paris. After spending hours talking with me, Madame Marquand began pulling Chanel clothes out of her closets and having me try them on. By evening's end I was decked out in a sleek cream tweed coat (circa 1958) with Coco's own white mousseline scarf tied dashingly (by Lilou) around my neck. Stylist that she still is in her late eighties, Madame Marquand insisted on taking photographs of me, and ran around her apartment adjusting the lighting and shouting posing instructions. I had the time of my life. As I left, Madame Marquand insisted that I keep the scarf, which Coco had made for herself out of the hem of one of her own chiffon evening dresses. I floated home through the streets of Paris, letting my sixty-year-old scarf fly out behind me in the night breeze. I had succumbed—not only to the charm of my interview subject and the eternal pleasure of dress-up games—but also to the idea that I was wearing a relic, an object of nearly religious significance, a piece of French civilization as foundational as the Arènes

de Lutèce, the stone ruins of a Roman arena hidden in Paris's fifth arrondissement.

The next day, realizing how easily ensorcelled I'd been by this bit of
Chanel mania, I rededicated myself to my goal here, which is to understand the process that had ensnared me: the mechanics behind this will to
copy and to be copied, the will toward emulation, the reverence for long-
dead charismatic individuals—in short, the uncanny historical reach of
Coco Chanel.

Given how meticulously Chanel effaced her "true" self, to write another traditional biography of her would be misguided, an exercise in
pinning down a ghost. After reading an early version of this manuscript,
my editor pronounced Coco "the hole in the center of her own story."
She was right. Chanel seems sometimes to recede, to disappear from the
grasp of those who try to explain her. Therein, though, lies the power of
her life. In her zeal to fit in, Chanel dissolved and re-created herself a
thousand times. But more important, she figured out a way to let other
women do that, too. The Chanel persona and design universe beckon us
to insert our own narratives into the blank space Coco left for us. That
hole where her life should be is actually a seductive invitation. Like the
painted pasteboard figures with cutout faces found at carnivals—behind
which tourists pose for novelty self-portraits, "disguised" as pioneer
wives or Victorian ladies—Chanel asks us to insert ourselves into her
persona, to meld our own biography with hers.

Chanel's close friend Jean Cocteau understood this phenomenon
perfectly. In 1933 he published a cartoon portrait of her for *Le Figaro illustré*, omitting her face entirely. Coco's identity communicates itself
through the casually regal pose of the body, the distinctively bobbed hair,
and, of course, everything she's wearing: the strands of pearls, the gathered bow of the blouse, the softly draped jacket, the knee-length skirt.
Cocteau's drawing brilliantly hints at Chanel's implicit invitation to
other women to insert their own faces into the blank space, to enter into
a dialogue or communion with Coco, without fear of losing themselves
completely—without "losing face." The longevity and appeal of Chanel's aesthetic depend, in fact, upon just how easy this process is.

Jean Cocteau's 1933 faceless portrait of Chanel

Mademoiselle

CHAPTER ONE

EARLY LIFE

> If there's one thing that interests no one, it's someone's life. If I wrote a book about my life, I would begin with today, with tomorrow. Why begin with childhood? Why youth? One should first offer an opinion about the era in which one is living—that's more logical, newer, and more amusing.
>
> **—COCO CHANEL**

Gabrielle Chanel turned her existence into a glamorous, cinematic soap opera that garnered near-constant chronicling by the press, but she always refused to offer concrete details of her earliest years. Instead, she chose to dispense occasional tidbits of truth, hidden amid the ever-changing fantasies she used to embellish the grim reality of her childhood and, perhaps, to soften for herself the legacy of a youth beset by poverty, tragic loss, and wounding betrayals by those closest to her.

Ferociously determined till the very end to obscure her true origins, Chanel lived in the present tense. Such insistence upon the "now," upon the "era in which one is living," as she put it, may help account for the saving grace of her life: her startling ability to interpret the moment, to create relevant fashion for most of sixty years. Perhaps if Chanel had had a more accepting relationship to her own nineteenth-century rural childhood, she would never have become a standard-bearer for twentieth-century urban womanhood.

But Chanel's modernist revolution and its ongoing power have their roots in that long-buried childhood of hers, in the flinty soil of France's Cévennes region where she was born, in her hardscrabble, peasant ancestors, and in the two major institutions that left their aesthetic, moral, and psychological stamp on her: the Roman Catholic Church and the military.

Chanel liked to tell people that she was a native Auvergnat, born in the south central region of Auvergne, in France's Massif Central—a gorgeous, still heavily rural area known for its agriculture, its myriad volcanoes—all extinct for thousands of years—and its highly mineralized water, reputed to hold curative properties. It was a slight untruth. Although Auvergne played a significant role in Chanel's life, and although her tempestuous nature often evoked comparisons with those many volcanoes, Gabrielle Chanel was actually born far from Auvergne's rugged beauty, in the northwest Loire Valley town of Saumur. The small lie was telling, though.

Auvergne was, for generations, home to the Chanel family—the region where her father, Albert Chanel, was born, the region where her grandparents eventually settled. Auvergne was also the place she was conceived. Claiming Auvergne as her birthplace, Chanel tried to knit herself a bit more tightly into her family history, into the clan that, for the most part, had severed its ties to her when she was a child. She later reciprocated the gesture.

In 1883, the year of Gabrielle's birth, the Chanel family's circumstances were bleak. Judged against even the modest standards of their rural peasant world, Gabrielle's parents, Albert Chanel and Jeanne Devolle, began their life together at a great disadvantage. At twenty-eight, Albert had little in the way of steady employment. With no trade, no particular skills, and owning almost nothing, he occupied one of the lowest rungs on the social ladder of nineteenth-century France: Like his father before him, he was an itinerant peddler. But unlike his father, Albert did not restrict his travels to the family's native area of southern France. Bolder, more adventurous, and quite comfortable out on his own, he peddled far and wide, moving north and west, riding a horse-drawn cart filled with small notions and household wares.

He gained his meager livelihood selling merchandise to the house-wives who gathered early in village squares on market days. Albert was well suited to his profession. While he may have been a gambler, a heavy drinker, and barely literate, he was also very charming. "The stands of itinerant peddlers were above all a show," as historian Eugen Weber has written, and Albert was a natural showman. An easy talker, quick with a joke or a deft compliment, he excelled at the kind of patter that could clinch a sale. It didn't hurt, either, that he was extremely handsome. Sol-idly built, with a glowing tan complexion, white teeth, a boyish snub nose, thick shiny black hair, and glittering dark eyes (Gabrielle resem-bled him strikingly), Albert Chanel knew just how attractive he was to women. By twenty-eight, he had evolved into an accomplished seducer.

What chance could a nineteen-year-old orphan girl ever have had against the onslaught of Chanel-style sex appeal? In 1881, Jeanne De-volle lived with her twenty-one-year-old brother, Marin, a carpenter who—in the absence of their parents—provided for his sister as well as he could. Vagabonding through the Auvergne town of Courpière, Albert befriended Marin and, as was his wont, sweet-talked the young man into renting him a room in the Devolle household for only a few francs. Once ensconced, it took him no time to set his sights on his host's pretty and lonely younger sister, a girl who wore her heavy, glossy hair in braids wound around her head. It was an easy conquest. Jeanne fell madly and instantly in love, and in a flash, she was pregnant. Just as quickly, Albert was gone, packing up and fleeing the menace of domestic shackles.

It was the oldest story in the world, but Albert hadn't counted on the tenacity of Jeanne's family. At first, a desperate Jeanne sought refuge with one of her uncles on her mother's side, Augustin Chardon, but when he discovered her condition he grew enraged and threw her out of the house. Marin intervened to help his sister, and after a time, their uncle took pity on the girl. The family resolved to track down the elusive Al-bert Chanel and hold him accountable. Saving Jeanne's honor became a cause célèbre. Soon another uncle got involved, and then even the mayor of Courpière joined in the mission. With the mayor's help, their little coalition succeeded in locating Albert's parents, Henri-Adrien and

Virginie-Angelina Chanel, who had settled in the nearby town Clermont-Ferrand, close to Vichy. Although still peddlers, Henri and Angelina had entered semiretirement and restricted their selling to the town where they lived.

The Devolle contingent arrived at the modest home of Monsieur and Madame Chanel and confronted the couple with news of Jeanne's pregnancy, along with a serious ultimatum: If the Chanels refused to divulge the whereabouts of their son or aid in finding him, Jeanne's family intended to pursue legal action. Seducing and abandoning a woman counted as a crime, and if convicted, Albert risked deportation to a forced labor camp.

Such a turn of events could hardly have surprised Albert's parents; shotgun weddings were a family tradition. Thirty years prior, the young Henri-Adrien—then a laborer on a silkworm farm—had also seduced and impregnated a local teenaged girl, sixteen-year-old Virginie-Angelina—Coco Chanel's grandmother. Then, too, outraged family members had intervened to coerce the perpetrator into marriage, after which the couple commenced their nomadic life as peddlers—a life made all the more exhausting and precarious by the nineteen children Virginie-Angelina would eventually bear.

Henri and Virginie-Angelina managed to scare up their wayward son, who had drifted to the eastern Rhône Valley town of Aubenas, where he was living in a room above a local cabaret.

It made sense that Albert Chanel, who would always aspire toward a finer life, had settled into quarters above a cabaret—it evoked an earlier, far more prosperous time for his family. Albert's grandfather, Joseph Chanel, had once owned a cabaret in the town of Ponteils, France, and the profession of *cabaretier* had, for a time, afforded Joseph a level of security and social stature rarely experienced by the Chanel family. "My father always wished for a larger life," Chanel told Louise de Vilmorin.

Later Albert would spin increasingly elaborate tales about fictional business ventures, and tell people that he, like his grandfather, owned a cabaret, or that he had bought a vineyard and become a wine merchant. But there was no hiding from reality when his parents and the Devolle-

Chardon family confronted him with Jeanne's pregnancy, now in its ninth month. Under duress, Albert agreed to recognize his child, but obstinately refused to marry Jeanne. Bitter quarrels ensued, but the young man held his ground. He found nothing so distasteful as the prospect of marriage. In the end, Albert wheedled his way into an odd arrangement that bespoke his penchant for dissembling: He would agree to pretend to be married to Jeanne, a charade that wound up involving even his boss, the cabaret owner, who played along and signed his name as a witness on the couple's faux marriage certificate.

This pretend marriage perpetuated another family custom, too: Chanel women resigning themselves to whatever commitment they could squeeze out of their shiftless men. Barely twenty years old, penniless, dishonored, and about to be a mother, Jeanne had little choice but to enter into this nonmarriage. Despite everything, she loved Albert with all the passion of an inexperienced young girl. Playing house with him and their new baby seemed like a good-enough consolation prize—far better than losing her handsome boyfriend forever to a far-off labor camp.

Baby Julia Chanel was born just days after her parents' play-acted wedding, and not long after that, Albert prepared to take to the road again—alone. Jeanne, however, would have none of it. Knowing she could not survive on her own and equally sure she could not return—disgraced anew—to her uncles in Courpière, she packed up her infant daughter and hit the road right alongside Albert, clinging to him, all pride cast aside. It was to be the tableau that defined the rest of her brief life.

The little family wended its way up to Saumur in the Loire Valley, where they lived in a single room in a house occupying a dark side street lined with commercial shops. Saumur owed its bustle and hum to the division of the French cavalry garrisoned there. These soldiers cut elegant figures in their fitted, gold-buttoned riding jackets, and were so important to the town that Saumur—unlike any other French city at the time—kept its stores open late into the night during the week to accommodate the schedules of military men who had no wives to take care of errands for them.

Although Jeanne had managed to travel to Saumur hanging on to Albert's coattails, she found herself largely alone upon their arrival. Albert had returned to peddling at regional markets and fairs, disappearing for long intervals. Now he was selling women's undergarments and flannels, which, of course, required many flirtatious encounters with the local ladies. Left to provide for their infant alone, Jeanne found work as a kitchen maid and laundress, scraping stale food off dishes, carrying heavy piles of dirty sheets, bending over tin washtubs, scrubbing. Such work—distasteful and exhausting for anyone—would have proved especially taxing for Jeanne who, in addition to having to tote a three-month-old everywhere with her, was also pregnant once more.

> Early happiness handicaps people. I do not regret having been profoundly unhappy.
>
> **—COCO CHANEL**

On August 19, 1883, Jeanne went into labor and, with Albert nowhere to be found, managed somehow to make her way to the local Catholic charity hospital, run by the Soeurs de la Providence. With no family or friends present, Jeanne gave birth to her second child, another girl. Hospital employees served as the witnesses on the birth certificate, but since none could read or write, they simply made their mark on the official documents. Two days later, the local vicar baptized the baby in the hospital chapel. Two local Good Samaritans, a man named Moïse Lion and a woman known as the Widow Christenet, were pressed into service as godparents of convenience. Convenience, too, dictated the child's name: Jeanne was too spent to think, so the nuns stepped in and christened the baby Gabrielle—meaning "God is my might" in Hebrew.

Only Lion could read or write at all, and with Albert missing and Jeanne unable to leave her hospital bed, no one corrected the small mistake on the baptismal certificate, which announced the birth of Gabrielle Chasnel—a misspelling of the last name that threw a near-permanent obstacle into the path of this baby's many future biographers.

Years later, Gabrielle added another alteration to her original name, claiming that her baptismal certificate read "Gabrielle Bonheur [Happiness] Chanel." The nuns, she said, had gifted her with this middle name as a good-luck charm. "Happiness" appears nowhere on those early documents. Chanel's invention of this unusual middle name, and her attributing it to the intervention of nuns, suggest an attempt on her part to offer her child self, ex post facto, a shred of the tender concern and warm parental regard so absent in the circumstances of her actual birth. "The child I was remains with me today.... I have satisfied her needs," Chanel told Louise de Vilmorin.

Such would be the pattern for the first decade of Gabrielle's life. Albert roved the countryside leaving Jeanne behind to care for their expanding brood. When she became pregnant for the third time, in 1884, Albert finally agreed to legitimize their union, marrying her on November 17, 1884, in Courpière. The nicety of a marriage certificate in no way altered their relationship, although it did provide a modest dowry for Albert from the Devolle family, in the sum of about 5,000 francs, or about $20,000 in today's dollars.

In 1885, Jeanne gave birth to her third child and first son, Alphonse— once more in the charity ward, once more without Albert. This scenario, too, was part of a Chanel tradition. Virginie-Angelina had given birth to Albert all alone in a charity ward, and her sisters-in-law had endured similar fates repeatedly. Henri's brothers, the Chanel boys, were well known for siring large families, but generally evinced little concern for either their many children or the exhausted women who bore them.

That year, the family made its home in the town of Issoire, in Auvergne, where Albert set up shop at the local markets. They rarely stayed in one place long, and sometimes moved even from street to street within a single town. Albert preferred to station the family on the outskirts of cities, where rents were lower and he had easy access to roads. Typically Jeanne would follow Albert to the fairs, carting her children with her. The toddlers ran about with little supervision.

The Chanel children did not attend school, but played together in and around the artisans' shops amid which they usually lived—tallow candlemakers, potters, and rope makers who wove skeins of hemp. Via the easy osmosis of childhood observation, Coco absorbed from these neighbors a love and knowledge of craftsmanship—an almost unconscious, physical understanding of how the human hand lends shape and purpose to raw materials.

Although largely absent and of no real help at home, Albert Chanel made his presence felt. Coco remembered her father as elusive but affectionate—a man who would come in, kiss her on the top of her head, and leave again, the clip-clop of his horse's hooves growing fainter outside the door. She recalled his great sensitivity to smells and his love of cleanliness, which made him something of an anomaly for his class and era. Not only was clean water scarce at the time; bathing itself tended to be viewed as something of a health hazard. Albert, though, according to his daughter, was ahead of his time in matters of hygiene, insisting, for example, that the children's hair be washed regularly with Savon de Marseilles, the traditional French soap made of Mediterranean seawater mixed with olive oil. Coco would develop a similar passion for freshness, and her preference for crisp, clean scents over heavy fragrances led to her later revolution of the perfume industry.

By 1887, when Antoinette, the fourth Chanel child, was born, Jeanne's health had begun seriously to deteriorate. She was what the French called at that time a *pulmonaire,* someone with lung trouble. Although Coco later said that her mother had contracted tuberculosis, claiming to recall bloodstained handkerchiefs, Jeanne more likely suffered from the less operatic but no less deadly condition of chronic bronchitis or asthma, aggravated by constant travel, exposure to the cold at those outdoor markets, fatigue, and back-to-back pregnancies. It ran in the family. Jeanne's mother, Gilberte—who had been a seamstress—had also suffered from pulmonary ailments and had died prematurely, when her daughter was only six, after struggling for years to catch her breath. This legacy weighed heavily on Coco, who always fretted over the state of her lungs and throat, tying scarves around her neck to ward off chills.

In 1889, after yet another pregnancy and the birth of baby Lucien, Jeanne packed up all five children and took them back to Courpière, to the home of her uncle Augustin Chardon—the man who had first thrown her out of his house and then relented and helped track down Albert. Taking pity again on his now-careworn niece, old before her time and wracked with an unshakable cough, Augustin agreed to care for the Chanel children so that Jeanne could set out on the road once more, trailing after Albert on his peregrinations. We can easily imagine what the Chardon relatives whispered about Jeanne and her blind devotion to the unscrupulous man who seemed to be slowly killing her. "I would hear people speak of my mother as, 'that poor Jeanne.'... My father ruined her," Chanel told journalist Marcel Haedrich, her friend and biographer.

But like Jeanne, Gabrielle never faltered in her fervent love for Albert Chanel. While she acknowledged his shortcomings—"My father was not very good.... I learned this later"—she stalwartly defended his behavior, inventing changing fictions to embellish his life and career. Sometimes she echoed his own preferred lies and said Albert had owned a vineyard. Sometimes, he was an elegant, worldly man who spoke fluent English and traveled to America to make his fortune. But whatever fantasies she spun about him, the essence of the story remained the same: Her father was a glamorous and charming man who loved her. "One has a father, one loves him very much, one thinks he is a good person.... He would say all sorts of tender and kind things to me, the things a father says to his daughter."

Julia, Gabrielle, Alphonse, Antoinette, and baby Lucien lived with their great-uncle Augustin Chardon for about two years—the most stable and secure time of their childhood. For the first and only time in their lives, the three eldest attended school together and had time to play in the fresh air. They didn't have to linger around their father's peddler cart or hear their mother gasping for air.

This temporary idyll ended abruptly when Jeanne returned alone to Courpière. Visibly weaker and more gravely ill than ever, Jeanne descended on her uncle's house with her usual proof of having once more located Albert: another infant in her arms—her sixth child, baby Augustin, named in honor of her uncle, the only man who had ever shown her any real compassion. The odds against this unfortunate baby proved too great however, and Augustin died at the age of only six months—perhaps from malnutrition, perhaps from infection.

Facing such tragedy, ground down by illness and poverty, another woman might have cut her losses and ceased running toward the husband who so consistently ran away from her. Not Jeanne. Soon after Augustin's death Albert sent word that he had established himself in the town of Brive-la-Gaillarde, about 150 miles from Courpière. Jeanne packed up and headed off again. With her she took her two eldest children, Julia and Gabrielle, tearing them away from school, their three younger siblings, and from the new home life in which they had just begun to flourish.

Jeanne moved back in with Albert who, while claiming to have become a gentleman innkeeper, was, in fact, a low-level employee working for an innkeeper, while still peddling. With the onset of winter, Jeanne's lung congestion worsened. She developed a dangerously high fever and could hardly breathe at all. This time, she was too spent to rally. On February 16, 1895, Jeanne Devolle Chanel died at the age of thirty-three. Albert was not present to comfort his wife in her last, suffocating moments, but we don't know the whereabouts of Gabrielle, then eleven, and Julia, just one year older. It is likely that they were there, watching helplessly as their mother gasped her last, and later sat vigil beside her body. If so, Gabrielle never told a soul about it.

Did the two motherless sisters run out of the house desperately looking for their wayward father? Did Albert Chanel return on his own? We don't know. It appears that Jeanne's brother-in-law, Hippolyte, arranged her funeral, and soon after, Albert came back, rounded up the rest of his children, and divested himself permanently of all five within days.

It is possible that Albert tried first to entrust his children to his parents. But Henri and Virginie-Angelina Chanel had little money and nineteen children, the youngest of which, their daughter Adrienne, was still a child, having been born just around the same time as their granddaughter Julia. (Adrienne was growing into an elegant and beautiful girl and resembled Gabrielle strikingly. Later this duo—more like sisters than aunt and niece—would become best friends and coconspirators.) Albert was certainly out of his depth in this dire situation, and so resorted to his usual solution—abandonment. Having fetched Antoinette from Courpière, he took all three daughters in his horse-drawn cart to the town of Aubazine, about fifteen kilometers from Brive-la-Gaillarde. No written documents remain to prove definitively what happened next, but it appears indisputable that Albert then deposited his children at the gates of the convent run by the Congrégation du Saint-Coeur de Marie, an order founded in 1860 to care for children and the poor—especially orphans—and housed in a massive medieval structure of high stone walls, which had once served as a Cistercian monastery. According to Edmonde Charles-Roux and other early biographers, a number of Chanel relatives distinctly recalled hearing at the time that "the girls"— Gabrielle and her sisters—were "at Aubazine." It was by far the most likely solution for Albert. Aubazine was the largest orphanage in the district, and Virginie-Angelina Chanel knew the nuns there, having worked as a laundress for the convent.

The Aubazine abbey, which housed the orphanage
where Chanel spent part of her childhood

Convent records for the period when the Chanel girls would have been admitted have been destroyed or otherwise lost, but, as Edmonde Charles-Roux astutely points out, this absence of documentation "might well confirm the hypothesis [of the girls' presence at Aubazine] rather than invalidate it," given Chanel's well-known penchant for effacing all evidence of her true childhood. Yet Chanel did permit herself, at least once, to make a veiled reference to this orphanage. She told Louise de Vilmorin that her grandparents sometimes sent her and her sisters away to a convent during several weeks in the summers: "a vast, ancient and very beautiful abbey…where the nuns…would stroll serenely. Their steps accompanied by the clicking of their long rosary beads hanging from their belts." (Years later, Chanel would acknowledge the abbey's importance to her when she commissioned an architect to copy some of its elements for the summer villa she built.)

Set in the lush, forested hills of the Corrèze Valley, Aubazine dates to the twelfth century. To this day, the Abbey of Saint-Etienne, which had been turned into a convent in the nineteenth century, remains the peaceful town's crowning glory. Devoid of nearly any adornment, save for its intricate mosaic floors and subtle, nonfigurative stained-glass windows, this somber, austerely beautiful place would be the girls' home for more than six years.

Albert earnestly promised to return for them soon, but Julia, Gabrielle, and Antoinette never saw their father again. "They tore everything away from me and I died," Gabrielle said in a rare moment of candor. "I knew that at twelve years old. One can die many times in the course of a life you know."

The Chanel sons fared even worse than their sisters. Albert had Alphonse, ten, and Lucien, only six, declared *enfants des hospices,* or "children of the poorhouse." With this, he effectively turned the boys over to whatever families agreed to take them, in exchange for a fee. Barely supervised, this system resembled nothing so much as a forced labor market for children. Treated often as free farmhands, such children rarely benefited from the payments disbursed to the caretaking families and almost never went to school. Few learned to speak or write standard French, but spoke mostly the various regional patois that had not yet been fully eradicated in France, and Lucien and Alphonse, no exception, knew their local dialect far better than they did French. Poorhouse children had no rights, and no social workers kept track of them. Abuse and beatings were routine, as was the most egregious kind of basic neglect. The Chanel boys endured these conditions until each turned thirteen, when both became peddlers, like their father and grandfather before, setting up their carts in the Auvergne town of Moulins, perhaps with some minimal help from Henri Chanel, who still worked in that region.

> At six years old, I was already alone. My father dropped me like a burden at my aunts' home, and left immediately thereafter for America, from which he never returned. . . . "Orphan"—that word has filled me with terror.
>
> **—COCO CHANEL**

As ever, Chanel doctored the facts slightly in this account. She was actually eleven at the time, not six; her father would never set foot out of France; and no aunts ever cared for these girls. Yet these remarks to writer Paul Morand convey with honesty the emotional tenor of Chanel's life after Jeanne's death. During this one brief period she lost in quick succession the congenial household she'd enjoyed in Courpière, the camaraderie of all her sisters and brothers, and her young mother. The cruelest blow, though, the one she could never assimilate, was her father's abandonment of the entire family. Ridding himself, with barely a backward glance, of all five young children, Albert seems to have shattered permanently Gabrielle's faith in human relationships. Surely by this age, she had seen enough of her mother's life to acquire a healthy mistrust of men, marriage, and motherhood. She had seen that, for women, love and attachment led to disgrace and humiliation. But Albert's betrayal was of another order of magnitude.

Although it seems that Albert never once visited his daughters at Aubazine, Coco did invent a memory of a single such visit. He returned once, she said, to the aunts' home, to bid her good-bye (siblings rarely figure in her memories—occasionally she would mention having had just one sister):

> A little before he left for America, my father brought me a dress for my first communion, in white crepe, with a crown of roses. To punish me for my pride, my aunts told me, "You will not wear your rose crown, you will wear a bonnet."...I threw myself on my father, "take me away from here." "Come my poor Coco, every-thing will be fine, I will come back, I will come back for you....We will still have our house." Those were his last words. He never came back.

As for what really became of Albert, it seems he continued his aimless life as a peddler in the region, and may have fathered at least one more child with another woman.

Chanel's retelling of her father's disappearance only throws its cruelty into starker relief. While softening her depiction of Albert—painting him as a generous man offering pretty gifts and affectionate nicknames (in reality, she became "Coco" only years later)—she can't sugarcoat her own experience of the situation. Even in this embellished memory, the child Gabrielle is desperately unhappy, begging her father to stay. And while there never was a special white dress or rose crown (although many Catholic girls would certainly have worn just such a costume for their First Communion), the description of her sense of deprivation likely stems from real-life memories as well. The fictional aunts' refusal to let Coco wear her fictional crown—the Catholic-tinged disapproval of the sin of pride—may well have been Chanel's fantasy translation of real treatment she received at the hands of the Sisters of Saint-Coeur de Marie. Nuns such as these would have been vigilant in stifling vanity or attachment to material goods. Late-nineteenth-century Catholic teach-ing manuals warned especially of the dangers inherent in a girl's love of beautiful clothes—a weakness feared to be the first step on the path toward fornication. It was even considered sinful for a young girl to look down at her own naked body while bathing.

Coco was eleven and a half—just on the cusp of womanhood—when she moved to Aubazine, likely feeling her body change, growing aware of her beauty, and surely already possessed of her exceptional instinct for style. How bitterly she must have borne the moral rebukes of the provincial nuns who controlled every aspect of her days. As if to prove how much it rankled, Chanel manufactured at least one other, similar memory, recounting to Paul Morand an episode when her "aunts" yet again coldly deprived her of a dress she adored—in this case, a formfitting, ruffled gown of violet taffeta. Chanel claimed that the violet dress had been designed for her by a local seamstress, but that her aunts, finding it too revealing, angrily confiscated it. Her story insists particularly on the aunts' grim, humorless nature: "In a normal family, where children are loved, we would have laughed about it. My aunts did not laugh at all." Although Chanel could never have owned this romantic frock, clearly she had dreamed of one, and clearly such longings were expressly forbidden—by the nuns.

Despite its near total alteration of the facts, Chanel's story of her father's last visit and disappearance sheds much light on her own subsequent life. Faced with Albert's blithe disregard, Gabrielle arrived at a terrible conclusion: She was utterly and permanently alone. She knew that the only way to cope with such pain, or to retain her dignity, was to make it seem logical or inevitable—to claim to agree with her father's decision, identifying herself with the powerful one in the situation: "I understand my father. Here was a man who wasn't even 30 when he left [he was actually 40]. He remade his life.... Why would he have worried? ... He knew [we] were in good hands.... He didn't care. He was right. I would have done the same." The remark reveals the final lessons Chanel absorbed from her father: that even the greatest emotional pain was unworthy of consideration, and that inflictors of such pain might still be worthy of admiration and imitation. Via such lessons, wounded children can grow up to be deeply wounding adults.

While many of Chanel's invented stories about her youth would change over time, the unyielding maiden aunts remained constant characters. Routinely, Chanel described for biographers and journalists the household of these sisters who raised her—cold and withholding, well-to-do but miserly. In Coco's account, the aunts were wealthy enough to keep servants, earning their income by raising fine horses that they sold to the military: "How I loved…the gentlemen officers…who came to see our horses," she told Morand. She even went so far as to claim that her aunts' prosperity—especially the lavish table they set—had prepared her for a luxurious adult life: "Eggs, chickens, sausages, sacks of flour and potatoes, hams, whole pigs on a spit. So much I grew disgusted with food.… When I lived in England in a luxury you cannot imagine…the most marvelous luxury…well that did not surprise me, because I'd spent my childhood in a fine house where we had everything we could ever need."

We don't know exactly what rations Chanel received during her years at Aubazine, but such fantasies of abundance sound like the inventions of a hungry child. Perhaps provisions at Aubazine were scarce. Perhaps Gabrielle dreamed that the nuns—the real "sisters" who raised her—might magically appear with heaping platters of sausages or roast pig. (Later in life, though, she carefully watched her slim figure and ate very sparingly, often only a bowl of soup for dinner.) Similarly, her remark about having been well prepared for future luxury only drives home how unprepared she really was.

Many people would be extremely proud to have overcome—and so spectacularly—such childhood challenges. But shame overshadowed Chanel's relationship to her past, and she made a life's project of concealing her years at Aubazine. She never mentioned the place or even uttered the word "orphanage."

Whatever their obfuscations, Chanel's descriptions of her early life always reveal more than they conceal. An intense fascination with death, even suicide, for example, recurs consistently in her accounts of the "maiden aunt" years. "I thought often of death," she told Paul Morand.

And she told several biographers of her youthful attachment to cemeteries—even prior to the loss of her parents. Coco frequently recalled that her favorite playground during her earliest years had been a cemetery. There, she said, she found her two "best friends"—tombstones of granite and basalt, overgrown with weeds, which marked the graves of two people she had never known. Gabrielle would visit the graves, bringing flowers and sometimes other offerings: "I would return in secret to my tombs, bringing crumbs from a cake, a piece of fruit, poisonous mushrooms that I thought were pretty. . . . I thought the dead appreciated my offerings, my love, my games; I still believe they protect me and bring me happiness."

For company, she also took her dolls to the graveyard—handmade rag dolls that she claimed to prefer to the expensive store-bought dolls she kept at home (which, of course, likely never existed): "I preferred my rag dolls, which everyone else found ugly and made fun of," she told Vilmorin. Even as a child, Chanel was driven by her creative convictions, it seems. And her love for humble rather than ornate dolls suggests the first stirrings of that famous Chanel style dubbed "luxurious poverty," which conjured elegance from the simplest of materials. Gabrielle and her misunderstood fabric dolls would sit and commune with their silent underground companions. "I was the queen of this secret garden. . . . The dead are not dead as long as we think about them, I would tell myself."

From these girlhood memories (authentic or embroidered) emerge clearly the two key sides of Gabrielle's personality: regal and determined, already fancying herself a "queen" in her little domain—and tragically bereft, a lonely child attempting to befriend death, trying to "think" the dead back to life. In her mother's worsening cough Gabrielle had probably already sensed death's looming shadow. As she acknowledged to Vilmorin: "Unlike children who could throw themselves into their mothers' arms and just express their joy, their anger or their tears, we could only walk near our mother on our tiptoes."

A few convent rituals offered a bit of solace to Gabrielle. She owed her lifelong love of music and singing to these years, and spoke sometimes of having sung in church, perhaps as a member of the convent choir. Later in life she showed a fond nostalgia for the pageantry of Catholic processionals of the sort in which she likely participated at Aubazine. But if she'd ever been a true believer, Chanel lost any real religious convictions early on, having found in the church a version of her own father's hypocrisy and dissembling. In conversation with Marcel Haedrich, she recalled her confusion when, for her First Communion, she was obliged to come up with a sin to confess. Not knowing what to say, she settled on a sin she'd heard about but only vaguely understood: "I said, 'Father I have had profane thoughts.' And he calmly responded, 'I thought you were smarter than the others.' And that was the end of confession for me. The priest knew therefore that it was me [despite being in the supposedly anonymous confessional booth]. I was furious. I hated him."

Still, Chanel formed bonds with the sisters who raised her, and maintained some contact with the congregation of Saint-Coeur de Marie for a time as an adult, writing to the *bonnes soeurs,* sending donations, and occasionally visiting them after she had become famous, arriving in a big black car that set the neighbors talking. "Woe to anyone who dared make any smart remark [to Chanel] about nuns," recalled Edmonde Charles-Roux. "She always retained immense gratitude toward them—thanks to them she learned to sew." And while no known correspondence exists between Chanel and the sisters who raised her, the archives of the Maison Chanel hold several letters written by Gabrielle in the 1930s to nuns of her acquaintance in southeastern France—the Dauphiné region. These brief notes, signed "G. Chanel," and not "Coco Chanel," display a softer, more respectful tone than do most other examples of Chanel's writing. The letters suggest an ongoing correspondence between Chanel and these sisters. In several, she thanks the nuns for their prayers and kind words and offers the same in return. In one, dated January 5, 1933, she invites her correspondent, a Sister Marie-Xavier, to "make use of her" should the necessity arise—presumably a politely veiled offer of funds.

Chanel did not continue to practice Catholicism actively as an adult, aside from attending the occasional Mass. Nevertheless, the ambiance—particularly the political atmosphere—of the Church during the Aubazine period found its way into Chanel's worldview in later years. It is worth pausing briefly to consider what Gabrielle would have experienced in a rural Catholic convent at this time, especially since between the ages of eleven and eighteen, Aubazine defined her entire existence, with no parents and little exterior life to counterbalance the opinions or practices she encountered there.

By 1895, when Gabrielle and her sisters entered Aubazine, France had already endured a quarter century of ongoing conflict between the government and the Roman Catholic Church. Although Napoléon's 1801 Concordat with the Vatican had established the Catholic church as a state institution in France, the Third Republic, inaugurated in 1870, strove to minimize religion's role in civic life, especially in education. The church reacted with outrage and hostility to this campaign of "de-christianization," as it was known. Anti-republican sentiment, along with monarchism, ran very high in Catholic circles, especially in the still heavily religious areas such as the Massif Central—where Chanel and her sisters lived. Later in her life, Chanel—despite her highly democratic sense of fashion—would evince great sympathy and enthusiasm for monarchical causes, and a distinct aversion to republicanism and democracy.

Along with her staunch anti-republicanism, Chanel's anti-Semitism may well find its earliest roots in these Aubazine years, when Catholic discontent acquired a distinctly anti-Jewish cast. For centuries, many European Catholics had mistrusted Jews as a matter of course, blaming them for the death of Christ. Now politics intervened. Seeking scapegoats to blame for their country's dangerous drift to secularism, many on the Catholic Right identified the usual culprits: Protestants, Freemasons, and especially Jews—whom they accused of inciting the moral decay of France. (The Right blamed those same groups for inciting the Paris Commune of 1870.) In a presaging of Nazi-inflected arguments that surfaced during the interwar years in France, influential Catholic political journals, such as *La Croix* and *Le Pèlerin*, condemned those groups it deemed "foreign" enemies of France, particularly those Jews and Protestants working in high finance.

Antipathy toward Jews in Auvergnat Catholic circles was likely exacerbated by perhaps the most momentous historical event to unfold in France during Chanel's Aubazine years: the highly polarizing Dreyfus affair. The 1894 arrest of Jewish army captain Alfred Dreyfus on the grounds of treason, his subsequent trial, conviction, and imprisonment, all seemed to validate France's deepest anti-Semitic prejudices. Dreyfus was vilified and depicted as an animal or subhuman monster, and his example served to justify increasingly institutionalized anti-Semitism. Not even the indisputable evidence later exculpating Dreyfus (leading to his retrial and pardon in 1899) could placate those factions who fervently believed in a conspiracy between the Republicans and the Jews.

No French citizen could avoid news of the Dreyfus case, which took on the quality of a national obsession. Given where she lived and with whom, Chanel would have been surrounded by powerful anti-Semitism during her time at Aubazine. We also know that her grandfather Henri Chanel, who lived nearby and with whom the Chanel sisters may have maintained some minimal contact, was an outspoken anti-Dreyfusard and passionate admirer of Emperor Napoléon.

Not all the lessons learned at Aubazine would necessarily have been this narrow-minded, however. The *bonnes soeurs* might well have exerted a progressive influence upon Gabrielle as well. To begin with, these sisters at Aubazine were technically *congréganistes* as opposed to *religieuses*—a subtle yet meaningful distinction. *Congrégations* represented a relatively new model of female religious order, which grew more popular as the nineteenth century progressed, partly in response to an increasing demand for social services. Unlike the more traditional *religieuses,* the *congréganistes* practiced "social Catholicism," and led an engaged community life—teaching, nursing, or helping the poor—which took priority over religious practices such as prayer or meditation. The congregations, furthermore, were far more diverse and egalitarian than were traditional religious orders, recruiting not only from more urban and educated social classes, but also from the rural peasantry—sometimes even for high-ranking positions. As historian Ralph Gibson points out, "The

congregations afford[ed] women unrivalled possibilities.... They provided a function in life ... for those unwilling or unable to marry."

This last point is key. In nineteenth-century France, these religious
orders stood alone in offering women—particularly peasant women—
a powerful alternative to becoming a wife and mother, one that did not
involve domestic or factory labor. At a time when nearly no professional
options existed for women, especially those of modest background, female congregations offered many types of employment, at all levels of
responsibility. And those at the helm, the mothers superior, wielded authority and commanded respect to a degree unheard-of for women at the
time, often supervising hundreds of women.

In other words, Aubazine presented young Gabrielle Chanel with a
picture of adult womanhood strikingly different from the memories of
her mother and other female relatives, whose lives hinged entirely on
their relationships to men. They worked—sometimes literally to
death—to support their many children, and they had no control over
their own futures. What a contrast Gabrielle must have noticed in the
lives of these *congréganistes*. Having largely renounced men and marriage,
these sisters did not "fall pregnant" (*tomber enceinte* in the French expression) or subjugate themselves to men. They exercised a socially relevant
profession. Most of us would see little freedom in nineteenth-century
rural convent life, but perspective is everything. For an observant and
imaginative girl, who had watched family life destroy her mother, these
bonnes soeurs, in their impressive starched white headdresses and flowing
black pleated skirts (Chanel's future trademark colors), all taking orders
from their mother superior—a female boss—might have struck a deep
chord. They were the first independent "career women" Gabrielle had
ever seen.

This is not to say that living at Aubazine brought Chanel happiness.
Although she always glossed over having lived in a convent, she
never described her childhood as anything but lonely and sad. Aubazine

is an imposing and severe venue, and Gabrielle was certainly not the type destined for religious vows. Apart from the domestic skills she learned there—especially sewing—what little instruction she received likely consisted of reciting aloud from prayer books—a method of rote learning permitting no questioning or interpretation. The church used this teaching method to create obedient Catholic wives, to tamp down individual personalities and homogenize the group as far as possible. Gabrielle surely chafed under such monotony, her lively mind resisting. "I have hated when people try to put order in my disorder or into my spirit," she told Paul Morand.

Blessed with a sharp eye for the workings of society, Chanel took the measure of her new surroundings and began coolly planning her escape. In her recollections, the "aunts" often taunt her with her low social class and poor prospects. Perhaps the nuns actually spoke to her this way; perhaps Gabrielle was simply watching the world around her. In either case, even as a child she understood and then rejected the ignoble rung she'd been assigned on the social ladder. The only way to outwit her fate, she grasped, would be to acquire her own wealth:

> I was a child in revolt. Proud people desire only one thing: freedom. But to be free, one must have money. I only thought of money as a way to open the door to the prison.... My aunts would repeat to me... "You will never have money. You will be lucky if a farmer will have you." Very young, I had already understood that without money, one is nothing, and that with money, one can do everything. Or that one had to depend upon a husband. Without money I would have had to remain sitting, waiting for a man to come find me. And if you don't like him? Other girls resigned themselves, but not me.... I repeated to myself: money, is the key to the kingdom.... It wasn't about buying objects.... I had to buy my liberty, to purchase it at any cost.

Trapped in a dreary convent, any lonely girl might have dreamed of riches. But only one in a million would ever have found a way to acquire them. It would be years before Gabrielle acquired her independence, but while she bided her time, she found some fuel for her fantasies: external evidence that change was possible and that miracles could occur. She found one of her most potent sources for fantasy in the sentimental novels she devoured in secret, particularly the melodramas of one of the most successful popular authors of the turn of the century, Pierre Decourcelle.

Chanel openly acknowledged loving Decourcelle—"I had a tutor, a sentimental hack, Pierre Decourcelle," she told psychoanalyst Claude Delay, her friend and biographer. "I lived my novels.... M. Decourcelle was very useful to me. I identified with his heroines," she recalled—although it is not entirely clear where she procured his books or the illustrated newspapers that serialized them. However she came by them, Gabrielle quickly became a passionate devotee of melodrama, or *les mélos,* and especially the work of Decourcelle.

A prolific writer of stage dramas as well as novels, Pierre Decourcelle (1856–1926) concerned himself less with style than with creating heart-pounding, emotional stories brimming with perfect love, tragic loss, mistaken identities, and implausible coincidence. Among the earliest authors to understand the power of cinema, he promoted the new art form vigorously and turned many of his own works into films.

Decourcelle particularly loved the motif of dramatic social reversal—stories in which the very poor suddenly grow rich or vice versa. Like a fin de siècle Danielle Steel, he churned out Cinderella tales of ravishing heroines triumphing over adversity. A quick look at just some of Decourcelle's titles reveals his typical preoccupations: *The Charwoman; The Two Marchesas; Brunette and Blonde; A Woman's Crime; Beautiful Cleopatra; The Queen's Necklace; The Working Girl; The Chamber of Love; The Woman Who Swallows Her Tears.*

Decourcelle was also something of a social critic, hinting at the arbitrary unfairness of social distinctions. In his one-act play *The Dancing Girl of the Convent,* for example, a rich and gorgeous star ballerina at the Paris Opéra renounces everything to become a humble nun. Before leaving for her cloister, the dancer bequeaths all her worldly goods to

Yvette—a beautiful peasant girl. Yvette travels to Paris to step into her new life, acquiring the dancer's fashionable wardrobe, priceless jewels, apartment, servants, and even—somehow—her many suitors. Although crude and uneducated, preferring cabbage soup (a lifelong favorite of Chanel's) to caviar, the girl takes to her new life quickly. Blessed with a brilliant mind and a knack for business, she makes fools of the hapless aristocrats around her by swiftly settling all their dilemmas—from adulterous lovers to stock market crises. Yvette then selflessly uses her new-found fortune to save her family farm from bankruptcy. When Decourcelle published this play in 1883—the year of Chanel's birth—such a tale of meteoric social ascent would have seemed outlandishly escapist. Peasant girls did not become millionaire Parisian femmes fatales and shrewd businesswomen—at least most peasant girls did not.

Similar twists of fate beset the heroine of Decourcelle's most famous novel, the 1880 *Two Little Vagrants*. In this potboiler, Hélène, a beautiful orphan raised in a convent, grows up to marry a wealthy count. She meets with misfortune when her husband, believing her unfaithful, gives their son away to an alcoholic drifter and banishes Hélène from their château. Once more penniless and alone, Hélène endures with Christian forbearance, devoting herself to charitable works, while searching for her lost son, Fanfan. In a parallel narrative, Fanfan, the once-pampered child, comes of age amid the itinerant underclass of rural France. Eventually, all is sorted out; mother and son are reunited, and Hélène returns to her picture-perfect life.

Chanel lost herself easily in such books, where the elements of life she knew all too well—convent orphanages, loneliness, peddlers, and poverty—hovered alongside their exact opposites: palaces, romantic bliss, aristocrats in elegant clothes (always described in detail), and boundless wealth. Gabrielle had yet to experience such heady pleasures, but reading of them ignited her imagination, stoking her hunger for not just a better life, but a spectacular one. Decourcelle made miracles seem possible.

Given the uncanny extent to which Chanel's eventual trajectory actually resembled a Decourcelle plot, we have to wonder whether that might have been her intention. Blessed as she was with a highly theatrical sense—an instinctive talent for emulation—young Gabrielle might consciously have set out to refashion herself as a Decourcelle heroine. "Those novels taught me about life; they nourished my sensibility and my pride," she confided to Paul Morand. Chanel even attributed her dreams of beautiful dresses to Decourcelle's novels. In later years, Chanel got to meet her favorite author when he was quite elderly. She told him of the lofty fantasies he'd inspired in her—and of the disappointment that came when she couldn't fulfill those fantasies as a young girl: "He was already an old gentleman and I said to him, 'Ah my dear, you have caused me...some very difficult months.'"

Gabrielle and her sisters remained at Aubazine until each turned eighteen. Thereupon, each girl faced the first major choice of her life: to stay at the convent and enter the novitiate or leave for the wider world. This was an easy one. Unlikely candidates for a nunnery, the Chanels agreed to be sent to nearby Moulins, to the Pensionnat Notre Dame run by the Chanoinesses de Saint-Augustin. Making this prospect more enticing, their aunt Adrienne had already enrolled at this pension. The girls would be with family. A modest version of a finishing school, the pension offered young women lessons in the domestic arts, including sewing, embroidery, child rearing, and thrifty housekeeping, turning them into good Catholic wives.

Aside from the presence of Adrienne, Moulins seemed to offer little to brighten Gabrielle's spirits. For one thing, the Pensionnat Notre Dame made her lowly social status painfully evident. Even convent schools such as this one upheld class distinctions among the students, and here the world split neatly into haves and have-nots. Those whose families contributed to their upkeep were the *payantes,* or paying girls; those who had no support were the *nécessiteuses,* or needy girls. Gabrielle and her sisters fell into the second category. They were the charity cases and, unlike the *payantes,* they had to earn their keep. The nuns soon put them to work peeling vegetables, scrubbing floors, and making beds.

The school also distinguished sartorially between the two groups: the *payantes* wore one uniform and the *nécessiteuses* wore another—a special

Chanel's convent school, the Pensionnat Notre Dame in Moulins

black outfit that immediately telegraphed their poverty. On Sundays, when the entire school would go to Mass, the *payantes* sat in the church's elevated center aisle, physically above the *nécessiteuses,* who made do with seats off to either side. As a teenager, then, Chanel learned a painful lesson she eventually turned to her own advantage: What you wear is who you are. She later redeemed the suffering caused by that uniform by inventing her own version of it, imposing it upon millions, and charging awfully high prices for it. A century later, latter-day *payantes* around the world still clamor to dress like the *nécessiteuses* of the Pensionnat Notre Dame.

Adrienne and Gabrielle were nearly the same age, and they resembled each other strikingly. Their temperaments, though, could not have been more different. Calm, self-possessed, and soft-spoken, Adrienne carried herself with the air of someone who'd been looked after, someone warmly connected to others. Although Adrienne hailed from the same humble Chanel family, she had never lacked for company or familial supervision—she still had both her parents, as well as eighteen older brothers and sisters. By the time Gabrielle joined her at Moulins,

Adrienne—who'd boarded there since the age of ten—had also developed affectionate relationships with several of the school's teaching nuns.

Trauma and loneliness had already hardened Gabrielle considerably. By her own account, she developed a rough, angry edge to her personality while still a youngster: "I was...a true Lucifer...nasty, enraged, a hypocrite," she told Morand. At Moulins, in the daily company of her more gentle, look-alike aunt, Gabrielle saw a vision of herself in an alternate reality.

And yet, things were changing. Moulins may have been a provincial town with a largely peasant population, but to a teenaged girl, newly sprung from a remote convent, it would have looked like a dazzling world capital. Brive-la-Gaillarde, home to the Aubazine congregation, lies in a deeply rural, desolate corner of France, which remains inaccessible by railway even today. Moulins, on the other hand, boasted a population of twenty-two thousand in 1900, and was a vibrant little city with its own train station. (Even into her old age, Chanel would always love trains, perhaps because of their early association with freedom and mobility.) Some of the town's energy derived from its hippodrome where, during racing season, elegant crowds from throughout France gathered to cheer on world-famous jockeys and their prizewinning mounts.

Moulins had horse racing in its blood, and many members of the local aristocracy were accomplished equestrians who raised thoroughbreds. The estates of these country gentlemen dotted the lush hills surrounding the town—stone châteaus with crenelated towers, sitting atop manicured gardens and sloping green pastures where horses grazed. Though many of them have since fallen into disrepair or been turned into tourist hotels, such provincial manors still radiate a powerful aura of ancient privilege. To Gabrielle, who could espy some of them on her walks to town, they were fairy-tale castles. These old country seats of Moulins provided her first glimpse into the world of the French upper class—outside the pages of her novels.

Her new home offered another considerable attraction for Gabrielle: like her birthplace of Saumur, Moulins was a garrison town. This meant that when the students of the Pensionnat Notre Dame walked to town for Mass, they had a good chance of crossing paths with the handsome young officers of the Tenth Light Brigade (Dixième chasseurs à cheval). Although quartered on the other side of Moulins, across the Allier River, these officers enjoyed strolling through town in their off-hours, striking in their gold-buttoned dolman jackets with goatskin closures. An evening might find the same cavalrymen at one of Moulin's café concerts, where they danced and drank and cheered when the performers took the stage—pretty local girls mostly, with dreams of big-city stardom.

Moulins offered exciting new possibilities, but obstacles remained. Gabrielle still lived under the supervision of Catholic nuns; she still toiled at dismal, unpleasant tasks. Although she loved being near the beautiful and charming Adrienne—whom she preferred over her own sisters—Gabrielle surely felt her isolation more keenly in Moulins, for it was here that she confronted the stark and disappointing truth about her family. At Aubazine, she had been aware she was a charity ward—aware that no one had rescued her or her sisters from their fate. But to a traumatized child living in a remote and isolated place, such facts, while painful, would have been abstract. Moving to Moulins brought Chanel and her sisters easily within the compass of their extended family. Henri and Virginie-Angelina Chanel had settled permanently in Moulins, and uncles Marius and Hippolyte lived nearby. Another relative, their aunt Louise—Adrienne's eldest sister—lived just twenty kilometers away in Varennes-sur-Allier. By far the most settled and prosperous member of the Chanel clan, Louise—unlike most Chanel women—had married well and happily. Her husband, Paul Costier, did not peddle trinkets, but earned a steady living as a railway stationmaster. The couple lived in a solid, comfortable home. Nineteen years Adrienne's senior, Louise had always been something of a second mother to the girl, and the two remained close while Adrienne boarded at Moulins.

Given Louise's age and respectability, the nuns felt comfortable entrusting all the Chanel girls to the Costiers' supervision for occasional visits. Aunt Louise would take the train into Moulins, pick up her sister and three nieces, and escort them all back to Varennes for some home-cooked meals and downtime away from the convent. At least one summer was spent entirely in Varennes.

Had such holidays been possible at Aubazine, they might have attenuated some of Gabrielle's anguish. Now, though, it must have felt like too little too late. Where had all these relatives been when she was contemplating suicide behind the stone walls of an orphanage? This belated reacquaintance with her family carried with it a bitter truth: Gabrielle had been abandoned not just by her blameless mother and the father she tried so hard to excuse, but by an entire clan of relatives who'd never been far away and who had been perfectly aware of her plight all along. Till the end of her life, she held herself at a great and chilly distance from nearly all of her Moulins relatives and their descendants. Family, she later told Morand, is nothing more than a series of "charming illusions . . . mirages that make you believe that the world is inhabited by other versions of yourself." A hardened cynic before she was even out of her teens, Chanel fell for no such illusions—although, arguably, she later populated the world with "other versions" of herself, creating a kind of global illusion of extended family.

Gabrielle did little to hide the disdain and anger she felt, openly telling Adrienne how much she disliked the Costier household and the little town of Varennes, which she claimed to find boring and bourgeois. And yet these family excursions held a certain charm for Gabrielle, since Aunt Louise was something of an amateur fashion designer. Possessing a version of the Chanel style gene, Louise had a quick, creative touch with fabrics, and a special flair for accessories. With a few deft stitches or some fancy scissor work, she could turn plain handkerchiefs into charming flowers to adorn a hat. In her hands, stray scraps of fabric morphed into fetching new bodices that revived old dresses. She added crisp white cuffs and collars to liven up blouses (details that would appear later in Chanel's own work).

When the four girls came down from Moulins, Louise would invite them to work alongside her. The Chanel women spent many hours together during those visits, lost to the pleasures of ribbons and bows, lace and velvet. Louise especially loved making hats, and Adrienne and Gabrielle would help her invent new designs. Such a pastime felt natural; all the girls sewed well—the nuns had seen to that. But for Gabrielle, this was more than an amusing hobby—she was developing her talent. In convents, the girls had learned practical sewing—to make bed linens or simple dresses. They learned to make perfect, even stitches. But with Aunt Louise, they stretched their imaginations.

In truth, her aunt developed Chanel's vision more than she did her craftsmanship. Gabrielle had a vivid imagination and a keen, original eye, but she never acquired the skills necessary for complex or ornate sewing. Nor did she ever learn to sketch her own patterns. In later life, Chanel would rely upon teams of experienced seamstresses to give life to her creations.

Helping Aunt Louise came with another bonus, too: the privilege of accompanying her on her annual trip to nearby Vichy to shop for sewing supplies. Vichy dazzled Gabrielle even more than Moulins had. The entire world flocked to this "thermal spa" town. Ever since the Romans discovered it in 52 B.C., Vichy had been enticing visitors with its spring water, whose medicinal powers remain legendary. In 1901, when Gabrielle discovered it, the city was reaching its peak of Belle Epoque glamour, known as France's premier water resort. Crowned heads of state, aristocrats, diplomats from all over—including Africa and the Middle East—and much of Europe's fashionable set descended every year on the town. As many as forty thousand visitors arrived annually, all seeking healing in the famous waters. (Instead of *touristes*, these visitors were called *curistes*.) With a grand, Art Nouveau–style casino and opera house, and a crop of newly built luxury hotels, turn-of-the-century Vichy glittered with a special luster. Gabrielle had never heard so many foreign languages—which she regarded as "passwords to a great secret club." She had never seen people of such diverse backgrounds and dress. She drank it all in.

. . .

Chanel (left) and her aunt Adrienne
on a trip to Vichy, 1902

Hard as they were, those two years at the Pensionnat Notre Dame afforded Gabrielle an important period of transition. She still lived in a convent but now enjoyed regular (if limited) access to a city. These years also cemented the bond with her boon companion, Aunt Adrienne, the only member of her family she had ever really enjoyed. Adrienne had an innate poise that seemed to awaken something in Gabrielle. Decades later, Chanel reminisced to Paul Morand about girlhood tea parties that Adrienne would stage for the two of them—parties at which Adrienne would insist they "play at being great [aristocratic] ladies" together.

In 1902, Gabrielle, then nineteen, and Adrienne, twenty, finally bade good-bye to convent walls. As was customary, the sisters of the school found a suitable "placement" for their students—in this case, work as seamstresses for a local Moulins establishment known as the Maison Grampayre, on the rue de l'Horloge, specializing in bridal trousseaus and layette sets for infants. Upon request, the shop also created outfits for women and girls. The locals soon took note of the lovely Chanel girls' marvelous way with a needle. Ladies began requesting their services specifically.

The girls began to taste some of the simple pleasures of independence. Out from under the nuns' watchful glare, they set up housekeeping together, sharing a rented furnished room on the rue du Pont-Ginguet.

A 1905 view of the Maison Grampayre, on the rue de l'Horloge, Moulins, where Chanel and her aunt Adrienne worked as seamstresses

To help make ends meet, they took in odd sewing jobs and began helping out at a tailor shop catering to cavalrymen—a setting, at last, with some real social possibilities.

The young officers of Moulins wasted no time chatting up the two new young and pretty seamstresses they discovered mending uniforms in the back of the shop called Modern Tailleur. The gentlemen began by inviting Adrienne and Gabrielle to accompany them on chaste outings—to take tea or enjoy fruit sorbets under the vaulted ceilings of the Grand Café or La Tentation, Moulins's historic watering holes. The girls soon found themselves at the center of a circle of aristocratic admirers. Tea dates turned into excursions to the Hippodrome to watch the races, and then into evenings at the café concerts. For most of her new gang, these little cabarets were just informal hangouts, places to catch some lighthearted entertainment. To Gabrielle, they meant something else entirely. This was her first experience of any kind of theater, and she felt drawn toward the stage. Here at last was an escape route. Gabrielle would become a star.

Local residents and former army officers who'd known Chanel as a young woman in Moulins recalled for decades thereafter her exceptional charisma. Rough around the edges, skinny, and flat chested, she hardly resembled the voluptuous beauties who were typically trailed by admirers. But even in her earliest youth, long before she'd made any mark on the world, Gabrielle knew how to captivate. This quality was not lost on the management of Moulins's most popular café concert, La Rotonde, which agreed to give Gabrielle her first onstage gig. She became what was known as a *poseuse,* one of a group of girls who "posed" onstage in a semicircle behind the star, looking pretty. Between sets, the *poseuses* got the chance to sing a few songs. They received no regular wages but were permitted to pass through the audience to collect tips. It was a start.

Despite her very modest singing talents, Gabrielle charmed the crowds at La Rotonde and soon became a favorite *poseuse,* raising cheers from the crowd for her renditions of the ditties that earned her her famous nickname. Gabrielle earned her new name by singing either "Ko-Ko-Ri-Ko" ("Cock-a-doodle-doo") or "Qui qu'a vu Coco?" ("Has anyone seen Coco?")—or possibly both—songs about a rooster and a lost dog, respectively. To French ears at that time, "Coco" sounded not like a woman's name but like an affectionate nickname for a pet or, by extension, like a diminutive of *cocotte,* the word that meant literally "small hen" and figuratively a sort of upper-level prostitute. Shouted night after night, the name stuck—perhaps with a little encouragement from Chanel, who would later prove quite adept at labeling new products.

But this Coco was no *cocotte*—at least not yet. While she loved the adulation of the men in the audience, her convent modesty ceded only slowly to the freewheeling ways of a cabaret dressing room. Other girls may have wandered around half-dressed backstage but not Coco. "She was a prude," according to a woman who'd known her in Moulins, "double-locking the door when she had to change." Traces of Chanel's sense of decorum about the naked body—her reluctance ever to reveal or exploit bare flesh—would remain visible as a signature element of her future style. But her personal discomfort with the looser mores of her new milieu began to abate under the admiring eyes of La Rotonde's handsome and distinguished patrons.

CHAPTER TWO

A NEW WORLD

Society women . . . I found hideous. [But] . . . the cocottes
were gorgeous . . . eccentric, very beautiful, appetizing.
They went well with my novels.

—COCO CHANEL

Life could be unforgiving for poor young women in fin de siècle
France. Girls like the Chanel foursome—pretty and charming
but lacking dowries or family connections—courted disaster in
their dealings with men. Yet men—particularly men of means—
presented one of the only possible escape routes, the hope of acquiring
some peace of mind and personal security. Although they attracted
plenty of attention among the wellborn young men in Moulins, the
girls' destitute backgrounds rendered them essentially unmarriageable.
They were simply unfit to enter society. Options, then, for finding a
husband were few indeed. They could marry peasants or peddlers, ensuring a life of backbreaking labor and dire poverty, or they could remain unmarried and brave the hard choices attending *that* decision.
The unmarried woman could eschew all sensual pleasures by entering
religious life, she could seek employment as a servant, or she could
negotiate the most treacherous territory of all: offering herself to men

outside of marriage, in exchange for varying degrees of comfort and respectability.

Common prostitutes occupied the lowest end of this spectrum, and at its uppermost reaches figured the courtesans, or *femme galantes,* women often connected to the theater. Also known as *cocottes* or—when involved with just one man at a time—as *irrégulières* (for their irregular social status), these were the glamorous women attached to wealthy and titled men, women whose beauty, style, and worldliness often put "respectable" wives to shame. At a time when virtuous young women were still being taught to regard bathing as a dangerous, immoral activity and were ignorant of virtually all sexual matters, *femmes galantes* bathed regularly, smelled wonderful, and knew their way around the bedroom.

Not just anyone could achieve *cocotte* status, of course. One had to be blessed with just the right combination of looks, charm, patience, guts, and savvy. But for those who managed to join the ranks, being a *cocotte* was not always such a bad career. Although dependent financially on lovers, if these "irregular" women were clever (and lucky) they might save enough to retire comfortably once they'd aged beyond their category. (In some cases, the former lovers actually paid out a kind of pension, in clear acknowledgment of the businesslike nature of these dealings.) Such success on the margins of society, though, was a rare and difficult accomplishment, and a *cocotte* virtually never wound up marrying a *fils de famille*—a society man. Life was a minefield.

While Gabrielle, Adrienne, and, for a time, Antoinette (who followed her sister to Moulins) survived their unmoored youth, Julia Chanel stepped on a mine. Like her mother before her, she succumbed to the charms of a local peddler and became pregnant. She had left the convent and run off with her young man, with whom she had a son—out of wedlock—on November 29, 1904. Julia christened the boy André Palasse, apparently after a certain Antoine Palasse of Moulins who, while not the child's father, agreed to accept paternity in exchange for payment. She and her lover moved in together, but their domestic arrangement collapsed. Julia then moved on to another disastrous love affair, this time with a young officer. When that officer also abandoned her, a desperate Julia added her name to the long list of Chanel family tragedies, taking her own life in 1910, at age twenty-eight.

Gabrielle later told people that Julia had killed herself by rolling repeatedly in deep snow until she froze to death—a story undermined by the fact that Julia died in the month of May. Perhaps Chanel had reason to obscure the details of her sister's death, for she might have felt some personal responsibility for it. On a few occasions, Gabrielle hinted that Julia's officer boyfriend had been so attractive that she had also fallen in love with him, raising the possibility that Gabrielle might have seduced her sister's lover, driving the bereft Julia to take her own life. While we can never know for sure, such behavior would not have been out of character for Gabrielle. Having been so forlorn as a child, she came to regard love as a zero-sum game, in which one woman's gain was always another's loss. Any other woman could be a potential rival, including members of her own family. This pattern would repeat itself often in Chanel's later life, which featured quite a track record of liaisons with married men—some of whom she seduced away from women close to her, including friends and clients.

Upon Julia's death, care of her orphaned six-year-old son, André, fell first to a local parish priest, who took the boy in for a time. But soon, his aunt Coco stepped in, unofficially adopting André and treating him as her own son. Chanel may simply have acted out of love and compassion for her nephew, or she may have devoted herself to him to assuage her guilt.

Biographers and journalists have often floated a third explanation for Chanel's lifelong attachment to André: that he was not her nephew, but her son. Rumors to this effect persisted for years, suggesting that Gabrielle, not Julia, had borne a child while in Moulins and then quickly hushed it up by arranging for the pliable Julia to care for the boy. No firm evidence will likely ever be found to corroborate this story. Gabrielle Palasse-Labrunie—André's daughter—says she never asked her aunt Coco about the past, knowing it would upset her. "She had a very motherly feeling for my father" is all Labrunie permits herself to say on the subject. If André really was Chanel's biological son, she never admitted it to a soul—not even the many friends who later suspected this and re-peatedly asked her about it. But whether he was her son or nephew, something about André allowed Chanel to welcome him (and later his children) into her life, even while she disavowed nearly every other member of her family.

If, in fact, André was Coco's son, there is one candidate most likely to have been his father: the first young man with whom Chanel permitted herself a relationship, one of her many admirers from La Rotonde, Eti-enne Balsan (1878–1953). A kind but unprepossessing man, not espe-cially handsome or tall, he hailed from the haute bourgeoisie rather than the aristocracy. Balsan was also jovial, easygoing, and very rich. He made for an ideal, even comforting, entrée into a new world. Coco was about to cross the border between her humble youth and an extremely upper-class adulthood. Balsan was her passport.

The Balsan family, from the central France region of Châteauroux, was known for both its immense textile fortune and its generations of expert equestrians. When Gabrielle met Etienne, sometime around 1904, he had recently left the army and, having lost both of his parents, was now free to enjoy his vast inheritance as he wished. Still in his twen-ties, independently wealthy, and seemingly unfettered by family obliga-tions, Balsan lived a life of many pleasures—chief among which were women, polo, and horses. Yet, despite his bachelor lifestyle, Balsan was actually a married man and father to a young daughter when he met Coco. According to his granddaughter Quitterie Tempé, when Balsan was in his early twenties, he married Suzanne Bouchaud—who was preg-nant at the time of their wedding with the couple's only child, daughter Claude. Suzanne and Etienne had almost immediately thereafter settled into amicably separate lives, with Madame Balsan "turn[ing] a blind eye to his mistresses," according to Tempé.

To provide an appropriate backdrop to his high living, Etienne was about to purchase his own country estate—the Château de Royallieu, in the town of Compiègne, originally a fourteenth-century monastery that had served as the royal residence of King Philip IV.

At the time Coco met Balsan, her burgeoning fame as a singer in

Etienne Balsan on horseback, 1900 (above). Chanel and Balsan riding donkeys with friends. Left to right: Maurice Cailloux, Mlle. Forchemer, Suzanne Orlandi, Baron Foy, Chanel, and Balsan

Moulins seemed to promise a better future for her. As precarious as her situation still was, she did have a few advantages—most important, her aunt Adrienne. Offering moral support and steadfast companionship, the lovely Adrienne served as Coco's "wingwoman." It is possible that the two girls took several train trips to Paris during this time. Chanel dropped hints of such excursions in conversations with Marcel Haedrich, but offered no details of what they did or whom they saw in the capital city. We can only speculate about how two lovely, unsupervised, poor young girls found the money to underwrite their time in the big city, and this is likely one of the times when Chanel tried her luck at some casual and discreet prostitution.

The bond between the two young women helped offset the pressures and risks they continually encountered. When, for example, Henri and Virginie-Angelina tried to force Adrienne into an arranged marriage with a local notary—a much older man she found repellent—Coco's presence helped her stand up to her parents. Without Coco, the meek Adrienne might never have found the strength to break off the engagement.

Freed from that constraint, Adrienne soon came to the attention of one of Moulins's most influential socialites, Maud Mazuel, a woman who'd made a career playing *salonnière* and chaperone (and, perhaps, madam) to legions of beautiful but socially marginal young women. Elegant and worldly, Maud held regular tea parties in her home where wellborn young men could mingle with her stable of beauties. Both Coco and Adrienne attended these events, but Adrienne fit into this environment especially well. A number of local aristocrats began vying seriously with one another for her favors.

Vichy . . . that doesn't exist.

—COCO CHANEL

Adrienne enjoyed, then, uncommon romantic success for a girl of her background. She would never weather the kind of personal tempests that would bring Coco so much heartache. But in the realm of ambition and hunger for the world, Coco was always one step ahead of Adrienne. Understanding that La Rotonde was a small-time establishment, Coco set her sights on the one glamorous city she knew, Vichy. She persuaded Adrienne to join her, and the girls set off to pursue Coco's dream of a career in operetta.

Balsan, who was already at this time a "special friend" to Coco, tried to convince her of the folly of her plan. While moved by her charm, Etienne had no illusions about Coco's unexceptional singing voice. "You won't get anywhere.... You have no voice," he told her. Nevertheless, he helped both girls prepare for their trip, paying for many of the provisions they would need and the fabrics from which they were sewing new travel wardrobes for themselves.

In Vichy, Coco and Adrienne—age twenty-two and twenty-three respectively—rented a tiny room together, as they had done in Moulins. Vichy, however, operated on another scale altogether. Here, charm and good looks only went so far. With little money and no connections, Coco and Adrienne foundered. Although Coco managed to score an audition at the famous Alcazar theater, which produced variety shows and operettas, the management there was unimpressed with her voice. Taking note of her charm, though, they encouraged her to take singing lessons and to return later. Adrienne was rejected out of hand and soon returned to Moulins and her bevy of suitors. Once back, she took up residence with her good friend Maud, moving into her villa in the town of Souvigny, a few miles west of Moulins. She continued to enjoy the amorous attentions of several noblemen, including the Baron Maurice de Nexon. Although Adrienne took her time selecting among her suitors, she eventually fell in love with Nexon, and the feeling was entirely mutual. Unlike most men of his class, the baron remained steadfast and faithful to his *cocotte* mistress, despite her unsuitability and his parents' adamant refusal to permit the couple to marry. Defying his parents' wishes, Maurice remained devoted to Adrienne for the rest of his life, later living with her outside of marriage for decades.

. . .

Coco was not yet ready to relinquish her Vichy dream. She knew she needed to make her own way, she knew she needed money, and she retained her passion for all things theatrical. Only one career seemed open to her—and she was determined to have it. She began taking singing and dancing lessons in Vichy, hoping to land the role of *gommeuse* at some theater. Like the *poseuses, gommeuses* were backup singers and dancers, eye candy in black sequined dresses who performed numbers between scenes. (Little black sequined dresses would later be an evening staple of Chanel couture.)

Coco was happy for a time in Vichy. She loved practicing singing and dance; she loved the hum and bustle of the international resort town. But her funds were running out, and no stage job materialized. Balsan probably helped her out somewhat, and she took in some odd sewing jobs. But to make ends meet, Coco needed more. At this point in her life, Chanel may well have once more allowed some men to pay for her favors—the quickest and easiest route to cash. According to Edmonde Charles-Roux, though, Coco soon found herself the most iconic position possible in Vichy: "water girl" at La Grande Grille, one of the city's premier thermal spas. Clad in white apron, matching cap, and little white boots, Coco would have joined the legions of young women dispensing glasses of warm mineral water to the *curistes* seeking relief for everything from hangovers to gallstones.

Standing for hours in a kind of circular well, surrounded by large faucets, several feet below where the customers walked and sat, the famous Vichy water girls were something of an amalgam of nurse, waitress, and showgirl. Such a job was a far cry from the stardom Coco sought, and she surely chafed at having to stand literally below her well-dressed customers. As the warm-weather "cure" season drew to a close, so did Chanel's Vichy adventure. Realizing she would never make a career of singing, and not planning on a career serving glasses of water, Coco returned to Moulins. As with every other episode she deemed shameful, this brief stint in Vichy disappeared from all official versions of Coco's life. She did recount having visited her grandfather at Vichy, when, she claimed, he was taking a cure. This is possible but not likely. "I think she closed all the doors to her past when she became Balsan's *irrégulière*," said Edmonde Charles-Roux. "She never again spoke of her mother, her father, or her brothers."

Returning to Moulins, Coco, now twenty-three, was somewhat at sixes and sevens. With Adrienne off at Maud's and in love with Maurice de Nexon, Coco understood that she, too, needed protection. She would not return to life as a seamstress in a rented room. Instead, she took a considerable leap—she moved into the Château de Royallieu, Etienne Balsan's vast stone property. It is worth noting that this is the first episode of her life that Coco seemed willing to acknowledge to her biographers. This is not to say that she told a single, coherent story about her Royallieu days, but rather that Balsan did not get expunged. He remained a clear, knowable character from her past, as well as a lifelong friend.

Balsan bought Royallieu in 1904 and turned it into a major center for breeding and racing horses, and for entertaining women. Balsan was an expert at all of these activities. In an era when "gentlemen riders" were ranked like tennis players, Balsan was considered a top seed, officially a "number one" rider, and—had such ratings existed—he would have earned similar marks in casual love. Along with the breeders, trainers, and jockeys who frequented Royallieu, Balsan hosted a constant stream of bachelor friends and beautiful *cocottes*.

As was typical for her, Chanel had multiple accounts of how she came to live with Balsan. She told Paul Morand that Etienne had helped her escape the evil clutches of her elderly aunts. In this version, she shaved years off her age, claiming that she was so young at the time—merely sixteen—that Balsan feared the police would arrest him. "His friends would tell him: 'Coco is too young, send her home,'" she told Morand. Chanel said she entered the Royallieu household after Balsan had broken off with the famous *cocotte* and Folies-Bergère dancer Emilienne d'Alençon—a voluptuous bisexual demimondaine.

The story Chanel told Claude Delay showcases more her love of horses and Balsan's easy charm. She recounted an afternoon she spent entranced, watching the trainers and jockeys exercise the horses in the Royallieu stables: "You could breathe in the fresh smell...the sunlight was golden...the jockeys and the grooms rode in a line....'What a beautiful life,' I sighed. 'It's mine all year round,' responded Etienne Balsan. 'Why don't you make it yours as well?'"

What rings most true in this version is Chanel's love for the beauty of the landscape, the animals, and the exhilarating freedom she sensed in country life. Royallieu enchanted her. She was a country girl and an athlete at heart, and fresh air and horses would always rank among her greatest passions. And whatever the original circumstances, Coco did wind up living in her own suite of rooms at Royallieu. Yet the claim that she had replaced Emilienne d'Alençon may not have been entirely accurate. In fact, Emilienne remained a constant visitor and sometime resident at the château. She had other lovers, including the famous jockey Alec Carter, but she and Balsan may well have fallen into bed together occasionally, given the relaxed, amorous atmosphere of Royallieu.

Coco was never Balsan's principal mistress. Her status was more on the order of amusing side diversion—one of many young women with whom Balsan dallied. Coco and Emilienne would become great friends for a time, but a remark made to Marcel Haedrich unmistakably reveals Coco's resentment toward a woman she clearly perceived as a rival: "Etienne Balsan liked old women, he adored Emilienne d'Alençon. Beauty, youth, those things didn't concern him." In 1906, the elderly Emilienne was thirty-six and ravishing.

Balsan hailed from a high-achieving family, whose fortune was already over a century old, dating back to the family's days supplying uniforms to Napoléon's army. By the age of twenty-four, Etienne's older brother, Louis-Jacques, had established himself as both a pioneer of aviation and a successful industrialist. Jacques would later join his family to one of America's greatest dynasties, marrying Consuelo Vanderbilt. Etienne evinced far less ambition. All he'd ever cared about was horses.

Whatever Etienne lacked in ambition, though, he made up for with personal charm and resourcefulness. He was what the French call *débrouillard*—someone who just gets things done. Perhaps this was part of what drew Balsan to Coco, whom he surely recognized as a fellow *débrouillarde*—having already propelled herself so very far from her origins.

Chanel was hardly a virgin when she arrived at Royallieu, but she was innocent of the ways of the leisured gentry. The exterior of the château may have looked reassuringly familiar to her—like Aubazine, it was a former abbey, a great medieval stone fortress—but what went on inside had little to do with religion. Balsan ran the estate like a kind of upscale fraternity house. No one had a job, everyone was young, and life revolved around horses by day and parties by night. When not in Compiègne, the gang traveled to other major horse-racing venues, including the Hippodrome de Longchamp and the Hippodrome de Vincennes, outside of Paris.

The women at Royallieu may have been "irregulars," but even within this group, Coco was an outcast. In addition to Emilienne, the celebrated courtesans frequenting Royallieu included dancer Liane de Pougy, beautiful singer Marthe Davelli (dark-haired and slim, she resembled Coco), and noted actress Gabrielle Dorziat.

These women had all been consorts to royalty or the haute aristocracy. Davelli, for example, was the mistress of sugar baron Constant Say. Pougy (born Anne Marie Chassaigne, in humble circumstances) had a long affair with the Viscount de Pougy, whose name she took, and later married Prince Georges Ghika of Moldavia, becoming a bona fide princess.

Not only were these women entirely at ease with wellborn men, they looked the part. These *grandes horizontales*—in the wonderful French expression—were professional beauties, experts in the art of self-presentation. They knew how to mold their generous figures with corsets. They wore their long hair in elaborate coiffures, topped with equally elaborate hats and veils. They traveled with trunks bursting with expensive dresses sewn from miles of silk and velvet, which they adorned with priceless jewels—badges of honor earned through distinguished service to "horizontality." And unlike society women, these ladies—who had real stage experience—knew all about makeup and didn't shy away from using it. In other words, the women of Royallieu were artists, and their masterpieces were themselves. They had learned long ago how to use their beauty to manipulate the world and one another. Many of them dabbled in lesbianism.

Chanel watched and learned. She found these women irresistible, if intimidating. But she had none of the right tools to emulate them—no fine wardrobe, no jewels, not even any curves to pour into a tightly laced gown. Boyish, slim hipped, and flat chested, Coco knew that copying Emilienne and the others would not suit her. Besides, although he was generous in many ways, Balsan was not given to lavish spending, and offered her no jewels or gowns. But *débrouillarde* as ever, Coco found her way.

Since most daylight hours at Royallieu were filled with equestrian activities, Coco focused on dressing for these. Aware that she looked especially fetching in schoolgirl or tomboyish styles, she created variations on these, often cadging items from Etienne's closets. Photographs from this period show Chanel in open-collared men's shirts worn with little schoolgirl ties, oversize tweed coats borrowed from Etienne, and simple straw boater hats, like the ones the men were wearing. These little boaters looked effortlessly chic next to the heavy and ornate concoctions typical of the period ("enormous pies balanced on heads, monuments of feathers, fruits, egrets," as Chanel described them).

And while Etienne did not offer to buy her fine clothes, he did arrange for her to visit a modest tailor in town, on the rue Croix-Saint-Ouen—where liveried servants and local groomsmen bought their clothes. Decades later, Chanel recalled the tailor's shock when she walked into his shop, which smelled, she said, like horses. No young ladies had ever sought his services before. But Coco knew what she wanted— a boy's riding costume with jodhpurs, like the ones worn by the English grooms she'd met at Royallieu. The tailor complied, and at such a reasonable price that Coco had enough left over for new riding boots.

The outfit was not just for show. Coco had figured out that success at Royallieu meant excelling at horsemanship. With the steely determination that would never desert her, Chanel took up riding. The result exceeded everyone's expectations. Etienne taught her to ride—and not sidesaddle, the way of delicate ladies in petticoats, but astride, like a serious male equestrian. Years later, in the salty language of stable workers, Coco confided the secret she'd discovered to maintaining a proper seat while riding: "You have to imagine that you have a precious pair of balls [here she made a cupping gesture] and that it would be out of the question to rest your weight upon them." For the rest of her life, Coco would benefit from this ability to think—and act—like a man.

Although Chanel rarely discussed her days at Royallieu, her stint there was extensive—probably close to six years. Aside from the parties, the riding, and the field trips to racetracks, château life for this cohort was fairly idle. Coco enjoyed walking the beautiful grounds and communing with the animals kept at the estate, especially one mischievous monkey that Balsan had adopted. The others relied upon social amusements, holding costume parties or playing practical jokes on one another. Balsan famously invited a bishop to dinner one night, exhorting his friends to dress modestly and behave correctly—no profanity, no sacrilege. The bishop arrived in full church regalia, but soon fell far short of all social or religious protocol. Drinking heavily, he proceeded to attack one of the housemaids and then began lewdly propositioning some of the men present. Balsan's dinner guests were horror-struck—until Etienne revealed that the bishop was actually an actor from Paris, and a friend of Marthe Davelli's. Etienne and Marthe had cooked up the entire scheme as a lark. Such were the high jinks Coco encountered at Royallieu.

Coco was shocked by this decadent atmosphere. Speaking to Louise de Vilmorin, she described life with Balsan's friends as a "vast game for the wealthy.... They were rich: they knew no hindrances. Money granted them freedom." Coco had no money of her own yet, but she did have leisure—which felt awfully good to her. She gained a reputation for lounging in bed for long hours every day, drinking café au lait and reading her cheap novels, sometimes not rising till past noon. And while Balsan and his friends were all young and relatively freethinking, certain social hierarchies still prevailed. Coco did not enjoy the same status as some of the other houseguests, and when more proper visitors arrived—say a married society lady—gamine orphans were invited to take their meals apart, with château employees. Even at the racetrack, whenever titled wives or parents were around, Balsan carefully kept Coco on the sidelines, with the bookies and the prostitutes. She was not permitted to enter the winner's circle. Such treatment surely rankled, but Coco never complained—either at the time or afterward. She expressed only gratitude for Balsan, with whom she remained friendly throughout her life.

But the languid habits of rich courtesans did not entirely suit Coco, and neither did the second-tier social status she had yet to shake. Chanel would never be mistress of Royallieu, and she knew it. Balsan was fond of her, and they surely slept together, but Coco and Etienne were not in love. They were more like erotic comrades.

The comforts of Royallieu, moreover, did nothing to attenuate Coco's yearning for independence. She was all too aware of the dangers of relying on men, and still burned to be special in some way. No longer hoping for a stage career, Coco sought another way to turn the spotlight on herself: "I wanted to escape, and to become the center of a universe of my own creation, instead of remaining on the margins or even becoming part of other people's universe."

Coco's escape path gradually came into focus. It lay, she discovered, precisely in her difference, in the unique style she was creating for herself out of necessity. The boyishly simple style Coco sported looked irresistibly fresh and modern next to the floor-sweeping skirts, petticoats, and corseted bodices of her colleagues at Royallieu. In following her own contrarian instincts and tricking herself out like one of Balsan's stable grooms, Coco set off her first fashion craze. Her little riding costume, man's overcoat, and cunning straw hats seemed to render obsolete all the heavy finery of Royallieu's feminine set. Chanel could see this herself: "The era of extravagant dressing of which I had dreamed, of dresses worn by heroines, was no more.... I knew that rich materials didn't suit me.... I stuck with my ... cheap clothes." Soon, the fabled beauties of Royallieu were trooping up the stairs to Coco's third-floor bedroom to try on her hats, jockeying for position in front of the mirror to admire themselves in her creations.

Aware that Coco was restless, Etienne encouraged her to try her hand at millinery. To him, making hats for her friends seemed like the perfect distraction for his bored pet. Chanel jumped at the chance. She set about buying dozens of basic straw hats (at Galeries Lafayette, during trips to Paris) and decorating them in her room, much as she once had while visiting her aunt Louise back in Varennes. The hats were a sensation, not least because they fit a woman's head. Coco had always worn her own hats low on her forehead, to keep them on in the wind, she said. But most ladies' hats at this time simply balanced atop their heads like plates, held on with pins and veils—a custom Chanel found absurd and impractical.

With the likes of Emilienne d'Alençon wearing Coco's creations, it was only a matter of time before other high-profile ladies started coveting her hats as well. At first, when asked where they'd procured their charming new headwear, Coco's friends would fib, vaguely citing Paris shops. Soon enough, however, Chanel's name was mentioned. Suddenly, she had a little business on her hands. Or rather, she almost did: A milliner can't operate out of a château bedroom. Chanel wanted her own store and approached the only benefactor she knew for help, Etienne.

This was more than Balsan had bargained for. It was one thing to encourage Coco's little hat hobby, quite another to support her in a serious business venture. Besides, women like Coco didn't work or own businesses. Balsan was more than skeptical, but did offer the use of his Paris *garconnière,* or bachelor pad, which he still kept at 160, boulevard Malesherbes, in the eighth arrondissement. He'd housed several mistresses there over the years, but never one with a hat shop. Coco began to travel back and forth from Royallieu to Paris.

It has often been speculated that, on one occasion in 1909, Coco sought special medical attention in Paris—of the kind offered by underground professionals known euphemistically as *faiseuses d'ange,* or "angel makers." Friends whispered for years that she had fallen prey to the fate of so many women in her situation—pregnancy. If Coco underwent an abortion, she did not speak of it, but biographer Marcel Haedrich, who interviewed many of Chanel's acquaintances, gives credence to this story. A backstreet abortion, furthermore, would explain Coco's lifelong inability to bear children.

From that point in 1909 onward, while Chanel continued to pursue her new career and her association with Balsan, she seemed to have changed—perhaps as a result of the abortion. She grew tired of the frivolities at Royallieu. Coco needed a more serious life and a more serious love.

CHAPTER THREE

DESIGNING TOGETHER

COCO CHANEL AND
ARTHUR EDWARD "BOY" CAPEL

The boy was handsome, dark, seductive. He was more than handsome, he was magnificent. I admired his nonchalance, his green eyes. He rode proud horses, and powerful ones. I fell in love with him. I had never loved [Etienne Balsan]. Between this Englishman and me, not one word was exchanged. . . . He was the only man I ever loved. He died. I have never forgotten him. He was the great chance of my life. . . . He was for me my father, my brother, my whole family.

—COCO CHANEL

Chanel's account of her first meeting with Arthur Edward "Boy" Capel might have been lifted from one of the sentimental novels she loved. Often, in recalling the details, she condensed months of her acquaintance with Capel into a moment of wordless mutual understanding, a *coup de foudre* when the pair locked eyes while riding horses in the southwestern French town of Pau. (Paul Morand saw the story's literary potential and fictionalized it in his novel *Lewis and Irene*.) According to Chanel, when Boy informed her that he would be leaving on the morning train for Paris, she dropped everything to follow him, showing up at the train station the next day, without so much as a suitcase. Seeing her there, an unsurprised Boy simply "opened his arms" to her, thus beginning their decadelong romance.

Arthur "Boy" Capel

While Coco doubtless embellished the details (and definitely brought a suitcase), the import of the story lies in the certainty it conveys. She met Boy when she was twenty-five, and his would always remain that pair of open arms she fell into effortlessly, the one perfect fit. Coco was right; Boy was the "chance of her life"—a potent catalyst setting off an astonishing reaction.

It is possible that the two did meet on horseback. It is just as likely that they met at Royallieu in 1908 when Boy, who knew Balsan through aristocratic polo circles, began frequenting the estate. And although the course of their early interactions may not have run as swiftly or as novelistically as Chanel would have it, theirs was a genuine and long-lasting love, by far the most important relationship Chanel ever had. "He gave birth to me," Chanel said of Capel and, metaphorically, it was so. Coco became "Coco" via Boy's love and tutelage. He awoke her mind, thrilled her body, taught her to think, inspired her business acumen, and introduced her to art, literature, politics, music, and philosophy.

Balsan had offered amiable companionship and some limited financial support—he had opened an important new window for Coco. But Boy flung open the doors. He could "see" Coco, looking beyond her façade of sharp-witted little seamstress to the hungry, brilliant, yearning spirit beneath. Boy and Coco's love affair lent shape not only to the rest of Chanel's personal life, but to the course of her global empire, engendering much of the liberating quality we still see in the Chanel aesthetic. Capel set Coco free and, in doing so, he set off a fashion juggernaut for women—a new approach to dress that contained within it an emancipatory impulse.

It was a philosophy inextricable from Boy's own highly considered and erudite views of international politics, to which Coco was exposed by virtue of his connections and influence. In fact, we can clearly see the early relationship between Chanel's fashion revolution and European politics in the course of her relationship with Capel. Coco Chanel owes her ongoing role as a revered figure of female freedom to the transformation she underwent—personally and professionally—from 1908 to 1918, the "Boy" years. New discoveries about Capel's mysterious life and work, moreover, help explain the unique bond that united this couple.

Deeply scholarly and intellectually voracious, Boy lived for ideas. He pondered questions of social justice, soul and spirit, economics, and foreign policy, and wrote two intriguing books on these subjects (the second published posthumously). He was also a true cultural hybrid, perfectly bilingual in the languages of his French mother and English father. Although educated in England, he was a longtime resident of Paris, and—unlike most of the crowd at Royallieu—completely at home amid the pulsing, vital culture of the capital.

But Capel distinguished himself most sharply from Balsan and company by virtue of his understanding of a concept unfamiliar at Royallieu: work. Balsan's male friends were either titled aristocrats or members of the long-standing haute bourgeoisie. Such men did not hold jobs or have professions. But the Capel family's fortune was new, barely one generation old. Boy's father, Arthur Joseph Capel, had been born to modest circumstances—his mother before him (Boy's grandmother) had been a lodging housekeeper from Ireland. Boy's father had made his fortune—in coal shipping and ocean liners—only within the years since his marriage to Boy's mother, Berthe Lorin Capel. Watching his father develop and nurture the family business, Boy acquired an entrepreneurial spirit. By 1901, Arthur Joseph Capel was retired and living comfortably on his investments. Boy, though, not content to live on family money, worked for his living and, in time, greatly increased the family's holdings and wealth.

While Coco fashioned her hats in Etienne's Paris bachelor pad at 160, boulevard Malesherbes, Boy stayed nearby in his own Paris apartment, just steps away at 138, boulevard Malesherbes. (It is not clear if Capel had chosen this apartment for its proximity to his friend Balsan, or to be nearer Coco.) He admired Coco and listened to her dreams. He began sending his glamorous lady friends over to Coco's studio to see her hats. Coco's charming designs and winning manner turned them all into devoted new customers.

Like the peddlers from whom she was descended, Chanel turned out to be a natural saleswoman. Soon her business had expanded to the point where she needed help. Her younger sister, Antoinette, was now living in Vichy and trying, just as Coco had, with little success, to become a cabaret singer. Aunt Adrienne (subsidized by her lover, Maurice de Nexon) had been helping Antoinette a bit financially, but now a far better prospect glimmered. Coco summoned her sister to Paris to help out on boulevard Malesherbes.

In the archives of the Maison Chanel, the first entry in the earliest available business logbook bears the date January 1, 1910. Carefully handwritten there, in fountain pen, is the name "Mademoiselle Chanel, Antoinette," described as a *vendeuse* (saleswoman), working on commission—earning 10 percent on all paid sales. Antoinette did not have Coco's talent or intense intelligence, but she had inherited other Chanel family virtues. She was indisputably pretty and engaging, and—most important—a hard and dedicated worker. She jumped at the chance to move to the capital.

Antoinette settled into the Malesherbes apartment. By day, she welcomed clients and helped them select hats, and at night, she slept in the back bedroom—which Coco had been using. This inconvenienced no one, though, since Boy and Coco were spending ever more time together, and on nights when she stayed in town, Chanel could be found down the street at Capel's apartment.

Etienne was not unaware of the situation. Technically, Chanel still "belonged" to him; she was his *irrégulière*. But as a man of the world, Balsan accepted Coco and Boy's romance, seeing it as little more than a harmless dalliance. He had more than enough young beauties to amuse him at Compiègne. And although skeptical of Chanel's business venture, he continued to provide her with some support. As Coco's business grew, she had begun selling clothes alongside her hats—simple jersey separates with a tomboyish feel—and so, in addition to lending her his Malesherbes apartment, Etienne arranged for Chanel to learn from a fashion expert, hiring accomplished Parisian seamstress Lucienne Rabaté.

Despite her youth—she was three years Coco's junior—Rabaté had already enjoyed a long career in couture. Unlike Chanel, she had undergone formal training in fashion and had risen in the ranks of the industry at the prestigious house of Chez Lewis, moving from apprentice up through such stages as *garnisseuse* (working with accessories, or "garnishes") and *aide-seconde*, before finally achieving the rank of *petite première*, charged with greeting clients and supervising their fittings. For an untutored novice like Coco, Lucienne was a precious asset. She brought with her not only her vast experience in both sewing and business management, but also two of her very capable assistants and many of her high-society and celebrity customers from Chez Lewis.

But life in the makeshift studio on boulevard Malesherbes bore little resemblance to the orderly, professional environment Lucienne had known. While sales were promising, Coco and Antoinette knew nothing about running a business or keeping books. And Coco, imperious by nature, resented Lucienne's attempts to intervene, and resisted ceding any authority or decision making to her. What's more, the Chanel girls lacked the discretion and decorum normally found in the best salons. Giddy with their new adventure, playing shop in a posh Paris bachelor pad, the sisters laughed and joked across the studio throughout the day, sometimes launching into the bawdy songs they'd learned as aspiring chanteuses. They ignored Lucienne's pleas for restraint, just as they ignored her attempts to weed out, or at least segregate, some of the less "desirable" customers—women she deemed too disreputable to mingle with their society customers. Coco flouted such notions regularly, seeing no problem in scheduling simultaneous fittings for both Henri de Rothschild's wife, the Baroness Rothschild, and his mistress, the beautiful actress Gilda Darthy. A frustrated Lucienne finally walked out—only to be lured back for a time by Coco, whose skills as a smooth-talking saleswoman grew sharper by the day.

After one year, with business thriving, Coco longed to expand beyond Etienne's apartment, but for that, she needed money and space. For the moment, neither seemed forthcoming. Balsan remained skeptical about Coco's real prospects, and put off her requests for a loan. Capel, though, thought Coco was onto something. He was falling in love with her, and he admired her ambition. He talked about Chanel's drive and ability with his childhood friend Elisabeth de Gramont, who recalled Capel's remarks: "You don't understand how much idleness can weigh on some women, especially when they are intelligent. And Coco is intelligent.... She has the qualities necessary for a businesswoman." As they fell deeper into their romance, Chanel prevailed upon Capel to approach Balsan on her behalf.

Balsan allowed himself to be won over. Together, the two men came up with a plan: Balsan would permit Coco to take full possession of his Malesherbes apartment as her atelier, and Capel would supply her with the additional funds needed. Coco was thrilled. With the entire apartment at their disposal for the business, the girls converted the bedroom into a second studio space. Antoinette would now work there during the days, but spend her nights in a newly rented room, nearby at no. 8, avenue du Parc Monceau. Coco had stopped using the bedroom entirely.

Under Boy's encouragement, Coco started to see herself in a new light, as someone with talent and a future, someone worthy of respect. "He listened to me and gave me the impression of having something to say," she confided to Vilmorin. For Boy, taking Coco seriously also meant subjecting her to some brutal honesty, calling her on her mean-spirited humor (she would defensively insult other women: "They're so ugly!... so dirty!"), her lack of education, even her poor eyesight. He talked to her of politics, and gave her books to read. She welcomed even his harshest criticism: "In teaching me, he didn't coddle me," she told Paul Morand. "He would critique my behavior, 'You acted badly,' 'you lied,' 'you were wrong.' He had the gentle authority of men who really know women, who love them without being blind." Boy didn't want Coco to be blind, either, and insisted she see an eye doctor about her severe myopia. Setting aside even vanity under Boy's suasion, Coco submitted to wearing the eyeglasses she had long needed badly. The new clarity of her vision proved a mixed blessing, given her critical nature. "I found people so ugly! For the first time, I was seeing them as they were, and not as I imagined them." (Later, Chanel convinced the world's women that spectacles—especially those in tortoiseshell frames like her own—were not a sign of a physical defect, but the chicest of accessories.) Slowly, Boy would sharpen her vision in countless other ways as well.

By 1910, Balsan could no longer ignore the obvious—his close friend had seduced Coco away entirely. Etienne finally confronted her, asking "Where are you and Boy these days?" to which she replied, "We are where men and women generally are together." Balsan then turned to Capel, who confirmed it: "I adore her," he told Etienne, upon which (according to most accounts), Balsan ceded gracefully. "If she loves you, she's yours." As amicable as this exchange sounds, some accounts suggest a tad more rancor was actually attached to the proceedings. Quitterie Tempé, Balsan's granddaughter, has said that Etienne suffered considerable pain upon losing Coco. And everyone agrees that shortly after the breakup, Balsan left on an extended trip to Argentina—perhaps to distance himself from his sorrow.

Thus began Coco and Boy's initial idyll together in Paris—a period that coincides precisely with the true start of Coco's business career. The two events, in fact, cannot be separated. Chanel owed her launch into the fashion world to Capel's love, his inspiration, and—not least—to his generous financial help.

Coco and Boy formed a highly unusual couple for their day. In 1910, no Parisian sophisticate would have batted an eye at a wealthy bachelor supporting a pretty, lower-class girl. But between Boy and Coco, more was happening. Capel was helping Chanel transform herself yet again, encouraging her as she turned from courtesan into something almost unheard-of for the era: a self-supporting businesswoman. At the same time, he was collaborating with her on an even more surprising venture: the birth of the *couturière*-celebrity, a fashion designer whose life as well as work would be accepted into society. We know the confluence of early events that drove Chanel in her ambition, but what accounts for Capel's open-mindedness?

Capel's background has remained relatively opaque, despite attempts by many Chanel biographers to clarify it. For nearly a century, persistent rumors have suggested that Boy was actually the illegitimate son of a powerful man—possibly one of the famous Péreire brothers, Isaac and Emile—two wealthy Paris-based Portuguese-Jewish bankers. (Paul Morand incorporated this possibility into his novel *Lewis and Irene*.) Rumors of that nature have served as partial explanations for Boy and Coco's special rapport—which makes sense. A shared bond of illegitimacy would certainly have enhanced mutual understanding and given Boy more sympathy for Chanel's painful childhood. Yet no evidence substantiates Boy's illegitimacy.

Newly discovered information, however, sheds light on the little-known maternal side of Capel's family. Edmonde Charles-Roux claimed that Capel never spoke of his mother, and until now, neither has anyone else. His mother's life, though, explains a good deal about Capel's attraction to Coco Chanel, and, by extension, what twists of fate led to the founding, against all odds, of the Chanel empire.

Although born in France in 1856, Berthe Andrée Anne Eugénie Lorin Capel spent at least part of her youth in London's posh Kensington district, as a boarder at a French Catholic convent school for upper-class girls. Serving as the school's "spiritual director" was none other than the handsome and glamorous Reverend Monsignor Thomas Capel, a well-known clergyman with a libertine private life—and the elder brother of Arthur Joseph Capel, Boy Capel's future father. The reverend, in other words, was Boy Capel's future uncle.

On July 24, 1873, the Reverend Capel officiated at the wedding of his younger brother, Arthur Joseph Capel, age twenty-five, and his former student, eighteen-year-old Berthe Lorin. Now unearthed, the marriage certificate provides vital and previously unknown information about Berthe.

After leaving secondary school, girls of the upper classes generally returned home to make their society debuts and find a husband. Yet upon graduation, Berthe Lorin did not return to France. The marriage certificate lists her address as 12 Scarsdale Villas, Kensington—a town house just blocks away from the convent school. Why did she not go home? It is possible she was not welcome.

That something was amiss in Berthe's family is confirmed by the marriage certificate: The space on the form reserved for the name of the bride's father has been left blank, which, according to Great Britain's General Register Office, "would suggest illegitimacy." Stranger still, no members of Berthe's family seem to have been present at the ceremony. Of the two witnesses required by law, contrary to convention, neither hailed from the bride's side, nor was there any signature granting the

Marriage certificate for Arthur Capel and Berthe Lorin, Boy Capel's parents

parental permission normally required to authorize the marriage of an underage girl.

Berthe Lorin clearly came from an affluent French family, yet, she did not marry into society. Her new husband, Arthur Joseph Capel, had worked as an office clerk and lived with his widowed mother. After the wedding, he and Berthe moved in with Monsignor Thomas Capel. This marriage, then, has the air of an expedient "arrangement." Some might guess at an unplanned pregnancy, but the evidence points elsewhere.

Despite his humble professional beginnings, by 1876, within three years of marrying his teenage French bride, Arthur Joseph Capel met with some real prosperity—via new French connections. He became a partner in Chamot and Capel, a shipping concern that acted as the London agent for the Paris-based French General Transatlantic company. A closer look at Capel's partner, Alexandre Chamot, reveals the likely source of those rumors about Boy Capel's provenance: Chamot was a brother-in-law of Jacob Péreire, founder of the Jewish banking fortune. Here, then, lies a link between the Capel family and the Péreires— although it exists one generation earlier than previously believed. Rather than the illegitimate son of a Péreire brother, Boy Capel may have, in fact, been an illegitimate *grandson* of this eminent clan.

Berthe and Arthur Capel postponed starting their family until they were financially stable. Not until 1877, four years into her marriage— and one year into her husband's new business arrangement—did Berthe give birth to daughter Marie, her first child (which likely dispenses with out-of-wedlock pregnancy as the reason for this union), soon to be followed by Edith, Bertha, and finally the couple's only son, Arthur Edward, or "Boy." In 1879, Chamot and Capel dissolved their partnership and Arthur founded a new business, listing himself as sole proprietor. From then on, his success accelerated, as he expanded his business internationally, branching out into coal, insurance, and transportation.

In the late 1880s, the family relocated to Paris, living on the avenue d'Iéna, in the very affluent sixteenth arrondissement. There, Berthe Capel blossomed into a celebrated society hostess, entertaining everyone from Russian dukes to performers from the Folies-Bergère. Society reporters chronicled her activities, noting her great beauty, fashionable clothes, and her connection to Monsignor Capel.

Arthur Joseph Capel was a smart, capable, and highly ambitious man, but it is obvious that someone was helping him from behind the scenes. In this case, coincidence may indicate causality. That is, it is logical to infer a connection between Arthur Joseph Capel's marriage to Berthe, a well-heeled but forsaken French girl, and the life-changing, lucrative partnership with affluent Frenchman Alexandre Chamot.

What is probable is that Berthe posed some sort of problem or inconvenience to her French family—perhaps illegitimacy—which led to her being sent abroad to England. Despite this, someone—who would not identify himself—was looking out for her, arranging a fine education and the chance for her to marry. Berthe was beautiful and accomplished, and as a dowry, Arthur Joseph Capel would have received a business partnership. The offer would have been irresistible. (Boy Capel would later write quite compellingly of the sexism inherent in society marriages and dowries.)

Berthe Capel died of unspecified causes at forty-seven, in Paris, on August 5, 1902. Her death certificate describes Madame Capel as "the daughter of a father and mother on whom we have no information." Newspaper accounts reveal that Berthe had some fortune of her own: She bequeathed to her son valuable shares in a coal shipping company, though it is unclear from whom she had acquired these.

These details about Berthe Lorin Capel grant us a fresh perspective on Coco and Boy's romance. Boy had been raised by a mother who'd spent her teens far from home, cared for and educated by nuns—a woman with no family present even on her wedding day—a woman not unlike Coco Chanel. While Berthe Capel clearly came from a social background far grander than Chanel's, she seems to have known what it meant to be alone in the world and to have something to hide. Growing up with such a mother would have sensitized Boy to an unusual story like Chanel's.

If Berthe Lorin enabled Boy to empathize with Coco, it was surely his father, Arthur Joseph, who'd taught him how to help her. Having watched his father develop his shipping empire, Boy knew what success looked like, and how to attain it. But Boy was far more than a canny businessman; he was learned. Berthe and Arthur Joseph had sent their only son first to a Paris Jesuit school, l'Institution Sainte-Marie, then to Beaumont, an exclusive Jesuit boarding school for boys in the English countryside, sometimes called "the Catholic Eton," and finally on to Stonyhurst, the most prominent and rigorous Jesuit institution in England. At both British schools, Boy had distinguished himself, winning several academic prizes. (All her life, Chanel kept in her library a beautifully illustrated book Capel had won as a prize at Beaumont in 1892, when he was twelve: *The Common Objects of the Seashore,* by J. G. Wood.) After his studies, he entered his father's business, while continuing to study philosophy, political science, history, and world religions.

Boy had traveled farther afield than did many in his cohort, spending extended periods at least twice in the United States, and possibly traveling to India as well. By the time Boy met Coco, he was a polished, erudite, and wealthy young man with a discerning eye. When he trained that eye on Coco, she became a project for him to nurture.

One of the first steps toward nurturing the Chanel enterprise entailed moving Coco and company out of their boulevard Malesherbes studio. In 1910, Boy subsidized Coco's move into new, more spacious commercial quarters. He helped her choose 21, rue Cambon for the site of her new boutique—an inspired location and just a few doors from where the Chanel store still stands today—at no. 31, rue Cambon. The rue Cambon nestles in the center of the first arrondissement, in the sanctum sanctorum of Parisian culture and luxury commerce, just steps from the Tuileries, the Louvre, the Palais-Royal, the Opéra, and the historic landmark and commercial mecca that is the Place Vendôme, home to the Ritz hotel—where Coco would later live for decades. Capel also helped her find a new studio head—or *première*—for Cambon, Angèle Aubert, a superb seamstress and manager who remained with Coco for years.

Together, Boy and Coco also moved their personal residence, leaving

Capel's Malesherbes apartment for a love nest on the avenue Gabriel, an elegant street that begins at the Place de la Concorde and runs parallel to the Champs-Elysées. (Boy retained ownership of the Malesherbes bachelor pad, though, as attested to by his use of letterhead stationery bearing that address, as late as 1915.) Living on the avenue Gabriel put the couple within a few meters of the Elysée Palace, home to the president of France, as well as several international embassies on the rue du Faubourg Saint-Honoré. Their apartment windows opened out over rows of classic Parisian chestnut trees, which bloom riotously pink in springtime.

On avenue Gabriel, Coco enjoyed that once-in-a-lifetime pleasure of decorating the first home one shares with a lover, reveling in being a grown-up, fully sexualized (if not, in this case, legitimately married) "we." Boy had already developed his own tastes in interior design and opened Coco's eyes to the beauties of his favorite antiques and offbeat *objets.* He introduced her, for instance, to his beloved Coromandel screens. These folding dark lacquered wood panels date back at least to seventeenth-century China (although they derive their name from the Indian region to which they were imported in the eighteenth century). Sometimes inlaid with jade, porcelain, or iridescent abalone, they feature delicately painted natural landscapes—birds in flight, trees, flowers, and snowcapped mountains—or decorative interior motifs depicting fans, palaces, and human figures in flowing Asian robes. Capel may have known and admired the beauty of Coromandel screens before Coco ever did, but they exerted an instant magnetic pull on her. She would spend a lifetime collecting them. "The first time I saw a Coromandel, I cried, 'How beautiful!' They play the role that tapestries did in the Middle Ages," she told Morand.

Chanel would come to be known for a fashion sensibility distinguished by modern, airy lightness, crisp lines, and sparse adornments, but under Boy's guidance (and with the help of his pocketbook), she indulged a somewhat different aesthetic sense at home. The avenue Gabriel apartment reflected Coco and Boy's love of deep, golden tones, ornate lacquered furniture, mirrors in gilt frames, floral designs, English silver, Oriental vases, white satin bedding, and sofas piled with soft, puffy cushions—all enclosed by those dark folding screens. Coco had the rugs dyed a deep beige, to give them, she said, an earthy color. The resultant décor communicated at once a warm, embracing feeling and a tasteful aura of privilege and old money. For the rest of her life, in every home she occupied, Coco would re-create for herself the look of this early apartment—the only place it seems she ever felt truly settled and at ease. She would also keep a white marble bust of a handsome young clergyman atop her mantelpiece. It was the focal point of her living room, and she told friends and visitors it was a distant relative of hers, the canonized Reverend Father Chanel, killed by "African natives" while doing missionary work in the nineteenth century. A closer look reveals that it is, in fact, Monsignor Thomas Capel, Boy's uncle. She had claimed Boy's family as her own.

Not even the delight of new love deterred Coco from pursuing, for a time, her earliest and most deeply held ambition: to become a star. Singing, she knew, was out, and so in 1911 she switched her focus to dance. Having been introduced to much of the Parisian avant-garde by Boy, Coco learned about the new "barefoot" dance of American sensation Isadora Duncan. A proponent of a free, less constrained form of dance, Duncan was drawn to the movement depicted on ancient Greek pottery and friezes, and had traveled to the Acropolis to stand among the ruins and commune with the Hellenic world, "inhaling inspiration," as she put it. Now she'd come to Paris with her troupe of young girls, known as the Isadorables.

Coco attended one of Duncan's salon performances on the avenue Villiers—at which the dancer appeared nude beneath her diaphanous toga—and claimed to be unimpressed. Coco never cared for nudity and dismissed Duncan as "a Muse for the provinces." But she was intrigued by another young dancer who traveled in modernist circles and was currently the mistress of actor Charles Dullin: Elise Toulemon, otherwise known by her Hellenic stage name, Caryathis. Although a classically trained ballerina, Toulemon practiced "eurythmics," a new, improvisational, natural approach to movement, invented by Swiss educator Emile

Jaques-Dalcroze. (Later, Caryathis—like Coco—would collaborate closely with the Ballets Russes.)

Coco began trekking up to the rue Lamarck in Montmartre for early morning class with Toulemon. Montmartre was already the simmering epicenter of modernist artists of every stripe, and several members of Chanel's future coterie were already living and working there, including Pablo Picasso, Max Jacob, and poet Pierre Reverdy. Though Coco was dedicated to her new pursuit, it was not to be. She had little appreciable talent for dance, and Caryathis told her so. Upon this, Coco—now twenty-eight—finally put away her stage dreams. She did, however, continue studying with Caryathis for a time, as a way of keeping her body toned and fit, she said. And the study of eurythmics may have benefited Coco even more than she realized. Her fresh modern fashion designs, which would bring Chanel the stardom she longed for, actually displayed some Dalcrozian qualities. In their striking ease, simplicity, and heightened sense of bodily awareness and harmony, Chanel clothes suggest, even now, a sartorial translation of some of the guiding principles of early modern dance.

Chanel's evolving fashion sensibility owed a good deal to Boy Capel's aesthetic influence as well. As she had with Etienne, Coco now regularly pilfered objects from Boy's closet—especially sportswear items such as the polo shirts he favored for beach weekends, English schoolboy-style blazers, and loose-fitting sweaters. And she continued to fancy masculine-style riding attire, too. Seeing this, Boy insisted her riding clothes be of the finest material and cut: "Capel said to me, 'I am going to have your clothes redone elegantly, by an English tailor.'" He sent her to the finest British menswear tailor in Paris and had a suit made for Coco that fit her to perfection—a long, slim, asymmetrical jacket and trousers, in a shimmering pearl gray. Coco wore the outfit when she and Boy visited Royallieu to go riding with Balsan—with whom they stayed on good terms. Coco's newfound elegance stunned the old gang.

While hats still made up the bulk of her business, a few of the tomboyish pieces she was now wearing found their way into her store—or rather into her *stores*. In 1913, Boy had the great foresight to encourage Coco to expand her Paris boutique and open a branch in the seaside resort of Deauville—where they spent summers, at the Hôtel Normandy. The new shop opened on the rue Gontaut-Biron, just across from Deauville's very grand casino. Chanel hired two local teenaged girls and hung out her first awning, on which black letters spelled out "Gabrielle Chanel," against a white background. The new store location proved as brilliantly chosen as the one on Cambon—rue Gontaut-Biron lay directly in the path of a constant stream of strolling aristocrats on holiday. Chanel and her staff had no qualms when it came to promoting their wares—as proved by an early article in the September 1913 issue of the woman's magazine *Femina*:

> *Deauville: At [Chanel's] "Frivolities" Shop, Rue de Gontaut Biron*. Every morning, at the chic time of day, groups form in front of this trendy new boutique. Sportsmen, foreign nobility, and artists call to one another and chat; some, friends of the establishment, approach passing ladies, inviting them to enter and select a hat, "Come dear Countess, a little hat, just one, for just five Louis!" And they enter, they chatter, they flirt, they show off their astonishing outfits.... Outside, it's a commotion, a double row of people sit and watch, contemplating, a double wave that rises ceaselessly toward the sea. It's Deauville passing by.

> Women: he wanted them all the time.... He wanted ... to study their profiles ... to cultivate their intelligence, to debauch them, to mould their characters, to get rid of them ... to stay in bed for days instructing them in strange literatures.
>
> **—PAUL MORAND, *LEWIS AND IRENE***

The years between 1910 and 1914, from age twenty-seven to thirty-one, were probably the best of Coco Chanel's life, bringing her fulfillment in the two realms Freud deemed necessary for happiness: love and

The fashionable crowds of the rue Gontaut-Biron, Deauville

work. Coco and Boy were not married, but together they enjoyed many domestic pleasures, including the pleasure of looking out for young André Palasse, Chanel's orphaned nephew. André had lodged with a country priest after the death of his mother, Julia, but by 1913, when André was nine, Coco and Boy had welcomed him into their home. They took him along when they traveled to Deauville, where he kept Coco company in her boutique.

The sight of the dark-haired little boy at Chanel's side invited gossip and speculation, despite Coco's repeated explanation that André was her nephew, not her son. (Capel's sister, Berthe, liked to bruit about that André was Coco's child by Boy, though she knew this to be impossible logistically.) And although he was assuredly not the child's father, Capel grew close to André, calling him "son," and taking an interest in his future. "Boy knew my father very well," recalled André's daughter Gabrielle Palasse-Labrunie. For a time, the little trio of Coco, Boy, and André Palasse looked and functioned much like the kind of nuclear family that Coco had never had before—and never would again.

But André did not fit perfectly into his aunt's elegant world. While he seemed to remember little of his mother, he still loved and missed the man he called "Monsieur le Curé"—the priest who'd been his guardian and sole tutor. The country cleric had not troubled about refining the boy's manners, and nine-year-old André evinced little interest in social decorum. His crude ways sometimes vexed Coco and Boy. Coco lamented, for example, André's audible burping at the table ("But Monsieur le Curé does it!" André would retort); and Boy balked when, while dining with him at the Rothschilds', the child mistook a finger bowl for a distasteful beverage and shouted, "I will not drink that!"

Deciding that her nephew had been "badly brought up," Chanel was adamant that André be turned into a gentleman. Her "son"—whether by nature or unofficial adoption—was a reflection of her, and would have to become learned, polished, courtly, and bilingual—as much like Boy Capel as possible.

With Capel's intervention, André was accepted into Beaumont College, Boy's Jesuit alma mater. The arrangement was ideal—Coco had neither the time nor, frankly, the inclination for the domestic duties of motherhood. She cared deeply for André, but she had a business, a love affair, and a social life to manage. Besides, at Beaumont, André would meet the right people and learn everything necessary to leap over many rungs on the social ladder, including perfect, unaccented English and the manners of an upper-class Briton. Still struggling to acclimate to her own dramatic social rise, Chanel was ensuring a far smoother ascent for her young charge—the greatest gift she could imagine giving him.

While André boarded away in England, Coco received instruction at home in Paris. Boy revealed to her the infinite joys of books and art, sharing with her his eclectic, even slightly mystical tastes. Like many progressive people of his generation, Boy had discovered theosophy—the movement devoted to investigating connections between humanity and the divine—propounded in the early twentieth century by Madame Helena Blavatsky and Rudolf Steiner, and studied by such modernist artists as Wassily Kandinsky, Piet Mondrian, and Kazimir Malevich. Coco joined Boy at the lectures on theosophy by Isabelle Mallet, at Paris's Société théosophique.

Chanel in her early twenties.
Coll. Taponier/Photo 12/The Image Works

The glamorous casino at Vichy

"Water girls" at La Grande Grille, the Vichy thermal spa
where Chanel may have worked

Chanel golfing, in her own sportswear, 1910. *Mary Evans/Epic/PVDE*

Three flowing jersey ensembles
by Chanel, as featured in
the magazine *Les Elégances
Parisiennes,* 1917. *Courtesy of Mary
Evans Picture Library/Epic*

Misia Sert, renowned patron of the arts and
Chanel's closest female friend,
in a 1907 portrait by Pierre-Auguste Renoir.
Roger-Viollet/The Image Works

Drawing of Chanel
beaded gown with
fringe, designed as a
stage costume for
Cecile Sorel, 1918.
Condé Nast

Chanel beaded evening dresses from the 1920s.
Collection of Phoenix Art Museum, gift of Mrs. Wesson Seyburn

Model in black Chanel
evening dress, 1928.
Courtesy of Mary *Evans
Picture Library/Epic/
Tallendier*

Chanel wearing her signature pearls backward,
the perfect symbol of social inversion, 1936.
Boris Lipnitzki/Roger-Viollet/The Image Works

Paul Iribe's illustration of fashions by Paul Poiret,
with furniture based on pieces designed by Iribe.
The Stapleton Collection/The Bridgeman Art Library

Iribe's vision of French arts
menaced by foreign, racially
"other" modernist influences,
1932

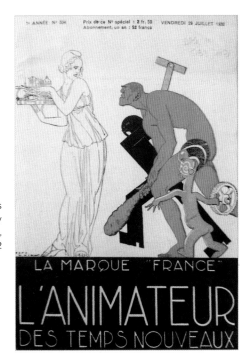

Coco as Marianne, bloodied and tormented,
as drawn by Iribe in *Le Témoin*

The side of Boy that drew him to such quasi-religious theories must have resonated with the peasant Catholic in Chanel. Like Boy, she'd grown up surrounded by the symbology of the church, but she'd also been steeped as a young child in the residual pagan beliefs of her rural ancestors—people who kept talismans and believed in curses. Her mystical side and his could commune over topics such as theosophy, and Capel's spirituality and Catholic training undoubtedly helped Coco to absorb and accept him as her teacher. Theosophy appealed to Coco, and in her later years, she referred to herself as "an old theosophist."

An ardent student of European philosophy, Boy read Voltaire, Rousseau, and Nietzsche; but he was equally drawn to Hindu theology, Old Testament exegesis, mathematics, science, east Asian history, and anything on art. He haunted art auction houses, with an eye especially for Chinese and Japanese art, and collected catalogs for these sales, which Coco kept in her own library for the rest of her life.

Boy also introduced Coco to poetry—especially Baudelaire's 1865 prose poem, "Knock Down the Poor!" ("Assommons les pauvres!") This still-shocking short piece skewers liberal pieties about the "deserving poor." In it, a man recounts beating an elderly beggar nearly to death: "I [broke] two of his teeth . . . grasped his throat . . . and began vigorously to beat his head against a wall." Just when the narrator believes he's killed the man, the tables turn: "[The beggar] hurled himself upon me, blackened both my eyes, [and] broke four of my teeth." This retaliatory violence thrills the (now-bloody) narrator, who believes he has "restored [the beggar] his pride and his life." Declaring, "Sir, you are my equal," the attacker then offers to "share his purse" with the beggar.

Chanel immediately grasped the poem's allegorical resonance for her life. Like Baudelaire's beggar, she shocked the world by aggressively avenging the wrong done to her, demanding that the privileged recognize her as an equal worthy of financial reward. Decades later, Chanel would tell an interviewer, "Boy Capel introduced me to 'Assommons les Pauvres!' . . . which informed my moral outlook. . . . I was that pauper whom Baudelaire needed to shake out of passivity."

That Boy pointed Coco toward the poem suggests that she had revealed to him her wretched early life and the bitterness it had sown in her. Perhaps he used it to urge her to action. Capel clearly saw himself as Chanel's teacher in myriad ways. He discouraged her, for example, from accepting conventional standards of beauty. While supremely attractive, Coco knew that her appearance did not conform to her era's notions of beauty. With her thin, boyish frame and long neck, "I didn't resemble anyone," she told Paul Morand. "I'm not pretty," she'd lament to Capel. But Boy had little patience for her insecurities: "Of course you're not pretty. But I have nothing more beautiful than you." It was effective. Coco tended to believe what Boy told her.

Actress Gabrielle Dorziat costumed in a Chanel hat and Jacques Doucet gown for *Le Diable Ermite,* 1913

According to Chanel, Boy also debunked some of her expectations of romantic love, finding them childish. When a petulant Coco, for example, whinged about not receiving flowers from him, Capel responded by having a bouquet delivered within the half hour. She was delighted. One half hour after that, another bouquet arrived, and then one more soon after. Coco grew bored and impatient with all the flowers—and that was the point. "Boy wanted to train me. I understood the lesson. He was training me in happiness," Chanel told Morand. "He was only happy in the company of the little provincial brunette, the undisciplined child I was. We never went out together (at that time, Paris still had certain rules). We put off such public expressions of sentiment for later, when we would be married."

Coco unquestionably wished to marry Boy. "We were made for each other," she said. But whatever he may have told her, Capel never intended to legitimize their union. For all his open-mindedness and genuine appreciation of Coco, Boy Capel was still a man of his times and class. He limited their appearances in public and introduced her only to some of his friends, mainly artists or intellectuals, including actress Cécile Sorel and newspaper mogul Alfred Edwards (whose wife, Misia, became Coco's lifelong best friend).

Theater artists like Sorel proved especially useful new friends, since Coco prevailed upon them to wear her hats in public and eventually convinced a few to wear her creations onstage. The lovely Gabrielle Dorziat—an acquaintance of Boy's whom Chanel had encountered at Royallieu—was among the first actresses to promote Chanel in this way. Starring in a 1912 adaptation of Maupassant's *Bel Ami*, Dorziat appeared in a Chanel hat, a simple broad-brimmed model adorned with a single dramatic plume. The rest of her costume had been designed by the most famous couturier in Paris, Jacques Doucet, who'd required some cajoling to permit his work to mingle onstage

Actress Cécile Sorel, costumed by Chanel in striped silk jersey for her role in *L'Abbé Constantin*, 1918

with that of a young upstart like Chanel. The following year, Dorziat sported a black satin hat by Chanel in a production of *Le Diable Ermite* (again paired with Doucet costumes). Chanel would continue providing hats, and soon entire costumes for theater (and later films) for the rest of her career.

Along with Boy Capel's artist friends, some of his more broad-minded British friends also met his new mistress. In their company, Boy and Coco would dine at Maxim's and the Café de Paris, visit art exhibitions, and attend the most glamorous musical and theater events. When Sergei Diaghilev shocked and dazzled Paris with his 1913 *Rite of Spring,* Coco attended opening night, escorted by power couple Charles Dullin and Caryathis. She seemed to be navigating perfectly through Parisian waters, with Boy removing most obstacles in her path. But this new freedom had its limits: Rarely, if ever, did Capel bring Coco into the drawing rooms of French society. France's titled class was not yet ready to welcome the likes of her, and Boy was clearly looking after his own interests. Introducing Coco into French salons might be a social gaffe from which an ambitious young man would never recover.

Coco tolerated such restrictions and—at least in retrospect—tended to put the best face on them. When she recalled, for example, how many evenings she and Boy spent home alone in their apartment, she claimed to have preferred this arrangement, giving the memory an exotic, slightly racy spin: "I have a harem woman side to me, which is quite happy with this kind of seclusion."

A classic example of the elaborate style Chanel rejected: a striped day dress by Charles Frederick Worth, 1900

The truth was, not only was Boy protecting his social reputation by hiding Coco, he was freeing himself to see other women. Capel loved Coco, but that did not hinder his pursuit of the many conquests that fell into his lap so easily. Any young man as handsome, charming, worldly, and rich as Boy Capel would have found it challenging to resist the seductions of Paris. But Boy was driven by more than pleasure. He had large-scale ambitions and clearly saw himself as a future world leader. He needed a suitable consort for such a life—not a seamstress, however dazzling.

Coco knew of Boy's other women but—at least in her recollection of these days—maintained an insouciant calm about it all. "He could sleep with all those ladies....I found it...a bit disgusting, but I didn't care," she recalled. She even claimed to have encouraged Boy to share the details of his conquests. In her telling, Boy rewarded her sangfroid with utter devotion, of soul if not of body.

> Deauville . . . was a perfect orgy of wealth and amusement.
> **—HELEN PEARL ADAM**

By the summer of 1914, the onset of World War I brought events far more momentous than Boy's indiscretions. When the German army invaded nearby Belgium and began making significant progress toward Paris, upscale French citizens sought refuge outside of the city. For many, Deauville beckoned as a safe haven, and Capel shepherded Coco up to the coast, insisting she stay there for her protection. Ever the businessman, he advised her to keep her Deauville shop open, which she did. The decision proved wise in several ways, for Deauville was becoming an outpost for wealthy women temporarily displaced from Paris. Deprived of their usual dressmakers and willing to pay highly inflated prices, these women needed more than just clothes—they needed a new style commensurate with a drastically changing world. Coco's fresh, minimalist style struck the perfect chord. The look she'd created for herself—born of her own limited funds, tomboyish temperament, social contrarianism, and instinctive desire for speed and freedom—now seemed to suit almost everyone. Somehow, through a kind of fashion alchemy, the Chanel look started feeling inevitable. A page had been turned.

> I became famous very suddenly, without realizing it.
> —COCO CHANEL

With her double status as fashionable boutique owner and companion of the dashing Boy Capel, Coco had become something of a personage in Deauville. While not yet accepted by society ladies, she aroused their curiosity. Count Jean-Louis de Faucigny-Lucinge, a long-standing acquaintance of Coco's, shared his mother's memories of Deauville, which sum up the contradictory nature of Chanel's renown at the time:

> A young designer established herself in Deauville, Gabrielle Chanel. She made ravishing hats that elegant women loved to order. She had been the mistress of Etienne Balsan and belonged, therefore, to a certain "class," or rather, she was *déclassée*. According to my mother, people visited [Chanel's] boutique out of curiosity or because they liked her clothes. But when she showed up at the Casino, on the arm of her English lover, whom everyone knew, Boy Capel, they'd "forget" entirely to greet her. She did not take offense, and played the game, aware that she belonged to the demi-monde. This ostracism . . . was, in truth, the spur of her irresistible social ascent.

The count was right—Coco was biding her time. Even while staying on the margins of society, she'd learned how to use that fact to attract attention. And Deauville, with its concentrated population of style mongers and people watchers, offered Chanel an ideal showcase for her unconventional look.

Coco developed a reputation for flouting convention. She thought nothing, for example, of going for a dip in the Atlantic Ocean—something society women rarely did. Odd as it seems to us today, only children, servants, and the occasional foreigner at Deauville and other resorts ever ventured into the sea; ladies merely gazed—fully dressed—upon it. Given the rarity of ocean bathing, Coco had little choice but to fashion her own swimsuits, which looked much like what men wore—two-piece ensembles consisting of knee-length jersey culottes and matching tank tops. Soon, though, as wartime rendered many such fine points of feminine decorum irrelevant, objections to women swimming fell away. When that happened, Chanel's bathing costumes (modest to our eyes but daring at the time) flew out of her boutiques, along with the head-hugging swim caps she'd also devised. The beaches were quickly covered with jersey-clad Chanel look-alikes.

Chanel's image came sharply into focus in wartime Deauville. By following her own instincts (and with Boy's ongoing counsel), she intuited the sea change in women's lives to be brought by the war. Coco came to represent a new kind of womanhood—breezy, athletic, and unfettered. Always her own best advertisement, she walked around town in the simple outfits she made for herself, outfits that conveyed at once an air of chic and great comfort: long, loose jackets belted low (and featuring large, menswear-style pockets), flowing straight skirts worn without corsets, polo shirts, and simple hats with broad brims—all in neutral colors.

"I was the person people talked about the most.... Everyone wanted to know me, to find out where I got my wardrobe," she said. Coco eschewed the fussy, complicated garments that encumbered women—fabric fortresses of whalebone and crinolines, enormous hats, and floor-sweeping trains. "Those dresses dragged all over the ground, picking up [debris]," she recalled with distaste. Coco saw the body as a moving, breathing, sexually alive entity, which needed to be dressed as such.

Chanel was doing more than inventing a new way of dressing; she was inventing a new way of *being,* and women clamored for a piece of the liberating fantasy she conjured. Wearing *a* Chanel was starting to meld into wearing *Chanel,* taking on the Coco persona itself. Chanel may have looked like no one else, but soon everyone else began to look like her. Four years after her start in business, a revolution had begun.

Coco described the powerful transformation she unleashed in Deauville:

> At the end of that first summer of war, I had earned 200,000 francs....What did I know of my new profession? Nothing. I didn't know there was such a thing as designers. Was I aware of the revolution I was creating? Not at all. One world was ending, another was being born. I was there, chance offered itself, and I took it. I am the same age as this new century, and it was therefore to me that it addressed itself for its sartorial expression. It needed simplicity, comfort, cleanness, I offered it all that, without realizing it.

Chanel's remarks here reveal something about her method. As she admits, she did not know much about designing. She had never formally studied fashion or apprenticed in a couture house. Her strength lay in imagination and instinct. Coco knew what she wanted to look like, and she understood how much her vision could appeal to other women.

Her other great attribute was a tremendous flair for the tactile, developed, perhaps, during early childhood when she lived among rural artisans who brought objects to life with their hands—candlemakers and blacksmiths. Like them, Coco had a deep, physical relationship to her materials, an innate sense of how fabric should drape and flow over a body. She threw herself physically into the act of creation.

"Chanel works with ten fingers, with her nails, the side of her hand, with her palms, pins and scissors, right on the dress...sometimes she falls to her knees and grasps it firmly, not to worship it but to punish it a little more," wrote the novelist Colette after watching Coco in her studio. In keeping with the laws of physics, the kinetic energy that went into the creative process emerged on the other end, in the final product. Chanel's clothes radiated life. For her, the female body was not something to be obscured or suppressed, but a source of vitality and energy—the spark that animates the clothes. There was virtually never anything revealing or overtly sexual about her clothes, but they were indisputably sensual— precisely because Chanel gave pride of place to the body's simple materiality: the flesh, muscle, and bone beneath the cloth. "For an outfit to be pretty, the woman wearing it must give the impression of being completely nude underneath it," she said.

It was a radical notion for the time. Critics sensed this, which is why even the earliest reviews of her work praise the beauty in the sway and texture of her fabrics. In this, Chanel resembled a sculptor, or even a choreographer, more than she did a traditional fashion designer. She could spend hours on her knees before a model, molding and pinning— and would continue to do this even into her eighties. She saw clothes and bodies in organic relation to each other, and knew how to cut garments to maximize movement. For Coco, the back, shoulders, and arms needed to be accorded their full range of motion:

No two women have the same arm circumference, the shoulder is never placed the same way, everything is in the shoulder, if the dress doesn't fit the shoulder well, it will never fit at all. The front doesn't move, it's the back that works.... The back must give, at least ten centimeters, it must be able to bend, to play golf, to put on one's shoes, one must measure the client with her arms crossed.... A garment must move with the body.

Chanel would maintain this focus on bodily freedom throughout her career. In this, she remains an outlier. Few other couturiers have ever cut jackets, for example, as perfectly as did Coco Chanel. Even today, to slide into a vintage Chanel jacket is to experience a welcoming, silky ease that defies description.

But vision and pinning alone do not suffice when founding a clothing empire. Someone needed to do all the work. Chanel quickly began hiring seamstresses—a situation that brought out perhaps her most useful talent of all: Coco was a natural commander, a leader of women, someone with no difficulty communicating her high standards for quality and low tolerance for error. In an interview, one of her first employees, Madame Montezin, recalled her experience at the Cambon atelier. Her remarks blend equal parts admiration and resentment: "Everything I know, I learned from Mademoiselle.... She possessed the art of giving orders and directing an establishment. Always the first to arrive and the last to leave, she ruled over the salon and the two large workshops in which she employed forty or so people. Difficult but just, Mademoiselle was horrified by mediocrity."

Later in life, Chanel acknowledged her own ignorance of fashion technique, while taking some subtle swipes at those more skilled than she: "I admire infinitely people who know how to sew, I myself never knew. I prick my fingers. Anyway today, everyone knows how to make dresses. Ravishingly handsome gentlemen...shaky old ladies know how...these are entirely nice people. I, on the contrary, am an odious person."

Chanel exaggerates here, as she did know how to sew—she'd learned in the convent, and her first job had been as a seamstress—and certainly could have refined her skills. But she chose not to. Gabrielle Palasse-Labrunie believed her aunt deliberately suppressed any early aptitude she'd had with a needle: "She refused to sew, not even a button. She used to sew when she was younger of course, but she'd forgotten it all." Instead, Coco dreamed up her creations, communicated her vision to the workers, and let them assume the responsibility of execution. She was a creative visionary—management not labor.

She makes the distinction clearly: "Nice" people sewed clothes, *she* was an "odious" person. Being odious set her apart from the worker bees and became a part of her professional demeanor—and little wonder. How else might Coco have accomplished all she did, while barely out of her twenties? Living in an era of rigid social hierarchy and lacking any precedent for what she was doing, Coco could hardly afford to be "nice."

She needed to establish her authority over her growing staff, and to overcome a thousand prejudices against her. This need to assert herself firmly, along with her indefatigable work ethic, the dyspeptic and wary temperament she'd developed, and her ongoing insecurity over her lack of a pedigree—in either fashion or society—combined to forge a professional personality befitting a young emperor. She was demanding, arrogant, unyielding, and hubristic—qualities that served her brilliantly, at least in her professional life.

Business continued to grow in Deauville, and Chanel kept pace by expanding rapidly. She incorporated more menswear-inspired items into her merchandise—sailor suits with patch pockets and three-quarter-length jackets; sweaters and caps inspired by those the local fishermen wore, pullovers like those worn by horse trainers—to which she added small feminine touches. One of her earliest innovations involved cutting open the front of men's sweaters and adding buttons or ribbon trim—thus giving rise to the precursor of the cardigan, which later became one of her staples. The origin of this idea had been simple: Coco disliked pulling men's sweaters, with their tight neck openings, over her head and mussing her hair. To remedy the problem, she simply took a scissors to the sweaters and cut them down the front, inserting herself into these garments in a new way. "I cut an old sweater....I sewed a ribbon [around the collar]. Everyone went crazy, [saying] 'Where did you get that?'" It was a perfect metaphor for her entire life: When Coco couldn't squeeze herself into something one way, she simply found—or created—another way, even if she needed a sharp instrument to do it.

Coco also took a scissors to her hair and gradually cut it shorter until it reached the chin-length bob level with which she is famously associated. "'Why are you cutting your hair?' [people asked me]. 'Because it bothers me.'" The new style was irresistible on Coco, setting off her fine, long neck and accentuating the natural curl of her nearly black hair. Immediately, her aunt Adrienne cut her own hair into the very same style, making her look even more like Coco. Soon fashionable women from Paris to Deauville were following suit, and, in no time, the centuries-old convention of elaborate coiffures had met its demise.

The foreign press noticed Chanel's influence before the French did. In July 1914, *Women's Wear Daily* ran an item about Chanel's sweaters:

Gabriel [*sic*] Chanel has on display some extremely interesting sweaters which embrace new features. The material employed is wool jersey in most attractive colorings as pale blue, pink, brick red and yellow. Striped jersey, one inch wide, in black and white or navy and white is also employed. They slip on over the head opening at the neck in front for about 6 inches and are finished with ball shaped jersey covered buttons; the buttonholes are bound with taffeta silk in the same shade as the jersey, thus they can be fastened up close around the throat or left open in a slight décolleté effect. The sleeves are wide enough to slip on easily over a shirtwaist though they fit snugly around the wrist and are finished with buttons and taffeta-faced buttonholes, the same as the front of the sweater.

Soon, the war reached Deauville. By September 1914 reserve troops arrived from Paris and a local hotel, the Royal, was repurposed as a hospital. Aristocratic ladies volunteered to serve as nurses. Tending to the wounded required simple clothes that permitted rather than hindered movement—precisely Chanel's strong suit. She began creating uniforms for these new, upper-class caregivers—crisp white blouses (not unlike those she'd worn at Aubazine), simple skirts, and white hats. She summoned Antoinette from Paris to help her and called upon her aunt Adrienne as well. All three Chanel women found themselves together again, and the clothes sold faster than they could restock them.

Chanel's sport costumes [are] increasing in popularity daily on the Riviera. . . . It is not unusual for smart women to place orders for three and four jersey costumes . . . at one time.

—*WOMEN'S WEAR DAILY*, 1916

To look once at a Chanel jersey costume is to desire it ardently.

—*VOGUE*, 1916

Beyond her stylish nurses' uniforms, Chanel was selling more and more of her separates. Her clothes offered the perfect solution for women dressing for a new world—for the war upended everything, not least gender roles. With an entire generation of European men torn from their normal lives and pressed into combat, millions of women stepped up gallantly to do the jobs they had left behind. For the first time in European history, upper- and middle-class women found themselves going to work every day. These new women workers flooded the streets, creating a sight unusual enough to startle passersby. They served not only as nurses, but as bus conductors, truck drivers, telephone operators, and office workers—freeing the men for military duty. Their clothes had to accommodate these women's newfound need to *do* rather than simply *be*.

Beyond sartorial concerns, a powerful shift in mentality accompanied this alteration in women's daily routines—a new way of thinking about women's lives. Prior to World War I, European women enjoyed few civil rights. They generally could not serve in the armed forces; they could not vote; they had only limited access to higher education and virtually no options for professional careers. The advent of war, however, seemed to harbinger change. No one could deny how brilliantly women were now succeeding in the working world. Performing their duties with grace, grit, and ability, Europe's female workers presented a seemingly airtight case for extending rights to women in all areas. And so amid the unspeakable bloodshed and destruction of World War I, glimmers of hope appeared in this one domain. A vision began to take shape of more equality between the sexes, and a world in which women's lives might expand beyond the confines of home and hearth. In this way, war proved enlightening to those women privileged enough to find meaningful work during these years (and those not requiring wages). Working-class women, however, suffered high unemployment and salary cuts during the war. Just as such changes provided fertile terrain and thousands of willing customers for Chanel's new and unusual look, they also eased the way for her somewhat new and unusual persona—the independent career woman.

Chanel's style and persona also dovetailed well with the logistical constraints imposed by war. With war obligations depleting fabric supplies, keeping clothing simple became a matter of exigency as well as of style. Coco herself suffered from shortages but met this challenge with her customary verve—and a little help from her friends. Etienne Balsan, whose family fortune came from textiles, helped her obtain silks and broadcloth from Lyon; Boy helped her import some tweeds from Scotland. But her mainstay during this period was simple jersey. In 1914, Chanel encountered textile manufacturer Jean Rodier, who was sitting on a surplus of machine-knitted jersey, a fabric used primarily at the time for men's underwear and nightshirts. But Coco saw its possibilities and, in a now-legendary stroke of foresight, bought out the entire stock—much to Rodier's surprise.

Jersey was an ignoble material, considered unworthy of being used for any garment seen in public. It came only in beige or gray; it shredded easily, showed any mistake or correction in sewing, and tended to pucker. In the hierarchy of fabrics, jersey occupied the lowest rung. Jersey was working-class. But Chanel knew something about making the most of humble circumstances. She turned those yards of jersey into tubular chemise dresses and skirts—garments that hung loose and straight, requiring a minimum of stitching and draping. She used it in its natural, undyed state, but she also started having the fabric dyed an array of beautiful colors in Lyon—France's textile capital. By necessity, since the fabric did not permit much tailoring, her jersey garments skimmed rather than defined the waist.

With this, Chanel confirmed and popularized a new feminine

silhouette—straight and sleek. She was not the first designer to experiment with suppressing the waist; Paul Poiret had accomplished that earlier in the century with his loose, uncorseted styles and "harem" pants. Nor would Chanel be alone in favoring this geometric, linear look. Madeleine Vionnet and Jean Patou—among others—created similar looks. But only Chanel embodied and publicized a concomitant lifestyle and growing personal celebrity, which echoed and underscored the social message of this new silhouette. ("Gabrielle Chanel . . . is known the world over," declared American *Vogue* in late 1916.) As a result, from the mid-teens onward, Chanel's name was associated with this new, freeing style that allowed women to dress and undress quickly and alone—no longer requiring a second pair of hands (be they a husband's or servant's) to hook buttons, lace a corset, and then hoist, smooth, and fluff yards of heavy fabric into the massive, sculptural outfits that entirely encased the female body.

It is a bit reductive, though, to insist that, by casting aside the corset, Chanel "liberated" women's bodies. The truth is somewhat more complicated. There is no question that wearing clothes without a corset felt deliciously freeing to some women who'd been raised in the rib-crushing undergarments. And the soft jersey fabric moving over the unbound body beneath added a sensual pleasure to Chanel's clothes, both for the wearer, who could enjoy the sensation on her skin, and for the viewer, whose eye could appreciate the clothes' modern, visual "speed." But Chanel's designs didn't only "free" women from corsets, they also "deprived" them of corsets. The Chanel customer had no choice. No one wearing a jersey dress could wear a corset, for the simple reason that every hook and stay would be visible under the thin fabric, as would the mounds of displaced flesh—bosom, back, or haunch—that tend to spill over and beneath the edges of corsets. Since Coco's slim, young body needed no corset, jersey suited her to perfection. But not all women could say the same. Chanel's clothes did not flatter all older women, or women with fuller figures, whose curves transformed into something more like lumps under Coco's sleek styles.

Such insistence upon youthful fitness early on distinguished Chanel from other designers. She was the first to turn the look of youth into a desideratum of fashion. To wear a Chanel successfully, it helped to be young or at least very slim. For those not so lucky, it required dieting and exercise—or "internalizing the corset"—in order to achieve a body more like Coco's. Of course, war brought shortages of food as well as fabric, which meant that everyone was eating less. In any case, the voluptuous beauties of the recent past were now refusing dessert under the diktat of the woman once deemed too scrawny to be classically beautiful. In this, Chanel imposed her own brand of stylish revenge on the world. She was, as always, completely aware of what she had done: "I created a brand-new silhouette, to conform to it, with the help of the war [when food supplies dwindled], all my customers became slim, 'slim' like Coco.... Women came to me to buy thinness. '*Chez* Coco, we look young, do what she's doing,' they told their seamstresses."

It was a truly serendipitous merging of one woman's talents and personality with the ethos of an exceptional historical moment. Chanel had created a persona that functioned like a looking glass held up to a changed era, showing women a new vision of themselves. As both a *couturière* and an emerging celebrity personality, Chanel seemed to be asking women to join her on the side of modernity, in the changed world of speed, airplanes, automobiles, and freedoms for women. "The creations of the Maison Chanel are having a tremendous vogue," declared American *Vogue* in 1916.

This modernity, of course, was emerging through the upheaval of war, and thus was shot through with shock, horror, and sorrow. During the four years of World War I, Europe witnessed violence, death, and destruction on a hitherto unknown scale. Nine million servicemen died, along with at least five million civilians, who succumbed to bombings, hunger, and disease. France alone lost 20 percent of its men of military age. And with account taken of disabled or disfigured survivors, only about one-third of all French soldiers made it through the war unharmed.

We can make sense of no phenomenon occurring in Europe during this time—including the rise of Coco Chanel—without considering it against the backdrop of this brutal, unrelenting massacre of young men. The persona Chanel crafted appealed so strongly and intuitively to women in part because it seemed to contain within it a shadow of those soldiers. (In 1915, she even introduced a new color: "soldier blue.") As a result of her own long early years of deprivation, sadness, and loss, the emotional affect of Coco's style had always been somber and restrained. It was, therefore, perfectly attuned to the reigning atmosphere during this terrible war.

Thin, androgynous, simply dressed in striped naval-uniform-style suits, or schoolboy sports clothes and blazers, the "Chanel woman" conjured the silhouette of the war's millions of soldiers—the young men dying just out of sight of the general population.

C oco had more than an abstract relationship to the war and the millions of young men in peril, for it took her beloved Boy away from her. While Chanel spent much of her time in the safety of Deauville, Capel had reported to the front by August 1914. He saw action immediately, taking part in the first major combat involving the English: the Battle of Mons, for which he'd been awarded the "Mons Star." But Capel was too ambitious to stay in the trenches long. Like Coco, he was benefiting from new opportunities afforded by the war, particularly a friendship he'd forged with a very powerful man: the seventy-four-year-old former prime minister of France, Georges Clemenceau—who would alter entirely the course of Boy's career. As Coco proudly told Morand, "He won the affection of old Clemenceau, who couldn't do without him."

In 1915, Clemenceau was serving as the president of the French Army Commission, and he met Boy during one of his regular inspection tours of the front. Almost immediately, the two men developed a deep rapport. Clemenceau was a serious Anglophile and fluent in English; he was also a true intellectual, a committed liberal, a lover of art and philosophy, and—in his day—a famous connoisseur of beautiful women. In Boy Capel, he surely saw a younger version of himself.

By 1915, Clemenceau (known as "the Tiger") had become an international statesman, devoted to strengthening France's alliance with Britain, working closely with his friend David Lloyd George, the liberal pacifist soon to become Britain's prime minister.

Aware of Capel's extensive experience in coal shipping, Clemenceau offered him an enticing opportunity: membership on the Franco-British Commission on Coal for the War—a post that would keep Boy safely away from the front. Coco, who had been frantic that he might be injured or killed, could finally relax. At the same time, Capel had ever less time for Coco. His new post effectively turned him into an unofficial diplomat, required to shuttle between London and Paris, and to socialize with the highest military and diplomatic circles. Such glittering circles often included young, aristocratic, and beautiful war widows, whom Capel did not fail to notice.

Boy's career rose meteorically. His newfound knowledge of wartime coal shipping needs allowed him to expand his own business dramatically, and he could hardly have chosen a more profitable commodity. Desperately needed for the war effort and in dwindling supply, coal—or "black diamonds" in the curiously inverted metaphor of the day—increased astronomically in value during the war. In response to the demand, Boy increased his fleet of freighters, which were contracted out to the French government for war use. He sold coal from his mines to French factories as well. These war contracts made Capel richer than ever. And his influence only increased when his friend Clemenceau was elected to a second term as prime minister in 1917.

While his attention was certainly divided, Capel had by no means forgotten Chanel. He visited her when he could and continued to advise her on business matters. He also remained the principal investor in her growing empire. Boy was profiting immensely from the new commercial possibilities brought by war, and he thought Coco should do likewise. He persuaded her that the best way to take advantage of the new markets and clientele opening up to her would be to expand again—this time to another resort location: Biarritz, on France's southwest coast. As with Deauville, the choice of venue was inspired.

Chanel with Boy Capel (with Constant Say, seen from behind),
on the beach at Saint-Jean-de-Luz, near Biarritz, 1917

Safely distant from the front and just over the border from neutral
Spain, Biarritz remained open for business to wellborn, pleasure-seeking
Europeans with cash to spare. And with no war blockades to impede the
transport of goods through Spain, Chanel could more easily procure raw
materials in Biarritz than in either Paris or Deauville. In the summer of
1915, Capel financed the opening of the third Chanel boutique, housed
this time not in a commercial building but in an actual villa they rented
out—the grand and ornate Villa Larralde, on Biarritz's fashionable rue
Gardères, which stands at the entrance to the beach and in front of the
casino. She hired sixty local workers, and asked her sister Antoinette—
who'd moved back up to Paris—to come down to direct the Biarritz
salon. Antoinette required coaxing; she enjoyed Paris, even in wartime.
Always persuasive, Coco lured her sister south by telling her how many
more eligible men she'd find in Biarritz (which was likely true, given the
many Spanish visitors to the town, as well as a growing coterie of exiled
Russian noblemen). Soon, a steady stream of young female Chanel em-

ployees was flowing back and forth between Paris and Biarritz. More experienced girls from the Paris atelier were invited to work at Biarritz, while new girls hired in the south traveled up north for training. When a few of these young women's parents objected to having their daughters uprooted thus, Chanel smoothly reassured them of the girls' complete safety. Besides, she told the anxious parents, it was patriotic to help support French business during wartime.

The store in Biarritz introduced Chanel fashions to customers from the neighboring Spanish cities of Bilbao and Barcelona, which increased sales so successfully that Coco had to open and staff an additional studio in her Paris offices, devoted exclusively to producing clothes for Spain.

In Biarritz, Chanel perfected her inspired publicity tactic of offering clothes free of charge to beautiful and well-connected women. When these women then wore Coco's clothes all over town to society parties, they became de facto house models—the most effective walking billboards imaginable. One of Chanel's first hires for the Biarritz branch, a twenty-one-year-old young woman named Marie-Louise Deray, recalled the studio atmosphere in these early days: "I heard a Parisian lady was opening a boutique in Biarritz, so I went there. Mademoiselle Chanel was not there. There was her sister.... I was hired and I became one of the mainstays of the firm. We immediately enjoyed a great success. Soon I had about sixty workwomen under me. I worked for very famous women who were often friends of Chanel, such as Marthe Davelli.... All of these ladies gave her a lot of publicity." Slim, long-limbed, with bobbed, wavy dark hair and a wide mouth, Marthe Davelli resembled Coco so strongly that when she wore Chanel clothes, she looked like a clone of Coco herself. Davelli was, therefore, one of Coco's favorite "unofficial mannequins," since she reminded the public not just of Chanel fashions, but of Chanel's charismatic personal image as well.

With branches now in three of France's choicest venues, Chanel's business began to acquire the aura of luxury and impeccable taste that would become its hallmarks. The new store was no mere hat shop that sold other items; it was a true fashion house that presented and sold entire collections—seasonal groups of coordinated designs, at couture prices. And money meant, at last, freedom. "I had founded a *maison de couture*," recalled Chanel. "It was not the creation of an artist, as it has become fashionable to maintain, or the work of a business woman. It was rather the work of a person who sought only her liberty."

In 1915, one of Chanel's simple jersey dresses sold for about 7,000 francs, or the equivalent of $3,700 in today's dollars. But it was hardly the materials or labor that made it so costly. Jersey was cheap; most pieces were unlined, and Chanel did not pay her seamstresses very much. It was the association with Coco herself, as she was quickly learning, that imparted value to the clothes. Their worth derived from the persona she was developing and the glamorous life she was leading. "People knew me, they knew who I was, nowhere could I pass unnoticed.... The curiosity to which I was subjected became insatiable and followed me constantly, and one could say it was one of the elements contributing to my success. I was my own advertisement, I always have been." An October 1916 article in *Women's Wear Daily*, with a Biarritz dateline, makes clear how deeply Chanel's renown wove itself into the allure of her clothes: "It would seem that the whole 'haute couture' of Paris is either here or represented for on the Plage the other morning.... Gabrielle Chanel passed attired in the long maroon-colored charmeuse cloak tipped with lapin dyed to match, which was such a success with American buyers at the Chanel opening in August." The article points out Chanel's canny use of fur in these early days. Many of her pieces, especially her jersey coats, sported fur collars and trim—even for spring and summer wear. But Coco used only the humblest pelts—usually dyed rabbit and sometimes beaver—in a move that perfectly sums up her aesthetic philosophy. "I had decided to replace rich furs with the most indigent skins.... In that way, I made a fortune for the poor, little tradespeople, the big [fur] retailers never forgave me for this," she told Morand.

Nothing telegraphs wealth and stature like a coat with a fur collar. But make that coat out of common jersey, and the fur collar out of cheap and lowly rabbit, and you've undermined the implied value of the coat.

Now, sell it at an exorbitant price, as if the coat were made of imported silk trimmed with sable, and you've arrived at the core of Chanel's business model, the essence of the style that Paul Poiret dubbed *"misérabilisme de luxe,"* or "luxurious poverty."

The clothes were humble, but conveyed—inversely—an aura of status. "Chanel is master of her art and her art resides in jersey," declared *Vogue.* Chanel had found a way to charge duchesses a fortune for the privilege of dressing in materials worn by their servants—the ultimate revenge for this *nécessiteuse*—this once "needy girl" from the provincial orphanage. Chanel was proud of this accomplishment, and of having communicated her principles to her customer. Coco enjoyed citing an American client who'd marveled at "[Having] spent so much money without it being visible!"

By the time Coco had opened her third boutique, she employed three hundred workers. She was becoming the style icon of a new generation, a famous and very rich woman. She played her new part to the hilt. "You had to see her arrive at noon, getting out of her Rolls, a chauffeur and a footman. She looked like a queen," recalled former Biarritz employee Marie-Louise Deray.

Chanel had craved wealth since her days at Aubazine, when she'd realized that money would grant her freedom. Other than that, though, she knew nothing of finances. When her early sales on rue Cambon had begun producing some revenue, Coco had gone wild, spending far more than she earned. But thanks to Boy, who had guaranteed a line of credit for her with Lloyd's of London, her checks never bounced. This gave her the illusion of infinitely available funds, and for a time, Boy let her go on believing in this fiction.

When Capel finally explained the reality of the situation, Coco was horrified. She described the revelation as a turning point in her career: "My heart contracted.... I looked at all the beautiful objects that I'd bought with what I had thought was my own money. And so all of this was paid for by him! I was dependent on him! ... I started hating this well-brought-up man who was paying for me. I threw my purse in his face and fled the apartment." Coco calmed down, but the next day she went to work armed with new purpose, announcing to her staff, "I am not here to have fun. . . . I am here to make a fortune. From now on, no one spends a centime without my permission."

"That day was the end of my unconscious youth," she recalled.

Chanel would never mismanage money again, and by 1916 she'd paid Boy back every penny he had advanced her. She even bought outright the Villa Larralde for the princely sum of 300,000 francs. (The same year, Chanel's last remaining ties to her peasant forebears were severed when both of her grandparents, Henri and Virginie-Angelina Chanel, died within months of each other. Aunt Adrienne traveled to Vichy to arrange their funerals.)

Chanel told Morand that Boy was shocked when she paid him back in full: "I thought I was buying you a toy, and discovered I was buying you your liberty," she reported him saying. While Boy had early on stopped seeing Coco's business as a toy, he was very serious when he spoke to her of "liberty." To Capel, helping Chanel found her empire was more than a matter of good business; it was a matter of conscience, for Boy Capel was passionately committed to equal opportunity for women. In an essay entitled "Necessary Emancipations," Boy wrote movingly of the obstacles impeding women: "For centuries, [women] have been considered . . . as inferior creatures. . . . The time has come to enfranchise them."

Such sentiments emerged naturally from Capel's deep interest in justice of all kinds. He mistrusted easy categorizations, decrying all labels—of sex, nation, class, religion, or race—that set up hierarchies among people. He held an almost mystical belief in an overarching connection among all peoples, which he called "the human family." Beyond the spiritual appeal of such notions, Capel saw the potential for real-world, political application—the basis of a progressive, internationalist philosophy of peace. Such a philosophy formed the core of the two books he authored: *Reflections on Victory and a Project for the Federation of Governments* (1917) and *De Quoi demain sera-t-il fait?* (What Will Tomorrow Be Made Of?), written apparently in French and published posthumously in 1939.

Reflections on Victory is astonishing in its prescience. With the outcome of the war still in the balance, Capel correctly guessed that Germany would suffer an ignominious loss that would incite it to terrible future violence: "Germany will take her revenge for what we propose to do to her." Capel also foresaw the coming power imbalance between the two nations: "In ten years' time...the German army will be three times as large as the French army.... How...can we expect to destroy or even dominate a strong, resolute, disciplined and organized mother-race like the Teuton race?"

To forestall the cycle of enmity, Capel proposed a solution: a collectivity, or "federation," of European states, in which patriotism and individual national interests cede to the greater good of all: "We [must] destroy the old fetish balance of power based on militarism, and firmly install federation in Europe.... The choice must be made between extinction and federation.... Militarism is the creed of those human reptiles whose business is war...who [act] in the name of country or national power."

For Capel, the key to building this "federation" lay in overthrowing Europe's "gerontocracy"—the old men who send young men off to die in war. Capel believed that handing the reins over to the idealistic younger generation would secure lasting peace. *The Times Literary Supplement* praised the book, while noting that some of its plans lacked practical details. Soon after *Reflections on Victory,* Boy nearly completed a companion volume (published only decades later), expanding on his vision for Europe's future. This sequel, What Will Tomorrow Be Made Of?, outlines Capel's notion of a democratic "City of the Future," where social class divisions fade away, and disenfranchised groups—especially women—enjoy equal freedoms. Capel devotes a section to the inequities of society marriages, and the mercenary practice of dowries.

Once Georges Clemenceau moved Boy Capel out of the trenches and into a diplomatic post, Capel was free to act on his many political passions. Until now, little has been known about Boy's wartime work, but a cache of letters uncovered in London's Imperial War Museum reveals a great deal about Capel's political role. While serving on the coal commission, Capel seems to have increasingly assumed additional—unofficial—responsibilities as a key liaison between the British and

French governments during the war, working directly under Sir Henry Hughes Wilson, British director of military operations during the war (and, as of 1918, chief of the imperial general staff). Correspondence between Wilson and Capel shows another side of Boy, who displays not only his genuine desire for peace and international understanding, but also his high-reaching ambitions and impatience with his lack of proper diplomatic rank and title.

The letters reveal Capel's interest in drawing Holland into the war (a plan that others also supported, but which ultimately failed), along with his idea of finding some Arab support to counter the recent entry of the Ottoman Empire on the side of the Central Powers. Cocky and conspiratorial, Capel's tone betrays a still-young man eager to prove himself a knowing insider:

> Dear General
> Mahomet has, I believe, plenty of relations & descendants.
> Could we not raise one of them to the Caliphate in Bagdad &
> make an ally of him? To regain "prestige in the East," "annoy"
> the Young Turks, and upset the *"Drang nach Osten"* [Germany's
> "push toward the East"]. The history of the Arabs is a proof that
> all similar ventures in the past have found plenty of followers.
> Seduce Wilhelmina [Holland] & flirt with Fatimah.

Boy's choice of metaphor here reminds us of his vast experience in seducing and flirting on multiple fronts at once. In another letter, Capel offers more details on how the British might "seduce Wilhelmina"— secure Holland's entry into the war—proposing himself as chief seducer:

> Re Wilhelmina, I am not looking for a "job," but to the *result*, so
> you can use me unofficially, if that is needed. I can open a house
> in Amsterdam and entertain lavishly at my own expense or take
> on a delicate negotiation which will be disavowed if
> unsuccessful. Freedom from responsibility often hastens
> conclusions.

Capel's assertion that he is not looking for a "job" would be more convincing were it not coupled so often with blatant attempts to angle for a specific, high-level diplomatic position.

In collaboration with Sir Henry, Capel had been devising a plan for a "War Council" of Allied nations, to be created independent of individual governments, with the goal of "balanc[ing] political and military elements," and remedying the "complete absence of cordiality or even understanding between our mixed bag of rulers."

Capel had been spending time in Paris and London, trying to win support for the concept. His letters mention meetings with French diplomat Jules Cambon, Georges Clemenceau, and Winston Churchill. Capel did not conceal his wish to be appointed the British representative to such a council, and never hesitated to tout his own expertise: "I think I know the political situation on this side...probably better than any other Englishman except you," he wrote to Sir Henry.

Initial attempts to form the war council met with resistance from many quarters, and it took months of negotiations to achieve any kind of consensus. Finally, in early 1916, a version of Capel's and Wilson's council received the green light. The new "Allied War Council" lacked many of the features Capel had hoped for, but was a success for him nonetheless. Two years later, in November 1917, a Supreme War Council was formed, which adhered more closely to the original plans. Boy continued on the Anglo-French coal commission, while serving as Wilson's unofficial representative in Paris, working with Clemenceau and Lloyd George. Ultimately, in 1918, when Clemenceau was once more prime minister, Capel was appointed political secretary of the British section to the Supreme War Council held at Versailles.

In his correspondence, Capel can sound callow and petulant. In one letter, he grouses about having to prepare a report, implying that such tasks were beneath him:

> I am now a clerk copying extracts.... Somebody must do that I
> suppose but it is a pity the supply of ammunition in France
> should suffer it, but there it is, I can't be a coal magnate & a 3rd

class agent at the same time & unless somebody shouts for me I must go on being a 3rd class agent.

But Capel's concern over status cannot be separated from his diplomatic effectiveness—in fact, the two elements of his personality are intertwined. His genius for public relations enabled him to sway heads of state on topics of world affairs, even while convincing those leaders to reward him personally. In myriad ways, Capel's letters reveal his nuanced understanding of the techniques of communication. He wrote about how to use the press to affect public opinion, about the importance of "prestige" ("The British have lost their initial 'prestige'—[we] need to 'counter-act' this"), and about how to influence high-ranking officers by appealing to their elitism ("Do not put Dukes in a troop with their butlers").

In his diplomatic correspondence, Capel is not the visionary, progressive intellectual of his published writings, but a crasser character, self-centered, and desperate for rank and status. Boy's erudition and sensitivity were genuine, but such attributes alone do not produce multimillionaire industrialists. He needed both sides of his personality to sustain his multifaceted, meteoric career—and to help Coco sustain hers.

Capel's ideas and guiding hand are clearly visible in Coco's own rapid and dramatic success during these years. Beyond the money he'd lent her, Capel offered Chanel something perhaps even more valuable: his intuitive sense of what today we call "branding"—the art of creating an ongoing, recognizable look and narrative around a product, person, or cause. Capel positioned himself as a key adviser to both France and England during the war, advising both governments on how to strengthen alliances, cultivate strategic friendships, and package their message attractively. Chanel shared many of his talents, and he encouraged her to use them in her own realm.

In truth, Chanel's and Capel's professions—fashion and backstage diplomacy—have much in common. Capel proved useful diplomatically because of his unique Anglo-French cultural fluency. Chanel, too, was a natural translator, a cultural hybrid. As someone so often uprooted and forced to remake her life in radically changing circumstances, Coco had finely honed her observational skills. Like a good diplomat, she carefully watched for cultural cues, and was adept at fitting into new environments quickly. She had not yet learned English (which she would later speak well), but in a mere few years, she had taught herself the language and habits of the upper classes, slipping into an entirely new world and making it her own (even forcing herself to eat oysters—which she found repugnant—after observing their popularity among the rich). She took those differences she could not hide and turned them to her advantage professionally, inventing a way of dressing that reflected her own modest background, the design elements she found around her, and her unusual tomboyish beauty. The result was sartorial diplomacy: She blended wealthy English schoolboy clothes with low-ranking French naval uniforms; she mixed masculine and feminine touches, cinching oversize menswear sweaters to show off dainty waists, adding bows or ribbons to schoolboy blouses. Chanel also recognized—as Capel did—the power of young people, and emphasized youth in all her creations.

As a couple, these two felt inevitable—even their names resembled each other. According to one theory, Chanel later created her famous double-C logo to interlock their two surnames. But Boy had ambitious plans that did not include Coco.

The Honorable Diana Lister Wyndham was the beautiful, tall, blond, blue-eyed daughter of Thomas Lister, the 4th Baron Ribblesdale (whose portrait by John Singer Sargent hangs in London's National Gallery). In 1913, at the age of twenty, Diana had married Percy Wyndham, a member of the British Expeditionary Force. By 1914, she was a war widow. Reserved, delicate, aristocratic, and—on her mother's side—the niece of Herbert Asquith, Britain's prime minister from 1908 to 1916, Diana was everything Coco Chanel was not. Born in 1893, she was also a decade younger than Coco. Capel had met Diana at the front, where she had volunteered as an army nurse and ambulance driver, like so many other wellborn women. When Boy began to court her, in 1918, Diana was just twenty-five, and few young women could have looked like more suitable wife material for a rising diplomat.

Chanel had long known of Capel's dalliances, and even claimed to accept them. But this one was different. Noting his increasing absences and his distracted air, Coco felt they were growing apart. Boy no longer spent all his military leaves with her.

But Boy and Diana's relationship was hardly smooth. Letters from Boy to Diana, recently uncovered, reveal his vacillating feelings toward her. Less than two months before Boy's wedding, even the Prince of Wales still knew that "Coco Chanel" was Capel's companion, mentioning their relationship in a letter to his own (married) mistress, Freda Dudley Ward:

> All you tell me about Capel is very interesting, no I've never met Gabrielle Chanel or "Coco" though she sounds as if she is worth meeting darling, another divine woman.

Those who knew Boy and Diana as a couple found them incompatible. In a diary entry of August 3, 1918, the British ambassador to France, Edward George Villiers-Stanley, who worked closely with Boy, refers to the rocky state of the couple's engagement: "Much amused to hear that the Capel-Wyndham marriage has still not come off although he telegraphed me to say he was being married on Wednesday.... I shall only believe it when I know the ceremony has actually taken place."

Diana, too, in a letter to her friend and former beau, Lord Alfred "Duff" Cooper, refers to the uncertainty of her future marriage and to the disapproval of her intimates, even while expressing delighted affection for Capel and his fortune:

> I think I'm going to marry Capel after all—so next time I see you, you'll be staying with me in my luxurious apartment, in the Avenue du Bois.

Global forces also intruded upon Boy's wedding plans. He had to put off his planned "marriage furlough" to contend with the grim realities of a war the Allies seemed on the brink of losing. Despite the hope offered by the entrance of the United States in April 1917, losses grew increasingly catastrophic for France and Britain in 1917 and 1918, as crushing defeats mounted. By March 1918, as Germany stepped up its attacks in what came to be called the Ludendorff Offensive, the Western Front was bombarded more heavily than it had been since 1914. Even Paris fell under siege from the massive German cannons that could fire from up to seventy-five miles away, sending Parisians diving for shelter.

An ancillary consequence of these bombings is worth noting here: Parisians were instructed to take cover in basements during shelling, and this led, curiously, to a business boon for Chanel. Finding that unexpected night bombings presented a fashion challenge, women guests at the Ritz hotel descended on the rue Cambon looking for chic but appropriate bomb shelter outfits. Chanel responded with a cache of men's jersey pajamas she'd recently purchased, which the women loved and snapped up at the usual high Chanel prices. A few years later, Chanel was re-creating these pajamas in raw silk and selling them as "resort wear." Thus did the emergency bomb shelter attire become Coco's famous "beach pajamas."

In late summer, once the Americans had helped push back the Germans, Capel was finally able to take his deferred leave from the war. He married Diana Lister Wyndham, who'd converted to Roman Catholicism for him, on August 10, 1918, at Beaufort Castle in Inverness, Scotland—the home of Diana's sister, Laura, who had married into Scottish nobility. The wedding announcement in *Le Gaulois* described Captain Capel as "descended of one of England's most ancient aristocratic families"—a misperception (or successful obfuscation) that suggests just how quickly Boy was benefiting from "nobility by association." The couple returned to Paris and settled into Boy's apartment on the avenue du Bois (now known as avenue Foch), bordering the Bois de Boulogne.

And where was Coco? Just blocks away in a new apartment, sick with grief. Although he had kept his wedding plans secret for several months, Coco had guessed the worst. "I knew before he told me," Coco told Claude Delay. Although she and Boy continued to see each other after his marriage, she could obviously no longer share his apartment. With the help of her new best friend, Misia Edwards, she found one at 45, Quai Debilly (now the avenue de New-York) in the sixteenth arrondissement, overlooking the Seine. Since Misia, about to marry her third husband, painter José-Maria Sert, wanted to hire new household staff, she encouraged Chanel to take on two of her former employees, butler Joseph LeClerc and his wife, Marie, a trained parlor maid. The LeClercs (along with their young daughter, Suzanne) moved into the Quai Debilly apartment with Chanel, and remained in her employ for many years.

With a heavy heart, Chanel accepted her new status. She would be Boy's *irrégulière*, forfeiting all hope of a more legitimate future together. Coco had beaten astronomical odds, crashing through countless social barriers to become the unusual creature she now was—rich, famous, successful, and moving in ever-higher circles. But Capel's marriage to Diana proved that some barriers remained insurmountable. Boy had, after all, met Coco when she was one of the *cocottes* in Balsan's stable at Royallieu. If Coco had not told him everything about her past, it is possible that Balsan filled in some details (including, perhaps, the abortion Etienne had helped her obtain). As progressive as he was, and despite his stirring essay on women's unequal marital rights, Arthur Edward Capel could not see his way clear to marrying a woman like Chanel. Keeping in mind that Boy's own pedigree remained somewhat overshadowed by mystery if not scandal, we can imagine why his ambitions ultimately trumped his principles, and, perhaps, even his feelings.

For a time, Coco fell into a paralysis of grief. In a letter to a friend and client, decorator Antoinette Bernstein, Chanel explains obliquely her inability to socialize, imploring, "pity me for I have just spent three very bad weeks."

The actual event of Boy's wedding galvanized Coco, though, driving her out of her lethargy and into what looks like revenge. Just one week after the Capel-Wyndham nuptials were announced, Chanel left Paris for the Alpine spa town of Uriage-les-Bains, in southeastern France. There, she openly conducted an affair with eminent playwright Henry Bernstein, the husband of the very friend in whom she had confided her worst sorrows, Antoinette. Beginning her career as a patron of the arts, Chanel even gave Henry a generous sum of money with which to purchase his own theater, the Théâtre du Gymnase.

Henry Bernstein had a long-standing reputation as a philanderer, and Antoinette seems to have accepted—or at least tolerated—his dalliance with her friend. When she and the Bernsteins' young daughter, Georges, visited Henry in Uriage, Coco was included in the family outings. And Chanel developed a great fondness for little Georges. The affair seems not to have put a crimp in Chanel's ongoing friendship with Antoinette, and their correspondence continued for years thereafter. During the affair, Coco wrote to Antoinette in flattering, solicitous if somewhat saccharine tones.

Chanel had known Antoinette Bernstein for years. They had met in Deauville when Antoinette and her mother had begun frequenting Coco's shop. Chanel had designed the blue jersey suit that Antoinette wore on the day she married Henry. Chanel also designed costumes for at least one of Henry's plays, the 1919 production of *The Secret*—about a vicious woman named Gabrielle who destroys other people's relationships by seeding mistrust between couples. And through it all, Antoinette continued to dress in Chanel couture. The two women "seem[ed] ... the best of friends ... wearing the same silk pajamas," as Georges remembered. (Apparently, Antoinette Bernstein was also abiding by Chanel's physical requirements for fashion. Georges describes her mother and Coco as "equally emaciated.")

Photographs from this period show Henry Bernstein walking with a radiant Coco who is holding the hand of little Georges, the trio looking for all the world like a happy family—with Coco standing in for the child's real mother. And that might have been the point. Having just lost her dream of becoming Boy's wife, perhaps of bearing his child, Chanel seems to have wanted to step into that fantasy some other way. By "borrowing" someone else's husband and child, she temporarily lived out this tableau. Coco would have a long pattern of inserting herself between couples in this way, most often while continuing to dress the wives of her paramours, creating odd little love triangles in which the two female "rivals" dressed alike. Even Diana Capel wore Chanel, both before and after her marriage to Boy.

After Uriage, Coco still felt the need to escape Paris, and rented a villa, known as "La Milanese," just west of Paris in the town of Garches. She went there to avoid the city, but not to avoid Boy Capel. Although wounded and angry, she remained as attached to him as ever (and he to her), and La Milanese provided a more discreet location for their ongoing affair. Coco and Boy still loved each other, but things were not the same. Although she never admitted it to anyone (and indeed never even spoke of Capel's marriage), Chanel had grown bitter. Capel—the man she'd thought of as her family, the first man she'd trusted since her father's abandonment—had pledged himself to someone else. The betrayal hit her to the core.

Diana Capel knew the reason for her husband's frequent absences, and started spending more time away from Paris herself, retreating to her native England. It was not uncommon for a wealthy man like Capel to have a mistress, but Diana found it hard to bear, perhaps because of all the sorrows she had already endured in her life—a tally that rivaled even Chanel's. In addition to the death of her young first husband, Percy, Diana had suffered the loss of two brothers and her mother, all by the time she was twenty-two. Now, her second husband seemed to be slipping away. Diana told friends that Boy spent hardly any time with her anymore, and barely spoke to her. She likely felt all the more vulnerable given that she became pregnant immediately after (or just before) her marriage. The Capels' daughter, Ann, was born on April 28, 1918. Prime Minister Georges Clemenceau graciously agreed to serve as the child's godfather. Boy and Diana's marriage may have begun to tarnish, but their social standing remained pure gold.

In the second half of 1918, the tide finally turned for the Allied powers, with Germany signing the armistice at Compiègne on November 11. After six long additional months of negotiations, on June 28, 1919, the Treaty of Versailles put an official end to France and England's war with Germany (other treaties dealt with other Central Powers). The same day saw forty-four countries sign the Covenant of the League of Nations, thus setting in motion the very sort of "Federation of Governments" proposed by Boy Capel in *Reflections on Victory.*

1919, the year I woke up famous and the year I lost everything.

—COCO CHANEL

As World War I ended, Boy Capel and Coco Chanel were reaching the first great peaks of their careers. Two gifted, driven, good-looking, and rich people in their midthirties, they had done more than survive the horrific war; they had managed to prosper and succeed through it. Chanel had redrawn the feminine silhouette for a new century; Capel had made himself indispensable to two major governments and seemed poised for a glorious political career. They remained deeply attached emotionally if not legally. In November 1919, when Coco's sister Antoinette married her much-younger wartime suitor, Canadian pilot Oscar Fleming (the bride in a white lace dress by Coco), Boy accompanied Coco to the wedding and served as a witness—in fine imitation of a dutiful brother-in-law. It seemed possible that Coco and Boy might become one of those enduring extramarital unions—of the sort that coexist for years in uneasy truce with foundering marriages.

Capel had risen diplomatically by excelling as a go-between, explaining England to France and vice versa. Now, he shuttled back and forth between a French woman and an English one, often driving long distances between cities in France. In December 1919, Boy made one of his hurried visits to Coco in her Garches villa. The next day, Monday, December 22, he left Paris in his chauffeured Rolls-Royce—his driver, Mansfield, at the wheel. His plan was to travel the 563 miles south to Cannes, to meet his favorite sister, Lady Bertha Michelham, for Christmas and later reunite with Diana, who would arrive from England.

The real reasons behind this trip remain unclear. Why would Capel abandon both Diana and Coco on Christmas? Some accounts suggest Capel intended to look for a secluded Mediterranean villa there, where he and Chanel could be alone; other sources suggest that Capel was planning to ask his wife for a divorce after the new year. In the end, the reasons do not matter, for the Rolls never reached its destination. In early afternoon, as the car rounded a slight turn on Route ND 7, outside the town of Puget-sur-Argens, one of its tires exploded violently, sending the car hurtling into a ditch where it burst into flames. Mansfield escaped with serious injuries; Boy was killed on the spot.

Capel's friend Lord Rosslyn, a Scottish polo player, telephoned a number of their intimates in Paris with the shocking news. When Count Léon de Laborde, an old friend from their Royallieu days (and another former lover of Coco's), heard what had happened he volunteered to tell Chanel immediately and drove out to Garches in the middle of the night. The house was dark and for a long time, no one answered the door. Persistent, Laborde pounded and shouted until her butler, Joseph, awoke and opened the door. Once apprised, Joseph wanted to delay telling Mlle. Chanel until morning. But Coco had heard the loud knocking and had padded down the stairs, still in her white silk pajamas. Seeing her, Laborde stammered to find the right words, but Coco had already grasped the truth. Silently, she went back upstairs, coming down minutes later, fully dressed and carrying a small suitcase. She asked Léon to drive her to Cannes, so she could see Boy one last time. They left at once.

Coco insisted they drive straight through to the coast, eighteen hours without stopping. She ignored Laborde's urging that they stop so she could rest during the night. When they arrived in Cannes the next day, Léon located Boy's sister Bertha—Lady Michelham—who was staying in a local hotel. Bertha invited them to her suite and offered Coco a place to rest. Again, Coco refused to sleep, sitting up all night in a chair, essentially reenacting the Catholic vigil over the dead—a ritual she'd known as a young girl, and likely performed nearly twenty-five years earlier beside the corpse of her young mother. For two days, no one in Cannes saw Coco cry.

Chanel never got to see Boy again. Burned beyond recognition, he had been placed in a sealed coffin right away. Chanel chose not to attend the funeral service held the next morning in Fréjus. Instead, she asked

Bertha's chauffeur to drive her to the site of the accident. It was easy to find—Capel's mangled, incinerated Rolls-Royce had not yet been towed away. Coco walked around the wreck, staring at it and running her hands over the twisted metal remains. Finally, she sat down by the side of the road and, according to the chauffeur who observed from a distance, burst into heart-rending sobs that lasted several hours.

Captain Arthur Edward Capel received full military honors at the Cathedral of Fréjus, the Riviera town just near the site of his accident. Several days later, on January 2, 1920, his body was transferred to Paris, where a second funeral was held at Saint-Honoré d'Eylau, on the Place Victor Hugo. Neither Chanel nor Diana Capel attended that funeral. Captain Arthur Edward Capel, recipient of the Légion d'honneur (awarded to him on July 6, 1918, for service as a foreigner in France), was laid to rest in Paris's Montmartre Cemetery.

The newspaper obituaries for Capel described him as one of the most famous Englishmen in France. They noted his diplomacy career, his excellence at polo, his marriage to Diana, and, not least, his great fortune. No mention appeared, naturally, of Coco Chanel—she lived in the background of his life. But in February 1920, when the London *Times*—as was customary—published the terms of Capel's will, Chanel emerged from the background. Of the 700,000 pounds totaling his estate (making him the equivalent of a multimillionaire today), 40,000 pounds were bequeathed to Gabrielle Chanel—a sign that Boy felt no need to conceal their relationship after his death.

If Chanel was surprised to find herself thus acknowledged by Boy, she was probably more surprised to learn that he'd left exactly the same sum—40,000 pounds—to another woman: twenty-seven-year-old Italian war widow Yvonne Viggiano, known also by her royal title, Princess Yvonne Giovanna Sanfelice. Somehow Boy might have managed to conduct not a double life, but perhaps a triple one. The rest of Capel's considerable fortune went to Diana and baby Ann.

At the time of his death, Boy did not know that Diana was pregnant again. The Capels' second daughter was born in June 1920, and christened June Capel, after her springtime birth month.

Chanel never breathed a word about the Princess Yvonne revelation, just as she never acknowledged Diana Capel to anyone. But Diana was clearly on her mind. Shortly after Boy's death, Coco moved from La Milanese to another rented villa close by in Garches, a house known as "Bel Respiro," which would remain one of her primary retreats for years. She brought with her Joseph, Marie, and Suzanne LeClerc, along with four dogs: two wolfhounds, Soleil and Lune, and the two dogs Boy had given her, Pita and Poppee. As soon as she moved in, Coco painted the exterior of the house beige and—in a gesture of mourning—had all the shutters lacquered in deepest black—a color scheme unusual for the neighborhood, and which later became a Chanel trademark combination.

From the outside, it looked as though Chanel had moved to flee her memories of Boy. On the contrary, she moved to be closer to Capel—but in a most curious way. The owner from whom Chanel rented Bel Respiro was none other than Diana Capel. Boy had purchased the house for himself and his wife shortly before his death, but when a bereaved Diana fled France afterward, she leased her house to Coco, for reasons unknown. Perhaps the unhappiness of Diana's brief marriage to Boy kept her from waxing sentimental about a house. Perhaps she was angry and wished to divest herself of the house, assuming that Boy had chosen a villa in Garches expressly to remain close to Coco. In any case, within a year, Chanel had bought Bel Respiro outright from Diana, using the money Capel had left her.

Coco's motivations for this transaction are a bit easier to fathom than Diana's. By inhabiting Bel Respiro, Chanel was absorbing the last traces of Boy Capel, while at the same time usurping one of his marital households. Coco had already long "inhabited" Boy in a metaphoric sense: She had worn his clothes, studied his philosophies, and launched an entire business empire under his guidance. Now she literalized the metaphor and moved into his home, occupying his space—and using his money to do so.

Capel's death devastated Coco, leaving her with a sense of emptiness comparable to what she'd felt upon the loss of her parents. "I won't prettify this memory," she told Paul Morand, nearly thirty years later.

"The death was a terrible blow for me. I lost everything losing Capel. He left in me a void that the years have not filled." Chanel was mourning another, secret void as well—the child she'd never been able to have with him. Although Coco told virtually no one about it, shortly before Boy's death, she suffered a miscarriage that required surgery and a brief hospital stay in Paris. The doctors told her she would never be able to have children—likely because of damage caused by her early abortion. Only in her later years did Chanel tell this story—to her friend Claude Delay.

But even in the depth of her despair and mourning, Chanel did not stop working. From Garches, she had her chauffeur, Raoul, drive her every day into the city, where she spent long days at her studio—which she had recently moved from 21, rue Cambon to more spacious quarters next door at 31, rue Cambon, where it stands to this day.

Since virtually everything about her work reflected his abiding influence, in some ways, Chanel's work was her memorial to Boy Capel—her ongoing tribute to him and to their time together. Coco also took comfort, or claimed to at least, in some of the spiritual beliefs she had acquired through Boy, particularly the theosophy-inspired concept of eternal life for all things. "I knew he had not really left me, and that he was simply on the other side," she told Marcel Haedrich. "This is how theosophy is indispensable. I just kept telling myself, 'He's there, he is waiting for me. We no longer exist on the same plane, but he is not leaving me. He wants my happiness.'" Chanel preferred to attribute such beliefs to the Eastern views she'd studied with Capel, but they owe at least as much to the tradition of the Catholic church in which she was raised.

A long Route ND 7 on the Riviera coast, between the towns of Fréjus and Puget-sur-Argens, just outside of Saint-Raphaël, stands a large cross in red stone. The inscription reads "In memory of Captain Arthur Capel, holder of the Légion d'Honneur, member of the [British] Army, who died accidentally on this spot, December 22, 1919." This

Memorial to Boy Capel, Fréjus, France

seems to be another memorial created by Coco in honor of the love of her life. Although it was erected anonymously, locals believe Chanel arranged to have it built. Given the discreet nature of their relationship and her later longtime residence in the area (she built her main vacation home in nearby Roquebrune), they are likely correct. For many years, during Chanel's lifetime, residents of Fréjus reported seeing bouquets of fresh flowers at the foot of this cross—but no one ever saw who left them there.

CHAPTER FOUR

GRAND DUKE DMITRI

C hanel's grief and sense of bone-deep loneliness were compounded in 1920 when news came of her younger sister Antoinette's death. Antoinette's brief marriage to Oscar Fleming had not been happy, and after a few awkward months with the Fleming family in Ontario, a distraught Antoinette had pleaded with Coco to pay her way home to France. Coco stalled, encouraging Antoinette to be patient, to try harder, and to work at promoting Chanel couture in Canada. But lacking Coco's inner steel and adaptability, Antoinette simply ran off with the first available man. She took up with a young Argentine, traveling with him to South America. There, it seems that, desolate over the failure of her new romance, Antoinette took her own life, though the Fleming family attributed her death to Spanish flu. She was thirty-three.

Antoinette was the second of Chanel's sisters to commit suicide after a failed love affair and the attendant social disgrace. In both cases, Coco was implicated in some way. If Chanel blamed herself at all for either death, she never admitted it, and she rarely spoke of the tragically short lives of the Chanel women. By 1920, Coco was the only female survivor of her family of origin, and determined to resist the sorrowful fates that had claimed Jeanne, Julia, and Antoinette. No man would rob her of her life. Work would save her. She told Vilmorin, "When I realized that my business had a life, my life, and a face, my face, a voice, my own, and when I realized that my work loved me, obeyed me, and responded to me, I gave myself over to it completely and I have had since then no greater love." Essentially, Chanel would marry her only faithful partner: work.

Along with love of work, Chanel remained more driven than ever by other desires: for stature, for influence, and for a place in the broad sweep of history. If anything, her growing cynicism about romantic love intensified her pursuit of these other, compensatory aspirations. The more unsatisfactory she found her own personal history, the more she sought a role in an abstracted, impersonal narrative, in History with a capital H. In 1921, History seemed to open its arms to her.

Chanel would later play down her two-year love affair with Grand Duke Dmitri Pavlovich Romanov, chalking it up to a kind of temporary exoticism: "The Russians revealed the Orient to me.... Every Westerner should get to know Slavic charm, to see what it's about.... I laugh about this adventure now." But Dmitri entered Chanel's life at a critical moment and exerted considerable influence over her. Through him, she encountered for the first time a certain stratum of European royal life—its design aesthetic, its powerful sense of history and capacity for nostalgic longing, and its reactionary political sympathies—all of which spoke deeply to Coco's own sensibilities and proved fundamental to her life and career. If she'd ever been drawn to Boy Capel's brand of progressivism, she turned firmly away from it now. Through Dmitri, Coco also grew acquainted with the Russian expatriate community of Paris—the aristocracy exiled by the Bolshevik Revolution—with which she would develop deep artistic ties.

Despite her protestations, Chanel was quite excited about her young lover, or at least by his role on the world stage and the possibilities he appeared to offer. She would ever after boast of her connection to Dmitri.

According to a close friend in later life, Jacques Chazot, even as an old woman, Chanel enjoyed regaling guests with tales of her Romanov lover: "She spoke often to me about the Grand Duke Dmitri with whom she had had a liaison.... Her stories fascinated me."

For a woman leery of attachments yet yearning for social advancement, little could have seemed more desirable than a superficial but well-connected nobleman, directly descended from the tsars. Moreover, from the duke's diaries—which have never been unlocked and read until now—we know that Dmitri thought obsessively about the possibility of a restored Russian monarchy, and about the likelihood of his assuming the throne as tsar. Many in his circle viewed Dmitri as the ideal candidate, and he began planning seriously for this eventuality. He attended meetings in Paris and traveled to other European cities to discuss the matter with supporters, sometimes with Chanel by his side. It required little stretch of the imagination for Coco to foresee the day when, married to Dmitri, she would naturally become empress of all the Russias.

Dmitri, then, fit perfectly into Chanel's worldview. She may not have fallen in love, but she did fall under a Romanov spell. In typical fashion, Coco subsumed his universe—in all its obsolescent splendor—and made it her own. She even claimed to discern a hidden ethnic bond between Slavic royalty and her own French country stock: "Inside every Auvergnat, there is an unacknowledged Oriental," she told Paul Morand, by way of explaining her ease with Dmitri's foreignness. She might as well have said, "Inside this peasant girl lives a queen." And she would have been right. While Coco did not, in the end, ascend the throne of Russia, the romance with Grand Duke Dmitri ennobled her in other ways.

From his earliest youth, a nostalgic melancholia hung over Dmitri Pavlovich Romanov. Born in 1891 to Grand Duke Pavel Alexandrovich and Duchess Alexandra Georgievna of Greece, Dmitri seemed destined for a life of triumph and pleasure. He was strikingly good-looking, tall, and athletic, with deep green eyes and the kind of chiseled profile associated with aristocracy. "Dmitri was extremely attractive,"

Grand Duke
Dmitri Pavlovich Romanov
as a cavalry officer

wrote his cousin and boyhood companion (and possible lover), Prince Felix Youssoupoff. "Tall, elegant, very *'racé,'* his look recalled the ancient portraits of his ancestors." Prince Felix grasped something essential here. Dmitri's role within the Russian nobility was always more abstract and historical—more about fitting into a portrait gallery—than it was human or personal. From the day of his birth, he confronted loss and abandonment, which left him with a permanent, nostalgic longing for family and—later—a fervent, somewhat grandiose nationalism.

Duchess Alexandra was seven months pregnant with her son when a boating accident sent her into premature labor. Soon after delivering Dmitri, Alexandra died, leaving behind the infant and his toddler sister, Princess Marie, not yet two years old. Alexandra and Pavel's marriage had been famously happy, and Pavel was too devastated by sudden widowerhood to take any pleasure in his frail new son. Care for Marie and Dmitri was left to a string of servants, including an English nanny who spoke to them only in her native language. The children's isolation intensified the bond between them, and they remained unusually close siblings all their lives.

Dmitri and Marie hardly knew their father. Duke Pavel spent most of his time traveling and in 1902, scandalized the Russian court by entering into a morganatic marriage, to Olga Valerianovna Karnovich Paley, a divorced woman. Knowing that such an irregular union would bring swift reprisals, Pavel married in secret, informing his children only after the fact, by letter. The duke's illegitimate marriage led to his banishment from Russia and permanent exile in France, whereupon his brother, Grand Duke Sergei Alexandrovich and his wife, Elizabeth (sister of Tsarina Alexandra), who had no children of their own, acquired official guardianship of Dmitri and Marie. Although privately devoted to his family, as the tsar's appointed governor-general of Moscow, Grand Duke Sergei was a severe, even sadistic, despot. In 1891, for example, under his reign, twenty thousand of Moscow's Jews were forcibly expelled from their homes during the brutal winter months.

On February 17, 1905, a member of the Socialist Revolutionary Party threw a nitroglycerin bomb into Duke Sergei's carriage, killing him instantly. His wife, Elizabeth, arrived to find her husband's body in fragments on the ground. Without weeping, the duchess knelt to retrieve shards of her husband's skull, shreds of his clothing, and one of his hands—still wearing its ring—from the bloodstained snow. By her side stood the teenaged Dmitri and Marie, bearing witness to the ghastly mutilation of the man they knew as a second father. Soon after the murder, Dmitri and Marie—orphans again—moved into the imperial palace, as wards of the tsar himself. Nicholas II proved a doting guardian and took a special interest in his nephew, whom he compared favorably to his own son, the tsarevitch Alexei, whose hemophilia had rendered him frail. Rumors even flew about Dmitri's replacing Alexei as heir to the throne, in a foreshadowing of later events in Dmitri's life.

Despite the tragic losses that beset his childhood, Grand Duke Dmitri passed the rest of his youth pursuing the pleasures and successes expected of a young Russian nobleman. He joined the Guards Regiment as a cavalry officer. He was an exceptional athlete and even competed in the 1912 Summer Olympics in Stockholm as an equestrian, finishing seventh. "No one had ever begun life with more ease or brilliance," wrote his sister, Marie, in her memoirs. "He trod a golden path, was caressed and feted by everyone. His destiny seemed almost too dazzling."

When you're a surviving member of the Romanov dynasty, life necessarily divides into "before" and "after." As Marie's wistful last sentence makes plain, she is looking back here, through the lens of her later expulsion from paradise, to a time before the slaughter of the rest of their family, before they had fled Russia forever, stripped of their fortunes and their titles. But the revolution was not the only historic cataclysm to divide Dmitri's youth.

Through boyhood years of shared adventures, Dmitri and his cousin, Prince Felix Youssoupoff, had cemented an abiding and loving friendship. When they were both young men, Felix—four years older and the more daring of the two—inducted Dmitri into his life of hedonistic exploits. Together, they explored the Gypsy camps outside of St. Petersburg, where prostitutes and drugs were readily available, and the opium dens of Paris's Montmartre district. Their exploits grew even more extravagant once the prince discovered his penchant for cross-dressing, and began a drag career as a nightclub "chanteuse."

Ignoring stern warnings from the tsar, Dmitri continued to fraternize with Felix, who gradually exchanged debauchery for mysticism, coming to regard himself as nearly supernaturally powerful. Dmitri's susceptibility to Felix's domineering influence would prove dangerous.

Although a semiliterate Siberian peasant, the megalomaniacal Grigori Rasputin had won great favor with the Russian royal family by styling himself a divinely inspired monk and religious adviser. The tsarina, convinced of Rasputin's ability to cure her son's hemophilia, ceded increasing authority to the monk, who was secretly plotting to seize power over the tsar, destroy the Duma, and replace all the cabinet ministers with his own appointees. With Russia's entry into World War I, the threat posed by Rasputin grew more serious, and many members of the court thought he would destroy the empire. Seeing no other options and convinced of his own, nearly mystical invincibility, Prince Felix decided to murder the monk, enlisting his impressionable cousin Dmitri.

On December 16, 1916, Felix, Dmitri, and a group of confederates attempted to kill Rasputin by feeding him tea cakes laced with cyanide. What followed has acquired the surreal aura of myth: According to Felix, Rasputin remained alive even after consuming the cakes, whereupon Felix shot the monk with Dmitri's revolver. Other accounts say that even after the men had thrown the monk's corpse into the Neva River, Rasputin emerged, unharmed, from the water, forcing them to shoot him yet again, this time fatally. This supernatural element of the story originates entirely with Prince Felix, who had a vested interest in depicting a demonic Rasputin.

What is certain is that the original poisoning plan failed (no poison was found upon autopsy), Rasputin was shot to death, and Dmitri, whether he'd handled the gun or not, was named accessory to murder.

Both cousins were sentenced to permanent exile, but while Felix was permitted a fairly gentle escape by ship, Dmitri was less fortunate. Thrown into an unheated freight train hurtling toward the Persian front of the war, Dmitri was expected to die either en route or soon afterward. Yet, while he suffered severely, Dmitri survived and made his way back to Europe, settling in Paris in 1920.

In murdering Rasputin, Felix and Dmitri had unknowingly saved their own lives. The chaos unleashed by the monk's death, and the subsequent unrest of Russia's so-called February Revolution of 1917, resulted in the abdication of Tsar Nicholas and the end of the Romanov dynasty. The replacement body, the "Provisional Government," lasted only until the November 1917 Bolshevik coup, which led famously to the slaughter of most remaining members of the imperial family.

Dmitri had escaped it all, but life as he knew it had vanished forever. He found himself bereft of fortune, rank, employment, family, and country. Dmitri had also severed all ties with his boon companion, Felix. Their joint participation in murder had taken a heavy toll on their friendship, which, judging from their correspondence, had, at times, veered into an erotic relationship.

I n Paris, Dmitri was utterly free but lacked both the means and the will to reshape his life. Even the city held few charms for him: "The social class which had money ... and which lived well ... is giving way *aux nouveaux riches*, of whom there are terribly many in Paris!"

Dmitri's Paris social circle consisted of his beloved sister, Marie, who had also managed to flee the Bolsheviks, and fellow expatriate Russians, many of whom were promoting a restored Russian monarchy. Dmitri was the prime contender in their eyes for emperor, preferred largely over the only other possibility, his cousin Grand Duke Cyril Vladimirovich Romanov. Though plans remained vague, the dream of becoming tsar occupied Dmitri entirely in the early 1920s. In long diary entries, he pondered how best to rule the new, modern Russia—how to be an enlightened emperor.

While he dreamed of the imperial palace, in real life, Dmitri was falling into poverty, borrowing heavily from friends, and doing little to pursue meaningful work. In this he was quite unlike his sister, Marie, who had begun a career in fashion, producing exquisite Russian embroidery. The few professional paths Dmitri did contemplate were hardly more practical than waiting to be tsar: "I will indeed be someone very great in Russia, but when? ... If I began to receive enormous sums of money for acting in the movies or if I became a professional dancer—that would go against my conscience." With little sign of imminent stardom (or tsardom) Dmitri compounded his troubles by turning to the only financial activity he knew: high-stakes gambling. His debts soon approached 100,000 francs.

Despite his difficulties Dmitri continued to live as a carefree socialite. His appointment book reveals long lunches and dinners enjoyed amid a constant stream of deposed nobility, reigning royals, ambassadors, and celebrities. The hotel letterheads atop his correspondence chart numerous trips to European capitals and posh resort towns.

Dmitri did consider one possible financial remedy: "The thought of marrying a very rich bride is less distasteful to me now than it used to be," the duke wrote in his diary on New Year's Eve, December 31, 1920, on page 71 of his journal. On page 82, an out-of-sequence entry appears, dated January 23, 1921. Dmitri has decided to add some recollections of a dinner party he'd attended the week before: "On that day I ate dinner with [French singer] Marthe Davelli. It was very pleasant.... Coco Chanelle [*sic*] [was there.] I had not seen her in 10 years. It was very nice to meet her again. Her face has not changed, but of course her looks are much more mature. She did not say a word about Boy Capell [*sic*]. The evening turned out wonderfully cheerful. We stayed until 4 in the morning. I was driven home by Coco, with whom I developed a surprisingly good relationship right away." This was one member of the deplored *nouveaux riches* Dmitri would learn to like.

A s Dmitri suggests, he had met Coco a decade earlier, almost certainly through Etienne Balsan, whom he knew through polo circles. Their renewed acquaintance quickly evolved into a romance. Dmitri was Chanel's physical type: Like Boy, he was handsome, athletic, and sure of his appeal to women. His eyes were even green, like Boy's. Coco swept in and, within days, Dmitri's diary mentions numerous visits to Chanel's home, drives in her car, and long nights.

Dmitri may have been drenched in nostalgia, but at thirty-seven, Coco Chanel faced squarely forward. She was a multimillionaire by today's standards, with three thriving boutiques in France, an international clientele, and a workforce of hundreds. Still grief-stricken over Boy Capel, she dated many men (and was sporadically seeing poet Pierre Reverdy at this time), but remained emotionally aloof, allowing work to define her existence. No success, though, fulfilled her need for the ultimate social status, the kind acquired usually only by birth. Chanel longed to be royal. Chanel's friend Lady Iya Abdy, herself of White Russian origin and an émigré from the Bolshevik Revolution, would later write, "Coco [was] always impressed by ... money and titles. She ... was ashamed of her roots. Instead of being proud of where she came from, she tried fiercely to hide her origins."

Chanel soon had Dmitri on an allowance, a small price to pay for bragging rights. Her police file suggests that she deliberately bruited about her relationship: "Information gathered allows us to establish that Chanel, today in possession of a fortune, provides financial support for her lover, with the unacknowledged goal of getting him to marry her and thus make her a Grand Duchess, or even Empress. It is said that she herself started the rumor of this marriage." We also know, from the stamped visas in her passport, that during her affair with Dmitri, Chanel traveled to Berlin with him, where he held meetings meant to plan his ascension to the throne.

In an attempt perhaps to live life more on Dmitri's terms, Chanel conducted the affair with uncharacteristic leisure, absenting herself from her studio longer than ever before. They traveled frequently and may even have lived together for a time, in Zurich, and later in adjoining suites (paid for by Coco) at the splendid Hôtel Le Meurice on the rue de Rivoli. After two months of dating in Paris, Coco urged Dmitri to accompany her to the Riviera, and the next day they drove in her new midnight blue Rolls-Royce (which she appears to have bought to tempt him) to the Côte d'Azur. (Dark-colored Rolls-Royces had been associated only with funerals, but once Coco put her stamp of approval on them, they became the fashionable car to drive—as she herself had predicted.)

On the Riviera, they spent three weeks in luxury hotels in Menton and Monte Carlo, golfing, shopping, dining, and visiting the casinos, with Chanel footing all bills. Chanel's chambermaid and Dmitri's valet, Piotr, came along to see to their personal needs. Coco said almost nothing about the tenor of their time together, but Dmitri's diaries describe the relationship as relaxed and companionable. He makes very clear, though, who was pursuing whom: "I ... gave in to Coco's passionate pleas to travel with her ... to bathe in the sun. ... She is extremely kind and a surprisingly dear and joyful companion. ... Time passes very quickly and pleasantly with her."

"Pleasant" falls far short of "passionate," and nowhere does Dmitri suggest any erotic interest on his part—quite the contrary: "I could not have chosen a better friend than dearest Coco to pass the time. We have the strangest relationship. I am far from being in love with her and never was. I fully realize that she is not even very beautiful, but nevertheless I am very attached to her. She herself, I don't know why, is astonishingly good to me, although she never brings up 'African' passions and does not ask about what is happening or about the future."

With the casual racism of his era and class, Dmitri here uses "African" as a synonym for "sexual," and suggests that their relationship may have been largely chaste. Chanel herself enjoyed intimacy with men, but Dmitri may have been more inclined toward male lovers (or, as he implies, was simply not attracted to her), although he certainly had dated women and later married, and fathered a son. Dmitri's account of their vacation suggests that Chanel was troubled by his ambivalence toward her. His description reveals her more vulnerable, even insecure side: "Coco is…sad…all the time thinking that I am most awfully bored and that I hated my time in Monte Carlo.... Though I [did] have a nice time, I am pleased to come back." However tepid their affair, Chanel wished to woo and please this man.

Other difficulties arose. Dmitri and Chanel were each anxious about the affair's potential effect on their reputations. Dmitri feared that being perceived as a kept man would harm him in the eyes of his monarchist supporters. "I personally have no illusions on this account.... They will spread the nastiest rumors among the Russian colony. They will go so far as to say that I am being kept by Coco."

Even worse, Chanel was a tradesperson, a commoner, which further threatened Dmitri's reputation. He had no thoughts of marrying her; he had his eye on a far more appropriate woman, Danish countess Marie-Louise Moltke, whom he had been cultivating for about a year. Surely recalling his father's banishment from court, Dmitri repeatedly describes his relationship with Coco using the highly charged word that besmirched Duke Pavel's second marriage: "I am not capable of living in such…falseness. After all…I have no experience with 'morganatic' relationships; I tremble at the thought of meeting acquaintances....I am completely incapable of such a *morganatic* relationship.... It is of course black ingratitude towards Coco, but I have had enough of gallivanting around France in a *morganatic* situation." (Emphasis is mine.) Chanel's private hopes notwithstanding, Dmitri—like Boy Capel before him—deemed her entirely unsuitable for matrimony.

Coco had her own cause for concern. In 1921, she was already involved with a besotted, highly jealous (and married) Igor Stravinsky, whose work for the Ballets Russes she was subsidizing while housing him and his entire family at Bel Respiro. Coco's sudden zeal for a seaside vacation with Dmitri may have stemmed simply from her desire to avoid Igor and his possessiveness. Chanel also likely worried that her dignity would suffer if her financial upkeep of another bankrupt Russian became public knowledge.

Even more than Dmitri did, Coco took pains to keep them shielded from the public on the Riviera. "I am not used to always thinking about whether or not I will meet acquaintances and to have to hide my location," wrote Dmitri. "It apparently also troubled Coco, since every time we entered a restaurant she asked me to go in first and see whether there were any acquaintances. It was absolutely clear that she did not particularly wish to be noticed. In general she was surprisingly naive about our trip, since she sincerely hoped that no one would find out about her leaving Paris, and especially with me." In one entry, Dmitri even describes Coco rushing to hide behind a wall in a restaurant upon catching sight of some friends.

Their attempts at secrecy failed. Stravinsky got wind of Chanel's escapades with Dmitri—probably via Coco's close friend and sometime rival, Misia Sert—and broke off their affair in a rage. It would have been impossible, in any case, for Dmitri to keep his personal life a secret, given the police surveillance that dogged him in France since his arrival in 1920. Police files contain careful records of Dmitri's varied residences, the hotels where he stayed in Paris and elsewhere, and the apartment he rented in Paris in 1920 on the rue de Miromesnil. The police kept track of Dmitri's social life, the *femmes galantes* he entertained, and the friends he frequented. Dmitri must have been keenly aware of being spied upon, for the file mentions that he had asked his concierge to keep his identity a secret (a request obviously disregarded).

It was perhaps this surveillance and the fear of prying eyes that prompted Chanel to install Dmitri at Bel Respiro after Stravinsky left. They took another extended vacation in 1922, when she whisked him off to Biarritz where she rented Ama Tikia, a white villa hidden by dunes, for two uninterrupted months—the longest vacation of Coco's life.

While clearly passive and dependent, Dmitri did wish to improve himself. One small notebook among his papers reveals that he sought inspiration in mysticism, perhaps inspired by his years with Prince Felix. Bearing the heading "Books I've read," the notebook contains a list of five volumes in the "self-help" genre: three by early twentieth-century mystic Hashnu O. Hara, and one each by spiritual gurus Lida Churchill and Flora Bigelow. Several of these volumes purported to teach a method for using the supernatural to "command luchre."

D abbling in the occult was so unexceptional among exiled Russian aristocrats that Dmitri's supporters even used spiritualism as a cover for their political activities, claiming that their meetings were séances. Chanel might well have attended some of these spiritual meetings with Dmitri. She was drawn to Christian mysticism and, since Boy, to theosophy and its offshoots. She also loved numerology and astrology, good luck symbols, and talismans. She kept tarot cards and a crystal ball in her apartment, and read the works of such authors as Joseph Péladan, the Rosicrucian novelist. Coco drew inspiration as well from Eastern religion and mysticism, referring often to one of her favorite texts, the Bhagavad Gita, to which Boy had introduced her.

It's easy to understand why the occult appealed to impoverished Russian monarchists. They all craved precisely what the occult promises: power and a way to manipulate one's environment. The occult and royalty have much in common: Both rely upon systems of signs, charged symbols of privilege—omens, secret numbers, royal insignias or jewels, titles—that grant power and knowledge to an elite, to those who can interpret or inherit them. Rasputin knew this; as a mere peasant, he had successfully harnessed the occult to counter the seemingly invincible power of dynastic royalty.

Chanel's interest in the occult stemmed from similar impulses. Psychoanalyst Claude Delay understood: "She was superstitious, and believed in the talismans of poor children." Gabrielle Palasse-Labrunie concurs: "Without symbols there was nothing. As a child she must have needed something to cling to. She constructed her own myth out of mysteries, signs, and symbols; she lived it and was imbued with it; symbols were everywhere in her beliefs, her apartment, her jewelry and her lucky charms, her style."

Any system of signs that conferred social power appealed to Chanel. Fashion is just such a system, of course—as Chanel knew long before social theorists such as Pierre Bourdieu examined the topic. "Where is the equivalent of [ancient magic] in our society?" Bourdieu asks in an essay on fashion and culture. The answer: "In the pages of *Elle*...in the couturier...who performs an act of transubstantiation."

From early in her career, Chanel had performed this kind of transubstantiation, by inventing her own talismans of power: design details that mimicked royal insignia or military medals and were intended to convey the transformative aura of social privilege. She routinely sewed heavy gilt buttons onto her simple jersey separates, for example, giving them the air of officers' uniforms, like the ones she had mended in Moulins. She would add further embellishment by embossing the buttons with elements borrowed from the occult, including astrological and folkloric symbols that resembled the identifying emblems of royalty: lions' heads (for her zodiac sign of Leo) and four-leaf clovers (for good luck).

The buttons looked remarkably like heraldic crests, and in a sense they were—they were the emblems of a new, parallel aristocracy, Chanel's self-created fashion elite. Rasputin had nothing on her.

Chanel's crash course in Romanov history furnished her with a new range of totems and icons of power, which she quickly subsumed into her aesthetic. Prime among these were her new Russian acquaintances themselves, especially Dmitri, of whom she made canny use at her salon.

"Dmitri was the *éminence grise* of Rue Cambon," wrote Claude Delay, referring to the Duke's habit of hanging around Chanel's studio, looking royal. Chanel enhanced the effect by hiring Dmitri's friend Count Koutouzov, former governor of the Crimea, as her *chef de réception*—the first person clients would meet—as well as some of Dmitri's young and pretty female acquaintances, who worked as models in her showroom. With all the Slavic aristocrats on display, kissing Dmitri's hand when he entered a room and referring to him pointedly as "Majesty," Chanel's boutique soon took on the air of a miniature Alexander Palace.

Along with all the Russian émigrés, the luxurious elements of Russian design invaded Cambon: brocade and tapestries, velvets, deep jewel tones, and fur. Though a departure from her humbler jersey styles, filtered through Chanel's social and aesthetic vision, these Old World, aristocratic details reemerged looking fresh, modern, and accessible. Her collections in the early 1920s featured sleek versions of typically Russian-style high-necked, embroidered, and intricately woven jacquard coats, red velvet gowns, and long tunics. Coco obtained much of her authentic Russian textile work from Dmitri's sister, Princess Marie, who—with Chanel's patronage—established her own embroidery business, known as Kitmir. "Grand duchesses did my knitting," Chanel later recounted with pride.

Through Dmitri, Chanel also encountered the sumptuous world of Russian imperial jewels. While such items might seem too Old World for Chanel's pared-down aesthetic, versions of them came to occupy an important place in her work, although often with a populist twist. We can trace most of what is still known as Chanel's signature jewelry pieces to this period, including the distinctive Maltese crosses of colored gems, which Chanel would later copy in inexpensive materials and pin to her suits; oversize emerald or ruby pins (again, often refashioned cheaply with colored glass stones); and the most iconic of all: long ropes of pearls. Dmitri had given Chanel one of the few heirlooms remaining to him: a strand of Romanov pearls. Rather than treasure this historic gift, Coco promptly had oversize paste copies made, and took to looping long garlands of them around her neck, sometimes irreverently mingled with the priceless originals. Somehow, instead of looking garish, the obviously

Three Russian- or "Byzantine"-inspired designs by Chanel, 1922: embroidered fur-trimmed coat, embroidered tunic top with Maltese cross motif, and beaded tunic dress

cheap beads seemed fresh and insouciant swinging against Chanel's neutral solid colors and tailored shapes. Layers of imitation pearls soon became one of the most famous and enduring trademark elements in the Chanel "lexicon"—a dense little symbol that neatly sums up the Chanel paradox, suggesting at once an ostentatiously democratic view of jewelry and a continuing love of the tokens of Old World inherited wealth. "One does not wear jewelry to appear rich, one wears it to be adorned. When costume jewelry is well made, it is meant to demolish real jewelry," observed Chanel.

.   .   .

C hanel's Romanov interlude also gave rise to the two innovations most crucial in securing her lifelong fortune and fame: her first perfume, Chanel No. 5, and the initial logo of interlocking Cs. Even before meeting Dmitri, Chanel had long intuited that a fragrance could serve as an anchor or linchpin of her design universe. She knew that women who could not afford her high-priced garments would likely spring for a small bottle of perfume, in order to enjoy a bit of her glamorous aura. "Fashion is in the air, borne upon the wind," Chanel said. A signature perfume would literalize the metaphor.

Uncertainty surrounds the creation of Chanel's signature perfume. Some accounts date its inception to 1920—one year before the affair with Dmitri began. Others insist that Dmitri first introduced Chanel to the man who would become her chief perfumer, Ernest Beaux—which would mean the perfume was launched at least one year later, in 1921. On these points, we must remain unenlightened, and accept what has likely been deliberate obfuscation on the part of the Maison Chanel, intended to maintain an aura of mystery around its most lucrative product.

However he entered Chanel's life, Ernest Beaux, former perfumer to the tsars, was the crucial catalyst for her perfume career. Beaux had been working for François Coty, but he agreed to take on Chanel's project, whereupon she traveled to his headquarters of Grasse, the fragrant town in the South of France, considered the perfume capital of the world. There, Coco spent days working with Beaux in his laboratory, proving herself as discerning of scents as she was of design. "In the lily of the valley they sell on the 1st of May, I can smell the hand of the kid who picked it," she liked to say. Beaux was impressed. Together, they hit upon the concept that eventually made Chanel a billionaire by today's standards: a perfume that evoked a new century and a new, modern kind of woman—a crisp scent to be marketed in a new way. While she was not the first couturier to create a fragrance—Paul Poiret had produced several, as had the Callot sisters—Coco revolutionized the concept entirely. Her perfume was to be an extension of her personal, highly modernist signature.

In 1921, perfumes were based on a set number of highly recognizable floral, herbal, or animal-derived essences, but Chanel insisted that hers have no overtly natural scent. "I don't want hints of roses, of lilies of the valley.... Perhaps a natural perfume must be created artificially," she said. To accommodate her wishes, Beaux combined floral and botanical essences (including ylang-ylang, neroli, sandalwood, vetiver, tuberose, and jasmine) with synthetic aldehydes, which made for a fresher, less recognizable scent, in which no one flower could be detected. Sounding like the modernist artist she was becoming, Chanel proclaimed that her perfume would smell like "a bouquet of abstract flowers." According to Beaux, the aldehydes added a note of clean northern air, the scent of Arctic snow, a "winter melting note." Of all the essences used in No. 5, jasmine predominates, although not noticeably so. Chanel insisted upon using a massive quantity of jasmine for one simple reason: Beaux had informed her that jasmine petals were impossibly expensive, and Chanel wanted to invent the "most expensive perfume in the world."

To package her perfume, Chanel again broke with tradition. Traditionally, perfumes came bottled in elaborate flacons bearing labels that evoked romantic or "Oriental" fantasies, such as "Nuit de Chine," "Forbidden Fruit," or "Lucrezia Borgia." Chanel had no patience for such exotic escapism. For her, only one fantasy was worth marketing: that of being—and smelling—like Coco Chanel. Accordingly, she eschewed a poetic title for the perfume, in favor of her own name—a first in the industry. The implication was clear: To wear the perfume was to wear Chanel herself, to take on a bit of her essence and mythic identity. Paradoxically, she had made borrowing that identity seem like the height of unique, modern individuality for all other women. "Women tend to wear the perfumes that men give them," she told Claude Delay, "but you must wear perfumes you love yourself, that are yours alone! When I leave behind a jacket, everyone knows at once [from its fragrance] that it's mine!"

Reinforcing the modernity of that Coco identity was the startling addition of a scientific-sounding numeral, the number "5," reputed to have been included because Chanel felt it was her lucky number. Perhaps she was remembering the five original children of her family, memorializing all but the youngest—baby Augustin—who'd died in infancy.

The bottle featured similarly modernist lines. Doing away with the usual decorative flacons, Chanel created the simple, sharp-cornered geometric container globally recognized to this day. The provenance of the bottle's design remains in dispute. It is possible that Chanel patterned it after one of Boy Capel's cologne flasks; it is possible that it was designed by Jean Helleu, who worked for Chanel for many years. But it is equally possible that, like so much from this period, the bottle owes its distinctive look to prerevolutionary Russia, since according to some sources it was actually designed by Dmitri, in imitation of the vodka flasks carried by officers of the Imperial Guard.

Chanel launched her perfume in the subtlest of manners, eschewing overt advertising. The very first night after she and Beaux settled on the formula, they dined out together with friends in Cannes. Having placed an atomizing flacon of the perfume on the table, Chanel surreptitiously spritzed every woman who passed by. "The effect was amazing," she later said. "All the women...stopped, sniffing the air. We pretended not to notice."

Back home in Paris, Chanel continued her campaign of subliminal seduction. Instead of putting her perfume on sale right away, she had her saleswomen spray the fitting rooms at Cambon throughout the day. When clients asked about the heavenly scent drifting around them, Coco would play dumb. "Perfume? What perfume?" she would ask, and then claim to recall a "little perfume" she'd "stumbled upon" while on vacation. Next, she began slipping bottles (she'd brought back hundreds from Grasse) to wellborn women of her acquaintance, as gifts—inciting the kind of word-of-mouth buzz that strengthened her clients' sense of belonging to a knowing elite. Finally, after a while, with no fanfare, the bottles began appearing discreetly on the shelves of her boutiques. By this time, demand had been whipped into a frenzy for this exclusive, mysterious product, and the staff could barely keep the store stocked.

In this way, much as perfume itself slowly unfolds and makes its presence known, the reputation of Chanel No. 5 expanded. It was to become the most successful perfume in the world, and its sales secured Chanel's fortune for the rest of her life. Chanel's intuition had been correct—perfume proved her most marketable and lucrative creation.

Chanel owed her great perfume success to more than just her good instincts. Within three years of launching this branch of her business, she dramatically enhanced its scope and profits through her professional collaboration with Pierre and Paul Wertheimer, the young German-Jewish brothers who owned Les Parfumeries Bourjois, the largest cosmetics and fragrance company in France.

It was Théophile Bader, owner of the Galeries Lafayette department store (where Chanel had once bought her stock of straw boater hats), who drew her to the attention of Pierre Wertheimer—the more charismatic of the brothers. Bader saw the potential of marketing Chanel No. 5 on a far bigger scale, and knew that the Wertheimers could provide Coco with the necessary financial backing and distribution network. In 1924, he arranged for them all to meet at the Longchamps racecourse (the Wertheimers were passionate racehorse owners), where a deal was quickly struck. Chanel sold Parfums Chanel to the Wertheimers, signing a contract that granted her a mere 10 percent of the enterprise. Théophile Bader received double that figure—20 percent—for having brokered the deal. And the Wertheimers, in exchange for developing the brand, distributing the perfume globally, and assuming all financial risk, kept 70 percent.

For decades thereafter, Chanel would claim to have been swindled in this deal that, admittedly, left her the smallest portion of the company. The truth was, the Wertheimers helped make Chanel one of the richest women in the world, and Chanel, in turn, helped the Wertheimers become far richer still. Their relationship grew only more complicated and tempestuous with time (and there were rumors of an intermittent love affair between Coco and the handsome Pierre), but when it began in 1924, all parties trusted one another so completely that they used the same lawyer. Pierre and Paul had instantly felt Coco's distinctive magnetism. Keen businessmen, they understood that they would be selling not only perfume, but also the captivating woman who'd created it.

To drive home the tight connection between the perfume and its creator, bottles of Chanel No. 5 were the first items ever to display the initial logo that Coco designed herself—the interlocking double Cs, which re-

The iconic bottle design
for Chanel No. 5, in its
most recent version

mains the company's trademark to this day. To wear Chanel No. 5 was to enter into Chanel's famous life, to take on her very essence, to be branded with, signed by, those interlocking Cs. The Cs represented the first use of a designer's own initials as an aesthetic motif in its own right.

The logo soon eclipsed all of Chanel's other motifs, appearing on jacket buttons, belts, shoes, and purses and acquiring enough cachet to turn into an abstract, impersonal status symbol, while still conjuring the person behind the initials. It became inextricable from the identity of the Chanel brand, appearing somewhere on nearly every accessory and all perfume packages. (Labels in her couture garments bore her entire name, "Gabrielle Chanel," instead of initials.)

Chanel now had her own sign system. Her identity, symbolized by those Cs, now conferred its special magic upon anyone who wore them. In a deft move, Chanel had turned initials—that highly individual sign of personal ownership—into a stamp of a privileged group identity.

Initialing garments held another, particular resonance for Chanel as well. In nineteenth- and early twentieth-century France, embroidering a young girl's initials on linens and lingerie was part of an important preparatory ritual for marriage: the creation of the trousseau. Growing up in an orphanage, Chanel surely did not have her own trousseau, but she cared enough about the symbolic weight of the ritual to claim that her "aunts" had forced her to prepare one: "Embroidering my initials on the tea towels of my future household; cross-stitching my nightgowns for a hypothetical wedding night, made me nauseous. I spit upon my trousseau in a fury." In the bitterness of this faux recollection, we hear the displaced anger of the girl deprived of such traditional rites of passage.

And so, instead of embossing her initials on her personal, household goods, Chanel figured out a grander plan: She would imprint her initials on the entire world. The double-C logo crystallizes the paradoxical brilliance at the heart of Chanel's empire: It granted prestige through uniformity, through mass identification with one idealized individual. Nearly everyone could own something with a Chanel logo, and nearly everyone wanted to. Coco had invented the cult of Chanel.

The provenance of the logo has sparked many stories and interpretations. Archivists at the House of Chanel have discovered that the sixteenth-century Catherine de Medici used a nearly identical emblem as her own identifying symbol, and it's perfectly plausible that Chanel fancied herself a latter-day Medici. Others have pointed to a similar linked-C pattern lurking in the stained-glass windows of Chanel's childhood orphanage at Aubazine. Chanel biographer Lisa Chaney has found a similar motif of entwined half circles (or "Cs") on the Arthur Capel Cup, a silver polo trophy presented by the Paris Polo Club, donated by Berthe, Boy's sister, with the likely (but unmentioned) support of Coco, who might well have designed the trophy's lettering. In this case, the first unofficial use of the double-C logo would have appeared, fittingly, on this object memorializing the life of Chanel's greatest love. Dmitri may have had a hand in the design as well: Some of the idle drawings decorating the margins of his diaries in the early 1920s recall Chanel's logo as well as her perfume bottles.

Finally, the C logo bears a resemblance to a four-thousand-year-old

Grand Duke Dmitri's diary drawings, including a sketch of
Coco's favorite number

Indo-European symbol of good luck—the swastika—adopted officially
by Germany's National Socialists in 1920, and an icon to which Chanel
and Dmitri would have had considerable exposure, given Dmitri's close
ties to Germany's Nazi Party and its White Russian supporters.

By the time Chanel's initial logo took shape, the swastika figured
widely on Nazi paraphernalia readily accessible to her and her social
circle, emblazoned on everything from uniforms to artillery. The swastika functioned in much the same fashion as did Chanel's Cs—as the
mark of a brand, betokening membership in an elite yet accessible community, the symbol of a highly attractive, demotic elitism. Nascent fascism and its symbols clearly appealed to Chanel, who went on to establish

her own close connection to the Nazi Party. Over time, she gravitated increasingly toward a reactionary, nationalist, and often deeply anti-Semitic social set, and her work continued to evolve into a curious blend of populism, militarism, and a kind of willed aristocratism.

Chanel's anti-Semitism must be read, in fact, in the context of her keen desire to manufacture a distinguished lineage for herself. Both Dmitri and Coco would have been inclined to distance themselves from the Jews, whom they regarded as a benighted, unaesthetic race lacking a country. Dmitri made the point most plainly in his diary, where he compared his plight with those of the Jews: "My God how much has happened since 1914! Papa is no more and there is not even that which only the Jews do not have—our motherland, our Mother Russia no longer exists."

To Dmitri, the Jews represented an orphaned people, a group with no parent country—an analogy that resonated politically for both him and Coco. These two—severed from home and family, eager for power and pedigree—both naturally gravitated toward theories that confirmed their own racial superiority while distancing them from such reviled orphans of history. With her new double-C insignia Chanel responded—consciously or not—to the heavy royalist nostalgia, militarism, and early fascism that saturated Dmitri's world, effectively inventing a new crest for herself—an emblem suggesting her command of a private fashion regiment of her own, or an alternative line of "family" descent through style.

Immersed in Romanov nostalgia and the symbology of a lost dynasty, this Auvergnat had found—or perhaps invented—the "Oriental" hidden within her after all. She had constructed her own personalized version of a dynasty, complete with its own tokens of power and prestige—all referring ultimately to her own re-created identity—a nonhistorical, nongenealogical form of royalty via fashion. The Romanov dynasty had begun its precipitous decline partly in response to the menace posed by Rasputin. While Dmitri had a hand in eliminating that one upstart peasant, he wound up abetting the imperial dreams of another. Through her liaison with Dmitri, Chanel gathered up the glittering remnants of Russia's defunct aristocracy and recycled them into the iconography of her own private empire. The Romanov dynasty had ended, but the House of Chanel had only just begun.

CHAPTER FIVE

MY HEART IS IN MY POCKET
COCO AND PIERRE REVERDY

A glass of papaya juice
and back to work. My heart is in my
pocket, it is Poems by Pierre Reverdy.

—FRANK O'HARA, FROM "A STEP AWAY FROM THEM," 1956

O nly very few among Chanel's intimates maintained close, un-broken relationships with her throughout her life. While she enjoyed a wide and diverse social circle, Coco tended to dis-connect herself from or simply lose those closest to her. She severed ties with most remaining members of her family; she had bitter feuds or out-and-out partings with many friends and associates; and she would suffer many abandonments and some real tragedies in her romantic life. She did stay on amicable terms with a number of former lovers, yet only one became a lifetime confidant and truly unwavering friend: French poet Pierre Reverdy, who loved her—largely from afar—for forty years.

Coco and Pierre met in 1919, when they were introduced by Misia Sert, who let no genius in Paris pass unnoticed (and was likely Reverdy's lover at some point). They began a romance the following year, when Chanel was probably also slightly involved with married playwright Henry Bernstein and shortly before her love affairs with Grand Duke

Poet Pierre Reverdy

Dmitri Romanov and—briefly—Igor Stravinsky. Busying herself thus with amorous activity, Coco seemed to be trying to push away her sorrow over Boy Capel, pursuing multiple erotic conquests in a manner we tend to associate with powerful men more often than with women.

Coco's two primary romances of the early 1920s could not have been more different. Chanel had fun with Dmitri but was well aware of his limitations. For her, the Duke's appeal lay in the glittering, external elements of his life. With Reverdy, she experienced just the reverse. Intense, passionate, spiritual, and brilliantly talented, Pierre spoke to the other side of Chanel—her country origins, her convent upbringing, her keen intelligence, and her intuitive interest in art. But Reverdy was also married and deeply conflicted—about his adulterous affair with Coco, about pursuing worldly success, and about anything that distracted him from his increasing religious devotion.

Born in 1889 (making him six years Coco's junior), Reverdy arrived in Paris at the age of twenty-one in 1910, having left his native Narbonne, a small, rural town in France's Languedoc region, near the Spanish border, just a few miles from the Mediterranean. In matters of family, Coco and Pierre had suffered similar trials, which left both with a lingering vulnerability. Like Coco, Pierre was born under the cloud of illegitimacy, the product of his mother's adulterous affair. His mother eventually divorced her first husband and married Pierre's father, but that marriage ended in divorce as well. Pierre's mother took his sister and moved away, leaving Pierre with his father. He never got over the loss. "I have always felt this sense of cosmic instability," he wrote.

The Reverdy side of the family consisted of artists and thinkers. Pierre's father was a progressive and refined man who encouraged his son's literary pursuits. The elder Reverdy's main occupation had been viniculture—working the rich soil of his vineyard in a part of France where wine was practically a religion. The Reverdy family also boasted a number of sculptors, men who shaped wood and marble into the edifices of many churches in the region. Pierre inherited his forebears' love of objects and woodworking and later imbued his poetry with a rich tactility resembling a sculptor's.

While not prosperous, the Reverdys enjoyed relative comfort until a catastrophic depression hit the wine growing industry in the early 1900s, which led to the "Winegrowers' Revolt" of 1907, when thousands staged mass protests against the policies that were slowly starving their region. The rallies led to violent showdowns with police, including the most notorious episode, which occurred in Narbonne. Angered over the arrest of one of their representatives, protesters attacked the police with stones. Police fired back. Soon the incident escalated and military troops fired on the crowds, killing five and wounding ten.

The killings devastated the community, raising specters of the 1871 Paris Commune when the government had also unleashed military violence against its own people. For the teenaged Reverdy, the violence resulting from the winegrowers' crisis signaled the end of his youth. He had participated in the protests and been horrified seeing friends and neighbors cowering in doorways, trying to dodge police bullets. His family lost its vineyard and sank into financial ruin. Pierre was left permanently disillusioned with life, government, and anything related to business, profits, or capitalism. He became a lifelong socialist.

After a brief stint in the army, Reverdy moved to Montmartre, where he quickly fell in with the leading lights of the cubist and surrealist movements: Picasso, Braque, Juan Gris, Apollinaire, André Breton, Cocteau, and Max Jacob. That same year, Pierre suffered the premature death of his father, a loss that devastated him.

Between 1915 and 1926, Reverdy wrote prolifically, producing at least twelve collections of poems and prose pieces, in addition to founding a highly regarded literary journal, *Nord-Sud* (North-South). But poetry didn't pay the rent. Pierre's wife, Henriette (a lovely seamstress he'd met in Paris and married secretly), was obliged to take in sewing. Pierre found a night job as a proofreader.

According to those who knew them both, Coco and Pierre fell hard and fast for each other. "Between Mademoiselle and the poet, it was love at first sight," wrote Maurice Sachs. He had a "devastating love" for Chanel, according to Jean-Baptiste Para. On her side, Chanel gravitated toward all the familiar traits she saw in Pierre. Although not classically handsome, his Mediterranean coloring—black hair and eyes, tan skin setting off unusually white teeth—recalled her own and that of her father and brothers. Reverdy also had an aura of rugged, peasant masculinity that appealed to Chanel, with a solid physique, expressive hands, and a very deep voice. A lover of beautiful women and good food and drink, Pierre exuded life and vitality. At the same time, sadness and existential despair were already eating away at him—caused in part by his very joie de vivre. His pleasure in life was, paradoxically, what tormented him. For Reverdy, vitality impeded the spiritual development he craved: "What encumbers me...is the health and robustness of my spirit, and it is in order to manage and control this health and this strength that I write."

Pierre cared little for restaurants, parties, and the glad-handing necessary for aspiring artists in Parisian society. "Life in society is a vast enterprise of thievery. One cannot get through it without becoming complicit."

And while Coco indulged in all of society's pleasures with gusto, she remained perfectly clear-eyed about that particular world. She told Paul Morand: "I employed society people...because they were useful to me....[But] they are irresistibly dishonest." Coco certainly admired high society and its alluring trappings, but the peasant girl within her longed to counter all the excess that surrounded her with simplicity, humbleness, and even austerity—the same qualities that Chanel imparted to her designs. She recognized a similarly controlled and restrained nature in Reverdy. "He was…severe with himself," she told Claude Delay. "He was an elevated soul."

We don't know if Coco and Pierre talked about their similar childhoods, their pain at losing their parents, or their shared experience as outsiders in Paris. We do know that Chanel took particular interest in Reverdy's stories of the winegrowers' revolt, since even decades later she would speak passionately of the young Pierre's participation in the protests, almost as if adopting his teenage memories as her own.

Chanel also took a deep interest in Reverdy's poetry and championed his cause in Paris. Knowing him too proud to accept her help, she secretly bought his manuscripts through intermediaries and then paid publishers to produce them, giving them extra money that she arranged to be paid to Reverdy in the guise of a "publishing stipend," without mentioning her name. She even gave Pierre marketing advice clearly based on her own experience: "If you write your poems on separate sheets of paper and sign each one, just as your artist friends do with their paintings, you will become as rich as they are, if snobbism has anything to do with it."

Although they spent many passionate moments together, Reverdy remained ambivalent about his affair with Coco and about his life in the world in general. Guilt about his infidelity to Henriette tormented him, as did his feeling that life in Paris was superficial and destructive. Typically, he would spend time with Chanel down in her elegant part of town and then rush off abruptly to Montmartre, disappearing for days at a time. Occasionally, he felt compelled to demonstrate the contempt he felt for Coco's decadent life, as he did memorably once during a reception at her home. As guests milled about in Chanel's beautiful garden, sipping cocktails, Pierre appeared with a straw basket on his arm. Greeting no one, he walked past the assembled company and knelt in the grass, clearly searching for something. Eyes strained to see what Pierre had begun dropping into his basket. Snails, as it turned out. Making great show of his indifference to the party, Reverdy had decided to go snail hunting at Chanel's reception, theatrically insisting upon his self-styled "country bumpkin" persona.

In May 1921, at the very height of his love affair with Chanel, Pierre took the dramatic step of converting to Catholicism. Max Jacob, himself a convert from Judaism, served as his baptismal godfather. Conversion turned out to be an imperfect path to virtue, however. The love affair between Pierre and Coco continued fitfully, even as Chanel pursued other men. He sent her every manuscript he wrote, and penned dedications to her in each volume.

The inscriptions' wide variation in tone testifies to Reverdy's ambivalence. In 1922, he produced his collection *Cravates de chanvre* (Cravats of Hemp—a reference to the ropes used in hangings). Chanel had subsidized the book's publication (albeit without Pierre's knowledge), and Picasso had provided the illustrations, making the volume a collector's item. In a handwritten dedication, Reverdy implies that he will back away from their romance: "Homage from the author, that imbecile, Pierre Reverdy.... Dear Coco I am your friend and have no other ambition than to be your best friend. Pierre." When Pierre inscribed his 1924 *Epaves du ciel* (Shipwrecks from heaven), though, he exercised far less restraint: "To my very great and dear Coco with all my heart until it beats its last." In the 1926 volume *La Peau de l'homme* (The skin of man) Pierre again reins in his emotions: "You do not know, dear Coco, shadow is the most beautiful setting for light. And it is there that I have never ceased nurturing for you the most tender friendship." Such vacillation defined their early relationship, a fact obvious to their friends. In a letter dated July 4, 1925, Max Jacob wrote to Jean Cocteau: "Reverdy converted on May 2, 1921. But ever since, he has been hesitating between uncertainty and disbelief, and between his wife and his stormy relationship with Coco Chanel."

For five years, Reverdy wrestled with his own uncertainty and inner anguish, sequestering himself for increasing periods in his Montmartre home, with the windows shuttered against the light, praying on his knees. He would even stop his clocks to silence his house completely and detach himself from the passage of earthly time. He continued to write, though, and beautifully, refining a spare, cinematic style tinged with an air of mystery that recalled his surrealist roots. The poems return frequently to images of windows, rooftops, or holes in walls—escape hatches to the natural world. Travel—another mode of escape or transcendence—also appears often in his poems, as in the very brief yet evocative "Departure":

> The horizon leans down
> The days are longer
> Travelling
> A heart leaps up in its cage
> A bird sings
> It is going to die
> Another door will open
> At the end of the corridor
> Lights up
> A star
> A dark-haired woman
> The lantern of the departing train

Reverdy was straining increasingly for escape—from Paris, from self-doubt, and perhaps from Chanel (the dark-haired woman?) as well. Through it all, Henriette seems to have maintained her composure and devotion, although she could hardly have been unaware of her husband's infidelity—of which all his closest friends were apprised. Finally, he could tolerate no more. In 1925, with a dramatic (some might say melodramatic) burst of self-abnegation, before a group of friends, Pierre set fire to a pile of his manuscripts and declared his imminent retreat from the world. He and Henriette would be moving to the village of Solesmes in Nord-Pas-de-Calais, a gray and chilly corner of northwestern France about one hundred miles from Paris. At thirty-seven, Pierre would enter life as a lay associate of the ancient Benedictine monastery there, the Abbaye de Solesmes, founded at the beginning of the eleventh century—a place not unlike Aubazine, Chanel's childhood home.

While Pierre did earn some money through his poetry, Misia Sert had helped finance the couple's move. ("You are a good fairy," he wrote to her.) He and Henriette settled into a small house on the grounds of the abbey, where they lived largely in solitude, amid a silence broken only by vesper bells. For the next thirty years, until the end of his life, Reverdy remained in Solesmes—the "horrific little village" as he called it—performing a self-imposed penance.

Pierre did permit himself some reprieves from his monastic regime and returned occasionally to Paris. No evidence suggests that Chanel ever visited Solesmes, but she did write and ask him to visit her at least once. His note of reply suggests his own desire to rein in his feelings: "I will come see you soon, but I will not stay long."

Reverdy continued to write voluminously and would send all his work to Chanel, each book or manuscript still bearing a handwritten dedication. His 1929 collection, *Sources du vent* (Sources of the wind), arrived with a note reading,

> Dear and admirable Coco . . .
> Since you give me the joy of liking something about these
> poems, I give you this book and hope it serves you as a soft and
> gentle bedside light.

In 1941 on a visit to Paris, Reverdy added a new inscription to Chanel's copy of his 1918 *Les Ardoises du toit* (Roof slates). In French, it was a rhyming verse:

> I add a word to these words so hard to reread.
> Since what is written is nothing
> But what I knew not how to say
> About a heart that loves you so much.

Chanel's personal library would eventually contain the complete published works of Reverdy, many in first editions, and virtually every manuscript. She read and reread these volumes, as evidenced by her handwritten pencil marks throughout. Chanel recognized Reverdy's genius and remained in contact with him throughout their lives. While she tended to be private about many of her lovers, she spoke openly about Pierre to friends, but usually only to praise his talent and lament his limited success.

Edmonde Charles-Roux recounts Chanel's frustration at Reverdy's obscurity: "Until her final years, Chanel would compare Reverdy, poor and little known, to other poets of his generation whose fame and fortune she felt were undeserved. 'Who were they? Who was Cocteau? A scribbler!' she would say, her voice choking with anger. 'A mere phrase-maker, a nothing. Reverdy, he was a poet! A visionary.'" Although Cocteau was also her good friend, Chanel here shows herself an excellent judge of literature. Reverdy's poetry was far richer and more sophisticated than Cocteau's. Her rage, though, was misplaced. Reverdy did not wish for fame and fortune, only for peace. But even peace eluded him. By 1928, after only two years at Solesmes, he felt he'd lost his connection to Catholicism and his faith. Yet he chose not to abandon his secluded life.

When Pierre made his infrequent excursions back to Paris, he reverted to his old, pleasure-seeking ways, visiting jazz clubs, staying out late, and drinking with old friends. But soon, inevitably, disgusted by his own pleasure, Reverdy would rush back to Henriette and his monastic world.

Chanel found something about Reverdy comforting and reassuring, and she turned to him whenever she encountered sorrow, even when that sorrow involved rejection by another man. In mid-1930, Coco would experience yet another rupture with a highborn lover, and reached out to Reverdy, who needed little coaxing to travel down to Paris for nights of dancing with Coco in Montparnasse. He even took the train all the way down to the Mediterranean, to stay with Chanel at her vacation villa, La Pausa. Neither Pierre nor Coco gave a thought to being discreet about their affair. Chanel even took Pierre on overnight visits to the home of her nephew André Palasse and his new family. (Palasse had married Catharina van der Zee in 1925 and lived, with their two young daughters, in a château Chanel had bought for them in Corbères, France.) This cozy phase of Coco and Pierre's relationship proved short-lived, though. Pierre returned to Solesmes, and Coco soon left for her stint in America as a Hollywood costume designer.

Pierre paid his most extended visit to Paris in 1938, when he accepted Coco's offer of a room at the Ritz. The late 1930s would be a difficult time for Chanel, who would lose another major lover in 1935, and then encounter a number of business challenges shortly thereafter. As always, when in pain or feeling lost, Coco turned to the ever-available Reverdy. When Pierre took up his brief residence at the Ritz, Coco had another lover, and Pierre and Coco might have kept their relationship platonic during this period, even while falling back into every other aspect of their former intimacy—talking for hours and seeing each other daily. The only hint that they may have strayed into bed during this time comes from a single remark about the 1938 visit from a friend of Reverdy's, the journalist Stanislas Fumet: "Pierre let himself be strangely seduced, a lot, it's true, a reaction to his overly austere life."

Shortly after Reverdy's return home from the Ritz, the Germans marched into France and established their occupation of the northern half of the country, which included Solesmes. Disgusted, Pierre sold his house and moved with his wife into a much smaller pavilion near the abbey. But the war galvanized Reverdy, and prompted him to join the French Resistance. He later learned of Chanel's involvement with the Nazis, but he seems to have forgiven her, believing that women in general were often weak and misguided in their political convictions.

After the war, Chanel and Reverdy maintained their correspondence and friendship. For Coco, Pierre felt like a "corrected" mirror image of herself, a shadow version of what her own life might have been had she turned away from fame and fortune and pursued instead only spirituality, art, and literature. Pierre even inspired Coco to try her hand at writing. Although she had no particular literary talent, from the late 1930s onward, she experimented with a series of aphoristic maxims—short, philosophical fragments contemplating morality and human nature, of exactly the sort Pierre often composed, following the grand French tradition begun in the seventeenth century by François de La Rochefoucauld, whom Reverdy instructed her to read. She would send these musings to Pierre, who would critique them and send them back to her. "I congratulate you on the three maxims you have sent me. They are very good," he wrote to her after one such exchange. That Chanel accepted—even pursued—this kind of interaction with Reverdy proves how completely she trusted him. Coco did not typically make herself this vulnerable to anyone.

Some of Chanel's writings were published in various women's or fashion magazines. Their wry, bemused tone reveals the unmistakable stamp of Reverdy's influence:

Lie if you must, but never in detail, or to yourself.

True generosity is to accept ingratitude.

Elegance is not the opposite of poverty. It is the opposite of vulgarity—and negligence.

Here, for comparison, are a few of Reverdy's versions of the genre, from his 1927 *Le Gant de crin* (Horsehair glove):

He who knows weakness is truly stronger than he who blindly believes in force.

We call traits that displease us in others "faults," and traits that flatter us, "virtues."

An opinion is a strictly personal sentiment to which we grant the importance of a universal truth.

Reverdy passed away in Solesmes on June 17, 1960, at the age of seventy. Chanel, along with most of his friends, learned of his death in the newspaper—he had confided in no one about his illness. Although most of their forty-year friendship took place only epistolarily and over a great distance, Pierre had served, in many ways, as Coco's conscience, her most constant guiding light. When asked why she thought he had faced death alone, contacting none of those closest to him, Chanel responded, "He never wanted to cede to anecdote." Her remark was apt, but also oddly reminiscent of Reverdy's dense, poetic style—a eulogy in a single sentence, itself resisting all anecdote.

CHAPTER SIX

WOMEN FRIENDS, MIMETIC CONTAGION, AND THE PARISIAN AVANT-GARDE

I n 1923, as Chanel's relationship with Reverdy continued in fits and starts, the affair with Dmitri petered out naturally, without acrimony. Nearing forty, Chanel had simply grown weary of supporting him. "Those Grand Dukes . . . looked marvelous, but there was nothing there," she told Claude Delay. As was her custom with former lovers, though, Chanel remained in friendly touch with Dmitri, after his marriage in 1926 to Audrey Emery, and up to his untimely death from tuberculosis in a Swiss sanitarium in 1942, at the age of fifty.

For a while, she also remained close with Dmitri's confidante, his sister, Princess Marie. This was typical for Coco, who often befriended couples and paid special attention to the women of the pairs. Sometimes, these couples consisted of her married lovers and their wives. Such was the case in 1918 when Chanel befriended Antoinette Bernstein, wife of her lover Henry Bernstein; when in 1921 she housed Stravinsky's ailing wife, Madame Yekaterina Stravinsky, and her children at Bel Respiro while dallying with Igor; and again in 1937 when she dressed socialite Mona Williams while conducting a flirtation (some say affair) with Mona's husband, Harrison Williams.

It is not clear whether the women always knew of Coco's involvement with their husbands. What is certain is that couples held a kind of negative fascination for Coco. "The worst is the couple," she told Paul Morand. "You might like them separately, but together, they are horrible."

By engaging both halves of a couple, Chanel could partake of the exclusionary solidarity she found so threatening; she could slip into the couple's sanctuary—just as she wished to gain entry into all clubs that excluded her. This pattern might have emerged in the aftermath of Boy Capel's marriage to Diana Wyndham, as Chanel's attempt to keep all potential "other women" safely within her grasp. It is also likely that Chanel found comfort in the familial trio she could form with couples, enjoying with them some faint shadow of that long-lost, most important couple in her life, her parents.

Giving the lie to her proclaimed disdain for couples, Chanel—like many children of absent parents—evinced great interest in reconciling separated couples. She delighted in advising her staff, for example, on their romantic woes and "always knew exactly what to do and what to say," according to her longtime assistant Lilou Marquand. "Mademoiselle adored repairing separated couples and was very good at it. She was like a fortune teller, a tarot card reader," says Marquand. (In her apartment, Chanel kept multiple figurines and sculptures of animals in pairs, as if surrounding herself with totemic figures of intact couples.)

Grand Duke Dmitri was unmarried when Chanel dated him, but he was very much half of a couple: His sister was closer to him than any wife could have been. (Claude Delay referred to the pair as *"un petit couple."*) Their early tragedies had bonded Dmitri and Marie, and their relationship had struck others as peculiarly entwined and mutually dependent, even when they were still living in Russia. According to a famous anecdote, during a formal ball at the imperial palace, Tsar Nicholas felt compelled to send a courtier to separate the siblings who danced conspicuously with only each other all night, refusing all other partners. Some believe Marie was pressured to marry Prince Wilhelm in order to detach her from her brother. Years later, when Chanel and Dmitri parted ways, he turned immediately to his sister for aid and comfort. And when he decided it was time for marriage, Dmitri chose Audrey Emery as his bride in close consultation with his sister. Upon Marie's death, she was buried, as she had requested, in a grave next to her brother.

Soon after Dmitri began seeing Coco, Princess Marie entered into a thriving business relationship with the House of Chanel. Even after Coco's rupture with Dmitri, Marie's atelier continued to furnish Chanel with embroidered and specially woven fabrics, until a dispute ended the friendship as well as the business partnership. They quarreled over Marie's breaking her exclusive arrangement with Chanel and acquiring other designer clients. Chanel feared that Marie would leak professional secrets to competitors.

Princess Marie in one of her own embroidered blouses

Until their falling-out, though, Chanel and Marie enjoyed an honest and intimate friendship. Unlike her brother, Marie adapted well to life in exile and harbored no monarchical aspirations of her own. Trading on the delicate hand embroidery skills she'd learned as a child from Russian nuns, Marie decided to launch a fashion career. Chanel was using a great deal of embroidery in her Russian-inflected collections at the time, and after Dmitri introduced the two women, Marie resolved to become Chanel's main purveyor of high-quality, low-cost piecework. It was an ambitious goal for a woman who had never been near a sewing machine, but Marie managed to succeed—even disguising her royal identity to take sewing machine lessons at the Singer store in Paris.

Marie's instincts proved excellent. She turned out to be a highly talented seamstress and quickly grew adept enough to impress the great Coco Chanel, who placed her first order with Marie for Russian-style tunics, blouses, and paletots. Soon, the fashionable women of Paris were clamoring for her stunning, intricately patterned designs.

Marie did not have Coco's flair for business, but Coco so admired her talent and drive that she helped Marie open her own atelier, Kitmir (named after a dog character of Persian mythology), which began hiring many of the princess's fellow aristocratic Russian émigrés, employing as many as fifty women at one time. Combining her new sewing skills with her love of fine art, Marie became a true virtuoso of the needle and found joy in such triumphs as seeing a model display her work on the runway or catching sight of a woman at the Ritz wearing a tunic she had embroidered.

Such were the pleasures of independent womanhood, which no one understood better than Chanel, who turned Marie into something of a protégée. In Marie, Chanel saw a version of herself: a woman deprived of social and financial means but dead set on using her own talents to reverse the situation. That Marie was a true duchess only enhanced Chanel's pleasure in being able to offer her largesse.

Coco did more than launch Marie's business; she transformed her personally. When thirty-one-year-old Marie arrived at rue Cambon, she looked, according to Chanel, "like a refugee . . . of over 40"—encumbered still by the elaborate coiffure and Old World, heavy-skirted dresses she'd worn in Russia. Chanel explained to her that, for business, Marie needed "to look prosperous." The princess needed a Chanel-style makeover. Marie was drawn in by Chanel's magnetism and accepted her transformative influence. "You were swept off your feet by the fierce vitality she exhaled, the quality of which was inspiring and infectious," she recalled. Smart and self-confident enough to accept even Coco's harshest criticisms, Marie allowed her new employer to work her magic.

Advised by Chanel that she was overweight and dowdy, Marie embarked on a diet and submitted to regular sessions with Coco's Swedish masseuse, who helped her shed pounds. Chanel dressed Marie (in Chanel naturally) and taught her to apply makeup—which Marie had never used. And when Coco informed the princess that her hairstyle resembled "a giant brioche on the top of her head," Marie did not resist as Chanel grabbed her head, tore all the hairpins out, seized a pair of scissors, and hacked off great fistfuls of Marie's hair, as if it were just another length of unruly fabric in her workroom. (When in a fever of creation, Coco often confused animate and inanimate objects. Her models complained that she routinely stuck her dressmaker pins right through their flesh during fittings, laughing when they yelped.) Although stunned by the violence of the gesture, and at first unhappy with her shorn locks, Marie kept her hair in a short bob, like Coco's, for decades thereafter. Dmitri might not have turned Coco into a duchess, but Coco turned a duchess into a "Coco." Chanel could now look upon this member of the Russian royal family, this once future queen of Sweden, and see... herself.

This was Coco's typical modus operandi: She would lure women to her charisma and then stamp them with her own distinctive image. For this reason, scores of photographs of Chanel and her women friends and associates look like pictures of twin sisters. Often, even the bodily postures of the women mimic Coco's, as if Chanel's physical attitude and stance were as contagious as her style. While she tended to absorb the men in her life, Chanel tended to *be* absorbed by the women.

Chanel owed her extraordinary success precisely to this mimetic contagion, to her power to elicit in women a deep desire to imitate her. Coco had crafted a role, her "wearable personality," complete with costumes, hair, and makeup, which other women longed to play. Her life was pure theater.

> Chanel confused herself with the female character she had imposed upon all of Paris.
>
> **—IRENE MAURY, FORMER CHANEL EMPLOYEE**

Theatrical creature that she was, Chanel felt a great attraction to the stage. She had taken her first steps toward metamorphosis, after all, on the little stage of a café concert in Moulins. But Chanel's real theatrical ambitions far exceeded the bounds of those early minor productions; her intention was to costume at least the entire female population of France. "Nations have a style," she told a journalist in later years. "You have a style when everyone on the street is dressed like you. I achieved this." She did not overstate. Coco knew that fashion is theater and—like a great playwright—she had invented an indelible character that women the world over longed to play.

At times, Chanel openly acknowledged her sense of herself as a dramatist, as when she turned her Cambon showroom into a theater with an actual stage, prompting *Vogue* magazine to title its review "Curtain Up, Fashion Appears." Occasionally, she compared herself overtly to a playwright, explaining to an interviewer: "The top of a dress is easy to create, like the first act of a play. The difficulty comes in the final act, and I alone know how to construct the skirt." Princess Marie likened Chanel's private fashion shows—held the day before a formal public show—to "dress rehearsal[s] of a play...The models were the actresses and the gowns the parts."

For Chanel, the 1920s brought confirmation that she indeed stood upon the world's stage. Her career success and her carefully crafted social persona had had their desired effect. Wealthy and prominent women wore her designs all over Europe and in America; many more wore cop-

Mimetic friendships: Chanel in her signature jersey and pearls, with Iya Abdy, 1929 (top). Chanel and the Duchesse de Gramont, St. Moritz, 1931 (bottom)

ies of her work. Coco had established herself as an icon of privileged chic in Paris, as close to self-made royalty as anyone could get. She sold Bel Respiro in Garches and took out a long-term lease on a historic town house, the Hôtel Montbazon-Chabot, 29, rue du Faubourg Saint-Honoré, a property with a vast garden.

Chanel's new neighbors included the Rothschilds and the president of France. In keeping with her penchant for pedigree, even Coco's house now boasted a royal lineage. The press reported that Mademoiselle's new home was "a famous old mansion whose history stretches far back into the eighteenth century." It had been constructed in 1719 for the Duchess Rohan-Montbazon of Brittany, and had subsequently housed many generations of French noblemen, including the nineteenth-century Count Antoine de la Panouse. Chanel furnished her new home lavishly, with crystal, velvet draperies, mirrors, the hand-painted Coromandel screens she loved, and carpets woven to her specifications. One of these carpets cost at least 100,000 francs (or about five times the price of a luxury automobile at the time), but Coco had no financial concerns. "I never discussed prices," she said.

This was to be the perfect backdrop for Coco's new, more prominent role on the cultural scene. To enhance her stature further, she hired a young writer, Maurice Sachs, a close friend and secretary of Jean Cocteau's, to fill her home with books she should read, paying him a generous monthly retainer to select just the right leather-bound classics. Some of these beautiful, gilded books can still be seen on the shelves of her apartment to this day, and just like the tomes in the study of Jay Gatsby, another mythic striver of the 1920s, many look virtually untouched. Later, when Pierre Reverdy inspected the book collection, he felt compelled to tell Coco how misled she had been. With all the money Chanel had paid him, Sachs had procured only poor-quality books of middling literary value. Chanel was furious and fired Sachs at once.

At the center of her outsized drawing room, Coco positioned two black grand pianos, suitable fixtures for the new social world she set out to conquer: Paris's theatrical avant-garde. For several years, she had been forging a tight friendship with the single best-positioned person in the world to guide her in this new endeavor: the Polish-born classically trained pianist—and famous beauty—Misia Sert.

Misia was doyenne of France's artistic elite and a true *salonnière* in the grand eighteenth-century tradition. She would provide the tutelage and all social introductions necessary to help Chanel transform herself yet again, this time from arriviste *couturière* into modernist artist. "It was about the music," Chanel told Delay years later, describing the atmosphere of that drawing room. "We would sit on the sofas, and I discovered the world of art."

> One should render homage to the profound and sparkling women who live in the shadow of the men of their epoch and who, within the artists' world . . . exert an occult influence. It is impossible to imagine the gold of José-Maria Sert ceilings, the sunlit universe of Renoir, of Bonnard, of Vuillard, of Roussel, of Debussy, of Ravel, . . . the Mallarmean prism . . . and the radiant dawn of Stravinsky, without seeing rise up the silhouette of the young, beribboned tiger, the soft and cruel face, like a pink cat, that belongs to Misia.
>
> —JEAN COCTEAU

Despite her sixty-year career devoted to dressing women, Coco claimed to hold her sex in very low regard. "A woman," she declared, "equals envy plus vanity plus chatter plus a confused mind." She made an exception, though, for the woman known as "the Queen of Paris," Misia Sert, née Marie Sophie Olga Zénaïde Godebska—twelve years older than Chanel, mercurial, cruel, self-absorbed, and the one close female friend she kept throughout her life, and even then, with some reservation: "I had only her as a friend, and in fact I appreciated more than liked her."

The unusual life of Misia Sert emerged from a concatenation of childhood sorrow, aristocratic privilege, sexual obsession and betrayal, and a nearly unbelievable parade of the greatest names in European modernism—with this last element being the most crucial. Although she possessed considerable musical talent herself, Misia earned her renown by virtue of the other people she ushered into history—the artists she discovered, nurtured, goaded, and promoted, among them Vincent van Gogh, Stéphane Mallarmé, Sergei Diaghilev, and Igor Stravinsky. Misia made a career of cultivating the talented luminaries of her era and offering them a sense of belonging to a select group. And though she came from great wealth, Misia was no snob. She could discern instantly the ineffable "x" factor of genius in people of any social class or background, as she would in Chanel's case.

Misia's lifelong friendship with Coco Chanel seems inevitable. When they met in 1916, Chanel was already glamorous and rich, yet longed for access to the highest levels of artistic society. Misia represented the dazzling apex of this society; she embodied social access. Marcel Proust referred to her as a "historical monument."

But like Chanel, Misia was needy. Her mother had died hours after giving birth to her, leaving Misia to endure a painful, lonely childhood. As an adult, Misia had a tendency to develop mad crushes on women whose love and approval she craved. When she met Coco at a dinner party, she immediately felt one of these crushes coming on.

The daughter of Cyprien Godebski, a renowned Polish sculptor with ties to the tsars of Russia, and Sophie Servais, a wealthy Russian Jew from a family of distinguished musicians, Misia was born into international artistic royalty. Her parents counted among their friends such luminaries as Franz Liszt, Gabriel Fauré, and Hector Berlioz.

Wealth and glamour could not keep the Godebskis' marriage from ending in tragedy. Long tortured by her husband's absences and infidelities, Sophie—nine months pregnant with Misia—made an epic trek across Russia to find him, traveling two thousand miles in the dead of winter. She finally located him, living with a pregnant mistress in St. Petersburg. Even worse, that mistress was Sophie's own young and beautiful aunt, Olga. The shock sent Sophie into labor, and she died the next day—of complications from the birth or perhaps just a broken heart. "The tragedy of that day left a deep mark on my destiny," Misia later wrote. That tragedy was compounded in the remaining years of Misia's childhood as she found herself shunted from one relative to another, eventually winding up at the Convent of the Sacred Heart in Paris, a cold, impersonal, and severely strict Catholic boarding school that she loathed.

We know that Chanel found Misia's story of her mother's death compelling, because later in Coco's life, she simply stole it and used it as her own. With all her usual fervor of imitation, she told Marcel Haedrich that her own mother had died after traveling a long distance to find her own wayward husband. It wasn't quite true, but it highlighted Coco's clear recognition of the similarity between her childhood and Misia's.

Misia Godebska eventually liberated herself from the convent, growing into a celebrated cat-eyed, voluptuous beauty who would inspire Renoir, Bonnard, Vuillard, and Toulouse-Lautrec (among others) to paint her portrait. After a brief career as a piano teacher in Paris, she began her real career as a *récolteuse de génies*—harvester of geniuses—as Paul Morand put it, unerringly collecting every promising writer, composer, choreographer, dancer, and painter in her path.

Misia often met her geniuses through her several husbands. Husband number one, Thadée Natanson, was a wealthy Jewish journalist and founder of the eminent journal *La Revue Blanche*. Through him, Misia befriended the most exciting figures of modern art and literature, including Leo Tolstoy, Anton Chekhov, Marcel Proust, Mark Twain, and Oscar Wilde. Claude Debussy played the piano in her drawing room; Henrik Ibsen escorted her to rehearsals of *Peer Gynt*.

In 1905, Misia divorced Natanson to marry Alfred Edwards, who was portly, asthmatic, and much older—but immensely wealthy and fond of bringing her precious jewels. They moved into a lavish apartment on the rue de Rivoli, facing the Tuileries, and went yachting on weekends. (Such luxuries may have helped Misia overlook Edwards's unconventional sexual proclivities; he was famously coprophilic.) With Edwards, Misia's salon grew only more dazzling. Renoir visited her apartment three times a week to work on his luminous portrait of her, which today hangs in London's National Gallery. When an envious Bonnard insisted on equal access, Misia sat for him as well.

After the Edwardses' marriage dissolved in 1909 (Alfred also had a fondness for young actresses), Misia, thirty-six, finally found the love of her life: the opinionated, passionate, and gallant Spanish muralist José-Maria Sert. They had a protracted affair for over a decade before Misia and "JoJo" Sert finally married in 1920.

When Sert introduced Misia to Russian impresario "Serge" Diaghilev (for whose Ballets Russes Sert had designed a number of sets), he inaugurated one of the most important artistic and business partnerships of the twentieth century. Like Misia, Diaghilev had lost his mother at birth; like Misia, he was born in St. Petersburg in March of 1872. They were kindred spirits and fell into an intense friendship at once. Diaghilev had only recently arrived in France in 1909, meeting Misia just at the moment when he began assembling his revolutionary troupe, Les Ballets Russes. With Serge, Misia assumed her greatest role—patroness of the Ballets Russes, the company that would permanently alter the course of theater, music, and, especially, dance.

Misia introduced Diaghilev to her young musician friends and regularly funneled money to him; her home provided the venue for Stravinsky to play his new score for *The Rite of Spring* (*Le Sacre du printemps*) for Diaghilev. Misia was among the very first to understand the complexity of Stravinsky's music. When Igor and Serge quarreled bitterly, it was Misia who brokered the peace between them. She counseled Diaghilev in his dealings with the erratic and brilliant Vaslav Nijinsky, with whom Diaghilev fell madly in love. She intervened on behalf of the young Jean Cocteau when he wanted to collaborate with Stravinsky; and after hearing an eighteen-year-old Francis Poulenc play his music at her home, she recommended him to Diaghilev, for whom Poulenc later composed the score of his ballet, *Les Biches* (on which Chanel would also collaborate).

Misia felt perfectly at home amid the world of the Ballets Russes; the group—which came to include Bakst, Fokine, Goncharova, Massine, Picasso, Satie, and Balanchine—provided the familial coterie she craved. She had assumed her role as godmother to this restive group when she met Coco Chanel in 1916, at a dinner given by actress Cécile Sorel in her Quai Voltaire apartment. Chanel was thirty-two and a rising young fashion star. The evening proved momentous for both women, but Misia was downright love-struck. The chapter in her memoirs dedicated to Coco begins with a description of that dinner. Coco insisted that this chapter be omitted from Misia's book, and it was published only years later by Misia's biographers:

> My attention was immediately drawn to a very dark-haired young woman. Despite the fact that she did not say a word, she radiated a charm I found irresistible.... Therefore I arranged to sit next to her after dinner.... I learned that she was called Mademoiselle Chanel and had a milliner's shop in the rue Cambon.
>
> She seemed to me gifted with infinite grace and when, as we were saying goodnight, I admired her ravishing, fur-trimmed, red velvet coat, she took it off at once and put it on my shoulders, saying with charming spontaneity that she would be only too happy to give it to me. Obviously I could not accept it. But her gesture had been so pretty that I found her completely bewitching and thought of nothing but her.... Sert was really scandalized by the astonishing infatuation I felt for my new friend.

As so often happens, the fine details of a first encounter augured the tenor of the entire relationship. After one dinner, during which they barely spoke, a virtually hypnotized Misia found herself wearing— however briefly—Chanel's velvet coat. While she may have declined Chanel's proffered gift, Misia was nevertheless soon enveloped in all things Chanel. ("Misia throughout her life was in search of tyrants," according to her biographer Arthur Gold.) The next morning she went straight to rue Cambon to see more of Coco's inventory and by day's end, Misia and JoJo Sert were dining chez Coco and Boy in the avenue Gabriel. Chanel's account of their earliest days together confirms Misia's intense interest: "She grabbed hold of me after dinner and has never left me since."

Misia had found another artist for her collection, and Coco had found precisely the kind of cultural mentor she sought. "Without Misia, I would have died an idiot," Chanel said. Misia even helped Coco refine her still-provincial accent, coaxing it into something more Parisian. She may have given her some rudimentary piano lessons, too. But the friendship with Misia was Coco's most reciprocal to date. While Misia would wield tremendous influence over Chanel's artistic and intellectual life, Coco held at least equal sway over Misia, molding her stylistically and socially, as was her custom with women friends. At forty-four, having weathered numerous marital storms, Sert was nearing the end of her career as a professional seductress. In Coco, she found a chic and beautiful woman whose distinctive, youthful style was specifically designed for sharing, offering a promise of renewed allure.

For Chanel, Misia represented not only incomparable cultural and social opportunity, but also another couple to befriend. Coco found JoJo Sert as compelling as Misia did. "One felt intelligent just listening to him," she told Marcel Haedrich. To Paul Morand she said, "Monsieur Sert was a personality, a character, much bigger than his painting. 'Admit that everything else seems dull in comparison to Sert,' Misia would say to me: it was true."

Coco and Misia (often with Sert as well) became inseparable partners in crime, dining out in Paris, attending the opera. When they appeared in public, Misia would usually be dressed in Chanel couture and, sometimes, to make a great theatrical show of their friendship, they would dress as twins, in identical Chanel outfits.

The friendship solidified three years after their first meeting, in 1919, upon the death of Boy Capel. "Coco felt this loss so deeply that she sank into a neurasthenic state," wrote Misia. "I tried desperately to think of ways to distract her." Misia devoted herself to Coco, inviting her to every society party she could find, although more than a few aristocrats were still loath to include a seamstress among their guests. When the Count and Countess de Beaumont refused to include Chanel at a masked ball at their home, Misia and JoJo refused to attend and, with Pablo Picasso in tow for good measure, escorted Chanel to the entrance of the Beaumont residence, where they mingled with the waiting chauffeurs and entertained themselves watching the costumed guests come and go.

Chanel (left) with Misia
Sert (center) and Hélène
Berthelot on the Lido,
c. 1930s

"Rarely have I been so amused," wrote Misia of that night. Etienne and
Edith de Beaumont rethought their guest list in the 1930s, when Chanel—
who by then had been employing Count Beaumont for some years as her
jewelry designer—became a regular at their soirées, and the countess's
favorite *couturière* for her own wardrobe.

In August 1920, Misia and JoJo finally married. For their honeymoon
they decided on a cruise to Venice aboard a private yacht; they also decided to take the still-despondent Chanel with them. Although she was
never JoJo's lover, Coco had infiltrated the couple's innermost sanctum.
The Serts had become her new family. That summer, Venice was filled
with French and Russian aristocrats, and Misia introduced Chanel to as
many as possible, making the trip one of Chanel's most definitive forays
yet into the beau monde. From within her new secure and privileged

position, Coco began planning her encroachment onto another part of Misia's territory—she, too, could become a patron and muse for the arts.

Diaghilev was also in Venice, complaining bitterly to Misia about his lack of funds to remount a new production of *The Rite of Spring*, for which Stravinsky's score required a full (and very expensive) orchestra. While privy to these discussions, Coco did not participate. Instead, once back in Paris, she discreetly betook herself to the Hôtel Continental on the rue de Castiglione (just two blocks from Cambon) to see Diaghilev, who barely recognized her name when she was announced. He soon snapped to attention, though, for Chanel had come on business. For years thereafter, she was fond of recalling this brief meeting that changed both their lives.

Asked by Chanel about his finances, Diaghilev explained that he had been soliciting donations from a variety of patrons, among them Nancy Cunard and Princess Edmond de Polignac, née Winnaretta Singer, American heiress to the sewing machine fortune. Chanel recalled their conversation thus:

DIAGHILEV: "I've been to see the Princess she gave me 75,000 francs."
CHANEL: "She is a grand American lady, I am only a seamstress. Here's 200,000."

With this, in the kind of social table turning she loved, the seamstress outstripped the grand American lady, writing out a check on the spot for a gift surpassing Diaghilev's wildest expectations. She had only one condition: that he tell no one of her generosity, especially Misia.

A secret among these three was very unlikely. Misia and Coco spoke every day by telephone and rarely made a move without consulting each other. Misia and Serge Diaghilev were also the closest of confidants. Nevertheless, Misia and Chanel never discussed that massive donation to the Ballets Russes. Its effect, however, was transformative for Coco.

With that stroke of her pen, the apprentice eclipsed the master. It was, as Arthur Gold wrote, "a gesture that combined generosity, bribery, and social maneuvering." Chanel wanted what Misia had—influence, acceptance, and respect within Diaghilev's circle—and she got it. She had also inserted herself once more between a pair of intimates, two best friends. Chanel was well aware of Misia and Serge's intense, intertwined relationship: "Misia never left Diaghilev," she told Morand. "Between them it was one of those devoted relationships of whispers—evil, tender, strewn with pitfalls." Now Coco had made sure that Serge owed more to her than he ever had to Misia. Chanel's donation catapulted her instantly to the highest patron status; she began attending every rehearsal of the Ballets Russes.

The backdoor transaction with Diaghilev was only the next step in Misia and Coco's intricate pas de deux—a mixture of love, emulation, and intense rivalry. When they met, a besotted Misia had stepped at once into Chanel's style; now Chanel had stepped just as smoothly into Misia's entire social and aesthetic world. Misia and JoJo had helped Chanel decorate her new townhome, which henceforth served as one of Paris's chicest gathering spots for all of Misia's best friends, particularly Cocteau and Diaghilev—who had become Coco's best friends, too.

Both women were aware of the tension, but Misia may have felt it more keenly. Coco was younger, on the ascent, gaining fame, and earning ever more money. Misia, over a decade older, had traded away her own musical career for a life of the kind of arts patronage at which Chanel seemed to excel effortlessly, without forsaking her own career. Taught from birth that people (especially women) were essentially pawns in a high-stakes social poker game, Misia now sought to outplay her protégée.

According to Chanel, when Edouard Vuillard, with whom Misia had had a bitter falling-out, asked Coco to pose for him, Misia instantly reconciled with the painter, "only to prevent him from painting me." Coco also believed Misia had similarly intervened to break off a nascent friendship between Coco and Pablo Picasso. In 1923, when Chanel briefly maintained simultaneous romances with Igor Stravinsky and Grand Duke Dmitri Romanov, Misia saw to it that Igor was apprised of his lover's betrayal, which devastated the jealous—albeit married— Stravinsky and sent him packing.

Chanel understood Misia's conflicting impulses: "[Misia's love for me] comes from a deep well of generosity mixed with a demonic pleasure in ruining everything she touches.... It's a loving spitefulness, seeing me makes her unhappy, but she is desperate if she does not see me.... I sometimes bite my friends, but Misia, she swallows hers." Yet Misia and Coco remained the best of friends, locked in an agon of mirror images. They were two hungry creatures, each ready to consume the other. Claude Delay called Misia "organically jealous." Such intense mutual need can create a certain erotic charge, and Misia may have succeeded in leading Coco into some Sapphic experiments, about which Chanel was completely silent and biographers have differed.

In their later years, Misia and Coco fell into the shared habit of injecting themselves with morphine. According to some accounts, Chanel made only limited use of this opiate, in the form of physician-prescribed Sedol, to help her sleep. Other sources insist that Chanel was seriously dependent on the drug as well. In either case, Misia most certainly became dangerously addicted to morphine and didn't hesitate to shoot up in cafés and restaurants, casually hiking up her skirt to inject herself in the thigh. Still a convent girl at heart, a scandalized Coco would beg her to stop, which led to some screaming public arguments between them, complete with hair pulling.

However vexed or amorous their friendship, it remained the one constant in both of their lives. When her beloved JoJo took up with the beautiful young Roussadana Mdivani, known as "Roussy," Misia turned to Chanel for solace. Coco moved her at once into a wing of her Riviera villa La Pausa, in 1927, continuing their shared tradition of rescuing each other from the catastrophes of love.

CHAPTER SEVEN

ANTIGONE IN *VOGUE*

CHANEL COSTUMES THE
MODERNIST STAGE

C hanel understood Diaghilev instinctively. In him she had found another eastern European refugee severed from home and steeped in melancholy nostalgia. Paradoxically, one of the most revolutionary aspects of the Ballets Russes would be their return to traditional Russian folklore and dance. Chanel said aptly that "Diaghilev invented Russia for foreigners." (Did she know she would later do the same for France?)

Diaghilev's Ballets Russes owed its success at least as much to business savvy and social climbing as it did to talent. He had invented a brand of seductive modernism that mingled high and commercial culture, and turned theatrical performances into prestige-conferring events—enticing spectators with accessible, popular references while presenting challenging new art. In *Rite of Spring*, for example, Vaslav Nijinsky infused his ballet choreography with moves borrowed from the low-rent, nightclub genre of apache dancing. Nijinsky's 1912 *Afternoon of a Faun*

mingled classical ballet with sensuous tango steps. Jean Cocteau's sce-
narios for Ballets Russes productions made use of everyday sights and
sounds such as typewriters clacking and phonographs playing, and borrowed elements from the circus (juggling, acrobatics), and from Hollywood cinema.

Diaghilev also made brilliant use of fashion to offer female supporters of his company the thrilling feeling of entering into a privileged "Ballets Russes world" of style. In 1912, for example, Ballets Russes costumer
Léon Bakst collaborated with renowned *couturière* Jeanne Paquin to
transform Bakst's sumptuous onstage creations into wearable, commercial designs available for purchase. For especially generous patrons of the
company, Bakst would occasionally fashion custom-made outfits patterned closely on his stage designs, sharing some stage-star glamour with
the "civilian" population.

Like Chanel, Diaghilev knew how to harness the marketing power of
celebrity. To give Ballets Russes performances the air of posh, A-list soirées, he lured the glitterati with free tickets. Chanel had done much the
same thing when she offered free clothes to aristocratic beauties who
became walking advertisements.

Chanel's first interaction with the Ballets Russes was financial, but
Diaghilev and his associates saw more in Coco than just deep pockets.
Gradually, Misia's friends—Diaghilev, Stravinsky, and especially Jean
Cocteau—recognized a kindred spirit and talent in Chanel. "By a kind of
miracle, she has worked in fashion according to rules that would seem to
have value only for painters, musicians, and poets," wrote Cocteau, who
was the first of the group to invite Chanel into their world as an artist. In
1922, while Coco was vacationing with Grand Duke Dmitri by the seashore, Cocteau phoned, asking if she would costume his new play, a radical adaptation of Sophocles's *Antigone*. That Picasso—who fascinated
her—would be designing the sets was argument enough for Coco. She
agreed immediately.

"I asked Mademoiselle Chanel to do the costumes because she is the
greatest *couturière* of our time," declared Cocteau. "And I cannot imagine
the daughters of Oedipus badly dressed." She had already conquered the

beau monde, but this was different. Now, the charmed circle of the French avant-garde opened to welcome Chanel, the first dressmaker of any stature to enter this exclusive club. Already something of a self-made mythic and royal character herself (and still faintly hoping for the title of tsarina), Coco would now dress the mythic royalty of ancient Greece. Her wardrobe choices for the characters reveal much about the mythology she was constructing for herself.

Cocteau inaugurated the wave of twentieth-century French playwrights who reconfigured ancient Greek drama for their own ends. A number of these modern dramatists returned repeatedly to Sophocles' *Antigone*. The final play in the Oedipus trilogy (although actually written first), *Antigone* is often understood to depict the struggle between *oikos,* the domestic realm of love and family obligation, and *polis,* the outer world of the state and adherence to its law. Its plot is deceptively simple: Creon, ruler of Thebes, forbids his niece, Antigone, to mourn for or bury her deceased brother, Polynieces, in a religious ceremony, because Polynieces is considered a traitor to the state. Antigone defies her uncle and buries her brother, whereupon Creon condemns her to being entombed alive and left to starve. By the time Creon finally relents, Antigone has already hanged herself in her crypt. Upon this, her fiancé, Creon's son, Haemon, commits suicide in despair.

Cocteau intended, he said, to strip *Antigone* of all excess and reveal the sleek, fast-moving play that lay beneath. He drastically cut the play's length. In other words, Cocteau performed a Chanel-style makeover on Sophocles, paring the play down to a sleekly modern version of its former self. The entire production lasted just forty minutes.

While not a Ballets Russes production, *Antigone* gathered an ensemble culled from Diaghilev's inner circle, including composer Arthur Honegger, Pablo Picasso, and Antonin Artaud. Cocteau reduced the chorus to a single part, which he played himself, speaking his lines through a hidden backstage megaphone.

Chanel's sleek and simple costumes further modernized the play. In this, her first official foray into costume design (a sideline she would continue to pursue for more than forty years), Chanel established her trade-

Génica Athanasiou
(right) as Antigone

mark approach to the stage: She preferred to put actors into highly recognizable versions of Chanel couture. Her creations for *Antigone*, which debuted on December 20, 1922, at the Théâtre de l'Atelier in Montmartre, resembled nothing so much as they did Coco's couture collections for fall and winter 1922.

Chanel embarked on *Antigone* during her "Russian" years, when she was involved romantically with Stravinsky and Grand Duke Dmitri. For winter 1922, Chanel's collection consisted of heavy woolen coats with jacquard woven patterns, Slavic-style tunics with rope belts, and large costume jewelry pieces, including brooches in the shape of Maltese (also known as "Byzantine") crosses. The ladies of Cocteau's *Antigone* looked like slightly muted, more stylized versions of the Chanel models depicted in that season's Paris *Vogue*. Chanel dressed Antigone and her sister, Ismene, in heavy wool garments in neutral tones of brown and white, soberly adorned with geometric jacquard patterns. Antigone, as protagonist and the fiercer sister, merited the more dramatic ensemble, featuring a specially made cloak that drew raves from reviewers: a hand-knitted wrap of undyed raw wool into which Greek vase motifs, in maroon and brown, had been intricately woven.

Ismene wore a simpler, shorter dress with a silvery tone, and no cloak. For Cocteau, the splendor of the sisters' costumes was proportionate to their nobility and purity of action: "Antigone has decided to act. She wears a coat of superb woolen weaving. Ismene will not act. She keeps her more ordinary dress," he wrote.

For Creon and Haemon, Chanel designed neutral-colored togas and leather sandals. She indicated their royal status by encircling their heads in hammered metal headband-style crowns, embossed with large gemstones arranged into a shape almost identical to the Byzantine crosses she was making that season in her costume jewelry line (inspired by Grand Duke Dmitri's royal family jewels), and which also figured as a decorative motif in some of her distinctive tunics.

C octeau received mixed reviews for the production. Many of the more enthusiastic responses came from conservative critics (including François Mauriac and Ezra Pound), who felt Cocteau had eliminated frivolous theatrical excess and created a respectful, even "virilizing" return to the classicism of Sophocles. *New York Times* theater critic Brooks Atkinson was less impressed, dubbing the play "a vest-pocket version of *Antigone*," which reduced Greek tragedy to "fiddle faddle."

In the end, Chanel's contributions outshone every other aspect of the play, garnering the most enthusiastic critical response. *The Christian Science Monitor* lauded the costumes for their seriousness, and for remedying a dangerous, "effeminate" trend in costuming classical tragedies:

Special attention must be called to the costumes. They are at the same time primitive and elegant. M. Dullin has resolutely discarded the supple woolens and the crepes de chine introduced by

Mounet-Sully [in an 1893 production of *Antigone*] ... [which can become] too luxurious, too refined, too effeminate [and] which did not become the tragic vigor of the piece. The costumes of *Antigone* at L'Atelier are inspired by the compositions which adorn amphoras. Cut with a refined gaucherie out of beautiful stuffs— heavy because rustic but fine because the matter is rare and well fashioned—enhanced with all the barbarian grace of the epoch, they delight the eye. The dressmaker, Mme Gabrielle Chanel ... must be greatly thanked for her artistic sense. The cloak of Antigone shaped like a sack and heavy with embroideries, and the dress with its fine folds and the silvery robe of Ismène—what marvelous discoveries!

Like those conservatives who praised Cocteau's "virile" approach, the *Monitor* applauds Chanel's apparent rejection of the feminine. Her fabrics are worthy for being stiff instead of supple, heavy instead of graceful—the reviewer might as well be talking about bodies, not clothes. The costumes seem to have acquired a manliness demanded by—and commensurate with—the gravitas of a classical Greek text. In the decades to come, this linking of Hellenism (especially Sophocles' character of Antigone) with masculine strength became a commonplace within a certain strain of European politics. Fascist propaganda routinely posited that the Aryan—the racially pure European man—found his roots in ancient Greece, birthplace of the athletic, superior civilization that had been lost through racial tainting and moral laxity.

Antiquity served the fascists as a handy aesthetic symbol of a fallen cultural elite, which they longed to reinstate. The story of *Antigone* lent itself especially well to this scenario, offering a young, virtuous heroine who refuses to compromise her principles. For the French right wing, Antigone became an allegorical figure of a purified France—like Marianne or Joan of Arc—young, inspirational, self-sacrificing, female but not feminine, a woman of manly virtues. Writers such as Jean Anouilh, and fascist supporters Robert Brasillach and Charles Maurras returned repeatedly to Sophocles' story, especially throughout the 1940s.

In 1922, Cocteau's politics were somewhat inchoate, and he had not yet acquired his reputation as an ardent nationalist and Nazi sympathizer. But his Antigone whispers an affiliation with the Antigones to come.

Chanel, too, would find her place among the extreme French Right, even becoming a kind of emblem for it. Coco was happy to assume this role, deeply drawn to any movement that seemed to offer membership in an elite and confirmation of her national and historic importance. In 1922, her political sentiments were still evolving, detectable more in her choice of lovers and friends than in her actions. But the critical reception to her *Antigone* costumes foreshadows Chanel's later popularity among the French nationalist movement, in that critics found her style lofty, monumental, and worthy of the association with France's grand, Hellenic past.

R eviewers consistently praised Chanel for her ease among the ancients, particularly the way her costumes bespoke high-culture seriousness. Her creations sent French *Vogue,* for example, into raptures: "These woolen dresses in neutral tones give the impression of ancient clothes rediscovered after centuries. Their cut adds to the character of each role, and the cloak seems to envelop strangely the daughter of the House of Atreus. Chanel has become Greek while remaining Chanel. Her unusual costumes prove this. Antigone's dress of coarse white wool woven with brown in places, is exactly the dress revealed to us by the friezes of Delphi: This is a beautiful reconstruction of an archaism, illuminated with intelligence."

The praise was well deserved. Chanel had, in fact, created beautiful and evocative costumes. But the extravagant attention paid to her contributions conveyed more than aesthetic approval; it proved the social and historic power of Chanel's "wearable personality." *Vogue* said it all: Chanel had become Greek while remaining Chanel. She had evoked ancient Greece but remained true to her own fictive universe and to "Coco"— a character more potent and identifiable than even Antigone. Instead of dressing actress Génica Athanasiou like Antigone, she had dressed her like a Chanel runway model for winter 1922, imprinting upon Sophocles' play the indelible Chanel fashion signature. "Becoming Greek" in this context meant "rising to the stature of myth"—a process Chanel had long been perfecting. Her designs, both on- and offstage, conveyed historical depth, gravitas, and even a touch of Byzantine royalty (via her well-known connection to a Romanov duke)—all characteristics associated with *Antigone*.

The classics of ancient Greece had always formed the cultural bedrock of European civilization, and Sophocles was part of the cultural pedigree of upscale, educated French audiences. By 1922, Chanel—the uneducated, orphaned peasant girl—had created a public identity and style adequate to the demands of illustrating such a high-cultural text. Her tireless campaign to refashion herself as a noblewoman with a prestigious pedigree had succeeded: Chanel couture could hold its own against the grandest and most ancient cultural backdrop imaginable.

Esteemed literary critic Roland Barthes agreed, declaring that Chanel ought to be considered a canonical French literary figure: "Today if you opened a book on the history of our literature, you should find the name of a new classical author: Coco Chanel. Chanel does not write with pen and paper...but with fabrics, forms and colors. Nevertheless...she has the authority and flair of a writer of the 'grand siècles'...Racine...Pascal...La Rochefoucauld...Mme de Sévigné....Chanel...endows [fashion] with all the classical virtues."

If Chanel's fashion signature sharpened and enhanced Antigone's nobility onstage, Coco's offstage celebrity enhanced the play's box office sales, and turned *Antigone* into something of a society happening. Reviews tended to focus on Chanel's costumes to the exclusion of every other aspect of the play. *Vogue* and *Vanity Fair* failed even to mention Honegger, Artaud, and Picasso. This didn't concern the play's producer, Charles Dullin (also the portrayer of Creon), who later wrote: "Society people came to the performances because of Chanel....Sophocles was only a pretext." Chanel, too, seemed convinced of her own importance in the production and tended to dominate rehearsals. When asked one day to step aside to allow the actors to rehearse with the text, she was reported to have said, in genuine confusion, "Text? What text?"

Antigone was so perfectly suited for Chanel's induction into the French avant-garde that one suspects Cocteau of choosing the play for that express purpose. Sophocles' Antigone is an unusual woman, an outsider who has lost her parents, defies society and its laws, and forgoes marriage and motherhood: "Not for me was the marriage-hymn.... My curse is to die unwed," she laments. While Chanel's life may fall somewhat short of the Sophoclean, a shadow of Antigone lived within her.

By all accounts, Athanasiou wowed the opening-night crowd with her magnificent cloak, but she was not wearing her intended costume at all. Instead, that first night, Antigone appeared onstage dressed in Coco Chanel's own coat, which had been flung about Génica's shoulders at the last minute. Minutes before the curtain was to go up, Chanel—in a foreshadowing of the peevish temper of her later years—noticed some small flaw and began pulling angrily at a thread on Antigone's cloak, ultimately unraveling it so badly that it became unusable. While the elderly costume assistant who had knitted the coat wept, Chanel threw her own dark brown jacquard-weave winter coat over Athanasiou and sent her out onstage to huge acclaim, confirming that "costumes" were not necessary here; Chanel's everyday couture was more than regal enough. "It's funny, the theater," Coco said later about the incident, "I threw my own coat over the actress' shoulders, well, that's what made the play!"

Chanel proved an excellent collaborator for the theatrical style of Diaghilev and company, and after *Antigone,* she worked on more productions. She costumed two more in Cocteau's series of Neohellenist dramas (which she called his "bazaar of antiquity"): *Orpheus* (1926) and *Oedipus* (1937), as well as his medieval drama *The Knights of the Round Table* (1937), on which she was assisted by a young Christian Dior. In the realm of dance, she entirely costumed Diaghilev's Ballets Russes seaside fantasy *The Blue Train* (libretto by Cocteau, sets by Picasso, and choreography by Vaslav Nijinsky's sister Bronislava Nijinska), in addition to contributing designs for various other Ballets Russes productions, including the mythology-themed *Zephyr and Flora* (1925, choreographed by Léonide Massine) and *Apollon musagète* (1928, score by Stravinsky, choreography by George Balanchine, starring Serge Lifar); as well as *Les Biches* (choreography by Nijinska, music by Francis Poulenc).

In nearly all cases, Chanel adhered to her ingenious practice of forgoing overt "costumes" in favor of tweaked versions of her own highly recognizable couture. For *Zephyr and Flora* (a story set on Mount Olympus), she translated anaphoric designs by set designer Georges Braque into garments. For Balanchine's *Apollon,* she redesigned earlier costumes by painter André Bauchant when the ballet reopened for its second run in 1929, dressing only the Muses, who each wore a typically Chanel-esque knit tunic cinched in three places by men's neckties from Charvet (the classic haberdashery on the Place Vendôme, once favored by Boy Capel). And in *Les Biches,* which featured a glamorous hint of lesbianism, the "flapper" character instantly telegraphed "Coco" by wearing a long strand of oversize pearls and carrying a cigarette holder.

While Chanel yielded somewhat to the demands of the historical period for certain productions, she always included enough of her signature style to conjure the classic "Chanel look." For *Knights of the Round Table,* for example, Chanel's fur and velvet fantasies looked more like medieval versions of couture than like costumes. As Cocteau said in an interview: "These are not...the costumes of a costumer. They are realistic, cut from fabrics of authentic opulence." The review in *Vogue* lauded the costumes for *Knights* as: "sumptuous...brocades, ermine and lame fabrics, evoking the most beautiful illuminated manuscripts of the past." In the novelist Colette's review of the play, Chanel's sometime friend wrote, "Thanks to [Chanel] the actors are as beautiful as princes in a tapestry, beautiful like the figures on tarot cards. One slightly monastic dress, in off-white, touched me like a line from a spiritual text."

.   .   .

Iya Abdy as Jocasta,
with Jean Marais
(far left)

For *Oedipus Rex,* Chanel dressed Jocasta (played by Iya Abdy) in a felt gown divided into geometric colored sections, flowing into a full skirt of multicolored accordion pleats. The bodice, with its diagonal V-shaped crossband, recalled an artillery magazine or the satin sash of Grand Duke Dmitri's army uniform. At least one critic espied this costume's Russian and eastern European influence: "Mme Abdy's costume consists of a Cossack's tunic over a skirt draped in the gypsy style, a ravishing picture."

Around her neck, Jocasta wore a long necklace that suggested an exaggerated version of Chanel's costume jewelry, made of wooden spools of thread swiped from a seamstress's worktable. (The spools also recalled the spinning threads of the three Fates of classical mythology.) Oedipus, played by Cocteau's strikingly handsome young lover, Jean Marais, wore the raciest costume Chanel ever dreamed up, consisting entirely of white elasticized bands wound around his naked body. The costume (and its variations worn by secondary male characters) scandalized some viewers, and blended overtones of S&M eroticism with a macabre reference to mummy wrappings, all while evoking Chanel's famous use of

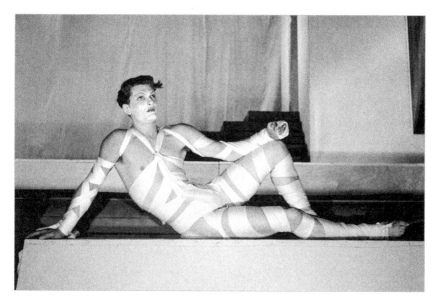

Marais as Oedipus

striped fabrics—with the elastic bandage material effectively "striping" the body.

For Cocteau's version of *Orpheus* (1926), which coincided with Coco's "English Country" phase, Chanel dressed the title character and his wife, Eurydice (played by the famous married couple of French theater, Georges and Ludmilla Pitoëff), in sporty British tweeds and golf sweaters (inspired by the casual clothes of Chanel's lover at the time, the Duke of Westminster). The character of Death, played by beautiful young actress Mireille Havet, wore a bright pink ball gown beneath a fur coat, prompting critic André Levinson to grouse, "Cocteau has supplanted Thanatos with a socialite dressed by Mademoiselle Chanel."

Levinson's remark speaks to the theatrical power of Chanel's work and its uncanny suitability to Cocteau's "lifestyle modernism." As was his custom, Cocteau removed the "patina of age" from the tale of Orpheus. Chanel's golf attire and ball gowns instantly updated the ancient Greek myth. Yet despite his modernizing alterations (and the several new characters he introduced into the story), Cocteau remained true to the spirit of Greek legend. His Orpheus is still a poet who travels to Hades to reclaim his wife, and is dismembered at the end. We learn nothing of the characters' psychology, childhoods, or family lives. These are not "real" people in a real world. Mythology does not concern itself with the vagaries of human nature, and neither did Cocteau. His Greek plays, like the ancient originals, live in a realm of timeless inevitability, devoid of personal psychology.

Therein lay antiquity's appeal for the French modernists, whose version of Greek mythology looked outward at broad social themes, rather than showcasing inward, intimate stories. The classics offered Cocteau and other writers a tool kit from which to pull ready-made plots and stock characters to be recombined in new ways.

Implicitly, Cocteau added one extra character to the legend of Orpheus: the character of "Coco Chanel." Although she did not appear onstage, Coco was palpably present. The world of golf sweaters, tweeds, and ball gowns was Chanel's world. Coco had become, in effect, her own stock character, as identifiable to audiences as were the legendary characters of Greek mythology. "Chanel" had become a latter-day mythological type—"a kind of strange goddess," as Maurice Sachs described her.

D iaghilev's 1924 pantomime ballet, *The Blue Train*, demonstrated that Chanel's mythic stock character worked just as effectively in non-Hellenic performances. Here, once more, through her non-costume costumes, she dominated the production with her celebrity presence.

For *The Blue Train*, Diaghilev gathered his most gifted collaborators: Cocteau wrote the libretto, Picasso painted the stage curtain—the largest work of his life at 10.4 by 11.7 meters; architect Henri Laurens designed the set, which featured cubist-inspired, tilting beach cabanas; Darius Milhaud composed the score, and Bronislava Nijinska served as choreographer.

Diaghilev said he wanted to cast off "the mists and veils of ballet"—

much as Cocteau had wanted to strip the "patina of age" from Sophocles. Accordingly, *The Blue Train* leavened its ballet with acrobatics, popular dance moves, satire, and broad pantomime.

As upper-class spectators would have known, the title was the nickname of the Calais-Méditerranée Express, a luxury train inaugurated in 1922, renowned for its all-first-class sleeping cars, which were painted deep blue with gold trim. Parisians boarded this evening train at the Gare du Nord, enjoyed five-star cuisine in the dining car, turned in for the night, and then awoke to the rocky cliffs, terra-cotta roofs, and glittering blue Mediterranean of Saint-Raphaël, Antibes, Nice, and Monte Carlo. The manifest for the Blue Train regularly included Winston Churchill, F. Scott and Zelda Fitzgerald, Cole and Linda Porter, Charlie Chaplin, and the Prince of Wales. Chanel and Cocteau were also regular passengers. The ultimate in modern celebrity glamour, the Blue Train figured often in the society and gossip columns.

Diaghilev's ballet brought those gossip pages to life, featuring a featherlight romance involving a group of leisured beachgoers, with nameless characters known only by their generic types—"handsome boy," "tennis player," "golf player," "bathing beauty," and so forth.

Instead of making "costumes," Chanel dressed the dancers in sportswear copied directly from her commercial line, altering the garments only minimally to accommodate the wear and tear of dancing. It was the first time that Ballets Russes dancers had ever appeared onstage in street clothes, and the crowds loved it.

Chanel dressed the entire cast in androgynous striped jersey, playing off her reputation for *garçonne* (tomboy) style. Dancers Anton Dolin (Cocteau's new lover at the time) and Lydia Sokolova ("handsome boy" and "bathing beauty") wore nearly identical versions of Chanel's hugely popular two-piece striped jersey swimsuit, consisting of fitted shorts and tank-style top. Sokolova sported one of Chanel's more practical inventions: a head-hugging rubber swim cap designed to permit women ease of movement in water. Fitted close to the head and hiding all of Sokolova's hair, the cap recalled Chanel's trademark little cloche hats while

Cast of *The Blue Train* (left to right): Léon Woizikovsky, Lydia Sokolova, Bronislava Nijinska, and Anton Dolin

underscoring the dancer's boyish (slightly "bald") appearance. As an added accessory, Sokolova wore oversize "pearl" stud earrings (made of wax-coated china), adapted from Chanel's costume jewelry line.

Two characters in *The Blue Train* did wear somewhat more specific costumes, for they were meant to evoke particular, real-life celebrities: The role of "tennis player"—performed by Nijinska—referred directly to French champion Suzanne Lenglen, an Olympic gold medalist and six-time Wimbledon winner. Like Chanel, Lenglen had earned a reputation as a "liberated" woman; she favored daringly bare tennis attire and was known to sip brandy between sets. The "golf player," played by Léon Woizikovsky, was modeled after Edward, Prince of Wales, famous for his love of the game and recently appointed captain of the Royal and Ancient Golf Club.

Nijinska wound up looking like a composite photo of Lenglen and Coco Chanel, in a two-piece all-white tennis outfit consisting of a long skirt, short-sleeved blouse, and mannish necktie, with her hair cut into a

French tennis sensation
Suzanne Lenglen, 1923

short "shingle" style adorned with a white head wrap. And in his tweed
plus fours and pullover sweater, the "golfer" unmistakably called to mind
photographs of the Prince of Wales in virtually the same outfit, although
Woizikovsky's featured Chanel's distinctive striping.

Coco was not overtly depicted onstage, but she might as well have
been. Her self-created mythic, "stock" character was palpably present.
This effect was intensified by a new development in Chanel's love life:
When *The Blue Train* premiered in June 1924, Coco was in the first flush
of her love affair with a well-known Riviera habitué, Hugh Grosvenor,
the Duke of Westminster. The duke was sometimes spotted at rehearsals
and was known to whisk Coco off for frequent yachting weekends in
Monte Carlo.

CHAPTER EIGHT

BENDOR
THE RICHEST MAN IN EUROPE

"Whose yacht is that?"
"The Duke of Westminster's I expect. It always is."
—NOËL COWARD, *PRIVATE LIVES*

Had she met him earlier, Chanel would not have been ready for Hugh Richard Arthur Grosvenor, the 2nd Duke of Westminster. While she may not have realized it initially, Coco had been training most of her life for her relationship with Westminster, which began in 1923, when she was forty and he forty-four. Among his many attractions, the duke was British, like Boy Capel, but even more crucial was the fact that, by startling coincidence, Westminster and Capel were actually related by marriage: Westminster's half brother, Percy Wyndham, had been the first husband of Diana Wyndham Capel, Boy's wife. The duke then belonged, indirectly, to the Capel family tree. This led Coco to a mystical interpretation: Westminster must be Boy Capel's gift to her from the beyond. "I am sure Boy sent Westminster to me," she said.

The duke had terrestrial charms as well. Not only was he the wealthiest companion she would ever have, he was the wealthiest man in Great

Britain, and possibly all of Europe, his inherited fortune consisting of vast international real estate holdings as well as the Eaton Railway. With Grand Duke Dmitri Romanov, Coco had dreamed in vain of becoming an empress. With Westminster, she saw the distinct likelihood of becoming a duchess. No revolutions had destroyed this duke's empire or deprived him of rank or title. No mishap had ever cut the golden threads that wove him into the tapestry of history. Westminster's birthright of tremendous wealth and power remained perfectly intact.

To friends and family, the duke had always been known as Bendor—Ben or Benny more casually. It was a prophetic nickname, auguring the Duke's lifelong affinities for ancient, aristocratic interests and values, as well as his powerful attachment to the Victorian era into which he was born. The word "Bend'or" derived originally from the royal motto—*azure à bend d'or*—meaning "blue with a band of gold," emblazoned on the fourteenth-century heraldic crest belonging to the duke's ancestors. The duke was not the first, though, to bear the name; that honor had gone to Bendor the horse—a thoroughbred belonging to the duke's grandfather Hugh Lupus Grosvenor (himself named after a wolf). Bendor I had distinguished himself by taking first prize at the Epsom Downs Derby in 1880, when his young, human namesake was but a year old.

Bendor the child was only four when his father, Earl Grosvenor, died. Four years later, his mother, Lady Sibell Grosvenor—then thirty-two—married twenty-four-year-old George Wyndham. Only sixteen years older than Bendor, Wyndham acted more as a genial older brother than as a father to the boy. It fell to Hugh Lupus Grosvenor, the 1st Duke of Westminster, to step in as a father figure and help raise his grandson. Very much a man of the nineteenth century, the 1st Duke of Westminster had earned fame for his great philanthropy, courage, and his famously close relationship to his godmother, Queen Victoria.

Hugh Lupus Grosvenor took pains to tutor the boy who would inherit his title. Classic paintings by masters such as Thomas Gainsborough, Joshua Reynolds, and Francisco de Goya lined the vaulted corridors of Eaton Hall, the gothic estate where Bendor grew up, including portraits of illustrious Grosvenor ancestors and their horses. As a boy, Bendor would gaze up at these paintings while his grandfather regaled him with stories of forebears both human and equine. He learned, for example, of the famous horse Copenhagen, ridden into battle at Waterloo by the Duke of Wellington, and of Macaroni, the family horse that had beaten all odds to win at Epsom, York, and Doncaster in the 1860s. So great was the Grosvenors' passion for the stables that, in addition to the paintings, actual bodily remnants of deceased thoroughbreds figured in their décor: Bones taken from some of the horses' skeletons were hung under the chandeliers at Eaton Hall. Given the zeal of this family preoccupation, it surprised no one when, as a toddler, Bendor asked, "Am I also a descendent of Macaroni?"

Growing up in this atmosphere had made Bendor something of a nobleman's nobleman. Striving all his life to live up to his grandfather's expectations, Bendor could never lapse in his devotion to title and legacy. Overshadowed thus by a larger-than-life figure from his family's past, the duke—although only four years older than Coco—seemed never fully to have entered the twentieth century. His concerns and surroundings remained far more rooted in the nineteenth.

Six feet two inches tall and robust, blond and blue-eyed, with a complexion weathered by sun and sea (Noël Coward described him as "floridly handsome"), Westminster excelled at polo, golf, and hunting, was a champion yachtsman, and had been a member of the 1908 British Olympic motorboat racing team. He evinced less aptitude, though, for academic matters. After a mediocre career at Eton, the duke put aside plans to stand for admission to Cambridge, setting his sights on the military instead.

Bendor was stalwart and exceptionally loyal, especially to the British Empire, and its global mission as he understood it. For Bendor, the imperial project was sacred and needed to be promoted passionately. Such beliefs led him to the political role that consumed much of his life: that of ardent disciple to Lord Alfred Milner (1854–1925). Milner, the German-born, Oxford-educated, charismatic founder of "New Imperialism," was one of the chief architects of the Boer War, a close collaborator of key British imperialist Cecil Rhodes, and a self-described "British race patriot."

The Duke of
Westminster in 1903

Milner had a tremendous gift for moral suasion, especially with
young men. After the Second Boer War brought South Africa under British rule, he formed a circle of such young men—mainly Oxford
graduates—who came to be known as "Milner's Kindergarten." This
group devoted itself to postwar reconstruction, and to creating a system
for controlling the black population, which developed into apartheid.
Bendor, who'd served as aide-de-camp to Milner in the Boer War, joined
the group, although he lacked the intellectual firepower of the other Kin-
dergartners and participated largely by making generous financial contributions. According to Westminster biographer Michael Harrison, the
duke became something of a groupie, maintaining an "emotional, semi-
mystical rapport" with Milner.

The duke had been a fine and admired officer during his first, teenaged stint in the military, in South Africa. Fifteen years later, he returned
to military service during World War I, rising to the rank of colonel. In
1914, at the age of thirty-five, he accomplished the most famous feat of
his military career: leading a fleet of armored cars (reconverted Rolls-
Royces whose configuration he had designed himself) across ninety-

three miles of Libyan desert, braving enemy fire, to rescue ninety-one stranded British prisoners of war.

He did not abandon his usual upper-class comforts—the caravan included his valet, several specialized mechanics, uniformed coachmen, and other servants who saw to his personal needs—but the duke saved all the prisoners, who were discovered nearly dead of thirst and starvation. He received the British Army's Distinguished Service Order for bravery.

Along with his athletic and military accomplishments, Bendor built a long and varied romantic career. His first marriage, to the beautiful Constance Edwina Cornwallis-West, known as Shelagh, lasted eighteen years (from 1901 to 1919) but had been often unhappy, marred by quarrels about the financial demands of the Cornwallis-West family, the duke's frequent infidelities, and, most dramatically, the tragic death of the couple's four-year-old son, Edward, after surgery for appendicitis. She did not bear him another son, nor did his second wife, Violet Mary Nelson, and by 1923 the British press was reporting that the second Duchess of Westminster had discovered her husband in flagrante with a certain Mrs. Crosby, at the Hôtel de Paris in Monte Carlo.

The Hôtel de Paris provided the backdrop as well to a more significant romantic encounter for the duke: his meeting with Coco Chanel. During the Christmas season of 1923, Chanel was vacationing on the Riviera, staying at the hotel with her friend and muse Vera Arkwright Bate—an English beauty widely acknowledged as the illegitimate daughter of a British prince. The two women complemented each other perfectly. Coco hungrily absorbed Vera's easy, joking manner with aristocrats, met her wellborn friends, and, frankly, cadged much from Vera's androgynous British style of dress. In exchange, she'd put the chronically strapped Vera on the Maison Chanel payroll, as a kind of style consultant and mannequin, paying her handsomely simply to wear Chanel outfits to society parties.

The duke first noticed Chanel at the Hôtel de Paris one night, sitting at a table with her Russian friend Lady Iya Abdy, Grand Duke Dmitri (with whom she had mostly broken off), and Vera. Westminster approached and asked Coco to dance. She accepted, leaving Vera and Iya to exchange glances—what might this mean? Bendor was Vera's first cousin, and she saw him often socially, so when, later that week, he begged to see the intriguing Coco Chanel again, she could not say no. Vera conveyed to Chanel the duke's invitation to dine aboard his yacht, *Flying Cloud,* which was moored—as it was often—in Monaco's harbor. (Chanel later hinted to Paul Morand that the duke had actually paid Vera to help him press his suit with Coco.) Westminster loved the Riviera, and frequently sailed down in *Flying Cloud,* a four-masted schooner with a crew of forty. It was the smaller of his two yachts; the other one, *Cutty Sark,* was an 883-ton converted Royal Navy destroyer and employed 180 people.

Chanel was reluctant. She was busy working, on her own collections and on Diaghilev's *The Blue Train.* Besides, she was familiar with Bendor's much-publicized infidelities and his string of mistresses, and felt no need to join the list. Still, to please Vera, she agreed. Perhaps to make a great show of her uninterest, though, Chanel brought a date along to her first meeting with the Duke of Westminster—Grand Duke Dmitri. Dmitri had wanted to see Bendor's famous yacht, and so Chanel arranged to have him invited, too.

That night, Bendor found himself captivated by Chanel. He had rarely met a woman of such fierce independence and charisma. Plus, she was what he called a "real person"—meaning a non-noble—a category he found most fascinating. After dinner, the party went ashore to go dancing at a nightclub in Monte Carlo. By evening's end, the duke was completely smitten.

The next morning Chanel's hotel suite overflowed with flowers—courtesy of the duke. When she returned to Paris, still more flowers began arriving regularly at her home in the Faubourg Saint-Honoré, along with extravagant gifts of jewelry—including a huge, uncut emerald. Even the duke's letters arrived with great drama: Rather than coming in the morning mail, they were personally delivered by couriers dispatched from England. The duke mistrusted the postal system and routinely used his considerable fortune to circumvent mailing any letters.

This was to be an all-out campaign. Despite the obvious appeal of such a worldly and ardent aristocrat, Chanel kept her distance. She remained leery of this still-married man with the terrible reputation. Coco knew what it meant to be a kept woman and had no intention of reverting to that life, no matter how grand the scale. "The Duke frightened me," she told Iya Abdy. The gifts continued. Bendor sent her fruit from his private orchards and rare orchids and lilies he'd picked himself in the hothouses of the Eaton Estate (where he employed hundreds of gardeners). He even sent fresh salmon, fished from his own streams in Scotland and shipped privately by plane to Paris.

The more Chanel demurred, the more Westminster pursued her. His pied-à-terre in Paris—a suite at the Hôtel Lotti, at 7, rue de Castiglione—was just a block from Place Vendôme, and Bendor tried to see Coco every time he came to town. He even attended rehearsals of *The Blue Train,* where his presence sparked the first press reports of a possible romance between them. Finally, Coco invited him to a dinner with her artist friends, including the Serts, Serge Lifar, and Maurice Sachs. The evening proved disappointing. The duke had little knowledge of modern art or music and much of the conversation eluded him. Not one to admit ignorance and not given to intellectual curiosity, Bendor turned condescending—suggesting that Cocteau write the history of his (Bendor's) dogs as a way of making extra money. Chanel's friends bristled at this new arrogant suitor.

Inevitably, though, Bendor's allure wore down Coco's defenses. When in the spring of 1924 he invited her again for dinner aboard *Flying Cloud*—this time moored near Biarritz—she accepted. There were one hundred guests in attendance that night but when the party ended, only ninety-nine went ashore. Bendor had his captain set off for a midnight cruise. Under the stars, he and Coco danced to the music of the private orchestra he'd paid to remain on the yacht through the night.

If Coco still had qualms about seeing a married man, she put them aside. Soon she was hosting social functions with the duke, even though Violet was still legally Duchess of Westminster. ("Coco is here in place of Violet," wrote Churchill to his wife after a salmon-fishing party with

Chanel and the duke.) Within a year the awkward situation resolved it-self, although not without some acrimony. In August 1924, *The New York Times* announced the impending divorce of the Duke and Duchess of Westminster, along with news that, pending a settlement, the duke had enjoined his wife Violet from even entering Eaton Hall. Violet lashed out at her adulterous husband in the press, declaring that he had rendered her "homeless." But once more Bendor had extricated himself from a marriage. His relationship with Chanel quickly attracted more attention from the press. On October 13, 1924, an article in Britain's *Daily Express* speculated that the next Duchess of Westminster could be a "clever and charming Frenchwoman who heads one of the big Parisian couture houses."

Although she did not speak of it, Chanel must have believed in the possibility of a marriage to Westminster. Why else would she have thrown herself into the life of a *châtelaine*? Being with Bendor meant accompany-ing him on his continual journeys on land and sea, from house to house, and honing the social and sporting skills of the British aristocracy. Just visiting his own properties took up much of the duke's time.

Among the properties they frequented most was the neo-Dutch style Château de Woolsack at Mimizan, perched on a lake in the Landes dis-trict of France, between Bordeaux and Biarritz. The woods were rich with wild game—especially boar—and Coco perfected her hunting skills, often alongside such illustrious guests as Salvador Dalí, Charlie Chaplin, Sir Anthony Eden, and David Lloyd George. It was here that Coco first met Winston Churchill, who'd befriended Bendor during the Boer War, and who remained close to him throughout their lives, despite their political differences.

Churchill was particularly fond of visiting the house at Mimizan. An amateur painter, he found the light there inspiring. Churchill found Cha-nel impressive, too, writing to his wife after a weekend, "The famous Coco turned up and I took a great fancy to her. A most capable and agreeable woman with the strongest personality Benny has yet been up against. She hunted vigorously all day, motored to Paris after dinner and is today engaged in passing and improving dresses on endless streams of mannequins." Chanel later said that with Westminster, she had "calmed down," but Churchill's letter gives us a good idea of the frenetic pace she had to keep up simply to maintain what amounted to a double life as Paris *couturière* and duchess in training.

Sometimes, though, her professional life merged with her country estate living. Along with Churchill and the other luminaries, Mimizan hosted visitors of more modest means: Chanel's workers. During his many visits to Chanel's studio, the duke had taken an interest in the seamstresses or *petites mains* (little hands) as they were called and, in the spirit of noblesse oblige, offered to let them use his house as a vacation retreat. Although she had rarely expressed especial interest in workers' rights, Chanel acceded, becoming one of the first couturiers to offer paid holidays. Throughout the years of her relationship with Bendor, Coco's senior seamstresses enjoyed two-week stints in the hunting lodge at Mimizan, marveling at the splendor of their surroundings and partaking even of the château's excellent cuisine, which showcased the region's wild game.

For northerly shore vacations, the duke would repair to his residence in Saint-Saëns, in Normandy, near Deauville, Chanel's old stomping ground. When he wished to travel there from Great Britain, he would have his private railway car attached to the fabled Orient Express after crossing the English Channel at Southampton on his boat train. To take in the Mediterranean sun he frequently rented villas on the Côte d'Azur and would yacht down to Cannes and Monte Carlo.

A sailor from childhood, Bendor had a special passion for the sea and tended to assess the mettle of his paramours by their reactions to boats. More than one lady friend had found herself banished permanently to shore for showing fear of squalls or succumbing to seasickness. Chanel had never learned to swim and she found sailing monotonous. But she found her sea legs quickly, apt as ever at grasping the requirements of a new social situation. Aboard *Cutty Sark* and *Flying Cloud,* Coco never faltered once, not even during severe storms. Impressed, the duke dubbed her his "favorite cabin boy."

Back in Britain, Coco would accompany Bendor as he traveled among

Chanel in fishing gear, c. 1930

his many residences. In London, they lodged at his palatial home, Bourdon House, on Davies Street, just off Grosvenor Square. In the Scottish Highlands, they enjoyed grouse hunting and salmon fishing in the River Cassley while staying at Rosehall House, a twenty-room mansion in the Sutherland region, fifty miles north of Inverness. The duke had bought this retreat soon after meeting Coco, and in a show of generosity and admiration for her talents, granted her carte blanche to redo its décor according to her taste. Soon the old rural estate bore the stamp of her distinctively modern sensibilities.

She removed all the ornate antique fireplaces in the house and replaced them with simple wooden ones; she recovered all the public reception rooms with wallpaper in neutral tones of cream, beige, and green; and she brought in hand-painted French floral wallpaper for the bedroom she shared with the duke. Coco brought another kind of French sophistication to the Highlands, too, installing what was reputed to be Scotland's first bidet, in the master bath of the second floor. How could she not have imagined herself as the future lady of this (and every other) manor?

Mainly, though, Coco and Bendor lived at Eaton Hall, his sprawling castle and accompanying grounds in Cheshire, England. There, Chanel completed an intensive apprenticeship in royal living. Eaton was "not a house, it's a town," remarked Loelia Ponsonby, who would later become the third Duchess of Westminster:

My general impression was of a conglomeration of buildings spreading in all directions, with a vast central block in the style of a French chateau and, towering over all, a campanile which seemed nearly as tall as Big Ben. In the middle of the courtyard was a colossal bronze horseman, falcon on wrist, mirrored in an ornamental pool, and the far side was enclosed by an ornate gilded screen and gates. Beyond the gates a double avenue of trees stretched into the distance, practically reaching to the town of Chester.... To my beglamoured eyes it all seemed like a story palace, complete with a Prince Charming living in it.

Perhaps because she, too, came from an aristocratic background, Ponsonby can admit here her own wonderment at Eaton Hall. Chanel, always more guarded, would not have likened the estate to a "fairy story palace," but she did describe it as evoking a "gothic style out of Sir Walter Scott." While Coco was well accustomed by this time to great privilege, life with Westminster existed on another scale altogether: "I knew with him a luxury the world will never see again," she said.

Entertaining at Eaton routinely involved sixty or more guests for dinner, followed by performances by comedians or ventriloquists, and then an orchestra for dancing. In this highly theatrical setting, Coco's recent work for the Ballets Russes came in handy. She had acquired a refined

Eaton Hall

appreciation for the power of costuming. For her new role as hostess at Eaton, she made herself a series of evening dresses designed for dancing—with multiple layers of silk fringes that floated in the air when she moved, giving her the air of a bird in flight. She had her *petites mains* sew versions of these dresses in solid black, white, red, and deep blue.

Among its hundreds of vast, stone corridors, Eaton featured a gallery of Roman busts, a gallery of horse portraits, and a library containing ten thousand books. The exquisitely manicured grounds included lakes, gardens, and wooded areas, along with the duke's prize hothouses filled with rare plants. Ever a diligent student, Coco would study the map of the estate but often found herself lost nevertheless. She didn't mind, however, since despite its splendor, Coco found a simple, rustic charm at Eaton. She loved taking long walks over the quiet grounds, rowing out onto the lake with the duke, or stopping to gather wildflowers. This kind of contemplative country living felt oddly familiar and comforting to her—it reminded her of her childhood at Aubazine.

Eaton Hall and the austere convent did, in fact, resemble each other. Both featured high stone walls, long, echoing marble corridors, and imposing medieval staircases, all set on acres of rolling green hills. To the shock of the armies of gardeners, Coco dared enter the hothouses and cut some of the flowers, arranging them in vases throughout the château—no one had ever thought to bring any of the flowers inside. She found a hothouse growing strawberry plants and brought the duke to join her in picking and eating them on the spot, outside in the sunshine. He'd had no idea that berries grew on his property. With the duke as proof of how very far she'd come, Chanel could indulge now in these humble pleasures. Often, she invited her nephew André Palasse—who was living in Mayfair and managing Coco's London-based business—and his toddler daughter, Gabrielle, to the château. Coco was the child's godmother, and the duke had agreed to be her godfather. Little Gabrielle, the peddler's great-granddaughter, gamboled over the green lawns at Eaton Hall, holding hands with her "Auntie Coco" and "Uncle Benny," as she called them in her fluent, upper-class English. The trio formed a charming and convincing family tableau. Bendor seemed entirely enchanted.

Chanel took pleasure in the easy, unregimented style of life enjoyed at Eaton Hall. This was a welcome contrast to her early experience of château living, at Balsan's Royallieu, where she had been something of an on-call concubine. It also differed sharply from the schedule kept at many of the country homes of other titled friends, where mealtimes were set in advance, along with tee times, tennis court appointments, and the like. At Westminster's estate, Coco enjoyed unstructured time.

"I had been living… with too much intensity.… With Westminster, there was nothing to do.… I lived life in the fresh air," she told Marcel Haedrich. And although she was not officially duchess, Coco was treated as absolute mistress of the manor by the hundreds of employees and servants. She grew comfortable with life at the estate and her new role there. She developed a particular fondness for an antique suit of armor that stood at the foot of one of the château's grand staircases—a relic, perhaps, from a long-ago battle fought by a Westminster ancestor. That empty metal suit came to life for Chanel, like a welcoming totem. "When I was certain no one could see me, I would approach and shake his hand," she told Charles-Roux. "He had become for me a sort of friend. I imagined him young and handsome." Projecting its living wearer back into the armor, Chanel was also projecting herself into this new, yet ancient, world. It was a romantic exercise. Rich, famous, independent, and well into her forties, Coco still craved a knight in shining armor.

Coco recognized a kindred spirit in Westminster. Having so thoroughly reinvented herself, she had little sense of belonging anywhere and was, at heart, very solitary. She found a similar quality in Bendor. "He doesn't like people very much," she told Morand, "and much prefers animals and plants." It was true. Westminster collected exotic animals, which he kept as pets at his various homes. A Brazilian guinea pig resided at Saint-Saëns, in Normandy, and Himalayan monkeys lived at his estate in Scotland. (All her life, Chanel would keep a white porcelain figurine of a monkey in her apartment, which she often picked up to hold and insisted be placed upon the table whenever she ate a meal. No one knew the monkey's significance, but it's possible it reminded her of Bendor's unusual pets, although Balsan had owned a monkey as well.)

Beneath her lover's eccentricities, Coco espied his loneliness. Bendor, she said, "[was] isolated by his wealth." Bored and impatient with the pretensions of his class, the duke was also not above inventing pranks to skewer his friends' hypocrisies. According to Loelia Ponsonby, Bendor would on occasion empty his bottles of fine, rare brandies and refill them with utter swill—leaving the original labels intact. He then amused himself watching his unsuspecting guests swoon over the "exquisite vintages" they were sure they were drinking. In this, the duke demonstrated yet another point in common with Chanel: They both understood how the right labels can govern desire. His aristocratic ennui meshed perfectly with her class resentment.

Bendor's politics would have appealed to Coco as well. Drawn to any philosophy that would balance the social scales by granting her some form of innate or "natural" superiority, Chanel would never have balked at the duke's adherence to Lord Alfred Milner's race-based patriotism. And her recent exposure to Grand Duke Dmitri's protofascism had familiarized her with the kind of casual, aristocratic anti-Semitism to which Bendor was also heavily inclined.

In 1927, for example, the duke sent one of his typical gifts of fresh Scottish salmon to his good friend Churchill and attached a brief letter noting that the fishes' "facial expression resembles some of our Hebrew friends." As often, though, such drawing room anti-Semitism shaded into a more disturbing kind. Ponsonby reported that Bendor kept a copy of a book called *The Jews' Who's Who*, which "purported to tell the exact quantity of Jewish blood coursing through the veins of the aristocratic families of England." According to Loelia, Bendor kept the book carefully hidden in a locked case: "I could never make out whether he thought that the Jews would send some burglar to steal it or whether, knowing that I did not share his anti-Semitic phobia, he suspected that I had designs on it."

Given the duke's interest in Jewishness as a blood-borne condition, it is not surprising that in the years leading up to the Second World War (he and Chanel had parted by then but remained on good terms), Bendor became closely involved with two pro-Nazi, virulently anti-Semitic British organizations, the Right Club and the Link. Both organizations were dedicated to promoting the notion that Jews were leading a financial conspiracy to drag Britain into war with Germany.

Bendor's pro-Nazi activities escalated throughout the 1930s, and by 1939 he had made common cause with a group of prominent Britons engaged in back-channel communications with the Third Reich, trying to ensure what they called "peace at any price," which included appeasing any and all German demands. Lady Diana Cooper, an old friend of Westminster's (and wife of "Duff" Cooper), recounts in her memoirs a scene in which Bendor shocked a group of his friends with his political and racial views: "He started by abusing the Jewish race, adding his praise for the Germans and rejoicing that we were not yet at war.... And when he added that Hitler knew after all that we were his best friends, he set off the powder-magazine.... The next day Bendor telephoning to a friend said that if there were a war it would be entirely due to the Jews."

When Churchill, then First Lord of the Admiralty, got wind of Bendor's freelance foreign policy work, he wrote him a letter of strong rebuke, warning him of the dangers and potential reprisals involved in countermanding the official actions of the British government. Bendor was haunted for the rest of his life by accusations of treason.

Bendor's politics were already quite well formed during his years with Coco, and we can safely assume Chanel had ample exposure to the duke's political opinions, which ultimately resembled Grand Duke Dmitri's. But Coco—with the rare exceptions of Boy Capel and Pierre Reverdy—was attracted by men who espoused the most antidemocratic, racially driven politics.

To fit more comfortably into the duke's elite world, Coco realized she needed to learn English. At first, when they were together, Bendor and Coco communicated mostly in French, which the duke spoke serviceably. Once ensconced at Eaton Hall, though, Chanel prevailed upon one of Westminster's secretaries ("an insignificant young man with a vague title," as she described him) to tutor her privately in English, imploring him to keep the lessons a secret from the duke.

Although nervous about the deception, the young man agreed and accepted payment from Coco for these sessions. To excel at language acquisition, especially as an adult, one needs a keen ear, a gift for imitation, and a quick mind. Chanel possessed all of these and rapidly learned a great deal of English. But, for months, she bided her time, hiding her increasing fluency from the duke and his friends. By feigning incomprehension during their conversations, she cleverly bought herself the freedom to study her new world without fear of making embarrassing grammatical—or social—gaffes. Eventually, Coco and Bendor communicated using a mélange of both languages: "We talked half in English, half in French," she said.

Chanel adopted English style as eagerly as she did the language. Westminster's world opened up to her the muted elegance of the British aristocracy, its genteel refusal of ostentation, its cozy fabrics, sports clothes, and reverence for tradition. In addition to his lavish gifts of jewelry (he favored Cartier), Bendor offered her more subtle presents, including three little enameled jewel boxes she would always keep on her dressing table. When opened, the boxes revealed that, beneath their enameled tops, they are made of solid gold—a fact undetectable on the outside. Exposure to such soft-spoken treasures taught Chanel the concept of *luxe caché* or "hidden luxury"—a philosophy she put into practice by sewing gilt chains inside hems, hiding luxurious fur inside simple trench coats, or inserting glossy, printed silk linings into basic wool jackets. "Luxury must remain nearly invisible, it must be felt," Chanel told an interviewer decades later. "Luxury is the coat a woman throws inside out over an armchair...and the underside is more valuable than the exterior." Adding hidden luxury to her designs allowed Coco to create a cognoscenti, an elite community of those who appreciated the subtle cues inaccessible to the less discerning. ("Hidden luxury" was also a fitting concept for the girl whose peasant exterior had hidden a startlingly rich and grand inner self.)

Bendor was comfortable only in age-softened, twenty-year-old tweeds and faded golf sweaters, and he opened Coco's eyes to the beauty of well-worn clothes. He preferred his oldest shoes, and required his valet to soak new socks in water for days to soften them sufficiently. Chanel claimed he'd worn the same jackets for twenty-five years.

Chanel's collections from 1924 to 1931 reflected the duke's inspiration, and featured man-tailored, sportswear-inspired tweed jackets, tartans, Fair Isle golf sweaters in heathered wools, houndstooth polo coats and shorter, nautical-style peacoats with gilt buttons—modeled closely after the one Westminster wore when yachting. Her new English country look was a big hit. The Baroness Edouard de Rothschild appeared in *Vogue* wearing a "natural-colored" Chanel suit in an article devoted to chic Scottish shooting parties in the Highlands. "Tweeds have made the practical beautiful and the beautiful practical," announced *Vogue* in 1928. That same year, *Time* magazine chronicled Chanel's growing success: "The Fame of G. ('COCO') Chanel has waxed since the war. Sweaters have made her name and her fortune, the light, boyish sweaters which form the sports costume of many an American and English woman. [But] the story of C. is shrouded in mystery." As ever, the fog surrounding Chanel's past life only enhanced her image.

Always enthusiastic about her business, the duke put a textile mill in the Highlands at Coco's disposal, where she negotiated the production of a new, softer, lightweight wool whose flexibility lent itself better to women's clothing, particularly her feminine sweaters. Coco's clients loved the new casual, "English" look, which they coveted even more after the June 1926 Paris opening of Jean Cocteau's much-heralded *Orpheus,* in which all the classical characters sported Coco's tweeds and golf sweaters. "Tweeds that I had imported from Scotland...dethroned silk crepe and chiffon," she told Paul Morand.

Coco looked down as well as up the social ladder for ideas. The distinctive striped uniforms of the Eaton Hall staff resurfaced on Coco's casual wool pullovers and some blouses. The bell-bottomed trousers worn by the crew of Bendor's yacht inspired Coco's first significant foray

Chanel in her own
English-style sweater
and pleated skirt,
with pianist Marcelle
Meyer, aboard
Westminster's yacht

into "slacks"—which became (and remain) a universal staple for women. She copied the sailors' hats too, and had her models (and herself) photographed wearing the caps and berets pulled down over their eyebrows, at just the angle she'd seen them worn on *Flying Cloud*. On the front of her own beret, she affixed a brooch bearing the Westminster royal insignia.

Attracted always by uniforms, Chanel also borrowed the fitted silhouettes of waistcoats worn by the butlers of Eaton Hall, adapting the style for her suit jackets; the footmen's starched collars and cuffs appeared on the blouses she designed for women, as did the color scheme of the butlers' vests. Filtered through Chanel's aesthetic, all these ultra-British, masculine style elements reemerged to look somehow French and feminine. With her easy glamour, Chanel made the transformation seem effortless.

Chanel also expanded her use of black during these years—a color

Chanel in nautical-style
flared trousers and
yachting-inspired cap,
on the Lido with her
friend Duke Laurino of
Rome, 1930

traditionally associated only with servants' uniforms or mourning. She had started creating black evening dresses around 1920, announcing that loud, theatrical colors made her ill.

"Colors are impossible," she said. "These women, I am going to put them in goddamned black." Just one year after the death of Boy Capel, then, Chanel turned the color of mourning into a global trend. By 1926, she had created an entire series of simple black dresses—in wool for daytime and silk or floaty chiffon for evening. The evening dresses featured rows of fringe or sequined beading.

The exquisite simplicity of the dresses drew admiration from the fashion press: "Chanel [is] famed for her black chiffons...a little bit of nothing, yet a masterpiece," gushed *Vogue*. Sleek, geometric numbers like these dresses had earned Chanel a place at the 1925 Paris Exposition internationale des arts décoratifs et industriels modernes, the definitive exhibition of Art Deco in every genre, including fashion. Chanel's boyish—*garçonne*—look helped cement her reputation as the epitome of modernity. And by October 1926, what we now call "the little black dress," that ubiquitous, infinitely reproducible, infinitely chic garment, was lauded by *Vogue* as "The Chanel 'Ford'—the frock that all the world will wear."

The remark was prophetic. *Vogue* had intuited the close relationship between Chanel's work and the automobile: Both conferred mobility upon women, both could be manufactured on a mass scale, and both would soon be indispensable. The little black dress turned the color associated with housemaids' uniforms and widow's weeds into a marker of privileged yet accessible—and somehow American (Ford-like)—freedom. Chanel summed up the phenomenon simply: "Before me, no one would have dared dress in black. For four or five years, I did nothing but black, with a little white collar, which sold like hotcakes, I made a fortune. Everyone wore a little black dress...movie actresses, housemaids."

The "little black dress," as it appeared in *Vogue*, 1926

Chanel herself continued to lead a life of mobility and luxury—precisely the virtues implicit in the little black dress. It is hard to know, though, if any of it made her happy. Little record remains of how she felt inwardly, of whether the dazzling successes of her midlife counterbalanced the earlier tragedies. This absence of documentation may itself be revealing: We may have few accounts of Coco's inner state partly because she had willed it out of existence, emotionally disappearing from her own life. Salvador Dalí took note of the "young and hard bitterness of [Coco's] unavowed sentiments."

Chanel occasionally admitted to unhappiness: "What followed [Boy's death] was not a happy life.... I don't like to become attached, because as soon as I care about someone, I become weak." By the time she was involved with Westminster, Coco was practicing detachment. Friends remarked that she had never really been enamored of Bendor, and her passion certainly seemed focused more on his manorial lifestyle than on the man himself.

Chanel now lived her life quite consciously for public consumption—from the outside in. Society columns breathlessly followed her activities—taking in the Grand National races in Liverpool, sunning herself on the Lido. If there had ever been a boundary between her private life and her fashion business, it disappeared completely once she met Westminster.

Chanel and the Duke of Westminster at the Grand National horse race

Her life was another commodity, a movie for the world to watch, with costumes available for purchase. Soon after a series of articles appeared about Coco's yachting expeditions with the duke, for example, Coco marketed her first line of cruise wear, based on the outfits she herself had worn in all the photos. Chanel herself was as watched and admired as were her aristocratic clients. *Vogue* reported approvingly sightings around Monte Carlo of "a striped costume of *tissu roulier* like the one that Chanel, the Duchesse de Gramont, and many others are wearing."

Through the duke, Coco vastly enlarged her circle of aristocratic clients, which now included such luminaries as Baba d'Erlanger, Princess Jean-Louis de Faucigny-Lucinge; the Honorable Daisy Fellowes, a fashionable socialite and heiress to the Singer sewing machine fortune; the Duchess of Sutherland; and the future queen consort of England, Elizabeth, Duchess of York (who had figured among Coco's initial clientele at Deauville but now became a regular customer). Chanel even opened a branch of her boutique in London's Davies Street in 1927, on Mayfair property lent to her by Bendor.

Coco had such an effect on fashion that even her skin tone could spark a lasting trend. For centuries, upper-class white women had cherished their pallor, shunning a tan as evidence of manual, outdoor labor. But when Chanel's olive skin turned bronze while sailing the Mediterranean, she unwittingly incited a craze for sunbathing and for the white beach pajamas she wore to offset her tan. "I was as tan as a gypsy from the cruise with the Duke. I who had always avoided the sun . . . had let myself go this time. That night, my color made my teeth shine, and I looked as if I were bursting with life. And that's when women began to sunbathe," she said later. In 1924, taking advantage of this new practice, the Maison Chanel introduced the first tanning lotion for women, L'Huile Tan. Later Coco would ask her chemists to add a sunscreen to the lotion. But Chanel had begun a trend that lasted for at least the rest of the twentieth century. Even now, talk of UV rays and cancer can barely squelch our collective fondness for a tanned appearance.

For a while, as Chanel worked to secure her position with the duke, she lived with him virtually full-time, staying for two to three weeks at a stretch and then commuting back to her business in Paris. Although Bendor would travel to Paris twice yearly to attend Chanel's runway shows, he did not enjoy spending time in rue Cambon, and took no pains to hide his impatience. He preferred to enjoy Coco's company on his own terms and on his territory. On one occasion, Chanel permitted the duke to ship all her seamstresses over to Eaton Hall so that she could work with them without having to leave his estate.

In general, Coco subordinated her schedule to the duke's, and traveled with him as much as possible. The truth was, despite her famously fierce independence, so admired by Bendor, Coco hesitated to leave him for long periods. She knew his reputation. She also hesitated to express the full force of her usually vibrant personality. While she recognized that he hardly compared to most of her friends in intellectual depth or brilliance, Chanel was uncharacteristically accommodating with the duke. "Coco was like a little girl before the Duke and was very careful not to contradict him," Lady Abdy told Pierre Galante.

She may have feigned childlike deference, but Chanel still had a multimillion-dollar empire to run, and that could not be done indefinitely from the English countryside. Coco moved back to the Faubourg Saint-Honoré, although she continued to visit England for weekends. In Paris, Chanel was now entertaining in a new more relaxed style, picked up during country weekends with the duke. "The greatest pleasure that I derived from him was merely to watch him live," she said of Bendor. Inspired, Coco threw large, buffet-style dinner parties, at which guests moved freely around. "Never a big, solemn dinner table," she said.

Their relationship remained the talk of the international press, and their marriage seemed a real possibility. Chanel never spoke of it, but her actions suggest that she still craved the legitimacy and security of marriage. Most of her friends, even the demimondaines, had found husbands by this point. Marthe Davelli had married Constant Say, heir to a great sugar fortune. The beautiful actress Gabrielle Dorziat—who'd worn Chanel's earliest millinery creations onstage—was now the Countess de Zogheb; and Vera had divorced Frederick Bate and in 1927 had married Prince Alberto Lombardi, a dashing Italian military man.

Chanel thought carefully about how to position herself to become the next Duchess of Westminster. Her family back in the provinces caused her particular concern, especially her brothers, Lucien and Alphonse. Lucien peddled shoes for a living and Alphonse ran a *café-tabac*. The duke knew little of her origins except the embroidered tales she told most friends, featuring a father off in America and two maiden aunts. She grew sick with anxiety at the thought of the press somehow uncovering her brothers and exposing the great Coco Chanel, future duchess, as the sister of uneducated, rural peasants. Coco must have heard the stories about the duke's contentious relationship with the demanding and cash-poor Cornwallis-Wests, his first wife's family, and surely assumed that Bendor would be disinclined to acquire any more impecunious in-laws.

Coco decided that, to clear the path to her future happiness, she had to prune her family tree. It took some convincing, but she got both Alphonse and Lucien to accept lifetime pensions from her in exchange for lying low. She even bought a palatial new home for Lucien and his family, hoping that, in the event he was discovered, the house would lend him an aura of respectability and prosperity.

At first, Lucien resisted his sister's offer; his wife found it too lavish and disapproved of her husband's retiring. Coco finally won Lucien over by promising that, when she retired, she would return to Clermont-Ferrand to live with him in the new house. The sweeter and more guile-less of the brothers, Lucien believed this and accepted her offer. The thought of his famous sister honoring him with her presence made him happy. The final term of her agreement displayed more cruelty on Coco's part: She extracted a promise from Lucien never to speak to or see Alphonse again. Alphonse was the crafty one and she didn't want him inciting his brother to any potentially embarrassing activities that could wind up in the press.

With increasing sureness, Chanel was navigating British society. When Bendor's daughter, Lady Mary Grosvenor, invited Chanel to her coming-out ball, to be hosted by her mother, the duke's ex-wife, Coco accepted, reciprocating the gesture by organizing a pre-ball dinner for Mary in London. That night, Chanel hosted Westminster; his ex-wife;

the Duchess of Westminster; both of his daughters, Ursula and Mary; and Winston and Clementine ("Clemmie") Churchill.

After dinner, as her guests prepared to leave for the ball, being held down the street, Coco went back upstairs, claiming she needed to change her dress. She would see them in a few minutes, she assured them, waving them off. Chanel then promptly undressed, took to her bed, and told her maid that she was unwell. Bendor soon noticed her absence at the ball and hurried back to Bourdon House. There he was told that Mademoiselle was ill and no longer receiving that evening. He went upstairs to find Chanel, her face ghostly white. She refused a doctor and when she embraced him, he found she'd left traces of white powder on his black coat. She had powdered her face with talc to appear pale with illness. Although onto her ruse, the duke was obliged to return alone to the ball.

Chanel had made a strategic move worthy of a great general. The king and queen were expected at the ball, and she knew that all of London society would be there lying in wait, longing to see her fail somehow, to watch her prove her unworthiness—the proper comeuppance for the duke's mistress, the brazen French parvenu. By not appearing, she had set them back on their heels. Everyone whispered about her absence all evening. Coco had become an advanced player.

But nature is harder to outwit than even the British peerage, and no matter how she tried, Chanel could not offer Bendor the one thing he desired above all: an heir. The duke had never recovered from the death of his son, Edward, and his unsuccessful marriage to Violet had only heightened his frustration at having no male child to inherit his title. While he seemed largely unconcerned with Coco's commoner status, the duke did not hide his interest in having another child.

In 1928, Chanel was forty-five years old. Most women would have trouble conceiving at that age, but in Coco's case, the odds may have been even longer—probably because of internal damage caused by an earlier abortion. Now, Coco turned her attention to combating biology, consulting doctors and midwives and gathering information on the limited fertility treatments available in that era. Her efforts—which involved performing what she called "humiliating gymnastics" during lovemaking—proved unsuccessful. "I always had the belly of a very young girl," she told Edmonde Charles-Roux, suggesting that somehow her slim figure was to blame.

W ith pregnancy eluding her, Chanel looked for other ways to create an enticing domestic, familial setting for herself and the duke, one that might encourage him to see a long-term future for their relationship. She decided to build an estate. The French Riviera had provided the backdrop for much of the couple's vacationing over several years, but they had always traveled there on Bendor's yacht and stayed in hotels or rented villas. In 1928, Chanel launched plans for her own Mediterranean retreat. She had certainly owned many impressive homes by this point in her life, and now she would build herself a palace to rival a duke's. As the lady of her own mansion, she would make a home for them both, where Bendor could relax completely. In the back of her mind, she might also have hoped that new, restful surroundings could be conducive to pregnancy. (She must also have been thinking of Boy Capel, who spent the last moments of his life driving along a stretch of Riviera coastline.)

Coco and Bendor scouted property on the Côte d'Azur, and in 1928, Chanel alone signed the deed on a tract of land in Roquebrune, France, paying 1.8 million francs. The property sat on the sloping hills of the Maritime Alps. On one side, it overlooked Monte Carlo and the Bay of Monaco; on the other, Menton and the Italian border town of Ventimiglia. In the late twenties, this region of coastal France was establishing itself as the most exclusive real estate in the world, home to European and American high society. Coco and Bendor would know many of their neighbors. Aviator and industrialist Jacques Balsan (Etienne's brother) and his wife, Consuelo Vanderbilt, had a home nearby in Cap d'Antibes, where they entertained Winston Churchill. Daisy Fellowes vacationed in the area, too, as did Viscount Esmond Rothermere, owner of the *Daily Mail* and *The Evening News,* who often hosted the Prince of Wales and Winston Churchill, who seems to have relished the role of houseguest. Along with the Ballets

Russes crowd, other famous artists and performers set up housekeeping on the Riviera, among them F. Scott and Zelda Fitzgerald; Cole and Linda Porter; Fernand Léger; and Ernest Hemingway.

Although for years many believed that Bendor had subsidized the Roquebrune estate, Coco alone undertook every expense for the project. After hearing Count Jean de Segonzac sing the praises of Robert Streitz, a promising young architect, Chanel interviewed the twenty-eight-year-old Streitz aboard *Flying Cloud,* asking him to submit a preliminary proposal for the design. Three days later he returned with his plans. Thrilled with his ideas, Coco and the duke hired him on the spot. It was Streitz's first major commission and he'd hit the jackpot.

At first, project engineer Edgar Maggiore tried to dissuade Chanel from building on the hillside site she'd chosen. The land consisted of mostly solid rock and clay pockets, inadequate support for the large and heavy construction planned. The hill, moreover, was out of plumb, rendering the site even more precarious. Chanel was adamant; she would build nowhere else. Finally, his objections overruled, Maggiore was obliged to construct a massive foundation for the house, with supporting beams more than a meter thick.

Chanel's choice of real estate had likely been prompted by more than just the spectacular views. This particular corner of Roquebrune boasted a serious, even sacred genealogy. The original house that had stood on the property was called La Pausa, a name with origins in Christian lore.

According to a Gallic legend, when Mary Magdalene fled Jerusalem after the Crucifixion, she traveled through Roquebrune, where a beautiful garden filled with graceful olive trees enticed her to stop and rest—to "pause." In the story, a chapel arose in the very spot where Mary Magdalene rested. In the fifteenth century, an actual chapel was built nearby to honor Our Lady of La Pausa, which remains to this day, adjacent to Chanel's property. For six centuries now, every August 5, believers make a pilgrimage from Roquebrune's Church of Sainte-Marguerite up to the chapel of La Pausa, carrying a statue of the Virgin Mary and enacting the Passion of Christ.

The site may have lacked solid geological foundations, but its grounding in Catholic history would have appealed powerfully to the convent girl in Chanel. Perhaps she was also recalling Pierre Reverdy's poem "Bande de souvenirs," which features a statue of Mary Magdalene, "in a chapel at the edge of the roads." In any case, as a woman who had risen above a compromised past, Chanel could not have found a home with a more apropos patron saint. Although she had the three houses standing on the property razed, she decided to keep the site's original name. Every year thereafter, on August 5, Coco showed her respect for the property's biblical past by placing roses at the portal of the public staircase used by the procession and setting out refreshments for the pilgrims—on a table covered with a white cloth.

Coco's Catholic childhood was, in fact, very much in her mind as she collaborated with Streitz on the design—perhaps because Eaton Hall reminded her of Aubazine, perhaps because of her new focus on domesticity. She wanted La Pausa to feel like a deeply rooted family home, and the only real family home in her own life had been her convent orphanage. Coco asked Streitz to take the abbey as a partial model, and had him travel to Aubazine to study the building—particularly the dramatic curving stone staircase that dominated it, which Coco called "the monks' staircase." While visiting the orphanage, Streitz met and spoke with the institution's long-standing mother superior. She remembered Gabrielle Chanel very well—"an illegitimate child born in the poorhouse." Times had changed.

La Pausa eventually cost Chanel a total of 6 million francs to build and would become a masterpiece of its genre, "one of the most enchanting villas that ever materialized on the shores of the Mediterranean," as American *Vogue* described it. Even with its ten thousand square feet set on nine acres, La Pausa managed to be warm and inviting. Built like a Roman villa, the house had three wings gracefully framing a central courtyard, which Chanel had paved with one hundred thousand specially sanded bricks. A white balcony ran the length of the house's interior face on the upper level, providing a stretch of private space for sunbathing. From within the open and airy central atrium, a majestic stone staircase arose—Streitz's homage to the central stairs at Aubazine.

Views of Chanel's villa La Pausa
on the Côte d'Azur

Chanel was deeply engaged in the creation of La Pausa, traveling down at least once a month from Paris to check on its progress. She would board the famous Blue Train to Monte Carlo, and, from there, hire a taxi to take her up the hills to Roquebrune. Sometimes she would return to Paris the same day. On one occasion, when Chanel had no time to spare for the commute south, Maggiore sent one of his stucco workers north to Paris, so that Chanel could consult with him personally on the exact color she wanted for her villa's exterior. She decided on a very soft gray, intended to melt into the tones of the weathered houses that dotted the seaside hills above Monte Carlo.

> On every slate
> sliding from the roof
> someone
> had written
> a poem
>
> The gutter is rimmed with diamonds
> the birds drink them
> **—PIERRE REVERDY, "ROOF SLATES," 1918**

Coco was equally exacting about the villa's roof, which was to be tiled in the fashion of traditional Mediterranean houses in the area. Although they were building from scratch, she wanted to endow La Pausa with an aura of history and tradition, to make it look as if it had always stood on that hill.

After studying local architecture, Chanel determined that she needed a particular kind of slightly curved, handmade tile whose warm terra-cotta color had been softened by the sun. La Pausa's vast roof would require twenty thousand such tiles, and they proved almost impossible to procure. And so Chanel had her contractor search the entire region for houses whose roofs featured these tiles. He then offered to pay the owners of these homes—many of them peasants—an exorbitant fee to allow the tiles to be stripped off their roofs and replaced with new ones. It was an arduous and costly process, but eventually, a sufficient number of the desired tiles were purchased and carted back to shingle the roof of La Pausa. The arrangement pleased everyone. Local residents were thrilled to have their roofs retiled at someone else's expense and to turn a handsome profit in the bargain. And Chanel achieved her goal: She had essentially "grafted" a feeling of august history onto a brand-new creation—exactly what she accomplished so often in clothing, and—arguably—with her own life story as well. (A few people were less excited about Chanel's choices for La Pausa: Her carpenters grew indignant when she demanded that they artificially "age" the perfect new shutters they'd built. They took pride in their pristine craftsmanship and had never heard of anyone simulating the appearance of wear and tear on a house.)

Wanting to give her house a lush and ancient-looking setting— perhaps recalling Mary Magdalene resting in her grove—and finding the vegetation a bit spare, she asked Maggiore to find additional olive trees of the right size and age. After much effort and expense, he managed to locate twenty olive trees, each at least a century old, in the neighboring town of Antibes. He then had these painstakingly transplanted onto Chanel's property. When *Vogue* later rhapsodized that "the house [was] set quite simply in the midst of a large grove of ancient olive trees," few readers would have imagined that while the *trees* were ancient, technically, the *grove* was not. Like the aged tiles on the roof, the ancient trees were brand-new transplants, put there to enhance La Pausa's glow of borrowed time. Ever masterful at inventing her own, fictional histories, Chanel had artificially added ancient splendor to her new setting.

A grand estate needs grand gardens. Moved by the wild beauty of the gardens at Eaton Hall, Chanel designed similarly free-form landscaping at La Pausa. Along with the olive trees, she had her gardeners plant groves of orange trees, fields of lavender, fragrant hyacinth, masses of purple irises, and rosebushes of every color, which climbed up the walls of the house.

In dramatic contrast to the lush and vibrant floral colors, the interior of La Pausa featured Coco's typical muted and restrained palette, with spare furnishings and nearly no knickknacks or *objets* of any kind. Antique cabinets, dark oak tables, and couches upholstered in mahogany leather stood against cream-colored walls. Thick carpets of a deep claret color were scattered throughout the main living space on the first floor, and heavy beige silk curtains framed the six sets of French doors opening onto the patio. Even the piano was beige. A vast library featuring handmade oak shelves and deep armchairs for reading stood off to one side of the atrium. And to enhance further the ambiance of an old country estate, outsize stone fireplaces were built into most rooms.

Upstairs, his and her suites for Coco and the duke stood separated by a white marble bathroom. Eager to provide Bendor with a familiar setting commensurate with his background, she once more "transplanted history," covering his bedroom walls in panels of eighteenth-century dark oak and arranging to have a sixteenth-century Elizabethan-era oak bed transported from one of Westminster's other homes. She even had the lights in the villa's entryway decorated with the crown from Westminster's coat of arms. Coco's own suite featured beige taffeta drapes and bedding, oak paneling, and an antique wrought iron bed. Suspended above both beds were curtains of gold netting, to repel mosquitoes in style.

If Bendor was to see La Pausa as an extension of his usual surroundings, it would need to be filled regularly with his friends and family. Coco had always been a world-class hostess, and to encourage visitors, she converted an entire wing of the house into a series of two-room guest suites that offered couples the feeling of private apartments. Chanel especially wanted Bendor's cousin and friend Vera Bate Lombardi to feel at home, so she offered Vera and Alberto use of La Colline, one of the guesthouses on the estate. Jean Cocteau also availed himself of La Colline, whose walls he decorated with some of his distinctive cartoon drawings.

Finished in 1929, La Pausa was a smash, becoming the hub of some of the most talked-about parties of Europe. Scores of British and French luminaries trained down for weekend parties of dinner and tennis hosted by Coco and the duke. Churchill grew fond of La Pausa and visited it when he was in the area. Few of their friends wanted to miss out on Chanel's legendary yet low-key hospitality, all organized by her house manager, Admiral Castelan—another one of the highborn Russian refugees she collected. (Chanel treated Castelan with great respect; he dined alongside all invited guests.)

Every morning, guests could press a button and within two minutes find breakfast waiting outside their door, including twin thermoses of coffee and warmed milk, all left discreetly by Coco's majordomo, Ugo. Visitors were left entirely undisturbed until lunchtime, when Chanel typically had her staff prepare an elaborate buffet. "La Pausa was the most comfortable, relaxing place I have ever stayed," said Bettina Ballard, a former *Vogue* editor who frequented Roquebrune in the 1940s and '50s: "The house was blissfully silent in the morning.... Lunch was the moment of the day when the guests met in a group and no one missed lunch—it was far too entertaining. The long dining room had a buffet at one end with hot Italian pasta, cold English roast beef, French dishes, a little of everything."

Westminster must have found La Pausa relaxing as well. He converted one of the smaller buildings on the property into a studio for himself, where he painted watercolors—perhaps inspired to take up this hobby by his friend and amateur artist Winston Churchill. Decades later, Churchill would wind up spending a lot of time at La Pausa, after Chanel sold it to his literary agent, Emery Reves.

From the outside, Chanel's life looked idyllic. She was more successful than ever, and she'd built a seaside palace fit for a duke and future duchess. But by the end of the 1920s, all was not well. Despite her new surroundings, Chanel had not conceived a child, to her great disappointment. And—as many guests at La Pausa could attest—peace did not always reign between Coco and Bendor. While the duke was clearly smitten with Chanel, he had always been a philanderer, and old habits are hard to break. Coco knew of his frequent infidelities, and they wounded her deeply. Visitors more than once reported overhearing bitter arguments and slamming doors at La Pausa. After such explosions, the duke would try to make amends, often with an expensive piece of jewelry. According to one account, during a yachting trip, Bendor tried to apologize for an indiscretion by giving Coco a priceless string of pearls. Coco accepted the gift, opened her fingers, and without a word, let the necklace fall into the sea. A nearly identical story exists about another affair, another apology, and Chanel dropping a priceless emerald into the waves.

The summer of 1929 brought another heartache as well. Serge Diaghilev, Chanel's and Misia's great friend, was gravely ill. At fifty-seven, he was suffering complications from the diabetes he had long ignored, often gorging himself on desserts or eating entire boxes of chocolates. Now he lay in a Venice hotel room, felled by a combination of meningitis and typhus. He had a telegram sent to Misia and Coco: "Am sick, come quickly." On August 17, the two women, who were sailing the Adriatic on *Flying Cloud,* disembarked on the Lido and hurried to the Grand Hôtel des Bains de Mer. There they found Diaghilev in the care of his lover Serge Lifar and Boris Kochno, the Ballets Russes dancer and librettist serving now as Diaghilev's secretary. Kochno and Diaghilev had also been lovers in the past, and Lifar and Kochno's bitter rivalry for Diaghilev's affections made the sickroom atmosphere tense.

Misia stayed behind, but Chanel sailed off later that day. She didn't get far. Consumed with worry for her friend, she turned back toward Venice. She arrived too late. Diaghilev passed away on Chanel's forty-sixth birthday, August 19, 1929. He died as he had often lived—penniless. Misia was ready to sell a diamond necklace to raise funds for his burial, but Chanel wouldn't hear of it. She arranged and paid for a funeral fit for a king.

As the sun rose over the Grand Canal on August 20, 1929, three gondolas sailed slowly away from Piazza San Marco toward the Isola di San Michele, Venice's cemetery island where the doges lie buried. The first boat, the funeral gondola carrying Diaghilev's coffin, bore a sculpted angel with golden wings on its bow. The next two carried four mourners: Diaghilev's former lover Boris Kochno; dancer Serge Lifar, Diaghilev's current lover; Misia; and Coco—the two women all in white. When they disembarked, the grief-stricken Russian men fell to the ground and began crawling to the grave site on their knees. An exasperated Chanel insisted they rise and walk normally. Even in sorrow, she remained her practical self—the crawling was melodramatic and taking too long.

Diaghilev's death signaled the end of a major chapter of European modernist dance and theater. Lifar and Kochno would try for several years to hold the Ballets Russes together, but it soon lost its momentum. And Chanel must have felt a personal chapter in her life ending as well. Diaghilev had welcomed her into his artistic world, recognizing her not only as a wealthy patron but as an artist—someone who could work alongside the likes of Picasso and Stravinsky.

Coco had remained forever a grateful admirer: "I loved him in his hurry to live," she said of Diaghilev. "He taught French audiences…that there were unknown enchantments on every street corner.…He looked for genius the way a bum looks for cigarette butts on the sidewalk." Her metaphor is as revealing as it is startling. She is referring to Diaghilev's famous eye for talented people, and also to his cubist-inspired penchant for incorporating unexpected, humble elements (jogging, sunbathing, folklore, newspaper headlines) into his productions. But as Chanel knew well, she herself fell into the category of street-corner enchantment or cigarette-butt genius. It had taken visionaries on the order of Diaghilev and his coterie to espy the serious artist that lay within a mere dressmaker. For Coco, Serge's death represented a great personal loss.

Losses were piling up. The relationship between Westminster and Chanel grew increasingly strained, and Bendor spent very little time at La Pausa during the late summer of 1929. Finally, a line was crossed. While both were aboard *Flying Cloud,* Coco discovered that the duke had invited a third party onto the boat—a pretty young interior decorator who had caught his eye. This was too much. Shocked by Westminster's indifference to her feelings, Coco demanded that the woman be escorted ashore at the next port. The duke complied, but Chanel had lost her tolerance for humiliations of this sort. The duke would never marry her, and his interest in finding a new wife to bear him a son was all too clear.

Chanel's relationship with the duke drew to a close in late 1929, although their rupture did not happen all at once. For a time, Coco found comfort in the arms of her former flame, the devout, ascetic, intellectual Pierre Reverdy—a man arguably the exact inverse of Westminster. When Bendor got wind of Chanel's renewed dalliance with Reverdy, he was shocked: "Coco is crazy! She's taken up with a priest!" Coco visited Eaton

Hall once more in mid-December. By Christmas, though, the fifty-year-old duke was engaged to the Honorable Loelia Mary Ponsonby, a twenty-seven-year-old English noblewoman he had met only two months prior.

If, after their six years together, Chanel felt shock and sorrow as Bendor replaced her so blithely—in a matter of weeks—she said little about it. She had encountered this particular heartache before. As she had with Boy, Chanel once more lost a lover to a woman of a higher, more suitable social position, and this time her rival was nearly twenty years her junior. Although she would later tell Paul Morand that she "had never tried to trap [Westminster]" and indeed had even "demanded that he get married" to someone else, Chanel's actions over the course of their years together prove just how serious she had been about becoming his wife. She'd grown entranced with his version of England, too, later insisting that "everything I liked was on the other side of the [Channel]."

Aggravating the humiliation of his swift engagement, Bendor insisted on presenting his new fiancée to Coco—as if seeking the Chanel stamp of approval. The only account of this meeting comes from Ponsonby's memoir. Her description makes clear that neither woman found the afternoon enjoyable:

> At the time, Mademoiselle Chanel had reached the pinnacle of fame. Her sober clothes, simple and uncomplicated, were considered the height of chic.... She sat down in an armchair.... She offered me a small footstool at her feet! I felt as though I were before a judge who was about to decide whether I was worthy enough to become the wife of her old admirer. I doubt very much if I passed the test.

Loelia and the Duke married on February 20, 1930, in what proved to be the society wedding of the year. Winston Churchill served as best man.

When Coco talked of her time with the duke years later, she rewrote history as liberally as she always did. It's painful to read the tale she concocted for Paul Morand, so much does it betray her need to save face. Even while insisting on her great boredom with Bendor, she turned their six years together into an entire decade. (She told Marcel Haedrich she had spent thirteen years with the duke. In a later interview, she increased it to fourteen.) "Salmon fishing is not a life.... Ten years of my life were passed with Westminster.... I've always known when to leave.... 'I've lost you, I can't live without you,' he said to me. I responded, 'But I don't love you. How can you sleep with a woman who doesn't love you?'... With me, [the Duke] couldn't have everything he wanted. Being 'His Grace' meant nothing, so long as a little Frenchwoman could refuse him. It was a terrible shock for him."

The denial and bravado only made it plainer: That old, familiar chasm between the royal realm she aspired to ("His Grace") and the peasant girl still within (the "little Frenchwoman") had come back to haunt her. Chanel's young niece, Gabrielle Palasse, spent the summer after Bendor's wedding with "Auntie Coco," and recalled the lyrics to a song Chanel sang over and over to herself during those weeks: "My woman has a heart of stone ... not human but with a heart of stone." In perfect keeping with the role-reversed account she had invented for Paul Morand, Chanel had chosen a "*she*-done-me-wrong" tune, singing from the perspective of a wounded man. Perhaps singing this, she imagined herself the stony inflictor of pain, rather than its victim. Or perhaps she sang the words as a mantra, hoping to harden her own heart in the process.

CHAPTER NINE

THE PATRIOTISM
OF LUXURY

CHANEL AND PAUL IRIBE

C hanel's romance with Paul Iribe coincided with a turning point, perhaps even the central pivot moment, of her life. When they met, in 1931, she was forty-eight—in the very middle of middle age—and had recently broken off with the Duke of Westminster. Many of her fondest dreams had come true, while others, she now realized, would have to be put aside forever.

Coco was, unquestionably, at the height of her fame, power, and influence. She had established herself as an arbiter of style, her classic look worn or emulated by millions. She was one of the richest women in the world, with a business grossing 120 million francs annually. She owned a perfume factory and a textile mill, and employed 2,400 workers in twenty-six different studios. Chanel's personal fortune was estimated at 15 million francs, with holdings and investments spread over several countries. "Chanel" had become a household word in Europe and the United States.

Coco had also reinvented herself as a legitimate artist, continuing to cultivate friendships and collaborations with the brightest lights of the modernist movement. While guarded and defensive in many ways, she was free and generous with money. Happy to play the grande dame with a ready checkbook, she supported her friends' artistic endeavors, and bailed them out personally when the need arose. "I prefer to give rather than lend money," she wrote. "It costs the same."

Weekends and holidays found her on the Riviera where house parties at La Pausa took place on a royal scale. After lavish buffet lunches featuring an array of world cuisines, guests could play tennis on the professional courts framed by yew bushes, wander the grounds, or be motored down the steep hill by one of Chanel's chauffeurs, passing through the olive groves and fragrant orange trees en route to Monte Carlo for an afternoon of shopping. No one's life could have been grander or more accomplished, but even so, certain hard truths were coming into focus.

The rupture with Westminster brought with it the sound of doors closing. Coco experienced a new kind of pain as she considered the options no longer possible for her. She would never have a child; she would never accede to royalty. Even worse, the second disappointment resulted from the first. Had she been able to conceive, Bendor, she was sure, would have married her and made her a duchess. (Loelia and Bendor did not have a child together and divorced acrimoniously after five years.) When he left her, the duke had taken with him Chanel's last chance for the kind of historic and familial legacies she craved.

On April 29, 1930, Coco's beloved aunt and longtime companion, Adrienne, finally married her long-term lover, Maurice de Nexon (after the death of his father, who had long opposed the union), making her the Baroness Nexon. Chanel would never have admitted it, but to stand by as the mild and unambitious Adrienne acquired an aristocratic title would surely have rankled. Some women might have talked it all over with their girlfriends, but the woman who sang of a "heart of stone" sought other ways. With Paul Iribe, Chanel would find another path to another glory.

Iribe was Chanel's first serious romance after the duke and clearly she had decided it was time for a change. In Iribe, Coco seemed to have chosen a lover more for his personal qualities than for what he could do for her. Iribe had no royal pedigree, and was far from wealthy. He was not particularly good-looking or athletic. He was even a bit pudgy and had false teeth. None of that, however, had impeded his success with women—including beautiful, and often very rich—women. They saw in him what Chanel would see: a talented designer and illustrator; a self-assured wit and—most crucially—a great admirer and connoisseur of womanhood, someone whose career in fashion, jewelry, and interior design seemed based on his sophisticated understanding of female beauty. "A woman is like a pearl," he told an interviewer in 1911. "Just as a beautiful pearl must never be carved or deformed by a setting ill-suited to its structure, so must each woman's body determine the lines and colors that complement its form. I would no more try to change the form of a pearl than I would dream of trying to alter the beauty of the feminine body."

As so many times before, when Chanel encountered a new potential lover, he was married—to his second wife, the beautiful American heiress Maybelle Hogan. His first wife, French actress Jeanne Dirys, died of tuberculosis shortly after their divorce in 1918. She had been among the earliest performers to wear one of Chanel's hats onstage, even appearing in it on a magazine cover drawn by Iribe.

Iribe had long been a part of Misia's and Cocteau's circle, so he and Chanel may have been acquainted prior to their first official encounter in 1931 when Maybelle Iribe, seeking to boost her husband's flagging career, arranged a commission for him to design some jewelry for Mademoiselle Chanel. Maybelle likely came to rue this helpful intervention. It's not known exactly when this business arrangement turned into a love affair, but in 1932, Chanel and Iribe announced—with much fanfare—their collaboration on a new, lavish diamond jewelry collection, and Maybelle moved out of the Iribe family apartment on the avenue Rodin. In 1933 she filed for divorce and moved back to the United States, taking their two children with her. In November of that same year, a *New York Times* headline read "Mlle Chanel to Wed Business Partner"—announcing the first and only time in her life that Coco was engaged to be married.

It had taken an exceptional confluence of circumstances to get Chanel, at age fifty, to the brink of marriage at last. Although his career was in decline and hers still on the ascent when they met, Iribe proved able to give Chanel something that she had been seeking since her first days in Paris, something loftier than money, artistic renown, or even a royal title: Paul Iribe transformed Coco into an allegory, an icon of historic importance. Nothing could have seduced her more.

Despite the power imbalance between them and Chanel's considerably greater fame and fortune, Iribe had her spellbound, entranced by the vision of herself that he reflected back to her. He knew just what kind of beautiful pearl she longed to be. He also understood her yearning for personal apotheosis via national glory. Iribe's hard-right, ultranationalist, xenophobic political views confirmed and reinforced Chanel's own opinions, crystallizing tendencies she had long harbored. Only Iribe could have yielded so much influence over Coco at this stage of her life.

He was her age exactly, born in Angoulême, France, in 1883, but he was not of French descent. His mother and father (who were unmarried) were Spanish and Basque, respectively. Yet in his youth, Paul's father, Jules Iribarnegaray (who later shortened and Gallicized the family name), wound up thrust into the spotlight during one of the most iconic moments in French history: the climax of the 1871 Paris Commune uprising. And strange as it may seem, sixty years later, via Jules's son, Paul Iribe, aftereffects of Iribarnegaray's strange role in this epochal event made themselves felt in the life of Coco Chanel.

The Commune, which seized governing control of Paris from March to May 1871, was born of the devastation, poverty, and famine engendered by France's humiliating defeat in the Franco-Prussian War. The ongoing privations of war, coupled with rising concern about a possible restoration of the French monarchy, fueled the founding of the commune—a largely proletarian committee that maintained leadership of Paris for seventy-one days. Replacing the French *tricolore* with the red flag of international socialism, the Communards agitated for secularism in schools and government, enhanced workers' rights, and equality for women. Throughout its brief rule, the Commune remained under consistent attack by the newly formed Government of National Defense, which governed the rest of the country from its headquarters at Versailles, under President Adolphe Thiers, known for his ruthlessness and brutality.

Within right-wing circles and even among some moderates, the Commune incited bitter invective infused with xenophobia and racism. The movement consisted nearly entirely of white French people, but to its angry critics, the Commune looked like an invading horde. Communards were depicted as dangerous, "barbaric," inferior, and racially other. The women participants, the *Communardes,* appeared in caricatures as grotesque, promiscuous hags.

For its most iconic act, designed to symbolize its utter rejection of French imperialism, the Commune chose to demolish the Colonne Vendôme, the enormous bronze obelisk at the center of the Place Vendôme, commissioned by Napoléon to celebrate his victory at Austerlitz and modeled after Trajan's Column in Rome. At the column's very top, majestically surveying the Place Vendôme, stood a statue of the emperor himself, dressed as Caesar, in Roman toga and laurel wreath, and holding a smaller statue representing Liberty perched upon a globe.

Today, the elegant Place Vendôme is home to some of the world's most exclusive shops and businesses—most famously Coco Chanel's boutique and the Ritz. But in 1871, the Place Vendôme was known more as a war memorial, and its column represented everything the Communards decried: imperialism, militarism, and the smug implication that France's imperial conquests were actually benevolent, bringing "liberty" to the world. With the column's demolition, the Communards intended to offer participants a cathartic, even festive moment. They even hired musicians to entertain the crowds.

On May 16, 1871, the appointed day, ten thousand people overflowed the Place Vendôme, which had been renamed the Place Internationale for the occasion. Tons of manure and straw had been laid to absorb the shock of the falling monument. But felling the column proved more challenging than expected. It took more than fifty men working for hours in the heat with chisels, ropes, and hammers to maneuver the monument into place. Leading the workers was Jules Iribarnegaray, Paul's father—a civil engineer hired by the Commune to ensure the day's success.

Under Iribarnegaray's direction, the workers finally managed to crack the tower precisely into three parts. It crashed to the ground with a deafening noise, sending up thick and fetid dust clouds as it hit the straw-covered manure. The impact decapitated Emperor Napoléon, whose laureled head rolled away from his body. Amid cries of *"Vive la Commune!"* and the strains of "La Marseillaise," spectators scrambled to spit on the fallen emperor or grab bits of his fractured stone body as souvenirs. As a special token of gratitude for Jules Iribarnegaray, who'd risked his life and freedom in service to the Commune, officials presented him with the little statue of Liberty atop the globe. He left the Place Vendôme that day six thousand francs richer (his fee), and in possession of the allegorical figure of liberty that had long nestled in the palm of Napoléon's hand.

The fall of the Colonne Vendôme during the 1871 Paris Commune

Soon after, the Commune met its demise in one of the bloodiest massacres of French history, with Adolphe Thiers's government sending in the military. More than twenty-five thousand French citizens were gunned down indiscriminately, and at least seven thousand others were deported to a wretched penal colony in New Caledonia.

Amazingly, Jules Iribarnegaray escaped execution and arrest, but, fearing for his life, went into self-imposed exile for ten years in Spain, where he met his future common-law wife and started a family. It is impossible to ignore the dramatic contrast between Paul Iribe and his father. Jules's role in the Paris Commune forged much of his adult life. He was obliged to go into hiding—eventually living in four different countries, uprooting his children repeatedly as he moved from place to place. He remained a liberal intellectual, joining the Freemasons and studying philosophy and science. As a Basque, he would have regarded himself as part of a culturally and ethnically distinct group, neither French nor Spanish. In other words, Jules Iribarnegaray was a nomadic internationalist and an intellectual—not unlike Boy Capel.

Jules's son, Paul Iribe, on the other hand, seemed determined to invert every aspect of his father's life, devoting himself to the most xenophobic, ardent versions of French nationalism and patriotism, insisting constantly on his Gallic bona fides.

By the early 1930s, when Chanel met Paul Iribe, his *pro patria* ardor had tipped over into zealotry. He was the Frenchest of Frenchmen, as much a pillar of chauvinism as was the Colonne Vendôme his father had laid low. Chanel was attracted to his passionate nationalism. French identity offered a consoling antidote to the lingering wounds of a rootless childhood for both Coco and Paul, and during her time with him Chanel grew more ardent in her own patriotism.

As an adult, Paul made little mention of his itinerant youth or his father's exile. But his past did not hold him back. By the age of seventeen, in 1900, he was working as an apprentice to architect René Binet assisting in designing the iconic Porte Binet—the vast, ornamental main entrance to the 1900 Paris World's Fair, adorned with a twenty-foot sculpture of a beautiful woman wearing a flowing dress and matching coat designed by

The grand Porte Binet entrance to the 1900 Paris World's Fair, topped by La Parisienne

celebrated *couturière* Jeanne Paquin. Sculpted by Paul Moreau-Vauthier, this figure was known as La Parisienne, and the tiara she wore represented the city of Paris.

Fair officials had permitted this substitution of a contemporary Frenchwoman for the more traditional mythological goddesses or feminine abstractions (Marianne, or "La Liberté," for example) commonly used for ceremonial statuary. La Parisienne effectively promoted the fashionable Parisian woman to the status of allegory. In 1900, thousands of tourists flocked to the World's Fair to marvel at France's achievements in every realm, from colonial expansion to technology and the arts—including haute couture, which enjoyed particular pride of place. Apprentice Paul Iribe took the image to heart.

Iribe's career as a popular magazine illustrator advanced rapidly, his work an amalgam of fashion, design, and ardent French patriotism. His career also benefited from his uncommon success with women, as when, at twenty-three, Iribe convinced a married woman to divorce her husband and then use her money to subsidize his first publishing endeavor: *Le Témoin,* a journal of art and politics, on which Jean Cocteau also collaborated. Iribe even founded his own advertising agency during these years, specializing in luxury goods. His signature logo motif—the delicate "Iribe rose"—appeared on products ranging from fine jewelry to fabrics to art books.

After *Le Témoin* folded, Iribe and Jean Cocteau launched a wartime journal, *Le Mot,* which ran for nineteen issues from 1914 to 1915, promoting French patriotism and cultural superiority, along with a strident anti-German stance. (Diagnosed with diabetes, Iribe was unable to enlist in the French Army during World War I.) Paeans to French heroes (Marshal Joffre, Joan of Arc) mingled on its pages with caricatures of sadistic and deformed Germans. While *Le Mot* did not display the rabid xenophobia and racism of Iribe's later years, it pointed clearly in that direction.

Iribe made his biggest splash as a fashion illustrator for such great turn-of-the-century couturiers as Jacques Doucet, Jeanne Lanvin (for whom Iribe designed the still-extant Arpège perfume logo), Jeanne Paquin—of Porte Binet fame—and Paul Poiret. Poiret's Orientalist, flowing couture was set off to excellent advantage by Iribe's sinuous lines and keen sense of color.

Iribe fast became one of the leading lights of the new Art Deco movement. Along with beautiful furniture and fabrics, he designed jewelry, clothes, and theatrical sets—all distinguished by his use of the finest materials (highly polished exotic woods and Chinese silks); vivid, saturated colors; sleek curvilinear shapes; and an elegant balance between the ornate and the restrained.

Iribe's career reached its apex, though, during the six years he spent in America designing costumes and sets for film director Cecil B. De-Mille. In Hollywood, Iribe enjoyed a larger-than-life, American-style celebrity, socializing with film stars and studio executives, teaching costume design at the Paramount Pictures school and becoming a regular contributor to *Vogue* magazine, and even traveling to New York City to costume Broadway plays.

It was in Hollywood that Paul met his second wife, heiress Maybelle Hogan. But Iribe was earning his own fortune—which he enjoyed with all the zeal of the convert. He drove a Cadillac that he christened "Fifi" and bought a yacht he called *Belle de Mai*. He hired a Japanese valet.

In 1922, DeMille promoted Iribe to artistic director for the epic film *The Ten Commandments*, for which Iribe created elaborate and lavish ancient Egyptian settings—aided by more than one thousand craftsmen. And so, although they did not yet know each other, in 1922, Coco and Paul were engaged in similar work: She was costuming Sophocles, he the Bible.

Iribe began work on DeMille's next monumental biblical project, *The King of Kings*, but success had gone a bit to his head. After arrogantly defying DeMille's wishes on several occasions, Iribe found himself out of a job and obliged to return to France with his family.

Paul did not cope well with his sudden career reversal. From the toast of Hollywood, he plummeted to a forgotten decorator in France. Feeling discarded and unappreciated, Iribe abandoned himself to extravagance, spending his way quickly through his entire fortune and much of Maybelle's as well.

> My growing celebrity eclipsed his declining glory . . . Iribe loved me with the secret hope of destroying me.
>
> —COCO CHANEL

Chanel had no illusions about Iribe's mixed feelings toward her. She recognized early on the sharp contrast in their careers at the moment they met. Yet, they had so much in common, including Chanel's recent experience in Hollywood. In February 1931, she left for Los Angeles at the invitation of Samuel Goldwyn, whom she had met in Monaco through Grand Duke Dmitri. With American cinema suffering in the aftermath of the Wall Street crash of 1929, Goldwyn was looking for new ways to lure audiences, especially women, back to the theaters. In Chanel he saw a golden opportunity to make his movies irresistible—they could double as Paris fashion shows! He offered Coco a guaranteed $1 million if she agreed to come to Hollywood twice a year, in spring and fall, to dress his stars both offscreen and on. He was specific on one point: Chanel was to put the actresses in styles "six months ahead" of fashion, in order to offset the inevitable delay between filming and release. Explaining his decision to *The New York Times,* Goldwyn said, "I think that in engaging Mademoiselle Chanel I have not only solved the difficult problem of how to keep clothes from being dated, but also there is a definite service rendered American women in being able to see in our pictures the newest Paris fashions—sometimes even before Paris sees them."

Chanel did not say yes immediately. She kept Goldwyn waiting an entire year—something no one else had ever dared do. She didn't need the money, and she already had a thriving clientele among America's wealthiest women, including many actresses who wore Chanel in their private lives. Eventually, though, Coco realized that Hollywood offered opportunity on a new, grander scale. All of America would come to know her look, which would then be copied by more manufacturers, who would all want to buy from Chanel's textile company Tissus Chanel, which she had founded in 1928.

In April 1931, Chanel set sail for the United States aboard the SS *Europa,* bringing Misia Sert along for company. Much cinematic hoopla attended Mademoiselle's first trip to the United States, and no expense was spared. In New York, Maurice Sachs joined them, and the three friends boarded a specially commissioned all-white luxury express train for California. Onboard, Chanel was treated like visiting French royalty, plied with champagne and flattered by the accompanying American journalists.

To fete her arrival in Los Angeles, Metro-Goldwyn-Mayer even trotted out Greta Garbo to welcome Coco with European-style kisses on both cheeks as she stepped off the train onto the station platform. The Hollywood press covered it as "The Meeting of Two Queens." Chanel stayed long enough to create costumes for three Goldwyn productions, *Palmy Days* (1931); *Tonight or Never* (1931); and *The Greeks Had a Word for Them* (1932).

But before the last two were even out of postproduction, Coco left Hollywood disenchanted. The outsized luxuries of Hollywood did not appeal to her. "Their comforts are killing them," she said of the Americans. She was also put off by Hollywood's high quotient of Jews (although the Jewish Goldwyn, apprised of her prejudices, had taken care to minimize her exposure to others of his faith). She did enjoy, however, one acquaintance she made in California, actor-director Erich von Stroheim, telling Edmonde Charles-Roux: "With him at least the extravagance had a purpose. He was taking on a personal vengeance. He was a Prussian who persecuted lower-level Jews. Since Hollywood was essentially Jewish...the Jews of Central Europe found in Stroheim a familiar nightmare. At least this was not fakery. Together they were living an old story whose aftershocks they knew in advance and to which they were all definitely rather attached."

It was an odd, but perspicacious, even psychoanalytic, interpretation of what she'd witnessed—but Coco did not have all the facts. In Hollywood of the 1930s, von Stroheim was known as an Austrian aristocrat, son of a count and a baroness, who had left Europe after a career as a military officer. In truth, this Prussian aristocratic officer was but another Jewish immigrant in Hollywood. Erich Stroheim—he added the "von" when he got to America—was the son of practicing Viennese Jews. His untitled parents had run a small millinery shop in Vienna, and Erich had neither attended the Austrian military academy nor had a distinguished military career. But von Stroheim had aspirations very like Chanel's, and when he arrived in the United States he had entirely shed his ethnic identity and fabricated an aristocratic past for himself. A good actor, he carried it off for years. In her acceptance and appreciation of von Stroheim's "performance" of Austrian nobility, Chanel may have intuited the

Gloria Swanson (right)
in *Tonight or Never*,
costumed by Chanel

deep similarity between them. They were both gifted poseurs who'd made careers out of their personal fantasies.

Chanel also chafed at being an employee, however grand, of a film studio. For their part, the Hollywood kingpins were less than thrilled with Chanel's work anyway. While stars such as Ina Claire and Gloria Swanson loved to wear her clothes in their private lives, the studios found that Chanel's muted tones and simple lines did not "pop" onscreen.

In the early years of the Depression, American movie plots tended toward escapist fantasies, and costume choices leaned more toward marabou stoles, flowing silk gowns, and diamond jewelry (worn even for daytime scenes) than toward tweed suits or jersey dresses. Chanel disdainfully referred to onscreen Hollywood fashion as "sartorial anarchy." But the anarchists rejected Chanel's brand of governance. "The most elegant Chanel ... was a washout on the screen," explained Hollywood costumer Howard Greer. "When you strip color ... and the third dimension from a moving object, you have to make up for the loss with dramatic ... contrast and enriched surfaces. ... Overemphasis was essential." *The New Yorker*

Chanel in her own clothes

put it more bluntly: "[Chanel] made a lady look like a lady. Hollywood wants a lady to look like two ladies." In 1932, when Katharine Hepburn, starring in *A Bill of Divorcement,* requested Chanel as her costumer, the producers flatly refused. Hollywood would later come to favor more restrained or realistic wardrobes for its stars, but in 1931, Chanel and Iribe would certainly have agreed on the frustrations of working in American films.

En route home from Hollywood, Chanel and Misia spent a few days in New York City, where Chanel discovered an American phenomenon far more attractive to her than Hollywood had been: S. Klein department store on Union Square. At this downscale emporium, Chanel found knockoffs of her own (and others') designs. While Americans had long been copying aspects of Chanel's styles, S. Klein was selling blatant replicas of her work, albeit in cheaper fabrics and at bargain prices. Most designers would have been furious; Chanel was delighted. Although she admitted to disliking the inelegance of discount stores like S. Klein, she recognized the value of such publicity.

When she returned to Europe, she set about organizing an event based on what she'd seen in New York. Prevailing upon her still-warm relationship with Bendor, she borrowed his town house in London to host a charity fashion show for more than five hundred society women and actresses, including fabled beauty Gertrude Lawrence. Chanel explicitly invited the ladies to bring along their seamstresses, so that they could make sketches and take notes. She was openly offering her clothes as models to be copied. "I prefer copying to stealing," she wrote years later. "Seriously, there are forty thousand little dressmakers in France. Where can they find their ideas, if not among us? Let them copy. I am on the side of women and seamstresses not the fashion houses."

"Mademoiselle Chanel has authorized being copied," wrote London's *Daily Mail* incredulously. Such practices would later enrage Chanel's couturier colleagues, who never shared her democratic view of fashion and did not fancy seeing their designs reproduced by others.

But for Coco, seeing copies of her clothes multiplied across the social spectrum and the world brought only pleasure—all the more so for her recent failure to win over the vast markets offered by Hollywood films. She remained as invested as ever in achieving ubiquity of style, a "nation" of style, "when all the people in the street are dressed like you," as she would later remark.

Coco was something of a style nationalist—the possibility of *her* look becoming *the* uniform for all of France (and beyond) excited her greatly. To dress an entire country, to become synonymous with its style, fed her yearning to belong. Chanel craved something beyond success, wealth, or fame. She wanted to be a symbol of and for France—to achieve the deeply rooted, almost genealogical, legacy that had been denied her by birth and by her several near misses at attaining aristocratic stature. She would not be tsarina of Russia; she could not produce an heir for a duke; but she could do better. She could engender a race of French (and European and American) women who all dressed exactly like her. In anyone else, such a plan might indicate madness; for Chanel, it was a plausible goal.

Fascinated as he was with nationalism and feminine style, Iribe was deeply drawn to Chanel, someone as invested as he was in *patrimoine*—the treasure trove of French culture. Though their relationship began as business, Chanel found Iribe charming and seductive. He even displayed some jealousy early on, asking her about her many former lovers. "My past tortured him," Chanel told Paul Morand, not without some pride.

Paul and Coco grew close as they planned their most significant artistic collaboration, a diamond jewelry collection for the De Beers corporation. De Beers, the South African gemstone company founded by British imperialist Cecil Rhodes (a close associate of Lord Alfred Milner's), saw its profits sinking during the first years of the Depression. Seeking to boost sales with an injection of Parisian glamour, they had approached Chanel about designing for them. Diamonds had never really interested Chanel, who famously preferred costume jewelry to the ostentation of expensive jewels, which she likened to "wear[ing] your checkbook around your neck." But Iribe sensed an opportunity and did his best to convince Chanel to accept De Beers's offer. She agreed—perhaps for the thrill of expanding into a new area of design, or—more likely—to please Iribe.

As independent and successful as Chanel was, one part of her always remained the *cocotte* careful to appease her man. Chanel attributed her surprising new interest in precious gems to the European economy. "During times when luxury is too readily available, I always found costume jewelry devoid of arrogance. This consideration disappears during periods of financial crisis, when the instinctive desire for authenticity returns." Starting to sound more like Iribe, Chanel resorted to the language of nationalism. Jewelry, she told an interviewer, was "a very French art," and her exhibition was intended to promote patriotism. Never be-fore had Coco attributed such motives to her work.

Whatever her initial motivations, Chanel enlisted Iribe's aide in cre-ating what proved to be one of her most enduringly beautiful collections of jewelry—costume or real. Coco did not sketch or draw, and much of her jewelry up to this point had been designed by others, including Fulco di Verdura and Count Etienne de Beaumont, so the designs were likely executed by Iribe, with extensive input by Chanel. Stylistically, the col-lection suggests a harmonious blending of both of them, featuring Iribe's ornate whimsy somehow contained within Chanel-esque simplicity.

Relying on three basic decorative shapes—a star, a bow, and a feather—the collection of all-white diamonds was sleek and modern. The settings—all in platinum—were rendered nearly invisible, so unob-trusive that the diamonds appeared to be floating. The pieces were clev-erly versatile: Earrings converted into hairclips; brooches could become necklaces. A meteor-shaped choker stayed on with no clasp at all, look-ing like a streak of glittering light across the neck.

Items from the De Beers jewel collection designed by Chanel and Iribe, displayed on a wax mannequin, 1932

Chanel debuted the collection for two weeks in her own home in the Faubourg Saint-Honoré, in November 1932. Members of the fashion elite, who had all received elegant engraved invitations, filed through Chanel's drawing room, marveling at the diamonds and the unusual way they were displayed. Instead of being laid out on velvet cases in vitrines, the jewelry adorned old-fashioned hairdresser's mannequins, whose life-like wax features wore lipstick and eye makeup. They created a slightly surreal lineup of bodiless heads, brilliant with jewels. Even more surreal, perhaps, was the sight of armed men in uniforms conspicuously circulating among the elegant guests. De Beers had hired security guards to protect the priceless gems. De Beers did not sell a single item, nor was that the intention. The company had commissioned the collection and exhibition entirely for publicity, to raise its profile via a new association with Paris and Coco Chanel. The results exceeded all expectations. Two days after Chanel introduced her collection, De Beers's stock rose twenty points on the London stock exchange.

Iribe saw his own stock climbing, too, as he stood beside Chanel and basked in her spotlight. He'd often depended on wealthy women, but Chanel was different from the heiresses he'd once pursued. She had earned her success, and it outstripped anything Iribe had ever achieved.

Paul tried to balance the scales by extracting an emotional toll from his benefactress. As a lover, he proved demanding and controlling, prone to harsh and contradictory judgments of her life. Having successfully persuaded her to work in the most expensive medium imaginable—diamonds—he was equally insistent that she lived too expensively herself, accusing her of extravagance. Iribe accused her of having too many possessions, dining too lavishly, of keeping too many servants.

Chanel was not blind to the hypocrisy of such reproofs coming from the owner of Fifi the Cadillac. But, to please Paul, she moved out of her town house in Faubourg Saint-Honoré—firing her devoted longtime butler, Joseph Leclerc—and into an apartment at the Ritz, which she completely renovated, covering the walls with her Coromandel screens, even putting in a new bathroom. (She stored her clothes in another apartment she kept above her offices at 31, rue Cambon.) The result was a

jewel box of an apartment, intimate, elegant, and—as usual for Coco—
furnished with more lushness and baroque detail than one would expect
from such a priestess of modernism. The Ritz would remain her primary
residence in Paris for the rest of her life.

Ever manipulative, Iribe was not placated. He preferred weekends at
her villa on the Riviera. "He dominated her," recalled Serge Lifar, "and
she hated it." While Chanel may have groused about Paul's demands to
Lifar, at some level she clearly accepted being dominated in this way, perhaps seeing it as an acceptable sacrifice for love. Coco was also all too
aware of Paul's discomfort with her greater wealth and success. In giving
in to him on every front, she may have been trying to spare his masculine
pride.

Among Chanel's many concessions to Iribe was her agreement to finance the resurrection of *Le Témoin,* the journal he'd founded twenty-five
years prior with the backing of an earlier mistress. (Chanel's library contained six first editions of the original *Le Témoin.*) This new version,
which premiered on December 10, 1933, ran for two years and served as
a weekly platform for Iribe's increasingly virulent xenophobia and hard-
right nationalism, which, for him, was deeply tied to the arts, fashion, and
design. Passionately concerned about France, he felt it was in decline and
greatly threatened by outside forces, including Freemasonry, Bolshe-
vism, the rising tide of fascism (Hitler had become chancellor of Germany in 1933), taxes, nonwhite peoples, and international modernism in
art.

In other words, with the exception of Germany, once more a potential common enemy, these were the very movements and forces associated with the Paris Commune. Iribe was allying himself with the very
same archnationalist, conservative politics that his own father had so
publicly opposed. Chanel's social circle was well aware of Iribe's father's
story, and warned her not to forget that "[Jules Iribe] brought down the
Column onto the straw," as if he might have bequeathed a subversive
streak to Paul. In fact, quite the opposite was true. Iribe wanted not to
revolutionize France but to preserve it in amber, and to repel the many
dangers threatening it.

Iribe understood these dangers primarily—and nearly exclusively—through their effects upon the French luxury industry. He felt that France risked losing the elite refinements that distinguished it as a country, and that the solution was to "make France French again," by restoring French perfume, jewelry, fashion, and furniture to their rightful dominance, and safeguarding them from homogenizing forces of modernist art and the machine aesthetic. "There is more authentic French art in the windows of a great perfume shop or a great shoe store, than in most exhibitions of paintings," he wrote in 1932.

Iribe had come to believe that the most important art movement of his time—modernism—was actually a conspiracy by leftists, foreigners, and nonwhite peoples to undermine the sanctity of France. Only the original "brand" of France, he insisted in several published articles, could fend off the attacks launched by the likes of Le Corbusier, Walter Gropius, Pablo Picasso (whose interest in African statuary disgusted Iribe), and Jewish playwright Henry Bernstein (perhaps also targeted for being one of Chanel's former lovers). Modern fashion and fabric were also anathema to Iribe; he ranted against "undistinguished," "machine-made" clothing, particularly those "in solid colors."

For Iribe, a proper "Defense of Luxury," as he put it, demanded a resurrection of prerevolutionary values. He lamented the death of the nobility and the concomitant loss of the "privileges...of...race." Within his curious logic, this aristocratic, or "racial," privilege was tied inextricably to French luxury manufacturing: "The prosperity and prestige of these industries is the prosperity and prestige of France." Luxury goods, moreover, were indistinguishable from their female consumers: "The supreme client of these industries is Woman." Iribe would dedicate the rest of his life to his vision of idealized aristocratic womanhood—a figure blending the patriotism of Marianne with the luxury boutique appeal of La Parisienne, the statue dressed in haute couture who reigned over the Paris World's Fair of 1900.

.   .   .

On November 27, 1933, *The New York Times* announced Coco's engagement to Paul Iribe. The headline, however, referred only to Chanel's relationship with another, more famous man: "Mlle Chanel to Wed Business Partner; Once Refused Duke of Westminster." The article goes on to describe Chanel as the "independent-spirited dictator" of fashion and a woman of "enormous personal fortune," and once more mentions that she was the former mistress of the Duke of Westminster. Anyone looking for information on the actual bridegroom would have found but one mention of him, seven lines into the first paragraph, identified simply as "Paul Iribe, painter and decorator."

With the launch of *Le Témoin* the following month, Iribe tried to reassert himself. Every issue's cover telegraphed its patriotism, resembling the French *tricolore,* in blue, white, and red. The words "Paul Iribe, *directeur,*" were printed clearly on the upper left-hand corner. Chanel's name appeared nowhere, although she had financed the entire operation.

Chanel was not acknowledged as *Le Témoin*'s publisher, though she did receive prominent exposure in the journal. Every issue included one or more political cartoons featuring Marianne, usually one on the cover and another as a centerfold. And this Marianne, who appeared hundreds of times in these pages, bore Coco's unmistakable face and figure. Week after week, Iribe made Coco *Le Témoin*'s top (and only) cover girl. He did not depict her wearing any of her trademark fashions—no jersey dresses, no suits, no cloche hats, no pearls; this version of Coco modeled only one outfit—a Phrygian cap and flowing robes. But with or without her name or famous accoutrements, and even transformed into a cartoon illustration, Coco was known by all at a glance. "It was her face!" as Gabrielle Palasse-Labrunie put it simply.

Iribe had turned the pages of *Le Témoin* into his own series of wedding announcements, symbolically righting the power balance between him and his world-famous fiancée. By suppressing her name and powerful role as publisher, and subsuming Chanel into Marianne, Paul made Coco

his creation, his symbol of the nation, essentially declaring himself betrothed to France herself. Iribe summed up his intentions for *Le Témoin*
with the motto he chose for the journal: "We speak French. Subscribe to
us."

Coco offered Iribe the ideal image for his project. She had become
the very embodiment of *francité*—the deeply rooted essence of national
culture and pride and, especially, of the feminized luxury trades that he
so revered. As John Updike would write, "Chanel...was in a way, France
itself—the ubiquitous name of French chic, its subtle, rational, penetrating glamour."

Although her classical garb recalled her symbolic role in the French
Revolution, as well as the Commune, Iribe's Marianne did not represent
democracy or egalitarianism (and certainly not socialism) so much as she
did a beleaguered elitism. To drive home the imperiled state of France,
Iribe subjected his Marianne to all manner of torments. She suffered
gunshot wounds, drowning, evil spells, criminal prosecution, and hanging. She appeared stripped naked, garroted, unconscious; her eyes gouged
out to bloody holes à la Oedipus; she was buried alive. Iribe even portrayed her nailed to the Cross. In every case, this tortured lady remained
recognizably Chanel.

Iribe depicted Coco flatteringly, even lovingly; her body long and
graceful, her face regal; and not all the Marianne drawings feature such
gore. But there is no denying the violence of dozens of these illustrations.
Whatever its patriotic intent, *Le Témoin*'s treatment of the Coco-
Marianne figure bordered on sadism. The resultant tone was a blend of
hero worship, fetishism, and cartoon snuff. Chanel was well aware of the
violent undercurrent of Iribe's feelings, telling Morand years later, "He
wanted to see me vanquished, humiliated."

I ribe did not rely on his Marianne alone to express his vexed and conflicted feelings toward Coco. He vented his animus against modernism
weekly on the pages of *Le Témoin*, targeting the Bauhaus and cubism, as
well as specific elements of contemporary women's fashion, all of which

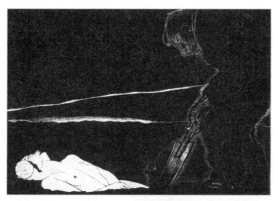

Chanel appearing as
Marianne in *Le Témoin*:
being interred, with eyes
gouged out, presiding over
an imperiled France turned
roulette table, and nailed to
the Cross

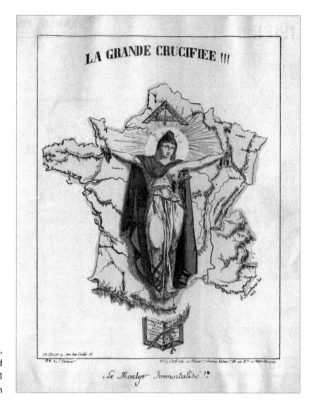

LA GRANDE CRUCIFIEE !!!

Le Martyr Immortalisé !?

The Paris Commune, figured as a crucified Marianne in an 1871 political cartoon

screamed their association with Chanel: costume jewelry, solid-color fabrics ("unfeminine"), British tweeds (not French), and military styles. "We have renounced French fashion in favor of the uniform," wrote Iribe. He also unleashed his contempt on a Coco trademark, the faux pearl necklace, opining that "[pearls] . . . available at any price range . . . signify nothing." But Iribe reserved his harshest criticism for another item instantly associated with Chanel: inexpensive couture knockoffs, which he dismissed as "leprosy on the clear complexion of Paris."

Iribe never mentioned Chanel's name in these diatribes, but he did not need to. By the midthirties, Coco enjoyed a long-established reputation for her use of solid colors; her textile factory was now producing the British tweeds that she had begun using—to great acclaim—during her Westminster years, and her suits had always been distinctly inspired by the military. While genuine political zeal may have driven Iribe, his public laments over modernism—especially in women's fashion—amount, in effect, to a thinly veiled attack on his own fiancée and primary source of funding. Clearly, Paul loved Coco best as a silent icon who could be beaten and battered week after week in the pages of *Le Témoin*.

The midthirties brought tremendous turmoil to all of Europe, and especially to Paris. The French economy grew perilously weak; unemployment soared; and, most frighteningly, violent antigovernment riots—provoked by the so-called Stavisky affair and organized by the burgeoning French pro-fascist movement—rocked France. This instability only stoked Iribe's and Chanel's anxiety about their country's decline, and hardened Iribe's stance in *Le Témoin*.

Protests against the government continued throughout January, with special vitriol from right-wing sectors reserved for both Prime Minister Edouard Daladier and his Socialist (and Jewish-born) deputy, Léon Blum (who later became prime minister). Paris boiled over on February 6, 1934, in one of the bloodiest riots seen in the city since the Commune. Demonstrators stormed the Palais Bourbon, home of the Chamber of Deputies (although all the deputies had fled); mobs streamed down the streets on both sides of the Seine. Right-wing leagues such as the pro-fascist Jeunesse patriotes (Patriotic Youth), in their paramilitary blue uniforms, and the similarly pro-fascist Action française and Solidarité française, marched in formation shouting "France for the French." As they had during the Commune, government troops, the Garde mobile, fired into crowds of French citizens, discharging as many as twenty thousand rounds of ammunition. The official death toll was between twenty and seventy, but many believed it much higher. More mass demonstrations and strikes followed. On February 12, more than a million workers descended into the streets of Paris during a general strike called for by the unions and the Socialist Party; thousands more marched in other towns.

Hundreds of such uprisings occurred regularly throughout the midthirties, organized by both ends of the political spectrum, leading many to fear France had plunged anew into a kind of violent, even revolutionary, upheaval. Journalists and publishers occupied center stage in much of the political drama, for the 1930s saw an explosion of mostly

right-wing, often anti-Semitic, periodicals. A great many of these journals received their funding from the luxury goods industry. Perfume
magnate François Coty owned three conservative papers, *Le Figaro*, *L'Echo
de Paris*, and the right-wing tabloid *L'Ami du Peuple*. Pierre Taittinger and
Jean Hennessy, of the champagne and cognac empires respectively, each
also owned right-wing papers. Taittinger had also founded the Jeunesse
patriotes.

As another multimillionaire in a luxury business, Chanel would have
found herself among peers in her new capacity as the publisher of *Le
Témoin*. But she was the biggest celebrity of the group, and surely the
only one underwriting a newspaper—and anonymously—to please a
boyfriend.

Chanel increasingly embraced her lover's worldview. "More than
ever before, I wanted to create aristocratic fashion," she wrote in August
1934, introducing her new collection. Through Iribe, she had acceded to
a status surpassing even that of duchess or tsarina; Chanel had become
the face of France. However much her cartoon doppelgänger suffered,
Chanel must have enjoyed Iribe's vision of her. She may even have appreciated the pain he inflicted on Coco-Marianne, seeing in it confirmation and cathartic reflection of her own many sorrows. For Iribe, Chanel
made grand-scale sacrifices: She moved out of her home for this man,
commissioned him to create print fabrics (which she rarely used in her
work), and diamond jewelry (ditto), and subsidized his journal. For a
brief time—quite uncharacteristically—she even ceded her business authority to him. It happened in the midst of a high-stakes argument with
the Wertheimer family, her partners in Parfums Chanel, the most lucrative division of her empire.

Chanel owed her fortune to her perfume business, in which she held
only a 10 percent interest, the rest belonging to Pierre and Paul Wertheimer, the founders of Bourjois cosmetics. But relations with the Wertheimers had always been vexed, since despite the tremendous wealth the
company had brought her, Parfums Chanel had made far more money
for the two Jewish brothers, who now held 90 percent of the business. In
1933, after Chanel's attorneys subpoenaed all the Wertheimers' financial

records, the brothers responded by trying to freeze her out as president. Chanel mounted suit against them.

In the midst of these negotiations, on September 12, 1933, Coco took the peculiar step of granting power of attorney to Iribe, transferring control to him and having him preside over a board meeting of Parfums Chanel. Never before had Coco abdicated responsibility so blithely. Iribe had never run a business, knew nothing of corporate law, and had demonstrated no particular gift for business diplomacy. And as Chanel might have predicted, he got nowhere in the meeting. Making matters worse, Iribe refused to sign the minutes at the end of the meeting—a necessary formality—whereupon the majority shareholders, who had tolerated his presence merely as a courtesy to Chanel, voted him off the board. The Wertheimers went ahead with their plans to reorganize the company, and Coco herself was ousted as president in 1934, after further disputes involving the Wertheimers' introduction—without Chanel's approval—of a Chanel brand cleansing cream. This step intensified the acrimony among them, though her 10 percent stake in the company continued to fill her coffers handsomely.

Chanel was far too smart to think Iribe a worthy proxy for herself in a business deal, so why would she have risked her fortune in this way? The only explanation is that Chanel yearned to disarm Paul, to attenuate his insecurities by allowing him to dominate her. She may have enjoyed the fantasy—however fleeting—of being able to rely on a man, of being the kind of protected woman she'd never been.

In at least one major way, Paul had provided her with a womanly status she'd never enjoyed: He had proposed. At last, Coco would have the status of wife. At the same time, Iribe's publishing venture assured her every week that she was France incarnate. While Boy Capel and Westminster had ultimately abandoned her to marry aristocrats, Iribe was different. He was prepared to marry Coco, not because he overlooked her commoner status but because he did not see it. For Iribe, Chanel *was* a kind of natural French aristocrat—a point he allowed Coco to make for herself on the sole occasion he permitted her a (discreet) byline in *Le Témoin*. On February 24, 1935, the regular column called Notre Mode

(Our Fashion) was signed by its guest contributor's initials "G.C."—clearly Chanel—and devoted to Iribe's favorite topic, "French luxury":

> I've always considered good manners, fine dining, and good humor in all social interactions to be the three essential elements of French luxury. These are more moral than superficial attributes and people who are very simple, very natural, and very refined acquire and keep them all their lives, without worrying about the state of their fortune, which has nothing to do with real elegance... thank God. For my part, and without any xenophobia, I believe that well brought up students have no need of foreign examples to know what is appropriate to wear to any social occasion they may attend.

The little essay summed up most of Chanel's and Iribe's philosophy.

As the populist uprisings of the midthirties spilled regularly into the streets, Coco's upper-class coterie began throwing ever more lavish formal, often masked, balls that transformed Paris town houses and Riviera villas into enchanted forests, African deserts, Mount Olympus, or the court at Versailles. Elaborate feasts were prepared, and guests vied with one another for the most original or historically accurate costumes. Among Paris's elite, an ambiance of decadence reigned during these prewar years, as if this group sensed imminent despair and privation. A distinctively *"après moi le déluge"* sentiment filled the air.

Chief among the festivities were the renowned masked balls organized by the Count and Countess Etienne de Beaumont, the very ones who had barred Chanel from their home back in 1920. Coco became a beloved regular, showing up bedecked in elaborate, beautifully made costumes of her own design, often captured by the society photographers. For the Masterpiece Ball, Coco became the androgynous, balletic fop of Jean-Antoine Watteau's 1716 portrait *L'Indifférent,* with silk cap, tights, and tunic. For Daisy Fellowes's Colonial Ball of August 1935, Chanel posed, with the thoughtless racism of her cohort, as a "humorous Negro sailor" (in blackface); for the Forest Ball given by André

Durst in 1935, she dressed as a leafy tree (in greenface); and for the
Waltz Ball of 1934, Coco became Queen Victoria (outshining even her
companions Napoléon III and Emperor Franz Josef), in full nineteenth-
century regalia: a black silk gown with a gigantic hoopskirt over layers
of starched crinolines—the very sort of garment she had rendered obsolete long ago.

The balls let Coco play at theatrical dress-up and offered a reprieve
from the austerity of her usual taste. In costume, Chanel could be outrageous for a few hours. She could allow herself to look like a queen who
ruled an empire. "The masked ball unmasks," Cocteau observed. Coco
even designed costumes for other guests, doing a particularly good job
for Serge Lifar and Daisy de Segonzac, who went as two eighteenth-
century figures—the court dancer Auguste Vestris and Marie Antoinette,
respectively—to a 1939 party thrown by the Marchesa Luisa Casati.
When Serge, Daisy, and other guests, all dressed as prerevolutionary

Chanel costumed as
Queen Victoria, 1934

noblemen, descended to the street, crowds of passersby grew incensed and hurled invective at them.

But Marianne was the ultimate costume for Chanel. She had always absorbed her lovers' ideas and styles, and since Iribe was already so much like her, it was very easy to relax into his worldview, which justified her own political prejudices while glorifying her personally. Iribe reflected and confirmed her version of elitism and racial superiority for which noble birth and inherited wealth were not required. In their shared philosophy, they both emerged at the top of the social heap. Such a democratized version of bigotry resolved the contradictions inherent in Chanel's aristocratic longings and contained within it an apologia for fascism, which Chanel would come to embrace.

Iribe absorbed Coco as well, subsuming her into a last attempt to resurrect his career, exploiting not only her money but her iconic status and even her physical likeness for his own purposes. Since Iribe viewed the Place Vendôme as a microcosm of all he valued in the French nation, then Chanel—with her apartment at the Ritz (15, Place Vendôme) and her main atelier just around the corner—was the new Napoléon atop the Colonne Vendôme, the dazzling imperial ruler of this "vitrine of France," as he'd dubbed the Place Vendôme.

C hanel's friends were aware of what was going on and expressed dismay. "I have just heard that Iribe is marrying Chanel. Aren't you appalled—for Chanel?" wrote Colette in 1933 to her friend Marguerite Moreno. After a dinner party at Chanel's, Paul Morand recounted to a friend that the moment Coco and Paul left the table, those remaining began gossiping about them, especially noting Iribe's girth: "Last night I was at dinner at Chanel's. She looked very nice with a little white barman's vest on. After dinner... they went off to play belote.... At the table, the rest of us could speak of nothing but his weight." Everyone knew of Chanel's intolerance for heavy people ("I detest fat," she was known to say); she had been trying to help Iribe slim down.

Chanel's nephew André Palasse also disapproved of Coco's relation-

ship with Iribe, whom he got to know quite well since, at Coco's suggestion, Iribe had hired the twenty-eight-year-old Palasse to help him with
Le Témoin. The two men spent long hours together working on article
texts and layout, and, according to Palasse's daughter Gabrielle Labrunie,
her father always felt uneasy with Iribe's treatment of Chanel, and worried especially about Paul's liberal use of Coco's money.

"[Iribe's unpleasantness toward her] was probably the biggest reason
why my father thought a marriage between them would never take place,"
Labrunie said. "My father found him very much an opportunist. Coco financed everything." For Labrunie, her aunt's attachment to Iribe was
driven more by the desire to be in a relationship than by desire for Iribe
specifically: "She…was…so attached to the idea of being in love again."

Coco's business was still thriving in the summer of 1935, but she was
nevertheless beginning to feel the pinch of Europe's economic crisis.
Chanel had also begun for the first time to worry about industry rivals,
particularly Elsa Schiaparelli, the Italian designer whose dreamlike,
surrealist-inspired creations, so unlike Coco's in style, were winning
great acclaim in Paris. Perhaps to avoid these anxieties, Chanel was
spending most of the season at La Pausa.

One mild September evening, Paul took the Blue Train down to
Roquebrune to visit her. Having slept soundly in one of the famous blue
and gold compartments, he arrived the next morning rested and ready
for tennis. Upon arriving at the villa he went immediately to change before Coco had come downstairs. When she appeared, he was already on
the courts, a white robe tied over his tennis gear.

Coco saw him and they moved toward each other for an embrace.
Before he reached her, Paul clutched his chest, his face contorted in pain,
and fell to the ground. He never regained consciousness. On September
25, 1935, in the Menton hospital to which Chanel had rushed him, Iribe
died of this massive heart attack. He was fifty-two.

Yet again, Chanel had lost the man in her life suddenly and tragically.
The shock was profound. "He died at her feet. That marks a person," said
Gabrielle Palasse-Labrunie.

The loss changed her permanently; she grew harder and more spiteful. Her racism and nationalist zeal had been ignited by Iribe, as had her sense of herself as a symbolic heroine of France. His mythmaking had jibed perfectly with her own and, upon his demise, Chanel was left alone again, her memory of Iribe entwined with his abstracted, nearly inhuman view of her. At fifty-two and after so many tragedies, Chanel must have known she would likely never marry now. She turned inward and more extreme in her opinions, subsuming perhaps the caricature into which Paul had already turned her.

CHAPTER TEN

THE PULSE OF HISTORY

CHANEL, FASCISM, AND THE INTERWAR YEARS

Underneath the glamour of Chanel beats the throbbing pulse of history—the history of fashion and the history of the world.

—MARIE-PIERRE LANNELONGUE

Why brilliant fashion designers—a notoriously nonanalytic breed—sometimes succeed in anticipating the shape of things to come better than professional predictors is one of the most obscure questions in history; for the historian of culture, it is one of the most central.

—ERIC HOBSBAWM

To delve into Chanel's life, relationships, and influence during the mid- to late 1930s, as war grew closer, is to approach volatile territory—to enter the debate about whether Chanel spent the war not merely as a Nazi sympathizer or collaborator, but as an enemy agent, a Nazi spy. From 2009 to 2011, no fewer than twelve books about Chanel appeared, and several broached this delicate topic with more candor than it had received before. Certain biographies made headlines with what appeared to be disturbing new information: that Chanel was, at best, what the French call a "horizontal collaborator," surviving the war using the courtesan's tactics she'd learned as a girl, or, at worst, an out-and-out Nazi agent.

The most inflammatory book, Hal Vaughan's *Sleeping with the Enemy*, confirmed more information than it revealed about Chanel's politics and her relationship to the occupying Germans. Vaughan focused his energies primarily on two areas of Chanel's life during the war: her love affair with Baron Hans Günther von Dincklage, an SS intelligence officer known as "Spatz" who was quartered at the Ritz during the war, and her involvement—via Spatz—in a failed spy mission for Germany known as Modellhut, or "model hat." Vaughan also wrote of Chanel's openly anti-Semitic views.

The world has long known of Chanel's dalliance with both Spatz and espionage. And she made little secret of her anti-Semitism, especially when in the company of her many like-minded friends. But Vaughan's access to previously classified intelligence documents provided long-missing, specific evidence not only of the extent of Chanel's involvement with the Nazis but also of how "official" her status really was—she even received a Nazi code name and agent number.

Some more sympathetic biographers, among them Justine Picardie (2010) and Lisa Chaney (2011), have argued that Chanel was guilty of little more than poor judgment, having fallen for a dashing younger man without regard for his nationality. Eager to protect its founder's good name, the Maison Chanel has hewn to this line as well. To dispel the accusations of anti-Semitism, the corporation has repeatedly pointed to Coco's many long-standing Jewish friends and associates, prime among these the Rothschild family and her business partners the Wertheimers. Some of her favorite billionaires, that is, were Jewish.

The moral lapses of brilliant, rich, and glamorous figures never fail to entice us, and the surprising extent of collaboration among midcentury Parisian notables—even such revered figures as Pablo Picasso and Gertrude Stein—has inspired considerable interest. But Chanel's relationship to fascism extends far beyond her amorous choices or her ill-conceived attempts at espionage—beyond even the realm of traditional biography.

By the midthirties, the name "Chanel" referred to something far more powerful than any one woman—"Chanel" had become a concept, a movement, a way of life, a vast constellation of visual associations and references instantly recognizable to millions of women in Europe and the United States. Although it had begun in the purely commercial, seemingly frivolous, world of female adornment, the Chanel empire now rooted itself in something deeper: a mythic underpinning, a *Weltanschauung*. Ultimately, this worldview, let's call it "Chanelism," became a political aesthetic—a system of readable symbols—whose scope resonated with and even perpetuated the ideological work of fascism. Yet Chanelism grew quite organically out of Coco's life, her psychology and taste, the company she kept, and the atmosphere in which she was steeped during the years leading up to the Second World War.

In the second half of the 1930s, Chanel's inner life was in turmoil. The months following Iribe's death were long and painful for her, and she took refuge at Roquebrune throughout the summer of 1935—leaving her business entirely in the care of employees for the first time in her life. Misia rushed down to La Pausa to support her grieving friend, but, characteristically, Coco refused to open up to her. Instead, as she had so many times before, she mourned a lost love inwardly, in silence. Plagued now by chronic insomnia, she began relying on Sedol, a prescription sedative with which she would inject herself nightly for the rest of her life—the likely provenance of her reputed reliance on another similar drug, morphine, to which Misia was already hopelessly addicted. In the fall, despite her sorrow and fatigue, Chanel returned to the Ritz and threw herself into her work.

No major love affair seems to have marked the years immediately following Iribe's death. But Chanel was rarely without a suitor of some kind. She may have had a brief affair in the midthirties with one of her most important jewelry designers, Count Fulco di Verdura, and her police surveillance file suggests that Coco was also involved at this time with the married Henry de Zogheb, an Egyptian-born banker and newspaper magnate, seventeen years her junior.

In 1935, Coco was also frequently seen in the company of the handsome twenty-nine-year-old Luchino Visconti, an Italian count by birth and fairly open about his homosexuality. We don't know if he made an exception in Coco's case, but Visconti's sister Uberta suggests the relationship was more of an intense friendship, dominated by Coco: "Chanel was fascinated by Luchino, but he was holding back.... He found her overwhelming and demanding. Chanel was in love with him, although to say 'in love' is such an approximation when one doesn't know the feelings of a woman who was more mature and accomplished than [he]. By then she was the queen, the undisputed authority in Paris. They [traveled]...Luchino always at her side. He went to stay at La Pausa." A recollection by Visconti's other sister, Ida, hints that, with Luchino, Chanel permitted herself some of the extreme, controlling behavior that later became routine for her: "[Chanel] would ring and [she] talked and talked; at times Luchino put the telephone to one side as she went on talking."

Part of Chanel's appeal for Visconti may have derived from her association with fascism, a movement to which he—like so many artists—was very attracted for a time: "When I was in Paris, I was kind of an imbecile, not a Fascist, but unconsciously affected by Fascism, 'colored' by it," he said. Visconti's was largely an aesthetic fascination. He loved the work of filmmaker Leni Riefenstahl, and after a visit to Hitler's Germany in 1934, had come away enamored of the parades of handsome young soldiers. Fascism also held social appeal, as one of Visconti's friends pointed out: "The elite people, like Coco Chanel, liked the Nazis."

Visconti's politics would change completely, thanks, ironically, to an acquaintance he made through Chanel. As discerning as ever of talent, Coco introduced Luchino to filmmaker Jean Renoir, who hired the young man as his assistant. Renoir was a committed leftist whose politics would deeply influence Visconti. Chanel, too, would collaborate with Renoir, making the costumes for two of his landmark films, both appearing in 1939: *La Règle du jeu* (*The Rules of the Game*), a satire of French social class hierarchies, and *La Marseillaise,* about the French Revolution. Renoir dedicated *La Marseillaise* to the recently fallen Popular Front government of Léon Blum. Perhaps tellingly, Chanel's contribution to the film was restricted to designing clothes for actress Lise Delamare, who played Marie Antoinette.

. . .

S till as vast an empire as ever, the House of Chanel employed four
thousand workers in 1935 and was turning out upwards of twenty-
eight thousand garments per year. Even so, Chanel felt some insecurity
in her professional life. The atmosphere in Paris seemed different to her
and she was now largely without a love life. The Depression had taken a
toll, and Chanel felt ongoing pressure from a number of rivals who had
gained momentum during her absence—designers such as Marcel Rochas, Mainbocher, and Italian Elsa Schiaparelli, who was collaborating
with Chanel's friends Jean Cocteau and Salvador Dalí to create fantasti-
cal surrealist garments that wowed Paris with their originality. Chanel
would also collaborate with Dalí, aiding him with the costuming of his
surrealist ballet *La Bacchanale* in 1939.

Throughout this period, Chanel played to her strengths. Her collections consisted largely of sleek, simple, elegant dresses and suits that eschewed ostentation in favor of such subtle details as jacket linings of
glossy printed silk and fine gilt chains sewn into hemlines to keep skirts
properly weighted. American *Vogue* characterized Chanel's 1937 spring
line as "dignified elegance...[which] brings us down to earth" and ap-
plauded her 1938 midseason collection for being "un-sensational, subtle,
wearable—[with] no tricks...short-jacket suits [in] wine, plum, navy
blue, brown; jackets fitted at the waist or belted in."

With another war looming, and Paris increasingly somber and anxious, Coco's trademark restraint seemed downright patriotic once again,
and she became something of a standard-bearer among her colleagues.
Taking the pulse of their clientele, French designers focused increasingly on wearability, practicality, even modesty—traits famously associated with Chanel. "The couture is swinging back to the great age of
Chanel simplicity," announced *Vogue* in 1937.

The grim external climate seemed to mirror the upheaval of Chanel's
personal world. The rocky period inaugurated by the stock market crash
of 1929 had not abated, and France faced continual crises both within the
nation and abroad. The birthrate had dropped precipitously, unemploy-

ment continued to rise, and nationwide strikes disrupted countless services and industries. France's instability was such that the country went
through five prime ministers in the four years between 1936 and 1940.
Above all, France watched with dread the encroaching menace of Italian
and German military aggression, as well as General Francisco Franco's
coup in Spain and the onset of the Spanish Civil War. Unstable domesti-
cally, and sensing a looming war for which it was ill prepared, France felt
dangerously adrift, demoralized. As often happens, such troubled conditions inflamed long-smoldering resentments and racial tensions.

For many years after the Second World War, popular wisdom held
that the French had heroically resisted their occupiers and Nazism in
general. The truth was far murkier. While France never tipped over entirely into becoming a fascist state, fascist ideology did find acceptance in
many sectors. In the later 1930s, Hitler's Final Solution and the Nazi
occupation were still several years away, but an ominous current of anti-
Semitism had already taken root in France, preparing the way for Vichy
and collaboration. Work by historians and critics from the 1970s onward,
especially Americans such as Robert Soucy, Eugen Weber, Alice Kaplan,
Jeffrey Mehlman, and Robert Paxton, has demonstrated the myriad ways
in which large numbers of French citizens accepted, even welcomed, an
alliance with Nazi Germany. Some people had purely practical reasons
for such views, seeing Hitler as the only alternative to communism. For
others, making common cause with Germany represented a last, desperate attempt to avoid revisiting the horrors of the first Great War. And
even when war did come, some degree of French collaboration consisted,
arguably, of sheer need—a desire to survive.

But many also felt deeply drawn to Nazism for political or philosophical reasons. "French fascism had generic roots.... There may have
been a native French fascism," wrote historian John Sweet. These generic
roots had been planted at least half a century prior, when the Dreyfus
affair plunged the country into years of bitter racial and political division. Hannah Arendt believed that the groundwork for Hitler and the
Final Solution was laid at this time, writing, "At the end of the Dreyfus
affair the slogans, 'France for the French,' and 'death to the Jews' were

seen to be almost magical formulas for reconciling the masses to the existent state of government and society."

Nearly fifty years later, fascism transformed the racial hatred and xenophobia behind such slogans into a coherent mythology whose appeal extended beyond Germany and into France. Fascism confirmed that, like Germany, France was a sick patient in need of care to nurse its body politic back to health. The treatment would restore Europe to an earlier and purer state, a prelapsarian golden—and Jewless—age. In the years just before the war, the political tumult in France awoke these long-standing tendencies, igniting France's domestic fascism. Of life in France in the years preceding the war, historian Tony Judt has written: "[It was] fundamentally nasty . . . [distinguished by] public hatred . . . personal attacks . . . [and] racial and xenophobic vitriol . . . hard to grasp today . . . and everywhere there was anti-Semitism."

The election in April 1936 of Léon Blum, the leftist candidate of the Popular Front and France's first Jewish prime minister, polarized the country, thrilling progressives but horrifying wealthy conservatives such as Chanel and her friends, stoking their anti-Semitism. Overt hatred of the Jews became commonplace, even in political discourse: "It is intolerable that our country should be represented by a Jew. We speak French not Yiddish," proclaimed one politician. "The soil of France is made to bear steeples not synagogues," intoned another. Chanel had long harbored similar sentiments and later admitted, "I am afraid only of the Jews and the Chinese, and far more of the Jews."

For Chanel, and thousands like her, "Jewishness" was a racial condition that could never be reconciled with "Frenchness." French chauvinism had begun justifying itself with genetic arguments. This was precisely the kind of thinking underpinning fascism, which constructed a story of biological greatness, according to which "myth becomes blood," as critic Philippe Lacoue-Labarthe has written.

In the 1930s the majority of Jews living in France were foreign born, so one easy way to limit their influence was through immigration law. In 1931, France dramatically tightened its once-liberal immigration policies, and by 1938, it enacted measures specifically restricting Jews.

The right wing was not alone in fomenting unrest in France during this time. In the two months before the Popular Front could take office, as many as two million French workers from every industry went on strike in an attempt to protect their new rights, which they feared would be revoked before even being granted. Chanel had been greatly unsettled by the violent, riotous strikes of 1934, but back then, Paul Iribe had been there to comfort her with his presence and bolster her worldview with his elitist philosophies. Now, just two years later, with Iribe gone and no one to take his place, Coco found herself entirely alone when the wave of strikes crashed right up on her doorstep.

On June 6, 1936, Chanel's entire Parisian staff walked out. Lining up

Chanel workers on strike, 1936

outside her boutique on rue Cambon, the employees—mostly women—brandished collection boxes and demanded shorter hours, collective contracts, the abolition of piecework, and higher wages in the form of weekly salaries. The sight of her employees on the street, disrupting the calm, elegant façade of her business, enraged Chanel. She could not tolerate the prospect of losing control of her empire and had no respect for business owners who compromised. "Consent to negotiations? Show your workers the books? Those men were crazy," she said of anyone who entertained the demands of labor.

Coco had no intention of altering her business practices. "I detest giving in, bending over, humiliating myself…conceding," she told Claude Delay.

Such rage was rooted partly in fear; since her work was her life, the strike threatened her very existence. Lashing out, she fired all three hundred employees immediately.

In Chanel's mind, the employees owed her their livelihoods and, therefore, their unquestioning loyalty and gratitude. The concepts of workers' rights and labor negotiations left her cold. Long ago, when the young Gabrielle had earned a pittance sewing clothes in a back room, striking had not been an option. No one had intervened to help her demonstrate for better working conditions. Chanel had climbed her own way out (albeit with the help of various wealthy protectors), and she expected others to do the same. She often advised the women who worked for her to find rich men to take care of them. With all the zeal of a convert, Coco, the former seamstress, identified only with management. She had fully adopted a ruling-class mentality, seeing herself as a kind of "divinely anointed" ruler.

But firing the staff accomplished little. The strikers did not disappear; on the contrary, they stayed on the premises. Staging a sit-in, they taunted Chanel, playing music and dancing in the workrooms, buoyed by a new sense of solidarity with all the other strikers around the country.

Coco realized she'd have to try another approach and came up with a new plan. Insisting that she simply did not have the capital to raise salaries, she offered instead a disingenuous nod to socialism: a plan to resign immediately and sell her business to the workers themselves, explaining that they could now assume all financial responsibility for the House of Chanel and pay themselves whatever they wished. She would stay on in the role of consultant.

The Chanel strike made headlines around the world. The usually liberal *New York Times* seemed largely sympathetic to Coco in its front-page story about the event: "With the same instinct she has shown in making for herself a leading place in the world of fashion, Gabrielle Chanel has acted boldly in the face of the advance of French socialism.... So far the workers' union has not accepted her offer [but] she will not compromise or bargain further... whatever the results."

Her workers, of course, could not buy Chanel out, and refused the offer. The shop and studios on rue Cambon remained closed for three weeks. Eventually, the overheated atmosphere in Paris calmed down and employers and workers began settling their feuds. Chanel finally put an end to her strike, acceding to some of her workers' demands. But she did so only grudgingly, after having publicly denounced her employees in a number of interviews. Chanel saw striking less as a political activity than as an illness, a collective madness. "You believe this was a matter of salary? Well, I can tell you it was the opposite.... Those people caught this like the Spanish flu, the way sheep catch gid." (Gid is a parasite that causes illness in sheep, making them spin wildly. In her distress, Chanel had let down her guard, permitting herself this farm animal analogy that clearly betrayed her peasant roots.) Even worse, in Coco's mind, striking was vulgar, unladylike behavior: "Imagine women... staging a sit down strike.... Very pretty. What idiots these girls were."

Other designers also coped with strikes. Coco's archrival Elsa Schiaparelli, for example, had suffered a walkout but emerged from negotiations on good terms with her workers. Chanel's imperious behavior left her relationship with her staff strained and awkward. They never forgot her disdain, or her blithe unconcern for the struggles of the people who'd helped make her one of the world's richest women.

Chanel's response to the strike revealed her increasing brittleness—how quick she was to anger and how little empathy she permitted herself to feel. Coco preferred to see herself as she had convinced the world to see her: an icon of belonging and connection on the grandest but least personal scale imaginable.

Ensconced permanently at the Ritz, Chanel occupied an insular, felted, and privileged world of aristocrats, multimillionaires, and proto-collaborators—a group to which she gravitated quite naturally. Such people confirmed her sense of belonging to an elite. Coco had long been at ease in the company of reactionary nationalists, even racists. With rare exceptions (Capel and Reverdy certainly), her lovers tended to hold the most archconservative views, their politics centered around protecting exclusivity and guarding treasure. Grand Duke Dmitri, with whom Chanel remained on friendly terms, joined the circle of Vasili Biskupsky, a known supporter of Hitler, and the führer himself had corresponded with Dmitri. The Duke of Westminster, like many members of the British royal family, had social ties to the Third Reich, and allied himself with pro-Nazi organizations.

His Royal Highness, Edward, Prince of Wales, known to his friends as David, was another intimate of Chanel's, introduced to her by her close friend Vera Bate, who was the prince's cousin. Always thrilled to be associated with royalty, Chanel never minded (and may actually have started) the rumors that His Highness had also pursued her romantically. "She did not mind dropping hints that, at one time, a very imprecise time, the Duke had courted her," recalled her friend Jacques Chazot. Edward, of course, as Edward VIII, was at the center of the world-rocking scandal of 1936 when he abdicated the throne of Great Britain to marry American divorcée Wallis Simpson. Once he had relinquished the throne, David and his wife, now the Duke and Duchess of Windsor, remained close with Chanel, who designed much of the famously chic Duchess's wardrobe. (A true acolyte of Chanelism, the Duchess of Windsor coined the adage "One can never be too rich or too thin.") After decades of rumors about the Windsors' Nazi connections, the couple's close relationship with the Reich is now a matter of historical fact. Not only were the

Windsors socially friendly with Hitler, visiting him in 1936 at his private Bavarian estate, Berchtesgaden, the duke was actually conspiring with the führer about a possible return to the British throne if Germany won the war.

Paul Iribe, of course, had been adamant in his Germanophobia, unlike many of Chanel's friends in the later 1930s. But had he lived longer, he might have softened his stance, for he embraced the same brand of outspoken anti-Semitism, racism, and nationalism that would lead many Frenchmen ultimately to make common cause with Vichy and the Germans. Paradoxically, the extreme Germanophobia of many nationalist French often coexisted peacefully with a pro-fascist mentality and sometimes slid gradually into outright support for the so-called *fascisme brun* (brown fascism), supportive of Germany.

Coco's friends largely resembled her lovers politically, and most of the artists close to her belonged to the conservative branch of modernism that allied itself with nationalism, classicism, and a lofty ideal of "French" purity and style. Cocteau figured prominently among those espousing this kind of "reactionary modernism," serving as the unofficial leader of a group of composers known as Les Six, who often worked with him on productions and whom Chanel also counted as good friends. They were Georges Auric, Louis Durey, Germaine Tailleferre, Arthur Honegger, Francis Poulenc, and Darius Milhaud. This group's abiding passion for Greek antiquity (Honegger had composed the score for Cocteau's *Antigone*) and for "purity" in French culture closely reflected the philosophies promulgated at the time by Action française and other nationalist organizations.

Although suspected of collaboration and briefly arrested after the war by an *épuration,* or "purification," committee (bodies set up by the government to investigate citizens suspected of having betrayed the nation), Cocteau never suffered any consequences; the government determined his actions amounted more to opportunism than to treason. The charges against him were dropped despite his many ongoing friendships within Hitler's inner circle and his very strong pro-German leanings. (These friendships were facilitated by Cocteau's fluent German, which he'd learned as a child from a German governess.) Some of Chanel's artist friends "leaned" so far that they tumbled right over into collaboration. Ballets Russes star Serge Lifar gained notoriety as one of France's most egregious collaborators, known to have visited Hitler on more than one occasion, and—most infamously—entertained Joseph Goebbels at the Paris Opéra Ballet. Prominent on this list as well was Maurice Sachs, who, although of Jewish descent, would register with the SS and work as a secret agent for the Reich.

Among the most publicly protofascist of all Chanel's intimates was Paul Morand—writer, diplomat, and, later, high-ranking Vichy official. Coco felt comfortable enough with Morand to grant him the series of 1946 interviews that later became *The Allure of Chanel*—one of the few biographies endorsed by the Maison Chanel. "They were very close," says Gabrielle Palasse-Labrunie. "She had confidence that he would re-produce what she said faithfully, even things that weren't true."

Chanel with
Serge Lifar, 1937

Paul Morand

Morand's strong racist beliefs make themselves clearly felt in many of his novels and travel essays. When it came to Jews, his tone could turn overtly murderous. In a 1933 editorial, Morand wrote, "At this time, every country except ours is killing its vermin.... Don't let us leave Hitler to pride himself on being the only person to undertake the moral rehabilitation of the West."

He went on to say that if Frenchmen had to die in the war so many feared, "we want clean corpses"—meaning those of untainted blood. Describing his dear friend Coco, Morand later recalled her as "the exterminating angel of nineteenth-century style"—a description that chillingly conflates Chanel's famous modernist streamlining of fashion with the kind of racial extermination Morand supported.

This was Coco's crowd: privileged, influential, accomplished, notoriously brilliant, and largely sympathetic to what we now consider some of history's most heinous philosophies. But their views were not out of keeping with those of many distinguished and powerful Frenchmen at the time. Chanel's cohort, in fact, reminds us of how alluring fascism proved to be, even to wealthy industrialists such as François Coty. The interests of multimillionaire businessmen might seem distinctly at odds with the tenets of National Socialism, a mass movement promoting state control, but French fascism's condemnation of capitalism was faint at best. And even during the war, Nazi officials did little to dismantle the profitable French companies sympathetic to Germany—including certain couture houses. On the contrary, such businesses looked to them like potential revenue sources for a Reich-controlled France of the future.

> The Nazi myth . . . is the construction, the formation, and the production of the German people in, by, and as a work of art. The mythic power is that of dreams, of the projection of an image with which one identifies. The absolute, in effect, is not something outside of myself, it is the dream in which I recognize myself.
>
> **—PHILIPPE LACOUE-LABARTHE**

Fascism's ingenious use of aesthetics resembled the inner workings of the fashion world to a startling extent. While it's true that many Parisians endorsed its principles over dinner at Maxim's, fascism at its core was a phenomenon for the masses, designed to appeal to and manipulate enormous crowds. Fascism worked a special, transformative magic upon crowds, granting them shape and purpose and conferring upon their thousands of participants—even those of the humblest social station—an ennobling sense of transcendence and belonging. The fascist images of history—the ones graven in our collective minds—all involve crowds: the Nuremberg rallies, the festival of Bayreuth, Hitler's speeches. Fascism choreographed vast seas of people into homogenous wholes, subsuming thousands into a single look, smoothly coordinated motion, and the harmony of cheers roared in unison: "massings of groups of people . . . uniformly garbed and shown in ever swelling numbers," as Susan Sontag wrote.

From such scenes emerged a distinctly paradoxical pleasure: The mass fascist spectacles insisted upon the essential superiority of all those present, their natural aristocracy of blood. But at the same time, the rallies and parades provided elitism's apparent opposite: the comfort of being entirely engulfed and dissolved in a vast, oceanic wave. Herein lies

Rows of SA
(Sturmabteilung)
standard-bearers at the
Nazi Party Congress in
September 1935,
Nuremberg, Germany

the movement's most irresistible seduction: Fascism promised acquirable greatness without the burden or loneliness of standing out, a way to transcend the masses while being held securely in their warm embrace—elitism and democracy in perfect equipoise.

Fascism's allure came beautifully packaged, too, presented with all the glossy appeal of a high-end advertising campaign. Like sophisticated marketing experts, Nazi propagandists "aestheticized politics," as philosopher Walter Benjamin declared.

Aestheticizing politics meant first aestheticizing the crowds, turning those enormous seas of people into thrilling mass spectacles. For pageantry, theatrical power, and awe-inspiring scale, nothing could compete with fascism. In the hands of master propagandists such as

Joseph Goebbels, the crowd itself became a totalizing work of art—a
Gesamtkunstwerk—in the manner of Richard Wagner. "The masses are
made to take form, [to] be design," as Susan Sontag wrote. Leni Riefenstahl's films of the crowds at the 1936 Summer Olympics in Berlin
indelibly demonstrate the excitement conjured in such settings.

To justify the massive scale of its project, fascism needed a story, a
unifying, lofty—if utterly fictional—narrative that could convince followers to subsume their individual lives to a larger goal, to accept "the
understanding of life as art, as well as the body, the people, [and] the
State as works of art." Accordingly, party officials crafted the "fascist
myth," a fairy-tale rewriting of history, infused with equal parts heroism
and regret. Hoping to cloak their political intentions in august drapery,

Adolf Hitler greets an
SA officer at a Reich
Party Day ceremony,
September 1934,
Nuremberg, Germany

they turned to antiquity, borrowing their myth from ancient Greece and allying themselves with its classical art and literature.

In the fascist reconstruction of history, the ancient race of Hellas represented the earliest incarnation of the superior white European, the Aryan. In their telling, Aryans descended directly from the ancient Greeks and were the world's last, noble vestiges of that advanced people. Curing Europe's malaise and restoring its long-lost vigor required a eugenics-based approach—repopulating the continent exclusively with Aryans and purging the polluting lower races. Europe would return to its earlier incarnation, as grand and racially pristine as it had been in antiquity.

Bolstered by the work of such intellectuals as Arthur de Gobineau, Georges Sorel, and especially, racial ideologue Alfred Rosenberg, this fascist myth took on the fervent quality of a new, secular religion complete with a story of a lost golden age and the promised reward of a new, fascist paradise, a "utopia of blood and soil."

Like all myths, this one inspired imitation in others, exerting its influence by provoking identification in the crowds and inciting them to emulate the story's heroic figures. Beautiful and invincible, the Greek-Aryan superman starring in this myth offered an uplifting and inspiring image.

This new origin story lent a patina of intellectual grandeur to what was essentially a massive landgrab fueled by murderous racism. The Greek-Aryan origin myth harnessed history, art, and literature to paper over the ghastly horror underlying fascism, granting it apparent cultural gravitas.

Despite its highbrow façade, fascism's methods were anything but lofty. Its techniques resembled nothing so much as the physical, visceral manipulations famously used in all forms of mass recreation: organized sports, cinema, and fashion. These phenomena all draw on the same elements: the lure of a privileged group of insiders (team members, stars, the chic); an insistence on youth, fitness, and physical beauty; a distinctly recognizable style; and powerful, charismatic personalities. Fascism, as Susan Sontag famously pointed out, was sexy.

For some of its glamorous trappings, fascism looked to Hollywood cinema, from which it borrowed the practice of relying on carefully stage-managed charismatic personalities. Mussolini, Hitler, Franco, and, later, Marshal Philippe Pétain in Vichy, all availed themselves of movie-star-style publicity techniques to hone their images and develop their cult followings. Benito Mussolini, for example, cultivated the aura of a rugged, perpetually young sportsman (despite being a grandfather), and staged photos of himself piloting a plane or skiing the Alps bare chested.

Adolf Hitler, unmarried and childless, acquired more the status of a religious idol—rigid, remote, omniscient. But his publicity machine worked as unrelentingly as Mussolini's. Hitler took on such iconic status that in 1936 it was decreed that the special black uniform jackets of his personal guard, the Leibstandarte, would boast cuffs embroidered with Hitler's entire name in silver thread, written in script as if he had person-ally signed each man's sleeve. In this, fascism combined the Hollywood motif of the star's autograph—the signature of the idol—with the haute

"Il Duce begins the threshing of the grain, June 1928"—a typical propaganda photograph of Benito Mussolini

Hitler inspects a locker while visiting his SS Leibstandarte, or bodyguard unit. Note the bands on the uniform sleeves, bearing Hitler's embroidered signature.

couture concept of the exclusive designer label that bears the magical name of the creator—*la griffe* (literally, "the claw," referring to the indelible sign of the artist, "scratched" into the garment)—confirming the elite status of both garment and wearer.

To balance, perhaps, Hitler's more hieratic, robotic charisma, Nazism offered up the considerable sex appeal of its central figure, the new "fascist man," modeled after the youths and warriors of classical statuary. The epitome of fascist principles, strong and beautiful, this Greek-Aryan warrior defined himself sharply against his physical and moral antitype, the people Paul Morand labeled "vermin": the Jews. Blond and blue-eyed, muscular and virile—fascist man was a paragon of masculine virtues.

Psychoanalytic theorists of fascism—notably, Klaus Theweleit—read this hyper-masculinity as a splitting of the self into a "(female) interior and a (male) exterior... [which] were mortal enemies." And it is true that most fascist propaganda offered an exaggerated stereotypical view of women, insisting upon their role as breeders and nurturers of children and relegating them to home and hearth. According to this interpretation, the muscular discipline of the fascist body represents the willed banishment of overwhelming, feminine characteristics. Once German fascism entered French culture full force, through Vichy and the occupation, similar urgings about exercise and fitness began appearing in popular magazines and in political messages.

Art of the era abounds with examples of the aestheticized fascist body—in Leni Riefenstahl's gorgeous photographs of Olympic athletes, and in the sculptures of Arno Breker, Jean Cocteau's close friend, whose marble monuments to the fascist male ideal earned him Hitler's passionate devotion, as well as a job as official sculptor of the Reich.

Germans were hardly alone in their appreciation of Aryan beauty. Breker's work found a large following in France, where he had lived for years before the war, and to which he returned regularly during the occupation. When in Paris, Breker frequently dined on the rue Cambon

Breker sculpture *Die Partei* (The [Nazi] party)

with Chanel and her friends, having been introduced to their circle by Cocteau. Cocteau even liked to compare his actor lover Jean Marais to a Breker sculpture come to life; decades later, in 1963, Breker created a bronze sculpture of a still very handsome Marais.

B reker's sculptures wore their nakedness majestically, but fascism gave equal time to the beauty of the *covered* body as well—to fashion. Keenly aware of the potent power of dress, the fascists created famously beautiful uniforms, especially for officers, which garnered acclaim beyond Italy and Germany. Even Americans found beauty in their enemies' uniforms.

Sleek and formfitting, fascist uniforms of both Italy and Germany showed to great advantage the hewn physiques beneath. Finishing touches provided by the high boots, the black leather trench coats, and an elaborate system of badges, armbands, and medals—all adorned with the ubiquitous swastika—made for a total look that bespoke military authority but also masculine beauty. Such attention to dress and accessories might seem to court charges of effeminacy, but the constant underlying threat of violence and destruction offset any potentially emasculating effect. "There is a general fantasy about uniforms," wrote Sontag. "They suggest community, order, identity (through ranks, badges, medals, things which declare who the wearer is and what he has done; his worth is recognized), competence, legitimate authority, the legitimate exercise of violence."

Sontag was right. Mere buttons and badges would have meant nothing without the tremendous power that clearly lay just beneath the glittering surfaces. But uniforms define more than their individual wearers; they also sculpt the *collective* body, unifying a group into a single whole— a sports team, an army, a nation. Though this is true of all uniforms, fascist uniforms were especially powerful, imbued as they were with the aura of myth—that compelling fascist narrative of a superior race, united under the mystical swastika. This underlying myth added ineffable allure to the uniform for those who watched and admired the soldiers, but also for those soldiers themselves.

Hitler's chief of foreign intelligence, the handsome and charming Walter Schellenberg (who was likely Chanel's lover later on), joined the SS in 1933 as a young law student, a decision explained in his memoirs:

> All young men who joined the Party had to join one of its forma-
> tions as well. The SS was already considered an "elite" organiza-
> tion. The black uniform of the Fuhrer's special guard was dashing
> and elegant, and quite a few of my fellow-students had joined. In
> the SS one found the "better type of people," and membership in
> it brought considerable prestige and social advantage.... I cannot
> deny that at age twenty-three such things as social prestige and,
> shall we say, the glamour of a smart uniform played quite a large
> part in my choice.

If such remarks make the brutally violent SS sound like a well-heeled college fraternity or a posh country club, that was precisely the point. The Nazis sought out recruits like Schellenberg, educated and polished men who not only could serve as glossy advertisements for the move-ment, but were themselves highly susceptible to the seductive elitism that came with the job. Another high-ranking Nazi official, Reinhard Spitzy, echoed Schellenberg's remarks when he was asked about his early induction into the SS: "[I]n the SS . . . we [understood that we were] . . . the future aristocratic spine bone of the German Nation.... And then the uniform was very beautiful. Black, no? Of course one liked the uniform and boots and all that."

Youth, virility, social status, national identity—in a kind of visceral alchemy, the fascist uniforms distilled these highly charged elements and conveyed their essence back to the wearers and even to civilian audi-ences. Private citizens could participate, since objects bearing the swas-tika insignia found their way into every aspect of daily life. A wide range of Nazi merchandise saturated the marketplace: watch fobs, lapel pins, matchbooks, pendants, jackets, banners, and lingerie, all emblazoned with the swastika and all for sale.

The swastika took on talismanic properties, tying the country together under a single graphic symbol. As a ubiquitous fashion accessory, the swastika permitted everyone access to the magic inner circle and telegraphed adherence to the sect. In its mass dissemination of this mystical-seeming symbol, Nazism proved it had become "a civic religion." The party went so far as to invent secular versions of Christian rituals, including a Nazi version of baptism, in which children were inducted into the party before an altar displaying Hitler's photograph instead of an image of Christ.

This promotion of mass national unification by means of icons, colors, objects, clothing, crowd formation, and so forth proved so essential to the Nazi machine that it earned its own name within the party's lexicon: *Gleichschaltung.* Meaning literally "same switching," the word has been translated as "coordination," "uniformization," or "bringing into line," and refers to the gradual tightening and centralization of control over all aspects of life—processes that lie at the heart of the totalitarian project. *Gleichschaltung* consisted also of political, cultural, and legal measures, among them: imposing compulsory membership in sanctioned cultural organizations, such as Hitler Youth, government takeover of sports and recreational activities (there was even a Nazi chess club), the suppression of trade unions, and the dismantling of all non-Nazi political parties. Over all of this vast process of "same-ification" loomed the swastika, the most powerful commercial logo ever invented.

The use of the swastika reminds us of just how closely Nazi propaganda methods resemble fashion branding techniques. In fact, in their similarities we find their parallel structures—what they share as means of social manipulation. Fashion has long been driven by some of the same mechanisms that propelled fascism. Certainly, fascism made expert use of the charms of well-cut clothes and eye-catching accessories. But the two systems also resemble each other on a deeper level. Both play upon the struggle between two basic and contradictory impulses: the desire to conform and the desire to be original. Both exploit the power generated when vast numbers of people imitate a given behavior.

The fascist movement shared certain core strategies with the fashion industry—including the marketing and manipulation of strong desires for adornment, for identification, and for a sense of transcendence, all of which led thousands of people to find meaning and beauty in fascist myth and iconography. Hitler himself had an eye for women's fashion and preferred to see the women in his life chicly dressed. Eva Braun raised party eyebrows with her exorbitant dressmaker's bills, but Hitler paid them without complaint. The uniforms worn by women under the Reich for sports teams, political leagues, youth groups, and the like displayed little of the high-fashion sensibility so evident in the men's military versions. Unhappy at one point with the plain uniforms proposed for the League of German Girls, Hitler insisted they be redesigned.

The topic of commercial women's fashion proved vexing to the fascists because Germany and Italy had long marched to the rhythm set by Paris. In the early 1930s, though, the fascists resisted permitting a rival country this degree of aesthetic influence. But French fashion proved too powerful to control. The Reich's multiple attempts to create a pure "German fashion" all failed. Upper-class German ladies, including many Nazi officers' wives, would not be deprived of Parisian style, and ultimately a number of French designers, including Jacques Fath, Marcel Rochas, and Nina Ricci, kept their own houses afloat during the war by transacting business with Berlin.

Even far chicer Italy failed in its attempt to create a pure "Italian" fashion purged of French influence. French couturiers—and especially Coco Chanel—dominated Italian couture until the second half of the thirties. Women's love of Parisian clothes consistently trumped government policy. Fashion, it seemed, would not submit to the process of *Gleichschaltung.* These failures, though, bespeak more than a misunderstanding of the workings of fashion. They point to a significant fault line running beneath the surface of fascism: its deeply contradictory view of women.

F ascist propaganda used sex to cleave the world in two. As much as it exhorted men to serve their countries through athletic and military prowess, it exhorted women to serve through motherhood and housewifery. Although Germany and Italy had differing versions of this restrictive stereotyping, the results were the same: Social progress for women in both countries was dramatically reversed.

All aspects of emancipated, modern womanhood came under attack. In Italy, abortion, birth control, and sex education for children were banned, and Italy's version of the Chanel-style flapper, *la maschietta*, was reviled for undermining the traditional feminine roles of wife and mother. Similarly, the Nazis established their famous "three-K model" for womanhood: *Kinder, Kirche, Küche* (children, church, kitchen), insisting on women's duty to repopulate the fatherland with Aryan children.

Fashion, of course, had no place in the virtuous woman's life. Nazi propaganda posters featured full-bosomed women—Aryan Madonnas— wearing the humblest clothes possible—the housewife's apron, the peasant's muslin dress, or, in the occasional nod to antiquity, a Grecian robe. The fascists may have lured male recruits with fashionable uniforms, but chic attire for women was morally suspect. Reinhard Spitzy, who admitted joining the SS for the uniform, recalled that, before his induction, part of the screening process including an interrogation of his wife about "whether she likes too much dresses or perfumes, or if she wants to be a perfect German wife."

But the fascists could never entirely squelch women's modernity, nor did they wish to. Despite the rhetoric of a return to home and hearth, fascism was invested in progress and technology. The modern world required (and already had) a modernized female population. Italy's fascist dictatorship even celebrated that avatar of national progress, the Nuova Italiana, or "New Italian Woman." Coherent social and national identities for women could never emerge from the illogic and hypocrisy of totalitarianism.

The political backlash against liberated women inevitably found its way to France. In 1935, France's population was only half that of the increasingly menacing Germany (forty million French to eighty million Germans)—a disparity that rekindled debates about population decline and spurred the creation of an antifeminist movement known as *retour au foyer* (return to the home), devoted to getting women out of the workplace and back to the nursery. A vocal right-wing group, the National

Alliance for the Growth of the French Population, launched massive propaganda attacks against *la femme moderne* for her interest in career, her unpatriotic neglect of child rearing, and her love of fashionable clothes. (Paul Morand figured among the many intellectuals who supported this movement.)

The French pronatalist, or pro-birth, movement especially scapegoated women's fashion—even as the thriving fashion industry was being touted as one of France's most precious remaining resources. Fashion was the province of the harlot; it lured women away from family life. In 1939, the Vichy-backed pronatalist women's magazine *Votre Beauté* attacked couturiers for reducing the contemporary woman to "a caricature, a sad doll that lives only for her body, her clothes, her sex appeal." Catholic philosopher Gustave Thibon lamented the poor moral character of young women who "read *Marie Claire.*"

If young women could be corrupted by *Marie Claire,* then Chanel was the devil incarnate, since no one's name graced the fashion pages more frequently than Coco's. Considered in the context of French interwar politics, then, Chanel was a paradox. Her personal beliefs put her squarely in the camp of the protofascists: She was a staunch nationalist, an archconservative, and a German sympathizer. She was a royalist, antiunion, anti-Semitic, antiparliamentarian, and had no patience for women's rights movements. Yet Chanel was also a never-married, (presumably) childless, professional woman, who lived openly with lovers. She virtually embodied the "sad caricature" lamented in pronatalist and fascist propaganda. What's more, she had founded a cult of imitators, branding women throughout Europe with her black-and-white letter Cs. Chanel was the patron saint—not to say one of the *creators*—of the fascists' reviled *femme moderne.*

On the surface, the paradox poses no dramatic historical problem. It mattered little that Chanel flouted entirely fascism's dictates for women—she hardly belonged to the targeted demographic. The rules for the masses do not apply to multimillionaires or global celebrities, which is also why Chanel felt no need to support feminist causes—*she* was doing just fine. At its highest social and cultural levels, fascism accommodated a spectrum of personal beliefs and private behavior. And in certain circles, fascism mingled comfortably with many facets of progressive modernism.

But Chanel cannot be reduced to a fascist fellow traveler with a privileged modern lifestyle. Her contradictory relationship to fascism worked itself out not in her personal beliefs or even in her professional activities, but in the way her movement, Chanelism, partook of fascism's tenets and aesthetics, participating in the "domestic" French version of fascism. Chanel actually built her global empire by using tactics and philosophy that deeply and startlingly mirrored the fascists', creating an odd symmetry between her movement and theirs. One could argue that Coco proved the more adept at wielding these tactics. After all, fascism ultimately met defeat, but Chanelism continues to this day, tapping into what Susan Sontag has called "the fascist longings in our midst."

> My epoch was waiting for me. I needed only to come, it was ready.
>
> —COCO CHANEL

At the zenith of her pre–World War II career, Chanel's public persona existed on a scale far beyond anything previously associated with a fashion designer or businesswoman. She was acquiring the aura of a world political figure. Her power, reputation, influence, and press coverage resembled those of the crowd hypnotizers amassing followings throughout Europe. She had become a symbol of the French nation and one of its wealthiest citizens. Millions knew her name and image at a glance; millions admired and copied her style.

And while the political turmoil of the 1930s distressed and unsettled her, like a good politician, Chanel knew how to benefit from the unrest around her. France's vexed climate and its culture wars wound up enhancing Coco's iconic stature. Music, art, theater, and literature all appeared susceptible to the taint of foreign (especially Jewish) influence, but haute couture still seemed securely homegrown. Fashion was the country's greatest native, commercial, and artistic treasure, a foundation stone of national identity, one of its key exports. In 1939, as war approached, *L'Art de la Mode* wrote, "France's Great Couturiers... through their ingeniousness, their taste, and their stature... wave high the banner of French glory throughout the four corners of the world. In the midst of our disappointments and political uncertainties, this is a fact that we must recognize."

Chanel's banner waved higher than anyone else's and she knew it. She was "a national icon of France at its most elegant," in the words of French historian Patrick Buisson. She represented the ne plus ultra of Parisian glamour, a guarantor of international prestige for France. "She was powerfully aware of her own importance to France," wrote Marcel Haedrich. In a 1931 interview with *Women's Wear Daily,* she loftily brushed aside the (accurate) assumption that she had reduced prices to improve flagging profits, insisting that she had done it out of civic-mindedness: The price cuts increased access to her designs, she claimed, preventing "poor reproductions of her work" from harming "the prestige of Paris."

Paul Iribe had had a point when he dubbed the luxury shopping district around Place Vendôme the "vitrine of France," its showcase to the world. As Iribe had known well, Chanel was the polished pearl at its center, shaping the world's view of her country. Jean Cocteau imagined Coco as a kind of pagan god, the genius loci of the first arrondissement. "Rue Cambon, Place Vendôme [are] sanctuaries where women prostrate themselves before the idol of Fashion," he wrote in his 1937 *Harper's Bazaar* profile of her.

Chanel's press coverage returned repeatedly to such imagery. *Le Miroir du Monde* lauded: "Gabrielle Chanel... to whom Paris owes, in the grace and beauty of the women, its indisputable glory." Commenting on the Grecian-style bas-relief that the Maison Chanel used as its icon at the 1939 World's Fair in New York, *Femina* journalist Martin Rénier referred to Chanel's business as "a temple of French taste, which she has demonstrated to us for so long." Chanel's choice of a Greek temple to represent her company was no accident; she saw her work as classic, timeless, mythic, and worthy of worshippers, a view that had been reinforced by her work costuming the great Greek myths for the French stage. Chanelism had become—and remains today—as much of a secular religion as fascism ever was. (In 2011, when asked to describe the Chanel worldview, a top Maison Chanel executive replied, "It's a religion.")

From national symbol it is but a small, conceptual step to compare her to a military commander, monarch, or even tyrant, and the press routinely likened Chanel to just such figures. In its account of her 1936 workers' strike, *The New York Times* positioned Chanel as both a guardian of the nation's patrimony and a totalitarian leader: "She will not abdicate but will continue to defend French fashions and the French taste.... Mademoiselle Chanel has long been famous as a dictator of fashions." Throughout the interwar years, *The New York Times* repeatedly described Chanel as the Parisian fashion dictator, and sometimes as the "leader of the cult of Chanel." The *Times* was not alone.

In 1933, a profile of Chanel for the magazine *Le Miroir du Monde* announced: "Gabrielle Chanel imposes fashion upon the feminine world like a dictator. She orders, one after the other, the wearing of jerseys, of costume jewels, of short hair; she demands complete luxury, gold, velvet, lace, and all women listen to her as if to an oracle!" That same year, American journalist and gossip columnist Elsa Maxwell—never one to mince words—imagined Chanel as the "miniature female Stalin of the Rue Cambon...imposing her imperious will on the countless armies of the world's women, whom, like a satirical and sinister Bo-peep, she has turned into willing sheep to baa at her commands." Winston Churchill described her as a "great and strong being fit to rule a man or an Empire." Even advertisements borrowed the lingo; "Chanel dictates," read the running header of a series of newspaper ads in *The New York Times* for knockoffs of Chanel accessories.

Fashion magazines painted Chanel as a heroic figure on the international political stage, someone advancing and protecting the cause of La Belle France. In 1938, when the countess Géraldine Apponyi—

future queen of Albania—commissioned her entire trousseau from Chanel, *Marie Claire* magazine recounted the transaction with the fanfare normally reserved for major political announcements. The article's title, printed in oversize, screaming block letters, declared: "A new treaty alliance has been signed between Albania and the Rue Cambon. German fashion to refuel here in Paris."

In 1935, *Femme de France* proposed fashion as the cure for France's spiritual malaise, and likened Chanel's contribution to a valiant military salvo: "It would be to misunderstand Paris to believe for one moment that it would … give in to discouragement. Our great designers continue to adorn our feminine beauty. … Mademoiselle Chanel *opens fire* [with] a varied collection … joining youth and femininity."

These were the voices issuing in the 1930s. They cast Chanel's authority and reign over European culture in terms that other contemporary voices used only for the decade's military leaders—and the phenomenon of fascism. Such language persisted throughout Chanel's life, used especially by anyone who had occasion to watch Coco in action at her studio. "She reigns with authority … over this army of workers. There on her battlefield, she has the audacity and spirit of a young general of the French Empire," wrote a journalist in *L'Express* in 1956, when the young general was seventy-three.

"The mood in the salon changes with Chanel's, as if it were the court of Louis XIV," wrote *The New York Times* in 1964. Chanel employee Marie-Hélène Marouzé recalled an atmosphere of "terror." Actress Jeanne Moreau remembered visiting rue Cambon and finding Chanel "[like a] spider in her web, magnificent … a royal princess."

"Many people feared her," according to former model Delphine Bonneval. "[When they knew she was about to arrive] the entire studio staff would stand at attention, hands on the seams of their trousers, like in the army."

Whether general, dictator, princess, or the Sun King himself, Chanel consistently inspired comparisons with leaders of a distinctly non-democratic kind—the sort growing more powerful throughout interwar Europe. Like them, she ruled alone, demanding absolute authority.

Chanel's longtime assistant Lilou Marquand recalled, "Mademoiselle put herself on a par with heads of state. She thought it was a pity that world leaders did not consult her." Describing her own career to Paul Morand, Chanel referred without irony to her "life as a dictator, success and solitude."

Like all charismatic dictators, Chanel had mastered her relationship to the crowd. But she did not need to stage huge rallies. *Her* crowds of women amassed themselves voluntarily all over the world, gathered together by fashion. Between 1923 and 1938, the Nazi Party convened annually for the Nuremberg rallies with their vast hordes of identically dressed participants. The year 1939 saw the biggest gathering of Italian fascist women, when seventy thousand uniformed female forces marched in Rome, an occasion that historian Victoria de Grazia has called a "[reconciliation] of fascist military aesthetics and female fashion consciousness." During those same years, Chanel cultivated her own following of clones. Throughout Europe and America, hundreds of thousands of women were striving daily to look like Coco, dress like Coco, smell like Coco, live like Coco, and wear Coco's own mystical symbol on their bags, scarves, jackets, and belts—that double-C insignia, created only one year after Hitler appropriated the swastika as his emblem.

Coco understood that as much as fashion is the most intimate of art forms, it is also the most public. Fashion borrows its shape from the individual bodies that wear it. A dress is but lifeless fabric until it is granted warmth and motion by the woman wearing it. Yet at the same time fashion *lends* shape to a group, stamping a collective visual "signature" on the world it encompasses, creating the look of a street, a city, a nation. Chanel grasped this essential paradox. Unlike any couturier before or since, she could tempt women to buy her clothes (and the many imitations of them) by persuading them that personal elegance could be found in mass uniformity. In Coco's eyes, crowds held a strange beauty, which she described quite philosophically to Paul Morand:

[No one] understands the concept of the mass. What makes the beauty of the *herbaceous border* [spoken in English] in an English

garden, is the mass; one begonia, one chrysanthemum, one del-
phinium, isolated, have nothing sublime about them. But twenty
feet deep, this floral unit becomes something magnificent. "But
that takes all originality away from a woman," [some might say].
Wrong: women keep their individual beauty by participating in a
group. Take a chorus-line dancer in a music hall, isolate her from
the rest and she's a hideous puppet; put her back in her row and
not only will she regain all her qualities, but, through comparison
with her fellow dancers, her own personality will stand out.

Her aesthetic appreciation of "the mass" was surely authentic, but her
claim that it enhanced "originality" was disingenuous at best—although
it remains one of the party lines promoted by the Maison Chanel. Employees there tend to speak of the way Chanel style "brings out each
woman's individuality." It may be true that the very sameness of the style
does highlight the personal qualities of the diverse women wearing it.
But that was not Chanel's primary concern. On the contrary, she consciously intended to create a world of replicas, perfectly aware that the
more simulacra of herself she created, the more original *she* would seem.
She acknowledged this plan overtly—and with considerable lyricism—
when speaking with Louise de Vilmorin:

As a child I had only two dresses. Perhaps this is why I created so
many later on, all conceived by me. As a child, I had only one
shadow, then I became a woman whose own shadow, for thirty
years, burst forth from her, thousands of times, via those thousands of dresses worn by other women. There was an era when
one had to be "Chanel." A Chanel dress, or more precisely, *the*
Chanel dress, seemed to have talismanic power, which could absolutely control [one's] destiny. My charm was perhaps that I resembled no one else.... This charm or privilege compelled a great
many women to want to look like me and marked them all with
the same appearance, while this repetition of my own fantasy left
me alone in my exceptionalism.

By the late 1930s, Chanel had made her fantasy come true. By dint of the nearly magical power of the clothes she called "talismanic" (the word reminding us of Coco's superstitious, mystical side), she could indeed see her own shadow cast by thousands of other women. "She is the image of what she has created," wrote a journalist for *Marianne* in 1937. Chanel's passion for self-replication remained undimmed throughout her life. She took great pleasure, for example, in outfitting in identical light gray Chanel suits the 130 women sent by France as guides for the 1961 Moscow Expo. "She couldn't believe that any woman would want to look any way except the way *she* looked," recalled famed fashion editor Carmel Snow.

Women no longer exist, all that's left are the boys created by Chanel.

—MARQUIS BONI DE CASTELLANE,
CELEBRATED PARISIAN DANDY

"Fashion," wrote Jean Cocteau in his 1937 profile of Coco, "is a nearly military discipline. It inflicts a uniform." In Coco's case, this was more than just a metaphor. From the earliest days of her career, when she coaxed fine ladies into little jersey sailor suits, Coco had drawn inspiration from military styles. Beyond just their clean lines and athletic ease, uniforms attracted Chanel with their aura of power and desirability— the same elements that spoke to men like Walter Schellenberg and Reinhard Spitzy.

By the interwar period Coco had long established many of the basics that make up the Chanel uniform to this day: skirt suits, slim-fitting blouses, boyish trousers, the signature tweeds and jerseys (made now in her own factories), ropes of costume jewelry, newsboy caps, medallion-like brooches, and, of course, the double-C insignia. And in the later 1930s, with war looming, Chanel's army-officer style seemed timelier and more pronounced than ever. She featured a number of overtly military-style suits, and went so far as to design red woolen ankle wraps modeled after soldiers' leggings. Even her designs for day dresses fell in

Chanel military-inspired suits, 1938 and 1939

line with this theme, as when she introduced a white canvas linen frock that *Vogue* likened to a "schoolgirl's uniform."

More than ever, the Chanel look was simple, sleek, and practical—and much copied by other designers as France grew increasingly somber. In 1939, *Marie Claire* enumerated the many military trappings popping up on different runways: "brass buttons, epaulets, Scotch caps, even top-coats cut in military manner... [and] English officers' polished boots." Even formal wear could incorporate military design elements. In 1937, Chanel produced an elegant evening pantsuit, covered in sequins.

Beginning in 1936, Chanel passed through a red, blue, and white period, perhaps in solidarity with her political cohort. After outbreaks of antistrike violence, the leftist Popular Front government had cracked down on the protofascist leagues and prohibited their use of emblems

Chanel sequined evening trouser suit and blouse, 1937-38

and banners. In response, extreme nationalists among the Paris bourgeoisie (a group that included many Chanel intimates) began ostentatiously displaying the French flag and its colors and wearing tricolor rosettes—appropriating these patriotic symbols as signs of resistance to the red flag of the Popular Front. Chanel's sudden interest in flying the national colors may have represented her contribution to the cause. And surely the tricolor palette reminded her of Paul Iribe, who'd telegraphed his ultra-patriotism by using only these colors for every cover of *Le Témoin*. In the wake of Iribe's shocking death, a still-bereft Chanel seemed increasingly to embrace Paul's politics and extremism, incorporating the absent lover. As Marcel Haedrich observed, "The ideas...of Iribe...comforted her after the explosions...of 1936."

Subtle military and patriotic touches turned up on Chanel's 1938 evening gown of red silk chiffon and satin grosgrain. Its tight bodice, fastened with hook-and-eye closures, looked like a short, military jacket,

while the red, blue, and white grosgrain ribbon shoulder straps and piping evoked both the French flag and the military decorations that often
hang from tricolor ribbons. The motif appeared as well on a 1939 evening dress made for Mona Williams (wife of American millionaire Harrison Williams, with whom Chanel had a flirtation), whose ruffled
bolero-like bodice featured tricolor striping floating over a skirt edged in
the same pattern—all embellished with rosettes. It's an unusually "busy"
and distracting print for a Chanel gown.

Just as Chanel was favoring a more spartan and military look, she also
seemed, oddly, to start favoring a distinctly different quality: frilly girlishness. From 1935 to 1939, she whipped up a series of uncharacteristically sweet dresses, frothy confections of lace, sequins, and full skirts,

Chanel's girlish ruffled evening dresses, pattern illustrations
from *McCall's Magazine*, April, 1935.

often in pastels. A few had flowing semidetached side panels meant to be draped over a woman's arms as she danced—the sort of fussy encumbrance Coco typically eschewed. The fashion press took note.

Femme de France magazine described Coco's 1935 spring collection as being "under the sign of youth and femininity." In March 1937, *Vogue* praised the "romanticism" of her "baby dresses"—a term never before applied to Chanel's typically very grown-up styles. In March 1938, she was lauded for putting "sugar and spice in the Paris collections," and later that year a white tulle Chanel dress trimmed with "baby lace bows"—suitable perhaps for a debutante ball—was crowned "glamour dress of the season." Even some day wear started prettying up, with floral print dresses appearing in 1939, along with little cloche-style silk hats, "smothered with flowers," prompting *Vogue* to declare that Chanel had acquired a new "Air of Innocence."

Chanel had always leavened her simple styles with outré feminine luxury touches such as lavish gemstone brooches and silk jacket linings in glossy prints. But this was different. She was tampering with the bones of her creations, wandering away from her structural abstemiousness, venturing past "youthful" and into territory bordering on "juvenile." As if to confirm this new attraction to girlishness, Coco herself took to wearing a startling and incongruous accessory for a woman over fifty: a big floppy satin bow tied around her hair. What accounts for this turn of events?

Claude Delay refers to this bow as "the ribbon of her past" (*le ruban de son passé*), a wonderful locution conjuring both the hair ribbon Coco might have worn as a schoolchild and the almost mythological image of a ribbon made of time itself, like the threads of destiny spun by the three Fates.

Delay was onto something. Having lost her only fiancé, facing the possibility of another war, Chanel took refuge in a wistful melancholy, a nostalgia for a younger, less dangerous time. She had sat out the last war secure in Deauville, in love with Boy Capel, designing whimsical sailor outfits. Now, twenty-five years later, she was far too established and mature to ignore the coming cataclysm, and too solitary to find refuge in anyone's arms. Bouncing between two opposing stylistic modes—cream puff and soldier girl—Coco's designs from this period suggest a conflicted inner state.

Yet these two stylistic genres are not as different as they seem. Both are about defying death. With the sweet dresses and her big bow, Chanel was thumbing her nose at age and other grim matters, digging her heels into lighthearted girlhood. (Chic as she was, she managed never to look ridiculous in that bow.) Her military style, too, crafted of sturdy wools, suggested a defense against death, evoking the protective, masculine force of the army repelling a murderous invader. Both styles, moreover, held a woman's sexuality somewhat at bay.

The nuns at her orphanage would surely have approved of Chanel's modest clothes, but more than her Catholic upbringing may have motivated Coco's sexually muted style. Downplaying the body may also have begun as a form of self-defense for Coco, a way to deflect sexual menace. After all, until at least her midtwenties, Chanel lived a life of extreme vulnerability: She was a pretty young girl, with neither money nor family to protect her. Surely during these early, precarious years, Chanel fell prey to the *wrong* sort of masculine attention, whether violent or merely menacing, and surely she considered how best to guard against it— including dressing unobtrusively.

An anecdote from Gabrielle Palasse-Labrunie—dating to the late 1930s, when Chanel's work grew especially modest and androgynous— confirms that Coco indeed imagined clothes as sexual protection. In the summer of 1938, after vacationing with Coco at La Pausa, the twelve-year-old Gabrielle needed a traveling outfit for the train ride home to Lyon. Always generous, "Auntie Coco" suggested a shopping expedition to Monte Carlo. The girl grew baffled, though, when Chanel steered her to the boys' department of a local haberdashery: "[Coco] chose…grey flannel trousers and a garnet-red [sweater], all quite chic but a bit surprising, as in those days, twelve-year-old girls didn't ever wear trousers. 'People look at you in a dirty way on trains,' [Coco] explained. 'Dressed like this you'll be decent.'... My aunt was always very strict with me."

We have here a partial explanation for Chanel's trademark boyish style: Masculine attire offered not only physical freedom and ease of movement, but a way to fend off male aggression. It's sexual armor.

Through the 1930s, even her fragrance business—the real source of her wealth—kept in step with this male/military theme, reflecting the times. In 1936, she and Ernest Beaux introduced Cuir de Russie (Russian Leather), a woman's perfume marketed with a masculine twist, via advertising featuring romanticized military images and other gender-bending details. A lengthy advertorial in *Votre Beauté* magazine for Cuir de Russie waxed positively Tolstoy-esque:

> Cuir de Russie evokes old billfolds forgotten in drawers.... Leather is one of the most luxurious scents in the world, conjuring well worn gloves, richly bound books, soldiers' dress boots...big armchairs.... It conjures the dashing officer packing his bags...Imperial Russia and the grand old hotels of Moscow, built for love and the good life, where Grand-Dukes drank French champagne.... It conjures old thatched cottages in far-flung corners of the Ukraine.... Cuir de Russie is a perfume for the slightly masculine brunette, the one who always wears a suit, even at Maxim's at midnight, one of those women who play poker and draw out of their fine leather bags the cash they've lost at the gaming table, separating banknotes from the love letters and stock certificates that scent the bills with their sharp, slightly savage fragrance, the scent of polished leather.

The prose here condenses much of Coco's own cinematic life into a paragraph. Those in the know would recognize the clues: ghosts of Chanel's former lovers—dashing officers, Russian grand dukes; money in casual abundance, and glamorous nightlife. And the heroine at the center of this romantic tableau? An androgynous brunette in a suit. As ever,

Coco plays a dual role, both creator and ideal customer. But in this case, something else happens: The idealized woman is practically a man. Cuir de Russie does not promise to help women *attract* Russian dukes or dashing officers in leather boots, but to help them become *more like* these alluring heroes. The perfume promises to endow women with the scent of manhood and, by extension, the privileges and protections it brings: wealth, nobility, travel, gambling, sex without shame or vulnerability (in hotels "built for love"), and military might. The message was simple: Wear the Chanel uniform—which includes the perfume—and step into this Cococentric fantasy of modern womanhood.

Chanel's "uniform," moreover, included more than just clothes and accessories. It included also those intangible, unbuyable elements that telegraphed "Coco" and her *garçonne* appeal: the bobbed hairstyle, the suntan, and—crucially—the "Chanel" body, modeled on her own— youthful, athletic, and boyish, without which nothing else looked right. Even into her old age, Chanel was fiercely proud of her fitness, often inviting friends to confirm for themselves the firmness of her tiny derriere.

And here once more, Chanel was treading on the fascists' aesthetic territory. Their ideal being, intended for mass reproduction, was a sleekly dressed, sun-bronzed, disciplined athlete-soldier; so was Coco's. If, in its association with physical perfection and flawless surfaces, the fascist (particularly, the Nazi) avatar suggested a gay or effeminate aesthetic (as many critics have noted), Chanel's imagined ideal featured a complementary tinge of androgynous, even lesbian chic—a look reminiscent of the 1920s flapper and still associated in the 1930s with independent, sexually ambiguous women.

And here lies the key to Chanelism's paradoxical relationship to fascism. While Chanel's lifestyle may seem to conjure the dangerous *femme moderne*, so vilified in fascist propaganda, Chanelism actually inducted millions into a kind of parallel army, stamping them with an aesthetic image, not of the ideal fascist woman, but of *the ideal fascist man*. Even as Chanelism countermanded principles of traditional womanhood as preached by the fascists, it simultaneously led women marching in lockstep to the aesthetic template of fascist masculinity, creating what amounts to an odd mirroring, the "fascist look" for men through the looking glass of women's fashion. As it turns out, the parallels between Chanelism and the fascist aesthetic universe proved deep and numerous.

The many interdependent components of Chanel style added up to what was called her "Total Look": an English term coined by the American press and adopted by the French to describe her revolutionary approach to fashion. Other designers had dabbled in accessories and jewelry (Poiret had even created furniture), but only Chanel achieved this kind of "totality" of vision, raising fashion to the status of an all-encompassing worldview, a *Weltanschauung*. French film star Romy Schneider understood this: "One adores [Chanel style] or one rejects it in its entirety. Because it is a coherent logical whole, 'ordered' in the sense of 'Doric order' or 'Corinthian order,' there is a 'Chanel order.' With its own reasons, rules, and regulations."

To find an analogy for Chanelism, in all its classical totality, Schneider turned to ancient Greece, to the Doric and Corinthian architectural orders. (Nazi intellectual Alfred Rosenberg specifically cited the Doric people for having "protected the [Aryans'] creative blond blood.") In its own way, Chanel's fashion revolution created a *Gesamtkunstwerk*, a complete mode of living, dressing, and looking that resembled a secular, aesthetic, nationalistic religion over which she reigned. Both Germany and Italy had failed in their attempts to standardize women's fashion and to create an aesthetic identity that appealed to modern European women. Coco, however, had managed it all on her own. She achieved sameification, the fashion equivalent of *Gleichschaltung*.

Like a charismatic fascist leader, Chanel founded her totalizing vision upon an origin myth, the story that unified her much-publicized life of luxury, her design universe, and the childhood she'd manufactured for herself. Gradually, as her personal life diminished, that glamour-girl myth seemed to overtake Chanel completely.

A 1934 profile in *Fashion Arts* magazine nicely outlined the Chanel myth, including a list of Coco's "typical" activities so extravagant and clichéd that the article reads like a parody: "Riding to hounds in the forest of Compiègne, lunching in the sunlit gardens of her villa at Roquebrune, a brilliant hostess in the spacious majesty of her great eighteenth century house in the Faubourg St Honoré, entertaining the smartest of women, imposing diplomats and international wits, Chanel is a true woman of the world." It sounded like satire, but it was all accurate. Chanel had seen to it that her life was indistinguishable from—fused with—the romance novels she'd loved as a child. It was this fusion of herself to her myth that she was really selling.

A 1937 advertisement for Chanel No. 5 explicitly invoked Coco's personal life as a template for other women's fantasies. Accompanied by a photograph of Chanel lounging at the Ritz, the highly theatrical ad read: "Madame Gabrielle Chanel is above all an artist in living. Her dresses, her perfumes are created with a faultless instinct for drama. Her perfume #5 is like the soft music that underlies the playing of a love scene. It kindles the imagination; indelibly fixes the scene in the memories of the players." The message was simple: Chanel's existence was a performance for which one could buy a ticket, not to sit in the audience, but to step onto the stage and get in on the act. Chanel's personal life was as much for sale as the perfume. To this day, Chanel boutiques all over the world are built as exact replicas of Coco's apartment, inviting customers to play at reincarnating the mythic heroine.

Coco's myth, of course, was born of her deep yearning to be seen and known, to belong. Although Chanel had always been independent, until Iribe's death in 1935, she still believed she might find stability or belonging as someone's wife. When that hope died on a Riviera tennis court, Chanel refocused all her energy on honing her iconic status. By creating her own cult, she could knit herself a group that she could not only join, but *rule*. In a rare moment of candor, Chanel told Louise de Vilmorin: "A loveless childhood developed in me a violent need to be loved. This need . . . explains, I think, my whole life. . . . I consider my suc-

Photo accompanying a 1937 advertisement for Chanel No. 5,
depicting Chanel in her Ritz apartment

cess as proof of love, and I like to think that, when people love what I create, they are loving me as well, loving me through my creations." Such was the indirect and impersonal human relationship for which Chanel settled: the love of customers for the commodities they purchased.

Following her habit of understanding her life in terms of French nationality, Coco explained to Vilmorin her long-standing sense that her
humble roots undermined her French identity, causing her a kind of national anomie: "In France, an unknown foreign woman is never suspect...but for Frenchwomen it is not the same: one must be known in
order to be recognized. That was not my case." Her solution to this problem of French anonymity was simple: "I wanted to escape and become
the center of a universe of my own creation instead of staying in the
margins or even becoming part of the universe of other people."

In this, she succeeded admirably, translating her "universe" into a
buyable luxury commodity. Fashion theorist Gilles Lipovetsky lays out
the process necessary for establishing a luxury brand: "The creation of a
luxury brand...[requires] building a myth. It is through references to a
mythified past, to origin legends, that great [luxury] brands are created.
Luxury is nothing...until it manages to recast its perishable goods in the
'timeless' realm of myth." This describes precisely how Chanel founded
her empire.

Lipovetsky also illuminates just how much Chanel's creation of her
luxury brand resembled the fascist project (this despite the fascists' ostensible rejection of capitalist consumption). In both cases, nationalist
fervor merged with a deliberately manufactured myth. Both offered an
accessible kind of glory and belonging, democratic elitism, created via
cults of personality and the canny use of branding, identification, uniforms, and magical symbols. Both lay claim to the creation of a new,
revolutionary kind of being: the "fascist man" and the Chanel woman.
And both beckoned followers with the trappings of aristocracy—insignia,
medals, uniforms—stripped of exclusionary requirements, creating an
aristocracy of nation. Finally, while the requirement of noble birth had
been explicitly obviated by both, in both cases a new demand replaced it:
that of youth and physical fitness.

Just when much of Europe, including France, felt most adrift, searching precisely for new national identities, Chanel offered women a story
of community and identity, a virtual nationality of fashion. From the
1920s through the dawn of World War II, a new kind of crowd was form-

ing in Germany, Italy, and France—drawn to the charismatic leaders Hitler, Mussolini, and Marshal Pétain, who all wove myths around themselves and their nations to attract and keep followers.

Like those men, Chanel was a charismatic leader offering an uplifting story, a story of glory by association. Just as she did routinely with the environments of her lovers and friends, Chanel absorbed and synthesized her political environment. Coming of age professionally just as those new mass movements took shape, she channeled her talents into a version of such a movement, which was heavily inflected by the beliefs and iconography of fascism, to which she was deeply attracted.

Coco may not have intended this to happen, despite her own right-wing, pro-Nazi worldview. Yet her fashion revolution wound up echoing and even, perhaps, abetting the social and psychological tendencies necessary to any mass political movement rooted in exclusionism, racism, fervent nationalism, and myth.

The Chanel revolution operated, then, on two distinct, seemingly contradictory levels. Unquestionably, it created a modernist, freeing, sexually exhilarating universe of desire and consumption for women. Both Chanel's independent personal life and her unfettered designs seemed to bespeak a progressive, even feminist worldview—a politics completely at odds with the retrograde vision of womanhood endorsed by the protofascists. Yet at the same time, Chanel's universe mirrored with startling precision many of the tenets and techniques of fascism—its nostalgia for a lost (or nonexistent) noble past, its democratic elitism, its creation of a secular religion, its insistence on athleticism and fitness, its glorification of youth, and even its dependence upon a cult celebrity figure. But—and herein lies the crucial element that renders the apparent contradiction possible—the fascist vision reflected in Chanelism was largely the version marketed for men, not for women.

Chanel had managed a historically unique trick: She succeeded in embodying the masculinist ideals of fascism while turning them into a liberating worldview for women. And just as Germany and Italy were devoting themselves to blotting out all traces of French influence in their fashion, Chanel was busy inventing a design universe that jibed perfectly with fascist ideology while also being inextricably bound to French identity.

It just may be, therefore, that Coco Chanel and her free-spirited fashions came along at exactly the right time to provide women—especially in France—with an alternate route to the manipulations of fascism, an ostensibly emancipatory worldview that seemed an appealing antidote to constraining sexism and reactionary politics, while achieving nonetheless the psychological goals of fascism. The high modernist style of Chanelism must be classed, finally, with the other modernist movements that coexisted with and even furthered the aims of fascism, all of which participate in what Roger Griffin calls "a complex causal nexus... [that] relates the strands of modernism concerned with aesthetic and social hygiene to the regime that attempted to enact the Nazis' eugenic and genocidal projects of Europe's purification."

Chanel never overtly acknowledged the deep parallels between her own revolution and the rise of fascism. She did not need to. The world she'd built around herself, her friends, lovers, lifestyle, and fashions had re-created a fascist universe in microcosm.

> I was the instrument of Destiny to effect a necessary cleansing operation.
>
> **—COCO CHANEL**

CHAPTER ELEVEN

LOVE, WAR, AND ESPIONAGE

Sustained romantic love had eluded Coco since the loss of Paul Iribe, but at the end of the decade another Spaniard in Paris drew Chanel into the last erotic partnership she would have with an artist: Catalan sculptor Apel-les Fenosa. Handsome, driven, and possessed of an arresting dark-eyed gaze, Fenosa was superbly talented, only erratically solvent, and a homeless refugee—a combination that proved highly attractive to Chanel. Like Iribe and Reverdy, Fenosa was an artist she could both subsidize and romance—an intriguing but seemingly controllable man. Their affair would last about a year, and while it followed some classic patterns for Chanel, it also cast light on how much she had changed.

Like Chanel, Fenosa had grown up an outsider, although they were poles apart politically. His progressive parents ("green anarchists" he called them) ran a hotel and vegetarian restaurant in Barcelona. "It was odd," he recalled. "I was a vegetarian until I was twenty, which made me

Apel-les Fenosa in his studio

see myself as very different, as if I were a Muslim." (In fact, Fenosa had cause to believe he might be of Jewish descent.) Apel-les was different physically, too—weak and of uncertain health. A childhood bout of encephalitis had left him with a permanent tremor in his left hand, but this handicap only strengthened his determination to become a sculptor.

Apel-les enjoyed defying expectations. Solitary and contrary, he had begun running away from home as a young child. At five, he was gone for three days before his frantic parents discovered him on the docks, being cared for by some kindly sailors. Fenosa turned out to have an innate talent for finding "rescuers"—people who would bail him out of trouble. This ability served him well when, at fourteen, he announced his refusal to take over the family hotel business and found himself thrown out of the house by his enraged father. Left penniless, Apel-les was forced to eke out his own existence, relying on odd jobs, generous friends, and the secret help of his more sympathetic mother. "I just threw myself into the adventure. I had no plans.... I still don't know how I managed it," he recalled. Yet manage he did, even enrolling from 1913 to 1918 at the Escola d'Arts i Oficis, where he studied sculpture and drawing.

In 1920, Fenosa was drafted into the army. A committed pacifist, the twenty-one-year-old Apel-les could not join the military he despised. Risking imprisonment, he decided to make a run for it. Along with his like-minded brother, Oscar, he fled across the border, into the French Pyrenees town of Bourg-Madame. Within hours, the French police arrested them, but not before the brothers had managed to meet and befriend two young local girls who turned out to have some influence. The girls intervened with the town's mayor, who arranged for the Fenosa brothers' release. Instead of deportation or a French prison sentence, Oscar and Apel-les received their liberty. They had successfully deserted the Spanish Army.

Oscar settled in Toulouse, but Apel-les traveled on to Paris, arriving in Montmartre on New Year's Day 1921 with eighty borrowed francs in his pocket. Soon enough, through friends, he wrangled an introduction to the man he would come to regard as an artistic father, Pablo Picasso. Quickly recognizing the younger man's talent, Picasso took Apel-les under his wing. He let Fenosa work beside him in his studio; he critiqued his sculptures; he even arranged his first Paris exhibition. "Without him I would have died having accomplished nothing," said Fenosa of Picasso. "He gave birth to me."

Fenosa blossomed in Paris, joining Picasso's circle and becoming especially close to Jean Cocteau. He worked prodigiously and managed to support himself—barely—by selling his busts and figurines of terracotta, bronze, and clay. His subjects tended to be minimalist female nudes with gracefully curved, elongated limbs. In their visual sleekness, Fenosa's sculptures conjure the early Constantin Brancusi, but their small size and delicate faces—framed often by long curls—suggest medieval statuettes. Fenosa was unconcerned with labeling his style. "All arts were modern in their time," he told an interviewer in 1968. "One mustn't worry about that."

Paris had become home, but in 1929, when a Barcelona gallery arranged an exhibition of his work, Fenosa dared to return to Spain. As a deserter, he had to reenter his home country on foot, surreptitiously, "hopping over the border like a rabbit," as he put it. But leaving the country the same way was impossible. Even a daredevil like Fenosa hesitated to tempt fate so brazenly. He considered his options. Spain seemed ready to turn a blind eye toward his transgressions, and his Paris bona fides brought him cachet in Barcelona. Although he had planned to be there for a week, Apel-les stayed in Spain for ten years.

Fenosa did not leave Barcelona again until May 1939, when he joined the nearly five hundred thousand other Spaniards fleeing the horrors of Franco's regime. Once more, Apel-les crossed the French border on foot, without proper papers. Once more he was arrested, and threatened with imprisonment or deportation. As always, Fenosa maintained his charm and sangfroid. While being held overnight by the border patrol, he talked his way into a card party with the French border policemen. They stayed up all night playing a raucous game of *belote*. When morning came, the guards felt so fond of their new prisoner-friend that they lent him money from their own pockets, doctored his visa, and waved him safely into France. The magic (or manipulation) had worked again. Fenosa had a genius for turning new acquaintances into devoted, even parental, protectors.

Back in France, that particular brand of genius continued to serve Apel-les well. Picasso gave him money, cooked him paella, bought his sculptures, and arranged a free apartment for him in Versailles, across the street from the Château—and just forty-five minutes by train from Paris. Boasting vast bay windows overlooking the famous Bassin de Neptune, the reflecting pool built for Louis XIV, the apartment was perfect for sculpting. Here, through the summer of 1939, Fenosa worked well and peacefully—all the more so since Jean Cocteau had called in a favor with the Foreign Office to obtain a legal visa for Apel-les.

If Cocteau played the role of guardian angel so well, perhaps it was because he had long enjoyed the attentions of one himself: his own patroness, Coco Chanel. Throughout their decades of friendship, Cocteau

Jean Cocteau with his
portrait bust by Fenosa

had turned to Chanel repeatedly whenever he found himself in need emotionally, medically, or financially. He'd often prevailed upon her to help his various friends and lovers as well. It seemed the most natural thing in the world to bring Fenosa to the Ritz, to meet the undisputed queen of his social circle.

Coco was approaching her fifty-sixth birthday that summer and had weathered some rough years personally and professionally. Apelles was not yet forty and embarking on a hopeful new phase of life. But the attraction between them was instant. Chanel was among those women who remain truly gorgeous into middle age, her carriage upright and regal, her gait supple, her famous figure as svelte as a girl's. She looked, in fact, not unlike the slim, elongated female figures Fenosa sculpted. And with her black hair and eyes, Coco had always had a Spanish air about her. She also had a profound and intuitive grasp of Fenosa's art form, since her own approach to fashion had always been deeply sculptural— tactile and three-dimensional—involving hours draping and pinning fabric on living models, rarely sketching or drawing her designs in advance. And although she had long harbored a crush on Picasso ("She was in love with Picasso," Fenosa told Josep Miquel Garcia, director of the Apel-les Fenosa Foundation and a friend of Fenosa's later years), nothing had ever happened between them—perhaps because they were too alike, both commanding and controlling presences, each quick to anger, each adept at seduction. "He fascinated me.... He frightened me," Coco had said of Picasso. Apel-les offered a more accessible Catalan conquest. She swept him into her orbit immediately.

By all accounts Apel-les and Coco were genuinely attached for a time. Fenosa admired Chanel and appreciated her savvy and generosity. "She was very intelligent, and she did a great deal for me.... She never did anything by chance." Chanel, charmed by Fenosa's talent and winning vulnerability, showered him with expensive gifts—a solid gold penknife, gold cuff links set with topazes, a set of silver hairbrushes.

Pencil sketch of Chanel
by Fenosa

Chanel and Fenosa had only been involved a few weeks when, on September 3, 1939, in response to Hitler's invasion of Poland, France and Great Britain declared war, beginning the strange period known to the British as the "phony war," and to the French as the *drôle de guerre*—the nine months of relative calm before the Allies took any major military action against the Third Reich. The lack of combat reassured no one, though, and the wariness of the preceding years in Paris escalated dramatically. In a frenzy to root out Communists, the French police conducted raids on suspected political organizations, seizing documents, books, even furniture. Newspapers and periodicals supporting Communism were abolished, and surveillance of suspected Communist sympathizers led to thousands of arrests and imprisonments.

Uneasy now in Versailles, Apel-les longed to be closer to his friends. He moved into his own room at the Ritz, courtesy of Coco.

Fenosa was not alone among Chanel's men living in the fabled hotel. Pierre Reverdy was there as well. Torn as ever between the two poles of his personality—ascetic Catholic mystic and worldly poet— Reverdy had temporarily swapped his monastery retreat for city life again (leaving his wife behind in Solesmes), and was living at the Ritz, on Chanel's tab. As usual, Coco continued to underwrite expenses for a man who routinely accused her—as had Iribe—of having too much money and leading an immorally lavish life. Now Pierre could argue with her from the comfort of a neighboring suite as they continued their platonic but intense friendship at the Ritz.

If Fenosa was perturbed by Reverdy's presence, he never said so. Both men were close with Cocteau and Picasso, and had likely met many times before. Chanel had no problem juggling the attentions of several men, particularly when she held the financial reins.

Outside the cocoon of the Ritz, Paris was grappling with the certainty of another European war. Inside the hotel, amid her Coromandel screens, thick Persian carpets, and oversize baroque gilt mirrors, Coco continued to hold court, perched upon the cushions of her impossibly soft quilted-suede sofa—designed in her signature beige. "I take refuge in beige, because it's natural," she told Claude Delay.

For the time being, Reverdy was able to tolerate the cognitive dissonance of being a leftist and devout Catholic ensconced among the glitterati as a Chanel "pensioner." Fenosa proved less flexible in his philosophies. Although Apel-les had long relied upon wealthy friends, he could not bear life at the Ritz circa 1939. "It bothered me to be at the Ritz.... It was opulence to a degree that made me crazy!... It was impossible. I had not been born to lead such a life." He shared his discomfort with Cocteau, and the two came up with a quick solution: Why not exchange apartments? Cocteau and Jean Marais occupied a small but lovely flat just west of Vendôme, in the Place de la Madeleine. Fenosa jumped at the chance and traded living quarters with the two men. Cocteau could now live even closer to his buddies Coco and Reverdy, and Fenosa could take some distance from the hothouse atmosphere of the Ritz.

But relocating to the Place de la Madeleine did little to lighten Fenosa's malaise and deepening guilt. His new apartment was mere steps from the Ritz, just down the street from Fauchon—Paris's most exclusive purveyors of truffles and foie gras—and within sight of the Eglise de la Madeleine, the splendid neoclassical temple built to honor Napoléon's army. He was earning good money now, sculpting busts of prominent friends, and he had a dazzling and famous lover. But he could not take pleasure in any of it. "He was desperate," according to Josep Miquel Garcia. "One day, he found himself at the Place de la Concorde, at the foot of the Obelisk, weeping; the disparity between the horrors of war which he had lived [in Spain] and this triumphant return to Paris was just too great."

Perhaps aggravated by his depression and the bitter winter of 1940—the coldest on record in France since 1893—Fenosa's faltering health weakened further. A bout of double mastoiditis brought high fever, extreme pain, and chills. Fenosa took to his bed, where he was attended by Chanel's personal physician. When he was hospitalized for several days, Chanel sent a handwritten note on Ritz stationery, inquiring about his health. It is signed "tenderly, Coco."

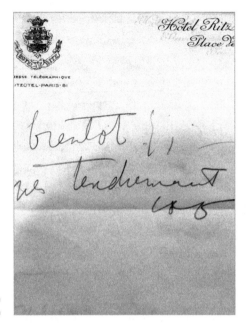

Handwritten note from
Chanel to Fenosa

That tenderness was real, but the relationship foundered. Fenosa found too much about Chanel's world repellent. Unlike most of her friends, he had an inner compass pointed always toward progressive causes, republicanism, and empathy. While clearly not averse to borrowed luxury, Apel-les could not tolerate the disjunction between the atmosphere on Place Vendôme and the war he could feel but not yet see. Life with Coco felt excessive. "Fifty-two Coromandel screens!" he exclaimed to Garcia. "Each one worth a million [francs]. . . . She covered me with gifts. She gave me for example an enormous gold bracelet. But I hid it. . . . It disgusted me to have a gold bracelet, I gave it back to her."

Beyond her personal excesses, Coco's response to the war would also have repelled Fenosa. Despite her much-touted patriotism, and her recent *tricolore* fashion palette, only three weeks after war was declared, she fired all 2,500 of her employees without warning and closed all her workshops. She also abruptly ceased the monthly stipends she had been sending her brothers, Lucien and Alphonse. To Lucien, she wrote:

I am very sorry to have to tell you this sad news. But with the Maison now closed, I find myself nearly in poverty. You can no longer count on anything from me as long as circumstances remain this way.

Taking her at her word, Lucien, now fifty-one and a retired peddler, sent a letter back to the Ritz (where he'd never been allowed entrée into Gabrielle's apartment), offering to share his own meager savings with his sister—this despite having retired years earlier only to please her. Alphonse, who ran a *café-tabac*, received a similar letter from Coco, but reacted differently: "My Gaby, So now you're flat broke. It was bound to happen."

Chanel responded to neither of them and would never see her brothers again. Lucien died in 1941, and Alphonse in 1953. From September 1939 onward, "Gaby" also severed all contact with her many nieces and nephews, remaining in touch only with André Palasse and her aunt Adrienne, the baroness. Chanel had always kept an aloof distance from the more hardscrabble branch of her family, but now she had decided, as Edmonde Charles-Roux put it, "to play dead."

Chanel played dead with her terminated employees as well. Shocked to be so swiftly deprived of their livelihoods just as husbands and fathers left for war, they tried to appeal her decision with the Confédération générale du travail, the French labor bureau. Negotiators were sent to reason with Chanel, imploring her to consider not only her employees but also her clientele, and the "prestige of Paris" with which she was so tightly allied. They could not move her. Like the Russian army retreating from Napoléon, Coco was practicing a "scorched-earth" policy, leaving nothing behind. Or almost nothing. Virtually empty, the Cambon boutique kept one counter open for selling perfume—the main source of Chanel's fortune, which she kept largely in Swiss bank accounts.

Chanel never offered a single coherent explanation for her decision to close her business. She told Pierre Galante and Claude Delay that she had simply been responding to the times. "I had the feeling that we had reached the end of an era. And that no one would ever make dresses again." She told Marcel Haedrich the implausible story that she'd had no choice, since her entire staff of thousands had all disappeared to bid farewell to family members being shipped off to war. "In a few hours the place was empty." Interviewed jointly with her close friend Serge Lifar, she maintained that she had intended her actions as a patriotic protest against the Germans—who had not yet occupied Paris—comparing herself favorably to other couturiers who kept their businesses open: "My dear, the only true *résistante,* was me!" Coco declared to Lifar (who after the war hid out in her closet at the Ritz, trying to evade his arrest for treason). Serge agreed emphatically.

Other possible explanations circulated: Perhaps Coco sought revenge against the employees who had enraged her three years earlier by striking. Perhaps the competition with Elsa Schiaparelli (now also living at the Ritz) got the better of her. The sheer number of contradictory hypotheses suggests that none was correct. Coco had never been idle a day in her life; early retirement did not seem a plausible choice for her. Another sort of employment may have awaited, however.

It is likely that Fenosa was deeply dismayed by Chanel's blithe dismissal of so many workers. Some of her other reactions left him cold as well. Coco could seem disdainful and snobbish. "I never really lived up to [her] expectations. What one must do, what one mustn't do." He recalled her reaction to a bottle of cologne he'd once bought. "She asked me to bring it to her and, right in front of me, she poured the entire bottle down the drain. The entire bottle."

Even more disturbing to him was what Fenosa called Chanel's serious drug habit. For five years, since the death of Paul Iribe, Coco had been injecting herself every night with Sedol, the morphine-based sleep medication. To the outside world she seemed unchanged, as productive and creative as ever. No record seems to exist of anyone else accusing Coco of outright drug abuse at this stage of her life. Aware of the Sedol habit, Claude Delay interpreted it as an antidote to loneliness, "the ferocious partner of her solitude."

According to Fenosa, though, Chanel's employees knew of her problem and hoped he might help her overcome it. "The workers were all very glad to see me with her, because she was doing drugs and that, I would not tolerate." Recreational drug use was not uncommon among Chanel's set. Misia, by this time, had already descended into her ruinous dependence on morphine, and recently suffered a heart attack and a severe retinal hemorrhage. And despite multiple stints in rehab (which Coco always paid for) Cocteau could not shake his love of opium, which he thought of in the most lyrical terms: "We all carry within us something folded up like those Japanese flowers made of wood that unfold in water. Opium plays the same role as the water. None of us carries the same kind of flower." More than once, Fenosa accompanied Cocteau to one of his opium dens. "I never [tried it], but...it was tempting," he admitted. Apel-les declined many kinds of pleasures offered to him by Cocteau, who addressed notes to Fenosa "my dear little squirrel."

No evidence suggests that Chanel smoked opium, and she did not partake of Cocteau's social drug world. As with most troubling aspects of her life, her drug use was kept entirely private; she injected herself at home. But Fenosa's account suggests that Coco's use exceeded any prescribed dose or medicinal purpose: "It was morphine, it was too much, you see. I was spent." Certainly, at whatever dosage, given the nature of the drug and the continued use over years, Coco must have been physically addicted. And as her lover, Fenosa would have seen the ill effects close up. He was adamant about the toll it took: "It was the drugs that separated us. When you love someone who takes drugs, either you start doing drugs yourself or the other one must stop." She did not stop, and Fenosa left, although the two remained on good terms.

Years later, when a fifty-year-old Fenosa finally decided to marry, he brought his beautiful twenty-year-old fiancée, Nicole, to rue Cambon. Chanel offered to design the young woman's wedding dress—which consisted of an eighteenth-century-style riding coat, with a fitted waist and flared panels. "She was brilliant, very brilliant," recalled Nicole Fenosa. Chanel had always delighted in taking the wives of her lovers or ex-lovers under her fashion wing. She did this out of generosity, to be sure, but dressing these women was also her way of leaving her mark upon them. Outfitting Nicole Fenosa on her wedding day allowed Chanel to be present at the altar—sartorially, at least—as yet another one of her lovers married someone else—in this case a girl easily young enough to be her granddaughter (Coco was sixty-seven by the time of Fenosa's nuptials, nearly half a century older than Nicole, the bride).

Chanel had spent a lifetime insinuating herself in this way into all sorts of privileged realms, from marriages to the upper reaches of the aristocracy to the art world. With lovers she had always been generous and accommodating, giving of herself while absorbing so much from them—social cues, aesthetic sensibilities, and political views. Initially, Chanel must have viewed Fenosa somewhat as she had Reverdy, and assumed she could "enter" his world as easily as she had Pierre's. Both men were emotional and driven artists; both held progressive and republican views. Both needed and accepted her financial support. But Pierre had his deeply mystical side—his fervent, if erratic, Catholicism. When they'd met, moreover, Coco was still a young woman, not nearly as battered and bitter as she was in 1939. Theirs had been a genuine passion, and it had appealed to the convent girl in her. Their connection remained the most permanent one of her life. Despite his marriage, and even his monastic retreat, Reverdy never fully left Coco. And despite their deep differences, he never rejected her. She regarded him as a lodestar of a purer time and life. His affection proved she was not all bad.

With Fenosa things were different. Apel-les was seventeen years her junior (Reverdy was only six years younger than she), and far more vital and socially integrated than the reclusive Pierre. Unlike all her many other ruptures with men, this breakup could only signal a rejection of Coco herself. Fenosa did not leave Chanel because of exigencies of social class. He had not died. Apel-les left Coco because of Coco—because her life, her habits, and her personality had become distasteful to him. The elegant world she had so carefully built felt tainted to him, and she knew it.

Fenosa's departure coincided with a major turn in Chanel's professional life. For the first time in more than thirty years, she was no longer designing couture. By closing her house she had removed herself from the creative process, save for a brief stint helping Dalí with his costumes.

She was still amassing a fortune from perfume sales, but only via an impersonal, commercial process in which she had little direct participation. There were no models to fit, no fabric to drape, no *défilés* to stage. Despite her generosity toward him, she had managed to drive away the first lover she had enjoyed in a long while. Coco had hardened considerably, as had her already-severe political opinions. Although she kept her coterie of friends, something in her had shrunk. The Sedol would only have intensified her detachment, numbing whatever empathy or self-awareness might have remained. Such was her state of mind as France slid into its darkest and most morally challenging times.

In May 1940, the phony war turned into a real one, as the Allies suffered a catastrophic loss in the thirty-five-day Battle of France. The Germans moved through the Ardennes and were making their way south. Air bombings destroyed the Allied outposts at Dunkirk; Neville Chamberlain resigned and Winston Churchill took the reins as prime minister, and French prime minister Edouard Daladier had been replaced by Paul Reynaud, for whom support was very weak. On June 10, just days after enemy bombs fell on the outskirts of Paris, the capital was declared an "open city" into which the Germans were free to march, unopposed. The unthinkable had happened: France had abandoned Paris. The members of Reynaud's government decamped from Paris to Tours. The Third Republic was ending, and enemy troops were fast approaching. This prompted one of the largest, most chaotic exoduses in modern history.

In terror, residents of Paris and surrounding cities scrambled to leave. The entire northern part of France emptied as citizens from all backgrounds tried desperately to escape south. Many of Coco's friends were among the fleeing crowds, including Cocteau, Jean Marais, Picasso, and Salvador Dalí and his wife, Gala. Fenosa left, too, for Toulouse, which his compatriots had long considered a part of Catalonia.

In the unusually high heat of several June days, the fragrant elegance of a Paris springtime disintegrated into filth, smoke, sweat, and despair. Apartments were packed up overnight, windows shuttered. Luggage and bedding were strapped to the roofs of cars, money and jewelry hastily grabbed. Store shelves were emptied of provisions. Theaters, libraries, and museums all closed. The Louvre took down nearly all its paintings. Friends and neighbors shared overcrowded cars that barely crawled along roads paralyzed by thousands of vehicles. Thousands more left in wagons, trucks, or on bicycles, some even on foot, trudging for miles in exhaustion. In all, about one-fourth of France's entire population took part in "l'Exode," nearly ten million people.

Chanel had no intention of remaining in the city under these conditions. She packed her trunks and, having lost her chauffeur to the exodus, quickly rounded up a friend of a Ritz employee to serve as a substitute driver. The new chauffeur, M. Larcher, counseled against driving Chanel's conspicuous Rolls-Royce, so with her longtime assistant Angèle Aubert and several other employees in tow they headed out in Larcher's own, more modest vehicle. Raids being launched on the Riviera by the Italian Army made La Pausa an unsafe option, and so Coco directed her driver to the southwest. They headed for the Pyrenees, to the town of Lembeye, where André Palasse lived. Palasse had been called up for military duty, but his wife and daughters still occupied the house Chanel had bought for the family through Etienne Balsan. (Balsan also owned property in the area, reviving the possibility that Balsan was André's biological father and wished to live near and help his son.) The Palasse family scrambled to make room for their new guests.

Momentous events unfolded at breakneck speed. The Germans entered a half-empty Paris on June 14, 1940. On June 16, the Reynaud administration disbanded, replaced by the rule of new premier Marshal Philippe Pétain, the eighty-four-year-old reactionary World War I hero. Two days later, Pétain requested an armistice from the Germans, and two days after that, on June 22, 1940, it was signed in Compiègne, the city where Chanel had once lived with Etienne Balsan. For his vice president, Pétain tapped Pierre Laval, the Auvergne-born former cabinet minister and self-made multimillionaire. Together they established l'Etat Français, "the French State," in the resort city of Vichy.

The armistice divided France in two: the occupied and unoccupied zones. The German military now commanded all French forces. Far from trying to protect France from the Germans, as they claimed, Pétain and Laval quickly set up an authoritarian regime largely in line with Hitler's. L'Etat Français replaced the country's national motto, *"Liberté, Egalité, Fraternité,"* with a new one, *"Travail, Famille, Patrie"* (work, family, fatherland). Pétain sought to establish himself as the leader of a messianic cult, after the manner of Hitler and Mussolini. On June 17, upon assuming power, he declared in a radio address, "I give to France the gift of my person to alleviate her misfortunes." An officially commissioned bust of the marshal would be distributed throughout the municipal buildings of France—the new required replacement for all statues of Marianne. The willowy, feminine allegorical figure of France, in her flowing robes, had morphed into an eighty-four-year-old man in military regalia.

Unlike the Nazis, who simply replaced religion with fascism, Pétain cloaked much of his repellent politics with doctrinaire Catholic pieties. France's defeat, he proclaimed, had resulted from the sins of parliamentary democracy. The country would serve penance for its moral decadence. In other words, democracy was to be replaced by a junta

Busts of Marshal Pétain made for town halls and prefectures

government that granted Pétain "almost all legislative, executive, and judicial powers." One of Pétain's advisers observed that the *maréchal* "now had more power than any French leader since Louis XIV."

Under Pétain, France would build dozens of internment and work camps to house anti-fascists, members of the Resistance, Jews, homosexuals, Gypsies, and anyone else deemed undesirable. Laval, too, proved exceptionally zealous, signing into law the deportation to German concentration camps of all foreign-born Jews found on French soil.

For vast numbers of people, France grew gravely unsafe as it disintegrated into a satellite of Germany, with ghastly new regulations taking hold. Jews lost the right to own a business. German censors carefully vetted all cultural materials, banning any works of art, literature, or theater by Jews, or anyone deemed anti-German. To pursue nearly any livelihood or profession—from running a store to composing an opera—meant transacting with the enemy. France wandered into a strange period of limbo. Much of the surface thrum of the quotidian continued, but bedrock assumptions about what it meant to be French had crumbled. "Everything we did was equivocal," wrote Jean-Paul Sartre. "A subtle poison corrupted even our best actions."

The "subtle poison" did not prevent occupied Paris from being restored very quickly—at least in appearance—to its usual, glittering self. The Germans surprised everyone with their good behavior. After moving into the city and requisitioning many of the best homes for their own quarters, they reopened cabarets, music halls, theaters, and restaurants. They behaved with impeccable grace and courtesy in a carefully orchestrated charm offensive. The Nazis didn't want to destroy Paris; they wanted to turn it into the jewel in their crown, while inciting the least resistance possible. To do that meant enticing its residents back to the city.

The Nazis succeeded in their plan. The population of Paris had plummeted in June, from two million to about seven hundred thousand. But by late July many thousands of Parisians had returned, including much of the social and cultural elite. Chanel prepared to return home

from Lembeye. While reassured by reports that Paris was again inhabit-
able, she was desperately worried now about her beloved nephew André,
who, she'd learned, had been taken prisoner and was languishing—sick
with tuberculosis—in a German detention camp.

Chanel was grief-stricken at the possibility of losing forever the
young man she considered (or who actually was) her son. She spoke
rarely of the depth of her attachment to him, but in a little-known 1944
interview with British journalist and former MI6 agent Malcolm Muggeridge, Coco let down her guard emotionally: "A close relative whom I
treated like my own son, and who was in poor health, had been taken
prisoner by the Nazis. . . . If that boy had perished in a Nazi compound I
could never have gone on living. I would have killed myself."

Gabrielle Palasse-Labrunie recalled her aunt saying much the same
thing: "[Coco] admitted to me that she could not have borne it if he had
disappeared, that she would have committed suicide." The threat of suicide was revealing. Many people Coco had loved had perished tragically,
but André was different. He was the only person for whom she'd ever felt
responsible, the one she'd always protected. The prospect of his dying appears to have provoked a different kind of sorrow—one tinged with self-
recrimination, with guilt that she would have proved unable to save him.
It was the reaction of a mother—a conclusion Malcolm Muggeridge
himself seems to draw during their conversation. Although Chanel carefully refers to André as a "close relative," Muggeridge pointedly ignores
this distinction and asks, "What happened to your son?" Chanel replies
without correcting the mistake, seeming to accept its implication: "He
was eventually released."

Nothing short of a DNA test could ever settle the question of André's
birth, but whatever the biological facts, André's illness and imprisonment
only intensified Coco's maternal attachment to him. (Gabrielle Palasse-
Labrunie recalls that, after the war, for the rest of Coco's life, she carried
in her wallet photographs of André in military uniform.) With a combination of grief and steely determination, Chanel set out to rescue
Palasse—a task that would entail cultivating and exploiting close contacts within the highest Nazi circles.

Saying good-bye to André's wife and daughters, Coco took to the road, along with her chauffeur, her employees, a woman doctor she'd encountered in town, and a friend she had also run into—the celebrated society hostess Marie-Louise Bousquet. Bousquet gained fame soon after for hosting weekly Franco-German luncheons, where Nazi officials mingled with French artists and aristocrats. After the war she became editor of *Harper's Bazaar* in Paris.

The Chanel caravan headed north in July. Coco sent a telegram to her recent ex, Fenosa, now in Toulouse. Bearing the date of July 13, 1940—Bastille Day Eve—the cable read:

> I will arrive Monday evening Toulouse. Try to find me a place to sleep. If not Monday, I will surely be there Tuesday.
>
>   Regards, Gabrielle Chanel.

They had clearly traveled a long emotional distance, and the days of "tenderly Coco" were over. Still, Fenosa would hardly have refused a request to help his former mistress.

The next stop for these reverse refugees was Vichy itself, where the new Pétain government had set up offices in the city's hotels. Lodging was very tight, and Chanel and Marie-Louise were obliged to suffer through the night in a stiflingly hot hotel attic. Amazingly, some of the crowds consisted of wealthy vacationers, taking the waters. Even amid all the political chaos, Vichy had maintained its upper-class resort ambiance that July.

"Everybody was laughing, drinking champagne.... I said, '*Tiens!* it's the high season,'" recalled Chanel. That exclamation, "*Tiens!*"—meaning "How do you like that?" or "Imagine that!"—contains Chanel's own acknowledgment of the situation's irony: How could people be enjoying themselves during such a crisis? But the French upper classes continued to disport themselves during Vichy and the occupation, Coco and Marie-Louise among them.

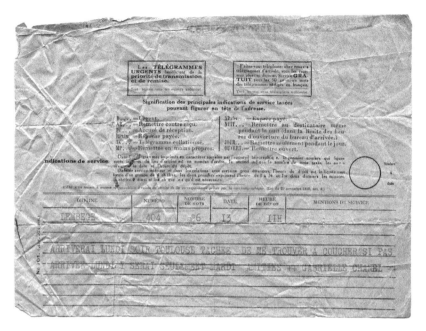

Telegram from Chanel to Fenosa

This quick overnight in Vichy reveals something key about Chanel's political status during these years. Biographers have paid scant attention to the trip. Axel Madsen notes only that "a government official" helpfully sold Chanel some gasoline. Hal Vaughan mentions that Chanel "visited friends" in Vichy. But who were these officials and friends, and what was the point of the visit? Vaughan believes that Chanel had gone to plead for the release of André Palasse, and that is probably correct. Elsewhere he points out (as does Pierre Galante) that Pierre Laval counted among Chanel's friends. But the extent and duration of this friendship merits further consideration. Vaughan believes that Coco had met Laval through her lawyer René de Chambrun, who was Laval's son-in-law.

The Chambrun marriage took place in 1935; therefore, in 1940, Chanel could only have had, at most, a five-year acquaintance with Pierre Laval, and even then, how close was she likely to be with her lawyer's father-in-law? In truth, Chanel and Pierre Laval had known each other far longer—for at least fifteen years. And their friendship existed independently of the Chambrun marriage. Proof of Chanel's long-standing acquaintance with Laval can be found in Elsa Maxwell's August 11, 1945, Party Line column, which she devoted to Laval:

> The first time I saw Pierre Laval, French Judas Iscariot and Hitler's lackey, was about twenty years ago. I had gone to tea with Chanel, the great French designer, and as I was ushered into her luxurious salon, I noticed there a squat, swarthy man dressed like an undertaker—all in black with the exception of a thin, white voile necktie. I mistook him for Pablo Picasso, the prominent Spanish painter, until Chanel entered and introduced the "Honorable" Pierre Laval, member of the French chamber of deputies. Chanel observed humorously that M. Laval, a country lawyer from her birthplace in the Auvergne, had been elected to the Chamber by the Labor vote.

Maxwell's piece confirms that in or around 1925, Chanel already knew Laval well enough to invite him to tea. Laval and Coco were exact contemporaries (he, too, was born in 1883) and his father owned a café in the region where Chanel grew up. She might have known him as a girl; she might also have met him through Etienne Balsan, since Laval seems to have had a connection to the prominent Balsan family, or she might have encountered him through the Duke of Westminster, her lover at the time of the Elsa Maxwell tea party. Finally, Chanel might easily have met Laval through his close friend Paul Morand. Paul and his wife, Hélène, had frequently hosted Laval at their Paris dinner parties.

Laval and Chanel were natural allies. Despite beginning his career as a socialist, as he amassed his fortune, Laval gradually moved to the Far Right. He owed his wealth, furthermore, to his investment in the Baccarat company—makers of fine French crystal. Involvement in this field would have placed Pierre Laval among the right-wing, pro-fascist luxury goods magnates of Paris (including Pierre Taittinger and François Coty) with whom Chanel socialized through the interwar years. Like a number of these men, Laval also owned a newspaper, *Le Moniteur.* That Coco, according to Elsa Maxwell, made a "humorous" remark about Laval's election by the Labor party proves her awareness of the irony of Labor supporting a politician who worked actively against the interests of workers. Maxwell goes on to explain:

> I thought him a slippery, unpleasant customer, and watched with amazement his remarkable rise to fame. He amassed a fortune of 80,000,000 francs in ten years and when I asked a French politician "How come?" he answered, "Why he plays both ends against the middle. He represents labor in the Chamber and in private life takes care of his rich industrial friends by settling their labor problems through political contacts."

This penchant for duplicity would emerge later, with far graver consequences, when Laval ruled Vichy.

It is highly likely then that Coco made a beeline for Vichy in July 1940 because she knew she could gain access to the new deputy prime minister. Undoubtedly she implored Laval's aid in liberating André Palasse, but subsequent events suggest that Coco was also looking after her own interests.

Chanel returned to Paris to find the Ritz transformed into living quarters for officers of the Reich. This quintessentially French luxury hotel—designed by Louis XIV's royal architect, Jules Hardouin-Mansart—now bore the Nazis' identifying logo; a swastika flag flew above the cream silk awnings. Uniformed sentries stood at the entrance.

No precise record remains of Coco's exchange with the officials guarding what had been her home, but somehow, she received permission to resume living at the Ritz, with one caveat: Chanel would have to trade her 1,700-square-foot two-bedroom with its view of the Place Vendôme for a couple of adjoining maids' rooms on the rue Cambon side, numbers 227 and 228, in the section for *Privatgast,* the private guests of the Nazis. Coco complied readily, although Misia scolded her for ceding too easily to these lesser quarters.

Almost all of the original long-term residents of the Ritz had been evicted by the Germans, and almost no "foreigners" (now meaning French people) could gain entry. Hermann Göring, head of the occupied territories, was living at the hotel, as would, at various times, Albert Speer, Nazi foreign minister Joachim von Ribbentrop, and Reich minister of the interior Wilhelm Frick. Aside from Chanel, only a handful of non-Nazi personnel enjoyed the privilege of living there—mostly supporters of the German cause. So how did Chanel get by the sentries and secure living quarters in what amounted to a very posh Nazi military barracks? It is overwhelmingly likely that Coco's German and Vichy connections, possibly Pierre Laval himself, had intervened. Such solicitude toward his old friend seems entirely in character for Laval. According to Pierre Galante, when Laval—already deputy prime minister of Vichy—ran into Serge Lifar at a reception in Paris, he admonished Lifar: "Insofar as you have any influence in Paris, protect the Auvergnats, and above all Chanel."

In moving to her new, smaller quarters, Chanel needed to relinquish most of her furnishings, which remained in her original suite. This caused her no distress; she was not overly attached to things, no matter how rare or priceless. "Wealth is not accumulation; it is the opposite," she told Claude Delay. There was one key exception: Chanel would not part with her Coromandels. Apel-les Fenosa had been outraged by the exorbitant prices of the screens, but their monetary value was not what Chanel prized. For her, the screens, with their painted flowers and exotic birds, conjured her love affair with Boy. Wherever she unfolded these large burnished wood panels, they instantly enfolded her in a cocoon of memories, obscuring whatever lay beyond. (In China, Coromandels had originally served as window coverings for royal ladies' quarters, since they allowed light to filter in while blocking the stares of outsiders.) The screens transformed any new space into a replica of the much beloved long-ago apartment she shared with Capel on avenue Gabriel. Now,

Coco folded up the Coromandels and moved them across the street to a small salon in her apartment above her atelier on rue Cambon. (She slept at the Ritz but entertained and dined on Cambon.) Like her itinerant peddler ancestors, Coco could essentially carry her home on her back, "like a snail," as she herself acknowledged. After all, she had learned early to adapt quickly to dramatic shifts of environment. During the war, this fluid relationship to the concept of "home" emerged in Chanel's highly mutable—not to say completely self-serving—notion of "home" in the national-political sense as well. Her allegiance, that is, turned out to be a function of purely personal expediency.

C hanel had long enjoyed a deep and symbolic relationship with French nationalism; she represented the utmost in French style and luxury and stood at the helm of one of France's most prestigious and lucrative commercial empires. But Chanel's Frenchness had always exhibited a strain of self-interest and expediency—a sense that she celebrated her nationality as a substitute for family lineage or for noble birth. With the German takeover of her country, the cracks in Chanel's patriotism began to show. The occupation engendered a thousand kinds of collaboration, most of which defy easy condemnation. But we now know that Chanel's was not the everyday kind of collaboration born of desperation, confusion, or even passivity. On the contrary, Chanel proved such an enthusiastic fan of the Nazis that she "unfolded her screens" on their side of the street, joining the payroll as an agent for the Reich.

It may not have been the first time she had played for the opposing team.

The dossier labeled "Gabrielle Chanel" at the Archives de la préfecture de police de Paris is thick and dates back to 1923. In that year, Chanel's relationship with Grand Duke Dmitri Romanov drew the attention of the authorities, who followed the couple closely in their travels throughout Europe. Although certain parts of the Chanel dossier contain some minor errors (in the spelling of names—including Chanel's—and sometimes the nationalities of parties involved), it appears reliable overall. Some of its information conforms to what we know through other sources. Where the police surveillance file offers new information, as below, the precision of the surrounding details lends credibility to its claims. An entry stamped "secret" and dated June 23, 1923, uncovers the real and startling possibility that Chanel had actually worked as a German spy or informant during the *First* World War:

> The Ministry of War (Second Bureau of the General Staff, Central Intelligence Section) has just communicated to my administration the following information:
>
> We alert you to the suspicious activities of a certain Miss Tchannen [*sic*], a fashion designer from Bahnhofstrasse in Zurich, who has been staying for a month in Paris at the Hotel Meurisse [*sic*], in the company of a Russian prince who calls himself a pretender to the throne of Russia.
>
> It seems that all of the couple's expenses are being paid by Miss Tchannen, who is not known in Zurich to possess a great fortune. One thing is however certain: the presence of this woman is not without interest for Germany and the German service of Lucerne is following very closely her activity in Paris. It would be, it seems, of interest to monitor the activities of Miss Tchannen and to investigate the origin of the funds at her disposal.
>
> The Tchannen sisters worked, during the war, for the German Secret Service. I respectfully request that you perform close surveillance of the above-named Tchannen and of the person who is accompanying her and communicate to me the results of your investigation.

The issuing authority for this document, the Central Intelligence Section (known in French as "SCR," for Section de centralisation du renseignement), was a division devoted to counterespionage work in the wake of World War I. While Chanel does not seem ever to have made Zurich her permanent residence in the 1920s, she did, in fact, open a boutique there, specifically at number 39, Bahnhofstrasse, where it still stands today. She and Dmitri did, furthermore, occupy adjoining suites at Paris's elegant Hôtel Le Meurice during this time, paid for entirely by Chanel, just as the report indicates. We also know that by the early 1920s, Dmitri had made common cause with members of Germany's National Socialist party, including Hitler himself, drawn to them by their shared interest in defeating the Bolshevik Revolution. What's more, Chanel's passport for this period shows that she traveled to both Zurich and Berlin, most likely accompanying Dmitri. The accuracy of all other information in this document lends credence to the charge that the "Tchannen" sisters engaged in wartime work for Germany (although the "sister" in question might be Chanel's aunt Adrienne).

During World War I, Coco divided her time largely among Deauville, Biarritz, and Paris, often in the company of Boy Capel. Capel would never have abetted or encouraged any treacherous activity on Chanel's part. But Boy was also an inconstant presence in her life, abandoning her for long stretches while he pursued his business interests, as well as his other romantic conquests. We don't know why Chanel might have worked for the Germans in those early years of her career. Perhaps she sought to undermine Boy's diplomatic war efforts, as revenge for his philandering? We do know that, during the Great War, when Coco was in her thirties, she was already more than influential enough to invite the interest of a foreign power looking to infiltrate the upper echelons of French society. And she already had a long history of feathering her own nest with whatever opportunity fate offered.

More than twenty years later fate provided another opportunity for Chanel to try her hand at espionage, and in this case, the documentation is overwhelming and irrefutable. As so often happened, seismic political events filtered into her life via a lover—in this case, the Nazi officer Baron Hans Günther Von Dincklage, aka "Spatz."

The divorced Dincklage was tall, blond, athletic, and handsome— a former professional tennis player according to Chanel; a polo player according to other accounts. In 1940, he was forty-four, thirteen years younger than Chanel (although he likely believed her to be ten years younger than she was—a lie supported by the passport she'd doctored, and her own youthful looks). Descended of a noble German family on his father's side and of an English mother, he was courtly, polished, and flirtatious. An accomplished polyglot, he spoke German, French, Spanish, and English fluently, and was apparently irresistible to women, with a long string of broken hearts in his wake. (Several accounts hint that he was especially adept in the bedroom.) According to Charles-Roux, Dincklage owed his curious sobriquet—Spatz, or "Sparrow"—to his extreme grace of manner—he was as light as a bird. Any inquiries about Dincklage usually drew from Coco the same two responses: "He was not German; his mother was English," and/or "When a woman my age is lucky enough to find a lover, she can hardly ask to examine his passport!"

Official biographies of Chanel continue to repeat—as does the Maison Chanel—that Mademoiselle had simply enjoyed the company of a dashing younger man and was completely unaware of his occupation. Some sources, including Gabrielle Palasse-Labrunie, claim that Coco had met Spatz twenty years before the war, in England, which is possible. Equally possible is that they had met in Paris, where Spatz had frequented elite social salons, or in the South of France, where he lived in the first half of the 1930s. He had gone to the Riviera to do more than play tennis.

Dincklage had begun his career as a lieutenant in the German cavalry, fighting with other noblemen on the Russian front during World War I. He later joined the Freikorps, a paramilitary group of war veteran officers from whose ranks later emerged many leaders of the Nazi SA (Sturmabteilung) and SS (Schutzstaffel), including Reinhard Heydrich and Heinrich Himmler. Composed largely of extreme right-wing anticommunists, the Freikorps was responsible, in 1919, for the murder of one of Germany's most famous antiwar activists and Marxist thinkers, Rosa Luxemburg, a leader of the Communist Party of Germany. Some sources suggest that Dincklage took part in that assassination. Other evidence points to his possible involvement in the 1934 joint assassinations of King Alexander of Yugoslavia and French foreign minister Louis Barthou.

Dincklage spent much of his long career as German agent number

8680F operating out of France (although also in Tunisia). In the early 1930s, Hans and his part-Jewish wife, Baroness Maximiliane von Dincklage, née von Schoenebeck (known as "Catsy"), lived largely on the Côte d'Azur, in Sanary-sur-Mer—a town with a substantial expatriate German colony. There they posed as a wealthy German wine merchant and his wife, while setting up a spy network to penetrate French naval secrets at the Toulon base nearby. Well-liked and charming, the couple socialized with the beau monde and recruited potential spies from among the French population.

In 1935, Germany passed the infamous Nuremberg Laws, which deprived Jews of citizenship and prohibited marriage between "Germans" (meaning Aryans) and Jews. Just three months prior to the enactment of the laws, and after fifteen years of marriage, Spatz divorced his wife. Although born into an aristocratic and very wealthy family, Maximiliane was now branded a racially undesirable Jew and, as such, posed a serious threat to her husband's career. Waiting until the last moment before the laws would take effect, the "sparrow" had flown lightly away in the nick of time. Despite this, Catsy and Spatz remained on friendly terms.

Shortly after Dincklage's divorce, French authorities exposed his identity as a Gestapo agent and a much-bruited article about him appeared in the journal *Le Vendémiaire* on September 4, 1935. His cover blown, Spatz fled and went into hiding in Switzerland. Catsy was less fortunate and was soon arrested as a foreign agent and interned in a French prison camp. In November 1939, the Swiss police picked Dincklage up in Bern and invited him to leave the country, which he did. He had kept himself out of prison but not out of the news. That same year, 1939, a right-wing journalist, Paul Allard, published a quickly high-profile book, *When Hitler Spies on France,* which named Dincklage as an agent of the Reich.

Somehow, Allard procured classified German documents consisting of Dincklage's correspondence with his superiors in Berlin. Most of Dincklage's reports reproduced in Allard's book concern themselves with appealing to "French taste" and "personality." Allard found Dincklage perceptive and an excellent judge of character, and deemed his reports "models of psychological tactics...masterpieces of the genre." He quoted large sections of them, showcasing Dincklage's advice from the field on how best to win the hearts of French citizens:

> My many society friends in France have allowed me to form an ever-growing group of French sympathizers, which will allow me, I believe, to do my best in the tasks entrusted to me.... Our influence will only spread slowly, and we will not see...immediate results. I ask you for articles in the major French newspapers about the "bourgeois life" of the SS. It would be good to include photographs showing, for example, [Nazi officers] doing their marketing, to prove with this that the S.A. [officer] is not a savage, but a citizen.

Unsurprisingly, given his famous romantic prowess, Dincklage had thought about how best to target French women: "I ask you once again for articles about...the German woman. They must be written in an accessible style...in French aimed at French women...articles likely to arouse the interest of the lady of the house in her German sister."

Rue de Rivoli during the occupation

By 1940, then, most French citizens who paid attention to current events would have heard something of the German spy and society hobnobber Hans von Dincklage—and that certainly includes the very well informed and socially connected Coco Chanel.

None of this mattered when Spatz returned to Paris, ostensibly as an attaché working in textile production for the war. The city now belonged to him and his compatriots. In addition to the Ritz, nearly every major public structure boasted a swastika flag: the Eiffel Tower, the Garnier Opera House, and the stone arches lining the rue de Rivoli, where Misia and JoJo Sert still lived.

In June 1942, a German officer approaches a young man and asks him, "Excuse me, sir, but where is the Place de l'Etoile?" The young man points to his left lapel.

—PATRICK MODIANO, *LA PLACE DE L'ETOILE*

"Le Juif et la France" (The Jew and France) poster for an exhibition devoted to "proving" how Jews had corrupted France

In September 1940 the so-called Jewish laws took effect, barring Jews from public office or other influential positions and forbidding them even to use public telephones. Thousands of Jewish businesses were seized; Jewish-owned art and property were repossessed, and, ultimately, nearly half of France's Jewish population was deported to Nazi death camps.

In March 1942, the Reich required all Jews in occupied France (including more than eighty thousand Parisians) to register with the police and identify themselves publicly by sewing to all their outer clothing a gold Star of David emblazoned with the word *Juif.* The "Jewish badge," as it was known, did not indicate a religious truth so much as a presumed "racial" one. Jewish-born poet Max Jacob, for example, Cocteau's and Picasso's close friend, had converted to Catholicism more than thirty years earlier, but was required to wear one.

Two Parisian women wearing Jewish stars, 1942

Oddly, the Jewish badge and the Nazi swastika had much in common, or, rather, they were like mirror images of each other. Each was a graphic symbol that created instant political identity: one denoting undesirability, the other, superiority. Historian Régis Meyran has written of the Nazis' "fantasy of total identification," the belief that individuals can be grouped into vast and simplistic categories, which then justify any atrocity. This concept of "total identification" owes something to the world of fashion and its marketing—an arena in which the Nazis showed particular savvy. Nazis understood how to dress and label things, concepts, and people—how to carve the world up into inner and outer sanctums with brutal clarity.

Chanel had always craved the inner sanctum, the right connections, access to the highest power. And she keenly understood how to conjure the same desire in others. Even Nazi soldiers, it turned out, were susceptible to Chanel's talismanic double-C logo. German military men lined up daily at the Cambon boutique to buy perfume for their wives and girlfriends, drawn at least as much by the packaging as by the fragrance. When perfume supplies ran out, the soldiers took to stealing the empty display bottles off store shelves. Their uniforms might have boasted swastikas, but that did not stop the German solders in their pursuit of something—anything—stamped with that *other* mystical symbol: the double-C insignia.

Just across from the boutique, Coco was ensconced in her new quarters at the Ritz. With a swastika adorning the hotel, living within its walls meant she had acceded yet again to the innermost sanctum, the new corridors of power. While Nazi soldiers eagerly sought out her label, Chanel showed equal eagerness to drape herself—metaphorically—with their swastika flag.

The story of Chanel's involvement with the Reich is dense and complicated, and she virtually never spoke of it. Although she lived in what amounted to a Gestapo barracks, Coco later insisted she never saw the Germans. But records exist documenting her surprisingly extensive connection to the Third Reich, and those who encountered her (including some who have kept silent until now) confirm Coco's active support of many aspects of Nazi policy.

We do not know how Chanel's affair with Dincklage began. She might have first approached Spatz on her own, in an effort to liberate André from the German prison camp. Or she might have been introduced by someone—perhaps Pierre Laval. In either case, Coco and Spatz fell into a romance quickly at the Ritz, and to friends it seemed as though Spatz spent all his free time in Chanel's suite at the hotel or across the street in the small apartment she kept above the Cambon studio.

The couple tried to be discreet. They socialized mostly at private dinner parties and avoided public places, especially upscale watering holes. Often, they stayed at home. Chanel had a small piano installed in her apartment, and she returned to practicing the light songs she had learned long ago. Dincklage would listen to her sing in her reedy voice. Spatz never wore his uniform, only elegant civilian clothes, and he and Chanel spoke in English when out in public. Their social circle included Misia Sert, her husband, JoJo (who was conducting a love affair with Marie-Ursel Stohrer, wife of Hitler's Spanish ambassador), Jean Cocteau, Serge Lifar, Paul Morand (now a Vichy ambassador), and Maurice Sachs (who was concealing his Jewish identity and working as an undercover Gestapo agent). They dined often at the home of Vichy's ambassador to occupied Paris, Fernand de Brinon—considered one of the architects of French collaboration. Other frequent dinner companions included the German ambassador to Vichy, Otto Abetz, and his French wife, Suzanne, née de Bruyker, and the many French aristocrats who had spent part of the later 1930s at costume balls, decked out as court figures from eighteenth-century France. Now the occupation seemed to be re-creating in real life the pre-democratic era they craved. Like royalty of the good old days, these die-hard noblemen and women could enjoy outrageous privilege, though misery lay just outside the gates.

Without her business to run, Chanel had little to do apart from these *mondanités,* but by late summer of 1941 she had found a new form of employment. Hal Vaughan and others contend that Chanel's work for the German secret service represented an exchange for the release of André Palasse, and this was likely the original impetus for her activities. But

Chanel went beyond the call of family duty in her efforts for the Nazis, probably because she believed in their cause.

Before she could be sent out on any missions, Chanel needed the approval of the higher-ups in Berlin. Dincklage served as the initial intermediary between her and Reich officials. In early 1941, Spatz traveled from Paris to Berlin, accompanied by a French aristocrat who had already turned into a Gestapo agent: the Baron Louis de Vaufreland (also known by his alias, "Piscatory"), who had been recruited by another German agent based in Paris, Hermann Niebuhr. In Berlin, Hitler and Goebbels personally met with Dincklage—proof that Spatz's star was on the rise. Whatever else they discussed, we know that Chanel's future role clearly figured on the agenda, since upon his return to Paris, Dincklage arranged a meeting between his travel companion, Vaufreland, and Coco.

Vaufreland explained to Chanel how much he could help her, provided she cooperated with him. He could have André Palasse liberated from prison camp and possibly also help Chanel wrest control of her perfume enterprise away from the Jewish Wertheimer family. Chanel must have evinced significant interest, since she next met with Vaufreland's superior, Hermann Niebuhr, who confirmed that André's release could be arranged. All Coco had to do was travel to Madrid to obtain information valuable for Germany. Having received her official agent number from the Nazis, F-7124, and her code name, Westminster (in honor of the duke, still her closest ally in the pro-German branch of the royal family), Chanel was ready.

The name "Niebuhr" (also rendered as "Nieuburg" and "Neubauer") appears several times in Chanel's police file. Document #5.455 RG 16.640 contains information obtained from the German secret service, Abwehr. It details an expedition to Madrid taken in late summer of 1941 by Chanel in the company of Baron Louis Vaufreland. On August 5, the two traveled by evening train across the border and on to Madrid. Abwehr officials in Paris had cabled ahead to ensure their safe and comfortable passage, and so they encountered no trouble at any checkpoint. Later, as Chanel settled into her luxurious suite at the Madrid Ritz (Vaufreland stayed elsewhere), she probably did not pause to consider what Apel-les Fenosa might have thought of her five-star visit to Franco's Spain, courtesy of the Third Reich. (Living out part of the war in Toulouse, Fenosa—unlike many of his fellow artists—refused to participate in any exhibition in France during its years of occupation.)

Records of Chanel's activities during her first trip to Spain no longer exist. Little documentation remains of this summer in Madrid apart from a few details surrounding a social visit made to a British diplomat's home—during which Coco made certain to mention her intimate friends Winston Churchill and the Duke of Westminster. But Chanel must have accomplished something, for by the end of 1941, André—still ill with tuberculosis—was back in France. "My joy was beyond words," said Chanel to Malcolm Muggeridge about André's release. "It was as though the bells you heard chiming throughout Paris were all pealing together within me."

But that joy was qualified; the war brought suffering on a global scale, and decline and death seemed to be stalking members of Chanel's closest circle. Misia, now seventy, was emaciated and nearly blind. André was home, but greatly diminished by four years in a POW camp. He lived in Paris while undergoing extended treatment for his TB—paid for by Coco. (He recovered slowly and imperfectly and was never again able to work full-time.) The winter of 1941 brought news that Grand Duke Dmitri was very ill with tuberculosis, for which he'd undergone two lung surgeries in Switzerland. The handsome young noble that Chanel had once whisked off to a Mediterranean tryst was succumbing to the same illness now ravaging André.

Faced now with this gradual shrinking of life, living through war yet again, Chanel must have felt some of her famous control slipping away. She had always responded to adversity by plunging more deeply into her work. In 1941, though, even "work" as she knew it had changed drastically. Having renounced—ostensibly forever—her career in couture, Coco had restricted her professional life to her stake in the lucrative Parfums Chanel and her new affiliation with the Nazis. Perhaps this is why those two elements came together to form her next project: to wrest control of the perfume business from the Wertheimer family using the Aryanization, or "Jewish," laws.

Chanel had long felt ill used by the Wertheimers, despite how wealthy she'd grown with their help. Her partnership with them dated to 1924, when they'd signed the deal that handed the reins of the company to the brothers and a 10 percent profit share to Coco. Over time, the original star fragrance, Chanel No. 5—later joined by No. 22, Gardenia, Bois des Iles, and Cuir de Russie—had become the best-selling perfume in the world. But even as the Chanel brand skyrocketed, Coco's proportionate share of perfume sales remained the same. To Coco, from within her protective bubble of the Ritz, this looked like the one war atrocity she needed to address.

Like many wealthy Jewish families, the Wertheimers had fled Paris before the Germans arrived, moving to New York City and setting up an independent subsidiary, Chanel, Inc. They built a perfume factory across the Hudson River in Hoboken, New Jersey, where they resumed manufacturing Chanel No. 5, selling it in the United States and in Europe at American PXs. This new corporation was earning large profits, but Chanel had no legal right to any of it. Furthermore, Coco, assuming that the Wertheimers could not procure the necessary flower essences in the States, feared that the new, rival version of the perfume was an inferior fake, consisting of ersatz ingredients. The idea that the Wertheimers were not respecting the sacred No. 5 formula, or that they were fabricating a lesser perfume under her name, enraged her still more. She wanted revenge.

Chanel called upon the aid Vaufreland had offered with the Wertheimer matter. Vaufreland sent her to Dr. Kurt Blanke, who dealt with the seizure of Jewish property under Aryanization laws in Paris. But the Wertheimers' foresight and business savvy proved greater even than the determination of the Third Reich.

The Wertheimers had long foreseen the peril Hitler posed to European Jews and had taken steps to protect their fortune. In late 1939, shortly before fleeing to the United States, they entered into business with a non-Jewish Frenchman named Félix Amiot, an aviation engineer who built and supplied bombers to France. Amiot received a payment of 50 million francs from the Wertheimers, and shortly thereafter, he apparently took control of Parfums Chanel. Via this arrangement, the business would remain in Aryan hands during the war, which protected it from precisely the plot that Chanel hatched.

Chanel tried to fight the Wertheimers, claiming that they, not Amiot, were still the owners of the business—which would render it susceptible to seizure by the Nazis. She was confident that her Nazi connections would win the day for her. As Patrick Buisson has written, "In a France subjected to the whims of the occupier, it seemed impossible that Mademoiselle would lose this unequal battle." But the Wertheimers were far from the underdogs here. As with all matters during World War II, battle lines among different factions could become blurry, and the Wertheimers had their own connections. In the eyes of the law, and thanks in part to some well-placed bribes to German officials and antedated stock transfers, Félix Amiot was now the legal owner of Parfums Chanel. The company was indeed safe from Nazi seizure. As one of the Wertheimers' lawyers later put it: "During the rest of the war, Mademoiselle Chanel had no further say in the matter." For good measure, the Wertheimers had also appointed to their board of directors Baron Robert de Nexon and several other prominent Gentile figureheads.

The addition of Robert de Nexon represented a Wertheimer coup de grâce. Not only was Nexon a member of Chanel's extended family by marriage—first cousin of Adrienne's husband—he was also a very old friend of Etienne Balsan's and someone Chanel had known in her long-ago past as a kept woman.

How had the Jewish Wertheimers managed to find their own German connection to bribe for this subterfuge? The answer is that, during World War II, Félix Amiot was an equal opportunity supplier of aircraft and armaments, transacting with Germany as well as with France. Put simply, the Wertheimers saved their company *from* the Nazis by paying off a French Nazi collaborator. Amiot had worked closely with Hermann Göring, commander in chief of the Luftwaffe, the German air force. No case better exemplifies this war's murky politics, the way it blurred the line between treason and patriotism, and, most striking of all, the power of money to short-circuit (sometimes) the Nazi machine.

The Wertheimers' new company, Chanel, Inc., continued to flourish in the United States, largely through its sales of No. 5, which, contrary to Coco's assumptions, still featured the finest floral essences from France and the all-important synthetic aldehydes. Proving yet again their astonishing talents for both business and backstage machinations, the Wertheimers had dispatched their own corporate spy to Grasse, France, to procure the jasmine, ylang-ylang, and other flowers needed for Chanel No. 5.

Through their daring, the Wertheimers had not only successfully escaped France with lives and fortune intact; they established a new, even more profitable American company.

As the New York division of Chanel, Inc., grew, Chanel's percentage of profits from sales of products bearing her name went ever downward. The Wertheimers owed 10 percent of their U.S. profits to Parfums Chanel, and 10 percent of *that* figure—hence only 1 percent total of U.S. proceeds—then went to Coco. Never did she acknowledge the implications of having tried to invoke the heinous Nazi Aryanization laws against her own business partners. That she had been outsmarted by these Jewish brothers in a financial matter could only have intensified her belief in Jewish avarice.

In his memoirs, Jacques Chazot reported a dinner party at which Coco indulged her animus against Jews, addressing herself to a female dining companion:

> [She said], "My dear, do you know why Jews love and understand painting so much better than they do music?" The woman was mutely astonished, a general silence fell. Chanel returned to her subject, sure of her dramatic effect, "Paintings sell better." She then continued along in the same vein: "Don't forget either that there are three categories: the Jews, who are my friends that I adore and I have proof of this! The Israelites—whom you must be very wary of and avoid like the plague, and the Yids, who must be exterminated altogether."

The last remark was hardly original. For many years, French anti-Semites had nuanced their bigotry with these famous "three categories" of Jews. In Chanel's case, the first, "acceptable" category would normally have included the Wertheimers, but at the time she spoke these words, even they would have fallen into one of the other, lesser categories.

Verbal anti-Semitism was not unusual among Chanel's set, but Coco tended to step over the line of genteel bigotry. More disturbing, though, are several instances of Coco's public behavior.

The dapper Prince Jean-Louis de Faucigny-Lucinge could trace his family back to the eleventh century. His wife, the angularly beautiful Liliane, or "Baba" (née Erlanger, of partially Jewish descent), had worked as a fashion model and was dressed by some of Paris's top couturiers, including Chanel. Together, the couple were glamorous fixtures of the Paris beau monde of the 1930s and '40s, and known for their lavish parties. Even their impeccable social status and wealth could not fully protect the Faucignys, though. The prince's autobiography, *Un gentilhomme cosmopolite (A Cosmopolitan Gentleman)*, contains a story hinting strongly that Chanel's idle dinner party anti-Semitism led, at least once, to real-world—and potentially horrific—action.

Faucigny recalled a Riviera evening during the war when he and his wife encountered their friends Stanislao Lepri, the Italian consul for Monaco, and Leonor Fini, the noted surrealist painter, who had just returned from a dinner at La Pausa. Visibly agitated, Lepri and Fini reported that throughout dinner Chanel had indulged in particularly vituperative remarks about the Jews and the war, claiming that "France had only gotten what it deserved"—a sentiment commonly voiced by the extreme Right, implying that the country's moral decline and passivity toward Jews and Communists had brought on its troubles. Lepri and Fini noted Spatz's presence at this dinner, referring to him as Chanel's "German lover," and added that even he was alarmed and "tried to moderate" her tone somewhat. Spatz was too polished an SS officer to permit himself such vulgarities.

Faucigny's story then takes a darker turn: The following day, his wife, Princess Baba Faucigny, and Chanel happened to cross paths in the lobby of Monte Carlo's Hôtel de Paris. Coco moved toward Baba to kiss her in greeting, but Baba, still deeply upset by what she'd heard of Chanel's anti-Semitic outburst of the previous night, turned sharply away, refusing the kiss. Soon after thus publicly snubbing Chanel, Princess Faucigny found herself hunted by the Nazis. She was obliged to flee her home and go into hiding for the remainder of the war. She successfully evaded the Nazis but died unexpectedly in 1945 at the age of forty-three. In his book, Prince Faucigny—who had once been a good friend of Chanel's—makes plain that he suspected a causal relation between his wife's encounter with Chanel and the Nazis' subsequent targeting of Baba:

> Gabrielle Chanel was not a woman to forget this sort of affront. But could her anger drive her to denouncing someone to the Nazis? The hypocritical ideology of the era, its moralism, chauvinism, anti-Semitism … encouraged Chanel to give these dangerous speeches. Where is the border between a sentence spoken into the air and a specific denunciation? A group of dubious people loitered around her, including a certain Vaufreland, the wayward son of a good family, a notorious collaborator believed to be a Gestapo informant. It is not impossible that Chanel … spoke imprudently about my wife [to Vaufreland] and that it was this parasite who drew the attention of the German agents to this supposed Jewish woman.

Faucigny never knew for sure whether Chanel had denounced his wife to Vaufreland, and he makes a grave accusation here. Near the end of his life, in 1990, Faucigny spoke to a journalist who asked him about Chanel. His response was a blend of anger tempered with psychological insight: "She was such a nasty woman, a horrible woman! And she conducted herself very badly during the war.… I recognize that she was very generous. She [was] a strange mixture of a woman, nasty, envious.… She had every kind of success, everything one could imagine, and yet she was very ill at ease [*mal dans sa peau*], keeping a sort of resentment and bitterness toward people, which came from her difficult youth."

Faucigny touches on an important quality in Coco—her inability to feel satisfied, her craving always for more—particularly for more security and more proof that she had arrived, that she was an insider. Paris during the war would only have aggravated this tendency in Chanel, since insiders and outsiders were so sharply delineated. By allying herself with the Germans, who looked for a time like the future masters of the universe, Chanel demonstrated that she had attained the ultimate status—she had entered the sanctum of the Reich.

This insatiable hunger for belonging may explain a story about Chanel's behavior during these years, which has never come to light before now. In 2011, James Palmer, a London-based attorney whose company, Mondex, specializes in the restitution of Jewish property stolen by the Nazis, contacted me with information about Chanel's surprising intervention in the life of a French-Jewish family during the war. Palmer put me in touch with two sisters, the late Viviane Forrester of Paris, eighty-six at the time of our conversation—a highly respected journalist and author—and Lady Christiane Françoise Swaythling, called "Ninette," then eighty-three, of London. Born into a German-Jewish family, the sisters bore the maiden name of "Dreyfus." Interviewed separately, they told exactly the same story.

Viviane and Ninette were young girls when the Germans invaded Paris and upended their comfortable life. They stayed in the city as long as they could, but eventually the family was forced to separate and go into hiding in the South of France to avoid arrest and deportation to the camps. In addition to constant fear, the sisters—like so many of their compatriots—endured terrible hunger, which Forrester described movingly in her memoir, Ce Soir, après la guerre (Tonight, after the war): "I was so hungry during that time that my teeth seemed to ache with the lack. In this time of rationing, to chew, to swallow—became an obsession. Ninette and I used to draw pictures for each other of our favorite foods."

The women's immediate family managed to survive, but not all their relatives were so fortunate. Their beloved Tante Louise, sister of their father, Edgar Dreyfus, was driven out of her home and into temporary

Viviane and Christiane
Dreyfus during their
family's exile from Paris
to Marseille to evade
deportation

quarters. Eventually she died in a tiny maid's room in exile. Another aunt, Tante Alice, was deported to a concentration camp where she, too, died. Coco Chanel played an odd role in the wartime story of the Dreyfuses. She stepped into their life through the front door of Aunt Louise's deserted apartment.

According to Forrester and Swaythling, the family's longtime chauffeur, Joseph Thorr, had been obliged to quit their employ once the occupation left them unable to pay his salary. With a heavy heart (and only after first asking M. Dreyfus's forgiveness and blessing), Thorr accepted a new job: driving Nazi officers around Paris. Still very attached to the Dreyfus family, the chauffeur later visited them in the South of France, bringing stories of his new job—including an anecdote regarding Chanel, which Forrester recounted—obliquely—in her memoir:

> I remember some of the stories Joseph told us. He talked about having driven a number of Nazi officials...including I believe, Goering.... He also confirmed that he had driven "that *couturière* whom Madame used to visit so often, in the rue Cambon." And that he had taken her to "rue Dumont-d'Urville to the home of

Monsieur's sister." To Aunt Louise's house! Where she no longer lived, having been forced out. "It's a very small world," Joseph remarked.... Aunt Louise, driven from her own home, now lived in a maid's room in the same neighborhood, who knows who put her there. She had become, like her sister Alice, powerless.... "And Madame Louise? Madame Alice? Do you know anything about them?" [we would ask]. Joseph knew nothing.

In personal conversations, the sisters filled in the details. Viviane Forrester confirmed that the *couturière* in question was, of course, Coco Chanel, who had dressed their fashionable mother for years. Whenever Madame Dreyfus had needed to go for a dress fitting, Joseph had driven her. He had seen Chanel herself many times.

But exactly what was the purpose of Chanel's visit to the deserted apartment? According to Swaythling, Thorr—who was of German extraction and spoke the language fluently—"was working for a German officer who was Chanel's lover. They drove to my father's sister's house, and the officer said, 'Here's a pencil and paper, go and make a list and you'll have it. It's yours.' She did it. She came out with a list, and that was it."

Chanel had been invited to make out a "shopping list"—to browse through Aunt Louise's home and choose anything she'd like to keep for herself from among the wealthy woman's furniture, artwork, and rugs. The German officer, presumably Dincklage, was allowing Coco to participate in the very-common Nazi practice of pillaging Jewish homes. (Hal Vaughan reported that Coco's attorney René de Chambrun decorated his home with valuable paintings stolen by the Nazis.) According to Joseph Thorr, in the Dreyfus sisters' recollections, Chanel selected a few pieces of antique furniture and arranged with her lover and Thorr to have the items delivered to her. She did not inquire about the owners of the apartment or why they no longer needed their possessions. She did not question (at least in front of Thorr) the implications of Gestapo agents entering someone's home on a whim. "I think she was very, very greedy," said Lady Swaythling.

Greed played a part in this transaction, certainly, but not greed for material things. An expedition of this kind would have appealed to Coco's hunger for unlimited access to the world. She could break into a stranger's home and traipse through it like a conquering Visigoth. Or rather, like the Visigoth's pampered girlfriend. At nearly sixty, she found herself once more receiving lavish gifts from a lover—the sexual glamour of the escapade no doubt enhancing the rush of implied military and political power. And as always in cases where Chanel sought to cement a bond with a man, the collateral damage was worth it to her.

In recounting this story, Lady Swaythling expressed her understandable sorrow and bitterness. She lamented the light punishments meted out to many collaborators: "People forgive everything." Our conversation ended, though, with a curious twist. Lady Swaythling returned to the subject of Chanel fashion. "I would never buy anything of hers," she declared, then added, "I was given a [Chanel] scarf and a bag, once. I gave the bag away, but I kept the scarf." With a brief laugh she explained that she would try to hide the double-C logo sometimes, but she did wear the scarf. "I liked it too much.... She had a chic. She made fashion very comfortable."

Lady Swaythling's laugh contained a trace of embarrassment, but it needn't have. That she kept and wore that scarf proves only that she belongs to her times and culture. Virtually no one, it seems, remains immune to the lure of the Chanel brand, which continues to triumph over any associations, no matter how personal or tragic. Like her mother before her, Lady Swaythling appreciates Chanel style, despite the grim story of Coco, Aunt Louise, and the apartment on rue Dumont-d'Urville, in the exclusive sixteenth arrondissement, just off the Place de l'Etoile.

As the Dreyfus family story demonstrates, Chanel was deeply ensconced within the Nazi inner circle, and before the war's end, she would be drawn one last time into active collaboration with the Germans—this time engaging in a complicated, far-fetched attempt to broker a separate peace between England and Germany.

The mission, known as "Modellhut" ("couture" or "model hat," in recognition of Chanel's profession), has been public knowledge since 1985 when Marcel Haedrich broke the story. Since then, new information has brought to light Chanel's access to high-level Axis officials—and her blithe disregard for the possible consequences of her actions.

From late 1942 and into the early months of 1943, the tide was turning against Germany. At the Casablanca Conference of January 1943, the Allies mapped out their strategy for winning the war and demanding unconditional surrender from the Germans. Allied forces had made great advances in North Africa, and General de Gaulle's Free French fighters were growing more powerful. As Germany lost ground, the Nazi hierarchy succumbed increasingly to internal feuds and conspiracies, including plots against Hitler's life and attempts to circumvent his authority. Operation Modellhut was one such attempt.

The goal of Modellhut was to bring the war to a close on German terms but behind Hitler's back, via an arrangement between Heinrich Himmler (Reich minister of the interior, director of the SS, and overseer of all extermination camps) and Winston Churchill. Chanel would serve as the prime intermediary, approaching her old friend Churchill on behalf of the Reich. The impetus behind this scheme remains unclear.

Some think that the mission originated with Major Walter Schellenberg, Himmler's chief of intelligence and Dincklage's direct superior. Others believe it all began with Chanel herself, who might have approached Captain Theodor Momm on her own with the plan. Hal Vaughan sees Modellhut as a joint venture, cooked up by Dincklage and Chanel out of fear for their own futures should Germany lose the war. According to Vaughan, Theodor Momm intended to transfer Dincklage to Istanbul, a dreadful prospect for Chanel, who "would have moved heaven and earth to keep Spatz close to her." Whatever its origins, we know that Modellhut involved Momm, Schellenberg, Dincklage, and Chanel.

After several failed attempts, Dincklage secured permission for Chanel's intervention in Modellhut in the fall of 1943 and was instructed to take Coco to Berlin to meet with Walter Schellenberg. In December 1943, Coco and Spatz went to Berlin and met with Schellenberg, who two years later offered details of their discussions as part of his Nuremberg testimony. According to the trial transcripts, Chanel assured Schellenberg that she could persuade her close friend Churchill to accept peace on Germany's terms. She proposed traveling to Madrid, where she would first meet with Sir Samuel Hoare, the British ambassador to Spain, whom she intended to persuade to grant her an audience with Churchill. Hoare was another old friend of Coco's and known for his pro-German sympathies. Churchill was expected to pass through Madrid in December after meeting with Stalin and Roosevelt at the Tehran Conference in Iran.

Adding more confusion to this already-baroque scheme, Chanel placed a curious condition on her offer: She insisted that her former style muse, Vera Bate Lombardi—whom she had not seen in four years— accompany her on the mission. Vera had taken Italian citizenship and was living in Rome with her husband, Captain Alberto Lombardi, a high-ranking member of the National Fascist Party. This last demand dismayed Theodor Momm—how could he trust an Englishwoman with matters of Germany's national interest? He had expected Chanel to go with Spatz.

Chanel had her reasons. She told the Germans that she needed Vera along simply to keep her company. In truth, Vera was being included for a far more important reason: It was she, not Coco, who enjoyed a real friendship with Churchill. Chanel planned to exploit Vera's high-level connections while taking credit for the mission herself.

After much intrigue, which included the Nazis' kidnapping Vera, briefly imprisoning her in a Roman jail, and then forcibly transporting her to Chanel's Ritz apartment, Coco got her wish. Vera Bate Lombardi would accompany Chanel to Madrid. Although Coco offered Vera a cover story for their trip (they were scouting locations for a new Chanel boutique in Spain, Chanel insisted), Vera, of course, knew better. She recognized that she was now part of a Nazi plan and would need to play along. In late December 1943, Coco and Vera, accompanied by Spatz, left for Spain, traveling by train on Nazi-issued passes.

They crossed the border at Hendaye where Spatz met with Schellenberg's representative, Captain Walter Kutschmann. Although he was undercover, posing as a border police commissioner, Kutschmann was, in reality, a chief in Himmler's spy service, and one of the war's most brutal criminals. Kutschmann "deliver[ed] a large sum of money to Chanel in Madrid," according to British agent Hans Sommer in his Nuremberg testimony.

Despite all the machinations, once Chanel and Vera Bate Lombardi arrived in Spain, Modellhut unraveled quickly. As soon as the women checked into the Madrid Ritz, Chanel sneaked off to the British Embassy to explain her plan to Ambassador Hoare. Churchill, she told him, would surely want to talk to her. She did not mention Vera Bate. Hoare quickly dashed her hopes: Churchill could see no one and was not coming to Madrid. He was ill with pneumonia and was remaining in Tunisia under medical supervision.

Unbeknownst to Chanel as she sat in Ambassador Hoare's office, Vera was also in the building—talking to a different British official. No sooner had Chanel left the Ritz than Vera had rushed off to the embassy, as well, seconds behind Coco. Schellenberg's testimony described what happened: "[Vera] denounced all and sundry [meaning, essentially, Chanel] as a German agent to the British authorities.... In view of this obvious failure, contact was immediately dropped with Chanel and Lombardi." This was true, but the mission did not end that neatly, especially not in Vera's case.

British Embassy officials found it suspicious that Coco and Vera had come separately to them, telling such divergent stories. They decided to keep both women under surveillance. Chanel was a world-famous and highly esteemed designer; could she be a spy? And if Coco was a spy, couldn't Vera be one, too? The embassy refused Vera's request for repatriation and assigned a British diplomat, Brian Wallace (whose code name was "Ramon"), to "assist" both women during their stay in Madrid.

Fearing she'd been betrayed by Vera, Coco dashed off a letter to

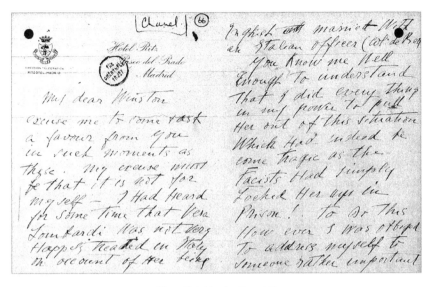

Chanel's letter to Churchill

Churchill attempting to exonerate herself. Written mostly in (surprisingly good) English, the letter tries to explain away her Nazi connections as the regrettable result of the exigencies of war. Coco carefully insists on her tender concern for Vera, and on how hard she had tried to "pull [Vera] out of this situation."

If Churchill ever saw Chanel's note, it was long after she wrote it, and no known response to it exists. Suffering from cardiac complications of pneumonia, he was believed near death at this time, and clearly his staff in London had no intention of perturbing the prime minister.

Despite the suspicion surrounding her, no one stopped Chanel from leaving Spain and returning directly to Paris in early January 1944. But Vera Bate Lombardi was held in Madrid for nearly a year, despite her repeated attempts to prevail upon her Allied connections for help.

Despite several inquiries into her case by Churchill himself, Vera remained tainted for months by her association with Chanel and Modellhut. Her luck finally changed after a top-secret document from Churchill's office noted that "Madame Chanel deliberately exaggerated her social importance in order to give the Germans the impression that she (Madame Lombardi) might be useful to them." This document cleared Vera's name sufficiently to permit her return to Rome, on January 4, 1945. She died only a few years later, in 1948, having never spoken to Chanel again.

Lost amid the secret letters, abductions, and betrayals is the presumed facilitator of the entire Modellhut mission: Spatz, who seems to melt away from the story. It is likely that he left Spain quickly as soon as the Gestapo learned of Vera's betrayal. But Dincklage had never been the ringleader of Modellhut—it had always been Schellenberg's project.

Chanel apparently returned one last time to Berlin after the anticlimactic end of Modellhut. She needed to account for the project's failure to Schellenberg. We don't know what they said to each other, but implausibly, inevitably, Chanel appears to have seduced Walter Schellenberg at some point in this process. True, she was twenty-seven years his senior, but Coco still enjoyed the attentions of younger men, including, of course, the forty-something Spatz.

Walter Schellenberg

Schellenberg's determination and high seriousness would have seemed to Coco a welcome change from Dincklage and his feckless, lightweight charm. And as Dincklage's direct superior, Schellenberg represented an advance in Chanel's access to power. She was betraying Spatz with his boss.

Besides, Chanel and Schellenberg were similar in some ways. They both had grand, even cinematic views of their own lives and power. They were both elegant and highly aware of fashion; they were both keenly conscious of their social status. Schellenberg had once confessed, after all, to joining the SS out of a desire to meet the "right sort" of people and wear the chic black uniform.

Thrown together by Modellhut, Chanel and Schellenberg would have discovered a shared appreciation for the thrilling rush of high-stakes espionage. Chanel had come out of retirement to play Mata Hari at the age of sixty, and Schellenberg, tall and handsome at thirty-three, not only resembled a spy from a Hollywood movie; he fancied himself one, too. Schellenberg "enjoyed to the full...the spurious glamour of...the secret agent," Alan Bullock writes in his introduction to Schellenberg's memoir, *The Labyrinth*. As evidence, Bullock points to the boastful enthusiasm in Schellenberg's descriptions of his office at the German Foreign Intelligence Ministry:

Microphones were everywhere, hidden in the walls, under the desk, even in one of the lamps.... My desk was like a small fortress. Two automatic guns were built into it, which could spray the whole room with bullets. All I had to do in an emergency was to press a button and both guns would fire simultaneously.... Whenever I was on missions abroad I was under standing orders to have an artificial tooth inserted which contained enough poison to kill me within thirty seconds if I were captured. To make doubly sure, I wore a signet ring in which, under a large blue stone, a gold capsule was hidden containing cyanide.

.   .   .

Perhaps he showed off these menacing toys to Coco. She would have enjoyed the poison signet ring.

Details of their affair are few but convincing. The most reliable witness is Reinhard Spitzy, who knew Schellenberg well. Argentine journalist Uki Goñi graciously shared with me the original transcript of his 1998 interview with Spitzy—who had fled to Argentina to evade capture—that uncovered the relationship. Amid exculpatory remarks and disavowal, the outlines of the Schellenberg-Chanel affair emerge.

> Schellenberg was a great man and a gentleman. It was unfair to attack him because he suffered a lot, dying from liver cancer probably brought on by despair after the war. He had a great love story with the great French fashion designer Coco Chanel. It was a fantastic romantic love story of Schellenberg with her. They both wanted to stop the war seeking contact with that idiot Churchill, the most guilty of them all. But Churchill refused.... Then Schellenberg fell ill with liver cancer, and Coco behaved wonderfully. She paid for his operation in Turin, then Schellenberg went to Rome and Coco Chanel placed her private plane at his disposal. Then he died and Coco Chanel paid for the burial. She behaved like a great lady. It was a fantastic and amusing story because Schellenberg and Coco Chanel were two very different people. But there were lots of stories like that in the war, where love and decency overcame all the terrible deeds of the shameless politicians.

Spitzy is not the only source claiming an affair between Schellenberg and Chanel. In 2011, I uncovered another source of information on the relationship. The Countess Isabella von Fechtmann, née Isabel Suarez Vacani, is descended from a well-connected Spanish family that had close ties to the highest levels of the Nazi Party. Currently preparing a biography of Reinhard Heydrich, chief of security for the SS, Countess Isabella claims to have learned of Schellenberg's affair with Chanel through several close family members and friends. She stopped just short of confirming definitively her main source, but left little doubt that it was her great-aunt Nini de Montiam, a Spanish actress and one of Franco's spies:

> One of [Chanel's] great loves was Walter Schellenberg.... He was handsome and loved women!...A tall, handsome Aryan...[he] was tender.... Dincklage was not as important to her as Schellenberg. I can't reveal my sources. But I will say that as a young girl... my aunt Nini Montiam (Isabel Montilla Contessa del Ampudia... she was Spanish) was Franco's best spy. She was my great aunt; her mother and my grandmother were first cousins. She knew the Windsors, she knew everyone.

Oblique as it seems, the reference is legitimate. Nini de Montiam had ties to high-ranking military officials, as well as to members of the British royal family, including the Windsors, who were famously frequent visitors to Franco's Spain and to Berlin. In his memoir, Schellenberg gives a detailed account of his own involvement with the Windsors, when he participated in an abortive attempt by Hitler to "kidnap" the duke, which really meant bribing him with more than 50 million Swiss francs to leave England and work for German interests.

No other details exist of Chanel's dalliance with Schellenberg. From Berlin she returned to Paris—and Spatz—without incident and never breathed a word about Modellhut to anyone (save one veiled reference in her interview with Muggeridge, who, as a former MI6 agent, had likely some prior knowledge of the affair). The entire episode evaporated nearly magically. Apart from Schellenberg's Nuremberg testimony, no other public discussion of Modellhut appeared for decades. No witness ever mentioned seeing the world-famous Coco Chanel in Madrid or Berlin during the months of the operation. No trace remained, despite all the people who surely dealt with Chanel—the countless hotel clerks, waiters, railway employees, and diplomats whose paths she crossed along the way. From this we may infer that Chanel had actually acquired some competence as a spy, learning to keep a low profile and avoid recognition, or that she knew how, if threatened with exposure, to use her fortune to smooth over a tight situation.

In retrospect, Modellhut seems at best a rather harebrained scheme. Why would high-ranking Nazi officials Walter Schellenberg and Theodor Momm entrust an espionage mission to a French fashion designer and one of her girlfriends? Why would these officers invest months in a plan that depended upon Coco Chanel to circumvent Hitler and save Germany? The answer is a combination of the true panic and desperation setting in among the Germans and the surprisingly influential position that Chanel had attained by the 1940s. However far-fetched it was, the fact that Chanel was permitted—even encouraged—to participate in Modellhut—under the code name "Westminster" no less—testifies to how closely she had allied herself with the pro-Nazi branch of the British royal family, many of whose members participated in other Anglo-German strategies to end the war on German terms.

On Coco's side, her willingness to serve as a paid intermediary between the Reich and England demonstrates how the war exaggerated some aspects of her personality. For someone as invested as she was in being a national icon, Modellhut would have seemed irresistible. Chanel surely assumed that the mission had the potential to turn her into a global heroine—the woman who helped end a world war. Success in this domain would have proved definitively that Chanel's influence—as commander of her own style regiment, as "dictator of fashion"—rivaled that of any actual military leader. Chanel disregarded the inconvenient fact that the mission's success would have annexed France permanently to the Third Reich. Patriotism had always meant less to her than power.

Chanel passed the remainder of the war in a more subdued fashion. She did no work save for a brief stint collaborating once more with Cocteau in 1944 on costumes for a revival of *Antigone*. She socialized with her usual set, seeing Lifar nearly every day. Although she had earlier served as "godmother" to French troops overseas, sending care packages, for example, to Jean Marais's unit, Coco held herself—with rare exceptions—aloof from the horrors of war.

In the winter of 1944, Jean Cocteau circulated a petition to release

Max Jacob, ill with pneumonia and in Nazi custody, but Chanel—who'd known Jacob well—refused to sign (as did, more shockingly, Picasso). Cocteau continued to work tirelessly for several weeks on Jacob's behalf. Finally, on March 16, 1944, the German Embassy announced that Jacob would be released from Drancy, the French internment facility for Jews en route to German concentration camps. The announcement came too late. Jacob, the devout Catholic convert, had died of pneumonia on March 5.

The occupation of Paris started to disintegrate when the Allied forces stormed the Normandy beach on D-Day, June 6, 1944. As the Allied armies drew nearer to Paris, Chanel and her *collabo* set began to lose their footing. No longer certain of being on the winning side, and growing anxious about reprisals, Chanel decided a preemptive strike was in order. She tried to switch sides and ally herself with the now-likely victors of the war.

She called the one member of the French Resistance she knew she could trust—Pierre Reverdy—and informed him of the whereabouts of a known Nazi collaborator, her own former houseguest and traveling companion, Baron Louis de Vaufreland. Reverdy acted on the tip and quickly arrested Vaufreland, who'd been hiding in the apartment of a French aristocrat, Count Jean-René de Gaigneron. Vaufreland was sent to prison and later to the camp at Drancy. He served six years. Chanel had sent one of her own accomplices to prison in an attempt to save herself.

But Vaufreland's arrest did not keep the French government from noticing Chanel's wartime activities. In mid-August 1944, as twenty thousand German soldiers and French fascists attempted to flee Paris in advance of the liberating Allied forces, Spatz begged Coco to leave with him, but she refused. In late August, two agents of the FFI (Forces françaises de l'intérieur; Coco called them the "Fifis") knocked on the door at the Ritz at eight o'clock in the morning to arrest her on suspicion of collaboration. Chanel, wearing only a light dressing gown and sandals, immediately followed them out silently, hoping that her regal dignity would keep them from searching the premises and finding the less-dignified Serge Lifar, who was hiding in her walk-in closet.

"Coco behaved like a queen, like Marie Antoinette being led to the scaffold," Lifar told an interviewer, recalling this set's fondness for pre-revolutionary France. Similarly, Theodor Momm likened Chanel's post-war stoicism to that of another famous French heroine of the Right: "Her heroic silence permits us to think that a drop of Joan of Arc's blood coursed through her veins." Momm keenly grasped Chanel's psychology. A remark of that sort, had it been made directly to Coco, would surely have propelled her into almost any folly.

Most suspected collaborators endured rough and humiliating treatment at the hands of the "*épuration*" or "purification" committees. Women were sometimes stripped naked, shaved bald, and paraded through Paris. But Chanel suffered no such indignities. She later complained that the worst part for her was the boorish behavior of the Fifis, who dared to use the informal pronoun *tu* to the doorman at the Ritz as they escorted her through the lobby. She was fingerprinted and released after only a few

Female collaborator taunted by members of the French Resistance, August 1944

hours of interrogation and permitted to return to the hotel. "They made me laugh," she scoffed about her interrogators.

Speculation abounds about how Chanel managed to avoid being indicted and tried as a spy, but she most likely owed her gentle treatment to intervention from her British connections, especially Churchill. Gabrielle Palasse-Labrunie recalls Chanel saying "Churchill had me freed." If that is so, the prime minister may have been concerned about the compromising material Chanel could divulge about certain members of the British royal family and their Nazi sympathies, prime among them Bendor and the Duke and Duchess of Windsor.

Mark Weitzman of the Simon Wiesenthal Center believes that Churchill feared specifically that Chanel would expose the details surrounding the Paris apartment kept by the Duke of Windsor during the war and paid for by Churchill himself. Keeping such a residence in enemy-occupied territory was an infraction of British law, which therefore meant the prime minister had served as accessory to a treasonous crime on behalf of the royal family.

While Chanel had landed on her feet, she knew better than to press her luck. She understood that she needed to disappear in order to avoid further investigation into her case, so she packed her bags to leave. But before she left town Coco engineered one last publicity move: In the window of her Cambon boutique she placed a sign offering free bottles of Chanel No. 5 to all American GIs. Just as the Germans had before them, the American soldiers happily queued up to nab these treasures for their sweethearts back home.

Chanel might have been trying to buy time with this perfume giveaway. Who would dare disturb the peace or safety of a benevolent French fashion icon making such a goodwill gesture? Or she might simply have wanted the Americans' last memory of her to be favorable. In either case, it was a brilliant decision. Despite the chaos all around her, Coco enjoyed two uninterrupted weeks in Paris to arrange her move.

In September 1944, Coco piled her luggage into her Mercedes and had her chauffeur drive her to Lausanne, Switzerland. She would remain there, in self-imposed exile, for eight years.

. . .

Although Chanel escaped all charges, the matter of her collaboration did resurface briefly after the war. In May 1946, Judge Roger Serre of Paris initiated a suit against Chanel on the charge of espionage and she was required to appear before the court. When confronted with the facts of Modellhut, as well as her attempt to use her Nazi connections to take Parfums Chanel away from the Wertheimers, Chanel simply denied everything. When pressed, she offered only transparent lies and excuses, insisting, for example, that she knew no one in the German military at all. The court was well aware of her untruths: "The answers Mlle Chanel gave to this court were deceptive," reads the transcript. But nothing ever happened. Chanel returned to Switzerland, unscathed. No press coverage of these proceedings exists.

For decades, no other accounts of Modellhut appeared anywhere else, either—a historical omission due at least partially to Chanel's liberal pocketbook. When Walter Schellenberg, suffering with terminal liver cancer, received a compassionate early release from prison in 1950, Coco paid all of his medical expenses. She continued to support Schellenberg (and his wife, Irene) for the remaining years of his life, which he spent in exile in Italy. When he died at the age of forty-two, Chanel paid all his funeral expenses. "Madame Chanel offered us financial assistance in our difficult situation and it was thanks to her that we were able to spend a few more months together," wrote Frau Schellenberg in a letter to Theodor Momm. After her husband's death, Irene published his memoir, *The Labyrinth*. It contained no reference whatsoever to Operation Modellhut or to Coco Chanel.

CHAPTER TWELVE

SHOWING THEM

CHANEL RETURNS

They said that I was old-fashioned, that I was no longer of the age. Inwardly, I was smiling, and I thought, "I will show them."

—COCO CHANEL

W hen Chanel left Paris for Switzerland in 1944, she disappeared from the world's stage as suddenly and completely as she had burst upon it thirty years earlier—entering a long and idle stretch of her life about which she later said little. Her official retirement from fashion had already begun, of course, five years earlier, in 1939, when she shuttered her couture house at the onset of World War II. For nearly fifteen years thereafter, from the age of fifty-six, Coco Chanel essentially vanished, abandoning both the practice of fashion and the high-profile life that had come with it. Voluntarily taking refuge in Switzerland, Chanel managed—with the likely help of well-placed friends—a graceful escape from the political repercussions that might otherwise have befallen her.

Coco melted into the expatriate circles of Switzerland, a discreet community of people who needed a quiet place to bide their time while waiting for the heat of the world's displeasure to cool. She bought a stucco three-story hillside villa in Lausanne, which she furnished in her usual style, outfitting it with Coromandel screens, gilt mirrors, Louis XV antiques, and lacquered furniture. But she spent the bulk of her time elsewhere, keeping the house largely to retain the tax privileges of Swiss home ownership.

In Switzerland, as in Paris, Coco preferred the life of a luxury hotel dweller. Although she had owned a number of very grand houses, hotels had always appealed deeply to Coco. Some advantages were obvious: Hotels were easy, offering round-the-clock staff, meals at any hour, and dining rooms and lounges for entertaining friends. Most important, hotels meant freedom, lightness, and the option of packing up and leaving on a whim—a benefit that still resonated for the girl once locked away in an orphanage. "Luxury is liberty.... I never settle in anywhere," Chanel told Claude Delay. "I've chosen liberty." And so she "camped out," as she put it, traveling among the wealthy resort towns of St. Moritz, Klosters, Lausanne, and Davos, taking up residence at her favorite hotels, the Lausanne Palace, the Central, or the Royal in Lausanne, the Beau-Rivage in Ouchy on Lake Geneva. Since she was not officially barred from France, she sometimes traveled back to spend time at La Pausa in Roquebrune. Occasionally, she made brief, discreet visits to Paris.

Coco was not alone, exactly. Until around 1950, Spatz, who'd escaped prosecution, remained her frequent and sometimes live-in companion. Even after he left her (apparently to paint nudes on an island off the coast of Spain), Dincklage continued to enjoy Chanel's largesse, supported by the generous lifetime pension paid to him through the trust Coco established after the war, known as COGA (for "Coco" and "Gabrielle").

Coco also took good care of André, who, still suffering from tuberculosis, could no longer work. Chanel made sure that Palasse and his family could stay near her, buying for them a series of three homes in Switzerland to which she would sometimes repair as well: a house in the wine region of Lavaux, an apartment in nearby Chexbres, and a villa in the woods of Lutry, in the canton of Vaud. No other member of the Chanel family benefited from such largesse, however. While all of Coco's siblings had died, a new generation of Chanel children had since been born into poverty.

Chanel with Spatz in
Switzerland, c. 1950

Yvan, the son of Coco's brother Alphonse, died, leaving behind several orphaned children. These children, Coco's great-nieces and nephews, were entrusted to the care of two of their aunts, Alphonse's daughters
Gabrielle and Antoinette—named, obviously, for the elder Chanel sisters. The children's situation offered an eerie parallel to the fictional tale
Coco had so often told of her own early life: orphans being raised by two
aunts. If she saw the similarity, it failed to move her. Chanel did nothing
to intervene or help. Aside from Aunt Adrienne, now the Baroness
Nexon, André Palasse, and his daughters, Chanel's extended family held
no interest for her. She had permanently severed all ties.

The companions of her years in exile included a few of her intimates
from France, among them writer and former Vichy official Paul Morand
and his wife, Hélène, whose reasons for fleeing to Switzerland were much
the same as Chanel's. Their financial situations, though, differed dramat-

ically. Chanel had always kept a large portion of her fortune in Swiss banks and elsewhere abroad. She remained independently wealthy. But Morand found himself nearly penniless, the French government having frozen his book royalties and revoked his civil service status. Always a generous friend, Chanel invited the couple to be her guests at the Badrutt's Palace Hotel in St. Moritz. There, in the winter of 1946, Coco and Paul sat down for the series of interviews that Morand hoped to turn into a biography of Chanel.

For some reason the transcripts of their conversations languished for nearly thirty years. In 1976, they finally appeared as *L'Allure de Chanel*— the oddly compelling book in which Morand cedes his own voice to Coco's, reproducing uncritically even her most far-fetched fabrications. Perhaps it was Morand's way of thanking Chanel for the friendship she offered during his period of disgrace. Morand later returned to France and reestablished his career.

Her old friend Luchino Visconti visited Coco in Switzerland, as did Misia Sert, who was deteriorating badly, falling ever more deeply into her morphine dependence. Misia came to Switzerland not only to see Coco but also to buy drugs. The 1945 death of JoJo Sert had taken a devastating toll on her. Despite their having divorced in 1927, when Jojo left Misia for the much-younger Roussy, he had always remained the love of her life. In the summer of 1950, Chanel was vacationing at Roquebrune and Misia came to visit. Then, on October 15, 1950, shortly after Misia's return to Paris, she died, at the age of seventy-eight. Upon hearing the news, Coco jetted immediately up to Paris.

Arriving at Misia's home, she insisted on time alone with her old friend, to prepare her for burial. Coco, the child who'd sought companionship amid the dead in cemeteries, felt completely at ease working with Misia's lifeless body.

Several hours passed; a crowd gathered outside the closed doors in the drawing room. Finally, the doors opened and Chanel emerged from the bedroom; the assembled guests peered past her and gasped. Lying in state upon her Louis XIV bed, which was covered with white flowers, Misia had traveled fifty years back in time. Resplendent in white lace, her hair loosely gathered in a chignon, her face smooth, Misia was once more the rosy young woman in Renoir's portrait. Coco had selected her dress and fitted it to her perfectly; she had colored and curled her hair, and applied her makeup; she'd even manicured her nails. "She did this out of affection—so that no one would see Misia looking ugly," says Gabrielle Palasse-Labrunie. But that wasn't all. Chanel had also performed a bit of makeshift plastic surgery, expertly pulling back Misia's jowls and loose facial skin, which she secured—like so much excess fabric—behind her ears with dressmaker's pins—a designerly gesture of mingled love and cruelty perfectly summing up the thirty-year friendship of two eternal *cocottes*. Unsurprisingly, Chanel sometimes told friends she might have liked to be a surgeon.

With Misia's death, Chanel lost an important part of herself. Misia had been her constant companion, the keeper of all her secrets. Misia had witnessed and nurtured Chanel's ascent in the world. Spatz's departure in 1950 had essentially marked the end of Chanel's romantic life with men. Now, with Misia's death, not only was Chanel without a lover; she had lost her best friend.

Misia's was not the only significant death among Chanel's closest circle during this time. The years between 1946 and 1956 claimed the lives of a startling number of Chanel's former lovers, friends, and associates. Vera Bate died in 1948, and Walter Schellenberg in 1952. Bendor, the Duke of Westminster, whom Chanel had hoped to marry and with whom she had always remained in close contact, died of a heart attack in 1953, at the age of seventy-four. Despite many attempts, Bendor had not produced a male heir. At the time of his death, he was married to his third wife, thirty-eight-year-old Anne Sullivan. Just one year later, in 1954, a traffic accident in Rio de Janeiro took the life of another major figure from Chanel's past: Etienne Balsan, the man who had moved her out of a rented room and into a castle. He, too, had remained in touch with Coco, perhaps because of his possible connection to André Palasse. It was Etienne who had introduced Coco to Boy Capel, and the fact that the two men died in such similar fashion must have seemed to her a particularly cruel irony. Finally, in 1956, Coco's softer, look-alike aunt, boon companion, and stalwart helpmeet of the early days, the lovely Adrienne Chanel de Nexon, died at seventy-four. Adrienne and Coco had been the only Chanel women of their generation to escape to a better life. When Adrienne died, so did Coco's last link to the past. Adrienne had been the only other person who truly knew how shockingly far Coco had come. The loss was "devastating," according to Gabrielle Palasse-Labrunie.

These years also ravaged the group of artists who had been attached to Cocteau and the Ballets Russes, all of whom Chanel knew well. Stage designer Christian Bérard, who had drawn fashion illustrations for Chanel, died in 1949, as did actor-producer Charles Dullin, who had starred in and produced Cocteau's 1922 *Antigone*. Vaslav Nijinsky, his genius long dimmed by schizophrenia, died in a London clinic in 1950; and composer Arthur Honegger, who had scored Cocteau's 1927 opera version of *Antigone*, passed away in 1955. The year 1954 saw the demise of writer Colette, with whom Coco had always had a respectful, if cantankerous, friendship. "I like Colette…but she was wrong to let herself get fat," Coco told Paul Morand. "Two sausages would have been enough for her, two dozen, that's just affectation," she added, channeling Oscar Wilde. Nevertheless, when apprised of Colette's decline, Chanel made a trip to the writer's bedside to pay her last respects. The brightest lights of her generation were dimming at an alarming rate.

Little in Switzerland could compensate for the loss of Chanel's community of artists. Her new Swiss social circle featured instead a variety of people who provided Coco with some kind of professional service. She spent a lot of time, for example, with her Swiss dentist, Dr. Felix Vallotton, and his wife. Asked by a reporter about her choice to live in Switzerland, Chanel proffered the improbable explanation "I'm here for the altitude and for my dentist. My dentist is the best in the world." Other companions included a rheumatologist, Dr. Theo de Preux (Chanel suffered increasingly from arthritis, especially in her hands), an ophthalmologist named Professor Steig, and a number of attorneys who managed her affairs. Such friendships—the kind sustained with individuals who are also on the payroll—are often the last resort of rich or famous people who mistrust the intentions of new acquaintances.

Chanel lived comfortably and well in Switzerland but was, in a sense, as unmoored as she had been during the dark days in Aubazine. She drifted about in a country not her own, without benefit of work, love, or most of her old friends. She lived under a cloud of political opprobrium.

In response, Coco retreated into herself. She took long walks in the woods, her chauffeur following slowly behind in her car until she was ready to be driven back to town. She spent long mornings in bed, reading novels or fashion magazines, just as she had some fifty years earlier when she lived as one of Etienne Balsan's stable of beauties. As during those years at Château de Royallieu, Coco endured a period of reclusive idleness. She had used the Royallieu years to divest herself of her peasant background, to draw a veil over her impoverished childhood, and to learn the ropes of upper-class life. Then, once she'd moved on, Coco had similarly drawn a veil over *that* period, willing out of existence her years as a rich man's courtesan. Now, all these decades later, Chanel once more took a time-out from the world, seeking to expunge yet another chapter from the book of her life: her affiliation with the Nazis.

For most women in their sixties, especially one tainted by suspicions of treason, such a period of inactivity would qualify not as a hiatus, but as permanent retirement. Yet as Chanel would later say, "Never was I in retirement in my heart." She had long experience in reinventing herself, and idleness had never suited her. Age didn't suit her, either, and so, somehow, she held it at bay, even as most others of her generation faded away.

When Michel Déon—a young journalist at the time—visited Chanel in Switzerland, he had plans of writing her biography. As was her wont, Coco would scotch these plans. But years later, in his memoirs, Déon beautifully evoked the woman he'd encountered in Switzerland, a still-vital Coco incongruously trapped among the decrepit, slightly louche crowd whiling away the time on Lake Geneva:

The Beau Rivage was an antediluvian hideout inhabited by troglodytes.... Mlle Chanel stood out for her energy and health. Her appearance at lunch, after her long preparations, was a theatrical entrance. If she had been forgotten by the crowd, her image, her allure, revived the memories of the Beau Rivage clientele: thirty years ago these dowagers in black lace, jowls held up with stiff velvet ribbons, had been dressed by her, skirts at the knee, and those old gentlemen, hobbling on their ebony canes, had once opened charge accounts for their girlfriends at Chanel.... And so when she crossed the lobby ... a murmur accompanied her. A fairy was passing, and they relived their youths, from Deauville circa 1910 to the last years between the wars.

As Déon makes clear, Chanel retained her iconic power in Switzerland. She had dropped off the world's radar screen, but in her limited new

Chanel with Maggie van Zuylen and Serge Lifar, mid-1950s

context, she still stage-managed her persona. And despite the grim collection of matrons around her, she found at least one vital new friend
with whom she could laugh and let loose a little: the Baroness Margarita
Nametalla van Zuylen, the Egyptian-born wife of the Belgian diplomat
Baron Egmont van Zuylen.

The baroness, or Maggie, as she was known, was a big, squarish, commanding woman who enjoyed a good time. Friends remember hearing
Maggie and Coco singing old cabaret songs together. According to a
source close to the Van Zuylen family, the baroness was an "obsessive
card player"—much like many other dowagers inhabiting Swiss hotels at
that time. Coco later disparaged the idle ladies of Switzerland and their
card games, but she and Maggie had something more important uniting
them: They had both taken a quantum leap from their social origins.

Although Van Zuylen was a titled noblewoman when Chanel met her,
the baroness came from a modest background. Born to Syrian parents in
Alexandria, she had received little education and spoke French with a
heavy Egyptian accent, rolling her Rs conspicuously. Some say that before she married the baron, she had made a living selling violets—a common flower girl. According to a friend of the family, Maggie seemed to
have read only one book in her entire life—a popular biography of
Cleopatra. Her interest in that ancient queen makes sense, for like Coco
(and Cleo), Maggie possessed an instinctive allure that drew rich and
powerful men to her. In this domain, she had even surpassed Coco,
achieving the one goal that had always eluded Chanel: marrying an aristocrat. It hadn't been easy. Maggie's marriage to Egmont had so enraged
the baron's father that he disinherited his son. For three years the young
couple cobbled together a livelihood, relying partly on Maggie's poker
winnings to sustain themselves. Eventually, the elder Baron Van Zuylen
relented—he, too, had fallen prey to Maggie's charm.

Coco would have felt very comfortable with Maggie van Zuylen—
a woman described as "unself-conscious, unconventional, and a
breath of fresh air in a pretty stodgy environment." Their closeness,

moreover, seems to have included erotic intimacy as well. Chanel and those close to her always denied rumors of her lesbianism. "Can you imagine? An old garlic clove like me?" Coco exclaimed when asked about women lovers. (Her word choice may have been telling though, since "garlic clove" was actually Belle Epoque French slang for "lesbian." Was this a private joke? An unconscious slip?) Gabrielle Palasse-Labrunie and Lilou Marquand similarly refuse to acknowledge Coco's likely bisexuality, Marquand dismissing the whole issue as "ridiculous." Renowned fashion photographer Willy Rizzo claimed never to have believed the "lesbian stories." And the Van Zuylen family never acknowledged the nature of Maggie's friendship with Coco.

Still, evidence points to the two women having slept together on many occasions. In his *Journal inutile,* Paul Morand wrote of Maggie and Coco "shar[ing] their private life" in Switzerland. "They didn't hide when I found them in bed together," he recalled. Whatever the exact details of their intimacy, the two women were deeply attached to each other. For most of the last years of her life, Coco wore nearly every day a gift that Maggie had given her: a gold Egyptian medallion on a very long chain, engraved in Arabic with the "Verse of the Throne," from the Koran. Sometimes, Coco would tuck the medallion into her jacket pocket, allowing only the chain of the necklace to show—as if to make a little secret of the pendant's poetry, held close to her body and hidden away.

Maggie was likely not Chanel's only female lover. As a young woman, Coco may have been tempted to experimentation while living among the demimondaines of Royallieu, women such as Emilienne d'Alençon and Liane de Pougy. At times, Misia Sert, too, may have been her lover. And with the advance of age, intimacy with women came to replace the many love affairs with men that had so defined Chanel's private world.

Not surprisingly, Chanel's earliest foray back into business took the form of an angry swipe at the Wertheimer family. New developments in their relationship left her enraged once more. Coco was well aware that, during the war, the Wertheimers had dramatically increased their fortune by selling Chanel perfumes in American PX stores around the globe. After the war, the Wertheimers returned to Paris, where they took back the shares of their company they had transferred to Félix Amiot. Amiot parted with the stock gladly, for, in exchange, the Wertheimers had arranged to shield him from prosecution by the French government for having sold his warplanes to the Germans.

Pierre Wertheimer visited Chanel in Switzerland and informed her of her share of the wartime perfume royalties. Since the Wertheimers had sold their shares of the original company, Parfums Chanel, and formed a new company, Chanel, Inc., Coco would receive only $15,000— a derisory fraction of what she knew to be millions of dollars. Even while siphoning off the lion's share of the profits, moreover, the Wertheimers continued to capitalize heavily on the Chanel brand. In advertisements and even their Christmas cards, they had been linking the Chanel and Les Parfumeries Bourjois company logos, exploiting her famous name without her permission. Coco planned her revenge.

Her first salvo came in 1946. Working with a small Swiss perfumer (whom she never identified), Coco invented a new perfume. Christening it "Mademoiselle Chanel," she began stocking it for sale in her rue Cambon boutique, the one venue she had kept open through the war. The Wertheimers reacted swiftly. Invoking their legal ownership of all Chanel perfume formulas, they had "Mademoiselle Chanel" perfume declared a counterfeit, and procured a court order to have all bottles seized from the shelves. Chanel had been angling for a fight, and she got one. When the court deferred ruling for two months, Chanel consulted her attorney René de Chambrun to help her devise a response.

Chambrun advised Coco to settle out of court peacefully and maintain her low profile—for her sake, as well as his own. As the son-in-law and former staunch defender of Pierre Laval—who was executed for treason—Chambrun was not inclined to mount a public legal battle. Chanel did not care. She countersued the Wertheimers for back royalties and damages, and for producing "inferior products" under her label. But her plan did not stop there. With Chambrun's guidance, she found a loophole to exploit in her contract with Chanel, Inc.

Although enjoined from *selling* perfumes independently of her agreement with the Wertheimers, Chanel remained legally free to create her
own perfumes and merely *give them away* to her friends. From Switzerland, she began work on a new series of beautiful fragrances, all of which
smelled strikingly like Chanel's top-selling perfumes—even better, according to some. They all bore the same names as Chanel's top perfumes,
with one small change: the addition of the word "Mademoiselle" in each.
Her new product line consisted of Mademoiselle Chanel No. 5, Mademoiselle Cuir de Russie, and Mademoiselle Bois des Isles. Chanel carefully observed the letter of the law. All the formulas differed slightly from
those of the original perfumes; all bottles and labels had been redesigned.

It remained only to give away these lovely new scents to a few
"friends": American industrialist Bernard Gimbel, owner of Gimbel's department store and Saks Fifth Avenue; Stanley Marcus, owner of Neiman Marcus; and, for good measure, Samuel Goldwyn, Hollywood
mogul. It was a brilliant move. The American perfume market had proved
a gold mine for the Wertheimers during their years in New York. Now
Coco was threatening their dominance in the United States by launching
(or threatening to launch) a line of rival products—all bearing the magical "Chanel" name that still carried so much resonance for retailers.
Coco herself might not have had the right to sell these perfumes directly,
but nothing could stop Mr. Gimbel and Mr. Marcus from buying the
formulas and then selling the new perfumes in their big American stores,
bypassing the Wertheimers completely.

Coco did not have to wait long to see the results of her gambit. The
American department store moguls had barely unwrapped the enchanting new perfumes when Pierre Wertheimer got wind of it and rushed up
to Lausanne, ready to settle out of court. After long negotiations in Switzerland between the Wertheimers and Chanel's lawyers, Coco obtained
a new and far more lucrative agreement. She was granted the right to
produce and sell her own perfumes, so long as she never used the number
"5" in their labeling; she would receive a onetime settlement of back
royalties totaling $326,000 (the equivalent of approximately $3.2 million
in 2013); and, most crucially, beginning in May 1947 (the year Paul Wert-

heimer died), Pierre agreed to pay Coco royalties of 2 percent annually on worldwide perfume sales, a figure worth at least $1 million a year (or close to $10 million in 2013). Toasting the deal with Chambrun, Chanel declared, "Now, I am rich."

Pierre Wertheimer had good reasons for yielding to Coco. However tumultuous and even vicious their relationship might seem from the outside, they remained curiously bound together, their fates inextricably linked. The last thing Pierre needed was the bad publicity of a drawn-out legal battle with Mademoiselle Chanel, the woman whose name guaranteed his family fortune. A lawsuit, furthermore, would only remind the public of the all-too-recent scandal surrounding Chanel's wartime activities. Pierre recognized that nothing good could come of fighting Coco. But more than logical business reasons motivated Pierre. Underneath it all, he maintained a powerful and abiding admiration—a kind of grudging love—for Chanel and her talents. The two were locked in a highly charged, passionate agon distinguished by bitter feuds followed by reconciliation and renewed collaboration—a pattern that lent weight to the persistent rumors of a long-ago love affair between them.

"Mademoiselle Chanel and Pierre Wertheimer were a mythic couple," observed Marie-Louise de Clermont-Tonnerre, director of international public relations for the Maison Chanel. In the years directly following the war, the ongoing saga of the Chanel-Wertheimer partnership reached mythic levels of intrigue: The Jewish billionaires who'd escaped from the Nazis with help from a profiteer who trafficked with Nazis now acceded to the financial demands of the woman who'd tried to seize their business using Nazi policies.

Although she'd won the right to manufacture her own line of perfumes in Switzerland, Chanel never exercised it. Those rival scents she'd created and sent to America had served their main purpose as a negotiating lever with the Wertheimers. Once she'd hammered out a new agreement with them, Coco seemed to put aside thoughts of returning to an active role in the perfume business. Fashion, however, was another matter. Coco had never stopped caring about design, and from her perch in Switzerland, she watched the Paris couture with increasing frustration.

Fashion, in her eyes, had taken a dramatically wrong turn since the Liberation. Before the war, a number of significant women designers had shared the limelight with the men. Names such as Madeleine Vionnet, Jeanne Lanvin, and Elsa Schiaparelli had appeared regularly alongside Chanel in the fashion press. By the late 1940s, though, most of the women had faded away, ceding the stage to new, male designers such as Jacques Fath, Pierre Balmain, and, most importantly, Christian Dior—who opened his own studio after working for designer Lucien Lelong. The names were new but the clothes emerging from their ateliers had a distinctively retro feel, featuring oversize skirts stiffened with crinolines, corsets, hemlines nearly to the floor, and big hats. The clothes were sculptural and beautiful but often impractical and cumbersome to wear. Paris couture had done an abrupt about-face, replacing the sleek, emancipatory aesthetic of modernism with an exaggeratedly hourglass silhouette.

The vision of womanhood appearing on runways now conjured an earlier, more traditional femininity, "suggesting something like a Gibson girl or whatever...grandmother should have worn," as one journalist wrote. French fashion had fallen into a nostalgic Belle Epoque dream, as if trying to turn the clock back to those last innocent years before anyone had ever imagined a world war. Leading this march backward in time was Christian Dior, a man whose mild manner and bland appearance contrasted ironically with the over-the-top glamour of his designs.

On February 12, 1947, Christian Dior's first collection hit the Paris fashion scene like a supernova. His ultrafeminine dresses, sculpted of dozens of yards of expensive fabric, bade a defiant farewell to wartime sacrifice and compromise, seeming to herald both a return to traditional femininity and a renewed prosperity. "Monsieur Dior, you've given us such a New Look!" exclaimed fashion editor Carmel Snow in the pages of *Harper's Bazaar,* and the term stuck. The style that harked back so clearly to an earlier century would be known, paradoxically, as "the New Look."

Fashion insiders were entranced. "A Paris sensation," hailed American *Vogue.* The Dior woman was a curvy ship of state, sailing into rooms with a voluminous, swaying skirt held out and away from the body by wide, padded hips—which seemed even wider in contrast with the corseted waist, cinched down to doll-like proportions. Dior dubbed these upside-down flower-skirted pieces his "corolla line." Boned and shaped bodices (the flowers' "stems") held the torso firmly in place, and stiff, padded bras molded breasts into conical shapes, positioned high on the chest. Some dresses even featured drapery in the back that created an unmistakable "bustle effect." High heels and wide-brimmed hats (or the precariously tilted, tricornered "tambourin" hats) completed the look. Encased in so much armature and fabric, a woman's body did not actively lend shape to a Dior dress (as it would in a Chanel) so much as passively surrender to it—held captive to a new, hyperbolic femininity.

It was an oddly perfect metaphor for the period of regression in women's political freedom in the years just following the Liberation. Although France had finally, in 1945, granted women the right to vote and run for public office, the onset of the Fourth Republic saw the rise of another natalist, or pro-birth, movement, which came with the usual lineup of conservative policies designed to encourage the "feminine mission" of baby making. The war had sent thousands of women venturing into the workplace for the first time, but upon the return of the soldiers, women were being encouraged to quit their jobs, exchange their trousers for dresses, and return home to the urgent task of rebuilding the French population, to producing the "twelve million beautiful babies in ten years" explicitly requested by General de Gaulle in a speech on March 5, 1945.

Along with its celebration of traditional femininity (with special emphasis on what are sometimes called "childbearing hips"), Dior also bolstered the country's ailing fashion industry, which had foundered badly since the war. His extravagant New Look proclaimed the return of French luxury and plenty.

Dior came naturally to his affluent aesthetic. He had been born into wealth (albeit of inelegant provenance—a family fertilizer business), and enjoyed the support of a rich patron, Marcel Boussac, whose investment in the Maison Dior was estimated at 700 million francs.

An elaborate
Dior gown, 1950

The fashion press welcomed Dior as the couture messiah. He became a household name virtually overnight, the artist of the new female silhouette. Carmel Snow could not resist a military analogy: "Dior saved Paris as Paris was saved in the Battle of the Marne."

But though his look was copied at every price point, and bargain shoppers at Ohrbach's could snap up "petal" dresses for $8.95, the truth was, Dior's style resisted low-rent imitation. Unlike Chanel, Dior relied on large quantities of expensive fabric, which demanded time-consuming stitchery. Attempts to achieve similar results using inexpensive synthetics sewn by machine resulted in visibly poor-quality garments. His style suited to perfection only those able to pay the highest prices, and in this, offered a compelling defense of real French haute couture, rapidly breathing new life back into the industry. Within two years, a staggering

75 percent of France's couture exports were Diors, which amounted to fully 5 percent of French export revenues overall.

The economic symbolism of his work did not escape Christian Dior. "Abundance was still too much of a novelty to reinvent an inverted snobbery of poverty," he recalled—taking a subtle swipe at Chanel. He also differed markedly with Chanel on the subject of imitations. Coco had loved to see her looks reproduced everywhere, but Dior had no patience for democracy in fashion. He strove openly to keep his couture exclusive, and in 1948, went so far as to prohibit legally the use of his name on any reproductions retailing below $69.95 for dresses, or $135 for coats (or approximately $694 and $1,260 respectively in contemporary currency). Like Chanel's long-ago love Paul Iribe, Dior subscribed to a patriotism of opulence. "In an epoch as somber as ours, luxury must be defended inch by inch," he declared.

Over the next decade, Dior produced some of couture's most gorgeous clothes. Keeping silhouette his primary focus, he drew and redrew the outline of the female figure, moving from the "corolla" look to the "Zigzag" (with a pronounced décolletage); the "Oval" (spotlighting rounded hips); the high-necked "Tulip"; and more—all of them crafted of the finest materials, tailored for maximum drama. He used jeweled beads, mink, and gold lamé. He created billowy "leg o'mutton" sleeves, vast skirts too wide to fit into taxis, and ultra-narrow "hobble skirts" (a turn-of-the-century style), which made walking nearly impossible. This opulent if impractical vision set the tone for couture, and Jacques Fath, Pierre Balmain, Cristóbal Balenciaga, and other designers produced similar visions of Cinderella glamour in the late forties and early fifties.

Dior expanded his business at an unheard-of rate. By 1957, his sales grossed more than $15 million per year (or the equivalent of $120 million today).

Of course, not everyone loved Dior. In 1948, in what soon became a famous incident, a group of angry older women dressed in pauper's rags set upon several younger women wearing Dior, literally ripping the dresses off their bodies—a staged protest against what the older women deemed a disrespectful and shocking waste of materials. With the travails of wartime still fresh in people's minds, Dior's excesses felt like a bitter slap in the face to some. Similar sentiments arose in America and Canada, where disgruntled women formed groups with names such as "the Women's Organization to War on Styles" (or WOWS), and the "League for the Prevention of Longer Skirts," in an attempt to forestall the new expensive, uncomfortable, and retrograde fashions. In California, one group of shapely *provocatrices*, dressed only in revealing swimsuits, picketed a dress shop, holding signs with slogans, including "Do we need padding?"

Chanel felt about ready to join the picket line. She could hardly believe the turn fashion had taken, how far it had strayed from her own vision. "Fashion has become a joke, the designers have forgotten there are women inside the dresses.... Clothes must have a natural shape." Asked specifically about Dior (whom she'd met when he assisted her back in 1937, on costumes for Cocteau), she exploded, "Dior? He doesn't dress women, he upholsters them!" Restless, bored, and dismayed at the work of her new Paris colleagues, Coco began thinking about the unthinkable: a return to an active designing career in Paris—a comeback.

Financial concerns played a role in her considerations—although Chanel later denied this. The latest deal with the Wertheimers had left her quite rich, but in the summer of 1953 Pierre Wertheimer came to the Hôtel Beau Rivage to announce to Coco that, for the first time in thirty years, perfume sales were lagging. While the perfume division was (and remains) the most lucrative arm of the Maison Chanel, its success had always depended partly on the reflected prestige of the couture line and Coco's personal visibility. But there had been no new Chanel fashions for fourteen years, and Chanel herself had been in exile for nearly a decade. With Coco's name fading from public consciousness, the brand was losing much of its cachet.

Coco proposed to Pierre that they market a new fragrance to revive business, but Wertheimer thought the idea too risky. When she accepted his decision without argument, Pierre assumed that Coco intended to remain permanently in retirement. Those who knew her in Switzerland assumed the same thing. They had all misread her completely.

Chanel seized this moment to act upon her growing intuition that she could do it all again—return to fashion and succeed. It wouldn't be easy. She was seventy years old, tainted by her Nazi affiliations, and had been off the cultural radar screen for fourteen years. But Coco had always flown the highest when defying expectations. Within a few days of her meeting with Pierre Wertheimer, she returned to the apartment she still kept at the Ritz.

Her new life would be sparer and more focused than ever before. Knowing she'd need money and having had her fill of "vacationing," Chanel sold her beloved villa La Pausa. The buyer was literary agent Emery Reves, whose most famous client, Winston Churchill, wound up writing much of his memoirs while relaxing at the house, which he had visited decades ago when Chanel lived there with Westminster.

Chanel next turned to her friends in America, who had been so useful in her perfume wars with the Wertheimers. She contacted powerful editor Carmel Snow and told her that she was seeking an American manufacturer to reproduce Chanel models for the United States ready-to-wear market. Coco's business instincts were still sharp. Americans were now the world's heroes, their economy was booming, and its ready-to-wear industry was growing exponentially—it was the perfect place for her re-entry into fashion. As expected, Carmel Snow responded with alacrity. On September 24, 1953, she sent a telegram to Chanel reading in part:

> Know first-class ready-to-wear manufacturer interesting in reproducing your line.... When will your collection be ready?... Happy to help you.

Chanel responded in a letter drafted with the help of lawyer René de Chambrun, in which she offered her reasons for returning:

> I got the idea it would be fun to go back to work, because work is all my life.... The current climate in Paris in which more and more women are shown collections they cannot afford is pushing me to do something completely different. One of my primary

goals is to have an American manufacturer produce a ready-to-wear line on a royalty basis. I feel that this would arouse considerable interest throughout the world. My first collection will be ready on November 1.

Contacting New York was only part of the plan. Chanel made sure that news of her proposed comeback and of her correspondence with Snow was leaked to Pierre Wertheimer, who, as Coco surely expected, wanted in immediately. In a meeting with Pierre, Chambrun, and Parfums Chanel CEO Robert de Nexon, Coco obtained a financial commitment from the Wertheimers: They agreed to back her new venture, footing 50 percent of all expenses related to her fashion launch. Pierre knew well that a successful Chanel couture collection (and subsequent American copies) would only enhance perfume sales.

In the late summer of 1953, Chanel plunged back into her working life, reopening two of the dusty, deserted workrooms on the third floor of 31 rue Cambon and renovating the still-functioning perfume boutique below. As part of her new austerity mode, she sold off the adjoining buildings on Cambon that she owned. For reinforcements, she summoned some of her former lieutenants, the women who'd helped run her empire before the war. "Come quickly," she told them, for she thought they would have no more than ten good years left to work (an underestimate, as it turned out). Lucia Boutet, known as Madame Lucie, was among the first to return to her role as *chef de cabine*. A plump woman with an authoritarian personality (and rumored to be another of Chanel's lovers), she knew how to keep things running smoothly and punctually—although some of the models found her overbearing. Madame Lucie had been Chanel's forewoman on Cambon, and, since the war, had been operating her own couture shop at 18 rue Royale. There, she and a number of former Chanel employees were continuing their mentor's tradition, turning out two-piece suits in a Chanel-esque style, as well as garments patterned after other couturiers. Madame Lucie leapt at the chance to return to Coco and closed up shop. She did not go alone. Accompanying Madame Lucie were about thirty of her employees, prime among them,

Manon Ligeour, who'd also started with Chanel, working for Coco as an apprentice in 1929, at the tender age of thirteen, and working her way up to *première*.

In 1946, when Manon had gone to work with Madame Lucie, she took with her some of the seamstresses left unemployed when Chanel had closed her doors. Now these same women agreed to work once more for the House of Chanel. Their return testified to both their personal loyalty and their trust in the durable magic of the Chanel name. "We were all greatly excited," Manon told Pierre Galante. "Mademoiselle had such guts!"

It posed no difficulty to hire middle-aged seamstresses and fitters whose careers had begun in the 1920s or '30s. Hiring runway models was another matter. Chanel needed a new crop of beautiful young women on whose bodies she would sculpt her designs directly. She knew the look she wanted—regal, confident, poised, refined, and not unlike Coco herself. "It was required that we resemble her a bit somehow," said one former model. Professional models would not do. In secrecy, Coco began hiring the debutante daughters of France's finest families, wealthy and titled young ladies like Princess Odile de Croy; Countess Mimi d'Arcangues; and the beautiful eighteen-year-old Marie-Hélène Arnaud, whose father was a director of the Rothschild Bank. Forty years before, the grandparents of girls like these would have been reluctant to acknowledge Chanel in the street.

Chanel had not lost her command of public relations. She allowed rumors of her return to circulate but refused all press interviews, trusting that she could create more and better buzz by remaining inaccessible. By December 1953, when she formally declared her intention, the fashion press was already writing articles devoted to Chanel. Since she had provided no new information about herself, journalists had to make do with the materials they could find. As a result, coverage consisted largely of old photographs and stories about Chanel as she had been: young, beautiful, and the most important designer in the world. She had, at least for the time being, presented an image of herself preserved in amber, willing the public to remember a Coco untarnished by either age or collaboration. There could have been no better publicity.

Such brilliant use of the press came at a price, though. By trading on her former reputation, Chanel was raising the ante in her own high-stakes game, inviting expectations perhaps too high to meet. On December 21, 1953, *The New York Times* announced Chanel's return in an article proving how high the bar was now set: "Chanel's re-opening is a real bombshell for the fashion folk, not only because of the nostalgia…but also because…her reappearance makes the big houses more than a little nervous." With a hint of *ressentiment,* French journalist Patrice Sylvain evoked the grandeur still attached to Chanel's name: "The news ran through Paris, Chanel was re-opening! … Chanel, with her legend of lavishness and wealth, her 150 million-franc profits, her fifteen studios, her yachts, her châteaus, and the magic of her expensive adventures, all of that was rising up out of a past still recent yet unbelievably far away."

At the start of her career, Chanel had contended with the rigid class hierarchy of France, along with obstacles to professional women too overwhelming to be contained within the modern term "sexism." Now, new hurdles awaited that were scarcely less daunting. Could Chanel overcome her political past, her advanced age, and the ghost of her own former glory?

No one knew what to expect of Chanel's new collection, but everyone clamored for an invitation to her first runway show, which promised to be the biggest event of the season. As she always had in the past, Chanel scheduled the show for the fifth day of the month, five having always been her lucky number. When the big day—February 5, 1954—came (several months later than Chanel had predicted to Carmel Snow), there were not enough gilt chairs to accommodate the hordes waiting in front of 31 rue Cambon—a mix of elegant former clients, assorted countesses, artist friends, and the entire international fashion press.

Louise de Vilmorin was there, as was Luchino Visconti, who'd brought the beautiful young actress Annie Girardot. Former Ballets Russes dancer Boris Kochno made an appearance. Many more tried to make their way into the overcrowded downstairs salon. "Two thousand people wanted absolutely to get in," recalled model Liane Viguié. "People were being trampled and pushed, some fell down the stairs, a baroness was wounded. They had to call the police to prevent a riot. Some of Mademoiselle's older clients couldn't even find a seat. It was frightening." Not even high priestesses of the fashion world Carmel Snow and Marie-Louise Bousquet could snag a chair; they were forced to perch on the last two unoccupied steps of the famous winding staircase—which had been commandeered as an impromptu bleacher section. George Salou, editor in chief of *L'Officiel de la Couture,* strained to see from his place in fashion Siberia—the eighth row. Together, all craned their necks, looking for Mademoiselle at the top of those stairs, her customary surveillance point in years past. But Coco wasn't there. Counting on the invisibility trick that had worked so well to that point, Chanel was hiding upstairs watching, but unseen.

Finally, a hush fell over the crowd as the first model made her appearance, wearing a cardigan suit of black jersey christened—in Chanel's customary manner—with a number instead of a name. The model wearing this simple outfit carried the small card that identified it—this was Chanel's only method for labeling garments; she offered no printed programs for her runway shows, unlike most other designers. Although the cardigan suit was the first offering of the day, it bore the title "Number Five"—again that lucky number.

But Coco's magic numeral had lost its power. The audience quickly understood that Chanel was offering nothing new. The show featured 130 items, including dozens of simple skirt suits in wool jersey and tweed (with slim skirts and square cardigan jackets), paired with blouses of white piqué or printed silk that matched the suits' linings, along with slender coats in neutral tones, several simple black dresses (one with sequins) with slightly flared skirts, and a few sheath dresses. In short, Chanel seemed to have put together a retrospective of her work from the 1930s.

· · ·

Perhaps nothing could have lived up to the fevered expectations of the crowd, but this collection brought a near-unanimous "tsk" of pity and disappointment. The models looked as they always had—like Coco; lithe brunettes all, with large bows worn atop low chignons. They presented the clothes as Chanel models always had, walking with hands in pockets and pelvises tilted forward, in deliberate, tutored imitation of Chanel's own gait. Each girl emerged about six steps after the one before her, with as many as seven or eight appearing on the floor at once. The salon's mirrored walls reflected their images infinitely around the space, creating the effect of a crowd of Chanel-like figures.

The clothes immediately announced a departure from the reigning aesthetic. Unlike the couture being turned out by Dior, Fath, Balmain, and company, Chanel's designs did nothing to accentuate the female form, but flowed smoothly, even modestly, over the body. The skirts stopped just below the knee. There was no revelation here, no exaggerated molding or extension of body parts, no décolleté, no drama at all.

The French fashion press corps was merciless. "In the play of mirrors, we did not see the future, but a disappointing reflection of the past," wrote the very influential Lucien François in *Combat*. Another journalist fumed, "All of Paris burned with impatience and curiosity for this...the biggest event of the season....God was it ugly! How could women ever have dressed like this?" *Le Monde's* review was similar: "Awaited with impatience, Chanel's return has disappointed her admirers. Her collection offers nothing and is a melancholy throwback to shapeless silhouettes, with no trace of bust, waist or hips. One had the impression of flipping through a slightly yellowed old family photo album."

More than a few reviewers shared *Le Monde's* displeasure, with many lamenting Chanel's neglect of the holy trinity of female assets: "[A collection] without breasts, waist, or hips...A melancholy retrospective," lamented one critic. "Chanel takes us back to yesteryear...no breasts, no waist, no hips," mourned another. Although the audience remained coldly silent during the presentation, when it was all over, some spectators did not hesitate to voice their contempt loudly as they exited, with a rudeness startling in the elegant setting.

What so repelled the French fashion critics seemed to be the anachronism of Chanel's clothes, along with her tacit rejection of the highly structured looks now dominating haute couture. Certainly, her collection had failed to deliver any novelty. But would these objections alone inspire such anger? The harsh, dismissive tone of so many reviews suggested that Chanel had hit a nerve, that her offense extended beyond the sartorial.

The key to Chanel's offense may have lain in a stray remark made by an unidentified countess in the Cambon audience, which was overheard and quoted by a journalist. "[These] are phantoms' dresses...very expensive for so much self-effacement," she said, poetically condensing the entire problem. Phantoms are the spirits of the dead that return to haunt the living. Chanel was drawing French ire by conjuring ghosts—not just of couture past, but of politics past—the ghosts of history. Her comeback felt eerily premature to the French. It was too soon for them to enjoy her nostalgic 1930s fashions, for they brought back a flood of unsavory memories—of war, of death, and of the guilt attaching to part of France's own population. Chanel was a phantom of collaboration and, to make matters worse, daring to charge her typically high prices, seeking profit despite her wrongdoing.

The countess dismissed Coco's simple style as expensive "self-effacement," implicitly comparing it to the ornate trappings of Dior or Fath. Ironically, though, the greater offense may have been Chanel's utter refusal to efface herself and the painful period she still evoked. She may have hidden upstairs, but Chanel had seen to it that her trademark image was stamped indelibly on the runway show, in the vast parade of models (and their infinitely mirrored reflections) who looked like Coco. It was the return of the repressed.

France's displeasure with Chanel's past was something of an open secret. Journalist Rosamond Bernier, who later founded *L'Oeil* magazine, interviewed Coco in 1953 for American *Vogue* and sensed the mood of lingering hostility. "I didn't know more than what people were saying...that she had behaved very badly.... There was still so much rancor, a desire to settle old scores. All of that overflowed onto Chanel. She had a very bad reputation at that time." In a private handwritten note unearthed in a Paris archive, American fashion writer and Elsa Schiaparelli biographer Palmer White recalled France's "antagonism" toward Chanel, incited by her "pro-Nazi activities."

Coco had felt the animosity within the first minutes of the show, and when it was over retreated upstairs to avoid visitors. "Mademoiselle is tired," her staff repeated to the friends and well-wishers who tried politely to greet her at the end. But while she'd been wounded, Chanel never doubted herself, and she conveyed that confidence forcefully to her staff. Manon Ligeour recalled vividly Chanel's refusal to bend to the criticism: "Mademoiselle was saying, 'They'll see! They'll see!'"

"She behaved as if others were wrong," marveled Robert Chaillet, a lawyer for Pierre Wertheimer. In one of her few interviews directly after the show, Coco told Simone Baron of *France-Soir,* "People no longer know what elegance is. When I work, I think of the women I try to dress, not the couture house.... Once I helped liberate women. I'll do it again." And she did, this time by maneuvering around France, by way of America.

While Europe insisted that Chanel was off her game, a pathetic Rip van Winkle of fashion, within a few weeks it became clear that Americans saw something else in her comeback: a fresh, modern, liberating way to dress that jibed perfectly with the United States' ethos of unencumbered, easy living. The Americans were also naturally less sensitive to the bad political memories that Chanel had revived in France. And so, while French buyers turned up their noses, the American buyers who had ordered Chanel models were quickly besieged with demands. Within weeks, more Chanel originals were being ordered for American boutiques, and Chanel-inspired designs were lining the racks of stores across the United States, from corner dress shops to big department stores. In March 1954, one month after the first runway show, *Life* magazine ran a large spread about the Chanel phenomenon, announcing, "At 71, she brings us more than a style—she has caused a veritable tempest. She has decided to return and to conquer her old position—the first." The commander in chief was back.

The Americans had not misunderstood Chanel's first return collection. They recognized it as a throwback—but this troubled them far less
than it did the Europeans. The *Los Angeles Times* condensed its dismissive
opinion of Chanel's comeback into the title of its review: "Chanel à la
page? [Chanel up to the minute?] But No!" *Women's Wear Daily* admitted
that the collection was "not going to break new fashion ground," but then
added, "the clothes are typically Chanel...graceful and easy"—and
therein lay the explanation for the Americans' interest.

Coco's comeback was not targeting the small and rarely profitable
world of haute couture, but the legions of ready-to-wear customers who
craved something "graceful and easy," a release from the constrictive
styles that had dominated fashion since the war. More than ever before,
Chanel was determined to confer her vision upon the multitudes: "I will
dress thousands of women," she told American *Vogue* magazine that February of 1954. "I will start with a collection, the same size collection I
used to make....It won't be a revolution, it won't be shocking. Changes
must not be brutal, must not be made all of a sudden. The eye must be
given time to adapt itself to a new thought."

By March of that same year, America's eye was adapting, and *Vogue*
was lauding Chanel's casual style, "the easy, underdone sort of clothes
that [are] the basis of Chanelism....Its influence is unmistakable....[Her]
suits are relaxing....Going easy on waists...they don't force." And in
July 1954, *The New York Times* ran a feature on the many Chanel-inspired
suits and dresses already being sold at Bullock's, Altman's, and Neiman
Marcus, announcing that "The spirit of Chanel has made itself widely
felt in the creation of the coming fall styles....Fashion was ready for
[Chanel's] direct approach."

Once the European press got wind of Chanel's success with the enormous and hugely important American market, its tone softened considerably. Complaints about Chanel's refusal to change her style turned into
paeans to her "consistency": "The inventor of the still-fashionable
sweater and the chemise dress of illustrious memory, Chanel, had retired
from the world. What would she bring us after her long absence? Why,

some Chanel of course! Cardigans, jersey suits, simple little dresses . . . the fashion press was disappointed, as if it had expected Chanel to become Dior or Fath!"

Many journalists praised Chanel for having made such swift inroads into the crucial United States market: "For six million Americans, Paris fashion is 'the Chanel storm'!" "Chanel's entire collection has been bought by the Americans!" Coco had recognized that her look would hold instant appeal to the United States, which she deemed a logical, athletic country: "They've been offering women idiocies which made it impossible to walk or run. American women refused these before French-women, because American women are more practical. . . . They walk, they run." On both sides of the Atlantic, reports of Chanel's calamity gave way entirely to buzz about her bold, successful, and influential re-turn to fashion.

One person not surprised by this turn of events was Pierre Wert-heimer, who had long profited from Coco's iron will and superb instincts. When he had gone to see her on Cambon soon after that first disastrous show, he'd found her slightly dejected but already at work on her new collection. "I want to go on . . . and win," she told him then.

"Yes, you're right to go on," he answered, indicating that he stood ready to help.

Things would get worse before they got better. Within one year, Cha-nel and her partners would lose more than 90 million francs. Most cor-porate backers would have walked away. Under the best of circumstances, couture is not a highly profitable venture, and Wertheimer owned only the perfume division, not Chanel's couture house. He had invested in Coco's comeback with an eye toward its potential for boosting perfume sales. Now, a number of his board members were explicitly advising him against any further investment in Chanel couture. But Pierre could see past the significant losses they'd incurred, past Chanel's advanced age and the initial bad reviews. Not only did he agree to continue backing her; he renegotiated their arrangement dramatically. On May 24, 1954, in a startling display of trust and foresight, Wertheimer agreed to buy Cha-nel out entirely, acquiring (for an undisclosed price) the couture house,

Chanel's Cambon real estate, her textile mills, and even the Chanel publishing company, which had not produced anything since Pierre Iribe's
journal, *Le Témoin,* in the 1930s.

In short, Parfums Chanel, the Wertheimers' business, purchased the
rights to all things Chanel—everything bearing her name or those famous initials. What did he give Coco in exchange for all that? In addition
to whatever initial payment he made to her, and the perfume royalties
(2 percent of profits annually) that he would continue to pay her, Pierre
agreed to underwrite all of Coco's business and personal expenses, including the cost of producing her collections, all employee salaries, her
apartment at the Ritz, her personal servants, travel, meals, entertainment, and her Rolls-Royce and chauffeur. No expenditure was too
minor—Wertheimer even agreed to pay Coco's telephone bills and buy
her postage stamps. At the same time, Chanel would retain total artistic
control over her collections. She could now devote herself entirely to her
work. For the rest of her life, Coco would never have to think a single
thought about money again. She was free.

Did Chanel cede control of her empire so completely to Wertheimer
purely for financial reasons? Certainly, money alone might explain her
decision. She'd managed to find a way to return to her work without risking the life of luxury she so enjoyed. But in accepting this deal, Coco
revealed more than a concern for material comforts. Divesting herself in
this way of all practical, financial transactions, Chanel had, in a sense,
transformed herself from captain of industry back into a courtesan, entrusting virtually all responsibility for her life to a wealthy man. Coco
would finish out her career the way she'd started it, under the benign
control of an affluent protector.

In retrospect, it makes sense. At seventy-one, Coco was now more
alone than ever, with no significant lover in her life and little prospect of
one. At times, she seemed to seek out intimate companionship with some
of her models. Reports abounded of the amorous attention she paid to
some of these young women, although it remained unclear if such flirta-
tions led to consummation. "She was a seducer," recalls former Chanel
model Betty Catroux (using the masculine noun in French, *séducteur,* in-

stead of the feminine, *séductrice*). "To me, Chanel was not a woman, or a mother. We saw her as a potential boyfriend!" adds Catroux.

But such relationships could not counterbalance Chanel's loneliness, or her pain at watching those closest to her die. She had begun reflecting aloud on her regrets, repeating often that her career had not brought her happiness. "The function of a woman is to be loved.... My life is a failure," she told Claude Delay. "Women must show their weakness, never their strength.... A woman needs the regard of a man who loves her... without this gaze a woman dies." Sometimes, Coco was moved to denounce all women with careers: "Women are becoming crazy. Men are living off them. The women are working and paying. It's ridiculous. Women are becoming monsters because they want to be men."

Here, Coco was conjuring Boy Capel, who'd often chided her forty years earlier: "Do not forget that you are a woman." Now, Chanel ostensibly condemned other women with Boy's words, but the real target was surely herself. Chanel had, of course, tried—and failed—to be a more traditional woman, to marry and have a family. But when those opportunities slipped away, she had always found comfort in her work. Now that Coco had returned to work again, her solitude looked permanent, and she found it harder to ignore her doubts about the choices she'd made.

The new contract with Pierre Wertheimer offered Chanel a way to reconcile returning to her career with her bitter regrets about the "unwomanly" life she'd led. Despite the terrible battles they'd waged against each other, the one ongoing masculine presence in her life had always been Pierre Wertheimer, and Coco let herself fall into Pierre's strong, savvy, billionaire arms.

W ertheimer never had cause to regret his decision. Within one year, Chanel had firmly reestablished herself as the queen of fashion. Response to her second return collection, in the late summer of 1954, bore no trace of the venom or condescension apparent only six months earlier, and Chanel seemed once more an inevitable force. "Paris has rediscovered her Chanel!" trumpeted *L'Intransigeant.* "Chanel is once again Chanel!" proclaimed another headline. Even when Chanel did insert some daring new detail, reviewers praised not her innovation, but her inherent, perennial Chanel-ness. In 1955, for example, when Coco dabbled with leopard fur, American *Vogue* announced "the look is unmistakably 1955. But it is also unmistakably Chanel."

The rest of the fashion world now fell in step behind Chanel. The New Look faded away; waists were uncinched and returned to their natural place; the exaggerated hips returned to human proportions. "We've realized," wrote one journalist, "that fashion is immutable."

"Chanel has the secret of making those timeless clothes…which always look elegant," wrote another. By 1957, *The New York Times* could report: "This winter, everyone is imitating [Chanel's] designs."

Chanel regained her footing by relying on her signature ability to marry simplicity and beauty. Her chemise dresses were extremely comfortable without being shapeless—slightly fitted in the front, often tied low at the waist with a fabric half belt. Her suits remained casual, with unfitted, often open jackets paired with elegant mid-length skirts—all equipped with numerous, perfectly placed pockets, large enough to accommodate small items such as a cigarette lighter or a lipstick. (Chanel thought women's clothes should be as practical as men's.)

As always, Chanel's flair for color and texture lent her suits and dresses special luxury and interest. She continued to hew to her preferred neutral and soft tones, seeking to reproduce the natural tones she found during her walks in the country or the Bois de Boulogne. Sometimes she would return to the studio with leaves, branches, or bits of moss she'd gathered, to show her staff exactly the shade of soft green or brown she wanted to re-create. A textile artist hired by Chanel recalled a day when Coco tried to explain the particular color she was seeking for a fabric: "Mademoiselle…plucked a flower [from a vase], then another and still another.…She crushed the petals, mixed them all up, and showed me the result. 'That's what I want,' she said."

Chanel did permit herself one bright color—she showed a number of suits in a dramatic red, explaining that "it is the color of blood and we have it in the interior of our bodies, so we should show it a bit on the outside." She experimented with her classic fabrics, featuring, for example, a new, unusually soft, herringbone tweed in an exaggeratedly wide pattern, as well as Shetland sweaters whose open weave lent them a lighter, more feminine texture. Uppermost always in Chanel's mind was the importance of the woman's own, bodily experience of the clothes. The way a garment felt on the inside mattered at least as much as how it looked on the outside. She had no use for any fabric that could scratch or irritate, such as lamé.

These years also saw Chanel improving upon the construction of her designs. She had always fashioned her garments to maximize comfort and the wearer's range of motion. Now she continued that tradition with subtle new details that added to the "impeccable" look of a Chanel. In 1956, for example, Chanel started inserting elasticized waistbands into her blouses. These invisible strips of elastic anchored the blouse in place, keeping it from riding up or ballooning unevenly over the tops of skirts. In 1957, a new Chanel skirt appeared whose deep pleats began low on the hips, emerging from a tapered, flat waist. With this, Coco had solved the fashion conundrum of how to create an elegant, tapered skirt that is nonetheless comfortable and easy to walk in. She had produced pleated skirts as far back as the 1920s, but this one represented a distinct improvement.

Pleated skirts are comfortable and conducive to strolling, but can add unattractive bulk around the hips and waist (think of Catholic schoolgirls' uniforms). Narrow skirts (like Dior's "hobble skirt") have a slimming effect, but can be tight and hinder walking. But Chanel's inventive skirt managed to slim the hips and waist while allowing for a longer stride—her deep pleats providing a generous amount of room in which the leg could move forward.

The skirt was an instant hit, and manufacturers at every level scurried to run up copies of it. Few if any knockoffs, though, could re-create the elegance of the original, which depended entirely on Chanel's meticulous craftsmanship. An article offering advice on how to spot a fake Chanel skirt explained that "A real Chanel [skirt] 'falls' to give the walk a supple allure, at once dignified and dancing, which is inimitable." Princess Hélène Obolensky, who'd worked as a personal assistant to Chanel, elaborated on the same theme: "The purpose of the skirt tailoring is to minimize the hips, flatten the back, and, by lifting the skirt line in front, add a graceful swinging stance to the body."

That graceful swing propelled Chanel through the 1950s. And while she regained her footing in France, it would always be America to which she owed the success of her comeback. As a child Coco had imagined a father making his fortune off in America; now she was living out that dream for herself.

America formally hailed Chanel as its conquering fashion hero on September 9, 1957, when Stanley Marcus bestowed upon her the Neiman Marcus Award for Distinguished Service in the Field of Fashion, also known as "the fashion Oscar." Chanel flew to Dallas to receive the golden plaque, which bore the following citation:

> To the great innovator who emancipated the feminine silhouette . . . who was the first to recognize that the casualness of the twentieth century must be reflected in the clothes women wear . . . who elevated the status of costume jewelry to a position of fashionable respectability . . . who was the first to bring perfume from the chemists' shop to the couturier's boutique . . . who was never afraid of being copied . . . who as an ex-champion had the courage to stage a successful fashion comeback in 1954, whose past accomplishments have had a tremendous influence on present fashions . . . to Chanel for her contributions . . . past, present, future.

Coco groused her way through Texas. She complained about the long lines of people waiting to shake her hand, and about the chilly air-conditioned rooms. She disparaged Americans' excessive casualness, their lack of elegance: "They don't understand luxury, real luxury. A country that understands only comfort is screwed!" But in photographs from that day, Chanel's smile as she accepted the award from Stanley Marcus looks genuine. Coco was surely thrilled by all the accolades. She knew her second career was in some ways even more astonishing than her first. And it was precisely Americans' love of "comfort"—the very quality she disdained—that made it all possible.

One year earlier, the recipient of the Neiman Marcus award had been that apostle of *dis*comfort, Christian Dior, the man who'd seemed to herald Chanel's obsolescence. Now just one year later (and only three years after returning to work) Chanel had knocked her rival off his pedestal. America was confirming the rightness of her vision, declaring her once more the priestess of modernity. Dior himself would pass away one month after Chanel's trip to Dallas, in October 1957, to be succeeded by the young prodigy Yves Saint Laurent.

The press coverage of her trip to the States (which included stops in New York City and New Orleans) was one long love letter. Announcing the award on its front page, *France-Soir* called Coco "the magician of French couture." *The New York Times* called her return to work "the most incredible comeback in fashion history" and lauded her as the "ageless designer whose young look is America's favorite." Brendan Gill and Lillian Ross declared in *The New Yorker* that Chanel's "designs have begun to affect women's styles (and apparently their minds) every bit as powerfully as her designs of thirty odd years ago did." And like so many other journalists, Gill and Ross took note of Coco's youthful vigor and appeal: "At 74, Mademoiselle Chanel is sensationally good looking with dark brown eyes, a brilliant smile, and the unquenchable vitality of a twenty-year-old."

Chanel's appearance and youthfulness, which she'd likely helped along surgically, were hardly incidental to her comeback. Unlike virtually any other designer, Coco had created a persona inextricably woven into her designs, infusing her clothes with the glamorous narrative of her life. Wearing a Chanel had always offered the promise of acquiring a bit of Coco's own charisma. Very few women of over seventy, though, could have hoped to resurrect themselves as charismatic objects of emulation. But, at least for a time, Chanel pulled it off. She amazed observers by still telegraphing the youthful energy and appeal that had been her calling card. ("At 75, she is still a stunning woman," wrote *The New York Times* in 1958.)

Chanel's vitality, freedom, and athletic allure meshed perfectly with America's image of itself, especially after World War II. The United States was the world's hero now, the dominant force of roaring economic power and commercial influence, a young, can-do country unfettered by Old World rules. Somehow, Chanel's long-standing aesthetic—while born in pre–World War I Europe and long the quintessence of Frenchness—now seemed the inevitable, nearly Whitmanian expression of the American ethos. Chanel, the elderly collaborator barely back from exile, was gone, metamorphosed into an American heroine who made it all seem perfectly natural. "The youthful philosophy of dress originated by the French designer has come to be taken as the classic American look," explained *The New York Times*.

V*ogue* even connected Chanel with the American women's suffrage movement: "She was the first fashion naturalist, the first to design clothes with the freedom and understated elegance Americans like best.... Chanel began thinking that way in 1919, the year...that American women gained the vote.... Chanel's clothes have a natural immediate appeal to American women."

Chanel had not needed to do anything specific to appeal to Americans. Her success in the States required no publicity stunt, no special rejiggering of her look. On the contrary, there had always been something latently American in the Chanel aesthetic, in its unfussy, athletic version of femininity, its blend of democracy and elitism, and—especially—in its inherent myth of self-creation. Chanel style had always been a Horatio Alger story writ in fashion, the promise that elegance and status were within everyone's reach, and could be put on like a well-fitting jacket.

Chanel owed her American redemption not to the high-priced couture she created for socialites, but to her most practical, most reproducible, day- and sportswear: suits, sweaters, and easy dresses of tweed or jersey. These items compose what might be called the fashion unconscious of postwar America, the elements that held visceral appeal for women. "Her return collection was just what American women wanted," wrote one fashion journalist. "The essence of Chanel...[is] the classic American look," declared another. "Any woman...knows the Chanel signs...the dash, the sense of luxe in the colloquial, the overall sensibleness of the Chanel approach....American women look marvelous in...Chanel."

Chanel had always had a genius for absorbing and reflecting back the most desirable aesthetic impulses around her. Now, after fourteen years of inactivity, Coco focused on the elements of her style that had the most in common with America's, mirroring back to American women an idealized, irresistible version of themselves. "See?" she seemed to be saying. "Your taste is instinctively good—it matches mine!" "Most American women know that they owe [Chanel] a debt of gratitude," pronounced *The New York Times.*

Thus did Chanel entirely remake herself one last time. As if by sheer intuition, she attached herself to the most powerful ally available, blended into its culture, and then disseminated it around the world. The woman who had tried to help the Axis powers win the war was now squarely on the side of the victorious Allied forces. All was forgiven. Or just forgotten.

Yet, however American the Chanel brand increasingly seemed, Chanel herself remained unmistakably French. Ingeniously, she'd found a way to package her *francité* as a readily accessible attribute for Americans seeking a quick hit of refinement—the fashion equivalent of some other postwar rituals of feminine cultural improvement, like the college girl's semester in Paris or the housewife's French cooking class. Now, even more than before her retirement, Chanel represented the face of Parisian chic. And she knew it. "For many Americans," Coco told Paul Morand, "France is me!"

Chanel's prestige continued to grow throughout the 1950s and '60s.

Hollywood stars flocked to her studio, among them Grace Kelly, Lauren Bacall, Rita Hayworth, Jane Fonda, and Elizabeth Taylor—seeking to add refinement to their splashy American celebrity. Fonda was brought by her then husband, French director Roger Vadim, who was trying to lend her French cachet. And while Chanel appreciated Elizabeth Taylor's talent and beauty, she deplored that famously voluptuous figure, which Taylor liked to showcase and Coco felt ruined the line of elegant clothes. French cinema stars also made the pilgrimage to Cambon, including Jeanne Moreau, Romy Schneider, Catherine Deneuve, Anouk Aimée, and Brigitte Bardot (brought, like Fonda, by Roger Vadim, to whom she also had a brief marriage).

While Chanel helped young movie stars gain sophistication, she was just as helpful to older clients seeking youthfulness. The magic of Chanel seemed always to grant each group exactly its needed measure of glamour or gravitas. Political wives found, chez Chanel, a uniform that connoted power tempered with femininity. "When my wife dresses in your clothes, I feel reassured," President Georges Pompidou told Chanel. Madame Claude Pompidou, nearing sixty, looked slim and vital in her Chanels. The young American First Lady Jacqueline Kennedy looked more distinguished and polished in hers. The famous raspberry pink wool suit and matching hat worn by Mrs. Kennedy on the day of President Kennedy's assassination was a Chanel (or a Chanel-approved replica). When she insisted on wearing the blood-spattered outfit throughout the subsequent swearing-in of Lyndon Johnson, the suit became a symbol of Kennedy's martyrdom and the besmirchment of Camelot.

During these comeback years, Chanel went on to invent some of her most iconic garments, accessories, and details—features that still instantly say "Chanel." Prime among these is the wool bouclé suit (1954), whose jacket with braided trim—sometimes adorned with Brandenburg, or "frog"-style, closures—declared its clear descendance from the elegant French cavalry uniforms Chanel had observed in her youth.

Other comeback inventions include Chanel's 1955 quilted leather shoulder bag with the chain link strap and, in 1957, the cap-toed beige and black sling-back pumps, whose black toe area gives the illusion of a

Chanel runway show featuring hussar-style suit with "Brandenburg," or frog-style, closures, 1959

smaller foot. Such items were easily copied, and reproductions flooded the market at every price point. "Paris is filled with little Chanels," declared *L'Intransigeant* in 1961. Nothing could have pleased Coco more.

Copying and fashion piracy, though, had long been the bane of the couture industry, and frustrated designers continually sought to thwart this problem. The Maison Dior, for example, required fashion buyers to put down a very steep security deposit (or *caution*) before viewing collections—money withheld in the event of any illegal copying of the designs seen. But Chanel had no interest in security deposits, or in "security" of any kind. She welcomed copies of her work at all levels. "Fashion should run on the streets," she told a journalist.

Chanel's fashion did run on the streets—all over the world. Knockoffs of her suits were sold out of handcarts at weekend flea markets in Europe, and copied in sari material and sold in the bazaars of New Delhi. In

Iribe's patriotic view of Paris's luxury shopping district: the rue de la Paix, looking toward the Colonne Vendôme, as France's "display case"

For his Fall 2011 runway show in the Grand Palais, Karl Lagerfeld re-created the Place Vendôme, replacing Napoléon with a metallic statue of Chanel atop a replica of the Colonne Vendôme. *Photo by Michael Dufour/WireImage*

Chanel's "patriotic" dress in the colors of the French flag, 1939. *Courtesy of the Museum of the City of New York/© The Costume Institute of the Metropolitan Museum of New York*

A surrealism-inspired evening coat created by Chanel's archrival Elsa Schiaparelli in collaboration with Jean Cocteau, one of Chanel's closest friends, 1937. Such whimsical pieces, so different from Chanel's in style, won great acclaim in late 1930s Paris. *Philadelphia Museum of Art, Pennsylvania, PA, USA/Gift of Mme Elsa Schiaparelli/The Bridgeman Art Library*

Poster, "Neues Volk 1938" [New People 1938], for the calendar of the Racial Policy Office of the Nazi Party, 1938, depicting the idealized Nazi family. *The Mitchell Wolfson, Jr. Collection/The Wolfsonian-Florida International University*

Chanel at her dressing table, in her Ritz apartment, 1938.
Photo by Jean Moral, courtesy of Brigitte Moral

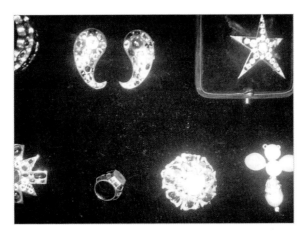

Chanel's personal jewelry case

A full-skirted,
fur-trimmed Chanel
evening dress, 1958.
*Boris Lipnitzki/
Roger-Viollet/
The Image Works*

Chanel leaving her rue Cambon offices, 1938.
Photo by Jean Moral, courtesy of Brigitte Moral

Chanel in her apartment surrounded by her models, 1959. *Willy Rizzo Studios*

Chanel in the Tuileries, 1957. *Willy Rizzo Studios*

Chanel at work, surrounded by fabric, 1959. *Willy Rizzo Studios*

Jacques Chazot (right) congratulating Chanel after a runway show, 1958.
STF/AFP/Getty Images

First Lady Jacqueline Kennedy
in a Chanel-designed suit:
Dallas, November 22, 1963.
*Photo by Art Rickerby/Time
Life Pictures/Getty Images*

Chanel's influence continues to surface in unexpected ways: above, a contemporary child appears costumed as Chanel for an art photograph; below, the French graffiti artist Zevs has repurposed the Chanel logo for an installation.
Courtesy of Jaime C. Moore (above); Courtesy of Zevs (below)

Egypt, the Nile-Hilton Hotel of Cairo outfitted its female elevator operators in copies of Chanel suits—substituting blue scarab buttons for the gold ones found on the originals. Coco reveled in this degree of imitation even though it flew directly in the face of many regulations imposed by the Chambre syndicale de la couture, the trade organization founded by Lucien Lelong. Devoted to preventing piracy, the *chambre* required couturiers to prohibit press photographers at collections, and to grant access only to "trade professionals," meaning buyers and journalists. Chanel disregarded such regulations and invited not only photographers into her runway shows, but also nontrade visitors, including private dressmakers whose avowed intention was to reproduce Chanel styles for their own customers. Once, she even opened her runway show to a contingent of nuns who directed a sewing workshop, surely recalling her own childhood guardians. On July 25, 1958, Chanel took a formal stand against the association's constraints and sent a letter of resignation to Raymond Barbas, president of the *chambre*. Now she was free to disseminate her designs as she saw fit. Inspired by Coco, Hubert de Givenchy and Cristóbal Balenciaga both followed her example and resigned from the *chambre*, prompting the organization soon after to drop its press embargo.

As in her earlier career, "copying Chanel" meant far more than merely copying specific designs. It meant copying—being like—Coco herself. Even in these elder years, Chanel imposed herself as an icon to be emulated by her customers and, more than ever, by her models and staff. As Coco's world of friends and intimates dwindled, she seemed to place ever more stringent demands on those near her, becoming increasingly domineering. With no one close enough to check her, she grew into a caricature of herself, both physically and emotionally.

"In the end, we are left with two mythic uniforms from this era," Claude Delay wrote. "Charlie Chaplin's and Coco Chanel's." It was an astute observation. Especially after the war, the Chanel uniform crystallized into a constellation of instantly recognizable parts: the straw boater; the bouclé, ribbon-trimmed skirt suit; the two-toned pumps; the quilted bag; the piles of pearls. But Chaplin's look belonged to his "Little Tramp" character, which was distinctly separate from Chaplin the man, offstage. The same could not be said of Coco's trademark look.

Chanel never "took off" her persona. She would wear the same (usually beige, ribbon-trimmed, bouclé) suit daily for an entire season (sometimes even wearing holes through the elbows). Her signature boater hat remained firmly on her head at all times, even indoors, to disguise her thinning hair, through which patches of her scalp were now visible. Refusing to go gray, she kept her hair an improbable jet-black color, dying it herself—perhaps to keep any coiffeur from seeing the extent of her hair loss. Blue-black bangs emerged from under the brim of that hat, which were either dyed or, as many thought, actually part of a hairpiece sewn into the hatband.

Keeping her slim figure remained paramount to Coco, who ate in-

Chanel in her apartment, 1956

creasingly lightly and weighed in at about one hundred pounds on her barely five-foot-three frame. But, as often is the case with older people, her thinness started looking like fragility. "She eats nothing," wrote Cecil Beaton of Chanel, "and one feels it is only her spirit that keeps her going." As if to compensate for her vanishing body, Coco began using a very heavy hand with makeup. Every day she redrew her sparse eyebrows with the thickest, blackest pencil and colored her wide mouth the deepest red.

As Chanel's personal appearance hardened into extremes, she required ever more confirmation and duplication of her image from her employees. These women, both staff members and models, did not necessarily dislike reproducing Chanel's style—many, in fact, looked up to her as a fashion icon. But whether they liked it or not, imitation of the boss was a job requirement. "When you had to go see her," recalled Delphine Bonneval, "you had to be perfectly coiffed and made up, and in your white blouse. I remember one day when [Mademoiselle] was going up the stairs and ran into a model on her way out for lunch whose skirt was too short or something. And she was dismissed."

When not modeling or preparing for a fitting, the models all wore a kind of uniform, including the same white blouse, beige-and-black Chanel shoes, and a blue or black suit. Many went beyond the call of duty, trying to mimic every distinctive "Coco" detail. Bonneval recalled that she imitated Chanel so well that she became a kind of "pastiche" of her, cutting her hair into bangs, and affecting a straw boater, scarf, cigarette, and pearls. Even outside of work, many of these women remained foot soldiers in Chanel's army.

"We wore nothing but Chanel," says Princess Odile de Croy. Manon Ligeour goes further, admitting, "I copied her a lot. I had her style.... I would never have worn something that was not in the Chanel style. I made myself suits in her style.... That way of being able to move, it was unique. The image people had of me on the exterior, my friends, my husband, my son, it was me in a Chanel suit." Born to poor parents—a chimney sweep and a laundress—Ligeour felt that she owed her escape from those humble roots to her association with Chanel, to her successful projection—and internalization—of a Chanelified image: "In my life as a woman, she [Chanel] changed many things. She granted me social ascension."

Chanel's stylist and assistant Lilou Marquand makes the same implicit connection between her own faithful imitation of Chanel's style and the profound changes Marquand experienced as a result of her career with Mademoiselle:

"I wore Chanel every single day. Everyone [at Cambon] wore Chanel. It was not possible to work at Chanel wearing anything other than Chanel.... If I have succeeded, it's because of her. Everything I know I learned from that woman," she says, adding, "She was a true Pygmalion." After Chanel's death, Marquand ran a boutique for a time selling her own knitwear copies of Chanel suits in the trademark neutral tones of beige and navy. Later, she became a highly accomplished textile and metal artist and, now in her eighties, continues to produce beautiful woven screens and wall hangings whose shimmering patterns of blended colors call to mind the nuanced tonal play of Chanel tweeds.

Chanel imposed her personality as strongly as she imposed her aesthetic. Her staff understood that they were to submit entirely to Coco's authority and caprices. With little or no personal life to return to after work, Chanel tended to vent her frustration and loneliness on those who worked for her. Employees quickly learned what was required of them in this luxurious yet severe environment.

While much of the staff reported to work at about eight thirty in the morning, Coco had never been an early riser and tended to show up hours later. When she did arrive, usually around one p.m., she was attended by a degree of fanfare befitting a five-star general or royal monarch. The moment Coco left her apartment across the street at the Ritz, hotel staff members would immediately telephone the operator at rue Cambon to alert her. A buzzer would sound throughout the studio to spread the word: Mademoiselle was on her way. Someone downstairs would spray a mist of Chanel No. 5 near the entrance, so that Coco could walk through a cloud of her own signature scent. "She was the first to have a perfumed space ... a divine scent," recalled actress Jeanne Moreau.

"When she entered the studio, everyone stood up," recalled photographer Willy Rizzo, "like children at school." Then, the staff would form a line, hands at their sides, "as in the army," employee Marie-Hélène Marouzé put it.

Once upstairs, Coco would loop over her head the ribbon necklace from which hung her indispensable scissors, indicating the start of serious work. From that point on, she addressed herself ferociously to creation, rarely even sitting down, although sometimes lying flat on the floor to check hemlines. She continued to design entirely without patterns and without wooden dress mannequins, and so spent long hours draping and pinning fabrics on live bodies—the models' bodies.

Although decades older than everyone around her, Chanel never tired. She could remain standing for nine hours at a time, without pausing for a meal or a glass of water—without even a bathroom break, apparently. She inflicted this schedule on others, holding them hostage to her energy and, in truth, her loneliness. Fueled by adrenaline and cigarettes, Coco kept her models standing while she fitted clothes on them for hours on end, rarely addressing the girls directly. The possibility that someone might need a respite from standing perfectly mute and motionless never seemed to concern Chanel.

By turns affectionate and callously manipulative, Coco kept her staff in a state of watchful anxiety. She played staff members off one another, "taking one person's ideas and giving them to another . . . playing on our nerves and creating competition," Manon Ligeour explained. She also tended to play favorites with her models, singling one out at a time for special treatment—generously lending her dresses or jewels, for example—and then abruptly changing course, freezing out her object of affection in favor of a new girl.

Yvonne Dudel offered a thoughtful interpretation: "She was so changeable, very difficult. She would . . . give . . . great privileges then take them away. . . . Was it perhaps meant to show people that they should never think themselves above her?"

Dudel may be right; Chanel certainly asserted an imperious dominance. But with such wounding, mercurial behavior Coco also

Chanel works with
model Paule Rizzo, 1959

reproduced—wittingly or not—the circumstances she'd endured in her
own life, in which loving attachments nearly always came to an abrupt
and painful end, either through abandonment or death.

That lifetime of loss weighed heavily upon Chanel in these years, but
her hardened exterior permitted little outlet for emotion. When Jean
Cocteau, a friend she had known for nearly fifty years, died in 1963, she
claimed to be unmoved by his death. "Jean, a poet? You make me laugh,"
she reportedly declared after Cocteau's funeral. Coco's misery expressed
itself obliquely. As her intimate connections fell away, she increasingly
filled her time with work and—especially—with talk, holding friends
and colleagues hostage to manic, torrential streams of one-way conversation from which no one could escape. Journalist Rosamond Bernier
found Coco highly frustrating to interview: "I must say, it wasn't a real
conversation.... She talked without stopping!"

"Chanel rattled on, her words ... like piercing machine gun bullets," wrote John Fairchild, former editor of *Women's Wear Daily*. "She would keep people standing talking for up to two hours," recalled Willy Rizzo.

Chanel used conversation to reel in her prey and hold it immobilized—in an attempt to forestall the crushing loneliness that overtook her the moment she stopped working. Above all, she dreaded weekends and holidays. "That word, 'vacation,' makes me sweat," she told Claude Delay. Her staff was keenly aware of Coco's fears: "[She] anguished at the idea of going home." said Gisèle Franchomme. At the end of even the longest workday, she had a habit of installing herself on the top step of her spiral staircase, subjecting any model trying to leave with an interminable monologue.

"She was exhausting," admits Lilou Marquand. "I would come home exhausted—she talked so much."

Sometimes, Coco would try to sweeten the captivity and offer her employees hospitality, inviting them into her rue Cambon apartment. There, Chanel called upon her great talents as a hostess, pouring the finest champagne and wines, still chattering nonstop. However grand the setting and refreshments, though, Coco's guests chafed under her regime of impromptu soirees. To them, these were lost evenings—time stolen from their family and friends. Dates had to be broken, boyfriends placated. But no one could refuse Coco's invitation, and although everyone but Chanel would have to be back at the studio by eight thirty the next morning, no one dared leave early.

Even those not in Coco's employ could wind up strong-armed into keeping her company. In these cases, Chanel's weapon of choice was guilt. In his memoir, Michel Déon recounts one Christmas Eve when Chanel invited him to dinner at the last minute, clearly afraid of spending the night alone. Christmas had brought her sorrow ever since Boy's death during that holiday season of 1919. Somehow, even though he had plans, Déon felt compelled to run over to the Ritz where he spent hours at dinner with Coco, drinking champagne. "I kept her company.... Left to herself she might have cried," he recalled. The girlfriend with whom Déon had planned to celebrate Christmas was left alone at a party, won-

Chanel holding court in her studio with models and staff, 1959

dering why she had been stood up. Coco had not been unaware of the couple's plans; she had, in fact, given the young woman a Chanel dress to wear for her night out with Déon. "Had she forgotten the dress she'd lent, or did she remember it and want to have some fun with me?" Déon wonders in his account. Even in her old age, Coco could not resist inserting herself between members of a couple, dressing the woman and "borrowing" the man.

Many of Chanel's guests noted the extent to which even her décor contributed to their sense of imprisonment: "The screens enclosed the space," recounts one former model. "When you sat on the couch, it felt like a cave.... It was dark at all hours." Even today, a visitor to Chanel's rue Cambon apartment can find the space disorienting. Coco used her

Coromandel screens as paneling, covering every square inch of the walls (even cutting holes into the valuable antique screens to accommodate light switches), including all doors. This made it next to impossible for visitors seeking an escape to find their way gracefully out of any room.

Implicit within all the talking were Chanel's rules about what she would *not* discuss. Her staff and even clients knew that Coco would brook no conversation about family life. Although many of the women around her were married and had children (even a number of the models, which was unusual for the profession), Chanel would tolerate no reference to these outside relationships. She preferred to preserve the fiction that everyone's life resembled hers—that those around her were as solitary as she.

Lilou Marquand felt that her marriage had deeply unsettled Chanel and discovered that Coco had begun spreading false and injurious rumors about her husband. Chanel also made it clear that no one could speak of personal pain or trauma. "We left our concerns outside, our sorrows, our personal losses. She would not tolerate that!"

What, then, did Chanel talk about? Often, her low opinion of others. Betty Catroux is one of many who remember Chanel's bitter view of the world. "She taught me to hate people and to trust no one," Catroux says. "Everyone except her was at fault," wrote Cecil Beaton. "When she talked about other people, it was always to speak ill of them," says Gisèle Franchomme.

Coco reserved some of her sharpest words for her fellow designers— except Cristóbal Balenciaga, whom she called "a great talent." As time passed, the free-spirited styles of the 1960s particularly enraged Chanel. She abhorred the miniskirt and any fashion she deemed immodest. Although she'd based her career on a model of independent, sexually liberated womanhood, Coco distinguished sharply between freedom and vulgarity in fashion. "They're showing the navel now," she complained. "That is not a woman's best feature. Pants below the navel with a blouse above it. It's so precious, the navel, that we have to put it in a shop window? Soon women will be showing their ass." She didn't mind Yves Saint Laurent too much, though, especially when he dropped his hemlines and created a simple, geometric black dress of wool and silk. "Saint Laurent has excellent taste. The more he copies me, the better taste he displays."

While Chanel was no doubt given to ill humor as she aged, some of the harshness of her tone might have been intended simply for shock value—to force people to hear her, to notice her, to feel her effect. Preserving her strong impact on others remained paramount to Chanel—it was her way of staying alive and relevant. At some level, Coco understood this, essentially admitting to Claude Delay that her constant talking was an attempt to forestall death: "If my friends tease me about my mania for nonstop talking, it's that they don't understand that I'm terrified of being bored listening to others. If one day I die [if!], I am persuaded that death will be nothing other than boredom."

Her frequent critique of other designers reassured her of her own dominance, her command over fashion. While she needn't have worried about the longevity of her influence, Coco's increasingly demanding, even despotic, behavior at work bespoke a deep anxiety about losing her control and authority.

No one who worked with her ever disputed Chanel's talent and vision. But producing a fashion collection requires a team effort, and Coco seemed reluctant to acknowledge the effort and gifts of her many employees. In 1960, more than three hundred people worked on the five floors of offices on rue Cambon. She had always been sharply critical, but now Chanel grew cold and withholding. Virtually never offering a word of praise, she responded to most of her employees' creations with stinging criticism, which sometimes took the form of her completely undoing—literally ripping apart—a newly sewn garment, insisting it be remade from scratch. The scissors always around her neck made Coco very quick on the draw.

Sometimes, Chanel's outbursts would reduce a seamstress to tears. "You'd arrive with a dress or a coat... and then a half hour later there'd be nothing left, everything demolished!" recalled Jean Cazaubon, a top Chanel tailor who specialized in suits. The staff smarted all the more under such arbitrary cruelty given the fact that they worked entirely without any drawn patterns. Their instructions consisted only of what Coco told them verbally.

The experts working for her knew how to design and sew Chanel garments, of course, and it seems that Coco's angry displays usually resulted less from genuine displeasure than from her unease that someone other than herself had created it. "It was all because she didn't want it said that it was us, that we were the ones who made it. When the girls cried, I'd tell them, 'If she ripped it up, that means she liked it!'"

Often, according to Cazaubon, the seamstresses would simply re-sew the destroyed garment without changing it at all, knowing there was a good chance that Coco would never mention the matter again. Sometimes Chanel would turn her destructive perfectionism against a random, non-Chanel item of clothing, tearing up the jacket of a visitor for example, simply because it seemed ill tailored.

Jean Cazaubon understood how ferociously Chanel wanted to hold on to her power, to her total ownership of the Chanel look, brand, and impact on the world. She had always had this kind of will—which had made the entire Chanel empire possible. With age making her more vulnerable, some of her inner desperation began to show. Coco grew less adept at couching her famous will in charm and seduction.

This is not to say that Chanel's charm had deserted her completely. On the contrary, she still exercised considerable fascination on those around her. She excelled, for example, at creating intimacy through private jokes, sometimes at the expense of a third party. Lilou Marquand remembers accompanying Chanel to an interview where Coco was asked her age. She was seventy-eight at the time but answered, "Eighty-seven," to which the credulous journalist replied, "Wow, you don't look a day over seventy-eight!" Under the table, Coco pressed Lilou's leg in a secret sign of complicity as the two women tried to keep from laughing. "Oh we had crazy laughs together," says Marquand. "Coco was enormously funny." Jeanne Moreau also remembers sharing lighthearted confidences with Chanel: "We spoke . . . of things I'd never discussed with anyone else in my life, and she would laugh!"

Along with her wit, Chanel also maintained her considerable seductiveness. Even into her eighties, men continued to find her alluring. "Oh, she knew how to be a coquette," recalls Willy Rizzo. Her ever-slim figure and great energy helped sustain this appeal. John Fairchild remembers catching sight, sometime in the 1960s, of "a Chanel [suit]. I thought it was a young girl. She walked rapidly with great paces, her head high, never looking to one side or the other. I took a second look. It was a Chanel, a real Chanel, Mademoiselle Chanel herself."

Lilou Marquand also attests to the elderly Chanel's startling effect on men, recounting a day when Chanel received an American journalist at her studio for an interview—a man in his early forties. According to Marquand, Chanel "worked her big charm number" upon this visitor, flirting, bantering, and joking. They talked for hours, and when he left, the journalist confided to Marquand in all seriousness, and with some confusion, "This is the most beautiful day of my life.... I am married, I have two children [but] I just fell in love with that woman." He had not forgotten that she was over eighty, but somehow her age did not impede

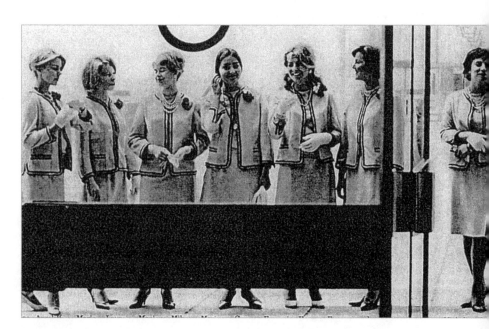

French guides for the 1961 Exposition Française in Moscow, in identical Chanel suits

her charm. "That was her extraordinary charisma," says Marquand. "She was seductive even then."

This rare combination of vision, will, and unusually enduring personal appeal allowed Chanel to impose her vision on the world for seventeen years after her return from exile. That vision communicated itself through her fashions, of course, but also through something more intangible—that Chanel persona and way of being. The "Chanel" name evoked a universe, a worldview, all of which stemmed from the woman herself. A Chanel press release put it this way in 1959: "You will not discover [Chanel] . . . if you try to look separately at a suit, a dress, a blouse, or a hat. . . . They are part of an 'atmosphere.'"

Chanel's overwhelming, even oppressive, personality with friends and colleagues was, in fact, another part of that "atmosphere"—or perhaps the force that sustained the atmosphere. Coco had an unquenchable need to see herself reflected everywhere around her—in mirrors, in the look-alike models she hired, in the uniforms she imposed on her staff and indeed on the world, in the millions of knockoffs she encouraged. And

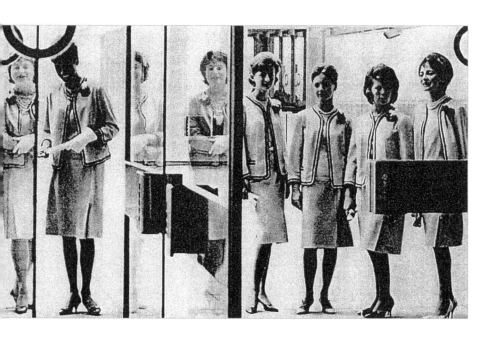

her self-centered, demanding behavior can be seen as an attempt to confirm just how deeply she could impress her will on others. Chanel even
took to scheduling her runway shows deliberately to conflict with President Charles de Gaulle's press conferences, ever eager to assert her dominance and, perhaps, her political importance.

World domination seemed within Chanel's grasp when, in 1961, she
was commissioned to design the uniforms for all the female interpreters
at the Exposition Française in Moscow, the largest exhibition of French
culture to date in a foreign country. From August 15 to September 15,
approximately forty-five thousand Russian citizens paid two rubles each
to stroll through forty thousand square meters in Sokolniki Park, near
Red Square, and peruse displays of French art, commerce, science, and
history. In addition to dressing the guides, the Maison Chanel presented
a runway collection at the expo.

Of course, no one expected the expo would open a new market for
French fashion. The Russians were decades away from having an economy strong enough for haute couture. But the point was not to sell
dresses, as Chanel knew well: "I find that this is a worthwhile experience.
I have always had but one goal in my life: to send my fashions down into
the street. And now here they will be, on Red Square, in Moscow." The
Russians had invited Coco to attend personally, but she found travel increasingly tiring and chose instead to send seven of her models to present her designs. Chanel knew she didn't need to appear in person to
make her mark on Russia. Her presence was felt powerfully enough via
the 130 female interpreters who flooded Red Square in identical Chanel
suits, ambassadors not only of their country, but of one woman's unmistakable identity—fused seemingly permanently to France's cultural
prestige.

G iven how indelible, ubiquitous, and theatrical a character she'd be-
come, it was hardly surprising that Broadway came calling for
Coco Chanel. Accounts differ, but perhaps as early as 1954, producer
Frederick Brisson approached Chanel with the idea of turning her life

story into a play and then a movie. Initially, Chanel refused Brisson's offer, just as she had turned down similar offers from Samuel Goldwyn in 1936 and again in 1940. Brisson, though, persisted for years, claiming he considered Chanel "the most fascinating woman on earth."

Finally, in 1962, Chanel agreed to a meeting in Paris with Brisson and his team: composer André Previn and Broadway lyricist Alan Jay Lerner (of the famous Lerner and Loewe, creators of *Brigadoon, My Fair Lady*, and *Camelot*, among others). Chanel did not recognize Lerner's name, but when she was told he had written the lyrics for *My Fair Lady*, she announced how much she had hated that play, particularly Cecil Beaton's costumes and sets—which she'd found inauthentic. Brisson knew better than to tell Chanel at that moment that Beaton was his first choice to design all sets and costumes for *Coco*, the musical, as well.

Coco had another reservation: She did not want her life portrayed as another rags-to-riches, Eliza Doolittle fairy tale. "I am not your 'Fair Lady,'" she reportedly chided Lerner. No, Coco saw herself as Pygmalion, not Galatea. In truth, she was both. Brisson reassured her that she would be pleased with the script.

Coco was finally won over after Previn played some songs for her on piano and Lerner sang. (Lerner's fluent French may also have impressed her.) Yet another obstacle remained: Pierre Wertheimer was refusing to grant permission for the commercial use of the "Chanel" name. Negotiations with the company dragged on for nearly three years, until Chanel threatened to shut down her couture house entirely if Pierre did not relent. Wertheimer gave in in 1965, approving the production with the proviso that there be no depiction of any Wertheimer family member or employee. Shortly after signing off on *Coco*, Pierre Wertheimer passed away at the age of seventy-seven, leaving another enormous gap in Chanel's life.

Brisson cast Katharine Hepburn as his leading lady—disappointing Coco, who'd initially thought he'd meant the far younger *Audrey* Hepburn. It was a counterintuitive move—Katharine Hepburn could neither sing nor dance, and had no interest in musical theater. She did have a long-standing interest in Coco Chanel, though, having tried and failed to get Chanel hired as costumer for Hepburn's 1932 film, *A Bill of Divorcement*. But the role of Coco Chanel would suit Hepburn for a number of subtle reasons.

By the late 1960s, Katharine Hepburn was easily as well known as Chanel, her distinctive persona indelibly graven into the American public imagination. Hepburn's famous face and voice instantly evoked a specific constellation of traits: intelligence, wit, WASP privilege, independence, and a certain androgynous charm, hinting at bisexuality. Hepburn had, in fact, been involved with a number of women lovers, in addition to her twenty-six-year relationship with Spencer Tracy, and rumors of her lesbian affairs had long plagued her. In other words, Katharine Hepburn offered Frederick Brisson a way to "translate" Chanel's iconicity for American audiences; Kate was Coco's Yankee doppelgänger.

Preparations proved arduous. Coco was unhappy that, to accommodate Hepburn's age, the story focused on Chanel's comeback years rather than on her romantic early days in Deauville. Chanel was most enraged, though, when Brisson refused to let her design the costumes and hired Cecil Beaton instead.

While Chanel might have seemed the ideal—or even the only—candidate for the job of costume designer, Brisson had his reasons. Cecil Beaton had an impressive track record. He'd already won two Oscars for costume designs he'd created for Lerner and Loewe films (in 1958 for *Gigi*, and again in 1964 for *My Fair Lady*). And Beaton was a crowd-pleaser. He made big, colorful, exaggerated designs that could be visually grasped in an instant. In this, his approach differed sharply from Chanel's costuming practice of more or less inserting her regular fashions into theatrical settings. Brisson was not looking for that kind of subtlety for his musical, and so he had Beaton create more than two hundred Chanel-*like* costumes for *Coco*—outfits reminiscent of Chanel's style yet completely devoid of their muted elegance. In the final scene, dozens of models appear wearing bright red evening dresses with big floating capes, trailing sleeves, and other extravagant details Chanel would never have permitted.

Opening night for *Coco*, on December 18, 1969, at the Mark Hellinger

Theatre, drew scores of New York luminaries all dressed to kill, many wearing Chanel, including Gloria Vanderbilt, Lauren Bacall, Martha Graham, Princess Lee Radziwill, and a very young Mia Farrow, then wife of André Previn. Beyond the theater, New York department stores had made a point to feature even more Chanel-inspired designs than usual, expecting (correctly) that the musical would boost sales.

With a production budget of $900,000, *Coco* was the most expensive show that had ever been produced on Broadway, yet reviews were tepid. Hepburn was hardly a musical star, and was talk-singing her lyrics (as Rex Harrison had in *My Fair Lady*). "Her voice is like vinegar on sand paper...a mixture of faith, love, and laryngitis," wrote Clive Barnes—not without affection—in *The New York Times*.

Coco disappointed even André Previn, who admitted, "*Coco* was not very good, I disliked it a lot." The play's choreography, by twenty-six-year-old Michael Bennett—who later created *A Chorus Line*—drew some plaudits, but the thin, clichéd plot depicted Chanel as the stereotypical frustrated and lonely career woman. In Hepburn's big finale number, "Always Mademoiselle," she tremulously talk-sang of a wasted (read: "unmarried") life:

Katharine Hepburn starring in the Broadway musical *Coco*

Dazzling Mademoiselle
in her golden shell
Life is such a very solitary holiday!

Not even the costumes escaped criticism. In *The New York Times* Marylin Bender attacked Beaton's designs: "Beaton's Chanels are as much like Chanel's Chanels as a jar of gefilte fish on a supermarket shelf is to *quenelle de brochet* [pike croquettes] at Grand Véfour [one of Paris's most exclusive restaurants, situated in the Palais-Royal and founded in 1785, before the French Revolution]." Bender's analogy was telling. She'd injected a distinctly Jewish element, likening Beaton's inadequate costumes to gefilte fish, while comparing real Chanel couture to the supposed opposite of that Passover staple: the refinements of Ancien Régime France.

Marylin Bender's remark recalls the extent to which Americans see French culture as a social elevator, an antidote for shame or perceived inadequacy, and how easily Jewishness is understood as one source of such shame. Bender suggests that Chanel offers a polished, "corrected" version of American Jewish identity—conveying a status superior by virtue of being more French, less vulgar.

The classic Chanel look and "atmosphere" felt familiar and attractive to postwar American women because they saw in it a version of their own famous "all-American" ideal: a sleek, athletic, slightly boyish creature, especially fetching in a uniform. In fact, though, the 1950s "all-American boy" look (for it starts with boyishness) is actually a distant cousin to the avatars promoted by fascists in both Italy and Germany. As historian George Mosse explains: "While most of the symbols and rituals of the civic religion of fascism vanished after the Second World War, its stereotypes are still with us.... There is little difference in looks...behavior, and posture, between Mussolini's New Man, the German Aryan, the clean-cut Englishman, or the all-American boy." Mosse is right. Even now, a whiff of racial hierarchy still clings to our idea of the "all-American" look, which conjures the blond hair, blue eyes, and sharp features typically associated with Northern European ancestry.

.   .   .

Fascism may have vanished, but a variant of those "symbols and rituals of a civic religion" live on in aspects of the Chanel phenomenon:
its creation of a self-enclosed universe, its panoply of branded, status-
conferring clothes and accessories, and its offer of membership in an elite
yet accessible community.

It only adds to the irony that Chanel owed her comeback to men with
names such as Stanley Marcus, Bernard Gimbel, and Nathan Ohrbach,
founder of Ohrbach's department store. But, of course, the Seventh Avenue "rag trade"—like the 1930s Hollywood studio system (incubator of
Katharine Hepburn)—was built largely by Jewish men: immigrants and
their sons who made their fortunes by selling back to America an impossibly glossy, idealized—and ethnically neutralized—dream of itself.

This is not to say that women were or are fascists for loving Chanel,
but rather that the mechanism that drove fascism taps into and manipu-
lates certain desires that never go away—a desire to outclass someone
else, to be more elegant, to be better dressed, to "pass," or to be, in some
cases, "more French." Fashion in general speaks to some of these desires,
but Chanel offered more than just fashion; she offered a world to inhabit
and a heroine to emulate.

By giving the role of Coco Chanel to legendary film star Katharine
Hepburn, Frederick Brisson confirmed that he grasped Chanel's implied
promise of social class enhancement and even ethnic leveling. Hepburn
never affected a French accent onstage, but instead spoke in her trademark lockjaw American style, which, coupled with her casually regal,
Bryn Mawr bearing, telegraphed an impeccable Anglo-Saxon pedigree—
the American version of aristocracy. That peculiar marriage of Coco's
and Kate's magic explains how *Coco* succeeded despite its myriad weaknesses. The play ran for a little more than nine months and 329 performances. Despite his detractors, Cecil Beaton walked away with the 1970
Tony Award for his costume work on the production.

The eponymous heroine of *Coco* never saw the play. By most accounts,
she had intended to attend opening night, and had even made herself a

white sequined dress for the occasion (perfect for being visible in a darkened theater). But in December 1969, shortly before the premiere, Coco suffered a small stroke that paralyzed her right hand. Instead of heading to New York, she checked into the American Hospital of Paris in Neuilly-sur-Seine for several days. Doctors predicted she'd make a full recovery if she followed a regimen of physical therapy for several months. But until then, Chanel would need to wear a black, elasticized brace to support her lifeless hand. She was horror-struck. Her hands were the source of all her creative activity; without them she could not work. "I'd rather have typhoid," she snapped to Claude Delay. She was naturally disappointed to miss seeing her story on Broadway, although she'd gotten wind of Beaton's distortion of her work: "He ruined the costumes, everyone has told me so."

Most of all, Coco feared that her stroke would make her seem old and feeble. Determined to keep up appearances, she hired a makeup artist to come to her apartment every morning to do her face. She would not be seen without her full Coco regalia.

Chanel did recover the use of her hand, although severe arthritis deformed the joints of both hands, rendering them partially numb and causing her to prick her fingers often with the dressmaker pins. Anxious always about losing her dexterity, Coco would play with a little rubber ball, turning it over and over to exercise her fingers. Sometimes she'd ask her niece Gabrielle to toss the ball back and forth with her to keep up her agility and reflexes.

During these years, Coco developed angina, and suffered as well from chronic insomnia, which she sometimes tried to alleviate by injecting herself with more than her usual nightly vial of Sedol. Coco's most troubling symptom, though, was her somnambulism—a nocturnal sleepwalking habit that she claimed to have suffered also as a child. Rising from her bed in the middle of the night, Coco was found several times by her maid Céline wandering her apartment. Once, Céline found her mistress immobile before the bathroom sink, compulsively running water over her hands. On a few other occasions, Chanel had to be kept from harming herself when she was found—still asleep—using her bedside scissors to shred her own nightgown.

Finally, when Mademoiselle Chanel was discovered one night partially undressed in the lobby of the Ritz, her staff took action. From then on, after Coco's nightly injection, Lilou and Céline attached her to her bed, gently tying her down. Chanel put up no resistance: "I used to do it all the time as a child. When I am like that, I must be attached," she told Claude Delay. And, like a child, Coco demanded that someone stay by her side until she fell asleep. Sometimes, Céline and another household staff member would play cards quietly in Chanel's bedroom until, seeing her drift off, they could tiptoe out. Coco felt especially vulnerable in sleep, the only time she was forced to abandon control. This was why she slept only at the Ritz, never in her Cambon apartment across the street. "I can't [sleep at Cambon], I'm too frightened!" Chanel told her niece Gabrielle. At a hotel, one is never alone, and Coco needed the presence of others around her—even strangers—at all times.

N either her growing fears nor various maladies slowed Chanel's daytime existence very much. Work remained Coco's lifeline to the world, and she clung to it fiercely, staying fit and active. Even well into her eighties, Chanel was flexible enough to bend over and place both palms flat on the floor without bending her knees. She continued to show up at the Cambon studio—fully dressed and made up—six days a week.

It was that seventh day that posed problems. The long solitude of Sunday grew unbearable for Chanel in her last years. Her social circle had shrunk to just a few companions, prime among these former dancer and television personality Jacques Chazot, journalist Hervé Mille, and psychoanalyst Claude Delay, and a handful of devoted employees—especially Lilou Marquand, and Chanel's household staff: her butler, François Mironnet, and the maid she hired in 1966, whose given name was Céline, but whom Chanel had, somewhat heartbreakingly, rechristened "Jeanne"—her mother's name. Céline accepted the new name with compassionate grace. Occasionally, Gabrielle Palasse-Labrunie or her sister, Hélène Palasse, would also visit.

Never having lost the need to be escorted by a gentleman, Chanel would often spend Sundays with François, the butler, strolling in the Tuileries and sitting with him on the garden's wrought iron chairs. Sometimes, she and Claude Delay would promenade on the Champs-Elysées or the Trocadéro. Other weekends would find Coco at the Longchamp Racecourse in the Bois de Boulogne. Racing was a passion she shared with the Wertheimers and in 1962 she had bought a thoroughbred, Romantica, whose jockey was the celebrated Yves Saint-Martin. Since cemeteries had always calmed her, sometimes Coco would have her driver take her to Père Lachaise—resting place of so many Parisian cultural stars, including a few of her own acquaintance, such as Isadora Duncan, Colette, and Francis Poulenc.

Despite her increasing ill humor, Chanel continued to bestow great generosity upon certain friends and associates. She supported her niece Gabrielle with a comfortable monthly allowance. When Lilou Marquand confided that her family needed money, Coco granted her an enormous raise immediately. (Marquand refused, however, Chanel's later offer to buy her a country home.) Sometimes, Coco let Jacques Chazot take her shopping at particular antiques stores whose owners, she knew, paid him a commission on any purchase she made—she didn't tell him she knew of his arrangement. She also granted Chazot an exclusive on-camera interview with her, simply to boost his television presenting career.

Mademoiselle reserved her greatest generosity for butler François Mironnet—one of the few people she trusted completely. Tall, strong, and charismatic, Mironnet was just thirty-three when Chanel hired him in 1965. Though of humble background—born to a peasant family in Normandy—he was said to bear a passing resemblance to the Duke of Westminster, which might account for some of Coco's attachment to him. Lilou Marquand remembers Coco's habit of leaning her head on Mironnet's shoulder and sighing affectionately, "Oh, François."

Over time, Chanel looked increasingly to Mironnet for companionship, care, and household management. She entrusted to him the responsibility of maintaining her house in Lausanne and all her financial transactions. She gave him the key to the hotel safe that held her jewel collection. Mironnet was the last man in Coco's life. "François calms me," she told Claude Delay.

In return for his calming attentions, and surely to encourage him to stay with her, Coco tried to elevate François's social condition. She invited him to put aside his butler duties and choose instead to work in any division of the Maison Chanel. Mironnet chose jewelry making, whereupon Chanel gave him private tutorials on creating costume jewelry, showing him her method of arranging imitation gemstones in modeling paste. When Mironnet created a convincing copy of a ruby necklace that Chanel had long ago received from the Duke of Westminster, Coco gave him the actual rubies as a "reward." When Coco's longtime friend Maggie van Zuylen died in 1969, François Mironnet accompanied Chanel to the funeral in Amsterdam, on a private plane. Coco bought François a new car. She even invited him to join her as a guest when she hosted a dinner for the Duke and Duchess of Windsor. Mironnet attended that party and when the woman seated next to him told him he looked "familiar," he startled the assembled company with his honest reply, "Yes, I used to serve at Mademoiselle's table." Coco was delighted—she liked nothing better than upending the social hierarchy.

But François had no aspirations to dining with royalty, nor would he bend entirely to Mademoiselle's caprices. One night, while dining in Switzerland with Coco and Lilou, Chanel, in all seriousness, asked François to marry her. Stunned, Mironnet stood up from the table and bolted from the restaurant, disappearing for days. Eventually, Lilou Marquand located him, holed up in a hotel in Lausanne, furious and wounded. In his mind, Chanel had mistaken him for a fortune-hunting gigolo, a man capable of marrying a woman nearly fifty years his senior simply for personal advancement. Lilou begged him to be generous, to understand that Chanel, in her heart, imagined herself a young girl, capable still of giving and inspiring love. François let himself be cajoled into returning to Mademoiselle's service. Chanel accepted his return and never mentioned the incident again.

In persuading François to stay, Marquand may have somewhat over-stated Coco's romantic notions. Chanel was no fool. Although she con-tinued to charm men of all ages well into her elder years, it is improbable that she thought Mironnet and she could conduct a "normal" marriage. More likely, she had hoped that their mutual affection and her continued generosity might suffice to keep François by her side for however many years remained to her—hardly a crazy idea. Countless rich and powerful men have acted upon similar impulses with no loss of dignity.

But Mironnet declined and tried to live his own life, discreetly. One weekend, though, François disappeared and did not return for four days. Chanel discovered he had gone off to get married without informing her, which so devastated her that she increased her dose of Sedol from one injection to four that night. We don't know whether, with this act, Coco was simply trying to ease her pain or end it forever. Whatever her inten-tion, Mademoiselle's iron constitution allowed her to wake up the next morning. She said nothing when Mironnet once more returned to work.

Chanel had no choice but to forgive François's "betrayal." She de-pended on him too much to cut him off. Instead, she redoubled her gen-erosity toward him, even buying and furnishing an apartment for him near the rue Cambon, to keep him that much closer to her. Mironnet was, in fact, one of the few people to whom Coco confided her anxieties about her failing health and her fear of losing her independence. She took great comfort in his promise that, should she become incapacitated, he would take her home to his parents' house in Cabourg, where his family would care for her (at last, the hope of caring parents). Coco even mapped out for François her somewhat ghoulish, even if tongue-in-cheek, wish for her last day. She would prefer, she told him, that upon her death, he and Lilou Marquand transport her corpse to Switzerland—seated upright in her private car. "Put me in the back of the car, between the two of you." Coco seemed to be imagining herself exactly where she always preferred to be: sandwiched between the two halves of a couple, like the cherished child she never was.

Inevitably, old age extracted its price from Coco. She grew physically weaker and unsteady on her feet, even while refusing to accept her limitations. When she fell while walking alone on the street near rue Cambon and cracked three ribs, it took stern convincing to get her to the hospital for X rays. Chanel also began exhibiting signs of slight cognitive decline—misjudging the exact location of a chair as she sat down, or climbing into the bathtub without realizing it had no water in it. She started forgetting appointments, or whether she had eaten lunch. Usually, though, Coco would catch herself in these moments and laugh.

Chanel also seemed to find the physical world around her increasingly intrusive or distasteful. Always fanatic about cleanliness and avoiding unpleasant odors, she now experienced smells so powerfully that she could hardly bear to eat in a public place, finding the aromas of other people's meals overwhelmingly repugnant. This may have been an inherited trait. Coco had always recalled her father's extreme sensitivity to smells. At the Ritz, she demanded a table at the farthest corner of the dining room, closest to the window and as removed as possible from other diners.

Beyond the infirmities and indignities of age, the question of her legacy consumed Chanel. Who would succeed her at the helm of the Maison Chanel? There was no obvious candidate; Chanel had never groomed a successor. She disliked sharing credit with the many talented people who worked for her, and so, at the end of her career, no one stood ready to assume responsibility for the house. Somewhat haphazardly, Chanel broached the possibility with a number of her friends and associates, including Marcel Haedrich, then director of *Marie Claire;* Hervé Mille, editor in chief of *Paris Match;* and Pierre Bergé, Yves Saint Laurent's business and life partner. None of these men was interested. The future of the Chanel empire remained an open question.

Yet Chanel showed little inclination to turn over the keys to the kingdom. Sustained by her small cadre of long-suffering and devoted intimates, she held illness, age, and anxiety at bay for a long time, continuing to create ceaselessly and to amass an ever-greater fortune. In 1970, the Maison Chanel employed a total of 3,500 people, spread over the four divisions of her company: clothing, textiles, perfume, and jewelry. Her 1970 sales were up 30 percent over those of 1969. She was more successful than ever, instantly recognizable to millions, and stopped in the street by admirers from every country. "I am more famous than I was before the war," she crowed to Marcel Haedrich. "The common people know me!"

Working at the pace she did past the age of eighty-seven, Chanel seemed for a time indestructible. It took a Sunday to bring her down. Coco spent the afternoon of Sunday, January 10, 1971, in the company of Claude Delay. They lunched together at the Ritz (a small steak, potatoes, a glass of Riesling, and coffee for Coco) and then drove in Chanel's Cadillac to the Bois de Boulogne, returning in the early evening. Coco repaired to her suite at the Ritz, fully planning to resume work the next morning on her collection.

A terrible fatigue overtook her that night, and at about eight thirty, Coco climbed into bed without even changing into her customary silk pajamas. Soon she was gasping for breath and crying out for "Jeanne," her maid, to open the window. When she fumbled with the vial of Sedol, unable to break it open and inject herself, Céline did it for her, administering Chanel's last dose of morphine. Relieved of the most intense pain of what was later adjudged an internal hemorrhage, Coco whispered, "So this is how one dies." By the time Céline rushed back to her side after frantically telephoning the doctor, Coco was gone. Her face was bathed in tears, according to Céline.

Before all the tributes and retrospectives attending the death of a global celebrity, there come first the ripples of reaction through the closest circle—family and friends, which tend to reflect the tenor of the deceased's personal interactions in life. In the case of Coco Chanel, her death predictably launched a series of bitter accusations, shifting stories, and misrepresentations. It seems indisputable that Chanel died alone save for the presence of her maid, Céline. Yet, perhaps wishing to confirm her special closeness with Chanel, Lilou Marquand claims to have rushed over at the last moment to hold Coco's hand as she died, then, by her own admission, removing from that hand—and keeping for herself—one of Chanel's rings.

We do know that Gabrielle Palasse-Labrunie arrived soon after Chanel's death and hurried everyone out, insisting that her aunt had expressly wished for no one to see her in death—a very plausible claim given Coco's embarrassment about her appearance in old age. Both Marquand and Jacques Chazot were angered by the way Labrunie stepped in to direct the proceedings, insisting that Chanel had never had more than minimal contact with her niece. "In fifteen years, I saw [Labrunie] there maybe three times," says Marquand, still angry forty years later that her intimacy with Chanel was not honored in the end.

Some of the infighting concerned, unsurprisingly, the distribution—or disappearance—of Chanel's personal property and fortune. The Chanel corporation, of course, was already entirely under the financial control of the Wertheimers. Premier jeweler Robert Goossens, who worked for Chanel as well as for Jacques Fath and Cristóbal Balenciaga, among others, has said that many of Chanel's most valuable jewels, precious stones given her by Grand Duke Dmitri or the Duke of Westminster and kept in a locked lacquered box, simply vanished after her death—and vaguely accuses Chanel's two great-nieces Gabrielle and Hélène of making off with the stones. Gabrielle Palasse-Labrunie completely contradicts Goossens, recounting that she arrived the morning after her aunt's death to find the jewelry box already nearly entirely empty. Labrunie, too, is still angry; she blames François Mironnet for the missing jewels. He had the key to the box, she says.

As for the devoted François, he placed himself in the eye of a legal hurricane immediately after Chanel's death by going to court to claim that Mademoiselle had bequeathed to him her home in Lausanne, all her jewels, and about 5 million francs in cash (about $6 million today). The case remained unresolved until one year later when a sealed handwritten letter fell out of a book found in Chanel's personal library. The letter, signed with Coco's name, detailed the legacy she'd promised to him, and appeared to legitimize Mironnet's claim. When handwriting experts could not confirm the letter's authenticity, Mironnet accepted an out-of-court settlement, and returned to his new life as a jewelry designer in Saint-Tropez.

W ho did inherit Chanel's personal fortune, whose estimated total ranged from 30 million francs to several billion? No one. At least, no one specific. In 1965, Chanel had formally declared that her sole inheritor was her foundation, COGA, in Vaduz, Liechtenstein—a venue chosen on the advice of her lawyers. The trust was administered by the Zurich law firm of Alfred Hier. Chanel might have stipulated a thousand possible uses for the trust, but she did not. Her entire will consisted of two sentences: "This is my last will and testament. I establish as my sole and universal heir the Coga Foundation Vaduz, Liechtenstein."

Apart from private instructions she left about bequeathing sums of money to various individuals who had been helpful to her, Chanel left almost no directions for her executors. She had perhaps spoken vaguely to her lawyers about COGA being used to help artists, but nothing in the legal documents required any particular disbursement of funds whatso-ever. For Coco, it seemed, COGA's mission was far less important than its discretion. She wanted to keep the foundation entirely shielded from public eyes, and in this, Mademoiselle succeeded entirely. Tiny Vaduz is home to more than fifty thousand holding companies, trusts, and foundations—none of which has any reason to be in Liechtenstein apart from the country's status as a tax haven and its policy of sepulchral si-lence about its investors and holdings. It is considered one of the most secretive tax jurisdictions in the world. The woman who strove so might-ily to obscure her origins in life had found the perfect place to hide the last vestiges of herself in death, burying her treasure without a trace.

Whatever the private chaos unleashed by Chanel's death among her intimates, the public received her passing with mournful respect and ad-miring tributes. On Wednesday, January 13, 1971, several hundred peo-ple filed into the grand marble Eglise de la Madeleine, just blocks from

Mourners at Chanel's funeral

the rue Cambon, for the funeral of Gabrielle "Coco" Chanel. Bowers of white flowers covered her simple oak casket, within which Coco, too, was all in white—the simple white bouclé suit in which Céline had dressed her for burial.

The mourners included many of the stars of the Paris fashion world: Yves Saint Laurent, Pierre Balmain, Cristóbal Balenciaga, André Courrèges, and Marc Bohan of the Maison Dior. Chanel had outlived many of her closest and most illustrious friends, but among those remaining to say good-bye were dancer Serge Lifar, Jacques Chazot, Salvador Dalí, Antoinette Bernstein, and Edmonde Charles-Roux—the friend whose plans to write Chanel's biography had so enraged her. Chanel's models paid tribute to their mentor with their gift of a white floral sculpture in the shape of a giant pair of scissors, which sat atop the coffin, too. Six of the models sat together in one pew, none of them wearing black. Instead, the young women had all dressed in variations of Mademoiselle's trademark suits of tweed or plaid, in light or pastel tones. In his eulogy, Father Victor Chabanis, vicar of the Madeleine, may have felt compelled to acknowledge—albeit subtly—Chanel's less-than-perfectly Catholic life: "It would take a greater voice than mine to describe this very Parisian, very human personality. She was universally respected."

Chanel was not buried at La Madeleine. After the funeral, a small procession of fifteen of her closest friends and family drove on to Lausanne, where in 1965, Coco had bought a plot in the beautiful, verdant Bois-de-Vaux Cemetery near Lake Geneva. There, in a very brief ceremony, Gabrielle was finally laid to rest.

The stone marking her grave was designed by sculptor Jacques Labrunie, her niece Gabrielle's husband, in close consultation with Coco. It is not directly above the grave, but off to one side, so that Chanel "could get out" if she wished, as she put it. Nearby stands a small bench, so that visitors might sit and converse with Coco, as she had so often with other graves during her lifetime. The stone bears only her name—Gabrielle

Grave of Gabrielle Chanel, Bois-de-Vaux Cemetery, Lausanne, Switzerland

Chanel (without "Coco")—and the dates of her birth and death. There is no quotation, no epitaph. Instead, a phalanx of bas-relief lions' heads keep watch over the woman beneath, born under the sign of Leo. Their manes fall into artful waves, as if arranged by a coiffeur, and their sculpted gaze mingles ferocity and an almost cartoonish sweetness. There are five of them.

AFTERWORD

I believe in the fourth dimension, and in the fifth, and in the sixth. . . . It is born from the need to be reassured, to believe that we never lose everything and that something exists on the other side.

—COCO CHANEL

Citing the Eastern philosophies she'd studied with Boy Capel, Chanel often insisted that death was not a final disappearance, but a mere crossing over—one passage among many. It's hard to know if this notion of "the other side" ever really convinced or comforted Coco, especially during her intensely lonely last few years.

But if Chanel had doubted the existence of an afterlife, events since her demise encourage the rest of us to believe in it, for Coco Chanel lives on with astonishing force and vividness, through the ubiquity of her signature style, the apparently endless fascination with Chanel herself, and the odd couple she makes with her successor, Karl Lagerfeld.

Chanel's afterlife passed through several phases. Immediately after her death came a period of respectful contemplation—in print as well as on the runway. Obituaries highlighted the epic story of the girl who'd transcended modest origins to become a fashion revolutionary, "the great spirit of the twentieth century," as Diana Vreeland put it. It would take years before some of the more accurate, gritty details about Coco's early life emerged, but most of the articles did acknowledge the mystery that had always attended Coco Chanel.

Just weeks after Chanel's death, her fashion house staged its first runway show without her, featuring the muted collection she'd been working on in her final days: bouclé tweed suits, unstructured coats and dresses, and the three white evening dresses with which Coco had always ended runway shows. Despite the subdued mood that afternoon, at the end of the show, audience members burst into unusually sustained applause, while craning their necks toward the celebrated spiral staircase, as if hoping to conjure Mademoiselle back to her usual observation post.

In the absence of any obvious successor, leadership at Chanel remained uncertain, and for more than a decade no one challenged the absolute authority of the house's deceased founder. In February 1971, the corporation tapped Gaston Berthelot, former designer of ready-to-wear at Christian Dior, as the new artistic "coordinator," tasking him only with perpetuating the extant Chanel style—not with creating any original designs. A few seasons later, Berthelot was replaced by former Chanel assistants Yvonne Dudel and Jean Cazaubon—with similar results: the impeccable reproduction of Chanel style, to the exclusion of all innovation.

While the Chanel brand remained as famous as ever, its air of luxury and exclusivity had begun to fade. Patronized throughout the 1970s largely by dignified ladies of a certain age—politicians' wives and wealthy grandmothers—the House of Chanel fell into a torpor. Once the epitome of youthful chic, the Chanel suit gradually morphed into a symbol of stodgy matronhood. Chanel No. 5 continued to generate tremendous revenue for the company, but by 1974, the famous flacon was being sold in thousands of corner drugstores across America, slumming alongside aspirin and shampoo—its magical allure all but evaporated.

Recognizing the problem, owner Alain Wertheimer (Pierre's grandson) took steps to restore the brand's cachet, hiring a Washington law firm to help him pull Chanel perfume out of low-market stores and developing a new line of cosmetics, Chanel Beauté, to be sold for high prices in a limited number of upscale locations. But shaking the Maison out of its deeper somnolence required a new vision, and Chanel's true renaissance did not begin until 1983, when Wertheimer appointed the fifty-year-old German-born Karl Lagerfeld as artistic director.

A prodigiously gifted couturier (who had never met Chanel), Lagerfeld had already enjoyed a thirty-year career in Paris, working for such houses as Patou, Fendi, and Chloé. He was also a true *personnage*—a self-styled dandy who spoke four languages, wore his hair in a small, low ponytail, and dressed like a Baroque nobleman, favoring brocade waistcoats, even a monocle. "The eighteenth century is my first love," Lagerfeld said, and the elaborate pageantry of his life confirmed this. In Paris, Lagerfeld resided in an eighteenth-century mansion, furnished with red damask draperies, gilded mirrors, and rococo furniture. He also maintained homes in Rome, Monte Carlo, Switzerland, and Brittany.

While his wealth was indisputable, its origins were not. Lagerfeld often hinted that his parents were leisured aristocrats, but in truth, he came from an affluent but solidly bourgeois family that had endured genuine privation, hunger, and fear during World War II. But Lagerfeld never admitted to any of the harder memories of his youth. For him, facts mattered far less than image, and he was a genius at creating his own myth. Wry, ironic, scathingly disparaging of anyone he deemed inelegant or boring, Lagerfeld had the *sprezzatura* to take on the ghost of Mademoiselle.

With his first Chanel runway collection, Lagerfeld walked a couture tightrope: While clearly acknowledging the Chanel tradition, he dared to look beyond the reigning classic tweeds and reached far back into the Chanel archives to revamp some of Coco's earliest, most beguiling ideas: the jersey suit, evening dresses with fluffy tulle boleros, and jewels sewn directly onto dresses.

Over time, Lagerfeld has made plain how little he cares to worship at the altar of Coco: "Respect is not creation. Chanel is an institution, and you have to treat an institution like a whore," he has declared. This iconoclasm has electrified and rejuvenated the house. Lagerfeld has lengthened jackets or nipped them at the waist, shortened skirts (sometimes to micromini dimensions), and incorporated a range of materials and cultural cues that would never have passed muster with Mademoiselle: leather, denim, hip-hop bling, sky-high heels, punk graffiti, surfer looks, S&M bondage details. "He has antennae everywhere," as Marika Genty, of the Direction du Patrimoine Chanel, puts it. Lagerfeld has sent models sashaying down the catwalk braless under see-through body stockings. He has tampered with the sacrosanct Chanel armhole, producing tighter, curvier, yet far less forgiving jackets. And he has even designed corsets to be worn visibly—as fashion, not undergarments—in flagrant defiance of Chanel's historic injunction against them.

Jettisoning Chanel's trademark understatement, Lagerfeld has produced—for more than thirty years now—consistently inventive, sensual, and lavishly beautiful clothes for the Maison, while at times designing for other labels as well. In his version of Chanel, women don't fit in, they stand out. Only newness interests him, and he claims to discard every garment and sketch after finishing a collection.

But despite his passion for the ephemeral, Lagerfeld never neglects the enduring features that make Chanel Chanel. He "speaks," that is, "fluent Chanel"—only in his own, distinct accent. Motifs such as quilted leather, imitation jewels, soft tweeds, chain link belts, gold-buttoned jackets, white collars and cuffs, and camellia flowers all float through his collections, looking familiar yet altered—as if plundered somehow from Coco's morphine-induced dreams: A suit jacket might be studded with faux pearls as big as Ping-Pong balls, pastel tweed fashioned into a cropped, boat-necked mini-blazer, or decorative fringe "buzz cut" so that its strands flutter outward from a dress instead of hanging straight down.

Accessories inspire special exuberance in Lagerfeld: A quilted leather shoulder bag might be blown up to the size of a hula hoop.

He has even designed a surfboard to resemble a giant Chanel slingback—in beige with a black "toecap," and stamped with the double-C logo. In a surreal photo shoot, models in classic Chanel skirt suits, pearls, and straw boaters toted the surfboards across a sandy beach.

Lagerfeld refines his own persona with similar self-aware wit. "I am my own marionette," he acknowledges. He dusts his trademark ponytail with dry shampoo to give it the look of a powdered wig, carries a fan, keeps his eyes hidden day and night behind massive black sunglasses ("I'm not a stripper!" he retorts when asked to remove them), and sticks usually to a uniform of bespoke white shirt with a high collar, tight black jeans and jacket, black tie with jeweled pin, fingerless black leather mitts, and heavy silver rings on every finger. The ensemble makes a postmodern pastiche of Goth, punk, the Prussian military (his press nickname is "the Kaiser"), the court of Louis XVI, and—in its black-and-white palette, modernist lines, and abundant jewelry—Coco Chanel. Lagerfeld also resembles Coco in his choice to keep two adjacent homes in Paris— one where he sleeps and sketches, the other for everything else. "They are very alike, these two people," says the director of international public relations for Chanel. Coco is also present in Lagerfeld's cultivation of a faintly royal bearing (he has staged runway shows at the Palace of Versailles), although he evokes nobility with a cool and knowing wink,

Karl Lagerfeld and his models in Saint-Tropez,
for the runway show of Chanel Cruise Collection, May 2010

never with aspirational longing. Via his nationality, Lagerfeld even manages to raise the specter of Chanel's relationship with Germany, only to exorcise it with his obvious preference for a safely pre-Nazi era.

Too self-ironic—and too male—to offer himself seriously as a role model for women, Lagerfeld relies on a different technique: By at once "channeling" Chanel, and caricaturing her, he keeps the myth alive while opening it up for others to share. Lagerfeld lends the Chanel persona to a changing cast of celebrities. With the Cambon studio, Chanel's suite at the Ritz, and other classic "Coco" locations as backdrops, he casts popular singers or actresses as latter-day Cocos, dressing them in Chanel couture, and having them reimagine famous portraits of Coco (pop icon Rihanna re-created a classic Horst photograph of Coco), or act out her life story. Actresses Keira Knightley and Geraldine Chaplin have both played Chanel in short films by Lagerfeld.

Lagerfeld has also infused the Chanel brand with the gravitas of high art. On his watch, exhibitions showcasing Chanel's life and work have been organized in major museums worldwide. Most dramatically, in a 2008 publicity campaign, the "Mobile Art Chanel Pavilion"—star architect Zaha Hadid's 7,500-square-foot portable gallery—toured the globe. Resembling a Chanel handbag transformed into a spaceship, and built at a reputed cost of 1 million euros, the pavilion traveled to Hong Kong, Tokyo, and New York—where it was erected on prime real estate in Central Park, at Sixty-ninth Street and Fifth Avenue. Once inside, visitors could view contemporary artworks purportedly inspired by Chanel's 2.55 quilted handbag, while marveling at Hadid's undulating, sci-fi structure.

However outré Lagerfeld, his couture, or recent Chanel publicity might seem, the generating force of this massive enterprise remains Coco Chanel herself. It's her classic style—the ribbon-trimmed tweeds, striped pullovers, long ropes of pearls, and two-toned shoes—that has never stopped being reproduced, her double-C logo that renders nearly any product a coveted status symbol. The ongoing love of these elements has helped Chanel grow to its current, vast proportions.

During the past three decades, the Chanel corporation (still held by the fiercely private Wertheimers) has expanded into nearly every country outside of Africa, and generates sales upwards of $11 billion annually. Yet Chanel employees at every level speak of their careers as a devotional, not a commercial, practice—as participation in an exclusive inner sanctum. "You've got to feel it in your gut," said a woman who helps manage the Chanel archives. "Chanel is a religion," says one executive. "You are inside it or you are not. It's a spirit."

Another high-level staff member, who deals with couture clients from the developing world, implicitly compared her work to a missionary's: "There are two kinds of clients: [those] who must be taught, and the cultivated, who already know." Employees, too, must be taught, and the Maison Chanel maintains training institutes in many world capitals, where new recruits learn not only about Chanel products, fashion, and business practices, but also about Coco Chanel, the woman. Studying the life of the founder (or an approved version of it) has proved an indispensable prerequisite for those who disseminate her image globally.

When I received permission to interview one of the most senior members of the Chanel team in Paris, I expected a very prepossessing figure. Not only was this woman a powerful executive, she was a celebrity, a jet-setting socialite, constantly photographed in the international press. She was also an aristocrat, bearing the instantly recognizable name of one of France's oldest, most historic families. Her presence continues Mademoiselle's practice of hiring members of the nobility.

An assistant escorted me into the office, where the lady—extremely slim and in her midsixties—was seated at her desk. She wore a cashmere sweater embossed with the double-C insignia, a Chanel tweed skirt, and Chanel pumps. Her dark hair was cut stylishly short. She looked up to greet me, and as she did so, she picked up an atomizer bottle of Chanel No. 5 sitting on her desk and quickly sprayed several circles of it around her head, creating for a moment a visible cloud. That mist soon evaporated, but its effect was long-lasting. As we talked that day, the scent never faded. Mademoiselle's aura stayed with us.

Chanel on her famous staircase, January 1, 1953

I have tried to be both invisible and present.

—COCO CHANEL

ACKNOWLEDGMENTS

The human, interpersonal aspect of research is, for me, the most gratifying. I treasure the new acquaintances I've made over these years, and look back with delight at the many interviews and conversations I've shared with them. I can but hope that the book does justice to all that has been given me during its creation.

France: I owe a debt of gratitude to the outstanding staff of the Direction du patrimoine de la Maison Chanel in Paris, especially Marika Genty and Cécile Goddet-Dirles. Thanks also to Odile Babin, Valérie Duport, and Marie-Louise de Clermont-Tonnerre for enlightening me about Chanel fashion, the history of the brand, its business practices, and its unique culture.

I am grateful to the staffs of the Musée de la mode de la Ville de Paris (Musée Galliera); the Musée de la mode et du textile; the Musée des Arts décoratifs; the Bibliothèque littéraire Jacques Doucet; the Bibliothèque Forney; the Bibliothèque historique de la Ville de Paris; the Bibliothèque de l'Arsenal; the Comité Jean Cocteau, especially Claudine Boulouque; the Archives de la préfecture de police de Paris, especially Emanuelle Broux-Foucaud; and the archives de la Société historique de Compiègne. Special thanks must go as well to Caroline Berton of Condé Nast, France.

For granting me personal interviews and sharing documents, photographs, and stories, I offer heartfelt thanks to Antoine Balsan; Philippe Carcasonne; Betty Catroux; (the late) Viviane Dreyfus Forrester and her sister, Dowager Lady Christiane Dreyfus Swaything; Philippe Gontier; James Palmer of Mondex Corporation; Danniel Rangel; Gabrielle Palasse-Labrunie; Lilou Marquand; Brigitte Moral Planté; and (the late) Willy Rizzo and his wife, Dominique Rizzo. For permitting me access to their mother's manuscripts, I thank Philippe de Vilmorin and Claire de Fleurieu. Thank you to French graffiti and installation artist Zevs, for granting me the rights to reproduce his work, and to Isée St. John Knowles of the Société Baudelaire.

For leading me to new information about Arthur "Boy" Capel, I thank Martine Alison, Daniel Hainaut, and Joseph Quinette of the Société de l'histoire de Fréjus.

Switzerland: I am grateful to Milo Keller and to Emile Barret of the Ecole cantonale d'art de Lausanne for help obtaining photographs.

Italy: I thank Countess Isabella Vacani von Fechtmann of Genoa for sharing her recollections of Chanel and for proposing intriguing new interpretations of certain events.

England: I am grateful to the staffs of the Victoria and Albert Museum, the Imperial War Museum of London, and the Churchill Archives Centre at Cambridge University. For his outstanding research help, I thank Marc Offord of Cambridge University. A special thank-you is due as well to Professor William Philpott of King's College, London.

Spain: Director Josep Miquel Garcia welcomed me most graciously to the Fundació Apel-les Fenosa in El Vendrell, Spain, shared his extensive archives with me, and even allowed me to view all the objects in an exhibition that had already been deinstalled.

United States: I thank Barbara Cirkva of Chanel, New York, for help-ing me gain access to the Chanel Archives in Paris. I am especially in-debted to Harold Koda, curator in charge of the Costume Institute at the Metropolitan Museum of Art, New York.

I am grateful to the staff of the Museum of the City of New York, particularly Phyllis Magidson, William DiGregorio, and Nilda Rivera, and to the staff at the Fashion Institute of Technology and the New York Public Library for Performing Arts. Thanks also to Leigh Montville of Condé Nast, New York.

The staff of Harvard's Houghton Library unlocked the diaries of Grand Duke Dmitri Romanov for me, and Philipp Penka, of Harvard's Department of Slavic Languages and Literature, translated those diaries with great subtlety and care.

Thanks go as well to the staff of the glorious Getty Research Institute, where I began this project; Rebecca Cape of the Lilly Library at Indiana University; Russell Martin of the DeGolyer Library at Southern Meth-odist University; the staff of the Wolfsonian-FIU Museum; the United States Holocaust Memorial Museum, especially Caroline Waddell; the Special Collections Department of Northwestern University; the Ari-zona Costume Institute; and the Harry Ransom Center of the University of Texas at Austin. Special thanks also to Uki Goñi for providing rare and important new materials, and to photographer Jaime Moore, who granted me rights to her work.

For sharing information and photographs of their historic family, I am grateful to their Serene Highnesses, Princess Anna Romanoff Ilyin-sky and Prince Michael Romanoff Ilyinsky.

To the many colleagues and friends who supported and encouraged me during this process, I want to express more than gratitude; I want to convey how lucky I feel to enjoy their company and innumerable talents. Thank you to April Alliston, Leirion Gaylor Baird, Kenneth Bleeth, Les-lie Camhi, Joy Castro, Mary Ann Caws, Anne Duncan (who helped with Greek translations), Caroline Evans of London's Central Saint Martins, Nancy Friedemann, Charley Friedman, Jane Garrity, Susan Gubar, Matthew Gumpert, John Habich, Richard Halpern, Glenn Kurtz (who read and commented thoughtfully on an early draft), Amelia Montes, Eugenia Paulicelli, Julie Stone Peters, Susan Poser (who also read and commented on every chapter), Nana Smith, and Willard Spiegelman.

Thanks to Maurice Samuels and Alice Kaplan for providing me an opportunity to present a part of this book at Yale University. I am, as ever, grateful to Andrew Solomon for his support, thoughtful critique, and amazing generosity.

Jaime Wolf was unstinting in lending me his legal expertise, as was his colleague Matthew Tynan.

For special research and technical assistance, I thank Bradley Cain, Robert Fuglei, Nahid Hassani, Jack Hill, Valérie Masson, Lisa Maurer, Paul Rubin, and Kenneth Seidel.

I have benefited from the support of administrators and colleagues at the University of Nebraska-Lincoln, especially James B. Milliken, Charles O'Connor, Harvey Perlman, William Nunez, Professor Susan Belasco, Professor Emerita Joy Ritchie, Petra Wahlqvist, Amy Ossian, and Lucy Buntain Comine. For their support of an earlier version of this project, I gratefully acknowledge the John Simon Guggenheim Memorial Foundation, the Dedalus Foundation, the American Council of Learned Societies, and the Getty Research Institute.

Scott Moyers believed in and nurtured this project from the very beginning and convinced me to trust my "biographer's yen." Andrew Wylie and his staff in New York and London provide a level of intelligent attention that can only be called "luxurious." Special thanks must go to Jacqueline Ko at the Wylie Agency.

For her rare combination of a brilliant critical mind and a very gentle, diplomatic style of persuasion, I am especially thankful for my editor, Jennifer Hershey. Associate editor Joey McGarvey combines keen insight and meticulousness with heroic levels of patience.

To my sister, Karen DeRubeis, thank you for being my most steadfast confidante. Thank you Alexandra and Dylan DeRubeis for your loving enthusiasm.

Finally, my husband, Jorge Daniel Veneciano, endured listening to nearly the entire manuscript read aloud, and dramatically improved it with his fine and astute suggestions. His vision never fails to surprise me, and through him, I learn to see the world in entirely new ways. His vibrant, learned, sophisticated yet joyful appreciation of design, art, culture, and life itself sustains me daily.

BIBLIOGRAPHY

ARCHIVES AND SPECIAL COLLECTIONS

Archives de la Préfecture de Police de Paris. Paris, France.

Archives de la Société Historique de Compiègne. Compiègne, France.

Balsan family archives. Private collection. Châteauroux, France.

Bibesco, Princess Marthe. Papers. Harry Ransom Center. The University of Texas at Austin. Austin, Texas.

Bibliothèque de l'Arsenal. Collection Auguste Rondel (materials on early twentieth-century French dance, drama, and musical performance). Paris, France.

Chanel, House of. Direction du Patrimoine (formerly known as the Conservatoire Chanel, archives pertaining to the life of Gabrielle Chanel and the Chanel Corporation). Paris, France.

Churchill, Sir Winston. Chartwell Papers. Churchill Archives Centre. Churchill College, Cambridge University. Cambridge, England.

Cocteau, Jean. Fonds Cocteau. Bibliothèque Historique de la Ville de Paris. Paris, France.

Cooper, Alfred Duff (1st Viscount Norwich). Papers. Churchill Archives Centre. Churchill College, Cambridge University. Cambridge, England.

Diaghilev, Serge. The Ballets Russes of Serge Diaghilev. Howard D. Rothschild Collection. Harvard Theatre Collection. Houghton Library. Harvard University. Cambridge, Massachusetts.

Fundació Apel-les Fenosa. Archive. El Vendrell, Spain.

Iribe, Paul. Fonds Iribe. *Le Témoin,* all issues. Bibliothèque Forney. Paris, France.

Northwestern University Library, Charles Deering McCormick Library of Special Collections, Siege of Paris Collection. Evanston, Illinois.

Romanov, Dmitri Pavlovich, Grand Duke of Russia. Diaries and Personal Record Books. Houghton Library. Harvard University. Cambridge, Massachusetts.

Swanson, Gloria. Papers. Harry Ransom Center. The University of Texas, Austin. Austin, Texas.

Vilmorin, Louise de. Fonds Louise de Vilmorin. Bibliothèque Jacques Doucet. Paris, France.

Wilson, Sir Henry H. Papers. Imperial War Museum. London, England.

WORKS ON CHANEL

Bott, Danièle. *Chanel.* Paris: Editions Ramsey, 2005.

Chaney, Lisa. *Chanel: An Intimate Life.* New York: Viking Press, 2011.

Charles-Roux, Edmonde. *Chanel and her World.* Translated by Daniel Wheeler. New York: The Vendôme Press, 1981. Originally published in French as *Le Temps Chanel.* Paris: Editions du Chêne, 1979.

———. *Le Monde Chanel.* Paris: Chêne/Grasset, 1979.

_____. *L'Irrégulière: l'itinéraire de Coco Chanel.* Paris: Grasset, 1974.

Cocteau, Jean. "Chanel, un projet romanesque." *Oeuvres romanesques.* Paris: Gallimard, 2006, 883–884 (original date of publication unknown).

Delay, Claude. *Chanel Solitaire.* 1974. Paris: Gallimard, 1983.

Fiemeyer, Isabelle. *Coco Chanel, un Parfum de mystère.* Paris: Editions Payot, 1999.

_____ and Gabrielle Palasse Labrunie. *Intimate Chanel.* Paris: Flammarion, 2011.

Galante, Pierre. *Mademoiselle Chanel,* translated by Eileen Geist and Jesse Wood. Chicago: H. Regnery Co., 1973.

Haedrich, Marcel. *Coco Chanel.* Paris: Editions Belfond, 1987, rep. 2008 Editions Gutenberg.

Kennett, Frances. *The Life and Loves of Gabrielle Chanel.* London: Gollancz Books, 1989.

Koda, Harold, and Andrew Bolton, eds. *Chanel.* New York: The Metropolitan Museum of Art, 2005.

Madsen, Axel. *Chanel: A Woman of her Own.* New York: Henry Holt, 1991.

Marquand, Lilou. *Chanel m'a dit.* Paris: Editions Lattès, 1990.

Mazzeo, Tilar. *The History of Chanel No. 5: The Intimate History of the World's Most Famous Perfume.* New York: HarperCollins, 2010.

———. *L'Allure de Chanel.* 1976. Reprint. Paris: Hermann, 1996.

Picardie, Justine. *Coco Chanel: The Legend and the Life.* New York: HarperCollins, 2010.

Ternon, François. *Histoire du numéro 5 de Chanel.* Paris: Editions Normant, 2009.

Vaughan, Hal. *Sleeping with the Enemy: Coco Chanel's Secret War.* New York: Knopf, 2011.

Vilmorin, Louise de. *Mémoires de Coco.* Paris: Gallimard, 1999.

Wallach, Janet. *Chanel: Her Style and Her Life.* New York: Doubleday, 1998.

OTHER WORKS

Adam, Helen Pearl. *Paris Sees It Through: A Diary, 1914–1919.* London: Hodder and Stoughton, 1919.

Alison, Martine. "Les Parents d'A. E. Capel." Unpublished article, 2008.

—————. "T. J. Capel." Unpublished article, 2008.

Allard, Paul. *Quand Hitler Espionne la France.* Paris: Les Editions de France, 1939.

Anthony, Noel. "Fern Bedaux Fights Back." *The Milwaukee Journal,* April 13, 1955.

Antliff, Mark. "Fascism, Modernism, and Modernity." *Art Bulletin* 84, no. 1 (March 2002): 148–69.

Arendt, Hannah. *The Origins of Totalitarianism.* 1948. Reprint, New York: Harcourt, 1968.

"Art de Vivre." *Madame Figaro,* April 17, 2009.

"Article on Moscow Exposition." *Le Patriote Illustré,* no. 32, August 6, 1961.

Atkinson, Brooks J. "The Play: Lunations of Jean Cocteau." *The New York Times,* April 25, 1930.

Baackmann, Susanne, and David Craven. "An Introduction to Modernism—Fascism—Postmodernism." *Modernism/modernity* 15, no. 1 (January 2008): 1–8.

Ballard, Bettina. *In My Fashion.* New York: D. McKay, 1969.

Balsan, Consuelo Vanderbilt. *The Glitter and the Gold: The American Duchess in Her Own Words.* 1953. Reprint, New York: St. Martin's Press, 2012.

Barbieri, Annalisa. "When Skirts Were Full and Women Were Furious." *The Independent,* March 3, 1996.

Bard, Christine. *Les Filles de Marianne.* Paris: Fayard, 1995.

Barnes, Clive. "Katharine Hepburn Has Title Role in 'Coco.'" *The New York Times,* December 19, 1969.

Barry, Joseph. "Chanel No. 1: Fashion World Legend." *The New York Times,* August 23, 1964.

—————. Interview with Chanel. *McCall's,* November 1, 1965, 172–73.

Barthes, Roland. "The Contest Between Chanel and Courrèges." In *The Language of Fashion,* translated by Andy Stafford and edited by Stafford and Michael Carter, 105. Oxford: Berg, 2006.

Baudelaire, Charles. "Knock Down the Poor!" Translated by Albert Botin. In *Baudelaire, Rimbaud, Verlaine,* edited by Joseph Bernstein. New York: Citadel Press, 1993.

Beaton, Cecil. *The Glass of Fashion.* New York: Doubleday, 1954.

—————. *The Unexpurgated Beaton: The Cecil Beaton Diaries as He Wrote Them, 1970–1980.* New York: Knopf, 2003.

Bedford, Sybille. *Quicksands.* Berkeley: Counterpoint, 2005.

Belle, Jean-Michel. *Les Folles années de Maurice Sachs.* Paris: Editions Bernard Grasset, 1979.

Benaïm, Laurence. *Marie Laure de Noailles: La Vicomtesse du bizarre.* Paris: Grasset, 2001.

Bender, Marylin. "The Challenge of Making Costumes Out of Chanel's Clothes." *The New York Times,* November 25, 1969.

Benjamin, Walter. *The Arcades Project.* Translated by Kevin McLaughlin. Cambridge, Mass.: Harvard University Press, 2002.

Berl, Emmanuel. "La Chair et le sang: Lettre à un jeune ouvrier." *Marianne,* June 24, 1936, 3.

Berman, Phyllis, and Zina Sawaya. "The Billionaires Behind Chanel." *Forbes*, April 3, 1989, 104–8.

Bernard, René. "La France frappe les trois coups à Moscou." *Elle*, August 11, 1961.

Bernstein, Henry. *Le Secret: Une Pièce en trois actes.* Ann Arbor, Mich.: University of Michigan Press, 1917.

Bernstein Gruber, Georges, and Gilbert Martin. *Bernstein Le Magnifique.* Paris: Editions JC Lattès, 1988.

Berthod, Claude. "Romy Schneider pense tout haut." *Elle* (France), September 1963, 130–32.

Berton, Celia. *Paris à la Mode: A Voyage of Discovery.* London: Gollancz, 1956.

Birchard, Robert S. *Cecil B. DeMille's Hollywood.* Lexington: University of Kentucky Press, 2004.

Birkhead, May. "American Women Dare Paris Riots." *The New York Times*, February 25, 1934.

———. "Chanel Entertains at Brilliant Fête." *The New York Times*, July 5, 1931.

Birnbaum, Pierre. *Un mythe politique: La "République juive."* Paris: Fayard, 1988.

Blet, Pierre. *Pius XII and the Second World War.* Translated by Lawrence J. Johnson. Mahwah, N.J.: Paulist Press, 1999.

"Bloc Notes Parisiens." *Le Gaulois*, December 6, 1885.

Bloch, Michael. *The Secret File of the Duke of Windsor.* New York: HarperCollins, 1989.

Bloom, Peter J. *French Colonial Documentary: Mythologies of Humanitarianism.* Minneapolis: University of Minnesota Press, 2008.

Bourdieu, Pierre. *Sociology in Question.* Translated by Richard Nice. London: SAGE Publications, 1993.

Boyd, Gavin. *Paul Morand et la Roumanie.* Paris: l'Harmattan, 2002.

Brantes, Emmanuel de, and Gilles Brochard. "Interview avec Jean-Louis de Faucigny-Lucinge." *Quotidien de Paris*, April 6, 1990.

Brasillach, Robert. "Journal d'un homme occupé." In *Une Génération dans l'orage: Mémoires*, translated by Mary Ann Frese Witt. Paris: Plon, 1968.

———. *Notre Avant-Guerre.* Paris: Plon, 1941.

Brubach, Holly. "In Fashion: School of Chanel." *The New Yorker*, February 27, 1989, 71–76.

Buisson, Patrick. *1940–1945: Années Erotiques*, vol 2: *De la Grande prostituée à la revanche des mâles.* Paris: Albin Michel, 2009.

Burton, Richard D. E. *Holy Tears, Holy Blood: Women, Catholicism, and the Culture of Suffering in France, 1840–1970.* Ithaca, N.Y.: Cornell University Press, 2004.

"Business: Haute Couture." *Time*, August 13, 1928, 35.

Butler, Judith. *Antigone's Claim.* New York: Columbia University Press, 2002.

Bytwerk, Randall L., ed. *Landmark Speeches of National Socialism.* College Station: Texas A&M University Press, 2008.

Cabire, Emma. "Le Cinéma et la Mode." *La Revue du Cinéma*, September 1, 1931, 25–26.

Capel, Arthur Edward. *De Quoi demain sera-t-il fait?* Paris: Librairie des Médicis, 1939.

———. *Reflections on Victory.* London: T. W. Laurie, 1917.

Carleston, Erin. *Thinking Fascism.* Stanford: Stanford University Press, 1998.

"Carnet Mondain." *La Nouvelle Revue*, July–August 1889, 207.

Carroll, David. "What It Meant to Be 'A Jew' in Vichy France: Xavier Vallat, State Anti-Semitism, and the Question of Assimilation." *SubStance* 27, no. 3 (1998): 36–54.

Chambrun, René de. "Morand et Laval: Une Amitié historique." *Ecrits de Paris*, no. 588 (May 1997): 39–44.

"Chanel: Ageless Designer Whose Young Look Is America's Favorite." *The New York Times*, September 9, 1957.

"Chanel à la Page, But No!" *Los Angeles Times*, February 6, 1954.

"Chanel Blousing." *Vogue*, March 15, 1956.

"Chanel Copies. USA—Daytime Programming." *Vogue*, October 1, 1958.

"Chanel Designs Again." *Vogue*, February 15, 1954, 82–85, 128–29.

"Chanel in Dig at Mrs. Kennedy's Taste." *The New York Times*, July 29, 1967.

"Chanel Is Master of Her Art." *Vogue*, November 1, 1916, 65.

"Chanel Is Returning to Dressmaking February 5." *The New York Times*, December 21, 1953.

"Chanel Offers Her Shop to Workers." *The New York Times*, June 19, 1936.

"Chanel Redevient Chanel." *République des Pyrénées*, October 14, 1954.

"Chanel reste fidèle à son style." *L'Aurore*, February 9, 1956.

"Chanel Resumes Easy Lines of the 1930s." *Women's Wear Daily*, February 8, 1954.

"Chanel's Exhibition Opened at 39 Grosvenor Square." *Harper's Bazaar*, May 1932, 67.

"Chanel Sport Costumes Increasing in Popularity Daily on the Riviera." *Women's Wear Daily*, February 28, 1916.

"Chanel Suit Casually Fitted." *Vogue*, September 15, 1957.

"Chanel Wants to Be Copied!" *The Louisville Courier Journal*, August 19, 1956.

Chanel, Coco. "Preface à ma collection d'hiver." Conservatoire Chanel, August 6, 1934.

———. Television interview by Jacques Chazot. *Dim Dam Dom*. 1968.

Chapsal, Madeleine. Interview with Coco Chanel, *L'Express*, August 11, 1960.

———. *La Chair de la robe*. Paris: Librairie Fayard, 1989.

Chazot, Jacques. *Chazot Jacques*. Paris: Editions Stock, 1975.

Churchill, Lida. *The Magic Seven*. New York: Alliance Publishing, 1901.

Clerc, Michel. "Chanel à Moscou." *Le Figaro*, July 27, 1961.

Cocteau, Jean. "A Propos d'Antigone." *Gazette des 7 Arts*, February 10, 1923.

———. "From Worth to Alix." *Harper's Bazaar*, March 1937, 128–30.

———. *Opium: The Diary of His Cure*. Translated by Margaret Crosland. 1930. Reprint, London: Peter Owen Publishers, 1990.

———. "Préface." *Orphée*. Paris: Editions Bordas, 1973.

———. *Théâtre*. Paris: Gallimard, 1948.

Colette. *Lettres à Marguerite Moreno*. Paris: Flammarion, 1959.

———. *Prisons et paradis*. Paris: J. Ferenczi et Fils, 1932.

———. "Spectacles de Paris." *Journal*, October 24, 1937.

Collins, Amy Fine. "Haute Coco." *Vanity Fair*, June 1994, 132–48.

Colón, Delin. *Rasputin and the Jews: A Reversal of History*. CreateSpace, 2011.

Cone, Michèle. *Artists Under Vichy*. Princeton, N.J.: Princeton University Press, 1992.

Conyers, Claude. "Courtesans in Dance History." *Dance History Chronicle* 26, no. 2 (2003): 219–43.

Cooper, Lady Diana. *The Light of Common Day*. Boston: Houghton Mifflin, 1959.

Cooper, Sandi E. "Pacifism, Feminism, and Fascism in Inter-War France." *The International History Review* 19, no. 1 (February 1997): 103–14.

Corbin, Alain. *Women for Hire: Prostitution and Sexuality in France After 1850.* Translated by Alan Sheridan. Cambridge, Mass.: Harvard University Press, 1990.

Cornwall, Tim. "£6m Facelift for Coco Chanel's Highland Love Nest." *The Scotsman,* July 1, 2012.

"Court Rejects Chanel Claim." *The Times* (London), May 31, 1973.

Cousteau, Patrick. "Ce n'est pas dans le film." *Minute,* April 9, 2009.

Coward, Noël. *Private Lives: An Intimate Comedy in Three Acts.* London: Samuel French, 1930.

Dalí, Salvador. *The Secret Life of Salvador Dalí.* Translated by Haakon M. Chevalier. 1942. Reprint, London: Dover Publications, 1993.

Dambre, Marc. "Paul Morand: The Paradoxes of Revision." *SubStance* 32, no. 3 (2003): 43–54.

Dank, Milton. *The French Against the French: Collaboration and Resistance.* New York: J. B. Lippincott, 1974.

Davis, Mary E. *Classic Chic: Music, Fashion, and Modernism.* Berkeley: University of California Press, 2006.

"Deauville Before the War." *Vogue,* September 1, 1914, 31.

"The Debut of the Winter Mode." *Vogue,* October 1, 1926, 69.

"The Decline of French Positivism." *Sewanee Review* 33, no. 4 (October 1925): 484–87.

Decourcelle, Pierre. *La Danseuse au couvent.* Paris: C. Lévy, 1883.

———. *Les Deux gosses.* 1880. Paris: Fayard, 1950.

De Giorgio, Michela. "La Bonne catholique." Translated by Sylvia Milanesi and Pascale Koch. In *Histoire des Femmes,* edited by Georges Duby and Michelle Perrot, 170–97. Paris: Plon, 1991.

De Grazia, Victoria. *How Fascism Ruled Women.* Berkeley: University of California Press, 1993.

Delange. "One-Piece Dress Wins Favor at French Resort." *Women's Wear Daily* 13, no. 88, 1.

Déon, Michel. *Bagages pour Vancouver.* Paris: Editions de la Table Ronde, 1985.

Dickinson, Hugh. *Myth on the Modern Stage.* Urbana: University of Illinois Press, 1969.

"Dior and Paquin Exhibit Fashions." *The New York Times,* February 19, 1947.

"Dior 52, Creator of 'New Look,' Dies." *The New York Times,* October 24, 1957.

Doerries, Reinhard. *Hitler's Intelligence Chief: Walter Schellenberg.* New York: Enigma Books, 2009.

Drake, Alicia. *The Beautiful Life: Fashion, Genius, and Glorious Excess in 1970s Paris.* New York: Little, Brown, 2006.

Dryansky, D. Y. "Camping with Coco." *HFD,* April 9, 1969.

Duchen, Claire. "Une Femme nouvelle pour une France nouvelle." *CLIO: Histoire, Femmes, et Sociétés* 1 (1995): 2–8.

"The Duke of Westminster Sues for Libel." *Gettysburg Times,* January 6, 1934.

Duncan, Isadora. *My Life.* New York: Boni and Liveright, 1927.

Dupont, Pépita. "Michel Déon Raconte Chanel." *Paris Match,* October 31, 2008.

Eckman, Fern Marja. "Woman in the News: Coco Chanel." *New York Post,* August 19, 1967.

Eco, Umberto. "Ur-fascism." Translated by Alistair McEwan. In *Five Moral Pieces,* 65–88. New York: Harcourt, 2001.

Emerson, Gloria. "Saint Laurent Does Chanel—But Better." *The New York Times,* July 31, 1967.

Engels, Frederick, translated by Anonymous, "Introduction," 9–22 in Karl Marx, *The Civil War in France: The Paris Commune* New York: International Publishers, 1968. Originally published in 1891.

Etherington-Smith, Meredith. *The Persistence of Memory: A Biography of Salvador Dalí.* New York: Da Capo Press, 1992.

Evans, Rob, and Dave Heneke. "Hitler Saw Duke of Windsor as 'No Enemy.'" *The Guardian,* January 25, 2003.

Ezra, Elizabeth. *The Colonial Unconscious: Race and Culture in Interwar France.* Ithaca, N.Y.: Cornell University Press, 2000.

Fairchild, John. *Fashionable Savages.* New York: Doubleday, 1965.

Falasca-Zamponi, Simonetta. *Fascist Spectacle: The Aesthetics of Power in Mussolini's Italy.* Berkeley: University of California Press, 1997.

"Farewell Glimpses of Parisians in Paris." *Vogue,* January 15, 1913, 96.

"Fashion." *Rob Wagner's Script,* May 1947, 31.

"Fashion: The New Line." *Vogue* 122, no. 3, August 15, 1953, 66.

"Fashions That Bloom in the Riviera Sun." *Vogue,* May 1, 1926, 56.

"Fashions: Yesterday, Today, and Tomorrow." *Vogue,* April 15, 1926, 83.

Faucigny-Lucinge, Jean-Louis de. *Fêtes mémorables bals costumés 1922–1972.* Paris: Herscher, 1986.

———. *Un gentilhomme cosmopolite, Mémoires.* Paris: Editions Perrin, 1990.

Fields, Leslie. *Bendor: The Golden Duke of Westminster.* London: Weidenfeld and Nicolson, 1983.

Fishman, Sarah. "Grand Delusions: The Unintended Consequences of Vichy's Prisoner of War Propaganda." *Journal of Contemporary History* 26, no. 2 (April 1991): 229–54.

Flanner, Janet. "Führer I." *The New Yorker,* February 29, 1936, 20–24.

———. "Führer III." *The New Yorker,* March 14, 1936, 23–26.

Forrester, Viviane. *Ce Soir après la guerre.* Paris: Fayard, 1997.

Fortassier, Rose. *Les Ecrivains français et la mode.* Paris: Presses Universitaires de France, 1988.

Fouquières, André de. "Grande Couture et la fourrure parisienne." *L'Art de la Mode,* June 1939.

Frader, Laura Levine. *Peasants and Protest: Agricultural Works, Politics, and Unions in the Aude, 1889–1960.* Berkeley: University of California Press, 1991.

François, Lucien. "Chanel." *Combat,* March 17, 1961.

———. "Chez Coco Chanel à Fouilly-les-Oies." *Combat,* February 18, 1954.

———. *Comment un nom devient une griffe.* Paris: Gallimard, 1961.

Frese Witt, Mary Ann. *The Search for Modern Tragedy: Aesthetic Fascism in Italy and France.* New York: Columbia University Press, 2001.

Fulcher, Jane. "The Preparation for Vichy: Anti-Semitism in French Musical Culture Between the Two World Wars." *The Musical Quarterly* (Autumn 1995): 458–75.

Fumet, Stanislas. "Reverdy." *Mercure de France,* January 1962, no. 1181, 312–34.

Garafola, Lynn. *Diaghilev's Ballets Russes.* New York: Da Capo Press, 1998.

————. "Diaghilev's Cultivated Audiences." In *The Routledge Dance Studies Reader*, edited by Alexandra Carter, 214–22. London: Routledge, 1998.

Garcia, Josep Miquel. "Biography of Apel-les Fenosa." El Vendrell, Spain: Fundació Fenosa, 2002.

Garcia, Xavier. "Interview with Apel-les Fenosa." *El Correo Catalán*, October 2, 1975. Fundació Fenosa Archives.

Geertz, Clifford. *Local Knowledge: Further Essays in Interpretive Anthropology*. New York: Basic Books, 1983.

Gellately, Robert, ed. *The Nuremberg Interviews*. New York: Knopf, 2004.

Gibson, Ralph. *A Social History of French Catholicism 1789–1914*. London: Routledge, 1989.

Gilbert, Martin. *The First World War: A Complete History*. New York: Henry Holt, 1994.

Gildea, Robert. *Marianne in Chains: Daily Life in the Heart of France During the German Occupation*. New York: Metropolitan Books, 2002.

Gill, Brendan, and Lillian Ross. "The Strong Ones." *The New Yorker*, September 28, 1957, 34–35.

Gillyboeuf, Thierry. "The Famous Doctor Who Inserts Monkeyglands in Millionaires." *Spring* (2009): 44–45.

Giroud, Françoise. "Backstage at Paris' Fashion Drama." *The New York Times*, January 27, 1957.

Godfrey, Rupert, ed. *Letters from a Prince: Edward Prince of Wales to Mrs. Freda Dudley Ward*. New York: Little, Brown, 1999.

Golan, Romy. "Ecole française vs. Ecole de Paris." In *Artists Under Vichy*. Princeton, N.J.: Princeton University Press, 1992.

Gold, Arthur, and Robert Fizdale. *Misia: The Life of Misia Sert*. New York: Morrow Quill, 1981.

Goñi, Uki. *The Real Odessa: Smuggling the Nazis to Peron's Argentina*. New York: Granta Books, 2002.

Gordon, Meryl. "John Fairchild: Fashion's Most Angry Fella." *Vanity Fair*, September 2012.

Grainvile, Patrick. "Coco Chanel: Une Vie qui ne tenait qu'à un fil." *Mise à jour* 10, no. 57 (November 27, 2008).

Grassin, Sophie. "L'Art de vivre." *Madame Figaro*, April 17, 2009.

————. "Chanel aurait été folle de vous!" *Madame Figaro*, April 9, 2009.

Griffin, Roger. *Modernism and Fascism: The Sense of a Beginning Under Mussolini and Hitler*. London: Palgrave Macmillan, 2007.

————. *The Nature of Fascism*. New York: Oxford University Press, 1991.

Grindon, Leger. "History and the Historians in *La Marseillaise*." *Film History* 4, no. 3, (1990): 227–35.

Guenther, Irene. *Nazi Chic? Fashioning Women in the Third Reich*. New York: Berg, 2004.

"A Guide to Chic in Tweed." *Vogue*, December 22, 1928, 44.

Hainaut, Daniel, and Martine Alison. "Société AJ Capel." Unpublished article, 2008.

————. "A La Mémoire d'Arthur Edward Capel." *Bulletin de la Société de l'Histoire de Fréjus et de sa Région* 9 (2008).

Hall, Lucy Diane. "Dalcroze Eurythmics." In *Francis W. Parker School Studies in Education* 6 (1920): 141–50.

Hanks, Robert K. "Georges Clemenceau and the English." *The Historical Journal* 45, no. 1 (March 2002): 53–77.

Hare, Augustus J. C. *Rivieras.* London: Allen and Unwin Press, 1897. Accessed at http://www.rarebooksclub.com, 2012.

Harrison, Michael. *Lord of London: A Biography of the Second Duke of Westminster.* London: W. H. Allen, 1966.

Harvey, David. "Monument and Myth." *Annals of the Association of American Geographers* 69, no. 3 (September 1979): 362–81.

Haury, Paul. "Votre Bonheur, jeunes filles." *Revue* 266 (September 1934): 281.

Hawkins, Dorothy. "Fashions from Abroad." *The New York Times,* August 1, 1956.

Hegel, G. W. F. *Phenomenology of the Spirit.* Translated by A. V. Miller. New York: Oxford University Press, 1979.

Hench, John. *Books as Weapons: Propaganda, Publishing, and the Battle for Global Markets in the Era of World War II.* Ithaca, N.Y.: Cornell University Press, 2010.

Herf, Jeffrey. *Reactionary Modernism: Technology, Culture, and Politics in Weimar and the Third Reich.* Cambridge: Cambridge University Press, 1984.

Higham, Charles. *The Duchess of Windsor: A Secret Life.* New York: John Wiley and Sons, 1988.

Hobsbawm, Eric. *The Age of Extremes: A History of the World 1914–1991.* New York: Vintage Books, 1996.

"Hold That Hemline: Women Rebel Against Long-Skirt Edict." *See Magazine,* January 1948, 11.

Horne, Sir Alistair. *The Fall of Paris: The Siege and the Commune.* 1965. Reprint, New York: Penguin, 2007.

Huffington, Arianna. *Maria Callas: The Woman Behind the Legend.* New York: Cooper Square Press, 2002.

Humbert-Mougin, Sylvie. *Dionysos revisité: Les Tragiques Grecs en France de Leconte de Lisle à Claudel.* Paris: Belin, 2003.

Inglis, Fred. *A Short History of Celebrity.* Princeton, N.J.: Princeton University Press, 2010.

"In Paris Church Chanel Rites Attended by Hundreds." *Los Angeles Times,* January 14, 1971.

"In the USA: Fashion Naturals by Chanel Who Started the Whole Idea." *Vogue,* October 15, 1959.

"Introducing the Most Chic Woman in the World." *Vogue,* January 1, 1926, 54.

"Iribe." *Proceedings of the Royal Geographical Society and Monthly Record of Geography* 10, no. 12 (December 1888): 813–48.

Iribe, Paul. "Le Dernier luxe." *Le Témoin,* November 4, 1934.

Jablonski, Edward. *Alan Jay Lerner: A Biography.* New York: Henry Holt, 1996.

Jackson, Julian. *France: The Dark Years: 1940–1944.* New York: Oxford University Press, 2001.

Jacob, Max, and Jean Cocteau. *Correspondance 1917–1944.* Edited by Anne Kimball. Paris: Editions Paris-Mediterranée, 2000.

Jaques-Dalcroze, Emile. *The Eurythmics.* 1917. Accessed at http://www.forgottenbooks.org/, 2012.

Jenson, Jane. "The Liberation and New Rights for French Women." In *Between the Lines: Gender and the Two World Wars,* edited by Jenson and Margaret R. Higonnet, 272–87. New Haven, Conn.: Yale University Press, 1989.

Judt, Tony. *The Burden of Responsibility: Blum, Camus, Aron, and the French Twentieth Century.* Chicago: University of Chicago Press, 1983.

———. "France Without Glory." *The New York Review of Books,* May 23, 1996.

———. *Postwar: A History of Europe Since 1945.* New York: Penguin Books, 2006.

Jullian, Philippe. "Reine de Paris pendant 40 ans." *Les Albums du Crapouillot,* no. 5 (undated).

Kaplan, Alice. *Dreaming in French: The Paris Years of Jacqueline Bouvier Kennedy, Susan Sontag, and Angela Davis.* Chicago: University of Chicago Press, 2012.

———. *Reproductions of Banality: Fascism, Literature, and French Intellectual Life.* Minneapolis: University of Minnesota Press, 1986.

Kershaw, Ian. *Hitler: 1889–1936: Hubris.* New York: Norton, 1998.

Koenig, René. *A La Mode: On the Social Psychology of Fashion.* Translated by F. Bradley. New York: Seabury Press, 1973.

Koepnick, Lutz. "Fascist Aesthetics Revisited." *Modernism/modernity* 6, no. 1 (1999): 51–73.

Koonz, Claudia. *The Nazi Conscience.* Cambridge, Mass.: Harvard University Press, 2003.

Koos, Cheryl. "Gender, Anti-Individualism, and Nationalism: The Alliance Nationale and the Pro-natalist Backlash Against the Femme Moderne, 1933–1940." *French Historical Studies* 19, no. 3 (Spring 1996): 699–723.

Koszarski, Richard. *Von: The Life and Films of Erich von Stroheim.* New York: Limelight, 2004.

Kurth, Peter. *Isadora: A Sensational Life.* New York: Little, Brown, 2001.

Lacan, Jacques. *Le Séminaire de Jacques Lacan, Livre VII.* Paris: Editions du Seuil, 1996.

"La Collection Chanel sortira le 26 janvier." *Nord Matin,* January 12, 1971.

Lacoue Labarthes, Philippe. *Heidegger, Art, and Politics: The Fiction of the Political.* Translated by Chris Turner. Oxford: Basil Blackwell, 1990.

Lacoue Labarthes, Philippe, and Jean-Luc Nancy. *Le Mythe nazi.* Paris: Editions de l'Aube, 2005.

Ladonne, Jennifer. "New Paris Boutique for Chanel." *France Today,* June 7, 2012.

"La Femme de la semaine: Chanel." *L'Express,* August 17, 1956.

Langlois, Claude. *Le Catholicisme au féminin.* Paris: Editions du Cerf, 1984.

Lannelongue, Marie-Pierre. "Coco dans tous ses états." *Elle* (France), May 2, 2005.

Laqueur, Walter. *Fascism.* New York: Oxford University Press, 1996.

———. *Russia and Germany.* New York: Transaction Books, 1965.

Larkin, Maurice. *Church and State After the Dreyfus Affair.* New York: Harper and Row, 1974.

LeCompte, Georges. "Clemenceau: Writer and Lover of Art." *Art and Life* 1, no. 5 (November 1919): 247–52.

Lees, Gene. *The Musical Worlds of Lerner and Loewe.* Lincoln: University of Nebraska Press, 1990.

Lelieur, Anne Claude, and Raymond Bachollot. *Paul Iribe: Précurseur de l'art déco.* Paris: Bibliothèque Forney, 1983.

"L'Empire revient." *Marie Claire,* March 4, 1938.

Leonard, Miriam and Vada Zajko, eds. *Laughing with the Medusa: Classical Myth and Feminist Thought.* New York: Oxford University Press, 2006.

"Le Rideau se lève, la Mode paraît, le point de vue de *Vogue.*" *Vogue,* April 1938.

Lifar, Serge. *Les Mémoires d'Icare.* Monaco: Editions Sauret, 1993.

Lipovetsky, Gilles. *Le Luxe éternel.* Paris: Gallimard, 2003.

Lipton, Lauren. "Three Books About Chanel." *The New York Times,* December 2, 2011.

"Lord Milner Wants Anglo-American Union." *The New York Times,* June 11, 1916.

Loselle, Andrea. "The Historical Nullification of Paul Morand's Gendered Eugenics." In *Gender and Fascism in Modern France,* edited by Melanie Hawthorne and Richard Golson, 101–18. Hanover, N.H.: University Press of New England, 1997.

Louvish, Simon. *Cecil B. DeMille: A Life.* New York: Thomas Dunne Books, 2008.

Louw, P. Eric. *The Rise, Fall, and Legacy of Apartheid.* Westport, Conn.: Greenwood Press, 2004.

"Lunch with Coco Chanel Biographer Justine Picardie." *La Chanelphile,* September 22, 2011.

Lupano, Mario, and Alessandra Vaccarri. *Fashion at the Time of Fascism: Italian Modernist Lifestyle 1922–1943.* Bologna: Damiani, 2009.

Macchiocchi, Maria-Antoinette. "Female Sexuality in Fascist Ideology." *Feminist Review,* no. 1 (1979): 67–82.

"Madame Chanel to Design Fashions for Films." *The New York Times,* January 25, 1931.

"Madame Chanel Welcomes Style Copies." *News Leader,* August 14, 1956.

"Magicienne de la couture française Coco Chanel va chercher aux USA l'Oscar de la Mode." *France-Soir,* August 31, 1957, 1–2.

Malraux, André. "Les Origines de la poésie cubiste." *Connaissance,* January 1920.

Mann, William T. *Kate: The Woman Who Was Hepburn.* New York: Picador Books, 2007.

Marais, Jean. *Histoires de ma vie.* Paris: Albin Michel, 1975.

Margueritte, Victor. *La Garçonne.* Paris: Flammarion, 1922.

Marx, Karl. Translated by Anonymous. *The Civil War in France: The Paris Commune.* New York: International Publishers, Co., Inc, 1968. Originally published in 1891

Mascha, Etharis. "Contradictions of the Floating Signifier: Identity and the New Woman in Italian Cartoons During Fascism." *Journal of International Women's Studies* 11, no. 4 (May 2010): 128–42.

Maxwell, Elsa. "Elsa Maxwell's Party Line: Laval Spelled Backwards." *Pittsburgh Post-Gazette,* August 11, 1945.

———. "The Private Life of Chanel." *Liberty Magazine,* December 9, 1933.

McConathy, Dale, and Diana Vreeland. *Hollywood Costume.* New York: Harry N. Abrams, 1977.

Mehlman, Jeffrey. *Legacies of Anti-Semitism in France.* Minneapolis: University of Minnesota Press, 1983.

Meltzer, Françoise. "Antigone, Again." *Critical Inquiry* 37, no. 2 (Winter 2011): 169–86.

Meyer, G. J. *A World Undone: The Story of the Great War 1914–1918.* New York: Delacorte, 2007.

Meyran, Régis. "Vichy: Ou la face cachée de la république." *L'Homme,* no. 60 (October–December 2001): 177–84.

Milligan, Lauren. "Not Coco." *Vogue* (UK), August 18, 2011.

"M. Iribe Has Been Appointed General Superintendant of the Panama R.R." *Engineering News and American Contract Journal* 67, no. 11 (February 9, 1884).

"M. Jean Cocteau's Modernist *Antigone.*" *The Christian Science Monitor,* January 29, 1923.

"Mlle. Chanel to Wed Business Partner." *The New York Times,* November 17, 1933.

Modiano, Patrick. *La Place de l'Etoile.* Paris: Gallimard, 1968.

Montboron. "Oedipe-Macbeth au Théâtre Antoine." *L'Intransigeant,* July 17, 1937.

Montgomery, Ann. *Another Me: A Memoir.* iUniverse, 2008.

Mont-Servant, Nathalie. "La mort de Mlle. Chanel." *Le Monde,* January 12, 1971.

Morand, Paul. *Black Magic.* Translated by Hamish Miles. New York: Viking Press, 1929.

———. *Journal d'un attaché d'Ambassade.* Paris: Gallimard, 1996.

———. *Journal inutile,* January 11, 1971.

———. *Lewis and Irene.* Translated by H.B.V. [Vyvyan Beresford Holland]. New York: Boni and Liveright, 1925.

———. *Hiver caraïbe.* Paris: Flammarion, 1929.

———. *Venises.* Paris: Gallimard, 1971.

Morris, Bernadine. "When in Doubt There's Always Chanel." *The New York Times,* May 14, 1970.

"Moscou: Tout est prêt pour l'exposition française." *Les Dernières Nouvelles d'Alsace,* August 12, 1961.

Mosse, George. "Fascist Aesthetics and Society: Some Considerations." *Journal of Contemporary History* 31, no. 2 (April 1996): 245–52.

———. *The Image of Man.* New York: Oxford University Press, 1996.

———. *The Nationalization of the Masses: Political Symbolism and Mass Movements in Germany from the Napoleonic Wars Through the Third Reich.* New York: Howard Fertig, 1975.

Mourgues, Renée. "Les Vacances avec Coco Chanel." *La République,* October 13, 1994.

Moynahan, Brian. *Rasputin: The Saint Who Sinned.* New York: Random House, 1997.

Muel-Dreyfus, Francine. *Vichy and the Eternal Feminine.* Translated by Kathleen Johnson. Durham, N.C.: Duke University Press, 2001.

Muggeridge, Malcolm. *Chronicles of Wasted Time: An Autobiography.* Vancouver, Calif.: Regent College Publishing, 2006.

———. Interview with Coco Chanel. September 1944. Accessed at http://www.chanel-muggeridge.com/unpublished-interview/, courtesy of the Société Baudelaire.

"Nécrologie." *Le Gaulois,* January 2, 1920.

Némirovsky, Irène. *Suite Française.* Translated by Sandra Smith. New York: Vintage, 2007.

Neruda, Pablo. "Je ne dirai jamais." In *Pierre Reverdy 1889–1960,* special issue of *Mercure de France,* no. 1181, January 1962.

Newman, Sharan. *The Real History Behind the Da Vinci Code.* New York: Berkley Trade, 2005.

Nicolson, Juliet. *The Great Silence: Britain from the Shadow of the First World War to the Dawn of the Jazz Age.* New York: Grove Books, 2010.

"No Dress Under $69.95 Will Bear the Name Dior." *The New York Times,* July 30, 1948.

Obolensky, Hélène. "The Chanel Look." *Ladies' Home Journal,* September 1964, 44–45.

O'Hara, Frank. "A Step Away from Them." Accessed at http://www.poemhunter.com/poem/a-step-away-from-them/.

Ollivier, Emile. *Le Concordat, est-il respecté?* Paris: Garnier Frères, 1883.

"On a tout vu." *Le Phare Bruxelles,* March 5, 1954.

Ory, Pascal, ed. *La France Allemande: Paroles du collaborationnisme français, 1933–1945.* Paris: Gallimard, 1977.

———. *Les Collaborateurs, 1940–1945.* Paris: Editions du Seuil, 1976.

"Out of the Paris Openings: A New Breath of Life—the Air of Innocence." *Vogue,* March 1, 1939, 1–24.

Oxenhandler, Neal. *Scandal and Parade: The Theater of Jean Cocteau.* New Brunswick, N.J.: Rutgers University Press, 1957.

Para, Jean-Baptiste. "Les propos de Reverdy recueillis." In *Pierre Reverdy.* Paris: Cultures Frances, 2006.

"Paris Carries On." *Vogue,* December 1, 1939, 86–87.

"Paris Collections: One Easy Lesson." *Vogue,* March 1, 1954.

"Paris Fashion Exhibitions at the Fair." *Vogue,* May 15, 1939, 60–63.

"Paris Lifts Ever So Little the Ban on Gaiety." *Vogue,* November 15, 1916, 41.

Paulicelli, Eugenia. *Fashion Under Fascism: Beyond the Black Shirt.* London: Berg, 2004.

———. "Fashion Writing Under the Fascist Regime." *Fashion Theory* 8, no. 1 (2004): 3–34.

Paxton, Robert. "The Five Stages of Fascism." *Journal of Modern History* 70, no. 1 (March 1998): 1–23.

Peeters, George. "How Cocteau Managed a Champion." *Sports Illustrated,* March 2, 1964.

"People." *Sports Illustrated,* April 20, 1964.

Perkins, B. J. "Chanel Makes Drastic Price Cuts in Model Prices." *Women's Wear Daily,* February 4, 1931.

Peterson, Patricia. "Paris: The Chanel Look Remains Indestructible." *The New York Times,* August 28, 1958.

Petropolous, Jonathan. *Royals and the Reich: The Princes von Hessen in Nazi Germany.* New York: Oxford University Press, 2006.

Philpott, William. "Squaring the Circle: The Higher Co-Ordination of the Entente in the Winter of 1915–16." *The English Historical Review* 114, no. 458 (September 1999): 875–98.

Picardie, Justine. "How Coco Chanel Healed My Broken Heart." *Mail Online,* September 29, 2010.

Pinkus, Karen. *Bodily Regimes: Italian Advertising Under Fascism.* Minneapolis: University of Minnesota Press, 1995.

Pochna, Marie-France. *Dior: The Man Who Made the World Look New.* Translated by Joanna Savill. 1994. Reprint, New York: Arcade Publishing, 1996.

Ponsonby, Loelia. *Grace and Favour: The Memoirs of Loelia, Duchess of Westminster.* London: Weidenfeld & Nicolson, 1961.

Pope, Virginia. "In the Chanel Spirit." *The New York Times,* July 11, 1954.

Porter, A. N. "Sir Alfred Milner and the Press, 1897–1899." *The Historical Journal* 16, no. 2 (June 1975): 323–39.

Pougy, Liane de. *My Blue Notebooks: The Intimate Journal of Paris's Beautiful and Notorious Courtesan.* Translated by Diana Athill. New York: Tarches/Putnam, 2002.

Pound, Ezra. "Paris Letter." *The Dial,* March 13, 1923.

Pratt, George C., Herbert Reynolds, and Cecil B. DeMille. "Forty-Five Years of Picture-Making: An Interview with Cecil B. DeMille." *Film History* 3, no. 2 (1989): 133–45.

Price, Roger. *A Social History of Nineteenth-Century France.* London: Hutchinson, 1987.

Pryce-Jones, David. *Paris in the Third Reich: A History of the German Occupation 1940–1944.* New York: Holt, Rinehart, and Winston, 1981.

Radzinsky, Edvard. *The Rasputin File.* Translated by Judson Rosengrant. New York: Nan A. Talese, 2000.

Rafferty, John. "Name Dropping on the Riviera." *The New York Times,* May 19, 2011.

Ramsey, Burt. *Alien Bodies: Representations of Modernity, "Race," and Nation in Early Modern Dance.* London: Routledge, 1998.

Reed, Valerie. "Bringing Antigone Home?" *Comparative Literature Studies* 45, no. 3 (2008), 316–41.

Reggiani, Andrés Horacio. "Procreating France: The Politics of Demography, 1919–1945." *French Historical Studies* 19, no. 3 (Spring 1996): 725–54.

Rémond, René. *The Right in France from 1815 to Today.* Translated by James M. Laux. 1954. Reprint, Philadelphia: University of Pennsylvania Press, 1966.

Rénier, Martin. "La Fleur du goût français à l'Exposition à New York." *Femina,* June 1939.

Reverdy, Pierre. *Gant de crin.* Paris: Plon, 1927.

———. *Nord-Sud: Self-defence et autres écrits sur l'art et la poésie.* Paris: Flammarion, 1975.

———. *Oeuvres complètes, tome II.* Paris: Flammarion, 2010.

———. *Plupart du Temps 1915–1922.* Paris: Gallimard, 1967.

———. *The Roof Slates and Other Poems of Pierre Reverdy.* Translated by Mary Ann Caws and Patricia Terry. Boston: Northeastern University Press, 1981.

Reves, Wendy and Emery Reves. The Wendy and Emery Reves Collection Catalogue. Dallas, TX: Dallas Museum of Art, 1985. Published to commemorate the opening of the recreated villa, La Pausa, in the Dallas Museum of Art.

Richardson, John. *A Life of Picasso: The Triumphant Years, 1917–1932.* New York: Knopf, 2010.

Ridley, George. *Bend'Or, Duke of Westminster: A Personal Memoir.* London: Quartet Books, 1986.

Robertson, Nan. "Texas Store Fetes Chanel for Her Great Influence." *The New York Times,* September 9, 1957.

Robilant, Gabriella di. *Una gran bella vita.* Milan: Mondadori, 1988.

Romanoff, Prince Michel. *Le Grand Duc Paul Alexandrovich de Russie: Fils d'empereur, frère d'empereur, oncle d'empereur: Sa famille, sa descendance, chroniques et photographies.* Paris: Jacques Ferrand, 1993.

Romanov, Grand Duchess Marie. *A Princess in Exile.* New York: Viking Press, 1932.

Rosenberg, Alfred. *The Myth of the Twentieth Century: An Evaluation of the Spiritual-Intellectual Confrontations of Our Age.* 1930. Reprint, Invictus Press, 2011.

Ross, David, and Helen Puttick. "Coco Chanel's Love Nest in the Highlands." *The Herald,* September 29, 2003.

Ross, Kristin. "Commune Culture." In *A New History of French Literature,* edited by Denis Hollier, 751–58. Cambridge, Mass.: Harvard University Press, 1989.

Ross, Nancy L. "Seeing Her Own Life: Chanel to Attend Coco Bow." *Los Angeles Times,* December 12, 1969.

Rousselot, Jean. *Pierre Reverdy.* Paris: Editions Seghers, 1951.

Rudnytsky, Peter. *Oedipus and Freud.* New York: Columbia University Press, 1987.

Rupp, Leila. "Mother of the 'Volk': The Image of Women in Nazi Ideology." *Signs* 3, no. 2 (Winter 1977): 362–79.

Sachs, Maurice. *Au Temps du boeuf sur le toit.* Paris: Editions de la Nouvelle Revue Critique, 1939.

Safe, Georgina. "Chanel Opens Shop in Melbourne." *The Sydney Morning Herald,* October 31, 2013.

Satterthwaite, P. H. "Mademoiselle Chanel's House." *Vogue,* March 29, 1930, 63.

Saunders, Thomas T. "A 'New Man': Fascism, Cinema, and Image Creation." *International Journal of Politics, Culture, and Society* 12, no. 2 (Winter 1998): 227–46.

Schaeffer, Marlyse. "Marlyse Schaeffer écrit à Chanel." *Elle* (France), 1962, 32.

Schellenberg, Walter. *The Labyrinth: Memoirs of Walter Schellenberg, Hitler's Chief of Counter-intelligence.* Translated by Louis Hagen. New York: HarperCollins, 1984.

Schouvaloff, Alexander. *The Art of the Ballets Russes: Serge Lifar Collection of Theater Designs, Costumes, and Paintings at the Wadsworth Atheneum.* New Haven, Conn.: Yale University Press, 1998.

"Scotland, the Happy Shooting Ground." *Vogue,* October 27, 1928, 46.

Sert, Misia. *Misia and the Muses: The Memoirs of Misia Sert.* Translated by Moura Budberg. New York: John Day, 1953.

Servadio, Gaia. *Luchino Visconti: A Biography.* London: Weidenfeld and Nicolson, 1981.

Sheppard, Eugenia. "Chanel for Men." *Harper's Bazaar,* December 1969, 158.

———. "Musical 'Coco' May End a Friendship." *Los Angeles Times,* November 23, 1969.

Silverman, Debora. *Art Nouveau in Fin-de-Siècle France.* Berkeley: University of California Press, 1989.

Simmel, Ernst. "Fashion." *International Quarterly* 10 (New York, 1904): 130–55.

Simon, John. "Theatre Chronicle." *Hudson Review* 23, no. 1 (Spring 1970): 91–102.

Singer, Barnett. "Clemenceau and the Jews." *Jewish Social Studies* 43, no. 1 (Winter 1981): 47–58.

Smith, Cecil. "Producer Brisson Bursting with Big Plans for 'Coco.'" *Los Angeles Times,* April 15, 1966.

Smith, Paul. *Feminism and the Third Republic.* Oxford: Clarendon Press, 1996.

Snow, Carmel, and Mary Louise Atwell. *The World of Carmel Snow.* New York: McGraw-Hill, 1962.

Sonn, Richard. "Your Body Is Yours: Anarchism, Birth Control, and Eugenics in Interwar France." *Journal of the History of Sexuality* 14, no. 4 (October 2005): 415–32.

Sontag, Susan. "Fascinating Fascism." In *Under the Sign of Saturn,* 73–108. New York: Picador, 2002. Originally published in *The New York Review of Books,* February 6, 1975.

Sophocles. *Antigone.* Translated by Elizabeth Wyckoff. In *Sophocles I,* edited by David Grene and Richmond Lattimore. Chicago: University of Chicago Press, 1973.

Soucy, Robert. *Fascism in France.* Berkeley: University of California Press, 1972.

———. *Fascist Intellectual: Drieu La Rochelle.* Berkeley: University of California Press, 1979.

———. "French Press Reactions to Hitler's First Two Years in Power." *Contemporary European History* 7, no. 1 (March 1998): 21–38.

Soulier, Vincent. *Presse féminine: La puissance frivole.* Montreal: Editions Archipel, 2008.

"Spain Prodded Again on Sheltering Nazis." *The New York Times,* June 19, 1946.

Spitzy, Reinhard. *How We Squandered the Reich.* Translated by G. T. Waddington. Norfolk, Va.: Michael Russell, 1997.

———. "The Master Race: Nazism Takes Over German South." *Master Race.* PBS television series. Directed by Jonathan Lewis. June 15, 1988.

"Sportswear Notes from Abroad." *Women's Wear Daily,* August 14, 1923, 3.

Spotts, Frederic. *The Shameful Peace: How French Artists and Intellectuals Survived the Nazi Occupation.* New Haven, Conn.: Yale University Press, 2009.

Stanley, Edward George Villiers. *Paris 1918: The War Diary of the British Ambassador, the 17th Earl of Derby, Edward George Villiers Stanley.* Edited by David Dutton. Liverpool: Liverpool University Press, 2001.

Steegmuller, Francis. "Cocteau: A Brief Biography." In *Jean Cocteau and the French Scene,* edited by Alexandra Anderson and Carol Saltus. New York: Abbeville Press, 1984.

Steele, Valerie. *The Corset: A Cultural History.* New Haven, Conn.: Yale University Press, 2003.

Steiner, George. *Antigones.* New Haven, Conn.: Yale University Press, 1996.

Sternhell, Zeev. *Neither Right nor Left.* Translated by David Maisel. 1983. Reprint, Princeton, N.J.: Princeton University Press, 1995.

Stewart, Amanda Mackenzie. *Consuelo and Alva Vanderbilt: The Story of a Daughter and a Mother in the Gilded Age.* New York: HarperPerennial, 2007.

Stravinsky, Igor. *Chroniques de ma vie.* Paris: Editions Denoël, 1935.

Stuart, Graham H. "Clemenceau." *The North American Review* 207, no. 750 (May 1918): 695–705.

Sweets, John F. *Choices in Vichy France: The French Under Nazi Occupation.* New York: Oxford University Press, 1994.

———. "Hold That Pendulum! Redefining Fascism, Collaborationism, and Resistance in France." *French Historical Studies* 15, no. 4 (Autumn 1988): 731–58.

Syberborg, Hans Jürgen. *"Hitler": A Film from Germany.* Translated by J. Negroschel. London: Little Hampton Book Service, 1982.

Theweleit, Klaus. *Male Fantasies.* Vol. 1, *Women, Floods, Bodies, History.* Translated by Stephen Conway. 1977. Reprint, Minneapolis: University of Minnesota Press, 1987.

Thomas, Dana. "The Power Behind the Cologne." *The New York Times,* February 24, 2002.

"Throwaway Elegance of Chanel." *Vogue,* September 1, 1959.

Trevières, Pierre de. "Paris et Ailleurs." *Femme de France,* no. 1035 (March 10, 1935).

Tual, Denise. *Le Temps dévoré.* Paris: Fayard, 1980.

Updike, John. "Qui Qu'a Vu Coco." *The New Yorker,* September 21, 1998, 132–36.

"Valet's £420,000 Claim on Chanel Will Come Before Court." *The Times* (London), March 22, 1973.

Veber, Denise. "Mademoiselle Chanel nous parle." *Marianne,* November 11, 1937.

Veillon, Dominique. *Fashion Under the Occupation.* Translated by Miriam Kochan. 1990. Reprint, New York: Berg, 2001.

Verner, Amy. "The Newest Chanel Boutique Is Like Stepping into Coco's Closet." *Globe and Mail,* May 26, 2012.

Viguié, Liane. *Mannequin Haute Couture: Une Femme et son métier.* Paris: Editions Robert Laffont, 1977.

"*Vogue*'s Eye View: First Impressions of the Paris Collections." *Vogue,* March 15, 1947, 151.

"Votre heure de veine." *Le Miroir du Monde,* no. 192 (November 4, 1933): 10.

Warnod, André. "Obituary for Paul Iribe." *Le Figaro,* September 29, 1935.

"Way of the Mode at Monte Carlo." *Vogue,* May 1, 1915.

Weber, Eugen. *Action Française.* Stanford: Stanford University Press, 1962.

———. *The Hollow Years: France in the 1930s.* New York: W.W. Norton & Co., 1994.

———. *Peasants into Frenchmen, 1870–1914.* Stanford: Stanford University Press, 1976.

Weiner, Susan. *Enfants Terribles: Youth and Femininity in the Mass Media in France 1945–1968.* Baltimore: Johns Hopkins University Press, 2001.

"What Chanel Storm Is About." *Life,* March 1, 1954.

"What Were They Expecting?" *Petit Echo de la Mode,* March 1954.

Will, Barbara. *Unlikely Collaborations: Gertrude Stein, Bernard Fay, and the Vichy Dilemma.* New York: Columbia University Press, 2011.

"Will Chanel Star in Stores?" *The New York Times,* December 19, 1969.

Wilson, Bettina Ballard. *In My Fashion.* New York: D. McKay, 1969.

Wilson, Colin. *Rasputin and the Fall of the Romanovs.* New York: Farrar, Straus and Giroux, 1964.

Wilson, Stephen. "The Action Française in French Intellectual Life." *The Historical Journal* 12, no. 2 (1969): 328–50.

Windt, Harry de. *My Note-Book at Home and Abroad.* London: Chapman and Hall, 1923.

Winegarten, Renée. "Who Was Paul Morand?" *New Criterion* 6 (November 6, 1987): 71–73.

Wiser, William. *The Twilight Years: Paris in the 1930s.* New York: Carroll and Graf, 2000.

Wollen, Peter. "Fashion, Orientalism, the Body." *New Formations,* no. 1 (Spring 1987): 5–33.

"Women at Work." *Time,* February 12, 1940.

Woolf, Virginia. *Mrs. Dalloway.* 1925. Reprint, New York: Harcourt, Brace, 1981.

———. *Three Guineas.* 1938. Reprint, San Diego: Harvest–Harcourt Brace Jovanovich, 1966.

Youssoupoff, Prince Felix. *Lost Splendor: The Amazing Memoirs of the Man Who Killed Rasputin.* Translated by Ann Green and Nicholas Katkoff. New York: Helen Marx Books, 2003.

Zeldin, Theodore. "The Conflict of Moralities: Confession, Sin, and Pleasure in the Nineteenth Century." In *Conflicts in French Society,* edited by Zeldin, 13–50. London: George Allen and Unwin, 1970.

NOTES

EPIGRAPH

ix **To know her:** Virginia Woolf, *Mrs. Dalloway* (1925; repr., New York: Harcourt Brace, 1981), 152–53.

INTRODUCTION

xiii **I dressed the universe:** Quoted in Paul Morand, *L'Allure de Chanel* (1976; repr., Paris: Hermann, 1996), 206.

xiii **What is Chanel?:** E.G., "La Femme de la semaine," *L'Express,* August 17, 1956, 8–9.

xix **Bowing to her wishes:** Michel Déon, *Bagages pour Vancouver* (Paris: Editions de la Table Ronde, 1985), 16–18; Pépita Dupont, "Michel Déon Raconte Chanel," *Paris Match,* October 31, 2008.

xix **insisted at the last minute:** Later, Arthur Gold and Robert Fizdale published the lost section on Chanel in their 1980 biography of Sert.

xix **Charles-Roux's biography:** An "irregular woman" is the antiquated French term for a woman who enters society through unorthodox means, through the back door—a woman of slightly imperfect virtue (similar to the English use of the term for damaged clothing or merchandise sold at a discount: "irregulars").

xix **this impossible injunction:** Despite knowing of Chanel's wishes, in 1990 Marquand published her own—largely flattering, and rather thin—memoir about her friendship with Chanel, *Chanel m'a dit* [Chanel told me] (Paris: Editions Lattès, 1990).

xx   **mysterious footsteps:** Justine Picardie, *Coco Chanel: The Legend and the Life* (New York: HarperCollins, 2010), 328; "Lunch with Coco Chanel Biographer Justine Picardie," *La Chanelphile,* September 22, 2011.

xx   **ongoing unearthly power:** Picardie also credits Chanel with helping her through her own painful divorce and has published articles comparing her own life's travails to Chanel's. See, for example: Justine Picardie, "How Coco Chanel Healed My Broken Heart," *Mail Online,* September 29, 2010.

1. EARLY LIFE

3   **If there's one thing:** Quoted in Marcel Haedrich, *Coco Chanel* (2008; repr., Paris: Belfond, 1987), 14.

5   **housewives who gathered early:** Edmonde Charles-Roux, *L'Irrégulière: L'Itinéraire de Coco Chanel* (Paris: Editions Grasset, 1974), 42–45.

5   **"The stands of itinerant peddlers":** Eugen Weber, *Peasants into Frenchmen, 1870–1914* (Stanford, Calif.: Stanford University Press, 1976), 408.

6   **restricted their selling:** Charles-Roux, 45–48.

6   **"My father always wished":** Louise de Vilmorin, *Mémoires de Coco* (Paris: Editions Gallimard, 1999), 19.

8   **pregnant once more:** Charles-Roux, 47–56.

8   **"Early happiness handicaps people":** Morand, *L'Allure de Chanel,* 24.

9   **good-luck charm:** Haedrich, 21.

9   **"I have satisfied her needs":** Vilmorin, 17.

9   **exhausted women who bore them:** Axel Madsen, *Chanel: A Woman of Her Own* (New York: Henry Holt, 1991), 7. "Disappearing was a practice at which all the Chanels excelled," notes Edmonde Charles-Roux, 65.

9   **The toddlers ran about:** Chanel never acknowledged her poor, itinerant roots, but on rare occasions, a tidbit about her peasant existence would escape her. She recounted, for example, this brutally vivid snippet about peddler-style dentistry: "[I recall] the tooth-extractors who traveled with a drummer and a trombonist in order to drown out the screams of the unhappy patient at the moment when his rotten tooth was being wrenched out." Quoted in Vilmorin, 27.

10   **something of a health hazard:** See Weber, *Peasants into Frenchmen,* for more on the scarcity of fresh water in much of late-nineteenth-century France. "If washing linens was rare, washing oneself was an exception .... Even in towns few made a habit of washing or bathing." Weber, 148.

10   **seawater mixed with olive oil:** Claude Delay, *Chanel Solitaire* (1974; repr., Paris: Gallimard, 1983), 19.

10   **suffered from pulmonary ailments:** Gilberte Devolle's death in 1869 on Geneanet: http://gw0.geneanet.org/bernard3111?lang=en&p=jeanne&n=devolle.

11   **tying scarves around:** Delay, 16.

11   **"I would hear people speak":** Haedrich, 23–24.

11   **"One has a father":** Ibid., 24.

12 **had just begun to flourish:** Charles-Roux, 70–75.

12 **Gabrielle never told a soul:** Claude Delay suggests that Chanel spoke of preparing her mother's corpse for burial and kissing her cold lips one last time. It is unclear if Delay inferred this or if Chanel actually admitted these facts to her. Delay, 71–72.

12 **their granddaughter Julia:** Claude Delay believes that Virginie-Angelina would have accepted the girls into her already-crowded home, but that Henri Chanel would not agree to it. Delay, 19.

13 **relatives distinctly recalled hearing:** Charles-Roux, 79. In an interview with Pierre Galante, a niece of Chanel's recalled, "I sometimes heard an uncle, an aunt, or a cousin ask: 'Where are the girls?' and my mother would answer, 'At Aubazine.'" Quoted in Pierre Galante, *Mademoiselle Chanel*, trans. Eileen Geist and Jessie Wood (Chicago: Henry Regnery Company, 1973), 14.

14 **penchant for effacing all evidence:** Charles-Roux, 79.

14 **"a vast, ancient and very beautiful":** Quoted in Vilmorin, 60.

14 **"They tore everything away":** Quoted in Charles-Roux, 79.

15 **minimal help from Henri Chanel:** Charles-Roux, 87–90.

15 **"At six years old":** Morand, *L'Allure de Chanel*, 13.

16 **"A little before he left":** Ibid., 24.

16 **fathered at least one more:** Years later, his son Lucien discovered Albert Chanel living with another woman, and reported back to his grandparents the lamentable state of his father's life. Still drinking heavily and in trouble with the law, Albert had taken to passing off dime-store household goods as the heirlooms of a bankrupt aristocrat in need of fast cash. Driving around in a finely appointed carriage he'd borrowed, Albert would claim to be a duke's personal valet, and talk guileless peasants into parting with large sums of money, convincing them that the worthless trinkets he was peddling offered a sound investment—that they were actually a duke's treasures being sold at steep discount. Upon receiving news of Albert's exploits, the entire Chanel clan—including even his own parents—broke off contact permanently with this black sheep of the family. Charles-Roux, 244.

17 **at her own naked body:** See Theodore Zeldin, "The Conflict of Moralities: Confession, Sin and Pleasure in the Nineteenth Century," in *Conflicts in French Society*, ed. Theodore Zeldin (London: George Allen and Unwin, 1970), 13–50. Historian of French Catholicism Ralph Gibson writes, "The body in the continuing Tridentine tradition, was regarded as the great enemy: at the end of the century, a sister would pass a dry chemise to a young boarder after a bath (which was also taken in a chemise), saying, 'Raise your eyes to Heaven, my child!' so that she would not see her own body." Gibson, *A Social History of French Catholicism 1789–1914* (London: Routledge, 1989), 119.

17 **"In a normal family":** Quoted in Haedrich, 33.

17 **"I understand my father":** Ibid., 24.

18 **"How I loved":** Morand, *L'Allure de Chanel*, 27.

18 **"Eggs, chicken, sausages":** Quoted in Haedrich, 28.

18 **"I thought often of death":** Morand, *L'Allure de Chanel*, 26.

19 **"I would return in secret":** Ibid., 17.

19 **"everyone else found ugly":** Vilmorin, 20.

19 **"queen of this secret garden"**: Morand, *L'Allure de Chanel*, 17.

19 **"Unlike children who"**: Vilmorin, 28.

20 **"I said 'Father'"**: Haedrich, 28.

20 **"Woe to anyone"**: Edmonde Charles-Roux, quoted in Sophie Grassin, "L'art de vivre," *Madame Figaro*, April 17, 2009.

20 **"make use of her"**: Gabrielle Chanel to Soeur Marie-Xavier, Conservatoire Chanel, Paris. Thank you to Cécile Goddet-Dirles for directing me to these documents and for her interpretation of both handwriting and the letters' tone.

21 **minimize religion's role**: The state pursued this goal via multiple avenues, including laws designed to secularize education and medical care—both of which had been heavily dominated by the church. Minister of Education Jules Ferry issued decrees in 1880 demanding the expulsion of any religious order running a school that lacked official government permission. The famous *lois laïques*, or secularization laws, of the 1880s banned clergy outright from teaching in state primary schools. By the century's close, many in the church felt that the spirit of the Concordat had been abandoned altogether. See Emile Ollivier, *Le Concordat, est-il respecté?* (Paris: Garnier Frères, 1883). Ollivier, a scholar and critic of the Académie française, reserved special disdain for the school system, which he felt had begun teaching "partisan books without conscience or intellectual probity, which denature facts and insult truth perpetually." Ibid., 25. Ollivier lamented particularly the lack of respect for France's monarchical and imperialist history, "that great French royalty," that "brought civilization to peoples throughout Europe." Ibid., 28.

22 **Dreyfus was vilified**: To promote its goal of purging the nation of such pernicious outsiders, *La Croix* even established a "Justice and Equality Committee," dedicated to blocking "Jews, Masons, and Socialists" in national and regional elections. The committee soon had a network of branches throughout the country. See Maurice Larkin, *Church and State After the Dreyfus Affair* (1973; repr., New York: Harper and Row, 1974), 24. See also Roger Price, *A Social History of Nineteenth-Century France* (London: Hutchinson, 1987).

22 **conspiracy between the Republicans**: See Larkin, 66; and Price, 283.

22 **outspoken anti-Dreyfusard**: Delay, 26.

23 **"unwilling or unable to marry"**: According to Gibson, "a third of the founders of successful congregations were the daughters of artisans, small traders, peasants, or salaried workers." Gibson, 118. See also Richard D. E. Burton, *Holy Tears, Holy Blood: Women, Catholicism, and the Culture of Suffering in France, 1840–1970* (Ithaca, N.Y.: Cornell University Press, 2004).

23 **female congregations offered many types**: In his landmark study of Frenchwomen in the Catholic church, *Le Catholicisme au féminin*, historian Claude Langlois attributes the success and growth of these congregations partly to women's desire for work and independence: "In the nineteenth century, congregations are practically alone in furnishing ... such varied types of female employment ... whence their success." Claude Langlois, *Le Catholicisme au féminin: les congrégations françaises à supérieure générale au XIXe siècle* (Paris: Editions du Cerf, 1984), 643.

23 **supervising hundreds of women**: See Langlois 643, and Gibson, 118.

23 **starched white headresses:** Edmonde Charles-Roux has remarked on the influence of the nuns' habit on Chanel's later fashions. Charles-Roux, 84.

24 **tamp down individual personalities:** Discussing the many restrictions imposed by Catholic orders, Gibson writes, "Convents and monasteries adopted the same techniques as did seminaries to control any kind of individuality or deviance .... The conventual rule prescribed the detailed control of bodily movements, down to the posture of head and torso, the direction of the eyes, the number of genuflections, etc.—a technique which we now understand was an essential part of subjecting individuals to authority. The religious habit itself was clearly designed to suppress individuality." Gibson, 132.

24 **"I have hated when":** Morand, *L'Allure de Chanel,* 66.

24 **"I was a child":** Ibid., 20.

25 **novels she devoured in secret:** The Catholic church had long disapproved strongly of novels, which they deemed a morally corrupting influence on girls and young women. But by the 1890s, the strict prohibitions against reading popular fiction loosened, and teenaged girls—even in a convent orphanage—would have been able to get their hands on such literary contraband. Michela De Giorgio traces the Church's response in France to the recreational reading of novels by young girls. Michela De Giorgio, "La Bonne Catholique," trans. Sylvia Milanesi and Pascale Koch, in *Histoire des Femmes,* ed. Georges Duby and Michelle Perrot (Paris: Plon, 1991), 170–97.

25 **"a sentimental hack":** Delay, 24.

25 **newspapers that serialized them:** Haedrich, 66.

25 **promoted the new art form:** With writer Eugène Guggenheim, Decourcelle cofounded the Cinematographic Society of Authors and Litterateurs (the Société Cinématographique des Auteurs et Gens de Lettres, or SCAGL, in French), established to adapt popular literature for the screen.

26 **uses her newfound fortune:** Pierre Decourcelle, *La Danseuse au couvent* (Paris: C. Lévy, 1883).

26 **mother and son are reunited:** Pierre Decourcelle, *Les Deux Gosses* (1880; repr., Paris: Fayard, 1950).

27 **"Those novels taught me":** Morand, *L'Allure de Chanel,* 20.

27 **"He was already an old":** Quoted in Haedrich, 34.

28 **seats off to either side:** Charles-Roux, 100.

29 **"a true Lucifer":** Morand, *L'Allure de Chanel,* 20.

29 **world-famous jockeys:** Charles-Roux, 91–114.

30 **jackets with goatskin closures:** Ibid.

31 **"charming illusions":** Morand, *L'Allure de Chanel,* 16.

32 **perfect, even stitches:** Charles-Roux, 96–100.

32 **medicinal powers remain legendary:** The great seventeenth-century writer Madame de Sévigné claimed to have cured a severe paralysis in her hands by taking the waters at Vichy, thus saving her literary career. Chanel's personal library contained the published letters of Madame de Sévigné—might she have known of Sévigné's connection to Vichy waters? Library inventory list, Conservatoire Chanel, Paris.

32 **"passwords to a great"**: Morand, *L'Allure de Chanel,* 30.

33 **"play at being great ladies"**: Ibid., 26.

35 **shop catering to cavalrymen**: Charles-Roux, 105–22.

36 **rooster and a lost dog**: We know of Chanel's early foray into cabaret singing from an interview conducted by Charles-Roux with Carlo Colcombet, who had been stationed near Moulins while in the army and had attended Coco's performances at La Rotonde. Carlo Colcombet remained a lifelong friend of Chanel's. Charles-Roux, 125.

36 **"She was a prude"**: Quoted in Charles-Roux, 124.

2. A NEW WORLD AND A NEW LIFE

37 **"Society women"**: Quoted in Haedrich, 51.

38 **never wound up marrying**: For a comprehensive history of every class of prostitution in France during this time, see Alain Corbin, *Women for Hire: Prostitution and Sexuality in France After 1850,* trans. Alan Sheridan (Cambridge, Mass.: Harvard University Press, 1990). Originally published in French as *Les Filles de noce: Misère sexuelle et prostitution aux 19è et 20è siècles* (Paris: Flammarion, 1978).

38 **off with her young man**: André's birthdate and other details are found in his police dossier at the Archives de la Préfecture de police de Paris. Hereafter cited as Paris police archives.

38 **paternity in exchange for payment**: André's daughter, Gabrielle Palasse-Labrunie, states, "What is certain is that Antoine Palasse was not the father: this is what I always heard my aunt and my father say." Isabelle Fiemeyer and Gabrielle Palasse-Labrunie, *Intimate Chanel* (Paris: Flammarion, 2011), 33.

39 **died in the month of May**: Isabelle Fiemeyer, *Coco Chanel: Un parfum de mystère* (Paris: Editions Payot, 1999), 53.

39 **driving the bereft Julia**: Lilou Marquand mentions Julia's suicide and Chanel's possible instigation of it. Marquand, 66.

39 **track record of liaisons**: In her later years, Chanel also became jealously possessive of her models and would often try to keep them from going home to their husbands and boyfriends, trying to "steal" them away from any other attachments. She never lost her hunger to "beat out" everyone around her in the race for love. This habit has been noted by a large number of former acquaintances.

39 **unofficially adopting André**: Fiemeyer and Palasse-Labrunie, *Intimate Chanel,* 33.

39 **Labrunie permits herself**: Gabrielle Palasse-Labrunie, conversation with author, March 2011.

40 **enjoy his vast inheritance**: Charles-Roux, 128.

40 **"blind eye to his mistresses"**: Quoted in Fiemeyer and Palasse-Labrunie, *Intimate Chanel,* 27.

42 **hints of such excursions**: Haedrich, 43.

42 **"Vichy ... that doesn't exist"**: Edmonde Charles-Roux reported that when asked about her time in Vichy, Chanel would grow ferociously angry and deny any connection to the city. Quoted in Sophie Grassin, "Chanel aurait été folle de vous!" *Madame Figaro,* April 9, 2009.

43 **"You won't get anywhere"**: Charles-Roux relates Balsan's remark, via the recollection of Carlo Colcombet. Charles-Roux, 128.

44 **from hangovers to gallstones**: Charles-Roux, 141–42; Madsen, 27ff.

44 **her grandfather at Vichy**: She told Morand about her grandfather's Vichy cure. Morand, *L'Allure de Chanel,* 29.

44 **"I think she closed"**: Sophie Grassin, "Chanel aurait été folle de vous! Edmonde Charles-Roux à Audrey Tatou," *Madame Figaro,* April 18, 2009, 84.

45 **"His friends would tell him"**: Morand, *L'Allure de Chanel,* 33.

45 **"bisexual demimondaine"**: Ibid. Immortalized by the likes of Henri de Toulouse-Lautrec and Jules Chéret, the self-named d'Alençon (born Emilie André, to a Montmartre concierge) had left a long series of illustrious lovers in her wake—including Leopold II, king of Belgium. She had also earned special fame for her ability to incite aristocratic men into frenzies of lavish spending, which had bankrupted entire families. Emilienne's most famous feat was having driven a certain Duke of Uzès into spending his entire family fortune on jewels for her. The duke's desperate mother had him shipped off to the Congo to keep him away from her, where he soon died of dysentery. Balsan, however, thrifty by nature, had managed to avoid ruining himself financially with Emilienne. Charles-Roux, 153.

45 **"You could breathe"**: Delay, 34.

46 **"Beauty, youth, those things"**: Haedrich, 47–48.

46 **marrying Consuelo Vanderbilt**: See Consuelo Vanderbilt Balsan, *The Glitter and the Gold: The American Duchess in Her Own Words* (1953; repr., New York: St. Martin's Press, 2012); and Amanda Mackenzie Stewart, *Consuelo and Alva Vanderbilt: The Story of a Daughter and a Mother in the Gilded Age* (New York: HarperPerennial, 2007).

47 **a bona fide princess**: After the prince's death, Pougy took the veil and lived out her life as Sister Mary Magdalene of the Penitence in a Swiss convent. See Claude Conyers, "Courtesans in Dance History," *Dance History Chronicle* 26, no. 2 (2003): 219–43.

48 **dabbled in lesbianism**: Emilienne d'Alençon was the author of a collection of lesbian poetry entitled *Sous le masque* (Beneath the Mask), published in 1918. See also Liane de Pougy, *My Blue Notebooks: The Intimate Journal of Paris's Beautiful and Notorious Courtesan: Liane de Pougy,* trans. Diana Athill (New York: Tarches/ Putnam, 2002). Originally published in French as *Mes cahiers bleus* (Paris: Plon, 1977).

48 **"enormous pies balanced"**: Morand, *L'Allure de Chanel,* 40.

48 **new riding boots**: Charles-Roux, 158–62.

49 **"You have to imagine"**: Ibid., 168.

49 **one mischievous monkey**: Galante, 23.

49 **entire scheme as a lark**: Charles-Roux, 203–4.

49 **"vast game for the wealthy"**: Vilmorin, 76.

50 **enter the winner's circle**: Madsen, 40.

50 **"I wanted to escape"**: Vilmorin, 77.

50 **"The era of extravagant dressing"**: Morand, *L'Allure de Chanel,* 43.

51 **visiting her aunt Louise**: Marcel Haedrich notes that Chanel purchased her straw hats at Galeries Lafayette. Haedrich, 52.

51 **Coco's lifelong inability:** Haedrich 45–46. According to Justine Picardie, "Several of [Chanel's] friends believed that she did [become pregnant by Balsan]." Picardie, 53.

3. DESIGNING A NEW WORLD TOGETHER:
COCO CHANEL AND ARTHUR EDWARD "BOY" CAPEL

53 **"The boy was handsome":** Morand, *L'Allure de Chanel*, 34–38.

53 **fictionalized it in his novel:** Morand's Irene was not a French fashion designer but a Greek banking mogul, a "modern young woman [who] went into business." Paul Morand, *Lewis and Irene*, trans. H.B.V. [Vyvyan Beresford Holland] (New York: Boni and Liveright, 1925), 97.

53 **their decadelong romance:** Vilmorin, 82.

54 **aristocratic polo circles:** Although not a titled gentleman himself, Capel traveled in heady circles. As early as 1907, the society column of *Le Figaro* mentions Capel's involvement in a polo-inspired charity ball, thrown by a committee consisting of Count and Countess Stanislas de Castellane; Grand Duchess Anastasia de Mecklenburg-Schwerin, the duc de Guiche (one of Capel's oldest friends), and A. Capel. *Le Figaro*, March 7, 1907, 2. Among the earliest mentions of Capel's name alongside Etienne Balsan's is one in *Le Figaro*, August 22, 1909, which announces a polo match featuring Capel, Balsan, and Prince Radziwill.

54 **"He gave birth to me":** Vilmorin, 83.

56 **living comfortably on his investments:** Daniel Hainaut and Martine Alison, "Société AJ Capel," unpublished article, 2008. I thank Daniel Hainaut and Martine Alison for their generous help in researching the background of the Capel family.

56 **on all paid sales:** Handwritten entries, original Chanel logbooks. Conservatoire Chanel, Paris.

58 **mistress, the beautiful actress:** Charles-Roux, 190ff.

58 **smooth-talking saleswoman:** Rabaté left for good in 1912, when she began working for the famous Maison Reboux in Paris, eventually taking over as its director. Charles-Roux, 190n1.

58 **"qualities necessary for a businesswoman":** Elisabeth de Gramont, quoted in Galante, 30.

58 **"He listened to me":** Vilmorin, 83.

58 **"They're so ugly!":** In conversation with Marcel Haedrich, Chanel recalled insulting women in this way, attributing it to her deep insecurity: "I was a little girl, frightened of everything, a little provincial who knew nothing." Quoted in Haedrich, 62.

59 **"He would critique my behavior":** Morand, *L'Allure de Chanel*, 40.

59 **"I found people so ugly!":** Chanel described to Claude Delay Boy's concern for her vision and subsequent prodding to see an eye doctor. Delay, 72.

59 **Balsan ceded gracefully:** Versions of this story appear in every biography. See Galante, 29; and Morand, *L'Allure de Chanel*, 39ff especially.

59 **Etienne suffered considerable pain:** Fiemeyer, *Intimate Chanel*, 28.

59 **extended trip to Argentina:** Ibid.; Delay, 53; Morand, *L'Allure de Chanel*, 39.

60 **Portuguese-Jewish bankers:** Other candidates for Capel's paternity included the Duke of Sussex and even King Edward VII. Charles-Roux, 222; and Haedrich, 55.

Claude Delay writes, "His most probable paternity was Péreire, the banker." Delay, 51.

60 **incorporated this possibility:** Describing the background of Lewis, the character based on Boy Capel, Morand wrote: "French on his mother's side, Lewis was the natural son of a Belgian banker who died before he left college, leaving him with not only very little money [and] a little Jewish blood; or so it was said." Morand, *Lewis and Irene*, 34.

60 **substantiates Boy's illegitimacy:** Both Isaac and Emile Péreire died before they could possibly have fathered Capel (Emile in 1875, Isaac in 1880). I have procured a copy of his birth certificate, which was filed in Brighton, England, in 1883, listing his parents, Arthur Joseph and Berthe Lorin Capel. A single irregularity on the birth certificate may explain the whispers about illegitimacy: While the certificate is dated September 8, 1883, it notes that Arthur Edward Capel was actually born two years earlier, on September 7, 1881. Capel's next oldest sister, Berthe, was born in 1880, yet her birth certificate, too, was delayed and filed in 1883. For some reason then, the Capel family put off registering the births of their last two children. This alone does not prove illegitimacy. The delay might have resulted from the family's moving from one town to another, or these certificates may represent emendations of earlier ones, which might have contained errors. With thanks to Martine Alison of the Société de l'histoire de la ville de Fréjus for her great assistance.

Arthur Edward was the Capels' fourth child, but their only son, and the early decision to call him "Boy"—the nickname appears on his birth certificate—suggests a father's exuberant delight at his first male child. Boy seems, moreover, to have enjoyed a close relationship with his father. In 1901, father and son even lived together in London, and Boy took over his father's businesses when Arthur Joseph retired around that same year.

60 **never spoke of his mother:** "The Lorins remain frustratingly mysterious," writes Lisa Chaney, with justification. Lisa Chaney, *Coco Chanel: An Intimate Life* (New York: Viking, 2011), 66.

60 **convent school for upper-class girls:** She is listed as living at the school's address, 23 Kensington Square, as of the 1871 London census. The Convent of the Assumption opened its doors in London in 1857. In the Catholic Directory of 1876, the Convent described its mission thus: "The Sisters of the Assumption receive a limited number of young ladies of the higher classes for education. French is generally spoken, and the pupils have every facility for acquiring a perfect knowledge of that language. They have also the advantage of the best masters for music, modern languages, singing, drawing, dancing; and, further, at the parent's desire, they can finish their education on the same system at the Mother House, Auteuil, Paris, or either of the Convents of the Assumption in the South of France." Quoted in Martine Alison, "T.J. Capel," 2008.

60 **Boy Capel's future uncle:** By 1873, the charming Thomas Capel, many years older than Arthur Joseph, had already established himself as a prominent figure in London. Martine Alison, "Les Parents d'A.E. Capel," unpublished article, 2008. Thomas Capel grew quite famous for ministering to the spiritual needs of royals, aristocrats, and beautiful young women. Benjamin Disraeli used him as the model for the char-

acter of Catesby in his 1870 novel, *Lothair*. But after weathering a series of mounting scandals involving pilfered church funds (discovered to have been redirected to Tiffany's) and liberties taken with pretty congregants, Monsignor Capel was defrocked, whereupon he set off for America to make a clean breast of it. Alison, "T.J. Capel."

61 **would suggest illegitimacy:** Information on marriage certificates accessed at www .gro.gov.uk/gro/content.

61 **neither hailed from the bride's side:** Both witnesses were British and connected to the Capels. The first, James Lacey Towle, was the groom's brother-in-law, married to Elizabeth Capel Towle. The second, James Foley, was the local parish priest.

62 **expanded his business internationally:** In 1881, Arthur opened a branch of his business in Cardiff, Wales, and by 1883, he had established himself in Spain and France.

63 **connection to Monsignor Capel:** In a December 1885 account of an opera gala, *Le Gaulois* reported, "In the Baroness de Poilly's box, an English beauty is visiting, and she is creating a sensation, like a star rising on the horizon. They call her Madame Capel. She is the sister-in-law of Monsignor Capel." "Bloc Notes Parisiens" *Le Gaulois,* December 6, 1885. The society column of *La Nouvelle Revue* mentions Berthe Capel's presence at a costume ball in 1889, "the very beautiful Madame Capel [was dressed as] a canteen girl during the Revolution." "Carnet Mondain," *La Nouvelle Revue,* July–August 1889, 207. "Madame Capel was deservedly popular," wrote explorer and travel writer Harry de Windt, "and 'Tout Paris' flocked to her delightful semi-Bohemian parties." Harry de Windt, *My Note-Book at Home and Abroad* (London: Chapman and Hall, 1923), 171. Thanks to Martine Alison for drawing my attention to this book.

63 **"we have no information":** Etat civil Paris régistre 16ème arrondissement V 4 E 10098, p. 11. Quoted in Alison, "Les Parents d'A.E. Capel."

64 **rigorous Jesuit institution:** Even as a young boy, at l'Institution Sainte-Marie, Boy distinguished himself. At only eight years old, he appears in *Le Figaro* among a list of Sainte-Marie's boys receiving prizes for the school year. Boy's prize was for excellence in "religious instruction." *Le Figaro,* August 12, 1889.

64 **several academic prizes:** Chaney, 67, 408n9. Excellent research by biographer Lisa Chaney has uncovered records of Capel at Stonyhurst as well as proof of his prizes and membership in a group known as the Gentlemen Philosophers of Stonyhurst— an elite within the elite.

64 *Objects of the Seashore:* Insurance inventory of Chanel's library holdings, Conservatoire Chanel, Paris.

64 **later live for decades:** Chanel told some people, including Marcel Haedrich, that she lived briefly at the Ritz in these early days with Etienne and Boy. It is possible one or both of them put her up at the hotel, but other sources say she stayed at Balsan's apartment when in Paris. It seems likely that if Balsan was supporting her, he'd save money by keeping her in his apartment, but if Capel was in charge of the bills, the Ritz was a possibility. "I was living at the Ritz Hotel. People were paying for me, they paid for everything." Haedrich, 56.

65 **use of letterhead stationery:** Correspondence between Boy Capel and General Henry Hughes Wilson, housed at London's Imperial War Museum, proves this.

65 **"The first time I saw":** Morand, *L'Allure de Chanel,* 60.

65 **dyed a deep beige:** Ibid.

66 **killed by "African natives":** Chanel told this outrageous lie to *HFD* [full title un-known] magazine in 1969. Clipping from Conservatoire Chanel. Monsignor Capel is in an October 29, 1911, *New York Times* article, whose accompanying portrait illustration proves he is the bust on the mantel.

66 **Boy's family as her own:** The bust has long been explained by the Maison Chanel as an antiques store purchase that Chanel passed off as a family heirloom depicting an ancestor of her own. In fact, it is unmistakably Thomas Capel, who was known for his distinctive good looks.

66 **"inhaling inspiration":** "I pass my day in the Acropolis … inhaling inspiration …. My dance at present is to lift my hands to the sky, to feel the glorious sunshine and to thank the gods that I am here," wrote Duncan. Isadora Duncan, *My Life* (New York: Boni and Liveright, 1927, 111), cited in Peter Kurth, *Isadora: A Sensational Life* (New York: Little, Brown, 2001), 6.

66 **never cared for nudity:** Charles-Roux, 200.

66 **invented by Swiss educator:** Eurythmics aimed to "put the completely developed faculties of the individual at the service of art," allowing the body to "become a marvellous instrument of beauty and harmony," in the words of its founder. Emile Jaques-Dalcroze, *The Eurhythmics* (London: Constable, 1912), 18. Reprinted by Forgotten Books, 2012. For an early discussion of the use of Dalcroze's method in elementary education, see Lucy Diane Hall, "Dalcroze Eurythmics," *Francis W. Parker School Studies in Education* 6 (1920): 141–50. See also Lynn Garafola, *Diaghilev's Ballets Russes* (New York: Da Capo Press, 1998); and Lynn Garafola, "Diaghilev's Cultivated Audiences," in *The Routledge Dance Studies Reader,* ed. Alexandra Carter (London: Routledge, 1998), 214–22.

67 **would collaborate closely:** Still later in her life, Caryathis would marry the openly gay writer Marcel Jouhandeau, with whom she adopted a daughter.

67 **keeping her body toned:** Charles-Roux, 202–10.

67 **sartorial translation:** Chanel was certainly not the only fashion designer of this period to make common cause with modern dance. Isadora Duncan found Paul Poiret's loose, "harem" style outfits perfectly in keeping with her aesthetic, and pronounced him a "genius." Duncan, 237. Paul Poiret provided costumes on occasion for the "Isadorables," and Duncan patronized him often for her own offstage wardrobe. See Kurth, 257.

Poiret also collaborated with the Ballets Russes, designing a line of women's fashions based on costumes that Léon Bakst had originally created for stage productions. Dance and fashion attracted increasingly similar audiences during these years, with women patrons of the Ballets Russes rushing to sign up for private dance lessons, and fashion designers taking their cues from dance costuming. "Ballet overlapped with fashion in recreation," Lynn Garafola observed in "Diaghilev's Cultivated Audiences." See also Garafola, *Diaghilev's Ballets Russes,* 291. Bakst also did dress design, a "conflation of categories that ended by fetishizing onstage costume as an object of private consumption for the Ballets Russes audience." New-style European celebrities wanted to dress to "create a theatrically conceived persona."

67 **stunned the old gang:** Charles-Roux, 225.

68 at the Hôtel Normandy: Galante, 29.

68 *Deauville: At [Chanel's]: Femina*, September 1, 1913, 462.

68 "Women: he wanted them": Morand, *Lewis and Irene*, 44.

69 impossible logistically: Delay, 59.

69 an interest in his future: Ibid.

69 André's daughter Gabrielle Palasse-Labrunie: Labrunie, personal conversation with author, March 2011, Yermenonville, France.

70 a distasteful beverage: Delay, 59.

71 lectures on theosophy: Fiemeyer and Palasse-Labrunie, *Intimate Chanel*, 47.

71 "an old theosophist": Haedrich, 117.

71 Chinese and Japanese art: Insurance inventory of Chanel's private library, Conservatoire Chanel, Paris.

71 "I [broke] two of his teeth": Charles Baudelaire, "Knock Down the Poor!" in *Baudelaire, Rimbaud, Verlaine*, trans. Albert Botin, ed. Joseph Bernstein (New York: Citadel Press, 1993), 161–63.

71 "Boy Capel introduced me": Chanel spoke of Baudelaire's poem in 1944 with former MI6 agent Malcolm Muggeridge in a little-known interview, whose authenticity I have verified. The interview has been made available online by the Baudelaire Society: www.chanel-muggeridge.com/unpublished-interview.

   Later in life, Coco would develop an interest in boxing, perhaps finding in it the same kind of vicarious thrill of violence that she seemed to feel reading this Baudelaire poem. In 1938, she (along with Jean Cocteau) helped subsidize the boxing career of "Panama" Al Brown, a black Panamanian American who reclaimed his title as the bantamweight champion of Europe. Soon after, Brown, with Cocteau's encouragement, switched careers and became a cabaret performer. Delay, 177; George Peeters, "How Cocteau Managed a Champion," *Sports Illustrated*, March 2, 1964; Peter J. Bloom, *French Colonial Documentary: Mythologies of Humanitarianism* (Minneapolis: University of Minnesota Press, 2008), 191.

72 "Of course you're not pretty": Morand, *L'Allure de Chanel*, 40.

72 "Boy wanted to train me": Morand, *L'Allure de Chanel*, 63–64.

72 "He was only happy": Ibid., 38.

72 "We were made": Quoted in Haedrich, 63.

73 a young upstart like Chanel: Charles-Roux, 212.

73 paired with Doucet costumes: E.G. "Farewell Glimpses of Parisians in Paris," *Vogue*, January 15, 1913, 96.

74 most glamorous musical and theater events: Galante, 29.

74 Charles Dullin and Caryathis: Charles-Roux, 215.

74 "a harem woman side": Morand, *L'Allure de Chanel*, 64.

75 "sleep with all those ladies": Haedrich, 64.

75 "Deauville ... was": Helen Pearl Adam, *Paris Sees It Through: A Diary, 1914–1919* (London: Hodder and Stoughton, 1919), 86.

75 pay highly inflated prices: Charles-Roux, 236.

76 "became famous very suddenly": Haedrich, 67.

76 "A young designer established": Jean-Louis de Faucigny-Lucinge, *Un gentilhomme cosmopolite, Mémoires* (Paris: Editions Perrin, 1990), 38.

77   **jersey-clad Chanel look-alikes:** Charles-Roux, translator Daniel Wheeler, *Chanel and Her World* (New York: The Vendôme Press, 1981), 116. Originally published in French as *Le Temps Chanel* (Paris: Editions du Chêne, 1979).

77   **"I was the person people":** Haedrich, 66.

77   **she recalled with distaste:** Ibid.

78   **"At the end of that first summer":** Morand, *L'Allure de Chanel*, 50.

78   **wrote the novelist Colette:** Colette, *Prisons et paradis* (Paris: J. Ferenzci et Fils, 1932), 161–62.

79   **"For an outfit to be":** Delay, 191.

79   **sway and texture:** A piece in American *Vogue* from September 1914, for example, took special notice of a "suede cloth" Chanel was using for a sports coat: "light weight ... with a nearly imperceptible twill. It has almost the texture of suede and is used with a raw edge." E.G., "Deauville Before the War," *Vogue,* September 1, 1914, 31.

79   **"No two women":** Morand, *L'Allure de Chanel*, 58.

79   **a welcoming, silky ease:** I must thank the staff of the Conservatoire Chanel for helping me experience different vintage Chanel garments and taking the time to point out their construction and the finer points of their design.

80   **"Everything I know":** Quoted in Galante, 31.

80   **"I admire infinitely":** Morand, *L'Allure de Chanel*, 59.

80   **"She refused to sew":** Fiemeyer and Palasse-Labrunie, *Intimate Chanel*, 98.

81   **"I cut an old sweater":** Haedrich, 68.

81   **"'Why are you cutting'":** Morand, *L'Allure de Chanel*, 54.

82   **convention of elaborate coiffures:** Chanel did not "invent" short hair; others— notably the models of Paul Poiret—had experimented with wearing a shorter style. But as so often, it was Chanel's example that sparked and then defined a trend.

82   **"Chanel has on display":** *Women's Wear Daily,* July 27, 1914, clipping from Conservatoire Chanel.

82   **permitted rather than hindered movement:** For more on the great sea change in women's work, especially of the upper classes, see G. J. Meyer, *A World Undone. The Story of the Great War, 1914 to 1918* (New York: Delacorte, 2007). Meyer points out that only upper-class women could afford the outlay of expense required for the uniforms necessary in their new jobs.

83   **"Chanel's sport costumes":** "Chanel's Sport Costumes Increasing in Popularity Daily on the Riviera," *Women's Wear Daily,* February 28, 1916.

83   **"To look once":** "Chanel Is Master of Her Art," *Vogue,* November 1, 1916, 65.

83   **to startle passersby:** See, for example, Adam, 99–100. A British journalist who spent the war living in Paris, Adam deftly evokes quotidian life during these years, taking special note of those spheres usually considered "feminine"—food, clothing, domestic supplies, etc. Of the huge numbers of working women, she writes, "The increasing appearance of women in civil life ... was very remarkable in France. Here ... there was even at one time an agitation to withdraw young girls from service in hospital wards, on the grounds that the sights they saw there were not fit for 'well-brought-up young girls.' ... After postwomen, tram conductresses, women ticket collectors, and so forth, Paris is seeing women in charge of hose-pipes."

84 **salary cuts during the war:** As historian G. J. Meyer observes, "For young women who had expected the future to be limited to marriage and childbearing, it all could be wonderfully thrilling." Meyer, 167. Lower-class women had always worked, of course, and often, the war put an end to their employment. In France, for example, women composed the bulk of the workforce of the garment industry, and thousands found themselves unemployed when factories shut down during the war. See Meyer, 667–70. And after the war, unfortunately, many of the promised and expected gains for women's rights failed to materialize. France did not grant women the right to vote until 1948.

84 **some tweeds from Scotland:** Madsen, 80.

84 **beautiful colors in Lyon:** Chanel's connection to fabric trade specialists of this sort came through Etienne Balsan. Madsen, 80.

84 **skimmed rather than defined:** Haedrich, 68–69; Morand, *L'Allure de Chanel*, 53–55; Charles-Roux, 262ff.

85 **declared American *Vogue*:** A.S., "Paris Lifts Ever So Little the Ban on Gaiety," *Vogue*, November 15, 1916, 41.

85 **rib-crushing undergarments:** Although even here, things are far from simple. As Valerie Steele points out in her excellent, nuanced history of the corset, many women were attached to their corsets, considering them necessary for health, good posture, a shapely figure, and more. See Valerie Steele, *The Corset: A Cultural History* (New Haven, Conn.: Yale University Press, 2003).

86 **youth into a desideratum:** "Previous to Chanel, clothes were designed for mature women," observed Cecil Beaton. "With Chanel's advent, they were all designed for youth. Or ... to make mature women look young." Cecil Beaton, *The Glass of Fashion* (New York: Doubleday, 1954), 194.

86 **a body more like Coco's:** I borrow the term "internalizing the corset" from Peter Wollen, who wrote aptly of this phenomenon: "[The Chanel look] involved adopting a new set of disciplines, internal rather than external: exercise, sports, diet.... Fitness and slimming mania simply replaced tight-lacing as forms of extreme artifice." Peter Wollen, "Fashion, Orientalism, the Body," *New Formations*, Spring 1987, 5–33.

86 **"I created a brand-new":** Morand, *L'Allure de Chanel*, 54.

86 **"The creations of the Maison Chanel":** A.S., "Paris Lifts Ever So Little the Ban on Gaiety," *Vogue*, November 15, 1916, 41.

86 **at least five million civilians:** See Martin Gilbert, *The First World War: A Complete History* (New York: Henry Holt, 1994), xv.

86 **made it through the war unharmed:** See Eric Hobsbawm, *The Age of Extremes: A History of the World 1914–1991* (1994; repr., New York: Vintage Books, 1996), 25–26.

87 **"soldier blue":** The color "soldier blue" first appears in an item about Chanel's jersey coats, and their popularity on the Riviera: "Chanel ... is showing jersey coats of white, mulberry, red and various shades of blue, including the new *bleu soldat*. They are buttoned down the middle front and they are loosely belted, quite long, and slashed to the belt on each hip." A.S., "The Way of the Mode at Monte Carlo," *Vogue*, May 1, 1915, 136.

87 **awarded the "Mons Star"**: Daniel Hainaut and Martine Alison, "A la Mémoire d'Arthur Edward Capel," *Bulletin de la Société de l'Histoire de Fréjus et de sa Région* 9 (2008). The Battle of Mons ended with the British forces retreating, after being confronted with far stronger and more numerous German troops.

87 **"He won the affection"**: Morand, *L'Allure de Chanel,* 64.

87 **surely saw a younger version**: Clemenceau had established his left-leaning bona fides early in his career, when as a delegate to the Paris Municipal Council he argued for amnesty for the Communards—the protesters in the 1871 uprising that ended with government troops massacring thousands of French citizens. Later, amid the anti-Semitic furor of the 1898 Dreyfus affair, Clemenceau once more declared his progressive politics, penning a series of articles arguing for the innocence of Captain Alfred Dreyfus. In fact, when author Emile Zola published his now-famous letter in defense of Dreyfus, it was Clemenceau—a friend of Zola's—who provided the document's defiant and unforgettable title: "J'accuse."

Prior to his first term as prime minister (1906–9), Clemenceau had enjoyed a long career blending politics, literature, and journalism. He'd lived in the United States—where he'd taught college French in Connecticut (marrying an American student); he'd edited and published several newspapers and journals. A great Anglophile and fluent in English, he'd translated John Stuart Mill's *Auguste Comte and Positivism* into French. He'd socialized with the cream of French artistic society (Edouard Manet figured among his intimates), been a great athlete, and—apparently—broken not a few feminine hearts. See Graham H. Stuart, "Clemenceau," *The North American Review* 207, no. 750 (May 1918): 695–705; Georges LeCompte, "Clemenceau: Writer and Lover of Art," *Art and Life* 1, no. 5 (November 1919): 247–52; Barnett Singer, "Clemenceau and the Jews," *Jewish Social Studies* 43, no. 1 (Winter 1981): 47–58; Robert K. Hanks, "Georges Clemenceau and the English," *The Historical Journal* 45, no. 1 (March 2002): 53–77.

88 **liberal pacifist soon to become**: See Hanks.

88 **beautiful war widows**: Charles-Roux, 222ff.

90 **producing clothes for Spain**: Charles-Roux, 258ff. See also Madsen, 81ff. Galante also cites former workers of Chanel's recalling how she used "patriotism" to convince them to stay on during the war. Galante, 38.

90 **"I heard a Parisian lady"**: Quoted in Galante, 37.

91 **coordinated designs, at couture prices**: Ibid., 36.

91 **"I had founded"**: Quoted in Vilmorin, 95.

91 **7,000 francs, or the equivalent**: Madsen, 82.

91 **"People knew me"**: Quoted in Vilmorin, 87.

91 **"It would seem that"**: Delange, "One Piece Dress Wins Favor at French Resort," *Women's Wear Daily,* vol. 13, no. 88, 1.

91 **"I had decided to replace"**: Morand, *L'Allure de Chanel,* 55.

92 **"luxurious poverty"**: Quoted in Delay, 74.

92 **"her art resides in jersey"**: "Chanel Is Master of Her Art."

92 **"[Having] spent so much money"**: Morand, *L'Allure de Chanel,* 62. French critic Lucien François later summed up the phenomenon: "When Mademoiselle Chanel gets

to heaven, she will surely impose her cardigans and little jersey shifts on the Princesse de Clèves and Marie Antoinette." Lucien François, "Chanel," *Combat,* March 17, 1961.

92   **she employed three hundred:** Madsen, 82.

92   **"You had to see her arrive":** Galante, 82.

92   **"My heart contracted":** Morand, *L'Allure de Chanel,* 50.

93   **every penny he had advanced:** Delay, 61.

93   **bought outright the Villa Larralde:** Madsen, 89.

93   **Aunt Adrienne traveled to Vichy:** Delay, 61.

93   **"I thought I was buying":** Ibid.

93   **the obstacles impeding women:** "The door to the City of the Future ... is still closed to women. For centuries, they have been considered ... as inferior creatures, as beasts of burden or of pleasure. The time has come to enfranchise them. They are already doing this themselves. Since the beginning of the Christian era, women's education has been limited to teaching them the art of pleasing men. In society ... a woman unable to please a man falls into a state of dependence and inferiority. Work has proven that the inferiority of women is nothing but an illusion created by the opposite sex. Today, work has given women the right to absolute equality with men." Arthur Edward Capel, *De Quoi Demain Sera-t-il Fait?* (Paris: Librairie des Médicis, 1939) 77–78.

93   **mystical belief in an overarching:** In this, he drew inspiration from nineteenth-century French occultist Alexandre Saint-Yves d'Alveydre and the eighteenth-century philosopher and Hebrew scholar Antoine Fabre d'Olivet. Fabre d'Olivet's universalist theory of "synarchy" held that every element of the world existed in deep relation to everything else. Capel, *De Quoi Demain,* 156.

93   ***Reflections on Victory* is astonishing:** Always abreast of scientific research, Capel anticipated the future military usage of radioactivity—still incompletely understood in 1917. In his second book, Capel predicted the economic rise of China and the danger of terrorism emerging among the impoverished and undereducated populations of Islamic nations.

94   **"Germany will take her revenge":** Capel, *Reflections,* 66.

94   **"In ten years' time":** Ibid., 51, 66.

94   **"We [must] destroy":** Ibid., 116–20. *Reflections on Victory* draws on Enlightenment figures such as Rousseau and Voltaire, but even more on the seventeenth-century Duke of Sully (whom Capel pressed Coco to read). In his *Memoirs,* Maximilien de Béthune, duc de Sully—prime minister under France's King Henry IV—argued for the creation of "The Very Christian Council of Europe"—a loose confederation of fifteen European nation-states, united in purpose and employing a common army. Several centuries ahead of its time, Sully's plan for a unified Europe, which he called "the Grand Design," prefigures not only the League of Nations, established after World War I, but even the contemporary European Union.

94   **plans lacked practical details:** "The book would gain in cogency if more attention were paid to the practical working out of the proposed scheme." "List of New Books and Reprints," *Times Literary Supplement,* May 10, 1917.

94   **mercenary practice of dowries:** Capel writes: "For the groom, the dowry plays a

primary role, so that rich little runts can marry the most beautiful girls, thereby degrading the finest products of our race. What becomes of love and virtue in such barters of beauty for gold? Is it not naïve to demand virtue of a young woman after you've exploited her ignorance in order to steal her only commodity: love? What support will she find in the vanity that was her downfall and the religion that betrayed her. The truth is, most often, discretion winds up replacing virtue." Capel, *De Quoi Demain,* 77–78. There is no mention of a translator; the bilingual Capel may have written the book in French. In 1918, Capel further demonstrated his interest in the struggles of young women by donating a substantial sum to found the Theatre Girls Home Club in Paris. Offering moderately priced room and board, a supervised common area for visitors, and a strict curfew of one a.m.—the dormitory-like club was designed to help protect aspiring (frequently teenaged) actresses who came to Paris from England, often without money or family. "The Week in Paris," *The Times,* October 7, 1918. One wonders whether Capel was responding to Coco's stories of her own difficult years trying to break into theater, or whether his own mother, Berthe, had had some connection to a vulnerable "theatre girl."

95 **"Mahomet has, I believe":** Arthur Capel to Henry Hughes Wilson, October 23, 1915, Imperial War Museum, London, HHW correspondence (cited hereafter as IWM), 2/82/7, letter 18.

95 **Re Wilhelmina:** Arthur Capel to Henry Hughes Wilson, October 20, 1915, IWM, 2/82/7, letter 15.

96 **"balanc[ing] political and military":** Arthur Capel to Henry Hughes Wilson, January 10, 1916, IWM, letter 33, and December 24, 1915, letter 30, respectively.

96 **French diplomat Jules Cambon:** "Winston in favour of War council," Capel writes to Henry Hughes Wilson on December 2, 1915, IWM, letter 25.

96 **"I think I know":** Arthur Capel to Henry Hughes Wilson, December 24, 1915, IWM, letter 30.

96 **achieve any kind of consensus:** In frustration at one point, Capel writes, "We asked for a Joint-War-Council in order to obtain—1. Unity of Direction. 2. Centralisation, which are indispensable to victory. What have we obtained? A Tower of Babel." Arthur Capel to Henry Hughes Wilson, October 23, 1915, IWM, letter 18.

96 **a Supreme War Council:** For a full account of the creation of both councils, see William Philpott, "Squaring the Circle: The Higher Co-Ordination of the Entente in the Winter of 1915–16," *The English Historical Review* 114, no. 458 (September 1999): 875–98. I am grateful to Professor Philpott for his guidance in researching this period and his help in accessing the archives of London's Imperial War Museum.

96 **"I am now a clerk":** Arthur Capel to Henry Hughes Wilson, February 2, 1915, IWM, 2/81/2.

97 **"Dukes in a troop":** Arthur Capel to Henry Hughes Wilson, February 1, 1915, IWM, 2/81. Capel even concocts a baroque scheme that involves befriending German Socialist leaders Karl Liebknecht and Rosa Luxemburg, in order to use them to seed antigovernment sentiment among German troops. Arthur Capel to Henry Hughes Wilson, undated, IWM, 2/81/7, letter 8.

97 **multifaceted, meteoric career:** Chanel does not figure in the Capel-Wilson correspondence, save possibly for one cryptic, slightly rhyming line. Capel writes to Wil-

son: "On Friday, I go to live (or die) with Coconeau, this may be of use for you to know." "Coconeau" could be a nickname for Coco, or for her home in Garches, which she nicknamed "Noix de Coco" or "coconut." "Chanel had baptized her house Noix de Coco," according to Henriette Bernstein. Quoted in Galante, 53. Capel might mean he is spending the weekend with Chanel. The "live or die" remark might refer to their tempestuous relationship. Arthur Capel to Henry Hughes Wilson, September 12, 1915, IWM, 2/81/15.

97 **Anglo-French cultural fluency:** Capel's letters, in fact, abound with observations about British and French national characteristics—the French are "fickle," the British "aloof."

98 **forcing herself to eat oysters:** Haedrich, 61.

98 **married Percy Wyndham:** By a striking coincidence, Percy Wyndham was a half brother of Bendor, the Duke of Westminster, with whom Chanel would have a very long relationship.

99 **all his military leaves:** Galante, 47.

99 **reveal his vacillating feelings:** Chaney, 130.

99 **"All you tell me about Capel":** Letter of June 26, 1918, in Edward, Prince of Wales, *Letters from a Prince: Edward Prince of Wales to Mrs. Freda Dudley Ward,* ed. Rupert Godfrey (New York: Little, Brown, 1999), 298.

99 **"being married on Wednesday":** Edward George Villiers Stanley, *Paris 1918: The War Diary of the British Ambassador, the 17th Earl of Derby, Edward George Villiers Stanley,* ed. David Dutton (Liverpool: Liverpool University Press, 2001), 119.

99 **"I think I'm going to marry":** Diana Capel to Alfred Duff Cooper, 1st Viscount Norwich, July 1918, Papers of Alfred Duff Cooper, Cambridge University, file DUFC 12/8. In her letter, Diana refers to Boy as "my darkie," clearly referring to his black hair and olive skin—qualities often cited as evidence of his Jewish heritage. Haedrich refers to him as having "the 'matte' complexion of an Oriental." Haedrich, 55. A colorful and multitalented character, Duff Cooper had a successful career in the British Foreign Office, served with distinction as an officer during World War I, and later became secretary of state for war. Despite all this, he was best known for sleeping with countless famous beauties (including Chanel's friend and biographer Louise de Vilmorin), both before and during his marriage.

100 **emergency bomb shelter attire:** Georges Bernstein Gruber and Gilbert Maurin, *Bernstein le magnifique* (Paris: Editions JC Lattès, 1988), 166; Chaney, 132.

100 **"nobility by association":** Wedding announcement in *Le Gaulois,* August 10, 1918. Reference courtesy of Martine Alison.

100 **"I knew before he told me":** Delay, 66. According to some accounts, Coco had known specifically of Diana and encouraged Capel to marry her, knowing he needed an upper-class wife, and guessing that Diana could never steal him away completely. Coco's friend Antoinette Bernstein recalled: "Chanel knew how insignificant the girl was and doubtless thought she would be able to keep a certain hold on Boy." Quoted in Galante, 48. But it is equally likely that Chanel invented this version of the story after the fact, to save her dignity.

101 **their young daughter, Suzanne:** Charles-Roux, 275.

101 **"pity me"**: Letter quoted in Gruber and Maurin, 166.

101 **had confided her worst sorrows**: Ostensibly enjoying a "thermal cure," Henry had rented a villa in Uriage, leaving Antoinette and their young daughter, Georges, behind in Deauville. They visited Uriage only occasionally during the summer. In late August 1918, Coco rented a villa adjacent to Bernstein's, and stayed with him most of the rest of the season. The couple seems to have cared little for discretion—according to Georges Bernstein's biography of her father, the affair was an open secret. Gruber and Maurin, 157. According to Axel Madsen, Chanel was also romantically linked to Argentine millionaire Paul Eduardo Martinez de Hoz about this time. Madsen, 94.

102 **to purchase his own theater**: "Chanel is the only woman who has ever given me money," Bernstein told a friend. Quoted in Gruber and Maurin, 167.

102 **great fondness for little Georges**: Letters from Chanel to Antoinette Bernstein from this period and into the 1920s routinely ask affectionately after Georges.

102 **correspondence continued for years thereafter**: "Whatever happened, that friendship existed [and] endured," writes Georges Bernstein in Gruber and Maurin, 166.

102 **Antoinette and her mother**: Speaking with Pierre Galante, Antoinette Bernstein recalled, "My mother and I often went to Deauville; that is how I met Chanel. It amused me to look at what she had in her shop. Then in Paris I went to see her. In the beginning our relations were purely professional and commercial. It is only after the war that we became fond of each other." Quoted in Galante, 31.

102 **the day she married Henry**: Gruber and Maurin, 157.

102 **seeding mistrust between couples**: Henry Bernstein, *Le Secret: Une Pièce en Trois Actes* (1913, repr. Ann Arbor: University of Michigan Press, 1917); accessed at http://babel.hathitrust.org/cgi/pt?id=mdp.39015033159727;seq=13;view=1up;num=5.

102 **"equally emaciated"**: Gruber and Maurin, 166.

103 **Even Diana Capel wore Chanel**: Marcel Haedrich mentions that Coco knew Diana and had dressed her, even after Diana married Capel. Haedrich, 72. Lisa Chaney points out that Diana Capel was seen after her marriage wearing a pair of chic gold trousers, which were most likely designed by Chanel. "Arthur saw nothing unusual in buying clothes for Diana from Gabrielle's salon in Biarritz, but once married, Diana began to object. Arthur overruled her. Why should she not be dressed by the most exciting designer in Paris? The long-standing tradition in Diana's family has it that she disliked Gabrielle." Chaney, 142–43.

103 **retreating to her native England**: Chaney, 143. It is possible that Diana Capel resumed her affair with her former beau Duff Cooper at this time, although this has been disputed by Lisa Chaney. Chaney, 412n17. "Lady Diana Cooper ... was sure [her husband, Duff] was seeking out that annoying Diana Capel, the woman whose husband was rumored to be having an affair with clothes designer Coco Chanel, leaving her free to spend time with her husband." Juliet Nicolson, *The Great Silence: Britain from the Shadow of the First World War to the Dawn of the Jazz Age* (New York: Grove Books, 2010), 148.

103 **Diana had suffered the loss**: See Charles-Roux, 282–83.

103 **Boy spent hardly any time**: Chaney, 144.

104 **"1919, the year I woke up"**: Quoted in Haedrich, 67.

104 **imitation of a dutiful brother-in-law**: Chaney, 143.

104 **later reunite with Diana**: In her late thirties, Bertha Capel had married Herman Stern, the 2nd Baron Michelham—a teenaged boy half her age who, despite his family's wealth, was considered unmarriageable by virtue of his being either mentally challenged or gay; both explanations have been offered. When the boy's father, Lord Herbert Michelham, became gravely ill, his much younger wife, Lady Aimée Michelham, learned that he had altered his will, reducing her share of his fortune. Wishing to retain control of her husband's money after his death, Lady Michelham had her dear friend (and possible lover) Boy Capel help coerce her sick husband into changing his will once more, with terms far more favorable to his conniving wife. In exchange for this assistance, Boy received a "gift" for his sister Bertha. She would marry Lady Michelham's young son Herman, thereby obtaining a noble title and a handsome lifetime income. Bertha Capel became Lady Michelham and was set for life. The only conditions were that she never cause a scandal and never bear a child. She agreed. This story has been told in fragments in multiple places, but I thank Martine Alison for consolidating and clarifying it all in her unpublished article, "Bertha Capel, Soeur d'A. E. Capel," 2008.

106 **burst into heart-rending sobs**: Charles Roux, 30ff; Delay, 66–73.

106 **his body was transferred to Paris**: Nécrologie, *Le Gaulois,* January 2, 1920.

106 **Neither Chanel nor Diana Capel**: In a letter to Freda Dudley, Edward, Prince of Wales, wrote of Capel's death and explicitly mentioned Capel's deteriorating marriage: "I heard this evening … that Boy Capel (Diana's second husband) has been killed motoring … on the Riviera …. I think she's d—d well out of it as he was a proper 'four-letter man' and she wasn't happy. But it's sad for her to become a widow a second time!!" Edward, Prince of Wales, 298.

106 **service as a foreigner in France**: Notices of Capel's death: *L'Eclaireur de Nice,* December 23, 1919; *The Times* (London), December 24, 1919; *The New York Times,* December 25, 1919.

106 **Boy felt no need to conceal**: Currency conversion and comparison to spending power calculated at http://www.measuringworth.com/ppoweruk/.

106 **but perhaps a triple one**: Lisa Chaney reports that Yvonne had a son, but it remains unclear who the child's father was.

106 **after her springtime birth month**: Three years after Boy's death, Diana married her third husband, Vere Fane, 14th Earl of Westmorland, with whom she had three more children. Diana, Countess of Westmorland, lived to the age of ninety—outliving her last husband by thirty-five years.

107 **Chanel had bought Bel Respiro**: Lisa Chaney has discovered this surprising turn of real estate events. Chaney, 150.

107 **"I won't prettify this memory"**: Morand, *L'Allure de Chanel,* 65.

108 **later years did Chanel tell**: Delay, 73.

108 **"I knew he had not really"**: Haedrich, 73.

109 **no one ever saw who**: Photo and information about the memorial are courtesy of the Société d'histoire de Fréjus et de sa région. I thank especially Daniel Hainaut and Martine Alison.

4. GRAND DUKE DMITRI

110 **promoting Chanel couture in Canada:** Charles-Roux, 298–301.

111 **"When I realized that my business":** Vilmorin, 94.

111 **"The Russians revealed":** Morand, *L'Allure de Chanel,* 95. According to Claude Delay, Chanel said, "These grand dukes, they're all the same, handsome but there's nothing in their heads .... They drink to quiet their fear ... Tall, handsome, superb, these Russians. But underneath, nothing!: just emptiness and vodka." Quoted in Delay, 109.

112 **"She spoke often to me":** Jacques Chazot, *Chazot Jacques* (Paris: Editions Stock, 1975), 81.

112 **Dmitri as the ideal candidate:** Excerpts of his diaries have been seen by a few people, but the bulk of them have been housed at Harvard's Houghton Library, where they were locked until 2010, when I had a paleographic locksmith open them, with the permission of the archivists.

112 **He attended meetings in Paris:** Chanel's passport records for this period show trips to Switzerland and Germany at the same times that Dmitri would have been visiting his supporters in those countries. Paris police archives.

112 **"Inside every Auvergnat":** Morand, *L'Allure de Chanel,* 95.

112 **"Dmitri was extremely attractive":** Prince Felix Youssoupoff, *Lost Splendor: The Amazing Memoirs of the Man Who Killed Rasputin,* trans. Ann Green and Nicholas Katkoff (1953; repr., New York: Helen Marx Books, 2003), 94.

113 **close siblings all their lives:** Prince Michel Romanoff, introduction to Jacques Ferrand, *Le Grand Duc Paul Alexandrovitch de Russie: Fils d'empereur, frère d'empereur, oncle d'empereur: Sa famille, sa descendance, chroniques et photographies* (Paris: Jacques Ferrand, 1993).

114 **forcibly expelled from their homes:** His tenure also saw the infamous Khodynka tragedy of 1896 in which more than 1,300 people were trampled to death in a mass panic at a public celebration for the coronation of the last tsar, Nicholas II. Sergei's security forces had been partly to blame for the disaster, having failed to control the surging crowds, but he refused all responsibility for the event, and declined to appear at the site of the accident or any of the victims' funerals.

115 **"He trod a golden path":** Grand Duchess of Russia, Marie, *A Princess in Exile* (New York: Viking Press, 1932), 74.

115 **drugs were readily available:** Youssoupoff, 94.

115 **penchant for cross-dressing:** Ibid., 87.

115 **exchanged debauchery for mysticism:** "The weakness of his character made him dangerously easy to influence," wrote Felix of Dmitri. Youssoupoff, 94. Princess Marie also cites her brother's immaturity at the time, mentioning their father's concern for Dmitri's future.

115 **destroy the Duma:** Youssoupoff, 214.

116 **depicting a demonic Rasputin:** Recent scholarship has demonstrated that Rasputin likely never ingested those poisoned cakes (he followed a strict diet and ate no sugar), never emerged from the river, and simply died as a result of multiple gunshot wounds. See Edvard Radzinsky, *The Rasputin File,* trans. Judson Rosengrant (New York: Nan A. Talese, 2000), 455–77.

116 **Rasputin was shot to death:** Radzinsky maintains that Dmitri fired the shot that killed Rasputin (Radzinsky, 482). Colin Wilson has written that the entire tea cake story is fictional, and refers to the murder of Rasputin as a "sordid and discreditable incident—the murder of an unarmed man by four terrified assassins." Colin Wilson, *Rasputin and the Fall of the Romanovs* (New York: Farrar, Straus and Giroux, 1964), 192.

117 **joint participation in murder:** In a letter dated February 26, 1920, Felix writes to Dmitri:

> Having come to know you, I loved you even more and my attachment to you became still greater. [The verb used here in Russian for "to know" suggests the more carnal, biblical sense of knowing, another indication of a possible intimate relationship between the two.] Please understand that I am not asking anything of you and that I am guided solely by the feeling of deep devotion to you and by a sense of sadness at the fact that you, whom I loved so fervently and in whom I believed so strongly, deserted me in my blackest moment.

Felix Youssoupoff to Dmitri, trans. Philipp Penka, February 26, 1920, Grand Duke of Russia Diaries and Personal Record Books, MS Russ 92, Houghton Library, Harvard University (hereafter cited as Dmitri Diaries), vol. 18.2, supplementary folder.

The following day, February 27, 1920, Dmitri writes to Felix:

> On December 24, 1916 we parted as friends. We met in May 1919 and only a memory was left of our friendship. Why? Because we view a single question with such different eyes and from such absolutely different perspectives—that this alone suffices to destroy any friendship. You understand perfectly well what I am referring to, of course. I am speaking about the murder of Rasputin. For me this incident always remains a dark stain on my conscience. I never speak about it. Why? Because I believe that murder will always be murder—try as you might to lend this fact mystical significance! ... Believe me that I would gladly look at you the way I did before December of 1916. But alas! It is impossible.

Dmitri to Felix Youssoupoff, trans. Philipp Penka, personal correspondence, February 27, 1920, Dmitri Diaries, vol. 18.2, supplementary folder (possibly unsent).

117 **"The social class which had money":** Dmitri Diaries, May 4, 1920, vol. 19.1.

117 **prime contender in their eyes:** "I am well aware that they desire a candidate with an uncorrupted conscience, and because of this everyone is turning away from Kirill and largely for this reason their choice falls on me," he wrote on February 28, 1921. Dmitri Diaries, vol. 23.1, 150. Dmitri's police surveillance file reads: "High society of the Russian colony in Paris consistently occupies itself with the re-establishment of the empire in Russia. The designated candidate at the present time for these Russian monarchists is the Grand Duke Dmitri." Paris police archives.

117 **the dream of becoming tsar:** "The people who visit me are of course all deeply convinced that Russia will be a monarchy and they all allude to the fact that I am a desirable pretender, but apparently nobody dares or is able to begin the preparatory work." Dmitri Diaries, May 4, 1920, vol. 19.1, 18.

117 **"I will indeed be someone":** Dmitri Diaries, February 28, 1921, vol. 23.1, 150.

117 **soon approached 100,000 francs:** "My old passion for gambling ... is stronger than I am.... There is not a single minute when I do not think about my debt, which is after all already nearing 100 thousand Francs." Dmitri Diaries, June 30, 1920, vol. 19.1, 155.

117 **reigning royals, ambassadors, and celebrities:** Names figuring in his visitor log include Rothschild, Windsor, Radziwill, Misia Sert, the American ambassador to France, Mrs. Cole Porter, and the Duchess of Northumberland. Dmitri, Visitors Book, Houghton Library.

118 **"The thought of marrying":** Dmitri Diaries, January 31, 1921, vol. 23.1, 71.

118 **"On that day I ate dinner":** Ibid., January 23, 1921, vol. 23.1, 82. According to Justine Picardie, Dmitri was having an affair with Marthe Davelli, who was more than happy to turn him over to Coco, complaining that he had become "too expensive" for her. Justine Picardie, *Coco Chanel: The Legend and the Life* (New York: HarperCollins, 2010), 128.

118 **he knew through polo circles:** Fiemeyer and Palasse-Labrunie, *Intimate Chanel*, 30.

119 **"tried fiercely to hide":** Quoted in Madsen, 145.

119 **"she herself started the rumor":** Police report, July 1923, Paris police archives.

119 **meant to plan his ascension:** Photographs of Chanel's passport at the Paris police archives prove that she traveled to Berlin several times during this period.

119 **the splendid Hôtel Le Meurice:** The Paris police archives suggest that Chanel and Dmitri lived together in Zurich on the Bahnhofstrasse, although no mention of this appears anywhere else. The police files also state that the couple took up adjoining suites at the Meurice, although Chanel would have had another apartment at the time.

119 **the fashionable car to drive:** According to Claude Delay, the staff at Rolls-Royce had tried to dissuade Chanel from purchasing the car in this color, but she had no doubts. "You'll see, everyone will soon want to order them." Delay, 67.

119 **Chanel footing all bills:** She loved to buy presents for friends and urged Dmitri to shop for a dog in Nice, although he seems not to have found one he wanted. Dmitri Diaries, March 30, 1921, vol. 25.1, 104.

120 **"I could not have chosen":** Dmitri Diaries, March 30 and April 15, 1921, vol. 25.1, 103–6.

120 **"Coco is ... sad":** Dmitri Diaries, April 16, 1921, vol. 25.1, 167.

120 **"I personally have no illusions":** Dmitri Diaries, March 31, 1921, vol. 25.1, 75.

120 **further threatened Dmitri's reputation:** Even the Paris police noted that Chanel's "liaison with the Grand Duke is badly looked upon by the White Russian party."

120 **Danish countess Marie-Louise Moltke:** "The more time passes, the more this Marie-Louise Moltke appeals to me." Dmitri Diaries, February 14, 1921, vol. 23.1, 113.

120 **"I am not capable":** Dmitri Diaries, April 15, 1921, vol. 25.1, 106–7.

121 **"I am not used to":** Ibid., 107.

121 **Stravinsky got wind of Chanel's:** Chanel later told Paul Morand that Misia Sert maliciously sent a telegram to Stravinsky reading, "Coco is a little seamstress who prefers grand dukes to Artists," inciting his rage. Sergei Diaghilev reputedly then sent a telegram to Coco reading, "Do not come [back to Garches]. He wants to kill

you." "I was angry for weeks with Misia after this treacherous telegram. She swore she'd sent nothing of the sort. Once again, I pardoned her." Morand, *L'Allure de Chanel*, 153.

122 **whisked him off to Biarritz:** Delay, 113.

122 **spiritual gurus Lida Churchill:** Dmitri, Private Papers, Houghton Library. The list included Hara's *Road to Success, Number, Name, and Color*, and *The Complection* [*sic*] *Beautiful*; Lida Churchill's *Magic Seven*, and Flora Bigelow Guest's *Casting Out Fear*. Hashnu O. Hara was the inventor of "psychometry," a theosophy-inflected form of extrasensory perception. His book *Number, Name, and Color*—which figures on Dmitri's list—purports to explain the magical powers of numbers and colors, including their ability to "command luchre." Hashnu O. Hara, *Number, Name, and Color* (London: L. N. Fowler, 1907), 3, accessed at http://books.google.com/books?id=5bf 1NyNUE5QC&pg=PA1&source=gbs_selected_pages&cad=3#v=onepage&q&f= false. Dmitri added a small annotation (in English) next to this title in his notebook: "Very difficult." Lida Churchill's *The Magic Seven* offers spiritual exercises designed to "center one's self," "concentrate the mind," and—the most urgent goal for Dmitri—"command opulence." Lida Churchill, *The Magic Seven* (New York: Alliance Publishing, 1901), accessed at http://www.surrenderworks.com/newthought library/Lida%20A.%20Churchill%20-%20The%20Magic%20Seven/The%20 Magic%20Seven%20Summary%20and%20Exercise.pdf. The techniques may have proved ineffective; "I didn't like it," notes Dmitri alongside this title.

122 **Dmitri's supporters even used spiritualism:** The Paris police were not fooled, noting in Dmitri's file: "The main Russian group meets at Auteuil under the pretext of doing experiments in spiritism. An undercover police commissioner attended one of these séances, posing as an expert spiritualist." Paris police archives.

122 **favorite texts, the Bhagavad Gita:** Fiemeyer and Palasse-Labrunie, *Intimate Chanel*, 47.

123 **"the talismans of poor children":** Delay, 90.

123 **"Without symbols there was nothing":** Fiemeyer and Palasse-Labrunie, *Intimate Chanel*, 60.

123 **signs that conferred social power:** Anthropologist Clifford Geertz explains the phenomenon of charismatic outsiders thus: "This is the paradox of charisma: that though it is rooted in the sense of being near to the heart of things, of being caught up in the realm of the serious ... [of] those who dominate social affairs ... its most flamboyant expressions tend to appear among people at some distance from the center, indeed often enough at a rather enormous distance, who want very much to be closer." Clifford Geertz, *Local Knowledge: Further Essays in Interpretive Anthropology* (New York: Basic Books, 1983), 143.

123 **"Where is the equivalent":** Bourdieu chose Chanel herself as his prime example of this near-religious process of transubstantiation:

> Take a supermarket perfume at 3 francs; the label makes it a Chanel perfume worth 30 francs.... [It is] now transmuted economically and symbolically. The creator's signature is a mark that changes ... the social nature of an object ... what is involved is not the rarity of the product, but the *rarity of the producer*. What makes the value, the magic, of the label is the collusion of all the agents of the

system of production of sacred goods. This collusion is, of course, perfectly unconscious.... Between Chanel and her label, there is a whole system, which Chanel understands better than anyone, and at the same time less well than anyone.

Pierre Bourdieu, *Sociology in Question,* trans. Richard Nice (1974; repr., London: SAGE Publications, 1993), 132–38.

124 **former governor of the Crimea:** Her employee logs show how valuable the Russian models were in particular—their salaries were often distinctly higher than those of the other models. Russian women's names start appearing in Chanel's employee records as of 1921 and many stayed in her employ long after the affair with Dmitri had ended. Conservatoire Chanel, employee register.

124 **a miniature Alexander Palace:** Delay, 113.

124 **"Grand duchesses did my knitting":** Quoted in Delay, 58. *Women's Wear Daily* reported on the Russian noblewomen working in textiles for Chanel, and the splash their designs were making: "The elaborately patterned jerseys which the Countess Orloff Davidoff makes for Chanel are immensely popular at Le Touquet. One of these, which attracted wide attention, is soft lemon in color, patterned in a darker green and has a collar and bindings of plain crepe to match the color of the finely pleated skirt.... Two piece coat and skirt costumes constructed of beige color wool with military braidings are also very much in evidence." "Sportswear Notes from Abroad," *Women's Wear Daily,* August 14, 1923, 3.

125 **"One does not wear jewelry":** Coco Chanel interviewed by Jacques Chazot, *Dim Dam Dom* television program, 1968. Democracy notwithstanding, Chanel would take pleasure all her life in trotting out her Romanov jewels to impress visitors: "All the good things in Chanel's life, though, have come from men.... The Grand Duke Dmitri of Russia hung such lavish jewels around her neck that when she opens her jewel box and spills them on a table to show friends, as she sometimes does, they can hardly believe they are real." Eugenia Sheppard, "Chanel for Men," *Harper's Bazaar,* December 1969, 158.

126 **around its most lucrative product:** Tilar Mazzeo is sure of this earlier date for the creation of Chanel No. 5. Tilar Mazzeo, *The Secret of Chanel No. 5: The Intimate History of the World's Most Famous Perfume* (New York: HarperCollins, 2010). Lisa Chaney writes, "Whatever has been written or said to the contrary, it is not actually known how or when Gabrielle Chanel met the gifted young perfumer Ernest Beaux. Even more significantly, no one really knows exactly when Chanel No. 5 was created." Chaney, 183.

126 **former perfumer to the tsars:** Ernest Beaux would serve as technical director of Parfums Chanel from 1924 to 1954.

126 **"In the lily of the valley":** Quoted in Mazzeo, 77.

127 **"I don't want hints of roses":** Quoted in Madsen, 133.

127 **"a bouquet of abstract flowers":** According to Jacques Polge—currently the master perfumer or "nose" for the Maison Chanel, "[Chanel Number 5]'s revolution in perfume is comparable to that of abstract art in painting." Quoted in François Ternon, *Histoire du numéro 5 de Chanel* (Paris: Editions Normant, 2009), 91.

127 **the scent of Arctic snow:** The remark comes from Beaux's protégé, perfumer Constantin Weriguine. Quoted in Mazzeo, 65.

127 **jasmine petals were impossibly expensive:** Quoted in Madsen, 134.

127 romantic or "Oriental" fantasies: Madsen, 134.

127 "Women tend to wear": Quoted in Delay, 112.

127 it was her lucky number: The number "5" might also have been selected to acknowledge that the formula represented Beaux's fifth attempt at mixing the fragrance.

128 Boy Capel's cologne flasks: Lisa Chaney reviews the possible theories of the bottle's
origins, but does not consider Dmitri as a source. Chaney, 190.

128 imitation of the vodka flasks: This theory is advanced by journalist Patrick Cousteau
in "Ce n'est pas dans le film," *Minute,* April 29, 2009. And the square-shaped doodles
that fill the margins of Dmitri's diaries for this period indeed suggest the bottle's
silhouette.

128 "The effect was amazing": Galante, 75.

128 its sales secured Chanel's fortune: Madsen, 130.

129 Keen businessmen, they understood: Mazzeo, 95ff. Chaney, 227–30. Phyllis Berman
and Zina Sawaya, "The Billionaires Behind Chanel," *Forbes,* April 3, 1989: 104–8.

130 Labels in her couture garments: I thank Bill DeGregorio of the Museum of the City
of New York for pointing out the couture labels on vintage Chanels and explaining
their evolution.

130 conferred its special magic: They became what fashion writer Lucien François
called "those fetish-objects that contain within them sorcery." Lucien François, *Comment un nom devient une griffe* (Paris: Gallimard, 1961), 35.

131 "Embroidering my initials": Morand, *L'Allure de Chanel,* 29–30.

131 lurking in the stained-glass windows: Picardie, 34.

131 life of Chanel's greatest love: Chaney, 191.

131 the margins of his diaries: Dmitri, Private Papers, marginalia.

132 its White Russian supporters: By 1920, Dmitri had been well ensconced among the
ultra-right-wing Germans who supported overturning the Bolshevik Revolution.
He cultivated friendships with the likes of White Russian generals Pyotr Nikolaye-
vich Wrangel and Vasili Biskupsky, both of whom collaborated closely with Hitler.
Dmitri writes of these alliances in his diaries: "It seems that the most serious political organization of a strictly party-related nature is the group of Markov II, the famous leader of the far right. I spoke with him, of course, and he made quite a good
impression on me." Dmitri Diaries, March 15, 1921, 25.1, 17–20.

Dmitri's diaries attest to visits to Berlin in the early 1920s, beginning at least in
March 1921. He was drawn to early fascism and eventually (several years after he
and Chanel parted) became a member of the Mladorossi, or the Union of Young
Russians, a group of expatriate Russians who "flirted with fascism," in the words of
Marina Gorboff, *La Russie fantôme: l'émigration russe de 1920 à 1950* (Lausanne, Switzerland: Editions L'Age d'Homme), 160–61. He even received an invitation from
Hitler to lead a group of exiled Russian aristocrats to fight with the German army
against the Bolsheviks. He declined, claiming he could not fight his compatriots,
even these. For more on Biskupsky, see Walter Laqueur, *Russia and Germany* (1965;
repr., New York: Transaction Books, 1990). Laqueur describes Biskupsky as a ma-
nipulator of the Russian monarchists, "playing one Grand Duke against another in
their ambitions for the throne," using them to gain allies in his own quest for power.
Laqueur, 120–21. But Dmitri's experience of Nazism and its symbols likely dates to

an earlier period in his life. The budding National Socialist Party and White Russians had long been ideological bedfellows.

132 **highly attractive, demotic elitism:** In explaining the function of the swastika symbol, psychologist Erik Erikson wrote, "The ceremonial permits a group to behave in a symbolically ornamental way so that it seems to present an ordered universe; each particle achieves an identity by its mere interdependence with all the others." Erik Erikson, *Young Man Luther* (1962; repr., New York: Norton, 1993), 186, quoted in George Mosse, *The Nationalization of the Masses: Political Symbolism and Mass Movements in Germany from the Napoleonic Wars Through the Third Reich* (New York: Howard Fertig, 1975), 12.

133 **a benighted, unaesthetic race:** Dmitri revealed the kind of offhand anti-Semitism that considers Jews unaesthetic in his diary entry of June 12, 1920: "In the evening I went to a housewarming celebration at the Iakovlevs. It was quite entertaining, I must say. Especially the people. There were a large number of Jews with the most surprising physiognomies." Dmitri Diaries, June 12, 1920, vol 19.1, 153.

133 **"Mother Russia no longer exists":** Dmitri Diaries, May 4, 1920, vol. 19.1, 8.

133 **reviled orphans of history:** Prince Felix Youssoupoff, closest companion of Dmitri's youth, believed in the anti-Semitic conspiracy theories commonly circulating among Russian aristocrats and promulgated in *The Protocols of the Elders of Zion*, the 1903 anonymous text first published in Russian and likely the work of Pyotr Rachovsky. *The Protocols,* later a key text for Hitler, claimed to uncover a secret Jewish plot to achieve global domination. Felix believed, for example, that Rasputin was in the secret pay of a group of Jewish conspirators. Some scholars suggest that Rasputin tried to fight the violence perpetrated against Jews in Russia, and that his advocacy for oppressed minorities in general drew the hostility that led eventually to his assassination. See, for example, Brian Moynahan, *Rasputin: The Saint Who Sinned* (New York: Random House, 1997), 261ff; and the self-published Delin Colón, *Rasputin and the Jews: A Reversal of History* (CreateSpace, 2011).

5. MY HEART IS IN MY POCKET: COCO AND PIERRE REVERDY

134 **"A Step Away from Them":** Accessed at http://www.poemhunter.com/poem/a-step-away-from-them/.

134 **was likely Reverdy's lover:** Galante, 110.

136 **"I have always felt this":** Pablo Neruda likened Reverdy's poems to "a vein of quartz." Hungarian photographer Brassaï thought they displayed "the transparency … and the purity of crystal." Pierre Reverdy to Jean Rousselot, May 16, 1951, quoted in Jean Rousselot, "Pierre Reverdy," in *Pierre Reverdy* (Paris: Editions Seghers, 1951), 15.

136 **rich tactility resembling a sculptor's:** Brassaï, "Reverdy dans son Labyrinthe," 159–268; Pablo Neruda, "Je ne dirai jamais," in "Pierre Reverdy 1889–1960," special issue of *Mercure de France,* no. 1181, January 1962, 113–14.

136 **troops fired on the crowds:** Laura Levine Frader, *Peasants and Protest: Agricultural Works, Politics, and Unions in the Aude, 1850–1914* (Berkeley: University of California Press, 1991), 139–45.

136 **He became a lifelong socialist:** "He seemed fundamentally shattered by life," wrote

Misia Sert about her early impressions of Pierre. Misia Sert, *Misia and the Muses: The Memoirs of Misia Sert*, trans. Moura Budberg (1952; repr., New York: John Day, 1953), 188.

137 **premature death of his father:** Quoted in Rousselot, 8.

137 **twelve collections of poems:** *Nord-Sud* featured Reverdy's work, as well as pieces by many of his cubist and surrealist associates, including Tristan Tzara and Louis Aragon. Adrienne Monnier, the esteemed French poet and translator, patron of modernists, and famed companion of Sylvia Beach, dubbed *Nord-Sud* "evidence of a serious and coherent mind." Quoted in Rousselot, 36.

137 **"Between Mademoiselle and the poet":** Maurice Sachs, quoted in Jean-Michel Belle, *Les Folles années de Maurice Sachs* (Paris: Bernard Grasset, 1979), 85.

137 **"What encumbers me":** Quoted in Benjamin Péret, "Pierre Reverdy m'a dit ..." pp. 227–233, in Pierre Reverdy, *Nord Sud: Self defence et autres ecrits sur l'art et la poésie* (Paris: Flammarion, 1975), 228. Originally published in *Le Journal littéraire*, October18, 1924.

137 **"Life in society":** Reverdy, "Le livre de mon bord," 645–806, in Pierre Reverdy, *Oeuvres complètes, tome II* (Paris: Flammarion, 2010), 791.

137 **"I employed society people":** Morand, *L'Allure de Chanel*, 157.

138 **"He was ... severe":** Delay, 244.

138 **adopting his teenage memories:** Chanel spoke to Charles-Roux of Reverdy's experience of the winegrowers' crisis. Charles-Roux, 367.

138 **"If you write your poems":** Quoted in Haedrich, 115.

139 **self-styled "country bumpkin" persona:** Recounted in Charles-Roux, 381.

139 **Picasso had provided the illustrations:** "It is for Reverdy that I have illustrated this book, and with all my heart," wrote Picasso. I thank the staff of the Conservatoire Chanel for showing me the handwritten inscriptions in Chanel's books.

139 **"Reverdy converted":** Max Jacob and Jean Cocteau, *Correspondance 1917–1944*, ed. Anne Kimball (Paris: Editions Paris-Mediterranée, 2000), 323.

139 **periods in his Montmartre home:** "I have grown used to kneeling, it doesn't tire me," he wrote. Stanislas Fumet, "Reverdy," in "Pierre Reverdy 1889–1960," special issue of *Mercure de France*, January 1962, 327.

140 **the passage of earthly time:** Fumet, 327.

140 **recalled his surrealist roots:** "Reverdy subjected poetry to a surgical paring down," observed André Malraux in "Les Origines de la poésie cubiste," in "Pierre Reverdy 1889–1960," special issue of *Mercure de France*, January 1962, 27.

140 **windows, rooftops, or holes:** "Degrees of Spirituality. I don't feel I am planted in the earth, but neither am I in the stars. Only above the rooftops," wrote Reverdy, *Le livre de mon bord*, 173.

140 **"The horizon leans down":** Pierre Reverdy, *The Roof Slates and Other Poems of Pierre Reverdy*, trans. Mary Ann Caws and Patricia Terry (Boston: Northeastern University Press, 1981), 47.

140 **as a lay associate:** Reverdy, *Le Livre de mon bord*. Reverdy explained his choice of Solesmes in a letter to a friend, French writer Louis Thomas:

For many years, I knew Sarthe [the district where Solesmes is located] and made frequent trips there to a farm isolated from the world by profound poverty and bad roads. One day, a friend wrote to me about Solesmes, where he had gone on retreat, about his love of the chanting, of the liturgy, of the services. I went to spend a week there in the village. I went back, and I stayed. I live in retreat. I work the land, I grow vegetables, I raise Siberian rabbits that are as beautiful as Christmas toys. I harvest miraculous melons. I try, finally, to live in the healthiest way possible, the simplest way, and the most logical too, in accordance with the doctrine to which I have converted.

Louis Thomas, quoted in Jean-Baptiste Para, "Les propos de Reverdy recueillis," *Europe,* no. 777–78 (1928), reprinted in *Pierre Reverdy* (Paris: Cultures Frances, 2006), 64.

141 **"You are a good fairy":** Quoted in Sert, 191.

141 **"horrific little village":** Quoted in Rousselot, 22.

141 **"I will come see you":** Quoted in Haedrich, 116.

141 **"Dear and admirable Coco":** Quoted in Charles-Roux, 367.

141 **"I add a word to these":**

> J'ajoute un mot à ces mots si durs à relire.
> Car ce qui est écrit n'est rien
> Sauf ce qu'on n'a pas su dire
> D'un Coeur qui vous aime si bien.

Charles-Roux, 371.

142 **"Until her final years":** Quoted in Charles-Roux, 369.

142 **Henriette and his monastic world:** Jean-Baptiste Para writes, "Reverdy, nauseated by his own frivolity, would feel an overwhelming desire to flee and return to Solesmes." Para, 65.

143 **château Chanel had bought for them:** Fiemeyer and Palasse-Labrunie, *Intimate Chanel,* 35.

143 **as a Hollywood costume designer:** Delay, 146.

143 **"Pierre let himself be strangely seduced":** Fumet, 316.

143 **misguided in their political convictions:** Charles-Roux, 648. See chapter 11 for how Chanel's and Reverdy's paths crossed politically at the end of World War II.

144 **after one such exchange:** Quoted in Haedrich, 114.

144 **"Lie if you must":** Chanel, "Collections by Chanel," *McCall's,* June 1968.

144 **"True generosity":** "Maximes de Gabrielle Chanel," *Vogue,* September 1938, 56.

144 **"Elegance is not the opposite":** "Interview with Chanel," *McCall's,* November 1, 1965, 122.

144 **"a few of Reverdy's versions":** Pierre Reverdy, *Le Gant de crin* (Paris: Plon, 1927), 92, 95, 115.

145 **"wanted to cede to anecdote":** Edmonde Charles-Roux, "Hommage à Gabrielle Chanel," *Les Lettres Françaises,* January 20–26, 1971, 22–23.

6. WOMEN FRIENDS, MIMETIC CONTAGION, AND THE PARISIAN AVANT-GARDE

146 **"Those Grand Dukes . . . looked":** Quoted in Delay, 109.

147 **Mona's husband, Harrison Williams:** Paris police records also suggest that Chanel

might have had an affair with Alfred Edwards, Misia Sert's husband between 1905 and 1909.

147 **"The worst is the couple"**: Morand, *L'Allure de Chanel*, 166–67.

147 **"always knew exactly what"**: Lilou Marquand, personal conversation with author, March 2011.

148 **pressured to marry Prince Wilhelm**: Madsen, 123.

148 **Audrey Emery as his bride**: Grand Duchess of Russia, Marie, 246–47.

149 **from Russian nuns**: "My own thoughts were taken up solely with the idea of a paying occupation," she wrote. Ibid., 158.

149 **"catching sight of a woman"**: "I remember ... a light grey tunic embroidered in different shades of the same colour with dashes of red .... I saw it worn 'socially' by a woman lunching at the Ritz ... [and] had great difficulty in keeping myself from staring at her." Ibid., 171.

150 **"You were swept off your feet"**: Ibid., 159–60.

150 **once future queen of Sweden**: Marie, a keen observer of people, recognized Chanel's innate authority, suggesting that Coco's personality was even more commanding than that of some Russian royalty she'd known: "I had seen people occupying great positions at work ... had listened to orders given by people whose birth or position gave them the right to command. I had never yet met with a person whose every word was obeyed and whose authority had been established by her own self out of nothing." Ibid., 173.

151 **"Chanel confused herself"**: Irene Maury (former Chanel employee), quoted in Renée Mourgues, "Les Vacances avec Coco Chanel," *La République*, October 13, 1994.

151 **"Nations have a style"**: "Chanel Is 75," BBC interview, 1959.

151 **"Curtain Up, Fashion Appears"**: "Le Rideau se lève, la Mode paraît, le point de vue de Vogue," *Vogue*, April 1938.

151 **"The top of a dress is easy"**: Quoted in L. François, "Coco Chanel," *Combat*, March 17, 1961.

151 **"dress rehearsal[s]"**: Grand Duchess of Russia, Marie, 175.

153 **many generations of French noblemen**: May Birkhead, "Chanel Entertains at Brilliant Fete," *The New York Times,* July 5, 1931.

153 **"I never discussed prices"**: Quoted in Delay, 119.

153 **fired Sachs at once**: Max Jacob and Jean Cocteau, *Correspondance 1917–1944*, ed. Anne Kimball (Paris: Editions Paris-Méditerranée, 2000), 575.

154 **"It was about the music"**: Quoted in Delay, 120.

154 **"One should render homage"**: Jean Cocteau, "Introduction," in Sert, v.

154 **"A woman," she declared**: Morand, *L'Allure de Chanel*, 163.

154 **"I had only her as a friend"**: Ibid., 79.

155 **Marcel Proust referred to her**: Arthur Gold and Robert Fizdale, *Misia: The Life of Misia Sert* (1980; repr., New York: Morrow Quill, 1981), 6. Proust drew inspiration from Misia for two—quite different—characters in *A La Recherche du temps perdu*: the lovely Princess Yourbeletieff and the overbearing social climber Madame Verdurin.

155 **"The tragedy of that day"**: Sert, 11–12.

156 **clear recognition of the similarity**: Haedrich, 21.

157 **fell into an intense friendship:** "Of all my friends," wrote Misia, "Serge Diaghilev is certainly the one who came closest to me, and whose affection was most indispensable to me. . . . It is very rarely that a friendship that starts on a note of such profound exaltation . . . continues for more than twenty years, remaining just as intense. This, however, was the case as far as Diaghilev and I were concerned." Sert, 112–14.

157 **for whom Poulenc later composed:** Gold and Fizdale, 223.

157 **Sorel in her Quai Voltaire:** Paul Morand describes this same dinner party in *Journal d'un attaché d'ambassade*.

> Cocteau tells me of an amazing dinner, the other day, at Cécile Sorel's home. Present were the Berthelots, Sert, Misia, Coco Chanel, who is decidedly becoming a personage, Simone, Lalo, Bailby, Flament, and himself. "Enter conqueror!" exclaimed Sorel and seated Cocteau next to Lalo, who two days before had written in his journal, *Le Temps,* that "Parade" was "a pretentious niaiserie." Cocteau sees Cécile run her fingers through her new short hair, fluff it up and say, "It feels so cool like this, it's so convenient!" After dinner, they decide to cut Simone's hair with nail scissors. Madame Berthelot refused to sacrifice her own hair. Cocteau claims that this new style is actually devoted to charity and that all the hair cut is gathered by Bailby and resold for the war wounded. "This short style is not at all becoming to Sorel," he said. "When she had her long hair, from a distance, she looked very 'grand siècle,' but now she looks like the elderly Louis XIV without his wig!"

> Morand, *Journal d'un attaché d'ambassade* (1948; repr., Paris: Gallimard, 1996), 277–78.

158 **"My attention was immediately drawn":** Quoted in Gold and Fizdale, 197–98.

158 **a virtually hypnotized Misia:** The coat was most likely a version of the topcoats winning international acclaim for Chanel that year, executed mostly in wool jersey, here enhanced, for her personal use, with velvet. *Women's Wear Daily* of February 28, 1916, reported on the trend: "[Chanel's] jersey topcoat is in great demand. There is nothing smarter than these topcoats. Chanel's latest models are in 3/4 length, made with flaring skirt section cut separately and joined at the normal waistline. Sleeves are of Raglan type. Fronts fasten at the throat to be turned back forming revers if desired. These coats, like Chanel's sport coats, are unlined. Chanel always employs fur on wool jersey models." "Chanel Sport Costumes Increasing in Popularity Daily on Riviera, *Women's Wear Daily,* February 28, 1916.

In October of the same year, *WWD* again reported on Chanel's fur-trimmed coats, this time noting one that Chanel wore at Biarritz, which appears similar to the one that so impressed Misia: "Gabrielle Chanel passed attired in the long maroon colored charmeuse cloak tipped with lapin dyed to match, which was such a success with American buyers at the Chanel opening in August." Delange, "One Piece Dress Wins Favor at French Resort," *Women's Wear Daily,* October 6, 1916, 1.

158 **"Misia throughout her life":** Gold and Fizdale, 202.

158 **"She grabbed hold of me":** Morand, *L'Allure de Chanel,* 121.

158 **"Without Misia, I would have":** Quoted in Haedrich, 86.

158 **her still-provincial accent:** Frances Kennett, *The Life and Loves of Gabrielle Chanel* (London: Gollancz Books, 1989), 36.

159 **"One felt intelligent"**: Quoted in Haedrich, 87; Morand, *L'Allure de Chanel*, 73.

159 **"I tried desperately to think"**: Sert, 198.

160 **"Rarely have I been so amused"**: Quoted in Gold and Fizdale, 198.

160 **The Serts had become:** In Claude Delay's interpretation, Misia's motives in bringing the grief-stricken Chanel along on her honeymoon were less than altruistic: "Coco's tears held a primal allure … tears and melodrama having spurred Misia's own development, and formed her sexuality." Delay, 82.

161 **"I've been to see the Princess"**: Morand, *L'Allure de Chanel*, 103. In 1920, 200,000 francs equaled approximately $160,000 in U.S. currency today. Some put the figure at 300,000 francs, including Chanel herself, who changes the figure even within Morand's text.

161 **A secret among these three:** Gold and Fizdale assume Diaghilev phoned Misia the moment Chanel left. Gold and Fizdale, 229.

161 **"a gesture that combined"**: Ibid.

162 **"Misia never left Diaghilev"**: Morand, *L'Allure de Chanel*, 99.

162 **she began attending every rehearsal:** In his memoirs, Stravinsky adds that Chanel not only financed the production, but allowed the costumes for it to be fabricated in her studios. Igor Stravinsky, *Chroniques de ma vie* (Paris: Editions Denoël, 1935), 115.

"*Le Sacre* could only have been mounted with the aid of friends. I must above all cite Mlle Gabrielle Chanel, who not only came to our aid generously, but also participated herself in the reprisal by allowing the costumes to be executed in her couture workshop, whose reputation is universal."

162 **break off a nascent friendship:** Morand, *L'Allure de Chanel*, 82.

163 **albeit married—Stravinsky:** For more on Chanel's relationships with Duke Dmitri and Stravinsky, see chapter 5.

163 **"I sometimes bite my friends"**: Morand, *L'Allure de Chanel*, 83–84.

163 **some Sapphic experiments:** Misia's primary biographers, Arthur Gold and Robert Fizdale, seem convinced of an at-least-intermittent erotic relationship between the women.

163 **seriously dependent on the drug:** Former Chanel apprentice and assistant Manon Ligeour suggested in a 2005 interview that Chanel took morphine. Apel-les Fenosa, Chanel's lover in the late 1930s, claims he broke off with her because of her drug use. Prince Jean-Louis de Faucigny-Lucinge also chronicles Misia's drug use in *Mémoires d'un gentilhomme cosmopolite* (Paris: Editions Perrin, 1990).

163 **complete with hair pulling:** Gold and Fizdale suggest that Coco's addiction matched Misia's in intensity and that both women traveled regularly to Switzerland to procure illegal stashes of the drug. Gold and Fizdale, 300. Amy Fine Collins cites Georges Bernstein Gruber's account of a hair-pulling fight between Misia and Coco. Amy Fine Collins, "Haute Coco," *Vanity Fair,* June 1994, 132–48.

7. *ANTIGONE* IN *VOGUE*: CHANEL COSTUMES THE MODERNIST STAGE

164 **"Diaghilev invented Russia for foreigners"**: Morand, 101.

164 **accessible, popular references:** Lynn Garafola refers to Diaghilev's productions as "prestige commodities." Garafola, *Diaghilev's Ballets Russes,* 357.

165 **sensuous tango steps:** *Afternoon of a Faun* was based on a poem by Stéphane Mallarmé—an idea Misia suggested to Diaghilev. Similarly, the Texas Rag is danced in the 1913 ballet *Jeux*. See Burt Ramsey, *Alien Bodies: Representations of Modernity, "Race," and Nation in Early Modern Dance* (New York: Routledge, 1998), 29.

165 **sumptuous onstage creations:** Mary E. Davis, *Classic Chic: Music, Fashion, and Modernism* (Berkeley: University of California Press, 2006), 22.

165 **sharing some stage-star glamour:** Diaghilev also knew how to use his dancers as "brand ambassadors." In 1924, for example, when the women's magazine *Femina* sponsored a series of fashion galas, Diaghilev sent Ballets Russes soloists to perform as part of the program. When a new branch of the Galeries Lafayette department store opened, Diaghilev's dancers once again appeared to perform on site.

165 **he lured the glitterati:** As Garafola observes, "The commercial setting in which performances took place added luster to their component parts: the artwork itself became a prestige commodity.... The new art promoted by Cocteau and his group was a look, a style, a tone that could be adapted with equal ease to the walls of a nightclub, costumes for a fancy dress ball, and score of a ballet." Garafola, *Diaghilev's Ballets Russes,* 357.

165 **Cocteau, who was the first:** Quoted in Nathalie Mont-Servant, "La mort de Mlle Chanel," *Le Monde,* January 12, 1971.

165 **"And I cannot imagine":** Jean Cocteau, "A Propos d'Antigone," *Gazette des 7 Arts,* February, 10, 1923.

166 **drama for their own ends:** Ancient Greece entered the cultural atmosphere once more in France with the work of Freud, the surrealists—who made use of Greek myth—and with the 1921 publication of the French translation of James Joyce's *Ulysses.* French dramatists who returned to the Greeks, in the tradition of seventeenth-century authors such as Corneille and Racine, included Jean Anouilh, Jean Giraudoux, and Jean-Paul Sartre.

166 **adherence to its law:** Interest has never waned in *Antigone*'s levels of meaning. Philosophers from Hegel onward have turned to this play as a foundational text on the subject of law and the individual, sexuality, and the state. See G. W. F. Hegel, *Phenomenology of the Spirit,* trans. A. V. Miller (New York: Oxford University Press, 1979); George Steiner, *Antigones* (New Haven, Conn.: Yale University Press, 1996); Judith Butler, *Antigone's Claim* (New York: Columbia University Press, 2000); Françoise Meltzer, "Antigone, Again," *Critical Inquiry* 37, no. 2 (Winter 2011): 169–86; Jacques Lacan, *Le Séminaire de Jacques Lacan, Livre VII* (Paris: Editions du Seuil, 1996), chaps. 19–21.

168 **Antigone has decided:** Cocteau, "A Propos d'Antigone."

168 **frivolous theatrical excess:** See François Mauriac, *Les Nouvelles Littéraires,* January 6, 1923, quoted in Sylvie Humbert-Mougin, *Dionysos revisité: Les Tragiques grecs en France de Leconte de Lisle à Claudel* (Paris: Belin, 2003), 229–30.

   Ezra Pound devoted a long—largely laudatory—essay to the production in the English modernist journal *The Dial.* Ezra Pound, "Paris Letter," *The Dial,* March 13, 1923, 13.

168 **"fiddle faddle":** Brooks J. Atkinson, "The Play: Lunations of Jean Cocteau," trans. Francis Fergusson, *The New York Times,* April 25, 1930. For more on the production, see Denise Tual, *Le Temps dévoré* (Paris: Editions Brochés: 1980).

168 **"Special attention must be called":** S. H., "M. Jean Cocteau's Modernist *Antigone*," *The Christian Science Monitor,* January 29, 1923.

169 **racial tainting and moral laxity:** See Peter Rudnytsky, *Oedipus and Freud* (New York: Columbia University Press, 1987), on the history of German fascination with Hellenic painting and sculpture, beginning with Johann Joachim Winckelmann.

169 **of a fallen cultural elite:** "Athenian society … as an aesthetic ideal was wed to the modern pseudoscience of eugenics; Greece functioned as a mythic prototype for the fascist 'new man' who was destined to inhabit an industrialized Third Reich, devoid of degenerate races." Roger Griffin, *The Nature of Fascism* (New York: Oxford University Press, 1991), 25–31.

169 **Writers such as:** Robert Brasillach—who was eventually executed for collaboration—translated Sophocles' *Antigone* and devoted a poem to it. Charles Maurras, founder of the anti-Semitic Royalist collaborationist group Action Française, saw in *Antigone* the embodiment of "the very concordant laws of man, the gods, and the city," and devoted a poem to "Antigone vièrge mère de l'ordre" (Antigone, virgin mother of order). And Jean Anouilh's *Antigone* has inspired many conflicting interpretations, with some critics seeing it as a veiled attack on the Vichy government, others seeing in it a pro-fascist subtext. See Katie Fleming, "Fascism on Stage: Jean Anouilh's *Antigone*," in *Laughing with the Medusa,* ed. Miriam Leonard and Vada Zajko (New York: Oxford University Press, 2006), 163–188. See also Mary Ann Frese Witt, *The Search for Modern Tragedy: Aesthetic Fascism in Italy and France* (New York: Columbia University Press, 2001).

170 **the *Antigones* to come:** Cocteau cited as inspiration one of France's most zealous anti-Semites and champions of so-called ethnic nationalism (the xenophobic concept of "France for the French"), writer Maurice Barrès. Handwritten document, undated, at Fonds Cocteau (Bibliothèque de la Ville de Paris).

170 **becoming a kind of emblem:** Her close friend Paul Morand, for example, was an avowed proponent of eugenics; see chapter 10. See also Andrea Loselle, "The Historical Nullification of Paul Morand's Gendered Eugenics," in *Gender and Fascism in Modern France,* ed. Melanie Hawthorne and Richard Golsan (Hanover, N.H.: University Press of New England, 1997), 101–18.

170 **"These woolen dresses":** "Chanel devient grecque," *Vogue,* February 1, 1923, 28–29.

171 **"Today if you opened a book":** Roland Barthes, "The Contest Between Chanel and Courrèges," in *The Language of Fashion,* ed. Andy Stafford and Michael Carter, trans. Andy Stafford (Oxford: Berg, 2006), 105. Originally published as "Le Match Chanel-Courrèges," *Marie-Claire,* September 1967.

171 **"Society people came":** Dullin, quoted in Francis Steegmuller, "Cocteau: A Brief Biography," in Alexandra Anderson and Carol Saltus, *Jean Cocteau and the French Scene* (New York: Abbeville Press, 1984), 298.

172 **"Text? What text?":** Quoted in Tual, 354.

172 **induction into the French avant-garde:** Critic Rose Fortassier suggests that Chanel exerted tremendous influence upon Cocteau's theatrical imagination, and that he viewed her as his most important collaborator. Cocteau "worked through Chanel," she writes. Rose Fortassier, *Les Ecrivains français et la mode* (Paris: Presses Universitaires de France, 1988), 182.

172 **shadow of Antigone lived:** Sophocles, *Antigone,* trans. Elizabeth Wyckoff, in *Sophocles I,* ed. David Grene and Richmond Lattimore (Chicago: University of Chicago Press, 1954, repr., 1973), lines 813, 899–912. Critic Françoise Meltzer writes, "[Antigone] does not ... belong, hence her foreignness." Françoise Meltzer, "Theories of Desire: Antigone Again," *Critical Inquiry, 37* (Winter 2011): 176. "[Antigone]," writes classicist Valerie Reed "is ... a migrant ... always moving toward a home which itself is perpetually displaced or receding." Valerie Reed, "Bringing Antigone Home?" *Comparative Literature* 45, no. 3 (2008): 325.

172 **unraveling it so badly:** In an oral interview, longtime Chanel employee Marie Hélène Marouzé recounted a nearly identical story that took place more than thirty years later. Romy Schneider (who was costumed by Chanel in films such as Luchino Visconti's 1962 *Boccaccio '70*) stopped by Cambon, wearing a Chanel suit. After talking for a while, Schneider was about to leave when Chanel decided that the shoulder of Schneider's jacket was not quite perfect. Ignoring Schneider's protests that she was late and had to leave, Chanel set about destroying the sleeve and refashioning it completely, saying, "I cannot let you leave with a shoulder like that!"

172 **"I threw my own coat":** Quoted in Madsen, 124.

173 **Georges Braque into garments:** See Alexander Schouvaloff, *The Art of the Ballets Russes: Serge Lifar Collection of Theater Designs, Costumes, and Paintings at the Wadsworth Atheneum* (New Haven, Conn.: Yale University Press, 1998).

173 **haberdashery on the Place:** From Conservatoire Chanel, Chanel and Stravinsky file.

173 **Chanel's fur and velvet fantasies:** The October 1937 review in *Marianne* magazine praised the costumes lavishly: "Mlle Chanel dressed [the actors] with the simplicity and sumptuousness of poetry, the realism of playing cards, and the splendor of the velvets of Van Eyck." Playing card characters, fictional yet immutable, are not unlike the kind of "stock" character that Chanel herself invented: the "Coco" character.

173 **"These are not ... the costumes":** Interview with Cocteau, *Ce Soir,* October 9, 1937.

173 **"beautiful illuminated manuscripts":** "Sur la scène et l'écran," *Vogue,* December 1937, 49.

173 **"one slightly monastic dress":** Colette, "Spectacles de Paris," *Journal,* October 24, 1937.

174 **"Mme Abdy's costume consists":** Montboron, "Oedipe-Macbeth au Théâtre Antoine," *L'Intransigeant,* July 17, 1937.

175 **casual clothes of Chanel's lover:** "We must adopt the costumes of the era in which the tragedy is being presented," wrote Cocteau in the preface to the play. Jean Cocteau, "Préface," *Orphée* (Paris: Editions Bordas, 1973), 38.

175 **"Cocteau has supplanted Thanatos":** André Levinson. Review of Cocteau's *Orphée* in *Art Vivant,* August 1, 1926, 594. "A week ago you still thought I was a skeleton wrapped in a shroud, carrying a scythe," says Death ironically to one of her attendants. Jean Cocteau, *Orpheus,* trans. John Savacool, in *The Infernal Machine and Other Plays* (New York: New Directions Books, 1963, repr., 1967), 122.

176 **These are not "real" people:** "Jean Cocteau's characters are given, not organic. He sets them before us as recognizable modern types who will reenact the ancient myth as required," writes Neal Oxenhandler in *Scandal and Parade: The Theater of Jean Cocteau* (New Brunswick, N.J.: Rutgers University Press, 1957), 101.

176 **realm of timeless inevitability:** "In no sense is . . . the uniqueness of character important [in myth]." David Grene, introduction to *Sophocles I,* in *The Complete Greek Tragedies,* ed. David Grene and Richmond Lattimore (Chicago: University of Chicago
Press, 1992), 7.

176 **showcasing inward, intimate stories:** These French modernists differed markedly
from many of their contemporaries in twentieth-century Western drama. While the
Scandinavian modernists, such as Henrik Ibsen and August Strindberg, and the later
Americans such as Eugene O'Neill, Lillian Hellman, and Arthur Miller, reveled in
the nuances of individual story and character, French modernist playwrights looked
outward instead of inward, forgoing individual contemplation in favor of far broader
themes.

176 **ready-made plots and stock characters:** See Hugh Dickinson, *Myth on the Modern
Stage* (Urbana: University of Illinois Press, 1969), 76ff for a discussion of Cocteau's
use of myth and the absence of psychology in his work.

176 **"a kind of strange goddess":** Maurice Sachs, *Au Temps du boeuf sur le toit* (Paris: Editions de la Nouvelle Revue Critique, 1939), 123. Turning death into this couture-
clad woman, Cocteau slipped in a tart commentary on the seductive decadence of
fashion, and its proximity to death. "Fashion prostitutes the body to the inorganic
world and represents the rights of the corpse," philosopher Walter Benjamin observed. Walter Benjamin, *The Arcades Project,* trans. Kevin McLaughlin (Cambridge,
Mass.: Harvard University Press, 2002), 82.

176 **Picasso painted the stage curtain:** Picasso's curtain was an enlargement of a painting
he had done of Amazonian women running on the beach.

177 **Cocteau were also regular passengers:** The romance of the Blue Train attracted
other artists, too. The train figured in Agatha Christie's 1928 novel, *The Mystery of the
Blue Train,* as well as in Georges Simenon's *Mon Ami Maigret,* 1949.

177 **and gossip columns:** During the winter of 1922–23, *Le Figaro* devoted a half page
nearly every day to a section called *"Le Figaro* aux pays du soleil" (Le Figaro in the
land of sunshine), which detailed the galas and sporting events of vacationing luminaries. See Garafola, *Diaghilev's Ballets Russes,* 379.

177 **the wear and tear of dancing:** The dancers complained that the jersey fabric was too
flimsy to withstand balletic exertions—seams split and hems frayed. Finally Chanel
had her staff sew two complete sets of costumes in order to have replacements always at the ready.

177 **fitted shorts and tank-style top:** Despite his French name, Dolin was an Irishman
born Patrick Kay, who had become Cocteau's new lover after the death of Raymond
Radiguet. Sokolova was British, born Hilda Munnings, who also adopted a more
European-sounding stage name as was the custom for many in Diaghilev's troupe.
See Madsen, 143.

177 **trademark little cloche hats:** Chanel's 1924 sportswear couture line was described
by *Women's Wear Daily* thus on February 4, 1924: "The characteristic, youthful line is
again predominant in the opening models shown by Chanel, who features many
boyish tailored suits . . . straight in silhouette.

179 **not overtly depicted:** For some, Chanel's dominating presence rendered the production too commercial. *The New Statesman* wrote, "[The Blue Train is just] . . . an elabo-

rate mannequin parade of bathing and other fashionable seaside costumes by the House of Chanel." Quoted in Garafola, *Diaghilev's Ballets Russes,* 99.

8. BENDOR: THE RICHEST MAN IN EUROPE

180 **"Whose yacht is that?:** Noël Coward, *Private Lives: An Intimate Comedy in Three Acts* (London: Samuel French, 1930), 21.

181 **"Boy sent Westminster to me":** Delay, 125.

181 **as well as the Eaton Railway:** The duke had inherited at least six hundred prime acres of some of the world's most valuable real estate, in the heart of London's Mayfair and Belgravia districts, as well as approximately thirty thousand beyond it. Rents paid him by tenants on his lands in the United Kingdom alone (he owned property all over the world) were estimated at $1.2 million a year in 1934. "The Duke of Westminster Sues for Libel," *Gettysburg Times,* January 6, 1934.

181 **belonging to the duke's ancestors:** The Grosvenor lineage could be easily traced back at least this far. A family dispute and legal case involving the Grosvenors was documented by none other than Geoffrey Chaucer, in French. Quoted in George Ridley, *Bend'Or, Duke of Westminster: A Personal Memoir* (London: Quartet Books, 1986), 7. Other documents can trace the Grosvenors to the twelfth century.

182 **"a descendent of Macaroni":** Quoted in Charles-Roux 423.

182 **Olympic motor boat racing:** Noël Coward describes the duke in his preface to Loelia Ponsonby, *Grace and Favour: The Memoirs of Loelia, Duchess of Westminster* (New York: Reynal, 1961). Quoted in Madsen, 149.

182 **admission to Cambridge:** The duke needed special tutoring to prepare for the Cambridge examinations, and the plan was soon shelved. "He was not of the type which wins school prizes," biographer Michael Harrison notes. Michael Harrison, *Lord of London: A Biography of the Second Duke of Westminster* (London: W. H. Allen, 1966), 30.

182 **key British imperialist Cecil Rhodes:** "Lord Milner Wants Anglo-American Union," *The New York Times,* June 11, 1916; *The Times* (London), July 25, 1925. Quoted in Bill Nasson, review of *Forgotten Patriot: A Life of Alfred Viscount Milner, Journal of Modern History* 81, no. 4 (December 2009).

183 **which developed into apartheid:** See P. Eric Louw, *The Rise, Fall, and Legacy of Apartheid* (Westport, Conn.: Greenwood Press, 2004), 10. Of the need to maintain a white overclass in South Africa, Milner wrote, "Our welfare depends upon increasing the quantity of our white population but not at the expense of its quality. We do not want a white proletariat in this country. The position of the whites among the vastly more numerous black population requires that even their lowest rank should be able to maintain a standard of living far above that of the poorest section of the population of a purely white country." Quoted in Shula Marks and Stanlye Trapido, "Lord Milner and the South African State," *History Workshop,* no. 8 (Autumn 1979): 66.

183 **firepower of the other Kindergarteners:** Westminster particularly helped fund Milner's projects for tariff reform and "imperial preference" (economic measures designed to safeguard the empire by extending preferential taxation to constituent states).

183 **something of a groupie:** Harrison, 98. For a discussion on Milner's extremely canny

manipulation of press propaganda for himself and his causes, see: A. N. Porter, "Sir Alfred Milner and the Press, 1897–1899," *The Historical Journal* 16, no. 2 (June 1973): 323–39.

183 **ninety-three miles of Libyan desert:** See Harrison, 163ff.

184 **Distinguished Service Order for bravery:** Jack Leslie, who served under Bendor for this mission, wrote about his commander: "Nothing but [Bendor's] amazing confidence and innate optimism could have ever started off a convoy prepared to do 300 miles to find them. He would class with any general as a great leader of men, having extraordinary personality. The odds were considered about six to one against our getting [the prisoners]." Quoted in Ridley, 102.

184 **a certain Mrs. Crosby:** See Harrison.

184 **androgynous British style of dress:** Vera's daughter, Bridget Bate Tichenor, later clamed that much of Chanel's English style was taken directly (and without attribution) from Vera. Zachary Selig, "The First Biography of Vera Bate Lombardi," http://www.slashdocs.com/pkyzmz/the-first-biography-of-the-life-of-vera-bate-lombardi-by-zachary-selig.html.

185 **duke had actually paid Vera:** Morand, *L'Allure de Chanel*, 196.

185 **converted Royal Navy destroyer:** The massive *Cutty Sark* had a 263-foot hull and a 25-foot beam. It ran on four steam turbines. Bendor kept the boat until the beginning of World War II, when he donated it to the British government to be used as a destroyer. Ridley, 134–35.

185 **a non-noble:** "He only liked what he called Real People. Apart from a few exceptions chosen by himself, nobody well known in the world or having the misfortune to have a title could be a Real Person." Ponsonby, 196.

185 **duke mistrusted the postal system:** There seems no definitive explanation for the duke's fear of the mail. It may have been a mere eccentricity of his, or, given his penchant for adultery, he may have exercised particular caution to avoid having any epistolary evidence getting intercepted.

186 **"The Duke frightened me":** Quoted in Galante, 103. Abdy suggested to Marcel Haedrich that Chanel hesitated to see the duke because she felt only minimal physical attraction to him. "Their passion was not sensual," she said. Quoted in Haedrich, 98.

186 **The duke had little knowledge:** "All forms of modern music, painting and sculpture were intolerable and he would have liked personally to destroy them," wrote Loelia Ponsonby, who would be Bendor's third of four wives. Ponsonby, 198–99.

186 **this new arrogant suitor:** Madsen, 152.

186 **a salmon-fishing party:** Quoted in Ridley, 135.

187 **"clever and charming Frenchwoman":** Quoted in Galante, 100.

187 **Just visiting his own properties:** Morand, *L'Allure de Chanel*, 191.

187 **"The famous Coco turned up":** Quoted in Leslie Fields, *Bendor: Golden Duke of Westminster* (Littlehampton, U.K.: Littlehampton Book Services, 1986), 200.

188 **duchess in training:** Quoted in Haedrich, 99.

188 **let them use his house:** Westminster had gained a reputation as a fair and generous landlord, but politically he was ill disposed to any kind of social progressivism. In

the House of Lords, he fought ardently against social programs that he felt placed undue burdens on the rich.

188 **showcased the region's wild game:** This is mentioned in the duke's Paris police file, as well as elsewhere. At eighty-nine, seamstress Manon Ligeour, who was apprenticed to Chanel in 1929 at the age of thirteen and worked for the Maison Chanel for nearly forty years, still remembered those vacations fondly. Interview, July 8, 2005, Conservatoire Chanel.

188 **his "favorite cabin boy":** Galante, 116; Fields, 190.

189 **Scotland's first bidet:** David Ross and Helen Puttick, "Coco Chanel's Love Nest in the Highlands," *The Herald* (Scotland), September 29, 2003. In 2012, the estate underwent a massive renovation, with the goal of turning it into a boutique hotel, capitalizing on its connection to Chanel. See Tim Cornwall, "£6m Facelift for Coco Chanel's Highland Love Nest." *The Scotsman,* July 1, 2012.

189 **"My general impression":** Ponsonby, 157.

190 **"Sir Walter Scott":** Morand, *L'Allure de Chanel,* 191. Even Lady Iya Abdy found a storybook quality in Chanel's romance with Bendor. "With the Duke, she lived a fairy tale," she told Marcel Haedrich. Haedrich, 98.

191 **"I knew with him a luxury":** Haedrich, 106.

191 **these dresses in solid black:** Fields, 199.

191 **Coco was the child's godmother:** According to Gabrielle Palasse-Labrunie, although Bendor was her godfather, it was Etienne Balsan (her possible grandfather) who attended her baptism. Westminster was unavailable, and Balsan had remained sufficiently close to Coco to fill in for the duke. Fiemeyer and Palasse-Labrunie, *Intimate Chanel,* 27.

192 **Bendor seemed entirely enchanted:** A 1929 BBC documentary about Chanel was filmed on the grounds of Eaton Hall and featured a segment showing little Gabrielle Palasse with her great-aunt.

192 **"I had been living":** Quoted in Haedrich, 99.

192 **"When I was certain no one":** Charles-Roux, 444.

193 **Bendor's unusual pets:** Gabrielle Palasse-Labrunie discussed the mysterious monkey statue in a private conversation with the author, March 2011. On Balsan's monkey, see Galante, 23.

193 **"isolated by his wealth":** Morand, *L'Allure de Chanel,* 187.

193 **swoon over the "exquisite vintages":** Ponsonby, 201.

193 **"some of our Hebrew friends":** Duke of Westminster to Winston Churchill, June 29, 1927, CHAR1/194/57.

193 **"I could never make out":** Ponsonby, 200–201.

194 **leading a financial conspiracy:** See Fields, 262.

194 **"He started by abusing":** Lady Diana Cooper, *The Light of Common Day* (Boston: Houghton Mifflin, 1959), 261.

194 **potential reprisals involved in countermanding:** See Fields, 263.

195 **"We talked half in English":** Galante, 107ff.

Interviewed in her elder years by *McCall's,* Chanel said, "We talked half in English, half in French. 'I don't want you to learn English,' he said, 'and discover there is nothing in the conversation you hear around us.'" Joseph Barry, interview with Chanel, *McCall's,* November 1, 1965, 172–73.

195 **"Luxury must remain nearly invisible":** Quoted in "En Ecoutant Chanel," *Elle,* France, August 23, 1963.

196 **the same jackets:** Morand, *L'Allure de Chanel,* 188.

196 **chic Scottish shooting parties:** "Scotland, the Happy Shooting Ground," *Vogue,* October 27, 1928, 46.

196 **"Tweeds have made":** "A Guide to Chic in Tweed," *Vogue,* December 22, 1928, 44.

196 **"The Fame of G.":** "Business: Haute Couture," *Time,* August 13, 1928, 35.

196 **particularly her feminine sweaters:** Fields, 199.

196 **"Tweeds that I had imported from":** Morand, *L'Allure de Chanel,* 57.

198 **"Colors are impossible":** Ibid., 55.

198 **"Chanel [is] famed":** "Introducing the Most Chic Woman in the World," *Vogue,* January 1, 1926, 54.

199 **the epitome of modernity:** Janet Wallach, *Chanel: Her Style and Her Life* (New York: Doubleday, 1998), 83. The term *garçonne* meaning "tomboy," or, later, "flapper," came into vogue after the 1922 publication of the racy novel *La Garçonne* by Victor Margueritte, the story of a proper young woman who cuts her hair, stops wearing corsets, and plunges into the Parisian counterculture for sexual and social experimentation. The scandal surrounding the novel resulted in Margueritte's losing his Légion d'honneur.

199 **"all the world will wear":** "The Debut of the Winter Mode," *Vogue,* October 1, 1926, 69.

199 **"Before me, no one would":** Haedrich, 107.

200 **"young and hard bitterness":** Salvador Dalí, *The Secret Life of Salvador Dalí,* trans. Haakon M. Chevalier (London: Dover Publications, 1993), 383. Originally published as *La Vie secrète de Salvador Dalí* (New York: Dial Press, 1942).

200 **"What followed [Boy's death]":** Morand, *L'Allure de Chanel,* 66.

200 **his manorial lifestyle:** During their relationship, Chanel would describe the duke as "perfect for his type" but later admitted she'd found him somewhat lacking intellectually. Charles-Roux, 447.

201 **"a striped costume":** "Fashions That Bloom in the Riviera Sun," *Vogue,* May 1, 1926, 56.

201 **initial clientele at Deauville:** Baba de Faucigny figures in a disturbing incident in Chanel's later life, see chapter 11. And we know this future queen consort as the Queen Mother, Elizabeth.

201 **Mayfair property lent to her:** Madsen, 166.

201 **"I was as tan as a gypsy":** Quoted in Fields, 173.

201 **Coco would ask her chemists:** Danièle Bott, *Chanel* (Paris: Editions Ramsey, 2005), 124.

202 **ship all her seamstresses:** On Westminster's impatience, see Delay, 126; and Picardie, 168.

202 **Coco subordinated her schedule:** Picardie, 168–69.

202 **"little girl before the duke":** Charles-Roux says that long after her affair with Westminster, Chanel admitted his "intellectual insufficiency." Charles-Roux, 447; Abdy quoted in Galante, 107.

202 **"The greatest pleasure":** Morand, *L'Allure de Chanel,* 186.

202 **"Never a big, solemn dinner":** Delay, 135.

202 **dashing Italian military man:** Charles-Roux, 445.

203 **Alphonse was the crafty one:** Ibid., 450–53.

204 **Everyone whispered about her absence:** The story of Mary's coming-out party is recounted by Delay, 136–37; Galante, 107–8; and Madsen, 167ff.

205 **slim figure was to blame:** Charles-Roux, 448.

205 **restful surroundings could be conducive:** Madsen, 167ff.

205 **most exclusive real estate:** Monte Carlo had had some obstacles to overcome en route to stardom. In the earlier 1920s it experienced some economic problems, which were solved, according to Pierre Galante, by tart-tongued American journalist Elsa Maxwell. Galante reports that Prince Pierre, father of the late monarch Prince Rainier of Monaco, complained to Maxwell about losing tourism, and she pointed out that the area's rock-covered beaches discouraged tourists. She suggested bringing in sand, which the prince decided to do. Thereafter, Maxwell made a point of talking up the charms of Monte Carlo in her columns. Galante, 124–25.

206 **performers set up housekeeping:** Madsen, 170.

206 **more than a meter thick:** Galante, 118–19.

206 **Our Lady of La Pausa:** "Pour fêter l'ouverture de la Pausa recréee à Dallas," Wendy and Emery Reves Collection, Dallas Museum of Art, 1985, exhibition catalog, 42–49.

206 **enacting the Passion of Christ:** "On the festival of Notre Dame de la Neige, a very curious procession, dating from the Middle Ages, still takes place here, in which the Passion is represented—peasants gravely taking the parts of Pilate, Herod, SS. Veronica and Mary Magdalene, &c." Augustus J. C. Hare. *Rivieras* (London: Allen and Unwin Press, 1897), accessed at http://www.rarebooksclub.com, 2012.

207 **refreshments for the pilgrims:** Galante, 116–20.

207 **"born in the poorhouse":** Dallas exhibition catalog, 42–49.

207 **"one of the most enchanting villas":** P. H. Satterhwaite, "Mademoiselle Chanel's House," *Vogue,* March 29, 1930, 63. Back on the market in 2012, the villa was listed at 40 million euros, or about $52.5 million. See "Coco Chanel Riviera Villa for Sale," *The Riviera Times,* February 29, 2012, http://www.rivieratimes.com/index.php/provence-cote-dazur-article/items/coco-chanel-riviera-villa-for-sale.html.

209 **dotted the seaside hills:** Galante, 119.

209 **"On every slate":** Pierre Reverdy, in *The Roof Slates,* Caws and Terry, trans., 19.

210 **have their roofs retiled:** Apparently, Chanel set off a "speculative boom" in old tiles in the area. See Wendy and Emery Reves, *The Wendy and Emery Reves Collection Catalogue* (Dallas, Tex.: The Dallas Museum of Art, 1985) 44–45. (Published to commemorate the opening of the re-created villa, La Pausa, in the Dallas Museum of Art.), 41.

210 **the *grove* was not:** Satterhwaite, 63.

211 **Outsize stone fireplaces:** Ibid., 62–65, 86.

211 **entryway decorated with the crown:** See John Rafferty, "Name Dropping on the Riviera," *The New York Times,* May 19, 2011.

211 **his distinctive cartoon drawings:** Charles-Roux, 449; Galante, 127.

212 "La Pausa was the most comfortable": Bettina Ballard, *In My Fashion* (New York: D. McKay, 1969), 49.

213 dropping a priceless emerald: Charles-Roux, 454–55; Haedrich, 108.

213 "On August 17, the two women": Chanel recalls sailing with Misia when they heard from Diaghilev, in Chazot, *Chazot Jacques,* 96. Galante also describes this episode, 109.

213 bitter rivalry for Diaghilev's affections: John Richardson, *A Life of Picasso* (New York: Random House, 1991), 378.

213 the crawling was melodramatic: Charles-Roux, 458; Morand, *Venises,* 117–18.

214 "I loved him in his hurry": Morand, *L'Allure de Chanel,* 101–3.

214 The duke would never marry: This episode is recounted by Galante, 113.

214 "Coco is crazy!": Charles-Roux, 459.

214 visited Eaton Hall once more: Picardie, 186.

215 met only two months prior: Ponsonby, 150–51.

215 prove just how serious she: Morand, *L'Allure de Chanel,* 194.

215 his version of England: Haedrich, 111.

215 "At the time, Mademoiselle Chanel": Ponsonby, 167–68.

215 Churchill served as best man: Ibid., 177.

216 she increased it to fourteen: "I spent thirteen years with a man who lived in the country." Quoted in Haedrich, 100. To *McCall's* she said, "I was lucky to have known the Duke. Fourteen years, that is a long time.... I have never felt more protected." "Interview with Mademoiselle Chanel," November 1, 1965, 165.

216 "Salmon fishing is not a life": Morand, *L'Allure de Chanel,* 194.

216 "My woman has a heart": BBC interview with Gabrielle Palasse-Labrunie. Claude Delay mentions this song as something Chanel heard in Hollywood in 1931, but Pierre Galante mentions her going with her friends to the Paris club known as Le boeuf sur le toit for jazz, where she might well have first heard the song. Galante, 61.

9. THE PATRIOTISM OF LUXURY: CHANEL AND PAUL IRIBE

217 a household word in Europe: Figures come from "La collection Chanel sortira le 26 janvier," *Nord Matin,* January 12, 1971. See also Chanel's police file, especially section dated December 1930, Paris police archives.

218 bailed them out personally: She subsidized at least twice, in 1926 and 1928, Cocteau's extended clinic stays for drug rehabilitation, and paid entirely for Diaghilev's elaborate funeral in 1929. She was also known to give large sums to favorite employees in extremis, although she was notoriously stingy with salaries.

218 "I prefer to give": "Collections by Chanel," *McCall's,* June 1968. Chanel later confided to Claude Delay that she grew weary of the constant requests for money.

218 fragrant orange trees: Bettina Ballard Wilson, *In My Fashion* (New York: D. McKay, Co., 1969), 49; *Vogue,* July 1938, 64–65; *Plaisir de France,* February 1935, 18–19; *Harper's Bazaar,* April 1939, 65.

218 "the Baroness Nexon": Charles-Roux, 459.

219 "A woman is like a pearl": Quoted in Anne-Claude Lelieur and Raymond Bachollot, eds., *Paul Iribe: Précurseur de l'art déco* (Paris: Bibliothèque Forney, 1983), 64. Originally published as an interview in *Commoedia Illustré,* March 1, 1911.

219 **Coco was engaged to be:** "Mlle Chanel to Wed Business Partner," *The New York Times,* November 17, 1933.

220 **a largely proletarian committee:** The monarchists had recently captured a majority in the French Assembly.

220 **secularism in schools and government:** The politics of the Commune were not unilateral, though, and consisted of various strains, ranging from moderate to radical. See David Harvey, "Monument and Myth," *Annals of the Association of American Geographers* 69, no. 3 (September, 1979): 362–81.

221 **known for his ruthlessness:** Thiers planned to abolish the Commune, by "us[ing] the conservatism of the country to crush the radicalism of the city," in the words of historian David Harvey, harnessing the resentments of rural Frenchmen to incite their participation in raids against their own city-dwelling compatriots. Adolphe Thiers even negotiated with Otto von Bismarck to win the release of French prisoners of war, who were then inducted directly into the Versailles army and sent to Paris to attack their own compatriots. Thiers had been especially cruel in his suppression of the worker movement during his years as minister of the interior under Louis-Philippe. Harvey, 370.

221 **Communards were depicted as dangerous:** Novelist Alphonse Daudet described his city under the commune as "Paris controlled by the blacks." Edmond de Goncourt compared the workers to "barbarians." See Kristin Ross, "Commune Culture," in *A New History of French Literature,* ed. Denis Hollier (Cambridge, Mass.: Harvard University Press, 1989), 751–58.

221 **imperial conquests were actually benevolent:** To the Communards, the column stood as "a symbol of chauvinism and incitement to national hatred," as Frederick Engels wrote. Frederick Engels, "Introduction," 9–22, in Karl Marx, *The Civil War in France: The Paris Commune* (New York: International Publishers, Co., Inc, 1968), 15. Originally published in 1891.

221 **They even hired musicians:** Special permits were issued, printed like invitations, and stamped with a Phrygian cap, in keeping with the commune's extensive borrowing of iconography of the French Revolution. They also borrowed the revolutionary calendar, referring to "Floréal," and so forth.

222 **his fractured stone body:** See Sir Alistair Horne, *The Fall of Paris: The Siege and the Commune* (1965; repr., New York: Penguin, 2007), esp. 350–51.

222 **Liberty atop the globe:** We don't know when Iribe shortened and Gallicized his Basque name, but he is listed as "Iribe" in contemporary accounts of the Commune. *Proceedings of the Royal Geographical Society and Monthly Record of Geography,* n.s., 10, no. 12 (December 1888): 813–48. Accessed online.

222 **the palm of Napoléon's hand:** Some sources suggest that financial need and a desire to impress his girlfriend at that time, actress Mary Magnier, motivated Jules Iribe to help demolish the Colonne Vendôme. Lelieur and Bachollot, 19.

223 **one of the bloodiest massacres:** Marx wrote:

> To find a parallel for the conduct of Thiers and his bloodhounds we must go back to the times of Sulla and the two Triumvirates of Rome. The same wholesale slaughter in cold blood; the same disregard, in massacre, of age and sex, the same system of torturing prisoners; the same proscriptions, but this time of a

whole class; the same savage hunt after concealed leaders, lest one might escape; the same denunciations of political and private enemies; the same indifference for the butchery of entire strangers to the feud. There is but this difference: that the Romans had no *mitrailleuses* [machine guns].

Marx, *The Civil War in France*, 75.

223 **ten years in Spain:** Maria Teresa Sanchez de la Campa, an Andalusian girl twenty years his junior, became—eventually—his wife. Jules would go on to pursue his itinerant career, as a superintendent working on the Panama Canal and also living for a time, with his family, in Madagascar, training colonists. "M. Iribe Has Been Appointed General Superintendent of the Panama R.R.," *Engineering News and American Contract Journal*, February 9, 1884, 67.

223 **joining the Freemasons:** Delay, 154.

223 **not unlike Boy Capel:** He was even a member of the Positivist Club of Paris, a group devoted to scientific inquiry that followed the philosophies of August Comte. Other adherents included Georges Clemenceau. "The Decline of French Positivism," *Sewanee Review* 33, no. 4 (October 1925): 484–87. His membership is mentioned in one of those old journals.

223 **mention of his itinerant youth:** Although he claimed to have attended Paris's L'Ecole des Beaux-Arts, Paul had likely not even completed secondary school. "Nothing about him is certain," writes art historian Anne-Claude Lelieur, "since throughout his entire life, Iribe made sure to divulge nothing whatsoever about his education and his origins." Lelieur and Bachollot, 32.

224 **particular pride of place:** Twenty different French fashion houses exhibited at the Fair; and La Parisienne, in her Paquin gown, stood above it all, welcoming visitors at the gate. Vincent Soulier, *Presse Féminine: La Puissance Frivole* (Montreal: Editions Archipel), 40. See also Debora Silverman, *Art Nouveau in Fin-de-Siècle France* (Berkeley: University of California Press, 1989), 291.

225 **an amalgam of fashion, design:** Iribe worked for *L'Assiette au Beurre*, owned by Thadée Natanson, husband of Misia, as well as *Le Rire* and *Le Cri de Paris*. His sophisticated political caricatures won him acclaim early on. *L'Assiette au Beurre* sent him to Madrid in 1902, when he was just nineteen, to cover the coronation of Alphonse XIII.

225 **Jean Cocteau also collaborated:** This patron was Norwegian socialite Dagny Bjornson. *Le Témoin* ran for four years and showcased work by Iribe and the coterie of talented friends he had already amassed, among them Sacha Guitry, Juan Gris, Marcel Duchamp, and Jean Cocteau (who convinced him to devote an entire issue to the Ballets Russes).

225 **the delicate "Iribe rose":** "Let us recall the way that [Iribe] proved that commercial art is not necessarily a minor art." André Warnod, obituary for Paul Iribe, *Le Figaro*, September 29, 1935.

225 **rabid xenophobia and racism:** "The 'foreigner' cannot love our journal," declared one issue, using the French word *métèque* for foreigner, a strong racial slur indicating someone of Middle Eastern or Mediterranean descent. The journal aimed, it said, to rescue "modernism and imaginative creative endeavor from German affiliation." See Jane Fulcher, "The Preparation for Vichy: Anti-Semitism in French

Musical Culture Between the Two World Wars," *The Musical Quarterly,* Autumn 1995, 458–75.

225 **Iribe's career reached its apex:** After his fashion drawings for American *Vogue* caught the attention of Jesse Lasky, one of the founders of Paramount Studios, Iribe was introduced to Cecil B. DeMille, who hired him in 1920.

226 **Cadillac that he christened "Fifi":** Delay, 159.

226 **He hired a Japanese valet:** See George C. Pratt, Herbert Reynolds, and Cecil B. DeMille, "Forty-Five Years of Picture-Making, an Interview with Cecil B. DeMille," *Film History* 3, no. 2, 1989: 133–45. Iribe's film credits as costume designer include DeMille's *Don't Change Your Husband* (1919); *The Affairs of Anatol* (1921), starring Gloria Swanson (whom Chanel would dress for films ten years later); *Manslaughter* (1922); *Adam's Rib* (1923); and *Feet of Clay* (1924).

226 **lavish ancient Egyptian settings:** See Robert S. Birchard, *Cecil B. DeMille's Hollywood* (Lexington: University Press of Kentucky, 2004), 179ff.

226 **she was costuming Sophocles:** "There is no question that it will be seen by more people than any picture the world has ever had," said director DeMille about *The Ten Commandments.* See George C. Pratt, Reynolds, and DeMille, especially 140. See also Simon Louvish, *Cecil B. DeMille: A Life* (New York: Thomas Dunne Books, 2008).

226 **obliged to return to France:** See Louvish, 262.

226 **"My growing celebrity":** Morand, *L'Allure de Chanel,* 129.

227 **"I think that in engaging Mademoiselle":** "Madame Chanel to Design Fashions for Films," *The New York Times,* January 25, 1931.

228 **apprised of her prejudices:** Delay, 149.

228 **"With him at least the extravagance":** Charles-Roux, 475.

229 **both gifted poseurs:** For details on the life of Erich von Stroheim, see Richard Koszarski, *Von: The Life and Films of Erich von Stroheim* (New York: Limelight, 2004).

229 **chafed at being an employee:** See Delay, 149.

229 **"sartorial anarchy":** Quoted in Emma Cabire, "Le Cinéma et la mode," *La Revue du Cinéma,* no. 26 (September 1, 1931): 25–26.

229 **"When you strip color":** Quoted in Dale McConathy and Diana Vreeland, *Hollywood Costume* (New York: Harry N. Abrams, 1977), 28.

230 **"[Chanel] made a lady":** *The New Yorker,* December 22, 1931.

230 **starring in *A Bill of Divorcement*:** Celia Berton, *Paris à La Mode: A Voyage of Discovery* (London: Gollancz, 1956), 166.

231 **"I prefer copying to stealing":** "Interview with Mademoiselle Chanel," *McCall's,* November 1965, 172.

231 **"Mademoiselle Chanel has authorized being copied":** See Madsen, 192. See also "Chanel's Exhibition Opened at 39 Grosvenor Square," *Harper's Bazaar,* 1932, 67. "The public will be admitted on payment of a small entrance fee which will be devoted to a charity connected with the textile industry .... [Exhibit features] more than a hundred models, created exclusively in British materials, and are not for sale. Range from dresses for Ascot to suits for the Scottish moors."

231 **"when all the people":** "Chanel Is 75," 1959 BBC interview.

232 **"My past tortured him":** Morand, *L'Allure de Chanel,* 129.

232 **"wear[ing] your checkbook":** Morand, *L'Allure de Chanel,* 145.

232 **"During times when luxury":** Delay, 153–54.

233 **Never before had Coco attributed:** Quoted in Charles-Roux, 499. Interview originally in *L'Illustration,* November 12, 1932, no. 4680.

234 **hired security guards:** Ibid., 499.

234 **accusing her of extravagance:** Morand, *L'Allure de Chanel,* 127.

235 **The Ritz would remain:** Delay, 163.

235 **"He dominated her," recalled Serge:** Quoted in Galante, 140.

235 **quite the opposite was true:** Haedrich, 122.

236 **"There is more authentic French":** Iribe laid out his new political philosophy in two manifesto-like essays: "In Defense of Luxury" (May 1932), published as a freestanding booklet, and "The 'France' Brand" (July 1932), published as a special issue of the journal *L'Animateur du Temps Nouveau.* The essays announce the argument that Iribe would develop through all sixty-nine issues of *Le Témoin.* France was under attack by pernicious foreigners and racial inferiors who had targeted its very soul—that is, its luxury goods industry.

237 **Gabrielle Palasse-Labrunie put it simply:** Gabrielle Palasse-Labrunie, personal conversation with author, March 2011.

238 **"ubiquitous name of French chic":** John Updike, "Qui Qu'a Vu Coco," *The New Yorker,* September 21, 1998, 132–36.

238 **"He wanted to see me vanquished":** Morand, *L'Allure de Chanel,* 129.

240 **"leprosy on the clear complexion":** Paul Iribe, "Le Dernier Luxe," *Le Témoin,* November 4, 1934.

241 **the so-called Stavisky affair:** As historian William Wiser has written, "1933 was Year One of a sobering European malaise." William Wiser, *The Twilight Years: Paris in the 1930s* (New York: Carroll and Graf), 98.

    Serge Stavisky, a Russian Jew living in Paris, was a known embezzler and pyramid scheme artist with ties to a number of highly placed members of the Radical Party of Parliament. Despite his long and public criminal record, Stavisky continued to live lavishly and evade prosecution, enjoying what everyone assumed was government protection. (Officials postponed his trial nineteen times over a period of sixteen years.) On January 8, 1934, when Stavisky was found shot dead in Chamonix, virtually no one believed the official explanation of suicide. The prevailing opinion, especially on the right, was that Stavisky had been murdered by the government in an attempt to cover up its involvement in his corrupt enterprises. Throughout January and early February, a series of related scandals broke out, involving the dismissal of the Paris police commissioner, Jean Chiappe, and a kerfuffle over a production of Shakespeare's *Coriolanus* at the Comédie-Française (the choice of this play had inflamed everyone, appearing pro-communist to the Right, and pro-fascist to the Left). Prime Minister Edouard Daladier only aggravated matters when, in a misguided attempt to quell the discord, he fired Emile Fabre, director of the Comédie-Française, and replaced him with M. Thome, head of the French secret service.

    While Iribe was ardently anti-German, and staunchly nationalist, his politics had much in common with the Fascists. This blend of xenophobia with Fascist sympathies was common among the French right wing in the 1930s. With the approach of World War II, many of those on the French Right made common cause with the occupying Germans and supported the collaborationist Vichy regime.

241 **Hundreds of such uprisings:** See Wiser, and also Eugen Weber, *The Hollow Years: France in the 1930s* (New York: W. W. Norton, 1994), 141. "February 6th … aggravated and confirmed political polarization: the politics of either/or. For the next few years there would be no more constructive debate between people of different political stripe. Only clashes."

241 **much of the political drama:** In 1934, over two-thirds of all published journals supported conservative, often anti-parliamentarian causes; these right-leaning (and usually anti-Semitic) papers enjoyed eight times the circulation of those on the left.

242 **in August 1934:** Chanel, "Préface à ma collection d'hiver," August 6, 1934, typescript at Conservatoire Chanel.

245 **layers of starched crinolines:** See Prince Jean-Louis de Faucigny-Lucinge, *Fêtes Mémorables, bals costumés 1922–1972* (Paris: Herscher Publishing, 1986).

245 **"The masked ball unmasks":** Quoted in Prince Jean-Louis de Faucigny-Lucinge, *Mémoires d'un gentilhomme cosmopolite,* 113.

246 **"Aren't you appalled":** Colette, *Lettres à Marguerite Moreno* (Paris: Flammarion, 1994), 232.

246 **"Last night I was at dinner":** Delay, 169. Morand on September 14, 1934.

246 **help Iribe slim down:** Delay mentions Chanel's open dislike of overweight people. Delay, 233.

247 **"my father thought a marriage":** Gabrielle Palasse-Labrunie, personal conversation with author, March 2011.

247 **"She … was … so attached":** Fiemeyer and Palasse-Labrunie, 157.

247 **"He died at her feet":** Personal conversation with author.

10. THE PULSE OF HISTORY: CHANEL, FASCISM, AND THE INTERWAR YEARS

249 **"the throbbing pulse of history":** Marie-Pierre Lannelongue, "Coco dans tous ses états," *Elle,* May 2, 2005, 115.

249 **"most obscure questions in history":** Eric Hobsbawm, *The Age of Extremes* (New York: Vintage, 1994), 178.

250 **made little secret of her anti-Semitism:** Jacques Chazot, who befriended Chanel in her later years, reports that she "spoke of Hitler as a hero," often horrifying guests. Chazot, *Chazot Jacques,* 74. He also recounts her penchant for telling anti-Semitic jokes at dinners she hosted. The Comtesse de Noailles recalled Chanel in the 1930s as a figure "throwing Tarot cards and badmouthing the Jews." Laurence Benaïm, *Marie Laure de Noailles: La Vicomtesse du bizarre* (Paris: Grasset, 2001), 314.

250 **Some of her favorite billionaires:** In one of several similar responses to Vaughan's book, the Maison Chanel told British *Vogue,* "Such insinuations cannot go unchallenged …. She would hardly have formed a relationship with the [Wertheimers] or counted Jewish people among her close friends and professional partners such as the Rothschild family … had these really been her views. It is unlikely." See Lauren Milligan, "Not Coco," *Vogue,* August 18, 2011. Justine Picardie repeats this justification in her biography. Picardie, 272.

250 **surprising extent of collaboration:** See for example, Barbara Will, *Unlikely Collabora-tions: Gertrude Stein, Bernard Fay, and the Vichy Dilemma* (New York: Columbia University Press, 2011). Most recently, such interest in the treacherous affiliations of wealthy and successful individuals may be ascribed to the growing unease in the States about income inequality, the role of banks in the Great Recession, and in 2011, the widespread Occupy Wall Street movement, which singled out the top 1 percent of U.S. taxpayers. See my own interview on this subject in regard to Chanel biographies in Lauren Lipton, "Three Books about Chanel," *The New York Times,* December 2, 2011.

251 **Misia was already hopelessly addicted:** Misia's health began to decline seriously in the mid-1930s, perhaps because of her increasing drug dependence. Her eyesight began to deteriorate; she suffered a retinal hemorrhage, and in 1939 she suffered a heart attack, Delay, 181.

251 **the married Henry de Zogheb:** Zogheb also dabbled in literature and is the author of *Illogismes* and *Les Maîtres de l'heure.* His wife, Odette, née Trézel, was known as a very elegant woman whose photograph appeared often in fashion magazines and society columns. Paris police archives.

252 **"to stay at La Pausa":** Quoted in Gaia Servadio, *Luchino Visconti: A Biography* (London: Weidenfeld and Nicolson, 1981), 49.

252 **"[Chanel] would ring":** Quoted in Servadio, 63.

252 **"When I was in Paris":** Ibid., 59. Originally published in Lina Coletti, interview with Visconti, *L'Europeo,* November 21, 1974.

252 **parades of handsome young soldiers:** This comes also from his sister Uberta. Quoted in Servadio, 47.

252 **Fascism also held social appeal:** An anonymous friend, quoted by Servadio, 47.

252 **satire of French social class:** Chanel would later costume such classic films as Louis Malle's *The Lovers* (1958), Roger Vadim's *Dangerous Liaisons* (1959), and Alain Resnais's *Last Year at Marienbad* (1961).

252 **who played Marie Antoinette:** For more on *La Marseillaise* and its parallels between the fall of Louis XVI and the collapse of the Blum government, see Leger Grindon, "History and the Historians in *La Marseillaise*," *Film History* 4, no. 3 (1990): 227–35. Uberta Visconti recalls that Chanel, oddly, had once escorted Luchino to a meeting of the Popular Front, where Coco seemed distinctly out of place: "[She] was covered in fantastic jewels, and they had mixed with huge sweaty men." Quoted in Servadio, 59. Such an outing was most out of character for Chanel, who was perhaps curious about this organization or, more likely, simply accompanying a man she found compelling.

253 **"dignified elegance":** *Vogue,* December 1938, 154.

253 **The birthrate had dropped:** During the midthirties, the population of Britain increased by 23 percent, that of Germany by 36 percent, while in France the population increased by just 3 percent, and most of that was due only to immigration from Eastern Europe and elsewhere. See Tony Judt, "France Without Glory," *The New York Review of Books,* May 23, 1996.

253 **went through five prime ministers:** Léon Blum lost his position in 1937 after only one year. Radical Socialist Party member Camille Chautemps then took over as

prime minister for one year, his second stint at the post. Blum resumed control for a single month in 1938, after which Radical Socialist Edouard Daladier took over for two years, followed by Paul Reynaud for less than two months before Pétain took over as Vichy began.

254 **Franco's coup in Spain:** Mussolini marched into Abyssinia in 1935, and Hitler invaded the Sudetenland in 1938, occupying the rest of Czechoslovakia in 1939. In 1936, General Franco's coup established a military dictatorship in Spain. As Judt observes, "The mid-Thirties were also the nervously anticipated *années creuses* (Eugen Weber's title); a shortfall of military recruits resulted from the trough in the birth rate in the years 1914–1918. Hence the sentiment, shared by military planners and pacifists alike, that France simply could not fight another war." Judt, "France Without Glory."

254 **The truth was far murkier:** French historian René Rémond was the most famous of those to insist that France nearly entirely rejected fascism. His 1954 classic, *The Right Wing in France from 1815 to de Gaulle,* distinguishes between the many French right-wing leagues and what he sees as "true" fascists. "The "Vichyite right [was] by its very nature a minority," he wrote. Rémond, *The Right Wing in France from 1815 to de Gaulle,* trans. James M. Laux (1954; repr., Philadelphia: University of Pennsylvania Press, 1966), 327.

254 **preparing the way for Vichy:** "In this key period in the history of French society ... before Vichy and independent of any Hitlerian influence, political anti-Semitism had become visible." Pierre Birnbaum, *Un mythe politique: La "République juive"* (Paris: Fayard, 1988), 328–29.

254 **French citizens accepted, even welcomed:** Among the most groundbreaking studies of France's version of fascism are Eugen Weber's *Varieties of Fascism* (1964); Robert Soucy's *Fascism in France: Case of Maurice Barrès* (1973) and *Fascist Intellectual: Drieu La Rochelle* (1979); Zeev Sternhell's *Neither Right nor Left* (1983); and Jeffrey Mehlman's *Legacies of Anti-Semitism in France* (1983). Robert Paxton, too, in *The Anatomy of Fascism* (2004), argues that France was far more Vichyist than resistant. Literary critics such as Alice Kaplan in her 1986 *Reproductions of Banality* began in the 1980s to draw attention to the importance of fascist French writers such as Robert Brasillach, Pierre Drieu La Rochelle, and Charles Maurras.

254 **consisted, arguably, of sheer need:** Historian Pascal Ory, a student of Rémond's, said, "Every Frenchman who remained on territory occupied by the German army or that was under its control had to some degree 'collaborated.'" Pascal Ory, *Les Collaborateurs, 1940–1945* (Paris: Editions du Seuil, 1976), 10.

254 **"French fascism had generic roots":** John F. Sweets, "Hold that Pendulum! Redefining Fascism, Collaborationism and Resistance in France," *French Historical Studies* 15, no. 4 (Autumn 1988): 731–58.

255 **"magical formulas for reconciling":** See Hannah Arendt, *The Origins of Totalitarianism* (1948; repr., New York: Harcourt, 1968), 89–120.

255 **The treatment would restore Europe:** "France's anti-Semitism was somehow deeper but more about xenophobia," for Arendt.

255 **igniting France's domestic fascism:** It is crucial to acknowledge the many nuances involved in French right-wing politics of this era. Not all nationalists were inclined

toward fascism. Not all who supported fascism supported Hitler's monstrous activities. Even the distinction between "right" and "left," furthermore, must remain approximate when we speak of these years, since the ostensible goals of Germany's National Socialist Party started out appealing strongly to France's own socialists. The fascist PPF (Parti populaire français), for example, was founded by Jacques Doriot in 1936, and by 1937 boasted a quarter of a million members. Those who remained supporters of the Nazis usually came to renounce their own socialism however, becoming, de facto, rightists. Many traditional Catholic right-wing supporters, moreover, deplored fascism. The complexity of distinguishing right from left has been admirably explored by Israeli historian Zeev Sternhell. See Sternhell, *Neither Right nor Left*, trans. David Maisel (1983; repr., Princeton, N.J.: Princeton University Press, 1995). In fact, according to Sternhell, France's strong nonfascist right wing was largely responsible for preventing a total surrender to fascism. Sternhell, 118. See also Robert Soucy, *Fascist Intellectual: Drieu La Rochelle* (Berkeley: University of California Press 1979), 3.

Moreover, although by the mid-1930s a significant number of Frenchmen openly supported fascism and belonged to one of the several active native leagues, not all right-wing partisans followed this path.

255 **"[It was] fundamentally nasty"**: Judt, "France Without Glory."

255 **horrifying wealthy conservatives**: Tony Judt aptly termed Blum a "lightning rod for modern French anti-Semitism." Tony Judt, *The Burden of Responsibility: Blum, Camus, Aron, and the French Twentieth Century* (Chicago: University of Chicago Press, 1998), 19. On February 13, 1936, shortly after the elections, Blum was dragged from a car and beaten almost to death by the Camelots du roi, a group of anti-Semites and royalists. The right-wing, largely pro-fascist Action française league was dissolved by the government following this incident. See Birnbaum, 316.

255 **"It is intolerable that our country"**: Daudet, *l'Action Française,* March 9, 1926, and Jean Louis Legrand in *Le Défi,* March 20, 1938, quoted in Birnbaum, 243.

255 **"I am afraid only of the Jews"**: Haedrich, 119.

255 **"myth becomes blood"**: Philippe Lacoue-Labarthe and Jean-Luc Nancy, *Le Mythe nazi* (Paris: Editions de l'Aube), 61.

255 **way to limit their influence**: See Romy Golan, "Ecole française vs. Ecole de Paris," *Artists Under Vichy* (Princeton, N.J.: Princeton University Press, 1992), 85. Even Léon Blum became the target of this xenophobia. Blum was born French to French parents and grandparents. Birnbaum recounts that in June 1936 a rumor began circulating that he had been born in Bessarabia with the original name Karfunkelstein. Within two days the *Action française,* delighted, repeated the story. As late as 1959 the mistake was printed in the *Petit Larousse Illustré* in a biography entry on Blum, and had to be withdrawn "under the threat of legal action." Birnbaum, 139ff.

255 **measures specifically restricting Jews**: These new measures included quotas, civil restrictions, and the requirement to present identity papers upon demand. See Elizabeth Ezra for more on French immigration policies between the wars. "In 1931 the French government reversed its more open immigration laws, drastically curtailing immigration and expatriating many already in France. From 1921 to 1931 the immigrant population rose from 1.5 million to roughly 2.9 million; between 1931 and

1936, it decreased to 2.4 million." Elizabeth Ezra, *The Colonial Unconscious: Race and Culture in Interwar France* (Ithaca, N.Y.: Cornell University Press, 2000), 144. See also Golan, 87ff.

256 **entire Parisian staff:** About the 1934 riots, *The New York Times* had reported that Chanel "particularly deplored [them]" since they disturbed the wealthy American women who "had come with the evident intention of placing substantial orders, especially welcome after the long dry spell in the dressmaking world." May Birkhead, "American Women Dare Paris Riots," *The New York Times,* February 25, 1934.

257 **the form of weekly salaries:** See "Marseilles Strikers Win," *The New York Times,* June 25, 1936.

257 **"Consent to negotiations?":** Quoted in Charles-Roux, 520–23.

257 **"I detest giving in":** Delay, 178.

257 **adopted a ruling-class mentality:** Charles-Roux, 523ff.

257 **other strikers around the country:** Workers were emboldened by the terms of France's new Matignon Agreements, which granted a forty-hour week and paid vacations.

258 **"With the same instinct":** "Chanel Offers Her Shop to Workers," *The New York Times,* June 19, 1936; see also Emannuel Berl, "La Chair et le sang: Lettre à un jeune ouvrier," *Marianne,* June 24, 1936, 3.

258 **"You believe this was a matter":** Quoted in Charles-Roux, 523.

259 **ties to the Third Reich:** See chapter 4 for Dmitri's relationship to this group, and chapter 8 for more on the Duke of Westminster's politics in the 1930s and beyond.

259 **"She did not mind dropping":** See Hal Vaughan, *Sleeping with the Enemy* (New York: Knopf, 2011). According to Vaughan (as well as Edmonde Charles-Roux) Chanel—always deeply attracted to nobility and wealth—had had a flirtation with Edward when they first met, which was just prior to her meeting the Duke of Westminster. See also Chazot, *Chazot Jacques,* 77.

259 **world-rocking scandal of 1936:** In 1936, several months before Edward stepped down, Chanel hosted a dinner at the Ritz for Churchill, during which she and Winston and Jean Cocteau discussed the looming crisis of Edward's marriage. Vaughan, 98.

260 **return to the British throne:** Declassified British intelligence files have proved that these negotiations took place. Rob Evans and Dave Hencke, "Hitler Saw Duke of Windsor as 'No Enemy,'" *The Guardian,* January 25, 2003. According to the files, Hitler felt that the duke was the only Englishman with whom he could negotiate an armistice.

260 **make common cause with Vichy:** In France, the most anti-German members of the right wing were also those most susceptible to the same racially based arguments of the Nazis.

Robert Brasillach explains clearly the typical French fascist turn toward Germany: "I was not a Germanophile before the war, nor even at the beginning of the politics of collaboration; I was simply looking for the interests of reason. Now, things have changed. It seems to me that I have entered into a liaison with the German genius, and I will never forget it. Whether we like it or not, we have cohabited. Thoughtful Frenchmen during these years have more or less gone to bed with Germany, not without quarrels, and the memory will remain sweet to them." Brasillach, "Journal d'un homme occupé," in *Une Génération dans l'orage: Mémoires* (Paris: Plon, 1968), 487, entry dated January 1944. Quoted in Frese Witt, 154n36., trans. Frese Witt. Also in "Lettre à quelques jeunes gens," in Brasillach, *Oeuvres complètes,* vol. 12 (Paris: Club de l'Honnête Homme, 1963), 612, dated February 19, 1944.

260 **slid gradually into outright support:** Robert Soucy explains that French nationalists sought to "emulate" the new Germany of the Third Reich. "In this way," he writes, "France would also become strong, compelling Germany to respect her." See Soucy, *Fascism in France* (Berkeley: University of California Press, 1972), 18ff. Here he is paraphrasing the argument made by Philippe Barrès explaining his decision to join France's Faisceau, the first Fascist party, established by Georges Valois. Pascal Ory in *Les Collaborateurs* explains this most clearly in his early section about the years leading up to the war. He refers to the "slide" of the "nationalists and Germano-phobes" into becoming "sincere admirers of international fascism, even 'brown' fascism." Ory, 21. "Was the French fascist...supposed to embrace the German invaders in the name of international fascism...or to cling determinedly to a nationalist ideology for which Germany was the traditional arch-enemy?" asks Erin Carlston in *Thinking Fascism* (Stanford, Calif.: Stanford University Press, 1998), 27.

260 **Les Six, who often worked:** The term "reactionary modernism" belongs to historian Jeffrey Herf. See Herf, *Reactionary Modernism: Technology, Culture, and Politics in Weimar and the Third Reich* (Cambridge: Cambridge University Press, 1984). As art historian Mark Antliff observes: "Fascists, though opposed to enlightenment ideals... were eager to absorb aspects of modernism (and modernist aesthetics) that could be reconfigured within their antirational concept of national identity." Antliff, "Fascism, Modernism, and Modernity," *Art Bulletin* 84, no. 1 (March 2002): 148–69.

260 **Francis Poulenc, and Darius Milhaud:** Jane Fulcher explains how the Jewish-born Milhaud reconciled his ethnicity with his extreme nationalism: "Milhaud considered himself to be a thoroughly assimilated Frenchman, but at the same time a Jew, from Provence, and thus of Mediterranean culture. He soon developed an abiding passion for ancient Greek civilization and myth; as with Freud before him, it was a neutral cultural ground shared by both gentiles and Jews. Thus, in a sense...the passion for the classical and for ancient history was a viable path toward a kind of desired cultural assimilation." Jane Fulcher, "The Preparation for Vichy: Anti-Semitism in French Musical Culture Between the Two World Wars," *The Musical Quarterly,* Autumn 1995, 470.

260 **"purity" in French culture:** As Jane Fulcher observes: "Cocteau savvily promoted Les Six, attempting to associate their style with the dominant politicized cultural values. [He] presented Les Six as the modern incarnation of the French tradition...[seeking] to update or to 're-invent' French nationalism."

260 **friendships within Hitler's inner circle:** A Paris police report (number 09641) from February 3, 1945: "Jean Cocteau: collaborator and admirer of Germans, was producing propaganda."

260 **from a German governess:** Sharan Newman, *The Real History Behind the Da Vinci Code* (New York: Berkley Trade, 2005), 24.

261 **entertained Joseph Goebbels:** Although in his autobiography he vigorously denied having supported the Reich, Lifar's name became synonymous with "traitor" in postwar France. Lifar, *Mémoires d'Icare* (Monaco: Editions Sauret, 1993). Lifar's thick police file in the archives of the Paris police proves that he was under surveillance for his suspicious activities as early as 1937, concluding with "it is definitive then that the presence of Serge Lifar is of no value in our country."

261 **register with the SS:** Sachs fled France eventually and died during an air raid in Hamburg.

261 **"She had confidence":** Personal conversation with author, March 2011.

262 **Morand's strong racist beliefs:** Morand was especially drawn to the writings of Count Arthur de Gobineau, author of the 1855 "Essay on the Inequality of Races," which established the theory of a three-race hierarchy, in which White Europeans (especially Aryans) occupy the first, superior position, followed by Asians, and then, trailing far behind, the "Black race." Gobineau's influence is apparent in Morand's 1929 account of his diplomatic mission to Haiti, *Caribbean Winter,* for example, as well as in novels such as the 1928 *Black Magic.* See Marc Dambre, "Paul Morand: The Paradoxes of Revision," *SubStance* 32, no. 3 (2003): 43–54; Morand, *Hiver Caraibe* (Paris: Flammarion, 1929); and Morand, *Black Magic,* trans. Hamish Miles (New York: Viking Press, 1929).

262 **could turn overtly murderous:** He was a "militant anti-Semite," in the words of historian Pierre Birnbaum, 155.

262 **"moral rehabilitation of the West":** Morand's editorial appeared in the first issue of *1933,* a weekly journal edited by Henri Massis, a founder of Action française. "De l'air! De l'air!" *1933,* October 1933, quoted in Renée Winegarten, "Who Was Paul Morand?" *New Criterion,* November 6, 1987, 73.

262 **"we want clean corpses":** See Winegarten, 73. Although Morand had distinguished himself as a journalist and novelist, he was thrice denied entry to the Académie française (1936, 1941, and 1958), before finally being admitted in 1968, probably because of his suspicious political activities.

262 **description that chillingly conflates:** Morand, *L'Allure de Chanel,* 8.

262 **how alluring fascism proved to be:** In February 1933, writing in one of the right wing newspapers he owned, *L'Ami du Peuple,* Coty had expressed his great enthusiasm for Hitler, then newly elected chancellor of Germany: "For years, I have predicted that the day would come... when patriotic Germany would acquire the ineffaceable right to the gratitude of the world by extirpating from the planet [Communist and Jewish] men... of prey." François Coty, *L'Ami du Peuple,* February 7, 1933, quoted in Robert Soucy, "French Press Reactions to Hitler's First Two Years in Power," *Contemporary European History* 7, no. 1 (March 1998): 21–38.

263 **fascism's condemnation of capitalism:** One of the texts that highly influenced Mussolini is Georges Sorel's 1910 *Reflections on Violence,* which lauds Marx and Lenin. Susanne Baackmann and David Craven have written about the subtly pro-business slant of certain fascist supporters: "Richard Evans and [Robert] Paxton... have shown a related phenomenon. Despite the anti-modernization and anti-capitalist rhetoric of every fascist movement, something else obtained historically speaking, since 'whenever fascist parties acquired power [...] they did nothing to carry out

these anti-capitalist threats.' (Robert Paxton, *Anatomy of Fascism* [New York: Knopf, 2004], 10.) To the contrary, a decisive moment both for the German National Socialists (with its 'Night of the Long Knives' in 1934) and the Italian Fascists (with its 'March on Rome' in 1922) entailed the purging of precisely those radical members of their respective movements who were most implacable in their opposition to capital or to any fascist business alliances with the traditional elites." Susanne Baackmann and David Craven, "An Introduction to Modernism—Fascism—Postmodernism," *Modernism/modernity* 15, no. 1 (January 2008): 1–8.

263 **Reich-controlled France of the future:** "Although a fascist lifestyle meant rejection of consumerism with its cult of personal comfort and happiness, fascist aesthetics were steeped in consumer culture." Thomas T. Saunders, "A 'New Man': Fascism, Cinema and Image Creation," *International Journal of Politics, Culture, and Society* 12, no. 2 (Winter 1998): 227–46. Lutz Koepnick makes a similar point—that the Third Reich, contrary to its ostensible doctrine, held out a promise of commodity consumption. See Lutz Koepnick, "Fascist Aesthetics Revisited," *Modernism/modernity* 6, no. 1 (January 1999): 51–73, 52.

263 **"The Nazi myth":** Lacoue-Labarthe and Nancy, 54.

263 **"massings of groups of people":** Susan Sontag, "Fascinating Fascism," *The New York Review of Books,* February 6, 1975, republished in *Under the Sign of Saturn* (New York: Picador, 2002), 73–108.

264 **a way to transcend the masses:** Alice Kaplan brilliantly describes this paradox: "The bizarre combination of populism and elitism in fascism: a man rejoices as he disappears into a crowd, deems himself uniquely privileged for so doing. He is taking the crowd within him, absorbing its powers, just as he is rejecting, violently, the societal outcasts that allow him to define a privileged crowd in the first place." Kaplan, *Reproductions of Banality,* 6. In an essay on what he calls "ur-fascism" (which include Hitler's and Mussolini's versions as well as latter-day descendants), Umberto Eco succinctly explains the charm of this paradox: "Ur-fascism cannot do without preaching a 'popular elitism.' Every individual belongs to the best people in the world, party members are the best citizens, and every citizen can (or ought to) become a party member." Eco, "Ur-fascism," in *Five Moral Pieces,* trans. Alistair McEwan (New York: Harcourt, 2001), 65–88, originally published in *The New York Review of Books,* June 22, 1995.

264 **Nazi propagandists "aestheticized politics":** For Benjamin, the only way to counter fascism's aestheticized politics was to "politicize aesthetics." He wrote of this phenomenon in the landmark essay "The Work of Art in the Age of Mechanical Reproduction," 1935. See Philippe Lacoue-Labarthe's discussion of Benjamin in Lacoue-Labarthe, *Heidegger, Art, and Politics: The Fiction of the Political,* trans. Chris Turner (1990; repr., Oxford: Basil Blackwell, 1990).

Zeev Sternhell writes, "[The fascists] turned their movement into both an 'ethic and a system of aesthetics.'" Sternhell, 249. Virginia Woolf famously made the connection between advertising and fascism in *Three Guineas:* "With the example then that [Fascists] give us of the power of medals, symbols, orders, and even, it would seem, of decorated ink-pots to hypnotize the human mind it must be our aim not to submit ourselves to such hypnotism. We must extinguish the coarse glare of advertisement and publicity." Virginia Woolf, *Three Guineas* (1938; repr., San Diego: Harvest-Harcourt Brace Jovanovich, 1966), 114. I thank Susan Gubar for drawing this remark to my attention.

264 **nothing could compete with fascism:** Historian Fred Inglis, who writes of fascism's relationship to celebrity, remarks: "These spectacles and performances...were not the adjuncts and externalities of power, they were as much Fascism in action as beating Jews in the street and fixing louvers to the tail-fins of Stuka fighter-bombers so that they howled when diving." Fred Inglis, *A Short History of Celebrity* (Princeton, N.J.: Princeton University Press, 2010), 169.

265 **"The masses are made to take":** Sontag, 97.

265 **Riefenstahl's films of the crowds:** Robert Brasillach wrote eloquently of these crowds, "where the rhythmic movements of armies and throngs seemed like a single heartbeat." Brasillach, *Notre Avant-Guerre* (1941), 282, quoted in Zeev Sternhell, *Neither Right nor Left,* 236. Lacoue-Labarthe explains, "The political model of National Socialism is the *Gesamtkunstwerk* because, as Dr. Goebbels very well knew, the *Gesamtkunstwerk* is a political project, since it was the intention of the Festspiel of Bayreuth to be for Germany what the Greater Dionysia was for Athens and for Greece as a whole.... The political itself is instituted and constituted (and regularly regrounds itself) in and as a work of art." Lacoue-Labarthe, *Heidegger, Art, and Politics,* 61. Mussolini spoke openly about imagining his power to "sculpt" the crowd as an artist would. See Simonetta Falasca-Zamponi, *Fascist Spectacle: The Aesthetics of Power in Mussolini's Italy* (Berkeley: University of California Press, 1997), 21, originally published in Emil Ludvig, *Colloqui con Mussolini* (Milan: Mondadori, 1932), 125.

265 **"the understanding of life":** Lacoue-Labarthe, *Le Mythe nazi,* 64–65.

266 **grand and racially pristine:** Theorist of fascism Alfred Rosenberg wrote, in *The Myth of the Twentieth Century,* "The great Aryans of Antiquity are the Greeks, that is, they are the people that produced myth *as* art." Quoted in Lacoue-Labarthe, *Le Mythe nazi,* 62.

266 **"utopia of blood and soil":** Gobineau was the author of the 1855 racist tract "An Essay on the Inequality of the Races." Sorel was famous for his 1908 anti-parliamentarian *Reflections on Violence.* The phrase "Utopia of blood and soil" belongs to George Mosse. See Mosse, *The Image of Man* (New York: Oxford University Press, 1996), 167.

Umberto Eco refers to fascism's use of this myth as a "cult of tradition," which was misremembered by means of a reinvented or "modernized" past. Eco, 78. Brasillach retained an impression of Hitler's Germany as "the surprising mythology of a new religion." Brasillach, *Notre Avant-Guerre,* 277–78, quoted in Sternhell, 250.

266 **emulate the story's heroic figures:** Lacoue-Labarthe, explaining the dangerous power of the Nazi myth, recalls that Plato famously banned the narration of most myths (those he deemed unsuitable, including much of Homer) from his Republic— precisely because of the risks of enticing spectators to imitate the corrupt behavior recounted:

[Plato's] condemnation of the role of myths presumes that we see in them in fact a specific function of *exemplarity.* Myth is fiction in the strongest sense, in the sense of active fashioning, or as Plato says, in the sense of "plasticity": it is therefore a fashioning whose role is to propose, if not to impose, models or types… which an individual, a city, or an entire people might seize upon and with which they might then identify themselves.… Mythic power is… that of the projection of an image with which one can identify.

Lacoue-Labarthe, *Le Mythe nazi,* 32, 35, and 54.

266 **the Greek-Aryan superman:** In his 1930 *Myth of the Twentieth Century,* Alfred Rosenberg explained how the myth justified the Nazi project of racial "cleansing":

This is the task of our century: to create a new human type from a new life-Mythus. Today an epoch begins in which world this story must be rewritten.… A life-feeling, both young and yet known in ancient times… a Weltanschauung is being born.… The dream of Nordic humanity in Hellas was the most beautiful of all.… Today a new belief is arising: the Mythus of the blood; the belief that the godly essence of man itself is to be defended through the blood; that belief which embodies the clearest knowledge that the Nordic race represents that which has overthrown and replaced the old sacraments.

Alfred Rosenberg, *Selected Writings,* ed. Robert Pois (London: Jonathan Cape, 1970), 34, 45, 47, 82. Originally published in 1938 as *Der Mythus des 20 Jahrhunderts.*

266 **apparent cultural gravitas:** Fascism, writes Robert Paxton, "is NOT a real 'ism', no doctrine, no manifesto, no founding thinker.… Their only moral yardstick is the prowess of the race, of the nation, of the community." Paxton, "The Five Stages of Fascism," *Journal of Modern History* 70, no. 1 (March 1998): 1–23.

266 **physical, visceral manipulations famously used:** On fascism's borrowings of commodity culture and its pleasures, Lutz Koepnick writes, "The Third Reich not only promised new career opportunities but also new tactics of diversion and commodity consumption. Apart from short periods of political euphoria, the allure of racing cars, radios, Coca-Cola… and Hollywood-style comedies—rather than the choreography of Riefenstahl spectacles—provided the stuff dreams were made of." Koepnick, 52.

266 **as Susan Sontag famously pointed out:** The sexuality was not openly acknowledged. All the nude male imagery was required to have a veneer of superhuman perfection intended to defuse the inherent sexual charge. Sontag was among the first to observe the sexual nature of fascist aesthetics, which she describes as "petrified eroticism" and "prurient." She points particularly to the homoerotic nature of fascism, with its muscular men and tight leather uniforms. To support her point she quotes a passage from Jean-Paul Sartre's 1949 novel, *Mort dans l'âme,* when the French protagonist, Daniel, watches with erotic delectation as the Germans march into Paris. Irène Némirovsky's novel *Suite Française* gives equal time to the erotic appeal of the German soldiers to French women. See Irène Némirovsky, *Suite Française,* trans. Sandra Smith (New York: Vintage, 2007).

267 **develop their cult followings:** German film director Hans-Jürgen Syberberg called Hitler "the greatest filmmaker of all time." Hans-Jürgen Syberberg, *"Hitler": A Film from Germany,* trans. J. Neugroschel (London: Littlehampton, 1982), 109.

267 **skiing the Alps bare chested:** "Mussolini became the living expression of the nation.

Mussolini's body, thus his virility, endlessly paraded in photographs, posters, news-reels, the press and advertising, as well as in public rallies, came to represent the social body as a whole." Saunders, 236. For an excellent study of Mussolini and the Italian fascists' use of media and the cult of personality, see also Falasca-Zamponi's *Fascist Spectacle* and Karen Pinkus, *Bodily Regimes: Italian Advertising Under Fascism* (Minneapolis: University of Minnesota Press, 1995).

267 **as unrelentingly as Mussolini's:** In fact, Hitler had studied Mussolini's rise to power and took him as his model. Hitler biographer Ian Kershaw writes, "Mussolini's tri-umph made a 'deep impression on' Hitler. Gave him a role model. Referring to Mussolini, less than a month after the March on Rome, Hitler reportedly stated: 'so will it be with us.'" Kershaw, *Hitler: 1889–1936: Hubris* (New York: Norton, 1998), 729, citing *Hitler: Samtliche Aufzeichnungen 1905–1924*, ed. Eberhard Jäckel and Axel Kuhn (Stuttgart: Deutsche Verlags-Anstalt, 1980). In her 1936 multipart profile of Hitler for *The New Yorker,* Janet Flanner captured this canny use of media:

"Though Hitler takes the worst photographs in the world, there are 70,000 of them, all different poses, in the Berlin files of *Reichsbildberichterstatter* Heinrich Hoff-mann, who is the official Nazi photographer.... Nazi Germany uses the camera lens more concentratedly and professionally than any other region on earth except Hol-lywood." Janet Flanner, "Führer III," *The New Yorker,* March 14, 1936, 23–26.

267 **personally signed each man's sleeve:** Flanner, 24.

268 **a paragon of masculine virtues:** Historian of fascism George Mosse writes, "Every man must aspire to a classical standard of beauty, and as he built and sculptured his body (and we must remember the part played by physical exercise in the aesthetics of fascism), his mind would come to encompass all the manly virtues which the fascists prized so highly." George Mosse, "Fascist Aesthetics and Society: Some Considerations," *Journal of Contemporary History* 31, no. 2 (April 1996): 245–52.

On the insistence of youth in fascist ideology, see also Walter Laqueur, *Fascism: Past, Present, Future* (New York: Oxford University Press, 1996): "Physical exercise played a crucial part in forming the fascist man; fascism accepted the by then tradi-tional notion that a fit body was the sign of a manly spirit. The insistence on youth was at least as emphatic. Nazism, like Italian Fascism, appeared as a movement of youth; to wit, the Italian anthem was 'Giovinezza.' Most Nazi leaders were in their late twenties and thirties. Goebbels was made head of the Nazi organization in Ber-lin at age 28 and became minister of propaganda at 36. Himmler became head of the SS at 29." Laqueur, 29.

"The liberty of the soul," wrote Alfred Rosenberg, "is Gestalt [form or figure]. Gestalt is always [delimited by form]. This limitation is determined by race. But race is the externalization of a particular soul." Rosenberg, 529. Rosenberg's em-phatic use of "Gestalt" here—meaning plastic form—draws a pointed contrast with the opposite concept it tacitly conjures: the deformity of the Jews, who were be-lieved to be so hyper-intellectualized that they devolved into useless, distasteful abstraction.

268 **"(female) interior":** Klaus Thevelveit, *Male Fantasies,* vol. 1, *Women, Floods, Bodies, His-tory,* trans. Stephen Conway (1977; repr., Minneapolis: University of Minnesota Press, 1987), 434.

269 **urgings about exercise and fitness:** Embracing the notion that national decay could
    be fought with a fit citizenry, Vichy in particular promoted renewed attention to
    sports. See Francine Muel-Dreyfus, *Vichy and the Eternal Feminine*, trans. Kathleen
    Johnson (Durham, N.C.: Duke University Press, 2001). See also Dominique Veillon,
    La Mode sous l'Occupation (Paris: Editions Payot, 2001): "Vichy, obsessed by the idea
    of physical decadence in French society, tries to develop a true politics of sports.
    Most women's magazines agree on one point. That one of the causes of France's
    degeneration is the forgetting or neglecting of the body. The national 'revolution'
    must be accomplished through a 'renaissance of the French body.'" Veillon, 229.

269 **Breker frequently dined:** Breker's solo exhibition at the Orangerie, which opened in
    Paris in May 1942, attracted more than eight thousand French visitors. George Mosse,
    The Image of Man: The Creation of Modern Masculinity (New York: Oxford University
    Press, 1995), 174. In a review of the exhibition, Abel Bonnard, Vichy's minister for
    education, gushed, "Monsieur Arno Breker, you are the sculptor of heroes.... The
    hero is Man revealed not only in his superiority, but in his plenitude. You reveal the
    effort of those who work and of those who struggle.... These grand statues stand like
    watchmen at the mast, contemplating the horizon of the centuries, while men exist
    merely within the horizon of days." Abel Bonnard review of Breker, reprinted in *La
    France Allemande: Paroles du collaborationisme français, 1933–1945*, ed. Pascal Ory (Paris:
    Gallimard, 1977), 226, originally published in *Nouvelles continentales,* May 1942.

270 **acclaim beyond Italy and Germany:** Artist and reserve SS officer Karl Diebitsch,
    along with graphic designer Walter Heck, created many aspects of the fascist rega-
    lia, including the all-black uniform. Umberto Eco puts fascist fashion in the grand-
    est possible company: "Italian Fascism was the first to create a... style of dress—
    which enjoyed greater success abroad than Armani, Benetton, or Versace today."
    Eco, 72.

270 **any potentially emasculating effect:** As Fred Inglis notes, "The accouterments of
    fascism as designed in Italy and Germany were characterized by terrific *style*. This
    expressed itself, on the one hand, by such flashy details as the big, contrastively co-
    loured lapels of senior officers' greatcoats, their polished riding boots, and their
    bowed riding breeches; on the other hand, this dandyism was placed beyond criti-
    cism by the brute power and mass of metal and thunderous noise commanded by
    the troops of tanks which were overture to the appearance onstage of a single, soli-
    tary, and heroic leader." Inglis, 166.

270 **"the legitimate exercise of violence":** Sontag, 97.

271 **"All young men who joined":** Walter Schellenberg, *The Labyrinth: Memoirs of Walter
    Schellenberg: Hitler's Chief of Counterintelligence,* trans. Louis Hagen (New York: Har-
    perCollins, 1984), 3–4. Originally published in German in 1956 by Harper and
    Brothers.

271 **early induction into the SS:** Reinhard Spitzy, *So haben wir das Reich verspielt* (Munich:
    L. Muller, 1987). Published in English as Spitzy, *How We Squandered the Reich,* trans.
    G. T. Waddington (Norfolk, UK: Michael Russell, 1997).

271 **"[I]n the SS":** Reinhard Spitzy, "The Master Race: Nazism Takes Over German
    South," *Master Race,* PBS television series, first aired June 15, 1998, produced and
    directed by Jonathan Lewis.

271 **even to civilian audiences:** The particular color of the Nazi uniform acquired symbolic, transmissible power, too. "Brown" and "Nazi" became interchangeable terms.
Crowds attending a Hitler rally were described in the press as a "brown mass," and
Hitler himself spoke of his "brown SA men," his "brown army," or "brown wall."
   "A female Nazi proudly defined herself as one of Hitler's 'little brown mice.' By
the summer of 1933 opponents spoke of the brown steamroller that had flattened
public life." Claudia Koonz, *The Nazi Conscience* (Cambridge, Mass.: Harvard University Press, 2003), 69.

271 **all emblazoned with the swastika:** See Koonz, 69. See also Irene Guenther, *Nazi Chic:
Fashioning Women in the Third Reich* (London: Berg, 2004), 136.

272 **under a single graphic symbol:** See Flanner, "Führer III," 26.

272 **"a civic religion":** The term belongs to George Mosse.

272 **displaying Hitler's photograph:** George Mosse, *The Nationalization of the Masses: Political Symbolism and Mass Movements in Germany from the Napoleonic Wars Through the
Third Reich* (New York: Howard Fertig, 1975), 206.

272 **heart of the totalitarian project:** Jacques Delarue translates the term as "uniformi-
zation," and writes, "Gleichschaltung…in other words the total Nazification of
Germany [consisted of] the submission of the people, and the subordination of the
State to the all-powerful Party." Delarue, *The Gestapo: A History of Horror,* trans.
Mervyn Savill (New York: William Morrow, 1964), 10. Originally published as *His-
toire de la Gestapo* (Paris: Librairie Arthème Fayard, 1962). See also Guenther, *Nazi
Chic.*

272 **suppression of trade unions:** Thomas Saunders defines *Gleichschaltung* as "a vision of
citizens and the economy harnessed in perfectly coordinated fashion to a national
purpose." Saunders, 237. Claudia Koonz writes, "The word adapted by the Nazis to
describe this unique process, *Gleichschaltung,* has no equivalent in other languages.
'Nazification' 'coordination' 'integration' and 'bringing into line'… The removal of
anyone who 'stained' or 'soiled' the nation was 'switching them off.'… A German
citizen, reporting anonymously for a London paper, captured both the mechanical
and biological overtones of *Gleichschaltung,* when he explained, 'It means that the
same stream will blow through the ethnic body politic.'" Koonz, 70, citing "Die
Erneuerung der Universität," *Spectator,* June 9, 1933, 831–32.

272 **mechanisms that propelled fascism:** Mario Lupano and Alessandra Vaccari explore
the deep connections between fashion and fascism in their beautifully illustrated
and provocative study, *Fashion at the Time of Fascism: Italian Modernist Lifestyle 1922–
1943* (Bologna: Damiani, 2009). They write of the "grounds for a comparison between fashion and fascism [and] their mutual interests… [which] include totalitarian
ambition, the sense of beginning, the epoch-making factor and an emphasis placed
on creation." Lupano and Vaccari, 8.

272 **Both play upon the struggle:** Georg Simmel, founding father of fashion theory, was
the first to articulate this dual purpose: "'Fashion is the imitation of an example.… At
the same time it satisfies in no less degree the need for differentiation." Georg Simmel, "Fashion," *International Quarterly* 10 (New York, 1904): 130–55, 296.

272 **imitate a given behavior:** Fashion theorist René König makes the connection quite
plain when he describes fashion as "a special form of regulated behavior… [in

which] imitation, starting from an initial triggering action, creates mighty currents which cause uniform action among the masses." René König, *A La Mode: On the Social Psychology of Fashion*, trans. F. Bradley (New York: Seabury Press, 1973), 128. He might as well have been recounting a Nazi rally.

273 **Hitler insisted they be redesigned:** Guenther, 120.

273 **kept their own houses afloat:** As early as 1933, the Reich founded an institute devoted to nationalizing women's style, the German Fashion Institute. But the institute foundered and succumbed to internal divisiveness, never succeeding in standardizing women's fashion in any way. In 1936, when Magda Goebbels, wife of the Reich's propaganda minister, initiated a patriotic boycott of French dress models, Hitler personally intervened to overturn it. Irene Guenther analyzes the discord and disorganization of the German Fashion Institute in *Nazi Chic*, 167–200. Janet Flanner in the first of her three-part profile of Hitler writes, "Hitler prefers the *Walküre* type of lady.... He also likes women who are well dressed. Though it would be officially denied, Hitler opposed Frau Goebbels's recent patriotic boycott of French dress models, a blacklisting which, since Germany has no dress designers, nearly ruined the foundation of Germany's ready-made garment trade.... Owing to Hitler's pressure, the ban was lifted and today one-third of the leading Paris couturiers model business is with Berlin." Flanner, "Führer I," *The New Yorker*, February 29, 1936: 20–24.

Hitler even expressed indulgent understanding of those German soldiers occupying Paris who ignored orders and bought silk stockings and other non-regulation French luxuries to send home to wives and girlfriends. Guenther, 141.

For the definitive study of French couture during the war and the relationship between designers and the Reich, see Dominique Veillon, *Fashion Under the Occupation*, trans. Miriam Kochan (1990; repr., New York: Berg, 2001).

273 **Women's love of Parisian clothes:** Famous Italian sportswear designer Countess Gabriella di Robilant, who opened her famous atelier "Gabriella Sport" in 1932, cited Chanel as one of her "spiritual masters." "From Chanel...I learned the science of dressing, I refined my taste and later...got to know many secrets of an art which up to then had been a prerogative of the French." Quoted in Lupano and Vaccari, 226. Originally in Gabriella di Robilant, *Una gran bella vita* (Milan: Mondadori, 1988). In December 1935 the Italian government established the National Board of Fashion dedicated to promoting and standardizing Italian design, but it did not accomplish its stated goals. The Italians even tried to police the *language* of fashion: French fashion terms used habitually in Italian were expunged and replaced with new Italian coinages. The *Commentario dizionario italiano della moda* (Commentary and Italian Dictionary of Fashion) by Cesare Meano, was published in 1936, with what Eugenia Paulicelli points out was the "paradoxical aim of both establishing and 'retrieving' a national tradition in the culture of fashion." Eugenia Paulicelli, *Fashion Under Fascism: Beyond the Black Shirt* (London: Berg, 2004), 57.

As in Germany, the Italian effort to eliminate foreign influence failed. "Fascist nationalism and its empty rhetoric could never construct an 'Italian national identity' closed in itself nor be a permanent and universal inspiration for an Italian fashion and style," writes Paulicelli, 15.

273 **contradictory view of women:** "Fascism had an ambivalent rapport with all models [of femininity]," Victoria de Grazia wrote. De Grazia, *How Fascism Ruled Women* (Berkeley: University of California Press, 1993), 73.

273 **through motherhood and housewifery:** In matters of sexual politics, the fascists looked to the early sexologist Otto Weininger, whose 1903 book, *Sex and Character,* laid out an extremely Manichaean view of human sexuality according to which men were logical, intellectual creatures, made for action and thought, and women, illogical, unconscious beings, best suited for mindless tasks and passive reproduction.

274 **Social progress for women:** This included ousting women from all civil service jobs and other forms of public employment, as well as drastically reducing many state-sponsored services for women and children. See Sandi E. Cooper, "Pacifism, Feminism, and Fascism in Inter-War France," *The International History Review* 19, no. 1 (February 1997): 103–14. Mussolini denied women the right to vote (after raising it as a possibility) and was responsible for establishing fascism's purely reproductive view of human sexuality, designed to limit women to the roles of wives, mothers, and widows. See Maria-Antoinette Macciocchi, "Female Sexuality in Fascist Ideology," *Feminist Review* no. 1 (1979): 67–82, 77.

274 **undermining the traditional feminine roles:** "Italy was uncomprehending of modern female roles," writes historian Victoria de Grazia. See de Grazia, 24. See also Etharis Mascha, "Contradictions of the Floating Signifier: Identity and the New Woman in Italian Cartoons During Fascism," *Journal of International Women's Studies* 11, no. 4 (May 2010): 128–42.

274 **duty to repopulate the fatherland:** "Woman's proper sphere is the family," proclaimed Joseph Goebbels in 1934. Quoted in Leila Rupp, "Mother of the 'Volk': The Image of Women in Nazi Ideology," *Signs* 3 no. 2 (Winter 1977): 362–79, 363. Originally quoted in Hilda Browning, *Women Under Fascism and Communism* (London: Martin Lawrence, 1934), 8.

Rupp discusses an interesting subgroup of feminist Nazis who agitated for women's equality. The party returned to this theme constantly: "We have given honor back to the housewife.... The work of the housewife ... is one of the most economically important factors in a nation," declared Gertrud Scholtz-Klink, head of the Nazi Women's League. Her speech, entitled "Duties and Tasks of the Woman in the National Socialist State," was delivered in October 1936 to a Nazi rally. Reprinted in *Landmark Speeches of National Socialism,* ed. Randall L. Bytwerk (College Station: Texas A&M University Press, 2008): 52–65, 59.

Hitler, who devoted a section of *Mein Kampf* to Germany's "fertility problem," even established a kind of paramilitary reward system for reproduction, bestowing medals to mothers of large families. Bronze stars went to women who had four children, silver to those with five, and gold to those with six or more. France had tried a similar system in the 1920s to combat the country's low birthrate. "The Führer decorates women with many children, just as he decorates the bravest soldiers," read a sample speech distributed to Nazi Party leaders for use on Mother's Day—a holiday celebrated with Christmas-like fanfare under the Reich. Such templates for speeches were distributed monthly to local and regional politicians to guide and standardize their rhetorical efforts. "Model Speech for Mother's Day," 1944, in Bytwerk, 144.

274 **"a perfect German wife"**: From PBS, *Master Race.*

274 **the Nuova Italiana:** Victoria de Grazia sums up the paradox neatly: "The constraints on women [were]...mystifying, insidious, and demeaning. [But] at the same time, the fascist dictatorship celebrated the Nuova Italiana, or 'New Italian Woman.'" De Grazia, 1. Germany fell prey to the same contradictions, having constructed an ideology based simultaneously on "a mythic past and a technological future," as Mark Antliff points out. Mark Antliff, "Fascism, Modernism, and Modernity," *Art Bulletin* 84, no. 1 (March 2002): 148–69.

274 **The political backlash:** At the same time, French feminists also responded to fascism's rise with increased activism, condemning Hitler's and Mussolini's militarism.

274 **back to the nursery:** See Christine Bard, *Les filles de Marianne* (Paris: Fayard, 1995). "Wherever economic crisis occurs," writes Bard, "women's right to work [outside the home] will be called into question." Bard, 313.

275 **unpatriotic neglect of child rearing:** The alliance had been established in 1896 by Jacques Bertillon. See Andrés Horacio Reggiani, "Procreating France: The Politics of Demography, 1919–1945," *French Historical Studies* 19, no. 3 (Spring 1996): 725–54. The Italians had a similar scapegoat: *la donna-crisi*—or "crisis woman"—the cosmopolitan and educated woman who refused traditional roles. See also de Grazia, 73. Alliance president Paul Haury denounced women who he felt denatured themselves, emasculated French men, and weakened the fabric of the nation. See Paul Haury, "Votre Bonheur, jeunes filles," *Revue 266,* September 1934, 281. Quoted in Cheryl Koos, "Gender, Anti-Individualism, and Nationalism: The Alliance Nationale and the Pro-natalist Backlash Against the Femme Moderne, 1933–1940," *French Historical Studies* 19, no. 3 (Spring 1996): 699–723.

275 **Paul Morand figured among:** Morand wrote an essay in 1944 blaming lack of procreation for France's political troubles.

In July 1935, Prime Minister Pierre Laval proposed a law designed to reduce state expenses—in households where both spouses worked for the government, the wife's salary was to be reduced by 25 percent. The same year, he also proposed that when both spouses worked as civil servants, the wife simply be fired, in order to save the state money and promote stay-at-home motherhood. Public outcry blocked passage of this law, but it resurfaced as a model for legislation successfully passed under Vichy. Bard, 317. See also Paul Smith, *Feminism and the Third Republic* (Oxford: Clarendon Press, 1996), 215. Laval would return to power as head of the Vichy government and be executed for treason in 1945.

Working women did not necessarily fare better under leftist governments. In 1939 under Prime Minister Edouard Daladier of the Radical Party, feminists lost a major battle upon passage of the Code de la famille, civil legislation that—among other things—replaced welfare subsidies for children with subsidies paid only to "the woman at home," effectively forcing mothers to forgo paid employment in order to receive benefits. See Smith, 249. The code outlawed abortion and placed new and extreme restraints on the sale of contraceptives. Those flouting the new law risked exorbitant fines and prison sentences of up to ten years. Although the Daladier government dissolved soon after the code was passed, its restrictions paved the way—and served as a model for—similar policies enacted by the Vichy regime, which severely restricted women's access to work, education, and reproductive freedom.

In 1939, Catholic playwright Paul Claudel wrote an ode urging Frenchwomen to heed Marshal Pétain's call to renounce worldly aspirations and return to motherhood and the home: "France, listen to this old man who cares for you and speaks to you like a father! Daughters of Saint Louis, listen to him and say: Haven't you had enough of politics?" Quoted in Muel-Dreyfus, 116.

France under Vichy embraced what Muel-Dreyfus has called "the eternal feminine," worshipping an extreme, nearly caricature-ish version of womanhood, embodied by the fecund housewife who strengthens the nation through procreation. In 1942, Pétain made abortion a capital crime. As Muel-Dreyfus points out, this philosophy co-opted women into the same rigid categories created by racism, producing "an amalgamation between sexual submission and social submission and, by celebrating national maternities, imposed its obsessions concerning the 'inassimilable.' French women, or rather, 'the' French woman, were inscribed by the power in its racist rhetoric." Muel-Dreyfus explains that for the Fascists, the subjugation of women amounts to a kind of "sexual racism, [which] feeds into [conventional] racism. Woman was never posited alone but with children, slaves, workers, Jews, the colonized, etc." Muel-Dreyfus, 6. Richard Sonn has studied the issue of women's reproductive rights during this era. See Sonn, "Your Body Is Yours: Anarchism, Birth Control, and Eugenics in Interwar France," *Journal of the History of Sexuality* 14, no. 4 (October 2005): 415–32.

275 **"a caricature, a sad doll":** *Votre Beauté,* quoted in Muel-Dreyfus, 107.

275 **Gustave Thibon lamented:** Quoted in Muel-Dreyfus, 25; originally in Gustave Thibon, *Retour au réel* (Lyon: Lardanchet, 1943), 66.

276 **fascism mingled comfortably:** As scholars such as Roger Griffin have demonstrated, fascism was not a monolithic structure, but rather more of a "syncretic" system that coexisted at times with progressive views on art, literature, music, and dance, and was neither exclusively reactionary nor anti-intellectual. See Roger Griffin, *Modernism and Fascism: The Sense of a Beginning Under Mussolini and Hitler* (London: Palgrave Macmillan, 2007). Not all supporters of fascism in France even shared its misogynist principles. Fascist sympathizer and Chanel friend François Coty, for example, expressed some approval for feminism in his newspaper, *L'Ami du Peuple.* Even Mussolini himself did nothing to prevent his daughter Edda from becoming one of the first women in Italy to wear trousers in public and to drive a car. George Mosse, "Fascist Aesthetics and Society: Some Considerations," *Journal of Contemporary History* 31, no. 2 (April 1996): 245–52, 250.

276 **"fascist longings in our midst":** Sontag, 97.

276 **"My epoch was waiting":** Quoted in Delay, 189.

277 **foundation stone of national identity:** William Wiser writes, "Fashion . . . had come to represent France as the ultimate in commercial creativity, a lucrative export—not even the advance of a world depression seriously diminished the demand for expensive dress wear, for the rich . . . are always with us." William Wiser, *The Twilight Years: Paris in the 1930s* (New York: Carroll and Graf, 2000), 141.

France was not the only nation aware of fashion's political importance. In Italy as well, fashion figured prominently in national conception, as Eugenia Paulicelli has pointed out. "Fashion is one of the key factors for understanding the manifold process of both personal and national identity formation as well as the complexity of identity's public performance and invention." In 1936, the National Fashion Body of Italy (the Ente nazionale della moda) published a dictionary of Italian fashion terms, whose goal was "eliminating French terminology from the language of fashion; and ... creating an Italian lexicon of fashion to plug the gap ... left by the purge of French terms." Eugenia Paulicelli, "Fashion Writing Under the Fascist Regime," *Fashion Theory* 8, no. 1 (2004): 3–34.

277 **"France's Great Couturiers":** André de Fouquières, "Grande couture et la fourrure parisienne," *L'Art de la Mode* (June 1939).

277 **"a national icon of France":** Patrick Buisson, *1940–1945: Années erotiques,* vol. 2: *De la grande prostituée à la revanche des mâles* (Paris: Albin Michel, 2009), 21–22.

277 **"She was powerfully aware":** Haedrich, 137.

277 **The price cuts increased access:** B. J. Perkins, "Chanel Makes Drastic Price Cuts in Model Prices," *Women's Wear Daily,* February 4, 1931.

277 **"women prostrate themselves":** Jean Cocteau, "From Worth to Alix," *Harper's Bazaar,* March 1937, 128–130.

277 **Grecian-style bas-relief:** Martin Rénier, *Femina,* June 1939. See also "Paris Fashion Exhibits at the Fair," *Vogue,* May 15, 1939, 60–63.

278 **"It's a religion":** This executive was then quickly corrected by a superior who asked that I remove the remark from my notes.

278 **"Gabrielle Chanel imposes":** "Votre heure de veine," *Le Miroir du Monde,* November 4, 1933, 10.

278 **"miniature female Stalin":** Elsa Maxwell, "The Private Life of Chanel," *Liberty Magazine,* December 9, 1933.

278 **"great and strong being":** Quoted in Ridley, 135.

278 **"Chanel dictates":** *The New York Times* advertisement, December 30, 1935.

279 **"A new treaty alliance":** Using similar military and political language, the same issue of *Marie Claire* announced the return to wide-skirted, crinoline-style dresses as proof of a "return to the Second Empire" and the style of "Empress Eugénie," warning furthermore that such aristocratic nostalgia in fashion risked inciting a "serious threat of a coup d'état." "L'Empire revient," *Marie Claire,* March 4, 1938.

279 **"It would be to misunderstand":** Pierre de Trévières, "Paris et ailleurs," *Femme de France,* March 10, 1935, 12. Emphasis added.

279 **"She reigns with authority":** "La femme de la semaine: Chanel," *L'Express,* August 17, 1956.

279 **"The mood in the salon changes":** Joseph Barry, "Chanel No. 1: Fashion World Legend," *The New York Times,* August 23, 1964.

279 **"[like a] spider in her web":** Marie-Hélène Marouzé oral interview; Jeanne Moreau oral interview transcript, April 22, 2006, Conservatoire Chanel.

279 **"hands on the seams":** Delphine Bonneval, interview, May 14, 2008, 5, Conservatoire Chanel.

280 **"Mademoiselle put herself on a par":** Marquand, 114.

280 **"life as a dictator":** Morand, *L'Allure de Chanel,* 87.

280 **"[reconciliation] of fascist"**: "The 'monumental gathering of the female forces' of fascism, rallying 70,000 women in Rome on May 28 1939, was, in the words of the official Stefani News Agency release, 'the most total and thrilling demonstration ever of the party's efforts toward forming a full-blown fascist and imperial consciousness... among its female forces.'" De Grazia, 225.

280 **the swastika as his emblem:** Chanel was introduced to German customers by 1926 at the latest, when a Berlin fashion show featured her work. Her designs continued to appear in all the top German fashion magazines until the official declaration of war with France.

280 **personal elegance could be found:** Designer Geoffrey Beene summed up the phenomenon neatly: "It's the first time I've seen women not objecting to another woman's wearing exactly the same thing they are.... The spirit of competition does not seem to exist in [Chanel's] case.... Chanel style... is beginning to take on the aura of a uniform." Quoted in Holly Brubach, "In Fashion: School of Chanel," *The New Yorker,* February 27, 1989, 71–76.

280 **"[No one] understands the concept"**: Morand, *L'Allure de Chanel,* 57. Her words echo those of the official magazine of the Nazis' League of German Girls, describing the new official uniforms: "The radiant white of the blouses, worn on the bodies of hundreds and even thousands of girls... brings great joy to the viewer." Quoted in Guenther, 121.

281 **"brings out each woman's individuality"**: Personal conversations with Marika Genty and Cécile Goddet-Dirles of the Conservatoire Chanel.

281 **"As a child I had only"**: Vilmorin, *Mémoires,* 52–53.

282 **"She is the image"**: Denise Veber, "Mademoiselle Chanel nous parle," *Marianne,* November 11, 1937.

282 **the 1961 Moscow Expo:** *Le Patriote illustré,* August 6, 1961.

282 **during her later years:** Carmel Snow and Mary Louise Aswell, *The World of Carmel Snow* (New York: McGraw-Hill, 1962), 55. In *La Chair de la robe* (The flesh of the dress), the distinguished French writer Madeleine Chapsal, who knew couture well (having worked for the great *couturière* Madame Vionnet) and who knew Chanel personally, echoes these sentiments: "I am conscious of this image, always identical, that Chanel has imposed for as long as she has worked in fashion, and well, it is the image of herself!" Madeleine Chapsal, *La Chair de la robe* (Paris: Librairie Fayard, 1989), 223.

282 **"Women no longer exist"**: Quoted in Madsen, 116.

282 **"Fashion," wrote Jean Cocteau:** Cocteau, "From Worth to Alix."

283 **"schoolgirl's uniform"**: *Vogue,* June 1937.

283 **"brass buttons"**: "Paris Carries On," *Vogue,* December 1, 1939, 86–87, 150.

284 **resistance to the red flag:** See Weber, 376.

284 **"The ideas ... of Iribe"**: Haedrich, 122.

285 **ribbon shoulder straps and piping:** This gown also partakes of Chanel's "Gypsy" style influence of the late 1930s, which included a number of tight little jacket and long skirt combinations.

285 **unusually "busy" and distracting print:** Chanel told Claude Delay that in 1938 Williams asked her to run off with him, complaining that his wife, Mona, was "just a

mannequin." "One year earlier, I would have followed him. He had a yacht, that's the best way to run away to begin a romance," she said, clearly recalling her Westminster days. Delay, 180.

286 **"sign of youth and femininity"**: Pierre de Trévières, "Paris et ailleurs," *Femme de France*, March 10, 1935.

286 **"sugar and spice"**: "Sugar and Spice in the Paris Collections," *Vogue*, March 1938.

286 **"glamour dress of the season"**: *Vogue*, August 1938.

286 a new **"Air of Innocence"**: "Out of the Paris Openings: A New Breath of Life—the Air of Innocence," *Vogue*, March 1, 1939, 1–24.

286 **a younger, less dangerous time:** There is also a visual echo here of Chanel's celebration of prerevolutionary France, in the elaborately ruffled costumes she designed in 1939 for Serge Lifar and Daisy de Segonzac (Nazi sympathizers both), when they attended a costume ball disguised as Auguste Vestris and Marie Antoinette. See chapter 9.

287 **"[Coco] chose...grey"**: Fiemeyer and Palasse-Labrunie, 169. Palasse-Labrunie goes on to explain that an anxious Coco later arranged for a male chaperon to accompany young Gabrielle on the train: fellow summer houseguest Pierre Reverdy, whose religious exile did not enjoin the occasional Riviera weekend.

288 **"Cuir de Russie evokes"**: "Advertorial" in *Votre Beauté*, February 1936, clipping from Conservatoire Chanel.

289 **firmness of her tiny derriere:** Personal conversations with Danniel Rangel.

289 **sun-bronzed, disciplined athlete-soldier:** Fashion historian Danièle Bott lays it out clearly: "Sport for [Chanel] represented a discipline and a strength synonymous with the virtues that she revered and demanded of herself." Danièle Bott, *Chanel* (Paris: Editions Ramsey, 2005). Eugenia Paulicelli discusses the importance of suntanning in the Italian fascist aesthetic of the body: "[A] suntanned body [had] started to become a synonym for being both sexy and modern. The link to sport...explains how this [tanning] had become one of the most important leisure activities encouraged by fascism." Paulicelli, 58–59.

289 **androgynous, even lesbian chic:** George Mosse has written of the way Nazis in particular strove to deflect any possibility of homoeroticism in their focus on male beauty. See Mosse, *Image of Man*. See also Carlston, *Thinking Fascism*. Carlston writes, "German fascist ideology and aesthetics make, in fact, what seem oddly contradictory uses of (homo) eroticism: creating a cult of virility that emphasizes male bonding while despising homosexual effeminacy." Carlston, 38.

290 **her "Total Look":** According to Marie-Louise de Clermont-Tonnerre, the term "total look" was invented in the early 1920s. Personal interview, May 2011.

290 **"One adores [Chanel style]"**: Claude Berthod, "Romy Schneider pense tout haut," *Elle*, September 1963: 130–32.

290 **"protected the [Aryans']"**: "The dream of Nordic humanity in Hellas was the most beautiful of all.... A true aristocratic, constitution-prohibited miscegenation. Nordic strength, diminished by continual struggle, was continuously revived through sea migrations. Dorians and then Macedonians protected the creative blond blood until even these tribes were exhausted." Rosenberg, 47.

291 **"imposing diplomats and international wits"**: Sylvia Lyon, "Gabrielle Chanel," *Fashion Arts* (Winter 1934–35), 28–29.

291 **"indelibly fixes the scene"**: Advertisement, *Stage* magazine, November 1937. The ad echoes Lacoue-Labarthe's explanation of how the Nazi myth operated: "[as] the understanding of life as art, as well as the body as art, the people as art…that is, as the accomplishments of will, as successful identifications with the dream image." Lacoue-Labarthe, 64–65.

291 **reincarnating this mythic heroine**: See, for example, Georgina Safe, "Chanel Opens Shop in Melbourne," *Sydney Morning Herald,* October 31, 2013; Jennifer Ladonne, "New Paris Boutique for Chanel," *France Today,* June 7, 2012; or Amy Verner, "The Newest Chanel Boutique Is like Stepping into Coco's Closet," *The Globe and Mail,* May 26, 2012.

291 **"A loveless childhood"**: Vilmorin, 40.

293 **"In France, an unknown"**: Ibid., 68.

293 **"I wanted to escape"**: Ibid.

293 **"The creation of a luxury brand"**: Gilles Lipovetsky, *Le Luxe éternel* (Paris: Gallimard, 2003), 93.

295 **"genocidal projects of Europe's purification"**: Roger Griffin, *Modernism and Fascism: The Sense of a Beginning Under Mussolini and Hitler* (London: Palgrave Macmillan, 2007), 59.

295 **"a necessary cleansing operation"**: Morand, *L'Allure de Chanel,* 178.

11. LOVE, WAR, AND ESPIONAGE

296 **"It was odd"**: Josep Miquel Garcia, *Biography of Apel-les Fenosa* (El Vendrell, Spain: Fundació Apel-les Fenosa), 2.

297 **might be of Jewish descent**: Ibid.

298 **"I just threw myself"**: Xavier Garcia, "Interview with Apel-les Fenosa," *El Correo Catalán,* October 2, 1975, Fundació Apel-les Fenosa.

298 **"Without him I would have died"**: Interview, Fundació Apel-les Fenosa.

298 **"All arts were modern"**: Rabat interview, quoted in Garcia, *Biography,* 77.

299 **a legal visa for Apel-les**: Josep Miquel Garcia, *Amic Picasso,* exhibition catalog (El Vendrell, Spain: Fundació Apel-les Fenosa, 2003), 41. In July 1939, Cocteau wrote a brief note to his old friend André-Louis Dubois, an official in Paris's Ministry of the Interior (the Foreign Office): "Permit me to recommend to you most highly, Fenosa. He is not 'a sculptor' but according to Picasso and myself, the only one that counts. Your kind attention will help us all in assisting him." Fundació Apel-les Fenosa. See also Fundació Apel-les Fenosa, *Cocteau-Fenosa: Relleus d'una Amistad/Reliefs d'une Amitié* (Barcelona: Ediciones Polígrafa, 2007), 19. Fenosa would later say that the contact with André-Louis Dubois made it possible for him to help countless other Spaniards fleeing Franco find safe haven in France.

301 **"He fascinated me"**: "I was swept away by a passion for [him]," Coco told Marcel Haedrich about her early encounters with Picasso. "He fascinated me. He would look at you like an eagle about to swoop down on his prey. He frightened me. When

he entered a room, even if I couldn't see him, I could feel his presence." Haedrich, 89. Chanel kept a room at her Faubourg Saint-Honoré apartment just for Picasso's use, and some accounts suggest that they did, in fact, have a brief dalliance. Picasso biographer John Richardson insists they did not: "Chanel was too much of a celebrity, and not submissive enough," he writes. John Richardson, *A Life of Picasso: The Triumphant Years, 1917–1932* (2007; repr., New York: Knopf, 2010), 190.

301   **"She was very intelligent"**: Josep Miquel Garcia, *Apel·les Fenosa i Coco Chanel*, exhibition catalog (El Vendrell, Spain: Fundació Apel·les Fenosa, 2011), 11.

301   **gold cuff links set with topazes**: Josep Miquel Garcia, interview with Nicole Fenosa, Fundació Apel·les Fenosa, 2005.

302   **nine months of relative calm**: Historian Julian Jackson dubbed the period "a parenthesis between war and peace." Julian Jackson, *France: The Dark Years: 1940–1944* (New York: Oxford University Press, 2001), 113.

302   **thousands of arrests and imprisonments**: See John F. Sweets, *Choices in Vichy France: The French Under Nazi Occupation* (New York: Oxford University Press, 1994). See also Jackson, 112–15.

303   **"I take refuge in beige"**: Delay, 192.

303   **ensconced among the glitterati**: See Meredith Etherington-Smith, *The Persistence of Memory: A Biography of Salvador Dalí* (New York: Da Capo Press, 1992), 235.

303   **"It bothered me"**: Garcia, interview with Nicole Fenosa, 59.

303   **"One day, he found himself "**: Garcia, *Biography*, 35.

303   **bout of double mastoiditis**: See Julian Jackson for a description of French conditions and morale during the *drôle de guerre*.

304   **"Fifty-two Coromandel screens!"**: Garcia, *Apel·les Fenosa i Coco Chanel*, 10.

304   **she fired all 2,500**: This irony was not lost on *Time* magazine: "Mme. Gabrielle (Coco) Chanel . . . now patriotically wears nothing but the French national colors— red, white, and blue—but less patriotically has closed her famous Paris style shop." "Women at Work," *Time*, February 12, 1940.

305   **share his own meager savings**: During her years with Westminster, Chanel had hoped that Lucien's retirement from peddling shoes would keep the press from uncovering the ignominy of having such a poor relation. She had also established Alphonse's pension at that time, hoping he, too, would stay away from reporters. See chapter 8.

305   **Lucien died in 1941**: Charles-Roux, *L'Irrégulière*, 536–38.

305   **"to play dead"**: Ibid., 533.

305   **They could not move her**: Madsen, 228–29.

305   **"I had the feeling"**: Galante, 170. The same words appear in Delay's biography as well.

306   **family members being shipped off**: Haedrich, 127.

306   **Serge agreed emphatically**: Ibid., 134.

306   **"I never really lived up"**: Garcia, *Biography*, 63; Garcia, *Apel·les Fenosa i Coco Chanel*, 12.

306   **"ferocious partner of her solitude"**: Delay, 176.

306   **"The workers were all very glad"**: Garcia, *Biography*, 59.

307   **"We all carry within us"**: Jean Cocteau, *Opium: The Diary of His Cure*, trans. Margaret Crosland (1930; repr., London: Peter Owen Publishers, 1990), 58. In a letter to Max

Jacob, dated December 16, 1928, Cocteau mentions having been in another three-month "cure" for opium addiction, and that Chanel had paid for it. Max Jacob and Jean Cocteau, *Correspondance 1917–1944,* ed. Anne Kimball (Paris: Editions Paris-Méditerranée, 2000), 575.

307 **"I never [tried it]":** Garcia, *Biography,* 69.

307 **"my dear little squirrel":** Fundació Apel-les Fenosa.

307 **Cocteau's social drug world:** Lisa Chaney believes otherwise. As evidence that Chanel smoked opium she cites *Hidden Faces,* Salvador Dalí's 1943 roman à clef, which includes a character, Cécile Goudreau, based on Coco. Cécile smokes opium in the novel, although this seems insufficient documentation. Chaney, 313. Fenosa is very clear that the drug in question is injectable morphine.

307 **"It was morphine":** Garcia, *Apel-les Fenosa i Coco Chanel,* 10.

307 **"It was the drugs":** Interview with Nella Bielski, Fundació Apel-les Fenosa.

307 **"She was brilliant, very brilliant":** Garcia, interview with Nicole Fenosa.

307 **the wives of her lovers:** Antoinette Bernstein wore a blue Chanel jersey suit on the day of her wedding to Henry, who was Coco's lover during the Bernsteins' marriage. "Coco would play a big role in our life," wrote the Bernsteins' daughter, Georges Bernstein. Georges Bernstein Gruber and Gilbert Marin, *Bernstein le magnifique* (Paris: JC Lattès, 1988), 157.

309 **thirty-five-day Battle of France:** During this battle, two million French soldiers were taken prisoner by the German army, "the largest number of prisoners ever captured in such a short period of time," or one in every seven Frenchmen between the ages of twenty and forty, according to historian Sarah Fishman. Fishman, "Grand Delusions: The Unintended Consequences of Vichy's Prisoner of War Propaganda," *Journal of Contemporary History* 26, no. 2 (April 1991): 229–54.

309 **decamped from Paris to Tours:** Historian Frederic Spotts captures the symbolic importance of these events: "The City of Light…incarnated not just France but modern Western culture. To seize this precious object, to take it from its people, to subject it to harsh foreign rule, was worse than mere occupation.… [It was] a stripping away of the very French-ness of France." Frederic Spotts, *The Shameful Peace* (New Haven, Conn.: Yale University Press, 2008), 10–11.

309 **Fenosa left, too, for Toulouse:** Spotts, 12–14.

310 **France's entire population took part:** Spotts, 6. See also Robert Gildea, *Marianne in Chains: Daily Life in the Heart of France During the German Occupation* (New York: Metropolitan Books, 2002). Author and reconnaissance pilot Antoine de Saint-Exupéry (*The Little Prince*), viewed the chaos from his plane and recalled seeing: "fires everywhere, supplies scattered helter-skelter, villages devastated, everything a shambles—a total shambles." Quoted in Spotts, 7.

311 **"I give to France the gift":** Quoted in Milton Dank, *The French Against the French: Collaboration and Resistance* (New York: J. B. Lippincott, 1974), 13. Originally published in Henri Amouroux, *La Vie des français sous l'occupation* (Paris: Fayard, 1961), 64.

311 **eighty-four-year-old man in military regalia:** Michèle Cone discusses "l'Art Maréchal," in *Artists Under Vichy* (Princeton, N.J.: Princeton University Press, 1992), 66ff. See also Julian Jackson on the Vichy department dedicated to creating and orchestrating images of Pétain. Jackson, 307.

311 **with doctrinaire Catholic pieties:** Pétain did not hesitate to compare himself, implicitly, to Christ. Vichy propaganda about Pétain's birthday, which was a holiday to be celebrated even by French soldiers in prison camps, referred to the festivities as if to a Catholic church ritual: "Our captive compatriots will also participate in this communion." Quoted in Fishman, 236.

312 **"almost all legislative, executive":** Quoted in Jackson, 133. Pétain played the role of "a military hero . . . a father-grandfather figure, and even a substitute king wrapped up in one," as Sarah Fishman has written. Fishman, 235.

312 **of all foreign-born Jews:** Although permitted by Germany to exempt Jewish children, Laval overrode this exception and insisted that all children be deported to the camps with their parents. Later, Vichy would begin reversing the naturalization papers for many Jews, stripping them of their French citizenship and thereby rendering them "foreign," and hence deportable.
    See Pierre Blet, *Pius XII and the Second World War,* trans. Lawrence J. Johnson (New York: Paulist Press, 1999), 232–34.

312 **ghastly new regulations taking hold:** For an excellent study of what historian Robert Gildea describes as "the grey areas," the countless compromises and nuances involved in living as an occupied nation during wartime, see his *Marianne in Chains.* Through his vast numbers of interviews with survivors of the era, Gildea discovered, for example, that many Frenchmen would take pains in public to praise the efforts of the Resistance, but in private reveal serious misgivings about the antifascist movement, whose actions often jeopardized the lives or livelihoods of local citizens. See also Julian Jackson on the problems of the "ordinary": "Was it possible to live outside politics in the peculiar conditions of the Occupation when 'ordinariness' has implications it would not have in other circumstances?" Jackson, 239.

312 **German censors carefully vetted:** Books by the likes of Thomas Mann, H. G. Wells, André Malraux, W. Somerset Maugham, Sigmund Freud, and Charles de Gaulle were destroyed, among thousands of others. See John B. Hench, *Books as Weapons: Propaganda, Publishing, and the Battle for Global Markets in the Era of World War II* (Ithaca, N.Y.: Cornell University Press, 2010), 30. See also Spotts, 57–59.

312 **"Everything we did was equivocal":** Quoted in Spotts, 4.

312 **a carefully orchestrated charm offensive:** "German soldiers . . . [behaved] less like foreigners than tourists," writes Frederic Spotts, "spending their time sightseeing, photo-snapping and shopping." Spotts, 18.

313 **"A close relative":** Interview accessed online at http://www.chanel-muggeridge .com/unpublished-interview/, courtesy of the Société Baudelaire. Muggeridge refers to this conversation of September 1944 in an unpublished letter to Jacques Soustelle, dated August 28, 1982, a copy of which was sent to me for authentication by Isée St. John Knowles of the Société Baudelaire; private correspondence with author, February 2013.

313 **"[Coco] admitted to me":** Fiemeyer and Palasse-Labrunie, 174.

313 **"What happened to your son?":** Muggeridge, interview with Chanel, September 1944.

313 **she carried in her wallet:** Fiemeyer and Palasse-Labrunie, 18.

313 **contacts within the highest Nazi circles:** It must be acknowledged, however, that

while her love for André was genuine, the only known time Chanel ever admitted to her dealings with the Reich (in her interview with Muggeridge), she disingenuously exploited her relationship with her nephew, using it to explain away all of her subsequent dealings with the Third Reich. The facts suggested otherwise.

314 **"I will arrive Monday evening"**: Fundació Apel-les Fenosa.

314 **a stiflingly hot hotel attic**: Hal Vaughan says that André-Louis Dubois (the official in the French Foreign Office who had helped Fenosa obtain a French visa, and a friend of Chanel's as well as Cocteau's) had given the ladies his own hotel room to use for the night. According to Vaughan, Chanel and Bousquet had met Misia Sert in Vichy and she, too, shared the hotel room with them. Vaughan, 124.

314 **"Everybody was laughing"**: Quoted by Haedrich,127.

316 **"The first time I saw Pierre Laval"**: Elsa Maxwell's Party Line: "Laval Spelled Backwards," *Pittsburgh Post-Gazette,* August 11, 1945.

316 **had frequently hosted Laval**: See René de Chambrun, "Morand et Laval: Une amitié historique," *Ecrits de Paris,* no. 588 (May 1997): 39–44. Morand also rushed to Vichy in the summer of 1940 and was quickly appointed ambassador to Bucharest. In April 1942, Morand wrote a letter to Josée Laval de Chambrun, expressing his desire to receive another diplomatic appointment: "Tell your father that…I consider it my duty to offer leaving France. I would like to show all my friends abroad that I stand behind your father, because there is no other policy for France." Quoted in Gavin Boyd, *Paul Morand et la Roumanie* (Paris: l'Harmattan, 2002). This letter is also reproduced in René de Chambrun's article above, p. 41.

317 **"I thought him a slippery"**: Maxwell, "Laval Spelled Backwards."

317 **when Laval ruled Vichy**: Laval had two stints under the Vichy regime. The first lasted only a year, after which his penchant for acting independently of Pétain led to dismissal from office. Laval returned to power in 1942. He was arrested in 1945 and executed by firing squad that same year.

318 **Misia scolded her for ceding**: Vaughan, 131, and Charles-Roux, 554.

318 **head of the occupied territories**: Vaughan, 131.

318 **the privilege of living there**: Nonmilitary guests at the Ritz included Madame Marie-Louise Ritz, wife of founder César Ritz; wine magnate and Nazi supporter Charles Dubonnet and his family; and American multimillionaire Charles Bedaux and his wife, Fern. The Bedauxes were also great admirers of Hitler and close to the Windsors. Vaughan, 131; Noel Anthony, "Fern Bedaux Fights Back," *The Milwaukee Journal,* April 13, 1955. See also Jonathan Petropoulos, *Royals and the Reich: The Princes von Hessen in Nazi Germany* (New York: Oxford University Press, 2006), esp. 210–12.

318 **"Insofar as you have any influence"**: Galante, 180.

318 **"Wealth is not accumulation"**: Delay, 147.

319 **"like a snail"**: Quoted in ibid., 226.

319 **function of purely personal expediency**: Marcel Haedrich writes, "With the helmeted sentries and barriers erected in front of the Ritz, she remained Mademoiselle Chanel, protected against everything by her genius, her glory, and also, by her money." Haedrich, 136.

320 **The issuing authority for this document**: The document was signed J. Nailier, director of National Security, Chanel dossier, Paris police archives.

322 **as light as a bird:** Charles-Roux, 545.

322 **took part in that assassination:** Lisa Chaney cites the memoir of Catsy von Dincklage's sister, Sybille Bedford, *Quicksands* (Berkeley: Counterpoint, 2005), 310–11, in which Bedford recalls hearing that Spatz had participated in the murder. Quoted in Chaney, 318. See also Vaughan, 15–19.

322 **King Alexander of Yugoslavia:** See Chaney, 318n11, referring to *Das Braune Netz*, 94.

323 **Dincklage as an agent:** Stephen Wilson notes Allard's participation in the early projects of Action française in "The Action Française in French Intellectual Life," *The Historical Journal* 12, no. 2 (1969): 328–50. Hal Vaughan mentions Allard's 1939 book as a source of information about Dincklage.

324 **"models of psychological tactics":** Allard, 38.

324 **"My many society friends in France":** All quotations from Dincklage's correspondence appear (translated into French) in Paul Allard, *Quand Hitler espionne la France* (Paris: Les Editions de France, 1939): 38–50.

325 **"In June 1942":** Patrick Modiano, *La Place de l'Etoile* (Paris: Gallimard, 1968), epigraph, p. 12. Modiano is playing on the fact that *étoile* means "star" in French.

325 **The Jew and France:** In the summer of 1940, Paris's Palais Berlitz cinema featured a special exhibition entitled "The Jew and France," which explained in detail the centuries of corrupt influence Jews had supposedly exercised over France. Over 500,000 people attended this exhibition, which then traveled to other cities.

 The statistic and description come from the Shoah Resource Center: http://www1.yadvashem.org/odot_pdf/Microsoft%20Word%20-%206328.pdf.

326 **barring Jews from public office:** Paris's Théâtre Sarah Bernhardt was renamed the Théâtre de la Cité, and all city streets named after Jewish people were relabeled. These and many other examples can be found in David Pryce-Jones, *Paris in the Third Reich: A History of the German Occupation 1940–1944* (New York: Holt, Rinehart, and Winston, 1981), 82ff.

326 **half of France's Jewish population:** Gradually, these anti-Semitic measures built a climate of terror and suspicion. By the end of the war, the Reich had seized more than twenty-one thousand Jewish-owned businesses, confiscated a fortune in Jewish-owned property—everything from middle-class home furnishings to the Rothschilds' art collection. See Spotts, especially pages 32–33. See also David Carroll, "What It Meant to Be 'a Jew' in Vichy France: Xavier Vallat, State Anti-Semitism, and the Question of Assimilation," *SubStance* 27, no. 3 (1998): 36–54.

326 **a gold Star of David:** The Roma people ("Gypsies"), homosexuals, Communists, and other groups were also forced by the Nazis to wear identifying badges.

326 **Cocteau's and Picasso's close friend:** Charles-Roux, 557.

327 **vast and simplistic categories:** See Régis Meyran, "Vichy: Ou la face cachée de la République," *L'Homme*, no. 160 (October–December, 2001): 177–84. Meyran points to the irony of the fact that the French Third Republic had, in fact, been responsible for the invention of Europe's first "identity cards," designed originally to ensure the security of French citizens. This political practice, based on a "logic of exclusion"—of foreigners or noncitizens, hence undesirables—was later turned against France by the German occupiers.

327 **military men lined up daily:** "A line formed every morning well before the store

opened, made up mostly of German soldiers," Chanel told Marcel Haedrich. Haedrich, 134.

327 **might have boasted swastikas:** See Charles-Roux, 559.

327 **she never saw the Germans:** Haedrich, 136.

328 **misery lay just outside:** Spotts, 20, 22.

329 **ally in the pro-German branch:** Vaughan, 142. Journalist Patrick Cousteau, editor of the Far Right French magazine *Minute,* believes that Niebuhr was also, at some point, Chanel's lover. While Niebuhr is mentioned multiple times in her surveillance file, he is not cited as a romantic interest of hers. I have found no evidence to support Cousteau's claim. Patrick Cousteau, "Ce n'est pas dans le film, Coco Chanel vue par les RG," *Minute,* April 2009.

330 **"My joy was beyond words":** Muggeridge interview with Chanel.

332 **"In a France subjected":** Buisson, 18–20.

332 **other prominent Gentile figureheads:** See Galante, 182–83. See also Vaughan, 151–52.

332 **past as a kept woman:** For Charles-Roux, this use of Nexon represents the Wertheimers' "refinement of cruelty"—a way to throw Chanel off guard by placing her in front of "the ironic gaze of a society man from a world she could never think of without bitterness…a witness from her past." Charles-Roux, 561.

332 **power of money to short-circuit:** The transaction and its implications have been discussed in numerous places, including *The New York Times.* See Dana Thomas, "The Power Behind the Cologne," *The New York Times,* February 24, 2002.

333 **the all-important synthetic aldehydes:** "No. 5 [was] probably the only perfume whose quality remained the same throughout the war," a company representative told Pierre Galante, 183.

333 **procure the jasmine, ylang-ylang:** This corporate "agent," Herbert Gregory Thomas, was an American-born international lawyer—fluent in French, Spanish, and German—who worked for the Wertheimers' main company, Bourjois. In the summer of 1940, disguised as a Spanish businessman and using a false passport, he traveled from New York to France via Spain, on a four-month mission for Chanel, Inc. During those months, he accomplished a series of seemingly impossible feats: He secured the secret "recipe" for Chanel No. 5; he smuggled out of Grasse a massive quantity of "natural aromatics"; and, with the aid of Félix Amiot, he smuggled Jacques Wertheimer, son of Pierre, out of Bordeaux, where he was hiding after escaping a German POW camp. Unsurprisingly, soon after returning from this mission, Thomas joined the Office of Strategic Services, which later became the CIA. After the war, he rejoined the Wertheimer organization, serving as president of Chanel, Inc., for twenty-seven years. Pierre Galante alludes to this story in his biography, but it is Hal Vaughan who put all the details together most clearly. Information on the story of Herbert Gregory Thomas also appears in Phyllis Berman and Zina Saway, "The Billionaires Behind Chanel," *Forbes,* April 3, 1989, 104–8.

333 **"[She said], 'My dear'":** Chazot, *Chazot Jacques,* 74–75.

335 **"Gabrielle Chanel was not":** Jean-Louis de Faucigny-Lucinge. *Un Gentilhomme cosmopolite* (Paris: Editions Perrin, 1990), 183.

335 **"sort of resentment and bitterness":** Emmanuel de Brantes and Gilles Brochard, "Interview with Jean-Louis de Faucigny-Lucinge," *Le Quotidien de Paris,* April, 26, 1990.

336 **Chanel's surprising intervention:** Palmer is an international consultant for Mondex Corporation of Toronto. He focuses on helping Jewish families recover assets looted from them during World War II, specializing in looted art.

336 **the maiden name of "Dreyfus":** This is the famous banking branch of the Dreyfus family, also known as the Louis-Dreyfuses, founders of the famous Dreyfus fund. American television actress Julia Louis-Dreyfus belongs to this branch of the family.

336 **"I was so hungry":** Viviane Forrester, *Ce soir, après la guerre* (Paris: Fayard, 1992), 62.

337 **"I remember some of the stories":** Ibid., 99–100.

338 **"was working for a German officer":** Lady Christine Swaythling, personal interviews with author, March 11, 2011, and August 5, 2012.

338 **practice of pillaging Jewish homes:** See Frederic Spotts on the practice of looting homes. "Less senior officials requisitioned family homes or confiscated those that had been abandoned by their rich British or Jewish owners.... Whole neighborhoods were sometimes taken over, owners thrown out.... The higher-ups helped themselves to furniture, kitchen equipment, linen, cutlery...and whatever else caught their fancy." Spotts, 32–33.

338 **paintings stolen by the Nazis:** Vaughan, 157.

340 **her blithe disregard:** Documentation of this spy mission exists in a number of venues, including the U.S. National Archives and Records Administration, which houses the Nuremberg trial transcripts of Nazi officials involved in Modellhut, the French army intelligence files, the British National Archives, and German intelligence archives.

340 **impetus behind this scheme:** Given how convoluted the story would become, its basic outline, as laid out in Nuremberg testimony, is deceptively brief:

"In April 1944 Staatsrat Schiebe [Walter Schieber], [Albert] Speer's right-hand man and one Rittmeister [Theodor] Momm mentioned to Schellenberg the existence of a certain Frau Chanel, a French subject and proprietress of the noted perfume factory. This woman was referred to as a person who knew Churchill sufficiently to undertake political negotiations with him, as an enemy of Russia and as desirous of helping France and Germany whose destinies she believed to be closely linked together." National Archives, Schellenberg testimony, deposed by Sir Stuart Hampshire, 1944, quoted in Reinhard Doerries, *Hitler's Last Chief of Foreign Intelligence: Allied Interrogations of Walter Schellenberg* (New York: Routledge, 2003), 108.

340 **approached Captain Theodor Momm:** Charles-Roux, 569.

340 **"keep Spatz close to her":** Vaughan, 159. According to Vaughan, Gabrielle Palasse-Labrunie confirms that her aunt wanted desperately to remain with Dincklage.

340 **Dincklage secured permission:** Vaughan, 160. Modellhut was exposed in April 1944 on page 65 of British Intelligence Report on the Case of Walter Schellenberg. Based on interrogations by agents of MI6, July 1945, at camp 020. It is stored as file xe001752: Walter S., Investigative Records Repository, Records of Army Staff, Record Group 319, National Archives at College Park.

341 **part of his Nuremberg testimony:** The U.S. National Archives house the transcripts of his testimony, which were declassified in 1985. Schellenberg was deposed by Sir Stuart Hampshire of the MI6, the British Secret Service.

341 **Hoare was another old friend:** In his biography of the Duchess of Windsor, Charles Higham cites Hoare's involvement in "discussing with [the Windsors] the potential of peaceful arrangements between Britain and Germany." Charles Higham, *The Duchess of Windsor: A Secret Life* (1988; repr., Hoboken, N.J.: Wiley, 2005), 334–35. According to Michael Bloch, Hoare was described as "the prime target for German peace feelers." Bloch, *The Secret File of the Duke of Windsor* (New York: HarperCollins, 1989), 108, quoted in Petropoulos, 211.

341 **Chanel placed a curious condition:** Vera would later say she had not seen Chanel in seven years, claiming in a letter to Churchill (dated August 8, 1944) that Chanel had "thrown her out" of her business in 1937. I have seen no other evidence of this, and Bate might be exaggerating in an attempt to distance herself even more from Chanel. The Churchill Archives Centre, Cambridge University.

341 **exploit Vera's high-level connections:** "Without Vera, the mission had no chance for success. Only Vera was close enough to Churchill." Charles-Roux, 579.

341 **part of a Nazi plan:** This is according to Charles-Roux, who interviewed Vera directly. Vera had attracted suspicion on both sides of the political divide. In the 1930s, French intelligence suspected her of spying for the fascists and kept her under extensive surveillance. French concerns about their activities were raised especially about Vera's second husband, Prince Alberto Lombardi, known to be a high-ranking member of the Italian National Fascist Party. Their file describes Lombardi as "disdainful and uncommunicative" and of uncertain occupation. The couple are described as "very suspicious." Paris police archives, report dated January 20, 1931, dossier 239.195.

342 **the war's most brutal criminals:** Uki Goñi reveals this in his book *The Real Odessa*. Goñi explains that Hendaye was the "French town where the Argentine diplomats in Spain who collaborated with the SD [German foreign intelligence service] went to deliver their reports." Uki Goñi, *The Real Odessa: Smuggling the Nazis to Peron's Argentina* (New York: Granta Books, 2002), 241.

342 **Sommer in his Nuremberg testimony:** This is reported in the testimony of Hans Sommer, quoted in Uki Goñi. Kutschmann, the Gestapo chief of Bordeaux at one time, was a notorious war criminal and, according to *The New York Times*, "boasted publicly of being responsible for the deaths of 15,000 Jews in Russia and Poland." "Spain Prodded Again on Sheltering Nazis," *The New York Times*, June 19, 1946. According to Goñi, Kutschmann managed to evade prosecution by fleeing to Argentina, disguised as a Carmelite monk. See Goñi, 241ff.

343 **"Pull [Vera] out of this situation":** CHAR 20/198A 66, Churchill Archives Centre. An embassy diplomat, Henry Hankey, sent Chanel's letter on to 10 Downing Street, where John Colville, private secretary to Churchill, forwarded it to his colleague Kathleen Hill, another Churchill secretary, with a note attached dated January 24, 1944. That note expresses skepticism about Chanel's claims of an ongoing close friendship with the prime minister. CHAR 20/198A 64, Churchill Archives Centre.

343 **prevail upon her Allied connections:** After nearly eight months in Spain, Vera wrote to Churchill on August 8, 1944, imploring him to rescue her and blaming Chanel openly:

Dear Winston,

I've never dared write and bother you about this interminable and nightmarish wait here to be allowed to repatriate after my escape from Coco and the Germans. . . . My conscience tells me your thoughts are far too precious to us all to be wasted on "old me" but on the other hand it does seem such a sign from heaven above [that Randolph Churchill advised her to write to his father] I've decided to act on it. . . . I was forcibly brought to [Chanel] in Paris in December 43 by her orders and by the methods of her German friends and my jailers. . . . I have written a report and given verbally all the information I can think of about the details of my imprisonment and kidnapping and I know no more. I found Coco very changed from seven years ago. . . . After all I had been thru for my fanatically British attitude that I could be suspected by my own people of doing something traitorish I can't believe it even now and beg to be allowed to defend myself. . . . Please let me go home to Albert and Tiger and work in the Cause you and I believe in I am getting old but I will do what I've always tried to do, my best its been no great shakes but I'm not a marvel but I am English and proud of it.

Your affectionate Vera

Still plagued by suspicions of espionage, Vera found herself once more a prisoner, albeit this time in far more luxurious quarters than she'd endured in her Roman jail. After moving out of the Madrid Ritz, she accepted the hospitality of the British diplomat assigned to "watch" her, Brian Wallace. Wallace had been sympathetic to Vera from the start, and had warned her to avoid being seen with Coco in Madrid.

343 **Vera remained tainted for months:** "I shall be glad to discuss with you the case of Vera Lombardi nee Arkwright who wishes to rejoin her husband in Italy," wrote Churchill to General Henry Wilson, supreme allied commander in the Mediterranean Theatre, on October 14, 1944. CHAR 20/198A/ 83, Churchill Archives Centre. A December 3 letter from a U.S. Army officer to Churchill's London office explains that the "case of Madam Vera Lombardi [is] delayed owing to the fact that madam Chanel who apparently instigated the special facilities afforded by the German Gestapo to Madam Lombardi is still being interrogated in France."

344 **This document cleared Vera's name:** The telegram ending Vera's purgatory read simply: "Madame Lombardi is free to return to Italy." CHAR 20/198A/89, Churchill Archives Centre.

344 **never spoken to Chanel again:** Upon her return to Paris, Chanel did address an angry letter to Vera in Madrid, berating her for her "betrayals." Charles-Roux, 600.

345 **wear the chic black uniform:** See chapter 10 for Schellenberg's remarks on the allure of the Nazi uniform, and so forth.

345 **"Microphones were everywhere":** Quoted by Alan Bullock, in the introduction to Walter Schellenberg, *Hitler's Secret Service* [original title: *The Labyrinth*], trans. Louis Hagen (New York: Harper and Brothers, 1956), 8.

346 **"Schellenberg was a great man":** Transcript translated from the Spanish by Uki Goñi. Goñi, personal interview with author, June 12, 2011. The original tape of the conversation is held at the U.S. Holocaust Memorial Museum.

347 **one of Franco's spies:** Countess Isabella also hinted that she had heard some facts about the romance from Otto Skorzeny, a high-ranking Nazi agent who was a close

friend of Schellenberg's, with whom the countess had a brief friendship while still a teenager. Charles-Roux, 631, mentions Schellenberg's friendship with Skorzeny.

347 **"One of [Chanel's] great loves":** Countess Isabella Vacani von Fechtmann, personal interview with the author, Genoa, Italy, March 2011.

347 **work for German interests:** See chapter 11 of *The Labyrinth*: "The Plot to Kidnap the Duke of Windsor," 118–34.

348 **a rather harebrained scheme:** As Reinhard Doerries writes, "What Coco Chanel presented was a complicated hackneyed undertaking that had little or no chance of success." Doerries, 166.

348 **other Anglo-German strategies:** See Petropoulos, 211ff.

348 **"godmother" to French troops:** Jean Marais, *Histoires de ma vie* (Paris: Albin Michel, 1975), 171. In 1942, when Robert Streitz, architect of La Pausa, asked Chanel to intervene on behalf of his friend Professor Serge Voronoff, a member of the French Resistance who had been arrested by the Gestapo, she agreed, perhaps intrigued by Dr. Voronoff's research. He was a forerunner of modern endocrinology, experimenting with "rejuvenation" techniques involving transplanting animal testicles. Galante, 181; Thierry Gillyboeuf, "The Famous Doctor Who Inserts Monkeyglands in Millionaires," *Spring* 9 (2009): 44–45, accessed at http://faculty.gvsu.edu/websterm/cummings/issue9/Gillybo9.htm.

348 **petition to release Max Jacob:** In the 1920s, Chanel saw a great deal of Jacob and found him very amusing. They shared an interest in astrology and Max would do her horoscope and read her palm. Charles-Roux, 388.

349 **Jacob, the devout Catholic convert:** Jacob's last letter to Cocteau is dated February 29, 1944.

> Dear Jean:
> I write to you from a train car thanks to the indulgence of the guards who surround us. We will be at Drancy any minute. That is all I have to say. Sacha [Guitry], when they told him about my sister [who had also been imprisoned by the Nazis] said, "If it were him [Max], I could do something!" Well, it's me
>
> Love,
> Max

Reproduced in Jacob and Cocteau, 600. Charles-Roux details more of Cocteau's attempts and the details of Jacob's last days, 608–9.

349 **apartment of a French aristocrat:** Vaughan, 53.

350 **"Coco behaved like a queen":** Lifar later gave himself up but received the indulgent sentence of a one-year suspension from the Paris Opéra. Galante, 185–87.

350 **"Joan of Arc's blood":** Quoted in Haedrich, 140.

350 **the doorman at the Ritz:** Gold and Fizdale, 296. Cocteau also expressed snobbish disdain for the post-occupation atmosphere in Paris, complaining that the Americans failed to maintain the proper decorum of the Ritz dining room: "At the liberated Ritz American officers have lunch with whores off the street. The great joy one should feel has been negated by a feeling of malaise and sadness.... The organized disorder of the Americans contrasts with the style of German discipline; it is disturbing, it is disorienting." Cocteau, quoted in Spotts, 230.

351 **she scoffed about her interrogators:** Haedrich, 144.

351 **intervention from her British connections:** Charles-Roux claims to have evidence from witnesses that Churchill not only tried to reach Chanel repeatedly by telephone from London at war's end, but that, failing to reach her, he dispatched a young assistant to Paris to look physically for Chanel. Charles-Roux goes on to claim that the prime minister's aide found Coco eventually—hiding out just after the liberation in a small hotel on the outskirts of Paris. No other proof of this story exists, but if true, it points to just how anxious Churchill was about what Chanel might say to the authorities. Charles-Roux, 612–17.

351 **"Churchill had me freed":** Vaughan, 187.

351 **accessory to a treasonous crime:** Amy Fine Collins, "Haute Coco," *Vanity Fair,* June 1994, 132–48.

352 **only transparent lies and excuses:** Chanel offered the court a series of lies. She insisted she had traveled to Madrid on perfume business, and that she and Vaufreland had simply run into each other by chance on the train—directly contradicting Vaufreland's own sworn testimony. She denied knowing she had ever been registered as a German agent. She said she had never made the acquaintance of any SS personnel.

352 **well aware of her untruths:** Quoted in Vaughan, 198.

352 **a letter to Theodor Momm:** Schellenberg's battle with liver disease is discussed in *The Nuremberg Interviews,* ed. Robert Gellately (New York: Knopf, 2004), 415–32. It's unclear whether Irene Schellenberg had any knowledge of Chanel's affair with her husband. Countess Isabella Vacani von Fechtmann claims, though, that Irene was a fiercely jealous woman who, aware of her husband's multiple affairs, once flew into a rage and tried to throw acid in his face. Walter was saved when Reinhard Heydrich, his commanding officer, swiftly pushed him out of the way.

12. SHOWING THEM: CHANEL RETURNS

353 **"They said that I was old-fashioned":** Quoted in Brendan Gill and Lillian Ross, "The Strong Ones," *The New Yorker,* September 28, 1957, 34–35.

354 **"Luxury is liberty":** Delay, 229.

354 **the Beau-Rivage in Ouchy:** "Camping out" remark quoted in G. Y. Dryansky, "Camping with Coco," *HFD,* April 9, 1969.

354 **still suffering from tuberculosis:** Although debilitated by his illness, Palasse survived into old age, passing away in 1996 at the age of eighty-nine.

354 **an apartment in nearby Chexbres:** Galante, 189.

355 **permanently severed all ties:** Madsen, 269.

356 **having frozen his book royalties:** Ibid., 264.

356 **at the Badrutt's Palace Hotel:** Chaney, 336.

357 **"She did this out of affection":** Palasse-Labrunie, personal conversation with author, March 2011.

357 **friendship of two eternal *cocottes*:** Jullian, 46. Gabrielle Palasse-Labrunie disputes this story, claiming that Chanel merely pulled back Misia's skin which, slackened by death, had simply become more malleable. Private conversation with author, Yermenonville, France, March 2011.

357 **liked to be a surgeon:** Marquand, 104.

357 **accident in Rio de Janeiro:** Charles-Roux, 628.

358 **The loss was "devastating":** Palasse-Labrunie, 183.

358 **channeling Oscar Wilde:** Morand, *L'Allure de Chanel*, 166.

358 **"My dentist is the best":** Dryansky, "Camping with Coco."

359 **"Never was I in retirement":** Brendan Gill and Lillian Ross, "The Strong One," *The New Yorker*, September 28, 1957, 34–35.

360 **"The Beau Rivage was":** Michel Déon, *Bagages pour Vancouver* (Paris: Editions de la Table Ronde, 1985), 20.

361 **Egyptian-born wife of the Belgian diplomat:** Madsen, 272.

361 **Maggie and Coco singing:** Ibid., 274.

361 **both taken a quantum leap:** In his diaries, Cecil Beaton recalls Chanel dismissing women "who spent their lives like Maggie van Zuylen at the bridge table." Cecil Beaton, *The Unexpurgated Beaton: The Cecil Beaton Diaries* (New York: Knopf, 2003), 141.

361 **fallen prey to Maggie's charm:** See Arianna Huffington, *Maria Callas: The Woman Behind the Legend* (New York: Cooper Square Press, 2002), 233ff.

361 **"unself-conscious, unconventional":** Personal conversation with a source close to the Van Zuylen family, February 2013.

362 **asked about women lovers:** Haedrich, 178. Lilou Marquand mentions that certain medications Chanel took actually gave her a faint garlic scent, which made Coco very self-conscious, whence probably her description of herself as "an old garlic clove." Marquand, 158. I thank Judith Thurman for pointing out the slang meaning in French of "garlic clove" or "*gousse d'ail.*"

362 **fashion photographer Willy Rizzo:** Willy Rizzo, private conversation with the author.

362 **"They didn't hide":** Paul Morand, *Journal inutile*, January 11, 1971, quoted in Chaney, 337, and 420n8.

362 **secret of the pendant's poetry:** Fiemeyer and Palasse-Labrunie, 183.

363 **having sold his warplanes:** Madsen, 266.

363 **Coco planned her revenge:** Haedrich, 146–47.

364 **new series of beautiful fragrances:** Chambrun's wife, Josée de Chambrun, adored the new scents, as did the professional "nose" or perfume expert called in by René de Chambrun to assess the samples. Galante, 192–93.

364 **for good measure, Samuel Goldwyn:** Ibid. On Chanel's creation of competitive perfumes and the subsequent legal arrangements, see also Madsen, 267ff, and Phyllis Berman and Zina Sawaya, "The Billionaires Behind Chanel," *Forbes*, April 3, 1989, 104–8.

365 **royalties of 2 percent annually:** Historical currency conversion calculated at MeasuringWorth, http://www.measuringworth.com/uscompare/.

365 **"Now, I am rich":** Galante, 193.

365 **"Mademoiselle Chanel and Pierre Wertheimer":** Private conversation with the author.

365 **tried to seize their business:** The odd twists of this story lend some credibility to a theory proffered by historian Countess Isabella Vacani von Fechtmann, whose family had high-level Nazi connections. She believes that, even during the war, among

the wealthiest members of French and German society, Nazis and Jews brokered discreet, mutually beneficial deals among themselves, while maintaining a charade of enmity: "My contention is they [the Wertheimers] told [Chanel] to do that [make a public attempt to seize the Wertheimers' holdings using the 'Jewish laws']. To save the house! It worked! The perfumes kept selling. Everyone wanted Chanel, even during the war." Private conversation with the author.

366 **"suggesting something like a Gibson"**: "Fashion," *Rob Wagner's Script*, May 1947, 31.

366 **"A Paris sensation"**: "Vogue's Eye View: First Impressions of the Paris Collections," *Vogue*, March 15, 1947, 151.

367 **an unmistakable "bustle effect"**: "Dior and Paquin Exhibit Fashions," *The New York Times*, February 19, 1947.

367 **the "feminine mission" of baby making**: These included financial bonuses for women who bore a child within the first two years of marriage, and for families in which only one member of the couple (nearly always the husband) worked outside the home.

367 **requested by General de Gaulle**: Quoted in Jane Jenson, "The Liberation and New Rights for French Women," in *Between the Lines: Gender and the Two World Wars*, ed. Margaret R. Higonnet and Jane Jenson (New Haven, Conn.: Yale University Press, 1989), 281. In the same volume, historians Margaret Higonnet and Patrice Higonnet write of the frequent return, after wartime, to more rigidly enforced gender roles, in order both to accommodate the employment needs of returning soldiers and to counteract the implicit feminization of a country devastated by war: "Postwar rhetoric appeals to a positive reconstruction of a former order, which is presented as 'organic,' a golden age of 'natural' gender relations.... In the postwar period, the reconstitution of the nation required that society reintegrate returning soldiers." See Margaret R. Higonnet and Patrice Higonnet, "The Double Helix," in Higonnet and Jenson, 40.

    Historian Claire Duchen has written of the antifeminist policies (not unlike those of Vichy, albeit minus the fascism) resulting from postwar anxieties about population levels: "Public discourse on the question spoke in terms of the 'feminine mission' or 'feminine nature' and no noteworthy transformation occurred in [the focus] upon the maternal function of women." Claire Duchen, "Une Femme Nouvelle pour une France Nouvelle," *CLIO: Histoire, Femmes, et Sociétés* 1 (1995): 6. "Motherhood dominated the Fourth Republic's definition of women's roles in postwar society," agrees historian Susan Weiner in *Enfants Terribles: Youth and Femininity in the Mass Media in France 1945–1968* (Baltimore: Johns Hopkins University Press, 2001), 25.

367 **foundered badly since the war**: The war and its aftermath had dulled the luster of French haute couture. Many fashion houses had gone out of business; materials remained scarce, and the French economy was still suffering. Even once-loyal customers were defecting from couture, lured away by the attractive, well-made, and far less expensive garments being produced by America's burgeoning ready-to-wear industry. Christian Dior's "aggressively indulgent style [was] meant to contrast with wartime shortage[s]," Tony Judt observed in *Postwar: A History of Europe Since 1945* (New York: Penguin Books, 2006), 234.

367 **return of French luxury**: Dior biographer Marie-France Pochna writes, "The true

power of this new fashion was a catalyst for the universal longing for change, the need to forget empty bellies, run-down apartments and a general feeling of tedium." Marie-France Pochna, *Dior: The Man Who Made the World Look New*, trans. Joanna Savill (New York: Arcade Publishing, 1996), 138. Originally published in French by Flammarion in 1994.

368 **Dior's style resisted low-rent imitation:** Pochna, 183.

369 **"inverted snobbery of poverty":** Quoted in ibid., 144.

369 **retailing below $69.95 for dresses:** Values calculated at MeasuringWorth. The goal was clear, as *The New York Times* explained, citing an interview with counsel for the Maison Dior: "American customers of Christian Dior would be restricted to a small and select group of persons and concerns 'enjoying the highest reputation.'" "No Dress Under $69.95 Will Bear the Name Dior," *The New York Times,* July 30, 1948.

369 **"In an epoch as somber as ours":** Quoted in "Dior, 52, Creator of 'New Look,' Dies," *The New York Times,* October 24, 1957.

369 **similar visions of Cinderella glamour:** Couture is "shapelier than it's been in years, and the shape is perfect," trumpeted American *Vogue* in 1953, adding one proviso: "The only thing that the new line [relies] on is this: the absolute cooperation of corsetry." "Fashion: The New Line," *Vogue,* August 15, 1953, 66.

369 **$120 million today:** Values calculated at MeasuringWorth.

370 **felt like a bitter slap:** Annalisa Barbieri, "When Skirts Were Full and Women Were Furious," *The Independent,* March 3, 1996; Pochna, 139.

370 **one group of shapely *provocatrices*:** "Hold That Hemline: Women Rebel Against Long-Skirt Edict," *See Magazine,* January 1948, 11.

370 **"Fashion has become a joke":** Galante, 200.

370 **"Dior? He doesn't dress women":** Pochna, 146. In one possibly apocryphal anecdote, Chanel finds herself pushed to return to fashion by an episode involving Marie-Hélène van Zuylen, the daughter of her friend Maggie. According to Axel Madsen, Coco encountered Marie-Hélène in Switzerland when the younger woman had just bought a new ball gown in the style made popular by Dior: boned, corseted, with an enormous skirt. The dress so irritated Coco that she insisted on whipping up an alternative gown for Marie-Hélène. According to this story (which sources close to the Van Zuylen family cannot confirm) Chanel had no fabric and so resorted to using some crimson taffeta drapes she found at the Van Zuylen château. Out of this material, Coco created a youthful trademark Chanel-style gown for her young friend, which garnered such lavish praise at the ball that Coco was convinced to return to fashion. Madsen, 267. While the story may not be true, it has odd symbolic weight. Any movie buff will recognize the anecdote as recalling the famous scene in *Gone with the Wind* (1939) when a penniless Scarlett O'Hara tears down some velvet draperies to make a gown for herself. It is likely that Chanel, who enjoyed Hollywood cinema, circulated this story about herself—placing herself directly into American popular culture as a kind of latter-day Scarlett—a heroine who rises from abject poverty and reinvents herself several times.

370 **Financial concerns played a role:** Amy Fine Collins has suggested that the Wertheimers themselves approached Chanel about making a comeback, specifically to improve perfume sales. Lucien François reported Chanel's denial of any financial

motive. Lucien François, "Chez Coco Chanel à Fouilly-les-Oies en 1930," *France-Soir,* February 18, 1954.

370 **reflected prestige of the couture:** "High fashion itself is not immensely profitable... but couture can create a tremendous aura, an aura that reflects profitably on any product sold under the Chanel name." Berman and Sawaya, 106.

370 **name fading from public consciousness:** Madsen, 282.

370 **all misread her completely:** Galante, 204; Madsen, 266. Michel Déon writes that Chanel never spoke of returning to work, and that none of her friends seemed ever to suggest it to her. "She seemed to live in her past," he recalled. Déon, *Bagages pour Vancouver,* 24.

371 **"Know first-class ready-to-wear":** Madsen, 284.

371 **"I got the idea it would be fun":** Quoted in ibid.

372 **correspondence with Snow was leaked:** Haedrich, 199.

372 **the models found her overbearing:** Former Chanel model Ann Montgomery offers a description of Madame Lucie in *Another Me: A Memoir* (iUniverse, 2008), 143.

373 **agreed to work once more:** Galante, 201; Manon Ligeour interview, July 8, 2005, Maison Chanel archives.

373 **"We were all greatly excited":** Galante, 202.

373 **"It was required that we resemble":** Odile de Croy interview, April 22, 2008, Maison Chanel archives, 6.

373 **consisted largely of old photographs:** Galante, 200.

374 **"a real bombshell":** "Chanel is returning to dressmaking February 5," *The New York Times,* December 21, 1953.

374 **"The news ran through Paris":** Patrice Sylvain, "Le Roman de Coco Chanel," 1954, unidentified clipping, Maison Chanel archives.

375 **"Two thousand people wanted":** Liane Viguié, *Mannequin haute couture: Une femme et son métier* (Paris: Editions Robert Laffont, 1977), 190.

375 **his place in fashion Siberia:** François, "Chez Coco Chanel à Fouilly-Les-Oies."

376 **imitation of Chanel's own gait:** "We slouched and pouted. Coco had taught us how to walk—demonstrating herself the gliding gait with hips thrust forward, shoulders tilted back, level turns with hand on hip—a plausible imitation of the debutante slouch so popular in the twenties." Montgomery, 148.

376 **a crowd of Chanel-like figures:** "Chanel Designs Again," *Vogue,* February 15, 1954, 82–85, 128–29.

376 **"In the play of mirrors":** Ibid.

376 **"All of Paris burned":** L. Dehuz, "Chez Coco Chanel: Une mauvaise farce," Maison Chanel archives.

376 **"Awaited with impatience":** E. de Semont, "Chanel," *Le Monde,* 1954, Maison Chanel archives.

376 **"A melancholy retrospective":** F.B.C., "La Collection Chanel n'a pas soulevé l'enthousiasme," Maison Chanel archives.

376 **exited, with a rudeness startling:** Michel Déon reported on the vulgar remarks made by the crowd in "Un Flair sans piété," *Nouvelles Littéraires,* January 21, 1971.

377 **offense extended beyond the sartorial:** "Chanel nous ramène le flou d'antan," *La Lanterne,* March 25, 1954, Maison Chanel archives.

377 **"[These] are phantoms' dresses"**: "Chanel, apôtre de l'effacement," undated clipping, Maison Chanel archives.

377 **"had a very bad reputation"**: Rosamond Bernier interview, Maison Chanel, February 26, 2007, 3.

378 **Elsa Schiaparelli biographer:** Palmer White, private correspondence, Maison Chanel archives.

378 **tried politely to greet her:** Haedrich, 158.

378 **"Mademoiselle was saying"**: Ligeour interview, Maison Chanel archives.

378 **a lawyer for Pierre Wertheimer:** Quoted in Galante, 255.

378 **"People no longer know"**: Simone Baron interview, *France-Soir,* February 7, 1954, quoted in Madsen, 288.

378 **"At 71, she brings us more"**: "What Chanel Storm Is About," *Life,* March 1, 1954, 49.

379 **"Chanel à la page?"**: "Chanel à la page? But No!" *Los Angeles Times,* February 6, 1954.

379 **explanation for the Americans' interest:** "Chanel Resumes Easy Lines of the 1930s," *Women's Wear Daily,* February 8, 1954.

379 **"I will start with a collection"**: "Chanel Designs Again," *Vogue,* February 15, 1954.

379 **"the easy, underdone sort"**: "Paris Collections: One Easy Lesson," *Vogue,* March 1, 1954, 101.

379 **"[Chanel's] direct approach"**: Virginia Pope, "In the Chanel Spirit," *The New York Times,* July 11, 1954.

380 **"expected Chanel to become Dior"**: "What Were They Expecting?" *Petit Echo de la Mode,* March 1954; "Chanel reste fidèle à son style," *L'Aurore,* February 9, 1956.

380 **"For six million Americans"**: Untitled clipping, *L'Intransigeant,* March 8, 1954.

380 **"entire collection has been bought"**: "On a tout vu," *Le Phare Bruxelles,* March 5, 1954.

380 **"They've been offering women"**: Haedrich, 173.

380 **more than 90 million:** Galante, 207; Madsen, 285.

381 **She was free:** Upon her death, her share of the perfume royalties would revert to the Wertheimers' company. Willy Rizzo discussed the details of Chanel's renegotiated contract with the author in a personal conversation. The details of the contract also appear in Galante, 216–17; Charles-Roux, 643ff; and Berman and Sawaya, 107.

382 **"To me, Chanel was not"**: Betty Catroux, private correspondence with the author. Catroux later moved on from the Maison Chanel to become the muse and face of Yves Saint Laurent's studio.

382 **"The function of a woman"**: Delay, 251–53.

382 **"Women are becoming crazy"**: Haedrich, 184.

382 **"Do not forget that"** Morand, *L'Allure de Chanel,* 168.

382 **"Paris has rediscovered"**: "Chanel redevient Chanel," *République des Pyrénées,* October 14, 1954.

383 **bits of moss she'd gathered:** Fiemeyer and Palasse-Labrunie, *Intimate Chanel,* 98.

383 **"'That's what I want'"**: Quoted in Galante, 248.

383 **"it is the color of blood"**: Delay, 192.

384 **scratch or irritate:** Ibid., 191–92.

384 **ballooning unevenly over the tops:** "Chanel Blousing," *Vogue,* March 15, 1956, 88.

384 **the leg could move forward:** "Chanel Suit Casually Fitted," *Vogue,* September 15, 1957, 119.

384 **"at once dignified and dancing"**: "La Jupe Chanel descend dans la rue," *Le Nouveau Candide*, May 4–11, 1961.

385 **"The purpose of the skirt"**: Hélène Obolensky, "The Chanel Look," *Ladies' Home Journal*, September 1964, 44–45, 179.

385 **"To the great innovator"**: Quoted in Carmel Snow, *Harper's Bazaar*, September 10, 1957.

385 **"They don't understand luxury"**: Haedrich, 199–200.

386 **"the magician of French couture"**: "Magicienne de la couture française Coco Chanel va chercher aux USA l'Oscar de la mode," *France-Soir*, August 31, 1957, 1–2.

386 **"most incredible comeback"**: Nan Robertson, "Texas Store Fetes Chanel for Her Great Influence," *The New York Times*, September 9, 1957.

386 **"ageless designer"**: "Chanel: Ageless Designer Whose Young Look Is America's Favorite," *The New York Times*, September 9, 1957.

386 **"At 74, Mademoiselle Chanel"**: Brendan Gill and Lillian Ross, "The Strong Ones," *The New Yorker*, September 28, 1957, 34–35.

386 **hardly incidental to her comeback**: Some people noted that Chanel looked better after she returned from Switzerland than she had before going. Anonymous sources close to the Maison Chanel confirm Chanel's recourse to plastic surgery. And photo evidence also strongly suggests that Coco had undergone some surgical enhancement before returning to her career.

387 **"At 75, she is still"**: Patricia Peterson, "The Chanel Look Remains Indestructible," *The New York Times*, August 28, 1958.

387 **"The youthful philosophy of dress"**: "Chanel: Ageless Designer," *The New York Times*, September 9, 1957.

387 **"She was the first fashion"**: "Throwaway Elegance of Chanel," *Vogue*, September 1, 1959, 220.

387 **like a well-fitting jacket**: As Harold Koda, director of the Metropolitan Museum of Art's Costume Institute, observes, "If you come from a supposedly egalitarian society … a uniform that's in good taste and [that] everyone can wear … is a fashion you can embrace.… With Chanel, a casual cardigan suit, anyone could wear it, so [Americans] loved it." Harold Koda, interview with the author, February 2011.

388 **"Her return collection"**: Peterson, "Chanel Look Remains Indestructible."

388 **"The essence of Chanel"**: "Chanel: Ageless Designer," *The New York Times*, September 9, 1957.

388 **"American women look marvelous"**: "Chanel Copies USA—Daytime Programming," *Vogue*, October 1, 1959, 138.

388 **"a debt of gratitude"**: Dorothy Hawkins, "Fashions from Abroad," *The New York Times*, August 1, 1956, 20.

388 **the housewife's French cooking class**: For a nuanced look at the diverse cultural roles played by France in the lives of postwar American women, see Alice Kaplan's *Dreaming in French: The Paris Years of Jacqueline Bouvier Kennedy, Susan Sontag, and Angela Davis* (Chicago: University of Chicago Press, 2012).

388 **"France is me!"**: Morand, *L'Allure de Chanel*, 182.

389 **to lend her French cachet**: Maison Chanel archivist Cécile Goddet-Dirles says, "Vadim passed all his girlfriends through Chanel, where they became 'official.' They

all came out with the same beige-and-black shoes, the same quilted bag." Personal interview with author, December 2008.

389 **Coco felt ruined the line:** Former Chanel *première* Yvonne Dudel recalled Chanel's particular aversion to Elizabeth Taylor's figure: "But have you seen that bosom? Those two babies' heads? " Yvonne Dudel interview, June 15, 2005, Champigny-sur-Marne, Maison Chanel archives.

389 **measure of glamour or gravitas:** *Vogue* magazine observed, "Chanel...flatter[s] a girl of nineteen or a woman of sixty." "In the USA: Fashion Naturals by Chanel Who Started the Whole Idea," *Vogue,* October 15, 1959, 89.

389 **President Georges Pompidou:** Quoted in Haedrich, 11.

389 **The young American First Lady:** Given the pressure for First Ladies to wear American-made clothes, Jacqueline Kennedy's Chanels may have been copies made for her in America.

389 **the besmirchment of Camelot:** Karl Lagerfeld has said that Kennedy's suit was, in fact, a copy of a Chanel, made by her friend, designer Oleg Cassini. But Justine Picardie is probably more accurate when she opines that Kennedy's suit was actually an officially approved Chanel copy, using a method known as "line-for-line," invented by Chanel specifically for replicas of her work. Picardie believes that Kennedy's suit was "fitted and made for Kennedy at Chez Ninon"—one of the companies authorized to produce these suits. Picardie, 304. Although Jacqueline Kennedy continued to wear Chanel after this tragic episode, Coco critiqued her harshly several years later, when Kennedy wore a white Courrèges dress. "She's got horrible taste and she's responsible for spreading it all over America," Chanel said of Kennedy. "Chanel in Dig at Mrs. Kennedy's Taste," *The New York Times,* July 29, 1967.

390 **"Paris is filled":** *L'Intransigeant,* March 23, 1961.

390 **sought to thwart this problem:** On the various creative methods of fashion piracy, see Meryl Gordon, "John Fairchild: Fashion's Most Angry Fella," *Vanity Fair,* September 2012.

390 **event of any illegal copying:** Dior demanded an up-front deposit of 100,000 francs from European buyers and 350,000 from American buyers. Françoise Giroud, "Backstage at Paris' Fashion Drama," *The New York Times,* January 27, 1957.

391 **"Fashion should run":** Peterson, "Chanel Look Remains Indestructible"; "Mme Chanel Welcomes Style Copies," *The Richmond News Leader,* August 14, 1956; "Chanel Wants to Be Copied!" *Louisville Courier-Journal,* August 19, 1956.

391 **substituting blue scarab buttons:** Lilou Marquand recalled finding Chanel suits at a flea market. Haedrich, 171; Marlyse Schaeffer, "Marlyse Schaeffer écrit à Chanel," *Elle,* February 23, 1962, 32.

391 **organization founded by Lucien Lelong:** Haedrich, 171.

391 **recalling her own childhood guardians:** Charles-Roux, 222.

391 **president of the *chambre*:** Galante, 220; Madsen, 295.

391 **to drop its press embargo:** Madsen, 295.

391 **"In the end, we are left":** Quoted in Patrick Grainville, "Coco Chanel: Une Vie qui ne tenait qu'à un fil," *Mise à jour,* November 27, 2008.

392 **quilted bag; the piles:** Chanel had met Chaplin years earlier on the Riviera and re-encountered him in the 1950s in Switzerland, where he, too, sought exile from po-

litical woes—in his case the witch hunts of the McCarthy era. She asked him how he'd come up with his costume. Delay, 236.

392 **patches of her scalp:** Former Chanel model Delphine Bonneval interview, May 14, 2008:

> Mademoiselle wore the same suit all the time. It was off-white, trimmed with navy.... She wore it always with her hat, a silk or chiffon scarf, a necklace of big pearls, and on top of that, all her jewelry. She wore always many necklaces at the same time. Her suit, always the same, this season a beige wool, trimmed with navy.... Napoleon didn't change his outfit often either.... And a hat, Mademoiselle Chanel never takes off a hat that, one senses immediately, is her crown. In the midst of all her bare-headed subjects, Coco Chanel is the only one, always, whose head is covered.

> Madeleine Chapsal, interview with Chanel, *L'Express,* August 11, 1960, 15.

392 **part of a hairpiece sewn:** Odile de Croy interview, April 22, 2008, 6. Galante, 250, discusses Chanel's hair color, as does Charles-Roux, 215.

393 **thinness started looking like fragility:** Malcolm Muggeridge described her as "someone tiny and frail, who if one puffed at her too hard, might easily just disintegrate; her powdery frame collapsing into a minute heap of dust, as those frail houses had in the London blitz." Muggeridge, *Chronicles of Wasted Time* (1972; repr., Vancouver: Regent College Publishing, 2006), 515. *The New York Times* mentions Chanel's weight in Joseph Barry, "Chanel No. 1: World Fashion Legend," *The New York Times,* August 23, 1964.

393 **"She eats nothing":** Cecil Beaton, *The Unexpurgated Beaton,* 153.

393 **"When you had to go see her":** Bonneval, 5.

393 **including the same white blouse:** Delay, 196, Marouzé, 8.

393 **"We wore nothing but Chanel":** Odile de Croy interview, 5.

394 **"In my life as a woman":** Ligeour, 9.

394 **"She was a true Pygmalion":** Lilou Marquand, personal interview with author.

394 **"She was the first to have":** Moreau interview. Lilou Marquand writes in her memoir that Chanel No. 5 was sprayed in the morning at rue Cambon, but Cuir de Russie was sprayed in the evening. Marquand, *Chanel m'a dit* (Paris: Editions Lattès, 1990), 28.

395 **"as in the army":** Marouzé, 5.

395 **without even a bathroom break:** Marquand, 76.

395 **standing perfectly mute and motionless:** Chapsal, 15. During these interminable fittings, Chanel appeared "insensible to certain mute supplications" on the part of her models and staff, according to Madeleine Chapsal.

395 **"She was so changeable":** Dudel, 2.

396 **"Jean, a poet?":** Madsen, 301.

396 **"I must say, it wasn't a real":** Bernier, 4.

397 **"Chanel rattled on":** John Fairchild, *Fashionable Savages* (New York: Doubleday, 1965), 36.

397 **"She would keep people standing":** Rizzo, personal interview, 2011.

397 **"That word, 'vacation,' makes":** Delay, 202.

397 **"I kept her company"**: Déon, *Bagages pour Vancouver,* 10.

398 **"borrowing" the man:** Ibid., 10.

398 **"When you sat on the couch"**: Franchomme, 6.

399 **spreading false and injurious rumors:** "For a long time she denied the existence of my marriage.... She was jealous of it...[and took] vengeance...through [creating] rumors," writes Marquand, 45.

399 **"We left our concerns outside"**: Dudel, 7.

399 **"She taught me to hate people"**: Beaton, 153.

399 **"a great talent"**: Quoted in Fairchild, 42. Balenciaga returned the compliment. He alone among Chanel's colleagues had acknowledged how important her comeback would be. "Chanel is an eternal bomb. None of us can defuse her," he prophesied in late 1953, even sending her a bouquet of flowers to welcome her back. Balenciaga's flowers only enraged Chanel, who quipped, "Flowers for a coffin. They shouldn't be in such a hurry to bury me." Galante, 201.

399 **"They're showing the navel now"**: Haedrich, 188.

400 **"Saint Laurent has excellent taste"**: Quoted in Madsen, 298. Also, Gloria Emerson, "Saint Laurent Does Chanel—But Better," *The New York Times,* July 31, 1967.

400 **"If my friends tease me"**: Delay, 238.

400 **the five floors of offices:** Chapsal, 15.

401 **"It was all because she"**: Jean Lazanbon, interview, Maison Chanel, June 27, 2005, 1, 4.

401 **tearing up the jacket:** Madeleine Chapsal reported watching Chanel cut apart the London-made suit of a male visitor, after which Coco told him there was "no hope" of fixing the suit. Chapsal also recounts a similar episode in which one of Chanel's models came to work in a Chanel suit the model had purchased for herself. Coco saw something amiss and shredded the seams while the distraught young woman vainly tried to stop her. Chapsal, 15.

401 **"Oh we had crazy laughs together"**: Moreau, 1.

402 **"Oh, she knew how"**: Rizzo, personal conversation with author, March 2011.

402 **"I thought it was a young girl"**: Fairchild, 31.

402 **"This is the most beautiful day"**: Lilou Marquand, personal interview with author, March 2011. She also recounts a version of this anecdote in her memoir. Marquand, 156.

403 **"You will not discover"**: Quoted in *Vogue,* March 1, 1959, 97.

404 **eager to assert her dominance:** Fern Marja Eckman, "Woman in the News: Coco Chanel," *New York Post,* August 19, 1967.

404 **"I find that this"**: Galante, 272; René Bernard, "La France frappe les trois coups à Moscou," *Elle,* August 11, 1961, 22–23; "Moscou: Tout est prêt pour l'exposition française," *Les Dernières Nouvelles d'Alsace,* August 12, 1961; Michel Clerc, "Chanel à Moscou," *Le Figaro,* July 27, 1961.

404 **producer Frederick Brisson approached Chanel:** The impetus for the project may have come from Brisson's wife, Hollywood actress Rosalind Russell, who yearned to play the starring role. It would have been a good fit; Russell had the right kind of crackling energy to play Coco. She was known for her vivid portrayals of professional women and big personalities, having won acclaim in Howard Hawks's *His Girl*

Friday (1940) playing a quick-witted newspaper reporter opposite Cary Grant, and later starring in *Auntie Mame,* on both stage (1956) and screen (1958).

405 **Brisson, though, persisted for years:** Cecil Smith, "Producer Brisson Bursting with Big Plans for 'Coco,'" *Los Angeles Times,* April 15, 1966.

405 **particularly Cecil Beaton's costumes:** Chanel would have had occasion to see *My Fair Lady* in New York during her 1957 trip to the States.

405 **"I am not your 'Fair Lady'":** Joseph Barry, "Chanel No. 1: Fashion World Legend," *The New York Times,* August 23, 1964.

405 **Pierre Wertheimer passed away:** The Wertheimer business then passed to his son, Jacques, a man devoted mostly to breeding thoroughbreds. Few considered him equal to the task of running his father's empire.

405 **the far younger *Audrey* Hepburn:** See Edward Jablonski, *Alan Jay Lerner: A Biography* (New York: Henry Holt, 1996), 245ff.

406 **relationship with Spencer Tracy:** "Kate had clearly been chosen, at least in part, for the enigmatic sexuality she'd bring to the role," writes William T. Mann, Hepburn's biographer. Mann, *Kate: The Woman Who Was Hepburn* (New York: Picador Books, 2007), 444.

406 **He'd already won two Oscars:** *Gigi,* for which Lerner also won an Oscar, was based on a Colette novel that borrowed heavily from the life story of Coco's old friend Marthe Davelli, the singer and *cocotte* who married the titled heir to a great fortune.

406 **big floating capes, trailing sleeves:** Beaton explained his choices with a veiled critique of Coco: "Chanel's favorite color, 'porridge' [beige], would have been very un-dramatic.... Her understated clothes are very anti-theater stuff," he said, recalling the main reason Chanel had not succeeded as a Hollywood costume designer back in the thirties. Quoted in Nancy L. Ross, "Seeing Her Own Life: Chanel to Attend Coco Bow," *Los Angeles Times,* December 13, 1969. See also Eugenia Sheppard, "Musical 'Coco' May End a Friendship," *Los Angeles Times,* November 23, 1969. See chapter 9 for a discussion of Chanel's work for MGM studios.

407 **feature even more Chanel-inspired designs:** "Of course, everybody knew the best thing to wear to the play was a Chanel," wrote the *Times.* Ellen Brooke of Sportswear Couture told *The New York Times* that Bergdorf Goodman department store had pushed her to turn out more tweed suits and other Chanel-esque casual clothes, "to tie in with 'Coco.' ... It turned out to be a good idea." Bernadine Morris, "When in Doubt There's Always Chanel," *The New York Times,* May 14, 1970. Ohrbach's laid in a supply of all aspects of the Chanel look, from shoes to jewelry, reporting that "business was brisk." "Will Chanel Star in Stores?" *The New York Times,* December 19, 1969.

407 **production budget of $900,000:** Much of the money had been sunk into Beaton's extravagant sets. His rendering of Chanel's studio, for example, consisted of a giant mechanical staircase—a glittering, mirrored spiral affair that rotated slowly, in the manner of a Busby Berkeley backdrop. Some nights it simply stopped functioning entirely, forcing Katharine Hepburn to improvise a chat with the audience.

Talking came easily to her but singing was another matter. John Simon described her singing style with his own neologism, "Schreckstimme," a witty play on the opera term "Sprechstimme." John Simon, "Theatre Chronicle," *Hudson Review,* Spring 1970, 99.

407 **"Her voice is like vinegar":** Barnes disliked the script but so enjoyed Hepburn's strong and quirky stage presence that he had a suggestion: "Dear Miss Hepburn, perhaps they should have made a musical of your life [instead]." Clive Barnes, "Katharine Hepburn Has Title Role in 'Coco,'" *The New York Times,* December 19, 1969.

407 **"*Coco* was not very good":** Quoted in Gene Lees, *The Musical Worlds of Lerner and Loewe* (Lincoln: University of Nebraska Press, 1990), 269.

408 **"*Dazzling Mademoiselle*":** André Previn and Alan Jay Lerner, *Coco* (1970 Original Broadway Cast), 1997, 1970 MCA Records D1168202. Many critics felt Lerner had stripped Chanel's biography of all nuance and grandeur. "Coco"...does not have much story...and...is empty of plot," wrote John Simon, 99. "'Coco' seems more like a rag-trade saga...that might have been titled, 'I can get it for you custom-made,'" complained Marylin Bender in "The Challenge of Making Costumes Out of Chanel's Clothes," *The New York Times,* November 25, 1969.

408 **"Mussolini's New Man":** Mosse, 1996, 248–49.

408 **which conjures the blond hair:** For a more contemporary example of the lingering shadow of the fascist man in fashion, consider the brand universe created by the Bronx-born designer Ralph Lauren (né Lipschitz), in which athletic, mostly Aryan-looking models cavort through landscapes evoking American WASP privilege—country manors, tennis courts, or yachts off the coast of Maine.

409 **despite its myriad weaknesses:** As John Simon said, "Katharine Hepburn...alone sells tickets." Simon, 99. Hepburn was replaced in August 1970 by French actress Danielle Darrieux, who could actually sing but lacked Hepburn's star power and recognition in the States.

410 **Beaton's distortion of her work:** Haedrich, 236.

410 **without her full Coco regalia:** Delay, 257–62. According to the Maison Chanel, Coco refused to attend the musical because of her displeasure with its depiction of her humble background and its focus on her later years.

410 **her agility and reflexes:** Fiemeyer and Palasse-Labrunie, 166, 169.

411 **"I must be attached":** Delay, 257. Lisa Chaney mentions this episode of Chanel trying to seduce a Ritz employee, and attributes it to a "former Chanel model." I heard the same anecdote from Brazilian journalist Danniel Rangel, citing specifically Vera Valdez, who is indeed a former Chanel model. Rangel, personal interview with author, March 2011.

411 **Chanel told her niece Gabrielle:** Fiemeyer and Palasse-Labrunie, 163.

411 **Céline accepted the new name:** Delay, 257. It had not been uncommon in pre-war France for wealthy employers to rename their servants according to their own whims.

412 **a thoroughbred, Romantica:** Galante, 152: Madsen, 317. See also "People," *Sports Illustrated,* April 20, 1964, 47.

412 **such as Isadora Duncan, Colette:** Galante, 256; Delay, 280.

412 **her shopping at particular antiques stores:** Recounted by Robert Goossens, interview, April 7 and 11, 2006, Maison Chanel.

413 "François calms me": Delay, 262.

413 Chanel accepted his return: Marquand, 129.

414 keep him that much closer: Haedrich, 222–24.

414 "Put me in the back of the car": Madsen, 322.

415 and cracked three ribs: Ibid., 318.

415 Coco would catch herself: Chazot, *Chazot Jacques,* 87. Marquand, 157.

415 closest to the window: Delay, 264.

415 future of the Chanel empire: Madsen, 324; Haedrich, 222.

416 "I am more famous": Haedrich, 233.

416 fully planning to resume work: Delay, 280.

417 one of Chanel's rings: Marquand, 160.

417 "In fifteen years, I saw": Marquand, personal conversation with author. Axel Madsen, 323, also describes Palasse-Labrunie's relationship with Chanel as no more than "cordial." Jacques Chazot says he saw Palasse-Labrunie once in the eight years he visited Chanel many times a week. Chazot, *Chazot Jacques,* 101.

417 making off with the stones: Goossens interview, conducted by the Maison Chanel April 7 and 11, 2006, 5.

417 the key to the box: Palasse-Labrunie, personal conversation with author.

418 jewelry designer in Saint-Tropez: "Valet's £420,000 Claim on Chanel Will Before Court," *The Times* (London), March 22, 1973; "Court Rejects Chanel Claim," *The Times* (London), May 31, 1973.

418 Who did inherit Chanel's: François Mironnet believed that Chanel had left a multibillion-dollar fortune, while the Wertheimers maintained it was a far lower amount. Madsen, 333.

418 its policy of sepulchral silence: Madsen, 333.

420 "It would take a greater voice": "In Paris Church Chanel Rites Attended by Hundreds," *Los Angeles Times,* January 14, 1971.

420 other graves during her lifetime: Fiemeyer and Palasse-Labrunie, , 197.

AFTERWORD

422 "I believe in the fourth dimension": Haedrich, 118.

422 highlighted the epic story: Diana Vreeland, "Mademoiselle's Magic," *Herald Tribune,* October 20, 1986.

423 hoping to conjure Mademoiselle: "Coco Is Missed," *The New York Times,* January 27, 1971.

423 perpetuating the extant Chanel style: "New Boss at Chanel," *The New York Times,* February 17, 1971.

423 symbol of stodgy matron-hood: Nicholas Coleridge, *The Fashion Conspiracy: A Remarkable Journey Through the Empires of Fashion* (New York: Harper and Row, 1988), 187.

424 limited number of upscale locations: Berman and Sawaya, 108.

424 harder memories of his youth: Alicia Drake has done an admirable job of researching Lagerfeld's early years in *The Beautiful Life: Fashion, Genius, and Glorious Excess in 1970s Paris* (New York: Little, Brown, 2006), esp. 332–37.

424 **"Respect is not creation"**: Quoted in Jane Kramer, "The Chanel Obsession," *Vogue,* September 1, 1991, 512.

425 **"antennae everywhere"**: Marika Genty, personal conversation with author, May 2010.

425 **discard every garment and sketch:** Suzy Menkes, "The Man Who Takes Over from Chanel," *The New York Times,* January 25, 1983.

425 **size of a hula hoop:** Sarah Karmali, "Chanel Hula Hoop Bag—Karl Lagerfeld Explains," *Vogue,* October 4, 2012.

426 **"I'm not a stripper!"**: Quoted in Hadley Freeman, "The Man Behind the Glasses," *The Guardian,* September 17, 2005.

426 **international public relations for Chanel:** Marie-Louise de Clermont-Tonnerre, personal conversation with author, March 2011.

427 **Hadid's undulating, sci-fi structure:** Although this pavilion was intended to travel to more cities, a flagging global economy and a series of mocking press reviews convinced Chanel executives to end the Mobile Art campaign early. See Nicolai Ouroussoff, "Zaha Hadid's Chanel Pavilion: Art and Commerce Canoodling in Central Park," *The New York Times,* October 20, 2008.

429 **"both invisible and present"**: Vilmorin, 21.

ILLUSTRATION CREDITS

INDEX

Page numbers 455–545 refer to endnotes. Page numbers in italics refer to illustrations.

PHOTO: © AGATON STROM

RHONDA K. GARELICK writes on fashion, performance, art, literature, and cultural politics. Her books include *Rising Star: Dandyism, Gender, and Performance in the Fin de Siècle; Electric Salome: Loie Fuller's Performance of Modernism;* and, as coeditor, *Fabulous Harlequin: ORLAN and the Patchwork Self.* Her work has also appeared in *The New York Times, New York Newsday,* the *International Herald Tribune,* and *The Sydney Morning Herald,* as well as in numerous journals and museum catalogs in the United States and Europe. She is a Guggenheim fellow and has also received awards from the Getty Research Institute, the Dedalus Foundation, the American Council of Learned Societies, the American Association of University Women, and the Whiting Foundation. Garelick received her Ph.D. and B.A. in French and comparative literature from Yale University. She splits her time between New York City, where she is a visiting scholar at the CUNY Graduate Center, and Lincoln, Nebraska, where she is professor of performing arts and English and director of the Interdisciplinary Arts Symposium at the University of Nebraska–Lincoln.